A New Star-Rating System & Other Exciting News from Frommer's!

In our continuing effort to publish the savviest, most up-to-date, and most appealing travel guides available, we've added some great new features.

Frommer's guides now include a new **star-rating system.** Every hotel, restaurant, and attraction is rated from 0 to 3 stars to help you set priorities and organize your time.

We've also added **seven brand-new features** that point you to the great deals, in-the-know advice, and unique experiences that separate travelers from tourists. Throughout the guide, look for:

Finds	Special finds—those places only insiders know about
Fun Fact	Fun facts—details that make travelers more informed and their trips more fun
Kids	Best bets for kids—advice for the whole family
Moments	Special moments—those experiences that memories are made of
Overrated	Places or experiences not worth your time or money
Tips	Insider tips—some great ways to save time and money
Value	Great values—where to get the best deals

We've also added a **"What's New"** section in every guide—a timely crash course in what's hot and what's not in every destination we cover.

Here's what the critics say about Frommer's:

"Amazingly easy to use. Very portable, very complete."

—*Booklist*

"Detailed, accurate, and easy-to-read information for all price ranges."
—*Glamour Magazine*

"Hotel information is close to encyclopedic."

—*Des Moines Sunday Register*

"Frommer's Guides have a way of giving you a real feel for a place."
—*Knight Ridder Newspapers*

Other Great Guides for Your Trip:

Frommer's Exploring America by RV
Frommer's National Parks of the American West
Frommer's San Antonio & Austin
Frommer's USA

Frommer's®

Texas

2nd Edition

by David Baird, Edie Jarolim,
Don & Barb Laine, Eric Peterson
& Neil E. Schlecht

WILEY

Wiley Publishing, Inc.

Published by:

Wiley Publishing, Inc.

909 Third Ave.
New York, NY 10022

ISBN 0-7645-2460-7
ISSN 1532-9941

Editor: Myka Carroll
Production Editor: Donna Wright
Cartographers: Roberta Stockwell & Nicholas Trotter
Photo Editor: Richard Fox
Production by Wiley Indianapolis Composition Services

Front cover photo: A neon sign in Dallas
Back cover photo: Palo Duro Canyon State Park

For information on our other products and services or to obtain technical support, please contact our Customer Care Department within the U.S. at 800-762-2974, outside the U.S. at 317-572-3993 or fax 317-572-4002.

Wiley also publishes its books in a variety of electronic formats. Some content that appears in print may not be available in electronic formats.

Manufactured in the United States of America

5 4 3 2

Contents

List of Maps

About the Authors

David Baird is a writer, editor, and translator based in Austin, Texas. He was born and bred in Houston, though he spent part of his childhood in Morelia, Mexico. He has contributed to several works about Texas and Mexico, including *Frommer's Mexico*.

Edie Jarolim was a senior editor at Frommer's in New York before she indulged her Southwest fantasies and moved to Tucson, Arizona. She has since written about the Southwest and Mexico for a variety of national publications, ranging from *America West Airlines Magazine, Art & Antiques,* and *Brides* to the *New York Times Book Review* and the *Wall Street Journal.*

Don & Barb Laine have traveled extensively throughout the West, spending as much time as possible in the outdoors, particularly the Gulf of Mexico and the Rocky Mountains. In addition to this book, they have authored or contributed to *Frommer's Colorado, Frommer's Utah,* and *Frommer's National Parks of the American West.*

Eric Peterson, a Denver-based freelance writer, has contributed to *Frommer's Colorado* and has authored *Frommer's Yellowstone & Grand Teton National Parks.* When he's not on the road or writing about travel, Peterson covers Colorado's business scene and Denver's punk-rock underbelly.

Neil E. Schlecht was reared in North Dallas. He attended Plano Senior High School, returned for graduate school at UT–Austin, and married a Texan. Now living in northwestern Connecticut, he is the author and co-author of more than a dozen travel guides, including *Frommer's Peru, Spain For Dummies,* and *Frommer's Cuba.* His Texas heroes are Lance Armstrong, Stevie Ray Vaughan, and Jimmie Dale Gilmore.

An Invitation to the Reader

In researching this book, we discovered many wonderful places—hotels, restaurants, shops, and more. We're sure you'll find others. Please tell us about them, so we can share the information with your fellow travelers in upcoming editions. If you were disappointed with a recommendation, we'd love to know that, too. Please write to:

Frommer's Texas, 2nd Edition
Wiley Publishing, Inc. • 909 Third Ave. • New York, NY 10022

An Additional Note

Please be advised that travel information is subject to change at any time—and this is especially true of prices. We therefore suggest that you write or call ahead for confirmation when making your travel plans. The authors, editors, and publisher cannot be held responsible for the experiences of readers while traveling. Your safety is important to us, however, so we encourage you to stay alert and be aware of your surroundings. Keep a close eye on cameras, purses, and wallets, all favorite targets of thieves and pickpockets.

New! Frommer's Star Ratings & Icons

Every hotel, restaurant, and attraction listing in this guide has been ranked for quality, value, service, amenities, and special features using a star-rating scale. In country, state, and regional guides, we also rate towns and regions to help you narrow down your choices and budget your time accordingly. Hotels and restaurants are rated on a scale of zero (recommended) to three stars (exceptional). Attractions, towns, and regions are rated according to the following scale: zero stars (recommended), one star (highly recommended), two stars (very highly recommended), and three stars (must-see).

In addition to the rating system, we also use seven icons to highlight insider information, useful tips, special bargains, hidden gems, memorable experiences, kid-friendly venues, places to avoid, and other useful information:

(*Finds*   (*Fun Fact*   (*Kids*   (*Moments*   (*Overrated*   (*Tips*   (*Value*

The following abbreviations are used for credit cards:

AE	American Express	DISC	Discover	V	Visa
DC	Diners Club	MC	MasterCard		

FROMMERS.COM

Now that you have the guidebook to a great trip, visit our website at **www.frommers.com** for travel information on nearly 2,500 destinations. With features updated regularly, we give you instant access to the most current trip-planning information available. At Frommers.com, you'll also find the best prices on airfares, accommodations, and car rentals—and you can even book travel online through our travel booking partners. At Frommers.com, you'll also find the following:

- Online updates to our most popular guidebooks
- Vacation sweepstakes and contest giveaways
- Newsletter highlighting the hottest travel trends
- Online travel message boards with featured travel discussions

What's New in Texas

If you're planning your first trip to Texas, you'll enjoy the variety of diversions on offer from the big cities to the dusty plains. But even if you're a repeat visitor, Texas offers plenty of new discoveries, including recently completed and expanded world-class museums, chic restaurants, and high-tech sports arenas. Here are the highlights of what you can look forward to during your trip.

PLANNING YOUR TRIP TO TEXAS If you're planning to take a trip across the border to Mexico, the total value of merchandise for personal use that each U.S. citizen can bring into the United States without having to pay duty is now $800. See "Texas: Gateway to Mexico" in chapter 2 for more information.

DALLAS Exploring Dallas The Sixth Floor Museum, 411 Elm St. (© 214/747-6660), has added a seventh floor for rotating exhibitions, though the museum is stubbornly keeping its original name. (The sixth floor, of course, is the spot where Lee Harvey Oswald, according to the Warren Commission, acted alone in assassinating President John F. Kennedy.)

The **Nasher Sculpture Center,** which will show off one of the world's foremost collections of modern sculpture, is finally slated to open by fall 2003. Dallas, where Ray Nasher made his fortune in banking and real estate, won out over New York and several of the world's most prestigious museums—though the $50 million is project being entirely funded by the private Nasher Foundation. The site,

adjacent to the Dallas Museum of Art, will feature a structure designed by the celebrated architect Renzo Piano and an outdoor sculpture garden landscaped by Peter Walker. For updates on the center's progress, visit www.nashersculpturecenter.org.

The **Meadows Museum of Art,** 5900 Bishop Blvd. at Mockingbird Lane, next to the Ford stadium (© 214/768-2516), another impressive collection mounted by a Dallas businessman, moved to new much bigger quarters on the campus of Southern Methodist University, and is now able to display a much greater number of its terrific collection of Spanish masters both old and contemporary.

In the world of sports, the Dallas Mavericks basketball team and the Dallas Stars, of the National Hockey League, have made their home in the new **American Airlines Center,** designed by the same architect who built the Ballpark in Arlington for the Texas Rangers.

Dining Monica Green, who's had such success with her Deep Ellum restaurant Monica's Acá y Allá, has opened a new, upscale Mexican eatery, **Ciudad,** 3888 Oak Lawn Ave. (© 214/219-3141), which locals are calling the best Mexican food in Dallas. **Fishbowl,** 3214 Knox St. (© 214/219-2695), has now taken over completely from Aquanox, the upscale seafood restaurant it formerly shared space with. It's now an informal, hopping place, full of the young and fashionable quaffing exotic drinks and sampling Asian tapas. **Liberty Noodles,** 5600 Lover's Lane (© **214/ 350-1133**), has moved from its funky Lower Greenville location to a much larger, shopping center spot—but it's kept the same great noodle and Thai/Asian menu, as well as the superb wine list and happening vibe. The popular little Middle Eastern joint Ali Baba Café has opened a new North Dallas location, **Ali Baba Café & Market,** 19009 Preston Rd. (© **972/248-8855**), with an attached market to serve the residential community.

After Dark Dallas lost the mega-cowboy complex Country 2000, but a long-delayed local incarnation of Houston's renowned **Gilleys** (where John Travolta and Debra Winger got hot and sweaty with mechanical bulls in *Urban Cowboy*), finally opened in summer 2003 at 1409 S. Lamar, Loft 612, east of I-30 (© **214/428-2919**).

FORT WORTH Exploring Forth Worth New to the historic Stock-yards District is the **Texas Cowboy Hall of Fame,** 128 E. Exchange Ave., Barn A (© **817/626-7131**), a museum that celebrates the great rop-ers of Texas rodeo. Another new addi-tion to Fort Worth, **National Cowgirl Museum and Hall of Fame,** 1720 Gendy St. (© **817/336-4475**), pays tribute to the women of the Old West from Dale Evans to Georgia O'Keeffe, and is the first and only museum in the country dedicated to overlooked notable Western women. Train buffs, families, and folks nostalgic for the Old West will be glad to hear that the **Tarantula 1986 steam train**—engine #2248 of the old Tarantula Railroad—is back up and running. It travels to historic Grapevine and back from the Stockyards; call © **800/457-6338** or visit www.tarantulatrain.com for exact schedules.

The terrific **Amon Carter Museum of Western Art,** 3501 Camp Bowie

Blvd. (© **817/738-1933**) has reopened after a 2-year, $39 million expansion by the original architect, Philip John-son, tripling the size of its galleries. But the biggest cultural news in Fort Worth was the December 2002 inau-guration of the new **Modern Art Museum of Fort Worth,** 3200 Dar-nell St. (© **817/738-9215**), in a land-mark building by the famed Japanese modernist architect Tadao Ando. Along with Philip Johnson's Amon Carter Museum and Louis Kahn's Kimbell, the Modern gives Fort Worth one of the most notable archi-tectural and art triumvirates in the United States.

Accommodations The elegant **Ash-ton Hotel,** 610 Main St. (© **800/ 327-4866**), just off Sundance Square in downtown, is Fort Worth's newest and only small luxury hotel. Housed in restored historic buildings, it's a plush and eminently comfortable place to stay, whether you're in town on business or pleasure. The hotel also features the city's newest and best restaurant.

Dining The biggest news to hit the Fort Worth dining scene, where locals are usually nonplussed by anything that tries too hard ("That's too Dal-las," they'll say), is **Café Ashton,** 610 Main St. (© **817/332-0100**), a sleek and impressive small restaurant within the new Ashton Hotel. The nouvelle American bistro cuisine produced by a surprisingly young chef is outstanding.

The other big news is the return to the scene of two of the city's best known restaurants, each of which had been put out of commission (by natu-ral and manmade forces). **Reata,** 310 Houston St. (© **817/336-1009**), which formerly inhabited the Bank One Tower, destroyed by the great Fort Worth tornado of 2000, has come back to life in the spot where Fort Worth lost a cultural institution, Caravan of Dreams. It now features a large rooftop terrace. Having been displaced by a parking lot, the locally legendary **Sardines Ristorante Italiano,** 509 S. University (© **817/332-9937**), has moved to a new location but very successfully replicated its dark, funky feel, and jazz combos still play nightly.

After Dark The renovation craze that swept Fort Worth's museums also resulted in big changes at **Casa Mañana Theater,** 3101 W. Lancaster (© **817/332-2272**). The theater with the aluminum geodesic dome and productions in the round completed a costly renovation and is back in action. See chapter 4 for complete details.

HOUSTON Planning Your Trip Changing the face of downtown will be Houston's new **light rail,** slated to begin service in January 2004. Futuristic in appearance, it will run down the middle of Main Street, stopping at elevated platforms. The city is closing the 1000 block of Main Street to all traffic but the train in order to create **Main Street Square** (which is at the geographic center of downtown). City developers intend this to be the centerpiece for the new vision of downtown, an open space where the public can enjoy sculpture and a long reflection pool with 62 computer-controlled water jets. Cafes and shops will border the square, and the light rail will bisect the pool and run in coordination with the computerized water jets.

After passing through downtown the light rail will head south through midtown, the Museum District, Herman Park, the city zoo, and the Medical Center, finally passing by the new football field, Reliant Stadium, and the AstroWorld and WaterWorld amusement parks. The total time for the 7½-mile trip will be 29 minutes. The trains will run every 6 to 15 minutes depending on the time of day. The light rail will open in time for the

2004 Super Bowl, which will be held at Reliant Stadium. For updates and additional information, check www.ridemetro.org.

Accommodations A number of new hotels have opened in Houston, but the two getting the most buzz are both in the Uptown area near the Galleria: the attractive and comfortable **Hotel Derek,** 2525 W. Loop South (© **866/292-4100**); and the new **InterContinental Houston,** 2222 W. Loop South (© **800/327-0200**), with great service and the latest in guest room amenities. These two will be strong competition for the Westin Hotels in the Galleria, which, despite a $28 million refurbishing, are slipping in terms of comforts and amenities. Over the next 2 years, downtown Houston will see the opening of two new Marriott hotels, a large Hilton, and a couple of boutique hotels.

Dining Hugo's, 1602 Westheimer Rd. (© **713/524-7744**), a new upscale Mexican restaurant in the Montrose District, has raised the bar for other restaurants serving interior Mexican cuisine. It has made the biggest splash of any new restaurant and is getting a lot of credit for being the first to offer Houston diners some of the lesser-known dishes of classic Mexican cooking.

Exploring Houston Downtown Houston has endured both the collapse of Enron and a slow public works project that made a mess of its streets and major arteries. But neither of these events seems to have drained downtown of its vigor; it continues to reinvent itself at an ever-quickening pace. Once a ghost town at night and on weekends, it's now home to more and more condos, hotels, restaurants, performing arts venues, and nightclubs. Most observers credit this transformation to the rebirth of the historic Rice Hotel as a luxury condo tower;

the conversion of the old convention center into **Bayou Place** (© 713/230-1666), a center for restaurants, bars, clubs, and a multiplex cinema; and the construction of the downtown baseball park, **Minute Maid Field** (formerly Enron Field). A string of successes has followed, the most recent being the new **Hobby Center for the Performing Arts,** 800 Bagby (© 713/227-2001), in the theater district. Houston now has more theater seats than any city in America except for New York.

Slated to open on the north side of the theater district is **Landry's Downtown Aquarium,** which will be a family-oriented entertainment center with 500,000 gallons of aquarium space highlighted by a shark tank that can be viewed from a glass tunnel that crosses through its center. The aquarium will also include restaurants, a Ferris wheel, and an observation tower. The aquarium is located at I-45 and Memorial Drive (© 713/223-FISH; www.downtownaquarium. com).

Under construction next to the convention center is the **new 20,000-seat basketball arena,** which will open at the end of 2003. It will be home to the Rockets and the Comets, Houston's NBA and WNBA teams, and will function as a multi-purpose venue for public events. With the baseball and football stadiums, this arena becomes the third major-league sports venue to be built in this city in a span of 3 years. See chapter 5 for the latest on Houston.

THE TEXAS GULF COAST Corpus Christi Fans of dolphins are heading to the new **Dolphin Bay at Texas State Aquarium** (© 800/477-4853), a protected environment for Atlantic bottle-nosed dolphins that are unable to survive in the wild. Nearby, the **USS** *Lexington* **Museum on the Bay** (© 800/523-9539) has added a

state-of-the-art IMAX theater with a three-stories-tall screen, believed to be the first and only IMAX theater installed on an historic naval ship. See chapter 6 for more information.

SAN ANTONIO Accommodations The only new hotel to open on the River Walk in several years, the **Hotel Valencia Riverwalk,** 405 N. St. Mary's (© 866/842-0100; www.hotel valencia.com), wasn't completed in time for it to be reviewed in this edition, but, based on a hard-hat tour and model room peek (they're techno-chic), it looks like a winner. Restoring a historic building and adding all kinds of high-tech accoutrements doesn't come cheap: Lodgings with a river view at this boutique property run $375 and up.

Dining Dishing out regional Mexican cuisine rather than typical Tex-Mex, **Manduca,** 215 Losoya St. (© 210/475-9099), is a welcome addition to the generally touristy River Walk.

Exploring San Antonio Even with hotel construction on hold, downtown San Antonio never stays the same. With the stabilization of its foundation and improvement of its lighting and acoustics in 2002, the **San Fernando Cathedral,** 115 Main Plaza (© 210/227-1297), completed the initial part of its three-phase restoration. The most impressive new addition, a 24-foot-high gilded retablo, should be unveiled by the time you read this.

When downtown isn't restoring its old buildings, it's building huge new sports arenas. In October 2002—less than a decade after the debut of the Alamodome—the **SBC Center,** One SBC Center Pkwy. (© 210/444-5000), opened with a pre-season basketball game between the New York Knicks and the San Antonio Spurs. The high-tech stadium not only houses the Spurs, but, as of the 2003 season, it also hosts the San Antonio Silver Stars (the WNBA team formerly known as the Utah Starzz). See chapter 7 for complete details.

AUSTIN Planning Your Trip Frontier Airlines (© 800/432-1359) has initiated two daily nonstop flights from its home city, Denver, to Austin-Bergstrom International Airport. Direct service from Austin to Seattle and Reno/Lake Tahoe was also introduced.

As though the S×SW music extravaganza in spring wasn't enough, another major tune-up has been added to Austin's calendar. In September 2002, the first 2-day **Austin City Limits Music Festival** (© 512/478-4811 or 512/478-7211) was held, featuring Emmylou Harris, Jimmy Vaughan, Shawn Colvin, and other performers in a variety of genres—just like the acts on the long-running public TV show for which the festival is named.

Dining It's tough to keep track of the culinary comings and goings around town. Recent arrivals include **La Traviata,** 314 Congress Ave. (© 512/479-8131), a casual trattoria. Also relatively new to Austin, **Emilia's** lit up the city's dining scene with its dazzling New American cuisine before closing in early 2003, the victim of the economic downturn.

Side Trips from Austin The relatively rural region around San Antonio and Austin changes less readily and steadily than the big cities—except when it comes to **Fredericksburg,** the most popular of the Hill Country towns. A $1.1 million visitor center opened in early 2003 and includes a 46-seat theater that screens a historical video, as well as several computers where travelers can check their e-mail.

The art museum in downtown New Braunfels that formerly housed an extensive collection of Hummels moved to the adjacent village, Gruene, where it was reincarnated as the **New Braunfels Museum of Art & Music.** It now offers excellent Texas-themed shows and is blissfully Hummel-free. See chapter 8 for complete details.

WEST TEXAS   El Paso   Bad news for smokers, but good news for those who prefer breathing clean air: In 2002, a **smoking ban** went into effect for all of El Paso's restaurants and bars.

Marfa   The big news in the central west Texas plains is that after years of semi-hibernation, the glorious 1930s-era **Hotel Paisano,** at Texas and Highland streets (© 866/729-3669), was rescued in 2001, and after a comprehensive restoration project, the property has reclaimed its former status as the premiere hotel between El Paso and San Antonio. The building itself is stunning, a renowned hybrid of prairie and mission architecture, and the rooms balance history and modernity, with comfortable new furnishings and a myriad of arches, stained glass windows, and other subtle details. See chapter 9 for complete details.

BIG BEND & GUADALUPE MOUNTAINS NATIONAL PARKS Increased national security following the September 11, 2001, terrorist attacks has reached the U.S.–Mexican border in **Big Bend National Park** (© 915/477-2251), and the informal border crossings to several small Mexican villages on the other side of the Rio Grande are no longer permitted. Park officials say that anyone entering the United States from Mexico in the park is subject to a fine of up to $5,000 and imprisonment of up to 1 year. See chapter 10 for more information.

1

The Best of Texas

by David Baird, Edie Jarolim, Don & Barb Laine,
Eric Peterson & Neil E. Schlecht

Texans are a unique bunch, unapologetic in their swaggering embrace of the place they call home. "It's flat and dry," you say. "Yup, parts are," they reply. "It's hot," you say. "Hotter 'n hell," they confirm. "Texans talk funny," you say. "Y'all do too," they retort. Self-confident and independent almost to a fault, Texas seems to embody all that's good, bad, and especially big about the United States. The former independent Republic of Texas—which shook off the landlord claims of Spain, Mexico, France, and even the United States—has diehards who still wish Texas would suck it up and secede.

Texans don't seem to mind too much if outsiders get caught up in the myths and clichés about Texas (that way they get to keep the truth to themselves). A 10-gallon hat doesn't hold 10 gallons of anything, nor is Texas flat, dry, and featureless, filled with cowboys on the range, oilmen watching their backyard gushers spit up black gold, and helmet-haired beauty queens. But it's hard to compete with the state's image, the canvas for 100 Western flicks. The big-sky frontier of Texas and the West is the quintessential American landscape, the mythic cowboy leading his longhorn cattle on long drives a heroic figure. The outlaws who thumbed their noses at authority (behind the barrel of a gun) and the boomtown gamblers who struck it rich are also part of the romantic tale of Texas.

The cowboy still exists, but Texas is now decidedly more urban than rural. Three of the nation's 10 largest cities are here: Houston, Dallas, and San Antonio. Texas today is as much a leader of high-tech industries as it is an agricultural and ranching state. There are world-class art museums and collections in Houston, Fort Worth, and Dallas, where local philanthropists have used their money and influence to import the world's most celebrated architects to build some of the nation's most talked-about museums. Although Texas is by and large a conservative place, Austin has for decades supported thriving hippie and renegade musician communities, and Dallas is nipping at its heels with a thriving music scene. The state is a melting pot dotted by pockets of Czech, German, and Irish communities; bilingual populations in the lower Rio Grande Valley and border towns; and more than four million people of Hispanic descent statewide.

This enormous state also has immense geographical diversity. Cross Texas and you'll see desert plains in the Texas Panhandle, the Piney Woods in East Texas, beaches in the Gulf Coast, North Texas prairies, scenic wildflowers and lakes in central Texas Hill Country, desert canyons in Big Bend National Park, and the rugged Guadalupe Mountains.

Still, some of the clichés are true. Texas, the second-largest state in the United States in both land mass and population, is larger than any country in Europe. You can set out from Amarillo in your car and drive south for 15 hours and still not reach the Mexico border. And everything is bigger in Texas, of course: The ranches are bigger, the steaks are bigger, and the bigger and badder cars—Cadillacs with longhorns on the grille and monster pickup trucks with gun runs in back—really do exist. In Texas you can carry a concealed handgun even in church, and the state is known as the capital punishment capital of the world. "Don't Mess with Texas" is more than an effective antilitter campaign.

Texans, though, are startlingly friendly and hospitable folks. Deals are still completed with handshakes, and adults say "yes, ma'am" and "nossir" to each other. Also, Texans love their sports, especially football. This is a place where entire towns pack the bleachers for Friday night high school games and preachers mention the game in their sermons, praying for victory in a kind of gridiron holy war.

Former Texas governor and owner of the Texas Rangers baseball team George W. Bush, who delights in using the down-home moniker "Dubya," lost the popular vote but was elected the 43rd president of the U.S. in 2000. Bush regularly draws the national media corps to his sprawling ranch in Crawford, Texas, outside of Waco, when he takes long breaks from Washington "to get back in touch with real people." Bush, a savvy politician, straps on his cowboy boots and homespun airs, showing that he knows how to make the most of his transplanted Texan status.

It's hard for most people to be indifferent about Texas. It's a place to romanticize and ridicule, to dream about and dismiss. Texans can leave the state, but sooner or later they'll admit their weaknesses for Texas dance halls and Old West saloons, Tex-Mex and barbecue, cowboy boots, and country music. From the big sky and flat plains and the Hill Country highways lined by Texas bluebonnets to the larger-than-life personalities like LBJ and Willie Nelson: Texas stays with you.

—*Neil E. Schlecht*

1 The Best Luxury & Historic Hotels

- **The Adolphus Hotel** (Dallas; ② **800/221-9083**): A landmark beaux-arts hotel, built by beer baron Adolphus Busch, his namesake looks and feels like a European château. Luxuriate among dark-wood parlors, baroque art and antiques, and an opulent dining room, one of Big D's best restaurants. Rooms are English country style, and a three-course English tea is served in the lobby living room every afternoon. See p. 93.
- **The Mansion on Turtle Creek** (Dallas; ② **800/422-3408**): Repeatedly named one of the top five hotels in the United States, the Mansion draws movie stars, princes, presidents, and luxury mavens. Formerly the grand estate of a cotton magnate in the 1920s and 1930s, the Mansion is refined

and supremely elegant throughout, with service to match. The innovative Southwestern restaurant has slipped a notch, but is still among the most prized in town. See p. 93.
- **Stockyards Hotel** (Fort Worth; ② **800/423-8471**): Over-the-top luxury would be out of place in the old stockyards, so this extremely comfortable and authentic slice of the Old West qualifies as a Fort Worth indulgence: cowboy luxury. Outlaws on the run, cowpokes and their madames, and the C&W elite have all propped up their boots here. Cowtown's cattle-ranching and railroad past are effortlessly evoked in the rooms, each of which is different: Tie your horse to the post (okay, park the Taurus in the lot) and bunk in the Bonnie

& Clyde, Geronimo, or Victorian Parlor room. See p. 126.

- **Four Seasons Hotel Houston Center** (Houston; ✆ **800/332-3442** or 713/650-1300): Lots of space to stretch out in and lots of service so you don't have to stretch too far. This hotel surpasses all others in amenities and services, and has the best fine dining in downtown Houston. Within a few blocks are the baseball park, the new basketball arena, a shopping mall, and the convention center. A bit beyond that is the city's theater district and nightlife hub. See p. 150.

- **Lancaster Hotel** (Houston; ✆ **800/231-0336** or 713/228-9500): Personal service, charming rooms, and great location are the keys to this hotel's success. If there's one hotel that makes having a car unnecessary in Houston, this is it. A block away are the symphony, the opera, three theaters, and the ballet. Make things easy on yourself by getting the concierge to buy your tickets at the time you make your reservations. Also within a block or two are a multiplex cinema and several restaurants and clubs—you'll have the best part of the city at your feet. See p. 150.

- **Omni Corpus Christi Hotel** (Corpus Christi; ✆ **800/843-6664** or 361/887-1600): The two towers of the Omni overlook Corpus Christi Bay, and the floor-to-ceiling windows of the 20-story Bayfront Tower offer spectacular views of the Gulf, particularly from its upper floors. Pamper yourself with a massage from the in-house massage therapist or relax in the whirlpool. Then have dinner in their Republic of Texas Bar & Grill. See p. 205.

- **Radisson Resort South Padre Island** (South Padre Island; ✆ **800/333-3333** or 956/761-6511): From the high-ceilinged lobby to the beautiful landscaping around the swimming pools, this Radisson spells luxury. Many rooms have grand views of the ocean, and everything is at your fingertips. See p. 217.

- **Menger Hotel** (San Antonio; ✆ **800/345-9285** or 210/223-4361): Who can resist a place that's right across the street from the Alamo and still has the bar where Teddy Roosevelt recruited his Rough Riders? This 19th-century gem sparkles now as it did 100 years ago. See p. 243.

- **The Driskill** (Austin; ✆ **800/252-9367** or 512/474-5911): If you want to play cattle baron, you can't do better than stay in this opulent 1886 hotel, restored to its former glory at the end of the 20th century. See p. 284.

- **Camino Real Hotel** (El Paso; ✆ **800/722-6466** or 915/534-3000): El Paso's finest hotel, just 6 blocks north of the Mexican border, effortlessly meshes El Paso's past and present. Although it has undergone numerous renovations since its opening in 1912, the lobby retains its stunning Tiffany glass dome ceiling and the original stained-glass windows, and you'll still find the elegant touches that established the hotel as an Old West landmark. See p. 327.

2 The Best Bed & Breakfasts & Small Hotels

- **Hôtel St. Germain** (Dallas; ✆ 214/871-2516): Ever wanted to stay with your spouse at a plush bordello? This intimate boutique hotel and elegant, prix-fixe restaurant is about as close as you'll come to that fantasy. A gorgeous mix of early-20th-century France and New Orleans, the seven suites are so swank, with pampering features like wood-burning fireplaces, draped Napoléon sleigh beds, bidets, and soaking tubs, that you may not want to leave. But your budget may force you to. See p. 93.

- **The Ashton Hotel** (Fort Worth; ✆ 800/327-4866): Just off Sundance Square, this new boutique hotel—Fort Worth's only small luxury hotel—offers luxurious rooms and great service, as well as one of the best new restaurants in North Texas. It's the new place to be in Cowtown. See p. 128.

- **Etta's Place** (Fort Worth; ✆ 817/654-0267): A cozy and relaxing small hotel that feels like a B&B is just a heartbeat from Fort Worth's charming nightlife, shops, and restaurants of Sundance Square. It bears the name of Etta Place, the handsome girlfriend of the Sundance Kid, who no doubt would approve of the spacious, modern rooms with lots of light and Texas touches. Kick back in the clubby library and music rooms. See p. 128.

- **La Colombe d'Or** (Houston; ✆ 713/524-7999): Have a four-course French dinner served in your suite's separate dining room. With such personal service and with only five suites and one penthouse, there's no way you'll get lost in the shuffle. Occupying a mansion built for an oil tycoon in the 1920s, the hotel has uncommon architectural features, and is furnished with antiques. Its location in Houston's Montrose District puts it squarely in the middle of the hippest part of town. See p. 155.

- **George Blucher House Bed & Breakfast Inn** (Corpus Christi; ✆ 866/884-4884 or 361/884-4884): This wonderful B&B combines the ambience of an elegant historic home—it was built in 1904—with modern amenities. Breakfasts are served by candlelight; and you're just across the street from a prime bird-watching area. See p. 204.

- **Ogé House Inn on the River Walk** (San Antonio; ✆ 800/242-2770 or 210/223-2353): The King William area abounds with B&Bs, but the Ogé House stands out as much for its professionalism as for its gorgeous mansion and lovely rooms. You don't have to sacrifice service for warmth here. See p. 244.

- **Villa del Rio Bed & Breakfast** (Del Rio; ✆ 800/995-1887 or 830/768-1100): A luxurious Mediterranean-style villa—actually a mix of Italian and Mexican styles—built in 1887, the Villa del Rio gets our vote for the best place to stay in this area for anyone who appreciates old-world ambience and pampering and an exciting breakfast. See p. 362.

3 The Best Hotel Bargains

- **The Bradford at Lincoln Park** (Dallas; ✆ 888/486-STAY): A new residential-style hotel that primarily targets businesspeople, it's also superb for other travelers and families. The nicely styled and spacious suites have fully equipped kitchens, and there are a pool and small spa, exercise room, and business center, as well as free continental breakfast and local calls. See p. 96.

- **Miss Molly's Bed & Breakfast Hotel** (Fort Worth; ✆ **800/99-MOLLY**): Texas style and hospitality radiate from this small 1910 home and now B&B on the main drag of Fort Worth's Stockyards District. Cattle barons, railroaders, and cowboys have all rested their heads here, often on the lap of a local lady. For Old West romanticism, this Victorian house among saloons and Western shops can't be beat, especially for the price. See p. 127.
- **Grant Palm Court Inn** (Houston; ✆ **800/255-8904** or 713/668-8000): The economy hotel business is quite competitive; rarely does a guidebook writer come across a motel in this category with such a marked price advantage. Attractive, clean rooms, well-kept grounds, and a convenient location that's not on some ugly freeway all make this a great pick. Throw in a free continental breakfast, pool, and hot tub and you'll want to pinch yourself. See p. 154.
- **Best Western Sunset Suites** (San Antonio; ✆ **866/560-6000** or 210/223-4400): Low room rates, lots of free perks, and a convenient location near downtown—not to mention super attractive rooms in a historic structure—make staying here a super deal. See p. 244.
- **Austin Motel** (Austin; ✆ **512/441-1157**): Look for the Austin's classic neon sign in Austin's hip SoCo area. The rooms have been individually furnished, many in fun and funky styles, but the place retains its 1950s character and its lower-than-1990s prices. See p. 286.
- **El Paso Marriott** (El Paso; ✆ **800/228-9290** or 915/779-3300): After a major renovation in 2000, this modern hotel is a solid lodging option for those who want to be near the airport. Catering mostly to business travelers, it's a bargain on the weekends. See p. 327.

4 The Best Restaurants

- **The French Room** (Dallas; ✆ **214/742-8200**): This formal but thankfully not intimidating restaurant in the historic Adolphus Hotel is dreamy, like dining at Versailles. Indulge in superb classic French cuisine and museum-quality wines surrounded by a rococo-painted ceiling, flowing drapes, and crystal chandeliers. See p. 97.
- **Citizen** (Dallas; ✆ **214/522-7253**). This ultra-sleek and super-chic Eurasian restaurant, adopted by Big D's scenesters, dares to pull out all the stops. Only a few years back Dallas could never have supported such an audacious restaurant. From the dramatic decor to dishes like black cod with blonde miso and tuna tartare with caviar and crème fraîche, it's Dallas's way of saying New York and LA ain't got nothing on it. See p. 100.
- **Javier's Gourmet Mexicano** (Dallas; ✆ **214/521-4211**): The owners and devotees of this gourmet Mexico city restaurant will gently inform you that, no, this isn't Tex-Mex. Javier's serves deliciously prepared grilled fish and meat dishes and mesquite-smoked chicken in a Spanish colonial setting. Come for a top-shelf margarita at the clubby bar, but I guarantee you'll stay for dinner. See p. 101.
- **Café Ashton** (Fort Worth; ✆ **817/332-0100**): The creative New American bistro fare at this

swank new restaurant, in a boutique hotel of the same description, has quickly shot to the top of everyone's best-of lists in Fort Worth. Hotel dining is rarely this good or this intimate. See what all the fuss is about. See p. 131.

- **Mark's** (Houston; © 713/523-3800): No fussy French nouvelle here, and no boring steak and potatoes either. Mark's manages to serve up dishes that can satisfy at some deep subconscious level while they fulfill our eternal quest for something new. This is the New American cooking as it should be performed. See p. 164.
- **Cafe Annie** (Houston; © 713/840-1111): No other restaurant in Houston garners quite the attention that this place does from both food critics and the public alike. With its innovative Southwestern cooking, the best wine list in the city, and a master sommelier (the only "master" in Texas), the restaurant has its credentials. Chef/owner Robert Del Grande offers up wonderful dishes that show just how fertile the crossbreeding of Mexican and American cooking can be. See p. 168.
- **Silo** (San Antonio; © 210/824-8686): When we give the nod to the Silo as tops in American cuisine, we're not talking meat loaf and mashed potatoes (although versions of both dishes may turn up on the menu). Silo's New American recipes, which rely on fresh seasonal ingredients from the area, will dazzle those willing to expand their culinary horizons. See p. 255.
- **Café Central** (El Paso; © 915/545-2233): Well worth the splurge, Café Central is a sleek urban bistro serving sophisticated international cuisine. The menu changes daily, but always offers a wide range of standout fare—most notably creative Southwestern interpretations of traditional Continental dishes—such as guyamas shrimp with a zesty tequila-cilantro sauce. The wine list is one of the city's best, with nearly 300 bottles, and desserts include the best *leches* (Mexican milk cakes) in all of Texas. See p. 329.
- **Avanti Authentic Italian Restaurant** (Del Rio; © 830/775-3363): Who would ever dream of going to a West Texas border town for great Italian food? No one, until they've been to Avanti, which offers some of the best homemade northern Italian dishes we've tasted anywhere. There's also an excellent selection of northern Italian wines. See p. 362.

5 The Best Texan Dining

- **Sonny Bryan's Smokehouse** (Dallas; © 214/357-7120): Sonny Bryan's has been turning out sweet barbecue since 1910, and the little smoke shack out on Inwood has acquired legendary status. Salesmen perch on their car hoods with their sleeves rolled up and wolf down hickory-smoked brisket, sliced beef sandwiches, and succulent onion rings. Thinner sorts squeeze into tiny one-armed school desks and get ready to douse their brisket with superb, tangy sauce. A classic. See p. 102.
- **Bob's Steak & Chop House** (Dallas; © 214/528-9446): Bob's will satisfy the steak connoisseur—the real Texan—in you. With a clubby but relaxed mahogany look and behemoth wet-aged prime beef and sirloin filets, this is a place for the J. R. crowd. Even the accompaniments—"smashed"

potatoes and honey-glazed whole carrots—are terrific. And the meat-shy need not fear: The chop house salad is a meal in itself. Cigar aficionados should keep their noses trained for Bob's cigar dinners: Every course is served with a different cigar. See p. 100.

- **Lonesome Dove Western Bistro** (Fort Worth; ℂ 817/740-8810): The work of a daring young couple, this friendly and eclectic restaurant challenges Cowtown to broaden its horizons. The creative Southwestern menu at this Stockyards eatery successfully stretches the popular theme in new ways, adding unique Texas touches that are both avant-garde and comforting. Pop in for the cheap Stockyards lunch special or dive into a blowout dinner. See p. 130.
- **Angelo's** (Fort Worth; ℂ 817/332-0357): Fort Worth's classic Texas barbecue joint is as unpretentious as they come: Its wood paneling, mounted deer and buffalo heads, metal ceiling fans, and Formica tables might have come from a Jaycees lodge. That's kitschy cool to some, meaningless to everyone else. What is important is the fantastic hickory-smoked barbecue. See p. 133.
- **Fiesta Loma Linda** (Houston; ℂ 713/924-6074): Bursting the bubble of a perfectly puffed tortilla smothered in chile con queso is the moment where anticipation meets realization in the Tex-Mex experience. The aroma, the texture, the taste . . . Words fail me. You can scour the borderlands a long time before coming up with an old-fashioned Tex-Mex joint like this one. The restaurant even has its own special tortilla maker for producing these puffed up beauties. Also, of note are the perfectly seasoned classic Tex-Mex enchiladas with chili gravy. See p. 163.

- **Recio's** (Corpus Christi; ℂ 361/888-4040): South Texas is littered with *taquerias* (restaurants that specialize in *taquitos*—similar to a burrito but folded), and this is among the best. Locally owned and operated by Robert and Minerva Recio, this justly popular restaurant serves homemade cooked-to-order food in a pleasant, casual atmosphere. See p. 206.
- **Rosario's** (San Antonio; ℂ 210/223-1806): Not only is the food—both Tex-Mex and regional Mexican—fresh and tasty, but the lively atmosphere and colorful setting add that extra Texas zing. Kick back, ogle the faux Boteros, and sip a cactus margarita. See p. 252.
- **The Salt Lick** (Austin; ℂ 512/858-4959): You might not be able to convince every local that the Asian-influenced barbecue sauce served here is pure Lone Star, but no one's gonna argue that the kicked back country atmosphere—including the BYOB policy—could be anything but Texan. See p. 293.
- **L&J Café** (El Paso; ℂ 915/566-8418): An El Paso landmark since it opened its doors in 1927, the L&J is both inexpensive and offers some of the best Tex-Mex food you'll find anywhere. The chicken enchiladas, overflowing with fluffy meat and buried under chunky green chile and Jack cheese, approach perfection. It doesn't hurt that the salsa is spicy, the beer is cold, and the service is quick and friendly, even when the place is filled to capacity—as it is most of the time. See p. 330.
- **Texas Café and Bar** (Lubbock; ℂ 806/792-8544): This rowdy, smoky roadhouse, affectionately called "The Spoon" by locals, is pure Texas, from the local color

seated at the bar and weathered tables to the Lone Star neon signs, longhorn skulls, and politically incorrect wooden Indian. The

menu, too, is 100% Texas: The barbecue is made with turkey, ribs, beef, or sausage. See p. 414.

6 The Best Lone Star Experiences

- **Hopping Aboard the Tarantula Steam Train:** The Old West comes alive aboard the Tarantula Railroad. A nostalgic train (usually a restored 1896 steam locomotive) rumbles along the track from Stockyards Station in Fort Worth, tracing the route of the Chisholm Trail, to the Cotton Belt Depot in historic Grapevine, Texas, a town with 75 restored turn-of-the-20th-century buildings. See "The Tarantula Steam Train" in chapter 4.
- **Lassoing the Fort Worth Stock Show and Rodeo:** Fort Worth ain't called Cowtown for nothing. In late January and early February, the Southwestern Exposition and Livestock Show, as it's officially called, recalls the glory cowboy days with horse shows, auctions, and all sorts of livestock, from beef cattle to llamas and swine. The nightly rodeos are big draws. See "Fort Worth" in chapter 4.
- **Attending a Mariachi Mass at Mission San José:** The Alamo may be more famous, but hearing a congregation of San Antonians raise their voices in spirited prayer reminds you that the city's Spanish missions aren't just, well, history. See p. 259.

- **Smelling the Blue Bonnets at the Lady Bird Johnson Wildflower Center:** Few people remember that it was Lady Bird Johnson who started a program to beautify America's highways—and that she began practicing it in her home state. This flower-powered research center is a natural outgrowth of this first lady's lifelong efforts to beautify the state. See p. 296.
- **Running the *Other* River Walk:** Enjoy a stroll or jog along the Concho River's 4-mile trail, meandering among bountiful outdoor gardens and water displays. Gaze at a bronze statue of a mermaid, "Pearl of the Conchos," or take in the Bill Aylor, Sr. Memorial RiverStage, an outdoor performing arts venue. There's also a 9-hole golf course on the River Walk's acres. See p. 350.
- **Exploring Big Bend National Park:** Vast and wild, this rugged terrain harbors thousands of species of plants and animals—some seen practically nowhere else on earth. A visit can include a hike into the sun-baked desert, a float down a majestic river through the canyons, or a trek among high mountains where bears and mountain lions rule. See "Big Bend National Park" in chapter 10.

7 The Best Museums

- **The Nasher Sculpture Center** (Dallas): This world-class collection of modern sculpture is in the final stages of being mounted in the downtown Dallas Arts District. Ray Nasher and his wife

Patsy spent 4 decades assembling what has been called the finest private collection in the world (it includes superlative works by Miró, David Smith, Brancusi, Moore, Giacometti, Picasso,

Matisse, Calder, and many more). Designed by Renzo Piano, it's scheduled to open by late 2003, adjacent to the Dallas Museum of Art. See p. 82.

- **Meadows Museum of Art** (Dallas): Now in a new building with more room to show off the greatest collection of Spanish masters outside Spain, the Meadows was built by a Dallas oilman fascinated by Spanish art. The museum proudly displays a wealth of works by Velázquez, Goya, Ribera, Murillo, Zurbarán—just about all the biggies from Spain's golden era as well as the 20th-century masters Picasso, Dalí, and Miró. See p. 85.

- **Kimbell Art Museum** (Fort Worth): Probably the country's finest small museum, this masterwork by Louis Kahn is a joyous celebration of architecture and a splendid collection of art to boot. Kahn's graceful building, a wonder of technology and natural light, is now a chapter in architectural studies worldwide. The small permanent collection ranges from prehistoric Asian and pre-Columbian pieces to European old masters, Impressionists, and modern geniuses. The Kimbell also gets some of the world's most important traveling shows. See p. 120.

- **Modern Art Museum of Fort Worth** (Fort Worth): In a spanking new modernist building designed by the Japanese architect Tadao Ando, the new Modern—actually the oldest art museum in Texas—is now the nation's second largest dedicated to contemporary and modern art. The permanent collection includes works by Picasso, Rothko, Warhol, Rauschenberg, and Pollock. See p. 121.

- **Amon Carter Museum of Western Art** (Fort Worth): The newly expanded Amon Carter Museum is one of the finest collections of Western and American art in the country, including the most complete group of works by Frederic Remington and Charles M. Russell, two behemoths of Western art. It also possesses a great photography collection and important paintings by Georgia O'Keeffe and others. See p. 119.

- **Menil Collection** (Houston): One of the great private collections of the world, it could very well have ended up in Paris or New York, but was graciously bestowed by the collectors on their adopted city. To experience the Menil is pure delight; very little comes between the viewer and the art, which includes works by many of the 20th-century masters, classical works from the ancients, and tribal art from around the world. See p. 175.

- **Museum of Fine Arts, Houston** (Houston): With the addition of the Audrey Jones Beck Building, the Fine Arts museum has doubled its exhibition space and has especially put its collection of Impressionist and baroque art in the best possible light. The museum also has several satellite facilities and attracts major touring exhibitions. See p. 173.

- **The Center for the Arts & Sciences** (Brazosport): One of those rare entities that does a lot of things exceptionally well, The Center includes a terrific natural history museum, a delightful small planetarium, an attractive art gallery, two theaters for a variety of performing arts events, and a nature trail. See p. 220.

- **San Antonio Museum of Art** (San Antonio): Almost as impressive for its architecture as for its holdings, this museum combines several castlelike buildings of the

1904 Lone Star Brewery. The $11 million Nelson A. Rockefeller Center for Latin American Art is the most comprehensive collection of its kind in the United States. See p. 258.

- **McDonald Observatory** (northwest of Fort Davis): McDonald Observatory is considered one the world's best astronomical research facilities, and twice a day, visitors can glimpse sunspots, flares, and other solar activity. Additionally, nighttime "Star Parties" are held 3 evenings a week, when visitors can view celestial objects and constellations through the observatory's high-powered telescopes. See p. 337.

- **Panhandle-Plains Historical Museum** (Canyon): The largest history museum in Texas, this excellent museum is anything but a dusty collection of spurs and bits. Well-thought-out, engaging, and informative, it is largely hands-on—you can sit in a Ford Mustang and listen to Buddy Holly tunes or try out a sidesaddle. There are also comprehensive exhibits on the region's history in terms of petroleum, art, transportation, Western heritage, and paleontology/geology. See p. 402.

8 The Best Shopping

- **Neiman Marcus** (Dallas): Established in 1907, Neiman Marcus is intimately identified with Big D and its shopaholics. The luxury purveyor's annual holiday catalog, with his-and-her fantasies for the rich, has become an institution. The downtown store is classy and retro-cool, the best place in North Texas to drape yourself in Prada and Chanel. See "Dallas" in chapter 4.

- **NorthPark Center** (Dallas): Dallas loves to shop, and while there are more malls than most people (except Dallasites) know what to do with, NorthPark is the most traditional and elegant with a graceful layout that outclasses its garish competitors. Besides top anchor stores (Neiman Marcus, Tiffany's) it enjoys rotating pieces from owner Ray Nasher's spectacular collection of modern sculpture, on display throughout the mall. See "Dallas" in chapter 4.

- **Maverick** (Fort Worth): If you're looking for well-made Western duds—suits and shirts with elegant piping and embroidered yokes that would have made you a star in the Old West—Maverick has some of the best. And if a certain someone is taking too darned long, easy does it. Lean on the bar and have yourself a Lone Star longneck. See "Fort Worth" in chapter 4.

- **M. L. Leddy's** (Fort Worth): This Fort Worth classic with the big boot sign out front is the western Prada of Cowtown. Does that make sense? Maybe not, but this is definitely designer cowboy—top-quality hats, hand-tooled belts, and custom-made boots. It's the traditional place for dads to take their young ropers for that all-important first pair or boots or first kiddie Stetson. See "Fort Worth" in chapter 4.

- **Uptown** (Houston): In this one, relatively small district of the city you can find Houston's Galleria (with over 300 retailers including Saks, Neiman Marcus, Tiffany's, and Versace) and four other malls fronting Post Oak (including retailers like Cartier and FAO Schwarz). See "Shopping" in chapter 5.

- **Paris Hatters** (San Antonio): Pope John Paul II, Prince Charles, Jimmy Smits, and Dwight Yoakam have all had Western headgear made for them by Paris Hatters, in business since 1917 and still owned by the same family. About half of the sales are special order, but the shelves are stocked with high-quality ready-to-wear hats, too. See "Shopping" in chapter 7.
- **Capitol Saddlery** (Austin): The custom-made boots of this classic three-level Western store near the capitol, run by the same family for 7 decades, were immortalized in a song by Jerry Jeff Walker. Come here for hand-tooled saddles, belts, tack, and altogether unyuppified cowboy gear. See "Shopping" in chapter 8.
- **Fredericksburg** (Texas Hill Country): It's hard to say how a town founded by German idealists ended up being a magnet for Texas materialists, but Fredericksburg's main street is chock-a-block with boutiques. This is the place to come for everything from natural chocolate mint–scented room deodorizer to handmade dulcimers. See "Hill Country Side Trips from Austin" in chapter 8.
- **El Paso Chile Company** (El Paso): We love this shop for its tongue-searing delicacies, with fiery names like "Hellfire & Damnation," and all things spicy. See "El Paso" in chapter 9.

9 The Best Places for Boot-Scootin'

- **Adair's Saloon** (Dallas): Deep Ellum's down 'n' dirty honky-tonk is unfazed by the new wave discos, rock clubs, and preppy SMU students in its midst. It sticks to its down-to-earth anti-style, knee-slapping country and redneck rock bands, cheap beer, and tables and walls blanketed in graffiti. See "Dallas" in chapter 4.
- **Billy Bob's Texas** (Fort Worth): Kind of like a big-tent country theme park, Billy Bob's has it all: 40 bars, a huge dance floor for two-stepping and Western swing, pro bull riding, and live performances by some of the biggest names in country music. And of course dance lessons: shuffle and two-step like a Texan after a few hours with instructor Wendell Nelson. See "Fort Worth" in chapter 4.
- **Big Balls of Cowtown** (Fort Worth): If Billy Bob's Texas is all gloss and swagger, Big Balls—how 'bout that name?—is pure sweat. The hottest roper place in town is where studs in their best hats and tightest jeans and their gals (in pretty much the same duds) come for Western Swing dancing. This is a serious honky-tonk. See "Fort Worth" in chapter 4.
- **Blanco's** (Houston): This is one of those genuine honky-tonks where you go for the music and the dancing and not for dressing up in Western duds. It's strictly come as you are, and this place attracts 'em from all walks of life, from bankers to oil field workers. It's a small venue, but gets some of the best of Texas's country music bands. See "Houston After Dark" in chapter 5.
- **Floore's Country Store** (San Antonio): Not much has changed since the 1940s when this honky-tonk, boasting the largest dance floor in South Texas (half an acre), opened up. Boots, hats, and antique farm equipment hang from the ceiling of this typical Texas roadhouse. There's always live music on weekends; Willie Nelson, Dwight Yoakam, Robert

Earl Keen, and Lyle Lovett have all played here. See "San Antonio After Dark" in chapter 7.

- **Texas Hill Country** (San Antonio and Austin): The Texas Hill Country has some of the best honky-tonks in the state. In Gruene, just outside of New Braunfels, **Gruene Hall** is the oldest country-and-western dance hall in Texas and still one of the mellowest places to listen to music. Don't miss **Arkey Blue & The Silver Dollar Bar,** a genuine spit-and-sawdust cowboy honky-tonk on the Main Street of Bandera. When there's no live music, plug a quarter in the old jukebox and play a country ballad by owner Arkey. And look for the table where Hank Williams, Sr. carved his name. See "Hill Country Side Trips" in chapter 7.
- **Broken Spoke** (Austin): This is the gen-u-ine item, a Western honky-tonk with a wood-plank floor and a cowboy-hatted, two-steppin' crowd. Still, it's in Austin, so don't be surprised if the band wears Hawaiian shirts, or if tongues are firmly in cheek for some of the songs. See "Austin After Dark" in chapter 8.
- **Midnight Rodeo** (Lubbock): This place is a great spot for two-steppin' or line dancing to live and recorded country music. See "Lubbock" in chapter 11.

10 The Best of Natural Texas

- **Dallas Arboretum & Botanical Garden:** Who knew Dallas had more than dust, concrete, steel, and glass? This surprising oasis on the edge of White Rock Lake is a great spot to duck the Texas sun. Relax on 70 acres of groomed gardens and natural woodlands, interspersed with a handful of historic homes. The gardens are especially colorful in spring and fall. See p. 83.
- **Fort Worth Botanic Garden:** A rambling, spacious showcase of 2,500 native and exotic species of plants on 100-plus acres, this is the oldest botanical garden in Texas, created back in the late 1920s. The Texas Rose Garden, 3,500 roses that bloom in late April and October, and beautiful Japanese Garden, are terrific places to hide out from the world. Bring a picnic, a book, and a flying disk. See p. 119.
- **The Big Thicket:** It has been called "the American Ark" for its incredibly rich variety of plants and wildlife, all packed into 100,000 acres of watery bottom land in deepest East Texas. You can explore the area on foot or in canoe, and see first-hand how the woods grow so thickly here that they all but blot out the sun, and make trailblazing almost impossible. See "Side Trips to East Texas" in chapter 5.
- **Aransas National Wildlife Refuge:** A mecca for birders, with some 400 species sited here, the refuge is also home to a variety of frogs and other amphibians, plus snakes, turtles, lizards, and numerous mammals. But Aransas has become famous for being the main winter home of the near-extinct whooping crane, the tallest bird in America—5 feet high with a 7-foot wingspan. See "Rockport" in chapter 6.
- **Mustang Island State Park:** This barrier island has more than 5 miles of wide, sandy beach, with fine sand, few rocks, and broken shells, and almost enough waves for surfing. The park is one of the most popular of Texas state parks,

and is especially busy on summer weekends. See "Rockport" in chapter 6.

- **The Devil's Backbone:** Much of the gently rolling Hill Country is pretty, but San Marcos is a convenient jumping-off point for one of Texas's most breathtaking drives. Take R.R. 12 West to R.R. 32 to reach the Devil's Backbone, a 15-mile, switchback-filled route with spectacular views. See "Hill Country Side Trips from Austin" in chapter 8.
- **McKittrick Canyon:** The canyon is forested with conifers and deciduous trees. In autumn the maples, oaks, and other hardwoods burst into color, painting the world in bright colors set off by the rich variety of the evergreens. See "Guadalupe Mountains National Park" in chapter 10.
- **Palo Duro Canyon State Park:** This 60-mile canyon, sculpted by the Prairie Dog Town Fork of the Red River over the last 90 million years, is a grand contrast to the ubiquitous, treeless plains of the Texas Panhandle. Its 800-foot cliffs, striped with orange, red, and white rock and adorned by groves of juniper and cottonwood trees, present an astoundingly stark beauty. See "Canyon & Palo Duro Canyon State Park" in chapter 11.

11 The Best Historical Attractions

- **The Sixth Floor Museum at Dealey Plaza** (Dallas): The events of November 22, 1963, shook the world. John F. Kennedy's assassination in Dallas is remembered by everyone old enough to remember, and argued over still. Visitors can tour the sixth floor of the Texas School Book Depository, from where the Warren Commission concluded that a single sniper, Lee Harvey Oswald, felled the president. The museum also examines the life, times, and legacy of the Kennedy presidency, making it a place to revisit not only the tragic episode but also an era. A companion must-visit for cynics is the Conspiracy Museum, whose name says it all. See p. 80.
- **The Stockyards National Historic District** (Fort Worth): Still very much looking the part, this area north of downtown was once the biggest and busiest cattle, horse, mule, hog, and sheep marketing center in the Southwest. Put on your boots and best Western shirt and tour the Livestock Exchange Building; Cowtown Coliseum (the world's first indoor rodeo arena); former hog and sheep pens now filled with Western shops and restaurants; and Billy Bob's Texas, the "world's largest honky-tonk." Then grab a longneck at the White Elephant saloon—the oldest bar in Fort Worth and the site of the city's most famous gunfight in 1897—and check in at the historic Stockyards Hotel. To enhance the experience, check out "longhorn cattle drive" that rumbles down Exchange Avenue daily—or take the 1896 Tarantula Steam Train into Grapevine. See "Fort Worth" in chapter 4.
- **San Jacinto Monument** (Houston): Here on the battlefield of San Jacinto, a small army of Texans led by General Sam Houston charged the much larger, better equipped Mexican army and dealt them a crushing blow. The victory gave Texas its independence. A monument and museum occupy the battlefield to honor and

explain the history of the battle and its significance. See p. 169.

- USS *Lexington* Museum on the Bay (Corpus Christi): Exploring this huge World War II–era aircraft carrier offers non-naval persons the opportunity to get an idea of what it was like to live for sometimes months in the claustrophobic conditions of such a limited area. In addition to sleeping, dining, and cooking areas, the ship provided a hospital, rec room, and of course numerous necessary working areas. See p. 202.
- The Alamo (San Antonio): It's smaller than you might expect, and it sits smack in the heart of downtown San Antonio, but the graceful mission church that's come to symbolize the state is a must-see, if only to learn what the fuss is all about. See p. 256.
- San Antonio Missions National Historic Park: It's impossible not to remember the Alamo when you're in San Antonio; more difficult to recall is that the Alamo was originally just the first of five missions established by the Franciscans along the San Antonio River. Exploring these four missions, built uncharacteristically close to each other, will give you a remarkable glimpse of the city's early Spanish and Indian history. See p. 258.
- State Capitol (Austin): The country's largest state capitol, second only in size to the U.S. Capitol—but 7 feet taller—underwent a massive renovation and expansion in the 1990s, which left it more impressive than ever. See p. 296.
- New Braunfels: Trying to decide which of the Hill Country towns is the most representative of the area's rich German heritage is tough, but the *gemütlich* inns, history-oriented museums, and sausage-rich restaurants—not to mention the major celebration of Oktoberfest—make New Braunfels a standout. See "Hill Country Side Trips from Austin" in chapter 8.
- El Paso Mission Trail: Established in the 17th and 18th centuries, these three historic Spanish missions provide a link to El Paso's colonial past. They are among the oldest continually active missions in the country, and warrant a visit for their architectural and historic merit. Especially impressive is the large Presidio Chapel San Elceario, near the site of "The First Thanksgiving," said to have taken place in 1598, 23 years before the Plymouth Thanksgiving. See p. 320.

12 The Best Family Adventures

- Old City Park (Dallas): Dallas is determinedly modern, with gleaming skyscrapers and a love for newness, but its Western heritage lives on museum-like in this facsimile of the Old West, a 13-acre park of historic buildings. Mounted like a late-19th-century village, it has a redbrick Main Street, Victorian homes, train depot, general store, one-room church, schoolhouse, and bank, all relocated from the Dallas area. The "Living Farmstead" re-creates a 19th-century prairie with actors in period garb. See p. 85.
- Arlington: Sandwiched between Dallas and Fort Worth is a kids' suburban dream world, where youngins can stumble from the roller coasters at Six Flags Over Texas to the water slides at Hurricane Harbor, followed by a visit to Ripley's Believe It or Not and The

Palace of Wax, topped off by paying their respects to baseball's greats at the Legends of the Game Museum at The Ballpark in Arlington. See "Arlington" in chapter 4.

- **Space Center Houston** (Houston): Always the most popular attraction in the city, NASA's Space Center Houston is a joint effort powered by NASA technology and Disney know-how. It is the epitome of interactive display and simulation that manages to fascinate both kids and parents. During your visit, you can check out what's going on at the Johnson Space Center through a tram ride and video feeds. See p. 171.

- **The Gulf Side of South Padre Island:** Fine white sand and warm water lapping at your toes—what more do you want? Although the shore is lined with hotels and condos, the beaches are public and open to everyone. See "Padre Island National Seashore" in chapter 6.

- **Six Flags Fiesta Texas** (San Antonio): Major thrill rides, a huge swimming pool shaped like Texas, and entertainment/food areas with Texas history themes— there's something for every family member at this theme park, and it's even slightly educational. See p. 260.

- **The Austin Bats:** The majority of adults and kids alike tend to finds bats a bit creepy—until they learn more about them, that is. From March to November, you can watch thousands of bats emerge in smoky clouds from under the Congress Avenue Bridge, and find out why Austinites adore the little critters. See "Seeing the Sights" in chapter 8.

- **Balmorhea State Park:** This is one of the crown jewels of the Texas state parks and also one of the smallest, at 45 acres. The main attraction is the massive, 1.75-acre swimming pool—3.5 million gallons of water at a fairly constant 74°F (23°C). Not your usual swimming pool, it's teeming with small fish and laden with rocks. But swimming, snorkeling, and scuba diving are all popular. There's also a reconstructed *cienega* (desert wetland) where you might spot native wildlife such as a Texas spiny soft-shell turtle, a blotched water snake, or a green heron. See "Small Towns of Central West Texas" in chapter 9.

13 The Best of Texas Online

- **The Handbook of Texas Online** (www.tsha.utexas.edu/handbook/online): The Handbook is an encyclopedia offering concise entries that explain who's who, what's what, and where's where in Texas. It's easy to use and has information on just about everything, from the locations of towns and counties to explanations of some of the state's legends, to biographical data on the many characters who left their mark on Texas history.

- **Texas Department of Transportation** (www.traveltex.com): The state's official tourism website is practically the only site you'll need to type in—everything else will be a link. We especially like the section that offers easily printable discount coupons, primarily for lodging and attractions.

- **Texas Outside** (www.texasoutside.com): This is a great resource for planning outdoor activities for just about anywhere in the state. It breaks Texas down into different regions and has separate pages for Texas's largest cities. You'll find maps and information on all sorts of outdoor sports, such as hiking, hunting, fishing, biking, and canoeing.

- **Dallas–Fort Worth Area Official Visitors' Website** (www.visit dallas-fortworth.com): For purely practical matters, this frighteningly bureaucratic-sounding address gives you the lowdown on area events and even allows you to download coupons good for saving a few bucks at museums, theme parks, and other local attractions.

- **MySanAntonio.com** (www. expressnews.com): The website of the city's only mainstream newspaper, the *San Antonio Express-News*, not only provides the daily news, but also links to local businesses such as dry cleaners and florists (via its Power Pages) and to movie, nightlife, and dining listings and reviews.

- **Austin 360** (www.austin360. com): Movie times, traffic reports, restaurant picks, homes, jobs, cars . . . This site, sponsored in part by the *Austin-American Statesman,* the city's main newspaper, is a one-stop clicking center for a variety of essentials. It's easy to navigate, too.

- **Texas fun:** We all know the Internet's best for purely personal and marginal interests, so check out these sites once you're done with your trip planning. Visit **www. texascooking.com** for authentic Texas cooking, including recipes and discussions of mysteries like the Texas fruitcake subculture conspiracy. Then there's **www. texascooking.com/notable.htm**: Which is the best three in a row? Morgan Fairchild, Farrah Fawcett, and Freddy Fender, or George "Spanky" McFarland of "Our Gang," Larry McMurtry, and Meat Loaf? Finally, check out **www.tded.state.tx.us/admin/ trivia.htm** for Texas trivia, including a list of some of the state's biggest and best, as well as Texas firsts.

2

Planning Your Trip to Texas

by Don & Barb Laine

As everyone knows, Texas is big, really big. For vacationers this means that there are a vast number of things to do and places to see, as well as varieties of climate, terrain, and even cultures. Depending on where you choose to go, you can have a fun Old West adventure, a relaxing (or rowdy) trip to the beach, an exploration of some of America's finest museums, or some of the best birding or fishing anywhere. This chapter gives you the information you need to get started.

1 The Regions in Brief

You can plan your trip to Texas in a couple of ways. If you're interested in a particular activity, such as birding, you might choose two or three locations and divide your time among them. Conversely, you could first select a destination, such as one of the state's major cities or national parks, and then decide what to do while you're there.

This book is organized geographically, and because this is a big state many visitors will limit their Texas vacation to one or two regions. We've summarized our coverage of the state to help you decide what kind of Texas experience you want to have.

THE DALLAS–FORT WORTH METROPLEX Made famous by a TV show about a Texas oil family and infamous by the assassination of JFK, Dallas is a center of commerce, home to headquarters for numerous banking, insurance, and other businesses. Big D, as it's known to locals, is one of the most sophisticated cities in Texas, with excellent restaurants, glitzy shopping, and swank hotels. Dallas's unpretentious sister, Fort Worth, is equal parts Old West and "Museum

Capital of the Southwest." Longhorns still rumble through the Stockyards National Historic District, while the city attracts art lovers to its top-notch museums. Both cities make good bases for outdoor recreation, children's activities, and professional sports outings; the city of Arlington, sandwiched between Dallas and Fort Worth, is home to several theme parks and the Texas Rangers baseball team.

HOUSTON & EAST TEXAS The state's largest city (and the fourth most populated city in the United States), Houston is the heart of the nation's oil and gas industry. Although not a primary tourist destination, Houston offers an abundance of attractions, including numerous museums, performing arts such as the city's excellent symphony orchestra, and a variety of outdoor activities. Here you'll find NASA's Johnson Space Center, which has made Houston famous and is the city's most popular attraction; and the Astrodome, the first of the domed sports stadiums. Nearby, Galveston combines small-town easiness with a good mix of museums and children's activities, plus its beaches. East Texas, along the Louisiana border, is a prime destination for anglers, boaters, and other outdoor recreationists.

THE TEXAS GULF COAST   Quite different from the rest of the state, this is where you find the ocean—the Gulf of Mexico—and if, as the saying goes, "Life's a Beach," this is life. In addition to the usual beach activities of swimming, sunbathing, beachcombing, boating, and even some surfing (okay, it's no Hawaii, but you *can* surf here), the Texas Gulf Coast is among the nation's top bird-watching regions, and also offers superb fishing. There are also some good museums and an active art scene.

SAN ANTONIO   One of the most popular destinations for vacationers, the delightful city of San Antonio hosts the most famous historic site in Texas: the Alamo, where in 1836 Davy Crockett and about 187 other Texas freedom fighters died at the hands of the much larger Mexican army. San Antonio also offers numerous other historic sites, a delightful River Walk, fine cultural attractions, and a madcap schedule of festivals that make it a popular party spot. West and north of the city, the Texas Hill Country is one of the prettiest areas of Texas, dotted with lakes and rivers and picturesque small towns. There are numerous historic inns, antiques stores, small museums, and opportunities for watersports and other outdoor activities.

AUSTIN   The state capital, Austin is a laid-back but sophisticated small city with a distinct personality—a little unusual, a bit intellectual, and a lot different from other Texas cities of its size. In addition to museums, historic sites, and a wide range of outdoor activities, you'll find the best nightlife in the state, with live music practically everywhere—from country to blues to rock to swing. To the west, the Hill Country is easily accessible via day trips.

WEST TEXAS   In reality Texas is an urban state, but to those of us who grew up watching TV and movie westerns, this is the real Texas, a land of dusty roads, cowboys, and cattle ranches. Although the shoot-outs are now staged and the cattle drives are by truck and rail, this region retains much of the small-town Old West flavor, and even the region's biggest city, El Paso, is in many ways just an overgrown cow town. The area's history comes alive at numerous museums and historic sites, such as the combination courtroom and saloon used in the late 1800s by Judge Roy Bean, the self-styled "Law West of the Pecos." West Texas also offers some surprises, such as 67,000-acre Lake Amistad, a national recreation area along the U.S.–Mexico border.

BIG BEND & GUADALUPE MOUNTAINS NATIONAL PARKS   Among America's lesser-visited national parks, Big Bend and Guadalupe Mountains contain rugged mountain scenery the likes of which is found nowhere else in Texas, or even in surrounding states. There are spectacular and inspiring views from dizzying peaks, and hiking, rafting, and other outdoor activities. We also include in this section a discussion of Carlsbad Caverns National Park, just over the state line in New Mexico, an easy side trip for those visiting Guadalupe Mountains National Park.

THE PANHANDLE PLAINS   A mix of terrain and experiences await visitors to this vast, rugged region that occupies the northern reaches of Texas. Here you'll find small-town charm, good museums, fascinating historic sites, and one of the most outrageous steakhouses in Texas. The main cities—actually just big towns— are Amarillo and Lubbock, and each provides comfortable lodging and

The Regions in Brief

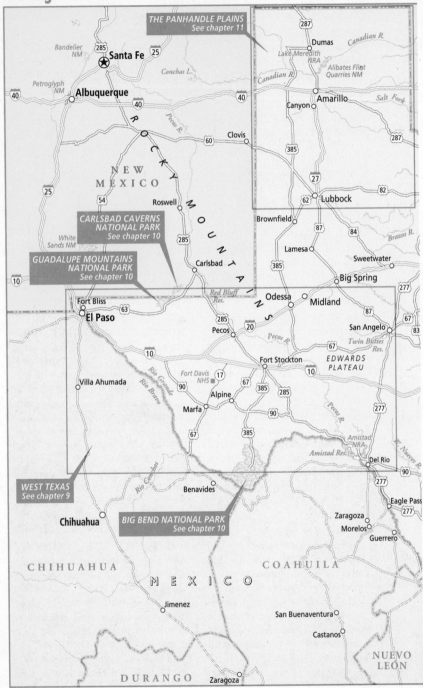

THE PANHANDLE PLAINS
See chapter 11

CARLSBAD CAVERNS
NATIONAL PARK
See chapter 10

GUADALUPE MOUNTAINS
NATIONAL PARK
See chapter 10

WEST TEXAS
See chapter 9

BIG BEND NATIONAL PARK
See chapter 10

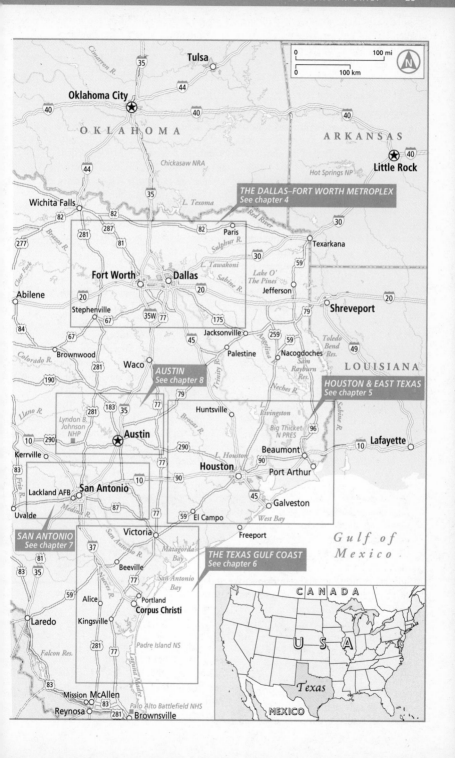

good eats. The region also offers plenty to do and see, with watersports on Lake Meredith National Recreation Area, and hiking, horseback riding, and some of the area's most spectacular scenery at Palo Duro

Canyon State Park. This is also home to a monument to rock 'n' roll pioneer Buddy Holly and a display of old Cadillacs, noses buried in the ground with their unmistakable fins pointed skyward.

2 Visitor Information

Contact the **Texas Department of Transportation,** Travel Division, P.O. Box 141009, Austin, TX 78714-1009 (© **800/888-8TEX;** www.traveltex. com), for a free copy of the official state vacation guide, which includes a state map and describes attractions, activities, and lodgings throughout Texas. The Texas Department of Transportation also publishes the *Texas Accommodations Guide,* which is usually sent along with the official state vacation guide, or can be ordered separately by calling © **800/452-9292.**

The nonprofit **Historic Accommodations of Texas** (© **800/428-0368;** www.hat.org) offers a free directory describing well over 100 member bed-and-breakfasts, country inns, unique hotels, and guesthouses. You can also get lodging information from the **Texas Hotel & Motel Association** (© **512/474-2996;** www.texaslodging. com).

The Texas Department of Transportation maintains a dozen excellent **Texas Travel Information Centers** around the state, offering free maps, brochures, and one-on-one travel counseling. Locations are as follows: **Amarillo,** I-40 East; **Anthony,** I-10 at the New Mexico state line; **Austin,** 112 E. 11th St., at the Capitol Complex; **Denison,** U.S. 75 at the Oklahoma state line; **Gainesville,** I-35 at the Oklahoma state line; **Harlingen,** U.S. 77 at U.S. 83; **Langtry,** off U.S. 90 on Tex. Loop 25; **Laredo,** I-35 North at U.S. 83; **Orange,** I-10 at the Louisiana state line; **Texarkana,** I-30 at the Arkansas state line; **Waskom,** I-20 at the Louisiana state line; and **Wichita Falls,** I-44 at U.S. 277/281. The centers are open daily from 8am to 5pm except on January 1, Easter Sunday, Thanksgiving Day, and December 24 and 25. For information, call © **800/452-9292.**

3 Money

Generally, Texas is not particularly expensive, especially compared to destinations on the East and West coasts. You'll find a wide range of prices for lodging and dining, and admission to most attractions is less than $10 (it's sometimes free, especially in the smaller towns). Prices in Dallas, Houston, and other major cities are mostly on a par with other Southwestern cities, such as Albuquerque and Phoenix. Those traveling away from the cities will discover prices in small towns usually quite reasonable, but resort areas such as Corpus Christi can

be a bit more expensive, especially during winter holidays. Traveler's checks and credit cards are accepted at almost all hotels, restaurants, shops, and attractions, plus many grocery stores; and ATMs are practically everywhere.

ATMS

The easiest and best way to get cash away from home is from an ATM (automated teller machine). The **Cirrus** (© **800/424-7787;** www.master card.com) and **PLUS** (© **800/843-7587;** www.visa.com) networks span the globe; look at the back of your bank card to see which network you're on, then call or check online for ATM locations in your destination. Be sure you know your personal identification number (PIN) before you leave home and be sure to find out your daily withdrawal limit before you depart. Also keep in mind that many banks impose a fee every time a card is used at a different bank's ATM. On top of this, the bank from which you withdraw cash may charge its own fee. To compare banks' ATM fees within the U.S., use www.bankrate.com.

TRAVELER'S CHECKS

Traveler's checks are something of an anachronism from the days before the ATM made cash accessible at any time. Traveler's checks used to be the only sound alternative to traveling with dangerously large amounts of cash. They were as reliable as currency, but, unlike cash, could be replaced if lost or stolen.

These days, traveler's checks are less necessary because most cities have 24-hour ATMs that allow you to withdraw small amounts of cash as needed. However, keep in mind that you will likely be charged an ATM withdrawal fee if the bank is not your own, so if you're withdrawing money every day, you might be better off with traveler's checks—provided that you don't mind showing identification every time you want to cash one.

You can get traveler's checks at almost any bank. **American Express** offers denominations of $20, $50, $100, $500, and (for cardholders only) $1,000. You'll pay a service charge ranging from 1% to 4%. You can also get American Express traveler's checks over the phone by calling ✆ **800/221-7282;** Amex gold and platinum cardholders who use this number are exempt from the 1% fee. AAA members can obtain checks without a fee at most AAA offices.

Visa offers traveler's checks at Citibank locations nationwide, as well as at several other banks. The service charge ranges between 1.5% and 2%; checks come in denominations of $20, $50, $100, $500, and $1,000. Call ✆ **800/732-1322** for information. **MasterCard** also offers traveler's checks. Call ✆ **800/223-9920** for a location near you.

CREDIT CARDS

Credit cards are invaluable when traveling. They are a safe way to carry money and provide a convenient record of all your expenses. Visa and MasterCard are the most widely accepted credit cards in Texas, followed by American Express and Discover.

You can also withdraw cash advances from your credit cards at any bank (though you'll start paying hefty interest on the advance the moment you receive the cash). At most banks, you don't even need to go to a teller; you can get a cash advance at the ATM if you know your personal identification number (PIN). If you've forgotten yours, or didn't even know you had one, call the number on the back of your credit card and ask the bank to send it to you. It usually takes 5 to 7 business days.

4 When to Go

As would be expected in a state as big as Texas, climate varies, sometimes considerably, by location; it can be snowing in one area of the state, such as Amarillo, while people are swimming at South Padre Island. High temperatures in the summer average in the 90s almost statewide, while average winter temperatures drop as you travel north. In addition, southern Texas is known for its muggy summers, which make it feel hotter than it really is, and which contrasts with the dryness of the West Texas deserts. The state's few mountainous areas have more extremes of temperatures, hitting the 80s and 90s during the day only to plunge into the 30s and 40s at night. All areas of Texas get more sunshine than most other parts of the United States.

The beaches along the Gulf Coast are busiest in winter, although they're seldom really crowded. But unless you're a college kid looking for some rowdy spring break action, you should avoid all resort areas, including the beaches and national parks, during March and early April.

Average Monthly High/Low Temperatures & Precipitation

	Jan	Feb	Mar	Apr	May	June	July	Aug	Sept	Oct	Nov	Dec
Dallas												
Temp. (°F)	54/33	59/37	68/46	76/55	83/63	92/70	97/74	96/74	88/67	79/56	67/45	58/36
Temp. (°C)	12/0	15/3	20/8	24/13	28/17	33/21	36/23	36/23	31/19	26/13	19/7	14/2
Precip. (in.)	1.6	1.9	2.4	3.1	4.3	2.4	1.7	1.8	2.9	2.8	2.0	1.5
Houston												
Temp. (°F)	62/43	65/45	75/53	79/61	85/67	90/73	92/75	92/75	88/71	81/61	72/53	65/45
Temp. (°C)	17/6	18/7	24/12	26/16	29/19	32/23	33/24	33/24	31/22	27/16	22/12	18/7
Precip. (in.)	3.2	2.8	2.4	2.5	4.4	5.3	3.9	3.8	4.9	3.4	3.6	3.0
San Antonio												
Temp. (°F)	61/38	66/41	74/50	80/58	85/66	92/73	95/75	95/74	89/69	82/59	72/49	63/41
Temp. (°C)	16/3	19/5	23/10	27/14	29/19	33/23	35/24	35/23	32/21	28/15	22/9	17/5
Precip. (in.)	1.2	1.5	1.2	2.0	3.5	3.0	1.2	1.8	2.6	2.6	2.3	1.0
Corpus Christi												
Temp. (°F)	65/45	69/48	76/55	82/63	86/69	90/73	93/75	93/75	90/72	84/64	76/56	68/48
Temp. (°C)	18/7	21/9	24/13	28/17	30/21	32/23	34/24	34/24	32/22	29/18	24/13	20/9
Precip. (in.)	1.7	2.0	0.9	1.7	3.3	3.4	2.4	3.3	5.5	3.0	1.6	1.3
Amarillo												
Temp. (°F)	49/21	53/26	62/33	72/43	79/52	88/61	92/66	89/64	82/56	73/45	60/32	50/24
Temp. (°C)	9/–6	12/–3	17/1	22/6	26/11	31/16	33/19	32/18	28/13	23/7	16/0	10/–4
Precip. (in.)	0.3	0.5	0.7	0.8	2.2	3.2	2.3	2.9	1.7	1.2	0.5	0.3

TEXAS CALENDAR OF EVENTS

January

- **Southwestern Bell Cotton Bowl Classic (& Parade),** Dallas. The annual college football bowl game, somewhat less prestigious than it once was, but still important in pigskin circles. Call ☎ 214/634-7525. January 1.

- **River Walk Mud Festival,** San Antonio. Each year, the horseshoe bend of the San Antonio River Walk is drained for maintenance, and San Antonians cheer up by electing a king and queen to reign over such events as Mud Stunts

Day and the Mud Pie Ball. Call ☎ 210/227-4262. Mid-January.

- **Super Bull,** Amarillo. Don't come expecting football—this is a bull-riding event at the Amarillo Civic Center. Call ☎ 800/692-1338 or 806/376-7767. Mid-January.

- **Southwestern Exposition and Livestock Show and Rodeo,** Fort Worth. Fort Worth's famous rodeo and livestock show is the nation's oldest, drawing nearly a million people to Will Rogers Memorial Center for 30 rodeo performances. It's kicked off by the All-Western Parade, the biggest horse-drawn parade in the world. Call ✆ **817/877-2400.** Mid-January to early February.

February

- **Stock Show and Rodeo,** San Antonio. San Antonio hosts more than 2 weeks of rodeo events, livestock judging, country-and-western bands, and carnivals at the SBC Center. Call ✆ **210/225-5851.** Early February.
- **Houston Livestock Show and Rodeo,** Houston. Billed as the largest event of its kind, the Rodeo includes all the usual events like bull riding and calf roping, plus performances by famous country-and-western artists. A parade downtown kicks off the celebration. Call ✆ **713/791-9000.** Mid-February.
- **Mardi Gras,** Galveston. The city's biggest party of the year, with parades, masked balls, and a live-entertainment district around the Strand. Call ✆ **888/425-4753.** Late February to early March.

March

- **South by Southwest,** Austin. The Austin Music Awards kick off this huge conference, with hundreds of concerts at more than two dozen city venues. Keynote speakers have included Johnny Cash. Call ✆ **512/467-7979.** Mid-March (during spring break at the University of Texas).
- **Dyeing O' The River Green and Pub Crawl,** San Antonio. Are leprechauns responsible for turning the San Antonio River into the green River Shannon? Irish dance and music fill the Arneson River Theatre from the afternoon on. Call ✆ **210/227-4262.** March 17.

April

- **Texas Hill Country Wine and Food Festival,** Austin. Book a month in advance for the cooking demonstrations; beer, wine, and food tastings; and celebrity chef dinners. For the food fair, just turn up hungry. Call ✆ **512/329-0770.** First weekend after Easter.
- **International Festival,** Houston. This festival highlights the culture, food, music, and heritage of a different country every year. Call ✆ **713/926-6368.** Last 2 weekends in April.
- **San Jacinto Festival and Texas History Day,** West Columbia. Highlights include a parade, talent show, arts and crafts show, and barbecue cook-off. The talent show, where you never know what's going to happen next, is the fun part. Call ✆ **800/938-4853** or 979/265-2508 or visit www. westcolumbiachamber.org. Mid-April.
- **Fiesta San Antonio,** San Antonio. What started as a modest marking of Texas's independence more than 100 years ago is now a huge event, with an elaborately costumed royal court presiding over 10 days of revelry: parades, balls, food fests, sporting events, concerts, and art shows all over town. Call ✆ **877/SA-FIESTA** or 210/227-5191. Mid- to late April.

May

- **Art Car Parade and Ball,** Houston. The parade of decorated cars is marvelous and hilarious and attracts participants from around the country. The ball—held in a large downtown parking garage—is guaranteed to be a spirited event. Call ✆ **713/926-6368.** Second weekend in May.
- **Tejano Conjunto Festival,** San Antonio. This festival celebrates the lively and unique blend of Mexican and German music born in south Texas. The best *conjunto* musicians perform at the largest event of its kind in the world. Call ✆ **210/271-3151.** Mid-May.

- **Return of the Chili Queens,** San Antonio. An annual tribute to chili, said to have originated in San Antonio, with music, dancing, crafts demonstrations, and, of course, chili aplenty. Bring the Tums. Call © **210/207-8600.** Memorial Day weekend.
- **Van Cliburn International Piano Competition,** Fort Worth. A prestigious competition, named for Fort Worth native and esteemed pianist Van Cliburn, which draws top classical pianists from around the world. Call © **817/738-6536.** Late May to early June (every 4 years, with the next one in 2005).

June

- **American Institute of Architects Sandcastle Competition,** Galveston. More than 80 architectural and engineering firms from around the state build sand castles and sand sculptures, taking this pastime to new heights. Call © **713/520-0155.** Early June.
- **Juneteenth Festival,** statewide. News of the Emancipation Proclamation didn't reach Texas until June 19, 1865—nearly 3 years after Lincoln signed it. This day is celebrated with blues, jazz, and gospel music, family reunions, and a variety of events. Houston has a major celebration; call © **713/284-8352** for more information. Weekend nearest June 19.

July

- **Gran Fiesta de Fort Worth,** Fort Worth. An outdoor festival celebrating Texas's Hispanic culture with Latin music, art, food, and parades. Call © **214/855-1881.** Third week in July.
- **Great Texas Mosquito Festival,** Clute. A joyous celebration to divert everyone from the annoying pest. See "The Great Texas

Mosquito Festival" sidebar on p. 221 for details. Call © **800/938-4853** or 979/265-2508. Late July.
- **Miss Texas USA Pageant,** Lubbock. This annual beauty contest takes place at Lubbock Municipal Coliseum and area hotels. Call © **800/692-4035** or 806/747-5232. Last week in July.

August

- *Austin Chronicle* **Hot Sauce Festival,** Austin. The largest hot sauce contest in the world features more than 300 salsa entries, judged by celebrity chefs and food editors. The music at this super party is hot, too. Call © **512/454-5766.** Last Sunday in August.

September

- **Fiestas Patrias,** Houston. One of the largest community-sponsored parades in the Southwest celebrating Mexico's independence from Spain. Houston's several *ballet folklórico* troupes twirl their way through downtown streets in a pageantry of color and traditional Mexican music. Call © **713/926-2636.** Mid-September (around the 16th).
- **Marfa Lights Festival,** Marfa. Celebration of the lights that inexplicably appear on the horizon just east of town. Expect street dances, live music, parades, and lots of food. Call © **800/650-9696** or 915/729-4942. Labor Day weekend.
- **Grapefest,** Fort Worth. Yes, Texas makes wine—some of it quite good. It flows freely at this, one of the country's biggest wine festivals. There's also live music and other entertainment. Call © **817/410-3185.** Early September.
- **Pioneer Days,** Fort Worth. A festival commemorating Fort Worth's early pioneer and cattle

rancher heritage with country music, rodeos, and Wild West shows. Call ℂ **817/336-8791** or 817/625-7005. Mid-September.

- **Bayfest!,** Corpus Christi. This huge festival fills Shoreline Drive from I-37 down to Bayfront Park with music, games, food, arts and crafts, and fireworks over the bay. Call ℂ **800/678-6232** or 361/881-1888. Late September.

- **State Fair of Texas,** Dallas. The nation's biggest state fair, held at the fairgrounds built in 1936 in grand Art Deco style. Call ℂ **214/565-9931.** Late September to third week of October.

October

- **Wings Over Houston Airshow,** Houston. This thrilling event usually features displays of current military aircraft and performances of aerial acrobatics. Call ℂ **281/531-9461.** Mid-October.

- **Commemorative Air Force Annual AirSho,** Midland. Come see vintage aircraft on display and strutting their stuff in flight. Call ℂ **800/624-6435** or 915/683-3381. First weekend in October.

- **Texas Jazz Festival,** Corpus Christi. This free and popular festival attracts hundreds of big-name musicians from across the United States. Call ℂ **800/678-6232** or 361/881-1888. Mid- to late October.

- **Halloween,** Austin. A hundred thousand costumed revelers take over 7 blocks of historic Sixth Street. Call ℂ **800/926-2282.** October 31.

November

- **South Padre Island Kite Festival,** South Padre Island. What could be more fun than flying a kite above blue waters? Or prettier to watch? For all those still young at heart. Call ℂ **800/678-6232** or 361/881-1888. Early November.

- **Lighting Ceremony and River Walk Holiday Parade,** San Antonio. Trees and bridges along the river are illuminated by some 80,000 lights, and Santa Claus arrives on a boat during this floating river parade. Call ℂ **210/227-4262.** Friday after Thanksgiving.

December

- **Christmas in the Stockyards,** Fort Worth. Cowtown's classic Old West corner is lit up even more than usual for holiday shopping and caroling with a Texas accent. Call ℂ **817/626-7921.** Throughout December.

- **Fiestas Navideñas,** San Antonio. The Mexican market hosts piñata parties, a blessing of the animals, and surprise visits from Pancho Claus. Call ℂ **210/207-8600.** Weekends in December.

- **Zilker Park Tree Lighting,** Austin. The lighting of a magnificent 165-foot tree is followed by the Trail of Lights, a mile-long display of life-size holiday scenes. Call ℂ **512/499-6700.** Sundays through December 24.

- **Harbor Lights Celebration,** Corpus Christi. The harbor is decked out for the holidays. There's an illuminated boat parade, fireworks, entertainment, and a visit from Santa Claus. Call ℂ **800/678-6232** or 361/881-1888. First weekend in December.

- **Dickens on The Strand,** Galveston. This street party in the historic district of the city features revelers dressed up in Victorian costume. There are parades, performers, street vendors, and lots of entertainment. Call ℂ **409/765-7834.** First weekend in December.

- **Las Posadas,** San Antonio. Children carrying candles lead a procession along the river, reenacting the search for lodging in a moving multifaith rendition of the Christmas story. Call

© **210/224-6163.** Second Sunday in December.

5 Insurance, Health & Safety

TRAVEL INSURANCE AT A GLANCE

Check your existing insurance policies before you buy travel insurance to cover trip cancellation, lost luggage, medical expenses, or car-rental insurance. You're likely to have partial or complete coverage. But if you need some, ask your travel agent about a comprehensive package. The cost of travel insurance varies widely, depending on the cost and length of your trip, your age and health, and the type of trip you're taking. Insurance for extreme sports or adventure travel, for example, will cost more than coverage for a cruise. Some insurers provide packages for specialty vacations, such as skiing or backpacking. More dangerous activities may be excluded from basic policies.

And keep in mind that in the aftermath of the September 11, 2001, terrorist attacks, a number of airlines, cruise lines, and tour operators are no longer covered by insurers. *The bottom line:* Always, always check the fine print before you sign on; more and more policies have built-in exclusions and restrictions that may leave you out in the cold if something does go awry.

For information, contact one of the following popular insurers:

- **Access America** (*©* 866/807-3982; www.accessamerica.com)
- **Travel Guard International** (*©* 800/826-4919; www.travelguard.com)
- **Travel Insured International** (*©* 800/243-3174; www.travelinsured.com)
- **Travelex Insurance Services** (*©* 888/457-4902; www.travelexinsurance.com)

THE HEALTHY TRAVELER

Vacationers in Texas generally need take no extra health precautions than they would at home. It is worth noting, however, that those hiking in the drier parts of the state, such as in the deserts of West Texas or the mountains of Big Bend and Guadalupe Mountains National Parks, should carry more water than they think they will need, and drink it.

When heading into the great outdoors, keep in mind that Texas has a large number of poisonous snakes and insects, and you should be very careful where you put your hands and feet. If you're hiking, stick to designated hiking areas, stay on established trails, and carry rain gear. When boating, be sure to wear a life jacket.

WHAT TO DO IF YOU GET SICK AWAY FROM HOME

If you worry about getting sick away from home, consider purchasing **medical travel insurance** and carry your ID card in your purse or wallet. Most health insurance policies cover you if you get sick away from home—but check, particularly if you're insured by an HMO. If you require additional insurance, try **MEDEX International** (*©* 888/MEDEX-00 or 410/453-6300; www.medexassist.com) or **Travel Assistance International** (*©* 800/821-2828; www.travelassistance.com).

The cost of travel medical insurance varies widely. Check your existing policies before you buy additional coverage. Also, check to see if your medical insurance covers you for emergency medical evacuation: If you have to buy a one-way same-day ticket home and forfeit your nonrefundable round-trip ticket, you may be out big bucks.

If you suffer from a chronic illness, consult your doctor before your departure. For conditions like epilepsy, diabetes, or heart problems, wear a **Medic Alert Identification Tag** (© 800/825-3785; www.medic alert.org), which will immediately alert doctors to your condition and give them access to your records through Medic Alert's 24-hour hot line.

Pack **prescription medications** in your carry-on luggage, and carry prescription medications in their original containers. Also bring along copies of your prescriptions in case you lose your pills or run out. Don't forget sunglasses and an extra pair of contact lenses or prescription glasses.

If you get sick, consider asking your hotel concierge to recommend a local doctor—even his or her own. You can also try the emergency room at a local hospital; many have walk-in clinics for emergency cases that are not life-threatening. You may not get immediate attention, but you won't pay the high price of an emergency room visit (usually a minimum of $300 just for signing your name).

THE SAFE TRAVELER

Most areas of Texas are as safe as any other part of the U.S.; in fact, residents of many of Texas's small towns never lock their doors. However, drug smuggling is common along the U.S.–Mexico border. To protect yourself from stumbling into a drug transaction or police raid, avoid hiking alone in isolated areas along the border and stay in the major tourist areas in border towns.

DEALING WITH DISCRIMINATION

Texas has a history of race-related incidents (like the 1998 murder of James Byrd Jr. in Jasper, Texas), but travelers of color will likely encounter few (if any) problems. African-American travelers might want to be cautious when traveling through the small towns of East Texas; see "Race Relations in East Texas" on p. 194. Also, around border towns, travelers of Hispanic descent or appearance may find that they are stopped by the border patrol more frequently than non-Hispanics, so be sure to carry a current, government-issued picture ID.

6 Tips for Travelers with Special Needs

TRAVELERS WITH DISABILITIES

Travelers with physical disabilities should find Texas relatively easy to explore. Although some older hotels and restaurants might not be wheelchair-accessible, newer properties, plus most major parks and historical monuments, are. To be on the safe side, call ahead to make sure facilities are suitable.

The U.S. National Park Service offers a **Golden Access Passport** that gives free lifetime entrance to U.S. national parks and other properties operated by the National Park Service for persons who are blind or permanently disabled, regardless of age. You can pick up a Golden Access Passport at any NPS entrance fee area by showing proof of medically determined disability and eligibility for receiving benefits under federal law. Besides free entry, the Golden Access Passport also offers a 50% discount on federal use fees charged for such facilities as camping, swimming, parking, boat launching, and tours. For more information, check www.nps.gov/fees_passes.htm or call © **888/GO-PARKS.**

The **Society for Accessible Travel and Hospitality** (© **212/447-7284;** www.sath.org) offers a wealth of travel resources for all types of disabilities and informed recommendations on destinations, access guides, travel agents, tour operators, vehicle rentals, and companion services. Annual membership costs $45 for adults; $30 for seniors and students. **The American Foundation for the Blind** (© 800/232-5463; www.afb.org) provides information on traveling with Seeing Eye dogs.

Mobility International USA (© 541/343-1284; www.miusa.org) publishes *A World of Options,* a 658-page book of resources for travelers with disabilities, and a biannual newsletter, *Over the Rainbow.* Annual membership is $35. *Open World for Disability and Mature Travel* magazine, published by the Society for Accessible Travel and Hospitality (see above), is full of good resources and information. A year's subscription is $13 ($21 outside the U.S.).

GAY & LESBIAN TRAVELERS

Texas is one of only four states (the others are Missouri, Kansas, and Oklahoma) that criminalize homosexual activity, with an anti-sodomy law that dates to the late 1800s. That law is occasionally enforced (two Houston men were arrested in 1998, spent a day in jail and paid fines), but a homosexual rights group is working to have the law overturned.

However, despite the official policy, most gay and lesbian travelers will find they are treated just like any other visitors to Texas, as Texans generally have a "live and let live" attitude. There are vibrant gay and lesbian communities in all of the larger cities, particularly Austin and Houston. A gay and lesbian–oriented weekly newspaper, *Texas Triangle* (© 877/903-8407 or 512/476-0576; www.txtriangle.com) is available at newsstands with state and national news, features, nightlife listings, a calendar of events, and classified ads. Information is also available from the **Lesbian/Gay Rights Lobby of Texas,** P.O. Box 2340, Austin, TX 78768 (© 512/474-5475; www.lgrl. org).

The International Gay & Lesbian Travel Association (IGLTA) (© 800/ 448-8550 or 954/776-2626; www. iglta.org) links travelers up with gay-friendly hoteliers, tour operators, and airline and cruise-line representatives. It offers monthly newsletters, marketing mailings, and a membership directory that's updated once a year. Membership is $200 yearly, plus a $100 administration fee for new members.

SENIOR TRAVEL

Mention the fact that you're a senior when you first make your travel reservations. All major airlines offer discounts for seniors; they also offer coupons for domestic travel for seniors over 60 years old. Typically, a book of four coupons costs less than $700, which means you can fly anywhere in the continental U.S. for under $350 round-trip. Many Texas hotels and motels offer discounts to seniors (especially if you're carrying an AARP card; see below), and an increasing number of restaurants, attractions, and public transportation systems do so as well.

Members of **AARP** (© 800/424-3410 or 202/434-2277; www.aarp. org) get discounts on hotels, airfares, and car rentals. AARP offers members a wide range of benefits, including a magazine and a newsletter. Anyone over 50 can join.

The Alliance for Retired Americans (© 888/373-6497; www.retired americans.org) offers a newsletter six times a year and discounts on hotels and car rentals; annual dues are $10 per person or couple. *Note:* Members of the former National Council of Senior Citizens receive automatic membership in the Alliance.

The **U.S. National Park Service** offers a **Golden Age Passport** that gives seniors 62 years or older lifetime entrance to properties managed by the National Park Service for a one-time processing fee of $10, which must be paid in person at any NPS facility that charges an entrance fee. Besides free entry, a Golden Age Passport also offers a 50% discount on federal use fees charged for such facilities as camping, swimming, parking, boat launching, and tours. For more information, click onto www.nps.gov/fees_passes.htm or call © 888/GO-PARKS.

Elderhostel (© 877/426-8056; www.elderhostel.org) offers several dozen programs throughout Texas, ranging from 4 to 12 days each (most are 6 days), on subjects and activities including birding, fishing, art, nature, and the state's history.

FAMILY TRAVEL

Texas is a family-friendly state, with lots of things for all ages to enjoy. Throughout this book you'll find numerous attractions, lodgings, and even restaurants that are especially well suited to kids. These include places such as the Dallas Zoo, Six Flags Over Texas in Arlington, the Children's Museum of Houston, and the Zilker Zephyr Miniature Trail in Austin. Look for the "Especially for Kids" sections in the city chapters. Additionally, state and national parks are great places for family vacations, and the national parks usually have excellent children's programs (be sure to ask about Junior Ranger programs).

One source of information on family travel is *How to Take Great Trips with Your Kids* (The Harvard Common Press), which is full of good general advice. Online, **Family Travel Network** (www.familytravelnetwork.com) offers travel tips and reviews of family-friendly destinations, vacation deals, and thoughtful features such as "Family Road Trips Made Simple" and "Kid-Style Camping."

STUDENT TRAVEL

The top spots for college students heading to Texas for spring break are **South Padre Island** for sun and fun and **Big Bend National Park** for serious hiking, but any of the beach areas and parks are popular.

For inexpensive accommodations in Austin, San Antonio, and Galveston, as well as the opportunity to meet other traveling students, join **Hostelling International** (© 202/783-6161; www.hiayh.org). A year's membership is free for those under 18, $28 for those ages 18 to 54. Other membership perks include discounts on car rentals, restaurants, and attractions and free basic travel insurance.

One of the best sources for information and bookings of discounted airfares and lodgings is **STA Travel** (© 800/781-4040; www.statravel.com). STA has offices in Houston, Dallas, and Austin.

TRAVELING WITH PETS

Many of us wouldn't dream of going on vacation without our pets. Under the right circumstances, bringing your pet along can be a wonderful experience for both you and your animals, and dogs and cats are accepted at many motels around the state. Throughout this book, we've noted the lodgings that accept pets. Some properties require you to pay a fee or damage deposit in advance, and most insist they be notified at check-in that you have a pet.

Be aware, however, that national parks and monuments and other federal lands administered by the National Park Service are not pet-friendly. Dogs are generally prohibited on hiking trails, must always be leashed, and in some cases cannot be taken more than 100 feet from established roads. On the other hand, U.S. Forest Service and Bureau of Land Management (BLM) areas, as well as many state parks, are pro-pet, allowing dogs on trails and just about everywhere except inside buildings. State parks require that dogs be leashed; regulations in national forests and BLM lands are generally looser.

Aside from regulations, though, you need to be concerned with your pet's well-being. Just as people need extra water in the desert, so do pets. We especially like those clever little no-spill pet water bowls available in pet stores (or online at www.vetvax. com). Also keep in mind that many trails are rough, and jagged rocks can cut the pads on your dog's feet. One final note: Never leave a dog or cat inside a closed car parked in the sun. The car heats up more quickly than you'd think—so don't do it, even for a minute.

7 Planning Your Trip Online

SURFING FOR AIRFARES

The "big three" online travel agencies, **Expedia.com**, **Travelocity.com**, and **Orbitz.com** sell most of the air tickets bought on the Internet. (Canadian travelers should try Expedia.ca and Travelocity.ca; U.K. residents can go for Expedia.co.uk and Opodo.co.uk.) Each has different business deals with the airlines and may offer different fares on the same flights, so it's wise to shop around. Expedia and Travelocity will also send you **e-mail notification** when a cheap fare becomes available to your favorite destination. Of the smaller travel agency websites, **SideStep** (www.sidestep.com) has gotten the best reviews from Frommer's authors. It's a browser add-on that purports to "search 140 sites at once," but in reality only beats competitors' fares as often as other sites do.

Also remember to check **airline websites**, especially those for low-fare carriers such as Southwest, JetBlue, or AirTran, whose fares are often misreported or simply missing from travel agency websites. Even with major airlines, you can often shave a few bucks from a fare by booking directly through the airline and avoiding a travel agency's transaction fee. But you'll get these discounts only by **booking online:** Most airlines now offer online-only fares that even their phone agents know nothing about. For the websites of airlines that fly to and from your destination, go to "Getting There," later in this chapter.

Great **last-minute deals** are available through free weekly e-mail services provided directly by the airlines. Most of these are announced on Tuesday or Wednesday and must be purchased online. Most are only valid for travel that weekend, but some (such as Southwest's) can be booked weeks or months in advance. Sign up for weekly e-mail alerts at airline websites or check mega-sites that compile comprehensive lists of last-minute specials, such as **Smarter Living** (www.smarter living.com). For last-minute trips, **Site59.com** (www.site59.com) in the U.S. and **lastminute.com** in Europe often have better deals than the major-label sites.

If you're willing to give up some control over your flight details, use an **opaque fare service** like **Priceline** (www.priceline.com; www.priceline. co.uk for Europeans) or **Hotwire** (www.hotwire.com). Both offer rock-bottom prices in exchange for travel on a "mystery airline" at a mysterious time of day, often with a mysterious change of planes enroute. The mystery airlines are all major, well-known carriers, and the airlines' routing computers have gotten a lot better than they used to be. But your chances of getting a 6am or 11pm flight are pretty high. Hotwire tells you flight prices before you buy; Priceline usually has

Frommers.com: The Complete Travel Resource

For an excellent travel-planning resource, we highly recommend Frommers.com (www.frommers.com). We're a little biased, of course, but we guarantee that you'll find the travel tips, reviews, monthly vacation giveaways, and online-booking capabilities thoroughly indispensable. Among the special features are our popular **Message Boards,** where Frommer's readers post queries and share advice (sometimes even our authors show up to answer questions); **Frommers.com Newsletter,** for the latest travel bargains and insider travel secrets; and **Frommer's Destinations Section,** where you'll get expert travel tips, hotel and dining recommendations, and advice on the sights to see for more than 3,000 destinations around the globe. When your research is done, the **Online Reservations System** (www.frommers.com/book_a_trip) takes you to Frommer's preferred online partners for booking your vacation at affordable prices.

better deals than Hotwire, but you have to play their "name our price" game. If you're new at this, the helpful folks at **BiddingForTravel** (www.biddingfortravel.com) do a good job of demystifying Priceline's prices. Priceline and Hotwire are great for flights within North America and between the U.S. and Europe. But for flights to other parts of the world, consolidators will almost always beat their fares.

For much more about airfares and savvy air-travel tips and advice, pick up a copy of *Frommer's Fly Safe, Fly Smart* (Wiley Publishing).

SURFING FOR HOTELS

Shopping online for hotels is much easier in the U.S., Canada, and certain parts of Europe than it is in the rest of the world. Also, many smaller hotels and B&Bs don't show up on websites at all. Of the "big three" sites, **Expedia** may be the best choice, thanks to its long list of special deals. **Travelocity** runs a close second. Hotel specialist

sites **hotels.com** and **hoteldiscounts.com** are also reliable. An excellent free program, **TravelAxe** (www.travelaxe.net), can help you search multiple hotel sites at once, even ones you may never have heard of.

Priceline and Hotwire are even better for hotels than for airfares; with both, you're allowed to pick the neighborhood and quality level of your hotel before offering up your money. *Note:* Hotwire overrates its hotels by one star—what Hotwire calls a four-star is a three-star anywhere else.

SURFING FOR RENTAL CARS

For booking rental cars online, the best deals are usually found at rental-car company websites, although all the major online travel agencies also offer rental-car reservations services. Priceline and Hotwire work well for rental cars, too; the only "mystery" is which major rental company you get, and for most travelers the difference between Hertz, Avis, and Budget is negligible.

8 The 21st-Century Traveler

INTERNET ACCESS AWAY FROM HOME

Travelers have any number of ways to check their e-mail and access the

Internet on the road. Of course, using your own laptop—or even a PDA (personal desk assistant) or electronic organizer with a modem—gives you the most flexibility. But even if you don't have a computer, you can still access your e-mail and even your office computer from cybercafes.

WITHOUT YOUR OWN COMPUTER

It's hard nowadays to find a city that *doesn't* have a few cybercafes. Although there's no definitive directory for cybercafes—these are independent businesses, after all—three places to start looking are at **www.cybercap tive.com**, **www.netcafeguide.com**, and **www.cybercafe.com**.

Aside from formal cybercafes, most **public libraries** across the world offer Internet access free or for a small charge. You can also log on in **hotel business centers,** though they sometimes charge exorbitant rates. Most **hostels** nowadays have at least one computer with Internet access.

Most major airports now have **Internet kiosks** scattered throughout their gates. These kiosks, which you'll also see in shopping malls, hotel lobbies, and tourist information offices around the world, give you basic web access for a per-minute fee that's usually higher than cybercafe prices. The kiosks' clunkiness and high price means they should be avoided whenever possible.

To retrieve your e-mail, ask your **Internet Service Provider (ISP)** if it has a web-based interface tied to your existing e-mail account. If your ISP doesn't have such an interface, you can use the free **mail2web** service (www.mail2web.com) to view (but not reply to) your home e-mail. For more flexibility, you may want to open a free, Web-based e-mail account with **Yahoo! Mail** (http://mail.yahoo.com) or **Fastmail** (www.fastmail.fm). (Microsoft's Hotmail is another popular option, but Hotmail has severe spam problems.) Your home ISP may be able to forward your e-mail to the Web-based account automatically.

If you need to access files on your office computer, look into a service called **GoToMyPC** (www.gotomypc.com). The service provides a Web-based interface for you to access and manipulate a distant PC from anywhere—even a cybercafe—provided your "target" PC is on and has an always-on connection to the Internet (such as with Road Runner cable). The service offers top-quality security, but if you're worried about hackers, use your own laptop rather than a cybercafe to access the GoToMyPC system.

WITH YOUR OWN COMPUTER

Major Internet Service Providers (ISP) have **local access numbers** around the world, allowing you to go online by simply placing a local call. Check your ISP's website or call its toll-free number and ask how you can use your current account away from home, and how much it will cost.

If you're traveling outside the reach of your ISP, the **iPass** network has dial-up numbers in most of the world's countries. You'll have to sign up with an iPass provider, who will then tell you how to set up your computer for your destination(s). For a list of iPass providers, go to www.ipass.com. One solid provider is **i2roam** (www.i2roam.com; © **866/811-6209** or 920/235-0475).

Wherever you go, bring a **connection kit** of the right power and phone adapters, a spare phone cord, and a spare Ethernet network cable.

Most business-class hotels throughout the world offer dataports for laptop modems, and a few thousand hotels in the U.S. now offer high-speed Internet access using an Ethernet network cable. You'll have to bring your own cables either way, so **call your hotel in advance** to find out what the options are.

Many business-class hotels in the U.S. also offer a form of computer-free Web browsing through the room TV set. We've successfully checked Yahoo! Mail on these systems.

If you have an 802.11b/**Wi-fi** card for your computer, several commercial companies have made wireless service available in airports, hotel lobbies and coffee shops, primarily in the U.S. **T-Mobile Hotspot** (www.t-mobile.com/hotspot) serves up wireless connections at more than 1,000 Starbucks coffee shops nationwide. **Boingo** (www.boingo.com) and **Wayport** (www.wayport.com) have set up networks in airports and high-class hotel lobbies. IPass providers (see above) also give you access to a few hundred wireless hotel lobby setups. Best of all, you don't need to be staying at the Four Seasons to use the hotel's network; just set yourself up on a nice couch in the lobby. Unfortunately, the companies' pricing policies are byzantine, with a variety of monthly, per-connection, and per-minute plans.

Community-minded individuals have also set up **free wireless networks** in major cities around the U.S. These networks are spotty, but you get what you (don't) pay for. Each network has a home page explaining how to set up your computer for their particular system; start your explorations at www.personaltelco.net/index.cgi/WirelessCommunities.

USING A CELLPHONE

Just because your cellphone works at home doesn't mean it'll work elsewhere in the country (thanks to our nation's fragmented cellphone system). It's a good bet that your phone will work in major cities. But take a look at your wireless company's coverage map on its website before heading out—T-Mobile, Sprint, and Nextel are particularly weak in rural areas. If you need to stay in touch at a destination where you know your phone won't work, **rent** a phone that does from **InTouch USA** (© 800/872-7626; www.intouchglobal.com) or a car-rental location, but beware that you'll pay $1 a minute or more for airtime.

If you're venturing deep into national parks, you may want to consider renting a **satellite phone** ("satphones"), which are different from cellphones in that they connect to satellites rather than ground-based towers. A satphone is more costly than a cellphone but works where there's no cellular signal and no towers. Unfortunately, you'll pay at least $2 per minute to use the phone, and it only works where you can see the horizon (i.e., usually not indoors). In North America, you can rent Iridium satellite phones from **RoadPost** (www.roadpost.com; © 888/290-1606 or 905/272-5665). InTouch USA (see above) offers a wider range of satphones but at higher rates. As of this writing, satphones were amazingly expensive to buy, so don't even think about it.

If you're not from the U.S., you'll be appalled at the poor reach of our **GSM (Global System for Mobiles) wireless network,** which is used by much of the rest of the world. Your phone will probably work in most major U.S. cities; it definitely won't work in many rural areas. And you may or may not be able to send SMS (text messaging) home—something Americans tend not to do anyway, for various cultural and technological reasons. Assume nothing—call your wireless provider and get the full scoop. In a worst-case scenario, you can always rent a phone; InTouch USA delivers to hotels.

Online Traveler's Toolbox

Veteran travelers usually carry some essential items to make their trips easier. Following is a selection of online tools to bookmark and use.

- **Visa ATM Locator** (www.visa.com), for locations of Plus ATMs worldwide, or **MasterCard ATM Locator** (www.mastercard.com), for locations of Cirrus ATMs worldwide.
- **Intellicast** (www.intellicast.com) and **Weather.com** (www.weather.com). Give weather forecasts for all 50 states and for cities around the world.
- **Mapquest** (www.mapquest.com). This best of the mapping sites lets you choose a specific address or destination, and in seconds, it will return a map and detailed directions.
- **Travel Warnings** (http://travel.state.gov/travel_warnings.html, www.fco.gov.uk/travel, www.voyage.gc.ca, www.dfat.gov.au/consular/advice). These sites report on places where health concerns or unrest might threaten American, British, Canadian, and Australian travelers. Generally, U.S. warnings are the most paranoid; Australian warnings are the most relaxed.

9 Getting There

BY PLANE

There are quite a few airports with commercial service in Texas, and choosing which one to fly to will depend on which particular airline you want to use and the part of Texas you plan to visit. The state's major airports are **Dallas/Fort Worth International, El Paso International, Bush Intercontinental** and **William P. Hobby** in Houston, and **San Antonio International.** Major airlines include **Air Canada** (© 888/247-2262; www.aircanada.ca), **American** (© 800/433-7300; www.aa.com), **America West** (© 800/235-9292; www.americawest.com), **British Airways** (© 800/247-9297; www.britishairways.com), **Continental** (© 800/525-0280; www.continental.com), **Delta** (© 800/221-1212; www.delta.com), **Frontier** (© 800/432-1359; www.frontierairlines.com), **Northwest** (© 800/225-2525; www.nwa.com), **Southwest** (© 800/435-9792; www.iflyswa.com), **United** (© 800/864-8331; www.united.com), and **US Airways** (© 800/428-4322; www.usairways.com).

GETTING THROUGH THE AIRPORT

With the federalization of airport security, security procedures at U.S. airports are more stable and consistent than ever. Generally, you'll be fine if you arrive at the airport 1 hour before a domestic flight; if you show up late, tell an airline employee and she'll probably whisk you to the front of the line.

Bring a **current, government-issued photo ID** such as a driver's license or passport, and if you've got an E-ticket, print out the **official confirmation page;** you'll need to show your confirmation at the security checkpoint, and your ID at the ticket counter or the gate. (Children under 18 do not need photo IDs for domestic flights, but the adults checking in with them need them.)

Security lines are getting shorter than they were during 2001 and 2002, but some doozies remain. If you have trouble standing for long periods of time, tell an airline employee; the airline will provide a wheelchair. Speed up security by **not wearing metal objects** such as big belt buckles or clanky earrings. If you've got metallic body parts, a note from your doctor can prevent a long chat with the security screeners. Keep in mind that only **ticketed passengers** are allowed past security, except for folks escorting passengers with disabilities or children.

Federalization has stabilized **what you can carry on** and **what you can't**. The general rule is that sharp things are out, nail clippers are okay, and food and beverages must be passed through the X-ray machine—but security screeners can't make you drink from your coffee cup. Bring food in your carry-on rather than checking it, as explosive-detection machines used on checked luggage have been known to mistake food (especially chocolate, for some reason) for bombs. Travelers in the U.S. are allowed one carry-on bag, plus a "personal item" such as a purse, briefcase, or laptop bag. Carry-on hoarders can stuff all sorts of things into a laptop bag; as long as it has a laptop in it, it's still considered a personal item. The Transportation Security Administration (TSA) has issued a list of restricted items; check its website (www.tsa.gov) for details.

In 2003 the TSA is phasing out **gate check-in** at all U.S. airports. Passengers with E-tickets and without checked bags can still beat the ticket-counter lines by using **electronic kiosks** or even **online check-in**. Ask your airline which alternatives are available, and if you're using a kiosk, bring the credit card you used to book the ticket. If you're checking bags, you will still be able to use most airlines' kiosks; again call your airline for up-to-date information. **Curbside check-in** is also a good way to avoid lines, although a few airlines still ban curbside check-in entirely; call before you go.

FLYING FOR LESS: TIPS FOR GETTING THE BEST AIRFARE

Passengers sharing the same airplane cabin rarely pay the same fare. Here are some ways to keep your airfare costs down.

- Passengers who can book their ticket **long in advance,** who can **stay over Saturday night,** or who **fly midweek** or **at less-trafficked hours** will pay a fraction of the full fare. If your schedule is flexible, say so, and ask if you can secure a cheaper fare by changing your flight plans.
- You can also save on airfares by keeping an eye out in local newspapers for **promotional specials** or **fare wars,** when airlines lower prices on their most popular routes. You rarely see fare wars offered for peak travel times, but if you can travel in the off-months, you may snag a bargain.
- Search **the Internet** for cheap fares (see "Planning Your Trip Online," earlier in this chapter).
- Join **frequent-flier clubs.** Accrue enough miles, and you'll be rewarded with free flights and elite status. It's free, and you'll get the best choice of seats, faster response to phone inquiries, and prompter service if your luggage is stolen, your flight is canceled or delayed, or if you want to change your seat. You don't need to fly to build frequent-flier miles—**frequent-flier credit cards** can provide thousands of miles for doing your everyday shopping.

For many more tips about air travel, including a rundown of the major frequent-flier credit cards, pick up a copy of *Frommer's Fly Safe, Fly Smart* (Wiley Publishing).

Travel in the Age of Bankruptcy

At press time, two major U.S. airlines were struggling in bankruptcy court and most of the rest weren't doing very well either. To protect yourself, **buy your tickets with a credit card,** as the Fair Credit Billing Act guarantees that you can get your money back from the credit-card company if a travel supplier goes under (and if you request the refund within 60 days of the bankruptcy). **Travel insurance** can also help, but make sure it covers against "carrier default" for your specific travel provider. And be aware that if a U.S. airline goes bust midtrip, a 2001 federal law requires other carriers to take you to your destination (albeit on a space-available basis) for a fee of no more than $25, provided you rebook within 60 days of the cancellation.

BY CAR

If you're planning a road trip, it's a good idea to join the **American Automobile Association** (© 800/336-4357; www.aaa.com). In Texas, AAA headquarters is at 3000 Southwest Fwy. in Houston (© 800/765-0766); there are also offices in Amarillo, Austin, Bedford, Conroe, Dallas, El Paso, Fort Worth, Laredo, Missouri City, Plano, and San Antonio. Members can get excellent maps, tour guides, and emergency road service; they'll also help you plan an exact itinerary. Members can get free emergency road service by calling **AAA's emergency number** (© 800/AAA-HELP).

More than 3,000 miles of interstate highways crisscross this huge state, connecting four major urban areas to each other and to cities in nearby states. Some relevant mileages: Houston to New Orleans, 350 miles; Houston to Phoenix, 1,180 miles; Dallas to Little Rock, 320 miles; Dallas to Kansas City, 550 miles; and Dallas to Denver, 880 miles.

BY TRAIN

Amtrak (© 800/USA-RAIL; www.amtrak.com) has several routes through Texas. The **Sunset Limited** has stops at Beaumont/Port Arthur, Houston, San Antonio, Del Rio, Sanderson, Alpine, and El Paso on its New Orleans to Los Angeles run; the **Heartland Flyer** stops in Gainesville and Fort Worth (where it connects with the Texas Eagle) on its run from Oklahoma City; and the **Texas Eagle,** which runs between Chicago and Los Angeles, stops at Texarkana, Mineola, Marshall, Longview, Dallas, Fort Worth, Cleburne, McGregor, Taylor, Austin, San Marcos, and San Antonio, where you can connect with the Sunset Limited.

10 Package Deals for Independent Travelers

Before you start your search for the lowest airfare, you may want to consider booking your flight as part of a travel package. Package tours are not the same thing as escorted tours. Package tours are simply a way to buy the airfare, accommodations, and other elements of your trip (such as car rentals, airport transfers, and sometimes even activities) at the same time and often at discounted prices—kind of like one-stop shopping. Packages are sold in bulk to tour operators—who resell them to the public at a cost that usually undercuts standard rates.

One good source of package deals is the airlines themselves. Most major airlines offer air/land packages, including **American Airlines Vacations** (© 800/321-2121; www.aavacations.com),

Delta Vacations (© 800/221-6666; www.deltavacations.com), Continental Airlines Vacations (© 800/301-3800; www.coolvacations.com), and United Vacations (© 888/854-3899; www. unitedvacations.com). Several big online travel agencies—Expedia, Travelocity, Orbitz, Site59, and Last-minute.com—also do a brisk business in packages. If you're unsure about the pedigree of a smaller packager, check with the Better Business Bureau in the city where the company is based, or go online at www.bbb.org. If a packager won't tell you where it's based, don't fly with them.

Travel packages are also listed in the travel section of your local Sunday newspaper. Or check ads in the national travel magazines such as *Arthur Frommer's Budget Travel Magazine, Travel & Leisure, National Geographic Traveler,* and *Condé Nast Traveler.*

Package tours can vary by leaps and bounds. Some offer a better class of hotels than others. Some offer the same hotels for lower prices. Some offer flights on scheduled airlines, while others book charters. Some limit your choice of accommodations and travel days. You are often required to make a large payment up front. On the plus side, packages can save you money, offering group prices but allowing for independent travel. Some even let you add on a few guided excursions or escorted day trips (also at prices lower than if you booked them yourself) without booking an entirely escorted tour.

Before you invest in a package tour, get some answers. Ask about the accommodation choices and prices for each. Then look up the hotels' reviews in a Frommer's guide and check their rates for your specific dates of travel online. You'll also want to find out what type of room you get. If you need a certain type of room, ask for it; don't take whatever is thrown your way. Request a nonsmoking room, a quiet room, a room with a view, or whatever you fancy.

Finally, look for hidden expenses. Ask whether airport departure fees and taxes, for example, are included in the total cost.

11 Getting Around

Texas is huge, so it's highly unlikely you'll want to try to see it all in one visit. Most visitors will be exploring either one or two cities or a relatively small section of the state. For those visiting major cities it's easy to fly in, use public transportation, and then fly or take the train to the next city (see the individual city chapters for airline and rail information). However, those who plan to see a variety of Texas locales will find that the most practical way to see Texas is by car.

BY CAR

Driving is an excellent way to see Texas in small chunks—roads are well maintained and well marked, and a car is often the most economical and convenient way to get somewhere; in fact, if you plan to explore beyond the cities—which we highly recommend—it's practically the only way to get to some places.

Fun Fact

Texas maintains 77,000 miles of roadways, including interstates, U.S. highways, state highways, and farm-to-market (designated FM on signs) roads. Furthermore, it has some 48,000 bridges on public roads—the most in the nation.

Texas Driving Times & Distances

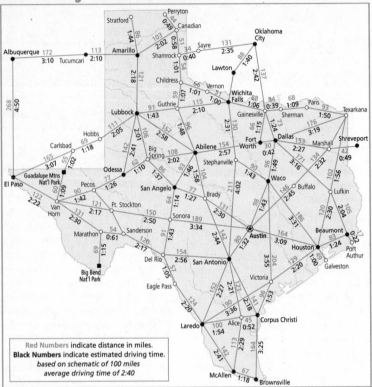

Red Numbers indicate distance in miles.
Black Numbers indicate estimated driving time.
*based on schematic of 100 miles
average driving time of 2:40*

Once you leave the interstates, there is a veritable spider-web of roads that will take you just about anywhere you want to go, at least until you venture into the vast emptiness of the southwest plains. This seemingly uncharted area contains two of the gems of the state however: Big Bend and Guadalupe Mountains National Parks. These two places make it worth the effort of finding a way to get there.

Traffic in major cities, such as Houston, can be a bit intense, especially at rush hour, but away from the cities you'll often find the roads to be practically deserted.

Because much of Texas has a relatively mild climate, snow and ice are not usually a problem. However, those traveling to or through Amarillo and other northern sections of the state in winter should check weather reports frequently—we were once stranded in the Panhandle for several days by an ice storm that left the highways a sheet of glass.

CAR & RV RENTALS National rental agencies readily available in Texas include **Advantage** (© 800/777-5500; www.arac.com), **Alamo** (© 800/462-5266; www.alamo.com), **Avis** (© 800/230-4898; www.avis.com), **Budget** (© 800/527-0700; www.budget.com), **Dollar** (© 800/800-3665; www.dollar.com), **Enterprise** (© 800/736-8222; www.enterprise.com), **Hertz** (© 800/654-3131; www.hertz.com), **National** (© 800/227-7368; www.nationalcar.com), **Payless** (© 800/729-5377; www.pay

lesscar.com), and **Thrifty** (© 800/847-4389; www.thrifty.com). Motor homes and campers are available from **Cruise America** (© 800/327-7799; www.cruiseamerica.com), which has outlets in Austin, Beaumont, Dallas, Fort Worth, Houston, and San Antonio.

INSURANCE   If you hold a private auto insurance policy, you probably are covered for loss or damage to the rental car, and liability in case a passenger is injured. The credit card you used to rent the car also may provide some coverage.

Car-rental insurance probably does not cover liability if you caused the accident. Check your own auto insurance policy, the rental company policy, and your credit card coverage for the extent of coverage: Is your destination covered? Are other drivers covered? How much liability is covered if a passenger is injured? (If you rely on your credit card for coverage, you may want to bring a second credit card with you, as damages may be charged to your card and you may find yourself stranded with no money.)

DRIVING RULES   Texas law requires all drivers to carry proof of insurance, as well as a valid driver's license. Safety belts must be worn by all front seat occupants of cars and light trucks; children under 17 must wear safety belts regardless of where they are in the vehicle; and children under age 4 or under 36 inches tall, regardless of where they're sitting, must be in approved child seats. The maximum speed limit on interstate highways is 70 mph; and the maximum on numbered noninterstates is 70 mph during daylight and 65 mph at night, unless otherwise posted. Motorcyclists are required to wear helmets, and radar detectors are legal.

THE "DRIVE FRIENDLY" STATE   For years the Texas Department of Transportation has been urging motorists to "drive friendly," and apparently many of them, especially in rural areas, have taken that message to heart. When you approach a vehicle from behind on a two-lane road, more often than not that vehicle will pull onto the shoulder, while maintaining speed, to let you pass without having to go into the oncoming lane. Fortunately, most Texas state highways have good, wide shoulders so there's little danger. We're not sure if this is technically legal or not, but everybody in rural Texas does it, including state troopers.

(**Fun Fact** **A Not-So-Safe Tradition Ends**

It took more than 10 years of legislative discussion, as well as the threat of a cutoff of federal road construction money, but Texas has finally joined most of the rest of the nation by banning the time-honored tradition of drinking while driving. In September 2001, a Texas state law went into effect that prohibits open containers of alcoholic beverages within reach of the occupants of a motor vehicle. Remember the movie *Urban Cowboy*, when John Travolta is cruising by Houston in his pickup truck, his hand wrapped around a longneck bottle of beer? Well, at least according to the law, those days are gone.

Texas: Gateway to Mexico

Many travelers believe that a vacation in western or southern Texas would not be complete without an excursion across the border into Mexico, to visit the picturesque shops, dicker for colorful pottery and handsome jewelry, and sample genuine Mexican food. In our experience, the shopping is especially enjoyable—you really can get some bargains—and the food is great, though we generally stay away from street vendors and patronize only the well-established restaurants. Mexican border towns welcome tourists and almost universally accept U.S. currency—in fact for many of these communities tourism is their primary source of income.

However, remember that a trip across the border, even if you just walk across for the afternoon, is in fact a trip to a foreign country, and the laws of Mexico, not the United States, apply. In addition, these border towns are often hotbeds of drug smuggling (see the section on Ciudad Juárez in chapter 9), so stick to the main tourist areas, and don't let anyone try to convince you to carry anything across the border for them.

U.S. and Canadian citizens should carry proof of citizenship, such as a passport or birth certificate, and a Mexican tourist card (available from Mexican officials at the border) is required for those going beyond the border towns into Mexico's interior, or those planning to stay in the border towns for more than 72 hours. Other foreign nationals will need a passport and the appropriate visas.

Travelers driving cars beyond the border towns will need vehicle permits, available from Mexican officials at the border, and those driving cars across the border for any distance at all should first buy insurance from a Mexican insurance company (short-term insurance is available at the border and at travel clubs such as AAA). If you're only planning to

MAPS   A good state highway map is available free at any state Information Center or by mail (see "Visitor Information," earlier in this chapter). Maps can also be purchased at bookstores, gas stations, and most supermarkets and discount stores.

ROAD CONDITIONS   Texas roads are among the best in the western United States, and the state's generally moderate weather keeps snow closures to a minimum. However, icy roads are fairly common in the northern sections of the state during the winter and hurricanes can cause flooding in late summer and early fall along the Gulf Coast. A recorded **24-hour hot line**

(© **800/452-9292**) provides information on road conditions statewide, and information is also available online at www.dot.state.tx.us/hcr/main.htm.

BY PLANE
A number of airlines offer flights between Texas's major cities; see the "Essentials" sections in individual destinations for airline information.

BY TRAIN
More than a dozen towns and cities in Texas are linked by rail, with mostly daily service from Amtrak. See "Getting There," earlier in this chapter, and individual destinations for more information.

cross the border, visit a few shops, maybe sample the Mexican food, and then cross back into Texas, consider leaving your car on U.S. soil and walking. This will save the hassles of getting Mexican car insurance and the red tape if you are involved in an accident; of course then you'll end up having to carry any purchases you make.

Warning: It is a felony to take any type of firearm or ammunition into Mexico (you could easily end up in jail and have your car confiscated). In addition, there are a number of regulations regarding taking pets across the border, plus fees, so it is usually best to board pets on the U.S. side.

When reentering the United States from Mexico you will be stopped and questioned by U.S. Customs officials, and your car may be searched. U.S. citizens may bring back up to $800 in purchases duty-free every 30 days, including 1 liter of liquor, 100 cigars (except Cuban cigars, which are prohibited), and one carton of cigarettes. Duty fees are charged above those amounts, and Texas charges a tax of about $1 per liter on all alcoholic beverages. Items that may not be brought into the United States, or which require special permits, include most fruits and vegetables, plants, animals, and meat.

The above is just a brief summary of the somewhat complex laws on traveling between the United States and Mexico. There are more details in the official state vacation guide available from the Texas Department of Transportation (see "Visitor Information," earlier in this chapter), and for complete information contact **U.S. Customs** (© **202/354-1000;** www.customs.gov) and the **Mexican Government Tourism Office** (© **800/ 446-3942** or 713/722-2581; e-mail mgtotx@ix.netcom.com). A good online source of information is www.mexonline.com.

12 The Active Vacation Planner

Texas is dotted with lakes, has numerous rivers, almost 700 miles of Gulf Coast, plenty of forest lands, and several mountain ranges. Its two national parks offer many hiking opportunities, and there are also scenic canyons, spectacular caves, and vast areas of rugged desert.

The **official state vacation guide** (see "Visitor Information," earlier in this chapter) is a good source of information for those planning outdoor recreation in the state. Information on fishing, hunting, and the numerous state parks in Texas is available from the **Texas Parks and Wildlife Department** (© **800/792-1112** or 512/389-8950; www.tpwd.state.tx.us). Reservations for camping at state parks can be made through the department's website or by calling © **512/389-8900.** General outdoor recreation information is also online at **www.texasoutside.com**.

Both RV and tent **campers** will find plenty of campsites throughout Texas, although tent campers will have fewer choices, especially along the Gulf Coast where numerous RV parks cater to "Winter Texans"—usually retired residents of northern states and Canada who spend winters in the sunny warmth of Texas and often arrive in plush motor homes or large trailers. The **Texas Association of Campground Owners** (© **800/657-6555** or

512/459-8226; www.texascamp grounds.com), offers a free booklet describing commercial campgrounds and RV parks in Texas and New Mexico. It's a generally good guide, with fairly complete information and directions, but unfortunately it does not include rates. However, it does include a "Texas Saver Card," for discounts of 10% or 15% at many facilities.

OUTFITTERS & OPERATORS

With a state as huge as Texas, you'd expect lots of outdoor adventures, and although there are lots of opportunities for outdoor activities in Texas, the state hasn't quite caught on with most of the major national adventure travel companies. However, we do recommend **GORPtravel** (© 877/440-GORP or 303/516-1153; www.gorptravel.com), which offers several Texas trips, ranging from rafting or canoeing the Rio Grande to Old West dude ranch vacations, where you get to play cowboy when you're not busy fishing, swimming, or just loafing. Another good national company that offers bicycling and multi-sport adventures in Texas is **Planet Earth Adventure** (© 800/923-4453; www.planetearthadventures.com); and multi-activity adventures in Texas are also available from **Tauck World Discovery** (© 800/788-7885 or 203/221-6891; www.tauck.com). The **Audubon Society** (© 800/967-7425; www.audubon.org) occasionally offers what it calls "nature odysseys" in Texas, with birding destination such as Big Bend National Park.

You can obtain information on the state's outfitters, including numerous hunting and fishing guides, from the **Texas Outfitters and Guides Association,** P.O. Box 33141, Kerrville, TX 78029-3141 (© **830/238-4207;** www.texasoutfittersguide.com).

ACTIVITIES A TO Z

There's a wide variety of outdoor activities in Texas, and moderate year-round temperatures in most of the state gives you more time to do them.

BIRD-WATCHING & WILDLIFE VIEWING Texas has some of the best bird-watching opportunities in the United States, especially along the Gulf Coast, where you often see colorful neotropical species found nowhere else in the United States. Check out the numerous national wildlife refuges, or stop practically anywhere along the coast—we like the Rockport area (see chapter 6). You can get bird checklists from most visitor centers and wildlife refuges, and online from the **Northern Prairie Wildlife Research Center** (www.npwrc.usgs.gov/resource/othr data/chekbird/r2/48.htm). Also, check with the **Audubon Society** (© **800/ 967-7425;** www.audubon.org) to see what the national organization and its various Texas chapters are offering by way of birding tours. Wildlife viewing is especially good at Big Bend National Park (see chapter 10).

BOATING Opportunities for boating are abundant along the Gulf Coast—there are boat ramps practically everywhere—but the state's many lakes also are ideal for boating. Especially good is Amistad National Recreation Area, a huge lake along the U.S.–Mexico border in West Texas; see "Del Rio & Amistad National Recreation Area" in chapter 9.

DUDE RANCHING As one would expect in a major cattle ranching state like Texas, there are ample opportunities for visitors to saddle up and hit the trail with genuine bow-legged cowboys (spitting chewing tobacco is optional). Close to 100 working ranches welcome guests. There are a number of ranches in the San Antonio area, and of course the West Texas plains has more than its share. A complete list of ranches, with contact information and other details, is available on the Texas Tourism website at **www.traveltex.com.**

FISHING & HUNTING   Texans love fishing and hunting, and you'd be hard pressed to find an area of the state without a popular fishing hole or nearby hunting location. The lakes of East Texas are especially good fishing spots, and the San Angelo area offers excellent fishing and hunting opportunities (see chapters 5 and 9, respectively). Gulf Coast towns such as Rockport, Corpus Christi, and South Padre Island have dozens of fishing boats available for bay and deep-sea fishing (see chapter 6). Hunting for birds, white-tailed deer, and even javelina is popular in many areas, including West Texas. For current license information, check with the Texas Parks and Wildlife Department (see above). Another good source of information is online at **www.texas huntingandfishing.com**.

FOUR-WHEELING   Visitors to Texas who brought along a street legal 4×4 will find miles of beach to explore at Padre Island National Seashore (see chapter 6).

GOLF   There are more than 900 golf courses in Texas, offering plenty of challenges and a wide variety of terrain. The best courses are near major cities such as Dallas, San Antonio, Houston, and Austin, but even out in the plains you're likely to stumble across an oasis of well-manicured green with a row of golf carts awaiting your tee time. Among top golfing destinations in Texas is the **Four Seasons Resort and Club at Las Colinas** (p. 96), in the Dallas–Forth Worth area, with two challenging courses, more trees than you can count, and a beautiful lake. In Houston (and with another course in the Dallas–Fort Worth area), **Tour 18** does a splendid job of capturing the feel and even look of some of the greatest and best-known golf holes in the country (see chapters 4 and 5).

HIKING   There are plenty of hiking trails in Texas, including those at the numerous state parks. Perhaps the most scenic trails are in the Big Bend and Guadalupe Mountains national parks—it's especially hard to beat the spectacular beauty of a fall hike in McKittrick Canyon at Guadalupe Mountains National Park (see chapter 10). Also very attractive are the hiking trails at Palo Duro Canyon State Park in the Panhandle Plains (see chapter 11). Hikers need to be prepared though; take plenty of water when hiking in the desert, watch for poisonous snakes and insects most everywhere, and use mosquito repellent in the Gulf Coast area.

WATERSPORTS   Swimming and water-skiing are practically year-round activities along the Gulf Coast and at Amistad National Recreation Area in West Texas (see chapters 6 and 9). The many lakes around the state—especially in East Texas and the Hill Country around San Antonio—also offer ample opportunity for a variety of watersports, especially canoeing and power boating. Rafters usually head to the Rio Grande near Big Bend National Park, where they can head downstream on their own or go with one of the local rafting companies (see chapter 10). For beachcombing, try Padre Island National Seashore (see chapter 6).

13 Tips on Accommodations

Texas offers a variety of lodging options, from typical American chain motels to luxury hotels, historic hotels and bed and breakfast inns, some pleasant and inexpensive mom-and-pop independent motels, cabins, and ranch-style resorts. To make your lodging an integral part of your Texas experience, we recommend choosing a historic property. There are quite a few historic bed and breakfast inns discussed in the following pages, and especially when you take into consideration the wonderful breakfasts prepared at most of them, the rates are fairly reasonable. Why spend $80 for a boring motel room and then another $10 to $15 for breakfast when for just a bit more you can instead sleep in a handsome inn, decorated with antiques, and be served a delightful home-cooked breakfast?

TIPS FOR SAVING ON YOUR HOTEL ROOM

The **rack rate** is the maximum rate that a hotel charges for a room. It's the rate you'd get if you walked in off the street and asked for a room for the night. Hardly anybody pays these prices, however, and there are many ways around them.

- **Don't be afraid to bargain**. Most rack rates include commissions of 10% to 25% for travel agents, which some hotels may be willing to reduce if you make your own reservations and haggle a bit. You may qualify for corporate, student, military, senior, or other discounts. Be sure to mention membership in AAA, AARP, frequent-flier programs, or trade unions, which may entitle you to special deals as well. Find out the hotel policy on children—do kids stay free in the room or is there a special rate?

- **Watch for coupon books and advertised discounts.** State welcome centers, community visitor centers, and a variety of businesses (but not hotels) distribute free booklets that contain discount lodging coupons. These are usually for chains, and almost always are for walk-ins only, so you won't be able to make a reservation. But if you can use one of these coupons you can often save 20% to 40% off the rack rate. These coupons are also available online at www.roomsaver.com.

- **Rely on a qualified professional.** Certain hotels give travel agents discounts in exchange for steering business their way, so if you're shy about bargaining, an agent may be better equipped to negotiate discounts for you.

- **Dial direct.** When booking a room in a chain hotel, compare the rates offered by the hotel's local line with that of the toll-free number. Also check with an agent and online. A hotel makes nothing on a room that stays empty, so the local hotel reservation desk may be willing to offer a special rate unavailable elsewhere.

- **Remember the law of supply and demand.** Resort hotels are most crowded and therefore most expensive on weekends, so discounts are usually available for midweek stays. Business hotels in downtown locations are busiest during the week, so you can expect big discounts over the weekend. Avoid high-season stays whenever you can: Planning your vacation just a week before or after official peak season can mean big savings.

- **Avoid excess charges.** When you book a room, ask whether the hotel charges for parking. Many hotels charge a fee just for dialing out on the phone in your room. Find out whether your hotel imposes a surcharge on local and long-distance calls. Finally, ask about local taxes and service charges, which could increase the cost of a room by 25% or more.

- **Consider a suite.** If you are traveling with your family or another couple, you can pack more people into a suite (which usually comes with a sofa bed), and thereby reduce your per-person rate.

Remember that some places charge for extra guests.

- **Book an efficiency.** A room with a kitchenette allows you to shop for groceries and cook your own meals. This is a big money-saver, especially for families on long stays.

- Join hotel **frequent-visitor clubs,** even if you don't use them much. You'll be more likely to get upgrades and other perks.

- Many hotels offer **frequent-flier points.** Don't forget to ask for yours when you check in.

14 Recommended Reading

Of the seemingly infinite number of books concerning the Lone Star State, there are a few novels this book's authors especially like, primarily for the view they provide into the soul of Texas (both the real and the mythical). Fans of James Michener will appreciate his historical novel *Texas.* Although a bit too wordy and involved for some of us, Michener is an excellent storyteller as well as historian, and brings the state and its people to life. (But couldn't he have done it in less than 1,344 pages?) The novels of Cormac McCarthy also bring Texas to life, especially its raw, violent ways. Especially recommended are *All the Pretty Horses,* a sort of coming-of-age story known for its magnificent prose, and his tense *Blood Meridian: Or the Evening Redness in the West.* You might also pick up a copy of Annie Proulx's latest, *That Old Ace in the Hole,* which is set in the Panhandle. For powerful, critically acclaimed short stories, try *Women Hollering Creek* by Texas author Sandra Cisneros. *The Gates of the Alamo* by Stephen Harrigan is a gripping, fictionalized version of Texas's most famous battle.

On the much lighter side, *Baja Oklahoma,* by Dan Jenkins, offers a funny, poignant, and somewhat raunchy look at what we might call classic modern Texans, at least the Fort Worth trailer-trash variety. The book was made into an equally good movie by the same name, starring Leslie Ann Warren and Peter Coyote, with a bit part played by a young actress you may have heard of—Julia Roberts. William Sidney Porter, better known as O. Henry, published a satirical newspaper in Austin and also worked in San Antonio in the late 19th century. A number of his short stories are set in the state, and can be found in *O. Henry's Texas Stories.*

Among nonfiction titles, serious history buffs may want to dip into Robert A. Caro's excellent multivolume biography of Lyndon B. Johnson, the consummate Texas politician whose career led him to the White House. For a quick and easy look at what Texas is all about, try *All Hat & No Cattle,* a collection of somewhat irreverent observations on Texas fashions, cuisine, music, animals, and the like by humorist Anne Dingus. Even readers who don't cook will enjoy *The Only Texas Cookbook* by Linda West Eckhardt. Interspersed among its 300 recipes—including classics such as Fuzzy's Fantastic South Texas Road Meat Chili and Bad Hombre Eggs—are numerous humorous anecdotes on food-related subjects. Those who savor biting political humor—and don't mind seeing every Texas Republican mercilessly skewered—will thoroughly enjoy any book of essays by newspaper columnist Molly Ivins, who is credited with bestowing the nickname "Dubya" on George W. Bush.

FAST FACTS: **Texas**

American Express There are branches throughout Texas; see "Fast Facts" in individual chapters for locations. To report a lost card, call ✆ **800/528-4800.** To report lost traveler's checks, call ✆ **800/221-7282.**

Business Hours Offices are usually open weekdays from 9am to 5pm. Banks are open weekdays from 9am to 3pm or later and sometimes Saturday mornings. Stores typically open between 9 and 10am and close between 5 and 6pm Monday through Saturday. Stores in shopping complexes or malls tend to stay open late: until about 9pm on weekdays and weekends, and many malls and larger department stores are open on Sundays. A growing number of discount stores (like Wal-Mart) and grocery stores are open 24 hours a day.

Car Rentals See "Getting Around," earlier in this chapter.

Embassies & Consulates See chapter 3, "For International Visitors."

Emergencies For an ambulance, the police, or the fire department, call ✆ **911.**

Holidays Banks, government offices, post offices, and many stores, restaurants, and museums are closed on the following legal national holidays: January 1 (New Year's Day), the third Monday in January (Martin Luther King, Jr. Day), the third Monday in February (Presidents' Day, Washington's Birthday), the last Monday in May (Memorial Day), July 4 (Independence Day), the first Monday in September (Labor Day), the second Monday in October (Columbus Day), November 11 (Veterans' Day/Armistice Day), the fourth Thursday in November (Thanksgiving Day), and December 25 (Christmas). Also, the Tuesday following the first Monday in November is Election Day and is a federal government holiday in presidential-election years (held every 4 years, and next in 2004).

Internet Access You'll have trouble finding convenient Internet access in the smaller towns, where you might have the best luck at the local library. Before you go, check for an Internet cafe in your destination at **www.cybercafes.com** or **www.netcafeguide.com/mapindex.htm.**

Liquor Laws The legal drinking age is 21, although minors can legally drink as long as they are within sight of their 21 or older parents or spouses. Where you can or cannot buy a drink, and what kind of drink, is determined in Texas by local option election, and so the state is essentially a patchwork of regulations. In most parts of the state you can buy liquor, beer, and wine by the drink. However, there are a few areas where you can buy only beer (which Texas defines as having no more than 4% alcohol; anything higher is "ale"), and others where you can purchase beer or wine by the glass but not liquor. There are also some areas that are completely dry—mostly in the Panhandle Plains and near the state's eastern border.

Lost & Found Be sure to contact all of your credit-card companies the minute you discover your wallet has been lost or stolen and file a report at the nearest police precinct. Your credit-card company or insurer may require a police report number or record of the loss. Most credit-card companies have an emergency toll-free number to call if your card is lost or stolen; they may be able to wire you a cash advance immediately or deliver an emergency credit card in a day or two. Visa's U.S. emergency number is ✆ **800/847-2911** or 410/581-9994. American Express cardholders and traveler's check holders should call ✆ **800/ 221-7282.** MasterCard holders should call ✆ **800/307-7309** or 636/ 722-7111. For other credit cards, call the toll-free number directory at ✆ **800/555-1212.**

Maps See "Getting Around," earlier in this chapter.

Newspapers & Magazines The state's largest daily newspapers include the *Dallas Morning News, Houston Chronicle, Fort Worth Star-Telegram,* and the *San Antonio Express-News.* Other cities and large towns, especially regional hubs, have daily newspapers, and many smaller towns publish weeklies. National newspapers such as *USA Today* and the *Wall Street Journal* can be purchased at newsstands in cities and major hotels; and you can also purchase two good monthly magazines, *Texas Highways* and *Texas Monthly,* throughout the state.

Pets See "Traveling with Pets," earlier in this chapter.

Safety See "Insurance, Health & Safety," earlier in this chapter.

Taxes Texans like to brag that the state is a great place to live because there is no income tax. However, money for government services has to come from somewhere, and one of those sources is you, the traveler. Texas lodging taxes are among the highest in the region, ranging from 10% to 17%, with the steepest rate in Houston. Sales taxes in Texas vary, but usually total from 7% to 8%, slightly higher than most surrounding states.

Time Zone Almost all of Texas is in the Central Standard Time zone (CST); the only exception is the state's far western tip, with observes Mountain Standard Time (MST). **Daylight saving time** is in effect from the first Sunday in April to the last Sunday in October.

3

For International Visitors

by Don & Barb Laine

Whether it's your first visit or your tenth, a trip to the United States may require an additional degree of planning. This chapter will provide you with essential advice about the more common problems that some visitors encounter, plus helpful tips on how things are done in Texas.

1 Preparing for Your Trip

ENTRY REQUIREMENTS

Check at any U.S. embassy or consulate for current information and requirements. You can also obtain a visa application and other information online at the **U.S. State Department**'s website, at **www.travel.state.gov**.

VISAS The U.S. State Department has a **Visa Waiver Program** allowing citizens of certain countries to enter the United States without a visa for stays of up to 90 days. At press time these included Andorra, Australia, Austria, Belgium, Brunei, Denmark, Finland, France, Germany, Iceland, Ireland, Italy, Japan, Liechtenstein, Luxembourg, Monaco, the Netherlands, New Zealand, Norway, Portugal, San Marino, Singapore, Slovenia, Spain, Sweden, Switzerland, and the United Kingdom. Citizens of these countries need only a valid passport and a round-trip air or cruise ticket in their possession upon arrival. If they first enter the United States, they may also visit Mexico, Canada, Bermuda, and/or the Caribbean islands and return to the United States without a visa. Further information is available from any U.S. embassy or consulate. Canadian citizens may enter the United States without visas; they need only proof of residence.

Citizens of all other countries must have (1) a valid passport that expires at least 6 months later than the scheduled end of their visit to the United States, and (2) a tourist visa, which may be obtained without charge from any U.S. consulate.

To obtain a visa, the traveler must submit a completed application form (either in person or by mail) with a 1½-inch-square photo, and must demonstrate binding ties to a residence abroad. Usually you can obtain a visa at once or within 24 hours, but it may take longer during the summer rush June through August. If you cannot go in person, contact the nearest U.S. embassy or consulate for directions on applying by mail. Your travel agent or airline office may also be able to provide you with visa applications and instructions. The U.S. consulate or embassy that issues your visa will determine whether you will be issued a multiple- or single-entry visa and any restrictions regarding the length of your stay.

British subjects can obtain up-to-date passport and visa information by calling the **U.S. Embassy Visa Information Line** (© 0891/200-290) or the **London Passport Office** (© 0990/210-410 for recorded information) or they can find the visa information on the American Embassy London's website at www.us.embassy.org.uk.

Irish citizens can obtain up-to-date passport and visa information through the **Embassy of USA Dublin,** 42 Elgin Rd., Dublin 4, Ireland (☎ **353/ 1-668-8777**) or checking the visa page on the website at www.us embassy.ie.

Australian citizens can obtain up-to-date passport and visa information by calling the **U.S. Embassy Canberra,** Moonah Place, Yarralumla, ACT 2600 (☎ **02/6214-5600**) or checking the website's visa page at http://usembassy-australia.state.gov/consular.

Citizens of **New Zealand** can obtain up-to-date passport and visa information by calling the **U.S. Embassy New Zealand,** 29 Fitzherbert Terrace, Thorndon, Wellington, New Zealand (☎ **644/472-2068**); or get the information directly from the website at http://usembassy.org.nz.

MEDICAL REQUIREMENTS

Unless you're arriving from an area known to be suffering from an epidemic (particularly cholera or yellow fever), inoculations or vaccinations are not required for entry into the United States. If you have a medical condition that requires **syringe-administered medications,** carry a valid signed prescription from your physician—the Federal Aviation Administration (FAA) no longer allows airline passengers to pack syringes in their carry-on baggage without documented proof of medical need. If you have a disease that requires treatment with **narcotics,** you should also carry documented proof with you—smuggling narcotics aboard a plane is a serious offense that carries severe penalties in the U.S.

For **HIV-positive visitors,** requirements for entering the United States are somewhat vague and change frequently. According to the latest publication of *HIV and Immigrants: A Manual for AIDS Service Providers,* the Immigration and Naturalization Service (INS) doesn't require a medical exam for entry into the United States, but INS officials may stop individuals because they look sick or because they are carrying AIDS/HIV medicine.

If an HIV-positive noncitizen applies for a nonimmigrant visa, the question on the application regarding communicable diseases is tricky no matter which way it's answered. If the applicant checks "no," INS may deny the visa on the grounds that the applicant committed fraud. If the applicant checks "yes" or if INS suspects the person is HIV-positive, it will deny the visa unless the applicant asks for a special waiver for visitors. This waiver is for people visiting the United States for a short time, to attend a conference, for instance, to visit close relatives, or to receive medical treatment. It can be a confusing situation. For further up-to-the-minute information, contact the Centers for Disease Control's **National Center for HIV** (☎ **404/332-4559;** www.hivatis.org) or the **Gay Men's Health Crisis** (☎ **212/367-1000;** www.gmhc.org).

DRIVER'S LICENSES

Foreign driver's licenses are mostly recognized in the U.S., including Texas, although you may want to get an international driver's license if your home license is not written in English.

PASSPORT INFORMATION

Safeguard your passport in an inconspicuous, inaccessible place like a money belt. Make a copy of the critical pages, including the passport number, and store it in a safe place, separate from the passport itself. If you lose your passport, visit the nearest consulate of your native country as soon as possible for a replacement. Passport applications are downloadable from the Internet sites listed below.

Note that the International Civil Aviation Organization (ICAO) has recommended a policy requiring that *every* individual who travels by air have his or her own passport. In response, many countries are now requiring that children must be issued their own passport to travel internationally, where before those under 16 or so may have been allowed to travel on a parent or guardian's passport.

FOR RESIDENTS OF CANADA

You can pick up a passport application at one of 28 regional passport offices or most travel agencies. Canadian children who travel must have their own passport; however, if you hold a valid Canadian passport issued before December 11, 2001, that bears the name of your child, the passport remains valid for you and your child until it expires. Passports cost C$85 for those 16 years and older (valid 5 years), C$35 children 3 to 15 (valid 5 years), and C$20, children under 3 (valid 3 years). Applications, which must be accompanied by two identical passport-sized photographs and proof of Canadian citizenship, are available at travel agencies throughout Canada or from the central **Passport Office,** Department of Foreign Affairs and International Trade, Ottawa, ON K1A 0G3 (✆ **800/567-6868;** www. dfait-maeci.gc.ca/passport). Processing takes 5 to 10 days if you apply in person, or about 3 weeks by mail.

FOR RESIDENTS OF THE UNITED KINGDOM

To pick up an application for a standard 10-year passport (5-year passport for children under 16), visit your nearest Passport Office, major post office, or travel agency. You can also contact the **United Kingdom Passport Service** at ✆ **0870/521-0410** or search its website at www.passport.gov.uk. Passports are £33 for adults and £19 for children under 16, with an additional £30 fee if you apply in person at a Passport Office. Processing takes about 2 weeks (1 week if you apply at the Passport Office).

FOR RESIDENTS OF IRELAND

You can apply for a 10-year passport, costing €57, at the **Passport Office,** Setanta Centre, Molesworth Street, Dublin 2 (✆ **01/671-1633;** www.irl gov.ie/iveagh). Those under age 18 and over 65 must apply for a €12 3-year passport. You can also apply at 1A South Mall, Cork (✆ **021/272-525**) or over the counter at most main post offices.

FOR RESIDENTS OF AUSTRALIA

You can pick up an application from your local post office or any branch of Passports Australia, but you must schedule an interview at the passport office to present your application materials. Call the **Australian Passport Information Service** at ✆ **131-232,** or visit the government website at www.passports.gov.au. Passports for adults are A$144 and for those under 18 are A$72.

FOR RESIDENTS OF NEW ZEALAND

You can pick up a passport application at any New Zealand Passports Office or download it from their website. Contact the **Passports Office** at ✆ **0800/225-050** in New Zealand or 04/474-8100, or log on to www. passports.govt.nz. Passports for adults are NZ$80 and for children under 16 NZ$40.

CUSTOMS
WHAT YOU CAN BRING IN

Every visitor more than 21 years of age may bring in, free of duty, the following: (1) 1 liter of wine or hard liquor; (2) 200 cigarettes, 100 cigars (but not from Cuba), or 3 pounds of smoking tobacco; and (3) $100 worth of gifts. These exemptions are offered to travelers who spend at least 72 hours in the United States and who have not claimed them within the preceding 6 months. It is altogether forbidden to bring into the country foodstuffs (particularly fruit, cooked meats, and canned goods) and plants (vegetables, seeds, tropical plants, and the like). Foreign tourists may bring in or take out up to $10,000 in U.S. or foreign currency with no formalities; larger sums must be declared to U.S. Customs on entering or leaving, which includes filing form CM 4790. For more specific information regarding U.S. Customs, contact your nearest U.S. embassy or consulate, or the **U.S. Customs** office (© **202/927-1770;** www.customs.ustreas.gov).

WHAT YOU CAN TAKE HOME

U.K. citizens returning from a non-EU country have a customs allowance of: 200 cigarettes; 50 cigars; 250 grams of smoking tobacco; 2 liters of still table wine; 1 liter of spirits or strong liqueurs (over 22% volume); 2 liters of fortified wine, sparkling wine, or other liqueurs; 60cc (milliliters) perfume; 250cc (milliliters) of toilet water; and £145 worth of all other goods, including gifts and souvenirs. People under 17 cannot have the tobacco or alcohol allowance. For more information, contact HM Customs & Excise at © **0845/010-9000** (from outside the U.K., 020/8929-0152), or consult their website at www.hmce.gov.uk.

For a clear summary of **Canadian** rules, request the booklet *I Declare,* issued by the **Canada Customs and Revenue Agency** (© **800/461-9999** in Canada, or 204/983-3500; www.ccra-adrc.gc.ca). Canada allows its citizens a C$750 exemption, and you're allowed to bring back duty-free

1 carton of cigarettes, 1 can of tobacco, 40 imperial ounces of liquor, and 50 cigars. In addition, you're allowed to mail gifts to Canada valued at less than C$60 a day, provided they're unsolicited and don't contain alcohol or tobacco (write on the package "Unsolicited gift, under $60 value"). All valuables should be declared on the Y-38 form before departure from Canada, including serial numbers of valuables you already own, such as expensive foreign cameras. *Note:* The $750 exemption can only be used once a year and only after an absence of 7 days.

The duty-free allowance in **Australia** is A$400 or, for those under 18, A$200. Citizens age 18 and over can bring in 250 cigarettes or 250 grams of loose tobacco, and 1,125 milliliters of alcohol. If you're returning with valuables you already own, such as foreign-made cameras, you should file form B263. A helpful brochure available from Australian consulates or Customs offices is *Know Before You Go.* For more information, call the **Australian Customs Service** at © **1300/363-263,** or log on to www.customs.gov.au.

The duty-free allowance for **New Zealand** is NZ$700. Citizens over 17 can bring in 200 cigarettes, 50 cigars, or 250 grams of tobacco (or a mixture of all three if their combined weight doesn't exceed 250g); plus 4.5 liters of wine and beer, or 1.125 liters of liquor. New Zealand currency does not carry import or export restrictions. Fill out a certificate of export, listing the valuables you are taking out of the country; that way, you can bring them back without paying duty. Most questions are answered in a free pamphlet available at New Zealand consulates and Customs offices: *New Zealand Customs Guide for Travellers, Notice no. 4.* For more information, contact **New Zealand Customs,** The

Customhouse, 17–21 Whitmore St., Box 2218, Wellington (② **0800/428-786** or 04/473-6099; www.customs.govt.nz).

HEALTH INSURANCE

Although it's not required of travelers, health insurance is highly recommended. Unlike many European countries, the United States does not usually offer free or low-cost medical care to its citizens or visitors. Doctors and hospitals are expensive, and in most cases will require advance payment or proof of coverage before they render their services. Policies can cover everything from the loss or theft of your baggage and trip cancellation to the guarantee of bail in case you're arrested. Good policies will also cover the costs of an accident, repatriation, or death. See "Insurance, Health & Safety" in chapter 2 for more information. Packages such as **Europ Assistance's "Worldwide Healthcare Plan"** are sold by European automobile clubs and travel agencies at attractive rates. **Worldwide Assistance Services, Inc.** (② **800/821-2828;** www.worldwideassistance.com) is the agent for Europ Assistance in the United States.

Though lack of health insurance may prevent you from being admitted to a hospital in nonemergencies, don't worry about being left on a street corner to die: The American way is to fix you now and bill the living daylights out of you later.

INSURANCE FOR BRITISH TRAVELERS Most big travel agents offer their own insurance and will probably try to sell you their package when you book a holiday. Think before you sign. **Britain's Consumers' Association** recommends that you insist on seeing the policy and reading the fine print before buying travel insurance. **The Association of British Insurers** (② **020/7600-3333;** www.abi.org.uk) gives advice

by phone and publishes *Holiday Insurance,* a free guide to policy provisions and prices. You might also shop around for better deals: Try **Columbus Direct** (② **020/7375-0011;** www.columbusdirect.net).

INSURANCE FOR CANADIAN TRAVELERS Canadians should check with their provincial health plan offices or call **Health Canada** (② **613/957-2991;** www.hc-sc.gc.ca) to find out the extent of their coverage and what documentation and receipts they must take home in case they are treated in the United States.

MONEY

CURRENCY The U.S. monetary system is very simple: The most common **bills** are the $1 (colloquially, a "buck"), $5, $10, and $20 denominations. There are also $2 bills (seldom encountered), $50 bills, and $100 bills (the last two are usually not welcome as payment for small purchases). All the paper money was recently redesigned, making the famous faces adorning them disproportionately large. The old-style bills are still legal tender.

There are seven denominations of coins: 1¢ (1 cent, or a penny); 5¢ (5 cents, or a nickel); 10¢ (10 cents, or a dime); 25¢ (25 cents, or a quarter); 50¢ (50 cents, or a half dollar); the gold "Sacagawea" coin worth $1; and, prized by collectors, the rare, older silver dollar.

Note: The currency exchange bureaus so common in Europe are rare even at airports in the United States, and nonexistent outside major cities. It's best to leave any currency other than U.S. dollars at home—it may prove a greater nuisance to you than it's worth.

TRAVELER'S CHECKS Though traveler's checks are widely accepted, make sure that they're denominated in U.S. dollars, as foreign-currency

> **⌢Tips Just in Case**
>
> Be sure to keep a copy of all your travel papers separate from your wallet or purse, and leave a copy with someone at home should you need it faxed in an emergency.

checks are often difficult to exchange. The three traveler's checks that are most widely recognized—and least likely to be denied—are **Visa, American Express,** and **Thomas Cook.** Be sure to record the numbers of the checks, and keep that information in a separate place in case they get lost or stolen. Most businesses are pretty good about taking traveler's checks, but you're better off cashing them at a bank (in small amounts, of course) and paying in cash. *Remember:* You'll need identification, such as a driver's license or passport, to change a traveler's check.

CREDIT CARDS & ATMS It is strongly recommended that you bring at least one major credit or charge card—**Visa** (Barclaycard in Britain) and **MasterCard** (EuroCard in Europe, Access in Britain, Chargex in Canada) are the most widely accepted in Texas, followed by **American Express** and **Discover.** You must have a credit card to rent a car, and hotels and airlines usually require a credit-card imprint as a deposit against expenses. There are, however, a handful of stores and restaurants that do not take credit cards, so be sure to ask in advance. Most businesses display a sticker near their entrance to let you know which cards they accept. (*Note:* Businesses may require a minimum purchase, usually around $10, to use a credit card.) In an emergency a credit card can be priceless.

You'll find ATMs (automated teller machines) on just about every block—at least in almost every town—across the country. Some ATMs will allow you to draw U.S. currency against your bank and credit cards. Check with your bank before leaving home, and remember that you will need your personal identification number (PIN) to do so. Expect to be charged up to $3 per transaction, however, if you're not using your own bank's ATM. Most ATMs also accept Visa, MasterCard, and American Express cards.

One way around the bank fees is to ask for cash back at grocery stores that accept ATM cards and don't charge usage fees. Of course, you'll have to purchase something first.

ATM cards with major credit card backing, known as "debit cards," are now a commonly acceptable form of payment in most stores and restaurants. Debit cards draw money directly from your checking account. Some stores enable you to receive "cash back" on your debit-card purchases as well.

SAFETY
GENERAL SUGGESTIONS Although tourist areas are generally safe, U.S. urban areas tend to be less safe than those in Europe or Japan. You should always stay alert. This is particularly true of Houston and Dallas, and in border towns such as El Paso. Avoid deserted areas, especially at night, and don't go into public parks after dark unless there's a concert or an event that will attract a crowd. If you're in doubt about which neighborhoods are safe, don't hesitate to make inquiries with the hotel front desk staff or the local tourist office.

Some additional advice: Avoid carrying valuables with you on the street, and keep expensive cameras or electronic equipment bagged up or covered when not in use. If you're using a map, try to consult it inconspicuously—or better yet, study it before you leave your room. Hold onto your pocketbook, and place your billfold in an inside pocket. In theaters, restaurants, and other public places, keep your possessions in sight.

Finally, always lock your hotel room door—don't assume that once you're inside the hotel you are automatically safe and no longer need to be aware of your surroundings. Hotels are open to the public, and in a large hotel, security may not be able to screen everyone who enters.

You may want to look into renting a cellphone, which can be useful in an emergency. One recommended wireless rental company is **InTouch USA** (© **800/872-7626**; www.intouchusa.com).

DRIVING SAFETY Driving safety is important too, and carjacking is not unprecedented. Obtain written directions—or a map with the route clearly marked—from the agency showing how to get to your destination. (Many agencies now offer the option of renting a cellphone for the duration of your car rental; check with the agent when you pick up the car.) And, if possible, arrive and depart during daylight hours.

If you drive off a highway and end up in a dodgy-looking neighborhood, leave the area as quickly as possible. If you have an accident, even on the highway, stay in your car with the doors locked until you assess the situation or until the police arrive. If you're bumped from behind on the street or are involved in a minor accident with no injuries, and the situation appears to be suspicious, motion to the other driver to follow you. Never get out of your car in such situations. Go directly to the nearest police precinct, well-lit service station, or 24-hour store.

Park in well-lit and well-traveled areas whenever possible. Always keep your car doors locked, whether the vehicle is attended or unattended. Never leave any packages or valuables in sight. If someone attempts to rob you or steal your car, don't try to resist. Report the incident to the police department immediately by calling © **911.**

2 Getting to the U.S.

Most international visitors will fly to Dallas/Fort Worth International Airport, El Paso International Airport, Bush Intercontinental or William P. Hobby airports in Houston, or San Antonio International Airport. Major airlines offering flights to Texas include **Air Canada** (© 888/247-2262; www.aircanada.ca), **American** (© 800/433-7300; www.aa.com), **America West** (© 800/235-9292; www.americawest.com), **Continental** (© 800/525-0280; www. continental. com), **Delta** (© 800/221-1212; www.delta.com), **Frontier** (© 800/ 432-1359; www.frontierairlines.com), **Northwest** (© 800/225-2525; www. nwa.com), **Southwest** (© 800/435-9792; www.iflyswa.com), **United** (© 800/864-8331; www.united.com), and **US Airways** (© 800/428-4322; www.usairways.com). International travelers can also take flights to O'Hare International Airport in Chicago, Los Angeles International Airport (LAX), and JFK International Airport in New York, and catch connecting flights to Texas.

British Airways (© **0845/773-3377** in London, or 800/247-9297 in the U.S.; www.britishairways.com) offers daily flights between London and both Dallas–Fort Worth and Houston. Travelers from the United Kingdom can also take British Airways flights to such cities as Philadelphia or Chicago and make connecting flights to Texas.

AIRLINE DISCOUNTS The smart traveler can find numerable ways to reduce the price of a plane ticket simply by taking time to shop around. Take advantage of the APEX (Advance Purchase Excursion) reductions offered by all major U.S. and European carriers. For more money-saving airline advice, see "Getting There," in chapter 2. For the best rates, be flexible with the dates and times of travel.

IMMIGRATION & CUSTOMS CLEARANCE Visitors arriving by air, no matter what the port of entry, should cultivate patience and resignation before setting foot on U.S. soil. Getting through immigration control can take as long as 2 hours on some days, especially on summer weekends, so be sure to carry this guidebook or something else to read. This has been especially true since the September 11, 2001, terrorist attacks, when security clearances were considerably beefed up at U.S. airports.

People traveling by air from Canada, Bermuda, and certain countries in the Caribbean can sometimes clear Customs and Immigration at the point of departure, which is much quicker.

3 Getting Around the U.S.

For specific information on traveling to and around Texas, see "Getting There" and "Getting Around" in chapter 2.

BY PLANE Some large airlines (for example, Northwest and Delta) offer travelers on their transatlantic or transpacific flights special discount tickets under the name **Visit USA,** allowing mostly one-way travel from one U.S. destination to another at very low prices. These discount tickets are not on sale in the United States and must be purchased abroad in conjunction with your international ticket. This system is the best, easiest, and fastest way to see the United States at low cost. You should obtain information well in advance from your travel agent or the office of the airline concerned, since the conditions attached to these discount tickets can be changed without advance notice.

BY TRAIN Amtrak (© 800/USA-RAIL; www.amtrak.com) connects Dallas, Austin, and several other Texas cities to both the East and West Coasts. International visitors (excluding Canada) can buy a **USA Rail Pass,** good for 15 or 30 days of unlimited travel on Amtrak. The pass is available through many foreign travel agents. With a foreign passport, you can also buy passes at some Amtrak offices in the United States, including locations in San Francisco, Los Angeles, Chicago, New York, Miami, Boston, and Washington, D.C. Reservations are generally required and should be made for each part of your trip as early as possible. Regional rail passes are also available.

BY BUS Although bus travel is often the most economical form of public transit for short hops between U.S. cities, it can also be slow and uncomfortable—certainly not an option for everyone (particularly when Amtrak, which is far more luxurious, offers similar rates). **Greyhound/ Trailways (© 800/231-2222;** www. greyhound.com), the sole nationwide bus line, offers an **International Ameripass** that must be purchased before coming to the United States, or by phone through the Greyhound International Office at the Port Authority Bus Terminal in New York

City (℃ **212/971-0492**). The pass can be obtained from foreign travel agents or through Greyhound's website (order at least 21 days before your departure to the U.S.) and costs less than the domestic version. You can get more info on the pass at the website, or by calling ℃ **402/330-8552**. In addition, special rates are available for seniors and students.

BY CAR   Unless you plan to spend the bulk of your vacation time in a city where walking is the best and easiest way to get around (read: New York City or New Orleans), the most cost-effective, convenient, and comfortable way to travel around the United States is by car. A car is also the best way to explore the state's rural areas, where public transportation is limited or nonexistent. The interstate highway system connects cities and towns all over the country; in addition to these high-speed, limited-access roadways, there's an extensive network of federal, state, and local highways and roads. Some of the national car-rental companies include **Alamo** (℃ 800/462-5266; www.alamo.com), **Avis** (℃ 800/230-4898; www.avis.com), **Budget** (℃ 800/527-0700; www.budget.com), **Dollar** (℃ 800/800-3665; www.dollar.com), **Hertz** (℃ 800/654-3131; www.hertz.com), **National** (℃ 800/227-7368; www.nationalcar.com), and **Thrifty** (℃ 800/847-4389; www.thrifty.com).

If you plan to rent a car in the United States, you probably won't need the services of an additional automobile organization. If you're planning to buy or borrow a car, automobile-association membership is recommended. The **American Automobile Association** (℃ **800/222-4357**) is the country's largest auto club and supplies its members with maps, insurance, and, most important, emergency road service. The cost of joining runs from $63 for singles to $87 for two members, but if you're a member of a foreign auto club with reciprocal arrangements, you can enjoy free AAA service in America. See "Fast Facts: For the International Traveler" below for more information.

 FAST FACTS: For the International Traveler

Automobile Organizations Auto clubs will supply maps, suggested routes, guidebooks, accident and bail-bond insurance, and emergency road service. The **American Automobile Association (AAA)** is the major auto club in the United States. If you belong to an auto club in your home country, inquire about AAA reciprocity before you leave. You may be able to join AAA even if you're not a member of a reciprocal club; to inquire, call AAA (℃ **800/222-4357**). AAA is actually an organization of regional auto clubs; so look under "AAA Automobile Club" in the White Pages of the telephone directory. AAA has a nationwide emergency road service telephone number (℃ 800/AAA-HELP).

Business Hours Offices are usually open weekdays from 9am to 5pm. Banks are open weekdays from 9am to 3pm or later and sometimes Saturday mornings. Stores typically open between 9 and 10am and close between 5 and 6pm Monday through Saturday. Stores in shopping complexes or malls tend to stay open late: until about 9pm on weekdays and weekends, and many malls and larger department stores are open on Sundays. There is also a growing number of discount stores, such as Wal-Mart, and grocery stores that are open 24 hours a day.

Currency & Currency Exchange See "Money" under "Preparing for Your Trip," earlier in this chapter.

Drinking Laws The legal age for purchase and consumption of alcoholic beverages is 21; proof of age is required and often requested at bars, nightclubs, and restaurants, so it's always a good idea to bring ID when you go out. Beer and wine often can be purchased in supermarkets.

Do not carry open containers of alcohol in your car or any public area that isn't zoned for alcohol consumption. And nothing will ruin your trip faster than getting a citation for DUI ("driving under the influence"), so don't even think about driving while intoxicated.

Electricity Like Canada, the United States uses 110 to 120 volts AC (60 cycles), compared to 220 to 240 volts AC (50 cycles) in most of Europe, Australia, and New Zealand. If your small appliances use 220 to 240 volts, you'll need a 110-volt transformer and a plug adapter with two flat parallel pins to operate them here. Downward converters that change 220–240 volts to 110–120 volts are difficult to find in the United States, so bring one with you.

Embassies & Consulates All embassies are located in the nation's capital, Washington, D.C. Some consulates are located in major U.S. cities, and most nations have a mission to the United Nations in New York City. Dozens of countries have consulates in Texas; most offices are in Houston, and some are in Dallas. Check the local phone book under "Consulates and Other Foreign Government Representatives." If your country isn't listed below, call for directory information in Washington, D.C. (© **202/ 555-1212**) or log on to **www.embassy.org/embassies**.

The embassy of **Australia** is at 1601 Massachusetts Ave. NW, Washington, DC 20036 (© **202/797-3000**; www.austemb.org). There are consulates in New York, Honolulu, Houston, Los Angeles, and San Francisco.

The embassy of **Canada** is at 501 Pennsylvania Ave. NW, Washington, DC 20001 (© **202/682-1740**; www.canadianembassy.org). Other Canadian consulates are in Buffalo (N.Y.), Detroit, Los Angeles, New York, and Seattle.

The embassy of **Ireland** is at 2234 Massachusetts Ave. NW, Washington, DC 20008 (© **202/462-3939**; www.irelandemb.org). Irish consulates are in Boston, Chicago, New York, and San Francisco.

The embassy of **Japan** is at 2520 Massachusetts Ave. NW, Washington, DC 20008 (© **202/238-6700**; www.embjapan.org). Japanese consulates are located in Atlanta, Kansas City, San Francisco, and Washington, D.C.

The embassy of **New Zealand** is at 37 Observatory Circle NW, Washington, DC 20008 (© **202/328-4800**; www.nzemb.org). New Zealand consulates are in Los Angeles, Salt Lake City, San Francisco, and Seattle.

The embassy of the **United Kingdom** is at 3100 Massachusetts Ave. NW, Washington, DC 20008 (© **202/462-1340**; www.britainusa.com). Other British consulates are in Atlanta, Boston, Chicago, Cleveland, Houston, Los Angeles, New York, San Francisco, and Seattle.

Emergencies Call © **911** to report a fire, call the police, or get an ambulance anywhere in the United States. This is a toll-free call. (No coins are required at public telephones.)

If you encounter serious problems, contact the **Traveler's Aid Society International** (© 202/546-1127; www.travelersaid.org). The Texas office is at the Dallas/Fort Worth International Airport (© 972/574-4420). This nationwide, nonprofit, social-service organization geared to helping travelers in difficult straits offers services that might include reuniting families separated while traveling, providing food and/or shelter to people stranded without cash, or even emotional counseling. If you're in trouble, seek them out.

Gasoline (Petrol) Petrol is known as gasoline (or simply "gas") in the United States, and petrol stations are known as both "gas stations" and "service stations." Texas often has some of the lowest gasoline prices in the United States; although prices fluctuate, at press time regular unleaded gas ranged from $1.30 to $1.50 per gallon, with the lowest prices in the Gulf Coast area. Taxes are already included in the printed price.

Holidays Banks, government offices, post offices, and many stores, restaurants, and museums are closed on the following legal national holidays: January 1 (New Year's Day), the third Monday in January (Martin Luther King, Jr. Day), the third Monday in February (Presidents' Day, Washington's Birthday), the last Monday in May (Memorial Day), July 4 (Independence Day), the first Monday in September (Labor Day), the second Monday in October (Columbus Day), November 11 (Veterans' Day/Armistice Day), the fourth Thursday in November (Thanksgiving Day), and December 25 (Christmas). Also, the Tuesday following the first Monday in November is Election Day and is a federal government holiday in presidential-election years (held every 4 years, and next in 2004).

Legal Aid If you are "pulled over" for a minor infraction (such as speeding), never attempt to pay the fine directly to a police officer; this could be construed as attempted bribery, a much more serious crime. Pay fines by mail, or directly into the hands of the clerk of the court. If accused of a more serious offense, say and do nothing before consulting a lawyer. Here the burden is on the state to prove a person's guilt beyond a reasonable doubt, and everyone has the right to remain silent, whether he or she is suspected of a crime or actually arrested. Once arrested, a person can make one telephone call to a party of his or her choice. Call your embassy or consulate.

Mail If you aren't sure what your address will be in the United States, mail can be sent to you, in your name, c/o General Delivery at the main post office of the city or region where you expect to be. (Call © 800/275-8777 or check the Web at www.usps.com for information on the nearest post office.) The addressee must pick up mail in person and must produce proof of identity (driver's license or passport, for example). Most post offices will hold your mail for up to 1 month, and are open Monday through Friday from 8am to 6pm, and Saturday from 9am to 3pm.

Generally found at intersections, mailboxes are blue with a red-and-white stripe and carry the inscription U.S. MAIL. If your mail is addressed to a U.S. destination, don't forget to add the five-digit postal code (or ZIP code), after the two-letter abbreviation of the state to which the mail is addressed. This is essential for prompt delivery.

At press time, domestic postage rates were 23¢ for a postcard and 37¢ for a letter. For international mail, a first-class letter of up to ½ ounce costs 80¢ (60¢ to Canada and Mexico); a first-class postcard costs 70¢ (50¢ to Canada and Mexico); and a preprinted postal aerogramme costs 70¢.

Measurements See the chart on the inside front cover of this book for details on converting metric measurements to U.S. equivalents.

Taxes The United States has no value-added tax (VAT) or other indirect tax at the national level. Every state, county, and city has the right to levy its own local tax on all purchases, including hotel and restaurant checks, airline tickets, and so on. Sales taxes in Texas vary, but usually total from 7% to 8%. An exception is the tax on lodging, which ranges from 10% to 17%, with the highest rate in Houston.

Telephone, Telegraph, Telex & Fax The telephone system in the United States is run by private corporations, so rates, especially for long-distance service and operator-assisted calls, can vary widely. Generally, hotel surcharges on long-distance and local calls are astronomical, so you're usually better off using a **public pay telephone,** which you'll find clearly marked in most public buildings and private establishments as well as on the street. Convenience grocery stores and gas stations always have them. Many convenience groceries and packaging services sell **prepaid calling cards** in denominations up to $50; these can be the least expensive way to call home. Many public phones at airports now accept American Express, MasterCard, and Visa credit cards. **Local calls** made from public pay phones in most locales cost either 25¢ or 35¢. Pay phones do not accept pennies, and few will take anything larger than a quarter.

You may want to look into leasing a cellphone for the duration of your trip.

Most long-distance and international calls can be dialed directly from any phone. **For calls within the United States and to Canada,** dial 1 followed by the area code and the seven-digit number. **For other international calls,** dial 011 followed by the country code, city code, and the telephone number of the person you are calling.

Calls to area codes **800, 888, 877,** and **866** are toll-free. However, calls to numbers in area codes **700** and **900** (chat lines, bulletin boards, "dating" services, and so on) can be very expensive—usually a charge of 95¢ to $3 or more per minute, and they sometimes have minimum charges that can run as high as $15 or more.

For **reversed-charge or collect calls,** and for person-to-person calls, dial 0 (zero, not the letter O) followed by the area code and number you want; an operator will then come on the line, and you should specify that you are calling collect, or person-to-person, or both. If your operator-assisted call is international, ask for the overseas operator.

For **local directory assistance** ("information"), dial 411; for long-distance information, dial 1, then the appropriate area code and 555-1212.

Telegraph and telex services are provided primarily by Western Union. You can bring your telegram into the nearest Western Union office (there are hundreds across the country) or dictate it over the phone (© 800/325-6000). You can also telegraph money, or have it telegraphed to you, very quickly over the Western Union system, but this service can cost as much as 15% to 20% of the amount sent.

Most hotels have **fax machines** available for guest use (be sure to ask about the charge to use it). Many hotel rooms are even wired for guests' fax machines. A less expensive way to send and receive faxes may be at stores such as The UPS Store, a national chain of packing service shops. (Look in the Yellow Pages directory under "Packing Services.")

There are two kinds of telephone directories in the United States. The so-called **White Pages** list private households and business subscribers in alphabetical order. The inside front cover lists emergency numbers for police, fire, ambulance, the Coast Guard, poison-control center, crime-victims hot line, and so on. The first few pages will tell you how to make long-distance and international calls, complete with country codes and area codes. Government numbers are usually printed on blue paper within the White Pages. Printed on yellow paper, the so-called **Yellow Pages** list all local services, businesses, industries, and houses of worship according to activity with an index at the front or back. (Drugstores/pharmacies and restaurants are also listed by geographic location.) The Yellow Pages also include city plans or detailed area maps, postal ZIP codes, and public transportation routes.

Time The continental United States is divided into **four time zones:** Eastern Standard Time (EST), Central Standard Time (CST), which includes all of Texas except its far western tip, Mountain Standard Time (MST), and Pacific Standard Time (PST). Alaska and Hawaii have their own zones. For example, noon in New York City (EST) is 11am in Dallas (CST), 10am in Denver (MST), 9am in Los Angeles (PST), 8am in Anchorage (AST), and 7am in Honolulu (HST).

Daylight saving time is in effect from 1am on the first Sunday in April to 1am on the last Sunday in October, except in Arizona, Hawaii, part of Indiana, and Puerto Rico. Daylight saving time moves the clock 1 hour ahead of standard time.

Tipping Tips are a very important part of certain workers' salaries, so it's necessary to leave appropriate gratuities. In hotels, tip **bellhops** at least $1 per bag ($2–$3 if you have a lot of luggage) and tip the **chamber staff** $1 to $2 per day (more if you've left a disaster area for him or her to clean up). Tip the **doorman** or **concierge** only if he or she has provided you with some specific service (for example, calling a cab for you or obtaining difficult-to-get theater tickets). Tip the **valet-parking attendant** $1 every time you get your car.

In restaurants, bars, and nightclubs, tip **service staff** 15% to 20% of the check, tip **bartenders** 10% to 15%, tip **checkroom attendants** $1 per garment, and tip **valet-parking attendants** $1 per vehicle. Tip the **doorman** only if he has provided you with some specific service (such as calling a cab for you).

As for other service personnel, tip **cab drivers** 15% of the fare; tip **skycaps** at airports at least $1 per bag ($2–$3 if you have a lot of luggage); and tip **hairdressers** and **barbers** 15% to 20%.

Toilets You won't find public toilets or "restrooms" on the streets in most U.S. cities, but they can be found in hotel lobbies, bars, restaurants, museums, department stores, railway and bus stations, and service stations. Large hotels and fast-food restaurants are probably the best bet for good, clean facilities. If possible, avoid the toilets at parks and beaches, which tend to be dirty; some may be unsafe. Restaurants and bars in resorts or heavily visited areas may reserve their restrooms for patrons. Some establishments display a notice indicating this. You can ignore this sign or, better yet, avoid arguments by paying for a cup of coffee or a soft drink, which will qualify you as a patron.

4

The Dallas–Fort Worth Metroplex

by Neil E. Schlecht

North Texas's two biggest cities, Dallas and Fort Worth, are often referred to as "DFW"—or, in a term that could only have been devised by so-called marketing geniuses, the Metroplex—as though they were closely intertwined twin cities. While unrelenting development has filled the flat land gaps between them and created a greater population of some four million, the fact is that the two cities remain 30 miles and worlds apart. Glitzy Dallas, home of the NFL's Cowboys, "America's Team," thrives on an identity of banking and business; it's "where the east peters out," in the words of Will Rogers. Fort Worth, the "Cowtown" of the old cattle drives and now the cultural capital of North Texas, has long identified itself quite differently: as the spot where the West begins. Much more laid-back than Dallas, Fort Worth might even be considered a bit pokey, except for its surprising roster of world-class museums and progressive civic-mindedness.

1 Orientation

ARRIVING

BY PLANE

DALLAS/FORT WORTH INTERNATIONAL AIRPORT Most visitors will arrive via DFW Airport (© **972/574-6000;** www.dfwairport.com), located midway between the two cities and one of the largest in the nation. The airport, the world's third busiest and larger than the island of Manhattan (take that, New York!), has four terminals connected by a "people mover." **DFW Airport Visitor Information** (© **972/574-3694**) provides hotel, sightseeing, and transportation information, and the **Airport Assistance Center** (© **972/574-4420**) offers crisis counseling, foreign language assistance, and car-seat rental. You'll also find currency exchange booths and ATMs in Terminals A, B, and E. All the major car-rental companies have representatives here.

Ground transportation to Dallas, Fort Worth, or the surrounding area is by Dallas Area Rapid Transit (DART) bus, airport shuttle, private car, charter limo, courtesy car, or taxi. Many hotels offer courtesy transportation to and from the airport; check to see if yours does. Transport by bus is the cheapest option, but the best value is taking the airport shuttle. For additional information on ground transportation, call © **972/574-5878** or 972/574-2227.

DART buses (© **214/979-1111;** www.dart.org) offer two means of travel between DFW Airport and downtown Dallas: the Trinity Railway Express (TRE) and DART Express Route 202. Passenger terminals at DFW Airport are served by two DART shuttles serving terminals A and C, and serving terminals B and E; both operate from CentrePort/DFW Airport Station. 202 Express

Buses depart from the DFW Airport ground transportation level in terminals A and E and travel directly to the West Transfer Center in downtown Dallas. The TRE does not run on Sunday; the 202 Express Bus runs hourly, 7 days a week, from 6am to 11pm. Single-ride fares on either are $2. A 202 Express Bus 1-day pass is available for $4 and is good for unlimited rides on DART and The T (including your return trip) until 3am the next day.

Another convenient mode of transportation to and from the airport is **Super Shuttle,** which can be reached 24 hours a day by calling © **800/258-3826** or visiting the website at www.supershuttle.com. A typical fare to downtown Dallas is $15 to $20, to Fort Worth $16 to $24. **The Airporter Bus Service** (© **817/334-0092;** www.the-t.com), operated by the Fort Worth Transit Authority, runs between downtown Fort Worth and DFW Airport (making 33 round-trips daily). It departs from the Airporter Park and Ride Lot, at 1000 E. Weatherford St. in Fort Worth, and Fort Worth's Ramada Plaza every half-hour between 6am and 10pm daily, and will even pick up at certain hotels ($10 per adult each way; $5 for seniors and free for children 16 and under when accompanied by a paying adult).

Taxis are also on hand at airport arrival gates. You can also make airport transportation reservations by calling **Checker Cab Co.** (© **817/469-8880**), **Yellow Cab Co.** (© **800/749-9422** in Dallas, 800/749-0900 in Fort Worth), or **Agency Limousine** (© **800/277-LIMO**). The taxi fare to downtown Dallas is about $38; downtown Fort Worth, $43.

Driving from DFW Airport   International Parkway connects directly to major freeways serving both Dallas and Fort Worth (Hwy. 114 and 635 north, and 183 and 360 south). Signs clearly indicate the route; each city is 17½ miles from the airport. Despite that seemingly short distance, the drive to downtown Dallas or Fort Worth in peak hours takes up to an hour.

LOVE FIELD   Love Field (© **214/670-6073**) is just 7 miles from downtown Dallas. After DFW Airport was built, Love Field became primarily a private plane and cargo airport for DHL and Federal Express. Southwest Airlines continued to operate out of it, and recently it has been resurrected as a commercial airport, with Delta and Continental Express building or revamping terminals. While you're hanging around in the Southwest terminal, drop in on the **Frontiers of Flight Museum** (© **214/350-3600**), open Monday through Saturday from 10am to 5pm, and Sunday from 1 to 5pm. Admission costs $2 for adults, $1 for children under 12.

All the major car-rental companies are represented here. The same ground transportation services for DFW Airport also travel to Love Field. A taxi downtown costs about $13; the Super Shuttle is $15, $6 for each additional passenger.

BY CAR

You'll almost surely need a car to get around Dallas–Fort Worth (unless you stick to the downtown areas), so it's not a bad idea to arrive in one. The major roads into Dallas are **I-635** (better known as LBJ Freeway), which goes from DFW Airport east to Dallas; **I-20,** which joins I-635 and heads west to Fort Worth; **I-35,** north-south from the border towns in south Texas, through San Antonio and Austin, Dallas, and all the way to Oklahoma; and **U.S. 75** (better known as Central Expressway), which runs north-south from downtown Dallas to the northern suburbs. From Houston, the drive to Dallas (or Fort Worth) is about 5 hours; from Austin, 4 hours. Dallas is about an hour from Fort Worth.

The Dallas–Fort Worth Metroplex

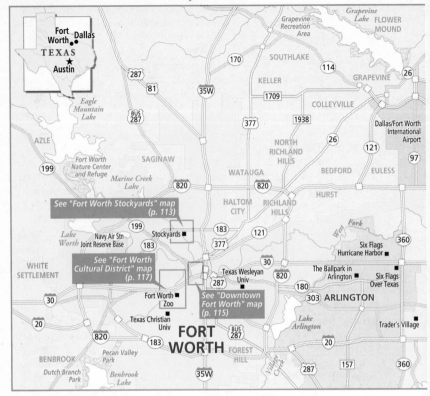

BY TRAIN

Amtrak's Texas Eagle serves Dallas's **Union Station,** 400 S. Houston St. (✆ **214/653-1101**), and Fort Worth's former **Santa Fe depot,** in the southeast corner of the city at 1501 Jones St. (✆ **817/335-3211**). Trains arrive from Chicago, St. Louis, Little Rock, San Antonio, and Los Angeles; Heartland Flyer trains serve Oklahoma City and Fort Worth. For more information and reservations, contact Amtrak at ✆ **800/USA-RAIL** or visit www.amtrak.com or www.texaseagle.com.

The **Trinity Railway Express (TRE)** travels back and forth between Dallas and Fort Worth; for more information, call ✆ **214/979-1111** or 817/215-8600 (www.dart.org or www.the-t.com).

2 Dallas

Known to locals as simply "Big D," this North Texas upstart doesn't lack for confidence. The indoctrination starts early. I grew up in North Dallas, and the refrain that all school kids had to parrot was from a little ditty that went "Big D, little a, double-l, a-s." Dallasites, like most Texans who are given to hyperbole when talking about their state, are proud to declare that their city is nicknamed "Big D" because, well, everything's bigger and better in Dallas.

Americans and people around the world have grown up with images of Dallas—some big, some not necessarily better. A sniper gunned down President

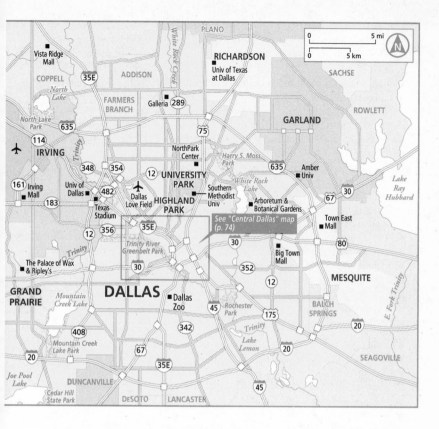

John F. Kennedy as his motorcade snaked through downtown Dallas in 1963; while the nation mourned, a local nightclub owner murdered the presumed assassin, Lee Harvey Oswald, right under the noses of local police. The Dallas Cowboys, a football club whose supporters had the audacity to call it "America's Team," won five Super Bowls and made scantily clad cheerleaders with big hair and big boobs a required accessory in professional sports. Bonnie and Clyde began their wanton spree of lawlessness in Dallas. J. R. Ewing presided over an oil empire in the TV soap opera *Dallas,* and propagated an image of tough-talking businessmen who wore cowboy boots with their pinstriped suits and had oil rigs pumping in the backyard. The irascible H. Ross Perot—remember him?—made a fortune in technology and thought he deserved to run the country.

Dallas has come to symbolize the kind of place where such larger-than-life characters live out the American dream, even if their versions are slightly skewed. Big D is about dreaming big, so the city, not much more than 400 square miles of flat prairie land broken up by shiny skyscrapers and soaring suburban homes, adopts all things big. Big cars. Big hair. Big belt buckles. Big attitude.

At just over 1 million inhabitants, Dallas now ranks as the eighth-largest city in the United States, but, flat and featureless, it has little in the way of natural gifts or historical precedents that would have predicted its growth. Yet the city grew from a little Republic of Texas pioneer outpost in the mid–19th century into a major center for banking, finance, and oil. It is a staunchly conservative city, and its residents' biggest passions seem to be making money and spending it, often ostentatiously. In the city that spawned Neiman Marcus, shopping is a religion, and mega-malls fan out in every direction, part of an endless commercial sprawl. Dallasites are also fiercely passionate about big-time sports, and not just the Cowboys. Just about every professional sports league has a franchise in Dallas, and there's also rodeo and the Texas Motor Speedway. This is a place where the top high school football teams routinely sell out playing fields that seat 20,000 and schedule their playoff games in Texas Stadium, home of the Cowboys, to accommodate a fan base that reaches far beyond parents and teachers. Dallas is also a place where Southern Baptist churches pack in nearly as many for Sunday services.

Dallas is the top business and leisure destination in Texas (and the second most popular convention site in the country). The city has grown more cosmopolitan in recent years, even though it's always been amazing to me how quickly newcomers from all over assimilate and begin to think Texan. The city can't yet boast a cultural life on a par with business opportunities, but a recent burst of arts philanthropy is finally allowing Dallas to play catch-up. Still, Dallas has plenty to entertain visitors, many of whom come on business: great hotels, eclectic restaurants, thriving nightlife, and even a pretty robust alternative music scene. And, lest we forget, shopping.

ESSENTIALS
VISITOR INFORMATION
Besides the DFW Airport Visitor Information (see above), there is a visitor information outlet at the **Old Red Courthouse** in downtown Dallas (at junction of Houston, Main, and Commerce sts.; © **214/571-1301,** 24-hr. hot line; open daily 9am–5pm). It has Internet terminals and touch-screen computer information kiosks. Before your travels, you might want to visit the website of the **Dallas Convention & Visitors Bureau** at www.dallascvb.com.

To get an immediate handle on what's happening in Dallas, check out the *Dallas Morning News* "Weekend Guide" (www.dallasnews.com) or *Dallas Observer* (www.dallasobserver.com), a free weekly paper with arts, entertainment, and dining information.

CITY LAYOUT
Dallas is extremely spread out, covering nearly 400 square miles. Traditionally, most people have worked in the downtown central business district and commuted to their homes in residential districts primarily north and east (but also south and west) of the city. New business attracted to the city has resulted in many more offices in outlying areas, particularly the corridor from Richardson to Plano, north of Dallas along U.S. 75 (Central Expressway) and west of the city in Carrollton and Irving/Las Colinas.

The West End Historic District, financial center, and Arts District are all downtown, just west of Central Expressway (though Deep Ellum, also part of downtown, is on the east side of U.S. 75). Central, in fact, divides east and west Dallas. LBJ Freeway, or I-635, runs through far north Dallas. It connects to I-20, which runs a loop south of the city. Irving, Grand Prairie, and Arlington are all due west, between Dallas and Fort Worth. I-30 leads directly west to Fort Worth.

THE NEIGHBORHOODS IN BRIEF

In addition to the six major neighborhoods discussed below, the city is surrounded by concentric rings of ever-expanding suburbs. (I grew up in one, Richardson, and went to high school in another, Plano, which remains one of the fastest-growing small cities in the United States.) In addition to ever-bigger homes, these areas are marked by scores of mega-malls, mini-malls, and strip malls of chain stores and restaurants that make the new developments very difficult to distinguish from one another.

Downtown Dallas This area encompasses the **Arts District,** the small nexus of downtown Dallas's fine and performing arts, including the Dallas Museum of Art, Nasher Sculpture Center, Meyerson Symphony Center, Crow Collection of Asian Art, and others; the **West End Historic District,** a former warehouse district and one of the oldest parts of the city transformed into a popular hotel, restaurant, nightlife, and shopping scene; and the core of downtown offices that extend east from **Reunion Arena** and **Dealey Plaza,** where the flagship Neiman Marcus store is the sole remaining department store. Though some urban-minded professionals are finally beginning to renovate residential loft spaces, downtown Dallas remains pretty much a ghost town after 6pm (except for West End). Still, it has a number of major hotels and makes a good place to drop anchor, especially for visiting businesspeople.

Deep Ellum Located east of downtown and bounded by Elm, Main, Commerce, and Canton streets, Deep Ellum is Big D's best impersonation of Austin, the live music capital of the Southwest (though locals contend that Dallas's music scene is actually hotter at the moment). Simultaneously ragged and chic, the former industrial district is the epicenter of the Dallas music scene, with alternative, blues, rock, and other music clubs interspersed with discos, honky-tonks, art galleries, furniture and second-hand shops, and upscale restaurants.

During the day the area is dead, but at night and on weekends it gets pretty rowdy. The name is said to be a southern drawl pronunciation of the main street, Elm.

Uptown & Oak Lawn Located northeast of downtown and promoted as "Uptown," **McKinney Avenue** and **Knox-Henderson** are chic restaurant rows and shopping meccas, one of the *in* places to live. McKinney Avenue, once the site of elegant old homes, is now the center of the Dallas art gallery scene, while Knox-Henderson is split right down the middle between trendy restaurants and upscale furnishings stores. **Oak Lawn, Cedar Springs,** and **Turtle Creek,** the heart of artsy gay Dallas, are also home to some of its finest hotels, restaurants, shopping, and the Dallas Theater Center, built by Frank Lloyd Wright.

Greenville Avenue & East Dallas The high point of Dallas nightlife, as it has been for decades, is this long strip located northeast of downtown Dallas, from LBJ Freeway south to Ross Avenue. Upper Greenville draws a slightly older and sophisticated crowd, while Lower Greenville (below Mockingbird) swims with nightclubs, bars both shabby and snooty, bohemian restaurants, vintage clothing stores, and resale furniture shops. East Dallas is home to the party district Deep Ellum, the Lakewood residential neighborhood, and old Dallas sites like the Cotton Bowl and Texas fairgrounds.

Central Dallas Accommodations, Dining & Attractions

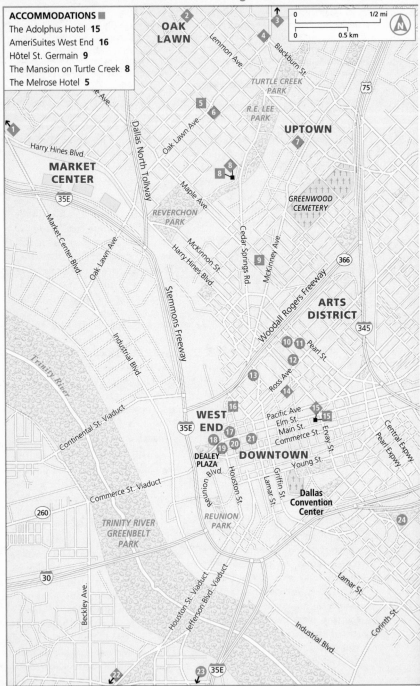

ACCOMMODATIONS ■
The Adolphus Hotel **15**
AmeriSuites West End **16**
Hôtel St. Germain **9**
The Mansion on Turtle Creek **8**
The Melrose Hotel **5**

OAK LAWN

Lemmon Ave.
Blackburn St.

TURTLE CREEK PARK

R.E. LEE PARK

75

UPTOWN

Harry Hines Blvd.

MARKET CENTER

35E

Dallas North Tollway

Oak Lawn Ave.

GREENWOOD CEMETERY

Maple Ave.

REVERCHON PARK

Market Center Blvd.

Oak Lawn Ave.

McKinnon St.
Harry Hines Blvd.

Cedar Springs Rd.

McKinney Ave.

366

Industrial Blvd.

Stemmons Freeway

Woodall Rogers Freeway

ARTS DISTRICT

345

Trinity River

Pearl St.
Ross Ave.

WEST END

35E

Continental St. Viaduct

Pacific Ave.
Elm St.
Main St.
Commerce St.

Ervay St.

Central Expwy.
Pearl Expwy.

DEALEY PLAZA

DOWNTOWN

Young St.

Reunion Blvd.

Houston St.

Griffin St.

Lamar St.

Commerce St. Viaduct

260

Dallas Convention Center

REUNION PARK

TRINITY RIVER GREENBELT PARK

24

30

Beckley Ave.

Lamar St.

Corinth St.

Houston St. Viaduct

Jefferson Blvd. Viaduct

Industrial Blvd.

22

23

35E

0   1/2 mi
0   0.5 km

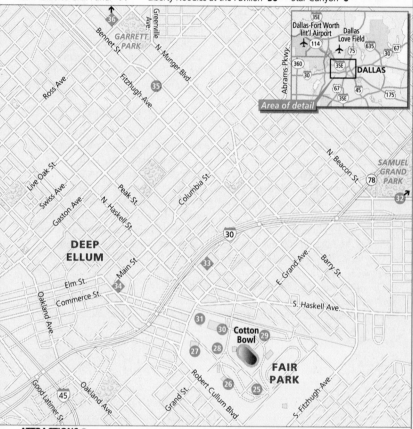

Park Cities The traditional haunt of the Dallas elite, Park Cities encompasses one of America's wealthiest residential districts, **Highland Park,** as well as the none-too-shabby **University Park** and the city's major university, preppy Southern Methodist University (SMU). Park Cities is located north of downtown and west of Central Expressway. Plenty of Dallasites tend to refer to the entire zone as Highland Park, if only to use the best-known district as shorthand.

North Dallas The northern edge of the city and southern edge of the suburbs is where the hardcore shopping begins (in places like the Galleria, Valley View, and Prestonwood malls in Addison). It is also home to an ever-growing contingent of hotels and restaurants away from the downtown business scene.

GETTING AROUND
By Public Transportation

Dallas used to be a typical Southern city where there wasn't a lick of public transportation, but things have really improved in recent years with **Dallas Area Rapid Transit (DART) buses and light rail,** which is constantly expanding out from the downtown area. Pick up a map at any visitor information center or virtually any hotel or major attraction. Single ride fare (no transfers) is $1 (50¢ for seniors, students, and children). Day passes are available for $2 ($1 for seniors, students, and children). Of particular interest to visitors in the downtown area is the free M-Line Trolley-Bus (Rte. 712), which travels from the Arts District to West End. For route and fare information, call ✆ **214/979-1111** or log on to www.dart.org.

The **McKinney Avenue Trolley,** a private, historic line of early-20th-century streetcars (and run entirely by volunteers) operates along McKinney Avenue from Uptown's Allen Street to downtown's Ross Avenue and St. Paul Avenue, next to the Dallas Museum of Art. It's a half-hour ride round-trip; the trolley fare is $1.50 for adults, $1 for children ages 2 to 12, and 50¢ for seniors and travelers with disabilities. Call ✆ **214/855-0006** for additional route information.

By Car

You can now actually get around Dallas without a car, if you stick to the major downtown sights, hotels, and restaurants. However, if you want to visit shopping centers in North Dallas or outlying areas, like Arlington and Fort Worth, most people will be better off with an automobile. Be advised, though, that if

---

(*Tips* **DART Rail Passes**

If you plan on doing a lot of hop-on, hop-off sightseeing and shopping, consider getting a day pass, good for all DART bus and light-rail travel. For local service, the 1-day pass is $2 ($1 for travelers with disabilities, students, and seniors); for premium routes, the 1-day pass is $4 ($2 discounted). For longer stays, the 11-ride Bonus Pak only saves you $1 off local and $2 off premium routes. You can purchase single tickets, day passes, and 11-ride Bonus Paks from the new Ticket Vending Machines (TVMs) on all rail station platforms.

> ### *Tips* Real Highway Names
>
> To get around Dallas, you'll need to know and adopt the colloquial names of the major local thoroughfares. As a general rule, numbers give way to proper names.
>
> | Official Name | Real Folks Name |
> |---|---|
> | U.S. Highway 75 | Central Expressway ("Central") |
> | Interstate 635 | LBJ Freeway ("LBJ") |
> | Northwest Highway | Loop 12 |
> | Interstate 35E | Stemmons |
> | I-35/U.S. 77/I-635/I-30 | R. L. Thornton |

your hotel doesn't have parking, street parking can be an expensive hassle in the downtown area.

The major car-rental agencies, which have outlets at DFW and Love Field Airports and at several addresses throughout the Metroplex, include **Alamo** (✆ 800/462-5266), **Avis** (✆ 800/230-4898), **Budget** (✆ 800/527-0700), **Dollar** (✆ 800/800-3665), **Enterprise** (✆ 800/736-8222), **Hertz** (✆ 800/654-3131), **National** (✆ 800/227-7368), and **Thrifty** (✆ 800/847-4389).

Note: Yellow lights do little to slow down drivers; even the running of red lights seems to have become epidemic in recent years, so be very careful before proceeding when the light turns green.

By Taxi

Don't expect to hail a cab as you would in midtown Manhattan, though you will find taxis parked in front of the bigger, upscale hotels and at the airports. Mostly, though, you'll need to call a cab. There are more than a dozen taxi companies, including **Big Tex Taxi** (✆ 214/350-4590), **Checker Cab Co.** (✆ 214/841-0000), **Cowboy Cab Company** (✆ 214/428-0202), **West End Cab** (✆ 214/902-7000), and **Yellow Cab Co.** (✆ 214/426-6262).

Fares are $2 (initial drop) and 40¢ each additional ¼ mile. Extras might include a $2 extra passenger charge, a $2.60 airport exit fee, and a 50¢ airport drop-off fee.

 FAST FACTS: **Dallas**

American Express There are offices at 8317 Preston Center Plaza (✆ **800/826-8759**; open Mon–Fri 9am–6pm), and at 13350 Dallas Parkway, Galleria Mall, Suite 3080 (✆ **972/233-9291**; open Mon–Fri 9am–6pm and Sat 10am–4pm).

Babysitters If your hotel doesn't offer babysitting services, contact **AAA Sitters** (✆ **972/272-8556**). Rates are about $8 an hour for up to two children (plus a one-time $20 registration fee and $10 transportation/service charge).

Dentists To find a local dentist, call ✆ **800/DENTIST.**

Doctors The **Doctor Directory** at St. Paul Medical Center (✆ **214/879-3099**) is a physician's referral service that can direct you to an appropriate health professional or specialist.

Drugstores There are 24-hour **Eckerd** drugstores located at 10455 N. Central Expressway at Meadow (© 214/369-3872), and 703 Preston Forest Center (© 214/363-1571). There's also **Kroger,** 17194 Preston Rd. at Campbell Road (© 972/931-9371), and **Albertsons,** 7007 Arapaho Rd. (© 972/387-8977).

Hospitals Major hospitals include the **Baylor University Medical Center,** 3500 Gaston Ave. (© 214/820-0111; for 24-hour emergency, 214/820-2501); the **Children's Medical Center of Dallas,** 1935 Motor St. (© 214/920-2100); and **Presbyterian Hospital of Dallas,** 8200 Walnut Hill Lane at Greenville Avenue (© 214/345-6789).

Internet Access The **Visitor Information Office** at the Old Red Courthouse (Houston, Main, and Commerce sts.) has computers with Internet access for an hourly fee. Decidedly hipper is **Main Street Internet,** 2656 Main St. (© **214/237-1121**); it's got a full bar, overstuffed couches, and occasional live music.

Maps The Visitor Information Offices at DFW Airport and the Old Red Courthouse (at Houston, Main, and Commerce sts.) have several maps of varying detail of Dallas and the surrounding area. If that's not enough, contact **MAP Dallas/Fort Worth** (© **817/949-2225**), which provides free street maps and visitor's guides.

Newspapers & Magazines Both the *Dallas Morning News* "Weekend Guide" (which comes out on Friday) and *Dallas Observer,* a free weekly, have plenty of current arts, entertainment, and dining information. *D Magazine,* a local monthly, has similar listings, as well as restaurant reviews. *Dallas Voice* is a free weekly serving the Dallas gay and lesbian communities, with listings of upcoming events.

Police For a police emergency, dial © **911;** for nonemergencies, call © **214/742-1519.** The main precinct headquarters is located at 334 S. Hall, in the central business district (© **214/670-5840**).

Post Office The central post office, 400 N. Ervay St. (© **800/275-8777** or 214/760-4700), is open Monday through Saturday from 8:30am to 5pm.

Safety In most areas during the day, Dallas is as safe as any big American city. You should exercise particular care, though, around Fair Park and after 7pm in downtown. Gay and lesbian travelers should exercise caution in the Oak Lawn section; even though it is the area of greatest concentration of gay residents and establishments, harassment has historically been a problem.

Taxes The general sales tax is 8.25%, hotel tax is 15%, and restaurant tax is 7%.

Transit Information For public transportation questions, call © **214/979-1111.**

Weather For weather information, call © **214/787-1111;** for current time and temperature, call © **214/844-6611.**

EXPLORING DALLAS

Dallas has long been better known for its business and banking instincts than its cultural treasures and must-see attractions—in fact, Fort Worth gallops fast ahead of it on the cultural radar (though the 2003 opening of the world-class Nasher Sculpture Center may finally put Dallas on the art map). Plenty of visitors simply come to Dallas and go native: shop during the day, eat and drink and attend big-time sporting events at night and on weekends. But Big D, a young city, can certainly entertain visitors for a few days or more: It has its infamous Kennedy legacy (which it has reluctantly decided to embrace), revitalized state fairgrounds, and a growing arts scene, plus a handful of parks and enjoyable places for the kids.

THE TOP ATTRACTIONS
Historic Downtown Dallas

Dallas County Historical Plaza   Just a couple of blocks from the spot where JFK's motorcade slowly rolled by the Texas School Book Depository is the heart of historic downtown Dallas—though nothing of permanence was built here until the 1890s. In the middle of the plaza is a reminder of Dallas's recent origins as a Western outpost: **John Neely Bryan Cabin,** a replica of the one-room log structure built by the Tennessee-born attorney credited with founding the city in 1841. The original cabin stood on the banks of the Trinity River.

Across Main Street is the **John F. Kennedy Memorial,** funded by private donations and designed by the famed architect Philip Johnson in 1970. The open-roofed square room, made of limestone, is a "cenotaph" (an empty tomb), according to Johnson. Unfortunately, the memorial is also empty of emotion—not the moving testament to a president and event that so marked the American national psyche. Inside the four solemn walls is a black marble slab, which looks like a low coffee table, engraved with the words "John Fitzgerald Kennedy." Johnson's intent was for the open roof to symbolize the "freedom of spirit of JFK," but I doubt that many visitors will feel their own spirits soar here.

Just west of the Kennedy Memorial, across Record Street, is the **Old Red Courthouse,** built in self-important Romanesque Revival style in 1890 on the site of the original log courthouse (property donated by city founder John Neely Bryan). The blue granite and red sandstone building today houses the **Dallas Visitors Center** (which has Internet access and plenty of sightseeing and hotel and restaurant information).

For those who miss the true nonbelievers that used to swarm around the Texas School Book Depository trumpeting wacky tales about the JFK assassination, Dallas now has **The Conspiracy Museum,** 110 S. Market St. (✆ **214/741-3040;** www.palladia.net/Conspiracy), brazenly located across the street from the Kennedy Memorial. Rejecting the conclusions of the Warren Commission Report and claiming "The Truth Shall Set You Free," the small, private collection of artifacts, photos, videos, and minutiae addresses the wealth of conspiracy theories, unsubstantiated but never let go of by a large segment of the population, that have swirled around the JFK assassination and other alleged cover-ups. A huge poster hanging from the ceiling proclaims that all the

---

⌐ Tips A Dollar Saved . . .

Look for $1 and $2 coupons for museums and other attractions in the *Dallas/Fort Worth Area Visitors Guide* and other tourism board publications (available free at the CVB office in the Old Red Courthouse as well as at some hotels and restaurants in Dallas).

Kennedy brothers were the victims of conspiracy. This is the kind of place where the staff, who call themselves "assassinologists," place an "Out to Lunch" sign on the door that says: "We look forward to seeing you (and that guy following you!)." The Conspiracy Museum is open daily from 10am to 6pm; admission is $7 for adults, $6 for seniors and students, and $3 for children. Allow a little less than an hour to visit the museum, unless you get caught up rehashing the assassination and reading all the minutiae. The staff offers free JFK historical walking tours, and they're pretty much rant-free.

Junction of Main, Market, Elm, and Record sts. No admission fees except for Conspiracy Museum. Open year-round daily 24 hr. DART Light Rail: West End station.

The Sixth Floor Museum at Dealey Plaza ★★ *Kids*   November 22, 1963, is a day Dallas can't live down and the world can't forget. A sniper's bullets assassinated the nation's 35th president, John Fitzgerald Kennedy, in Dallas as his motorcade traveled west on Elm Street. Whether or not there was a single shooter or more camped out on the grassy knoll below, and whether or not the Cubans or the Russians or the CIA were involved, the Warren Commission concluded that 24-year-old Lee Harvey Oswald fired his rifle at least three times from a window perch on the 6th floor of the Texas School Book Depository, killing JFK and critically injuring the Texas governor, John Connally. (Oswald had only days earlier secured a menial job at the School Book offices.)

The redbrick building overlooks Dealey Plaza, an otherwise unremarkable spot that is ingrained in the memory of most Americans and people across the globe. The museum, the top draw in North Texas, preserves the spot where Oswald crouched and fired his rifle (now encased in Plexiglas), but it also examines the life, times, and legacy of the Kennedy presidency. The exhibit provides a moment-by-moment account of the day of the assassination and a day-by-day recollection of that harrowing November week. The display, which includes documentary film footage and more than 400 photos, summons the "Camelot" White House before getting to the event that put Dallas on the quivering lips of people across the globe. On view are images from the famous Zapruder film, whose frames have been isolated and examined more than any footage in history. However, there is no original evidence on display; everything examined by the Warren Commission forms part of the National Archives in Washington, D.C. The JFK assassination has been so hashed over and occupies such a place in pop culture that few visitors are likely to discover much in the way of new information. It is, however, a place to revisit the tragic episode and recall (or tell your kids about) the impact it had on you and a stunned nation—as children's drawings from the period and visitor remarks inscribed in "Memory Books" at the museum's exit attest. Unless the information here is new to you or you want to relive the episode in great detail, spending no more than a couple of hours here should be plenty.

Dealey Plaza, which draws two million curious visitors annually, remains a stark public square at the junction of a triple underpass, virtually unchanged from 4 decades ago. A red X marks the spot on the asphalt of Elm Street where Kennedy was struck; incredibly, many visitors to Dallas feel compelled to dodge traffic and have their pictures taken while standing on the X as cars hurtle by. Unless you really want to follow in the footsteps of JFK, however, I strongly advise against such reckless participation in our nation's history.

411 Elm St. at Houston (entrance on Houston St.). *(C)* **214/747-6660.** www.jfk.org. Admission $10 adults; $9 seniors, students, and children ages 6–18; free for children under 6. Audio tours $3 extra (in 7 languages). Daily 9am–6pm. Closed Thanksgiving and Dec 25. DART Light Rail: West End station.

Moments At the Top of the Tower

Dominating the Big D skyline is sphere-topped **Reunion Tower** (© 214/ 651-1234; DART Rail: Union station), the top of which is lit up like a giant pincushion at night. The tower, located in Reunion Park at Reunion Boulevard, rises 50 stories, and the dome rotates very slowly (completing a single rotation in just under an hour), though imperceptibly to the naked eye. Take an exterior elevator to an observation deck for panoramic views of the city and surrounding plains, or have a drink at the Top of the Dome cocktail lounge, where you can blame your spinning head on something other than the libations in front of you.

The Arts District

Art lovers will want to spend the better part of a morning or afternoon in the Arts District, though you could do a drive-by through a couple of the museums in a little over an hour. To get there via public transport, take DART Light Rail to Pearl or St. Paul station.

Dallas Museum of Art ✲   Though a substantial notch below a world-class institution, this I. M. Pei–designed museum contains impressive collections of international art, especially from the Americas, Africa, and Asia and the Pacific. The Arts of the Americas section is the largest and most impressive, with valuable contributions from pre-Columbian lost civilizations of the Aztec, Maya, and Nazca peoples and Spanish colonial arts. The more limited Art of Europe gallery exhibits a handful of works by the biggies—van Gogh, Monet, Cézanne, Gauguin, and Degas—while the small 20th-century collection includes Picasso, Mondrian, and Giacometti, among others. The contemporary collection includes works by Mark Rothko, Jackson Pollock, the Texan Robert Rauschenberg, and Jasper Johns. In the Wendy & Emery Reves Collection is a curious re-creation of Coco Chanel's French summer home, complete with her collection of furnishings and paintings by French Impressionists like Monet, Toulouse-Lautrec, and Degas. The DMA puts on interesting occasional exhibits, such as the recent, colorful "Day of the Dead" installation. In the lobby, where jazz combos play for free on Thursday evenings, hangs a gorgeous, monumental blown-glass sculpture by Dale Chihuly. A couple of hours should be sufficient, unless you're a dedicated art hound.

1717 N. Harwood (at Ross St.). © 214/922-1200. www.dm-art.org. Free admission for permanent collection; for special exhibitions $6 adults, $4 seniors and students. Tues–Wed and Fri–Sun 11am–5pm; Thurs 11am–9pm. Guided tours Tues–Fri at 1pm, Sat–Sun at 2pm; gallery talks Wed at noon.

Trammell & Margaret Crow Collection of Asian Art ✲   This exceptionally displayed collection is the product of one of Dallas's best-known real estate developer's fascination with the arts of Japan, China, and India. The 500 pieces on display (taken from a collection of more than 7,000 objects) range from 1000 B.C. to the 20th century. The first floor is dedicated to the arts of Japan; its galleries hold Japanese scrolls and screens, as well as ceramics and bronzes. The Chinese galleries focus mostly on painting, sculpture, and decorative arts from the last Chinese empire, the Qing dynasty (1644–1911). Across a sky bridge is the third gallery, dedicated to Indian culture, with Hindu sculptures and features of Indian architecture, including a large residence facade in elaborately carved red limestone. There are also a number of sculptures from Cambodia—a standout

The Nasher Sculpture Center

Despite its status as the principal art museum in a city of considerable wealth, the rather modest permanent collection of the Dallas Museum of Art is proof that either north Texans don't collect much great art or they don't donate it on a grand scale to local institutions. One notable exception to that rule is Raymond Nasher, one of the world's foremost collectors of contemporary sculpture. A local businessman by way of New York who made his banking and real estate fortune in Dallas (with the shopping mall NorthPark Center, among other properties), Nasher finally decided, after years of being wooed by the Dallas Museum of Art as well as major institutions like the Guggenheim Museum in New York and the National Gallery of Art in Washington, D.C., to establish a public sculpture garden in his adopted city. The $50 million project is being entirely funded by the private Nasher Foundation.

The Nasher Sculpture Center ✮✮✮ is slated to open in fall 2003 on a 2½-acre site adjacent to the Dallas Museum of Art, in a glass-and-marble structure designed by the renowned architect Renzo Piano. The center is certain to change the way art fans think about Dallas. The collection, amassed over 4 decades by Ray and his wife Patsy, is considered by some art experts to be the finest private collection in the world. The 54,000-square-foot center will feature an outdoor sculpture garden landscaped by Peter Walker, with pieces from Nasher's immense collection exhibited both indoors and out. The collection includes some of the finest individual works from the likes of Joan Miró, David Smith, Constantin Brancusi, Henry Moore, Alberto Giacometti, Henri Matisse, Alexander Calder, Isamu Noguchi, Richard Serra, Mark di Suvero, and many others. With an auditorium and classroom, the center will also focus on the study of modern sculpture. Even though the Nasher Center is still in the works at this writing (only one major sculpture, by Richard Serra, a piece that previously announced the entrance to the Dallas Museum of Art, has been installed), I've seen much of Nasher's collection and interviewed him for an art magazine at his Dallas home, and I'm certain the new Nasher Sculpture Center—which has some of the biggest names in art and architecture attached to it—will quickly become one of Dallas's most highly prized treasures.

The Nasher Center is bounded by Woodall Rogers Freeway, North Harwood, Flora, and Olive streets. For more information, including hours and prices (the center had not yet been inaugurated at press time), see www.nashersculpturecenter.org.

is the pre-Khmer 7th-century figure of Vishnu—and Nepalese and Tibetan objets d'art. Allow an hour or two to see it all.

Crow's non-Asian sculpture collection is on display at the **Trammell Crow Center,** located at 2001 Ross Ave. at Harwood. It includes 19th- and

20th-century French bronzes (by Rodin and Maillol) throughout the office building and in the garden.

2010 Flora St. (between Harwood and Olive sts.). ℰ **214/979-6430**. www.crowcollection.com. Free admission. Tues–Sun 10am–5pm, Thurs till 9pm. Guided public tours Sat and Sun at 1pm. Audio tours ($5) also available and gallery talks ($10) regularly scheduled.

The Outskirts of Downtown: Historic Parks, Fairgrounds & Museums

The Dallas Arboretum & Botanical Garden ⭐   Dallas may not be celebrated for its cool green beauty, but the area around White Rock Lake, and more specifically the Arboretum and Botanical Garden, is a welcome oasis. Just 15 minutes from the gleaming skyscrapers of downtown Dallas are nearly 70 acres of carefully planted and groomed gardens and natural woodlands, interspersed with a handful of historic residences, that meander along the banks of the lake. The Jonsson Color Garden features one of the nation's largest collections of azaleas, which bloom spectacularly in spring, and nearly 6 acres of chrysanthemums in the fall. And while North Texas is not exactly New England, October and November are as ablaze in color as anything you'll see in this neck of the woods. If you find yourself in Dallas during the torrid summer (or spring and fall) months, the Palmer Fern Deli is a secluded, shady spot where mist-sprayers drop the temperature at least 10° to 15°—reason enough for a visit here. An hour is probably enough time to see most of the gardens, though it's a fine place to linger, read, and relax.

8617 Garland Rd. (Tex. 78). ℰ **214/327-8263**, or 214/327-4901 information hot line. www.dallasarboretum.org. Admission $6 adults, $3 children ages 6–12, free for children under 6. Daily 10am–5pm. Parking $3.

Fair Park ⭐   Fair Park, a classic conglomeration of Art Deco buildings and spacious grounds built for the 1936 Texas Centennial Exposition, is undergoing a renaissance. Built to commemorate the Republic of Texas's independence from Mexico, it is the only intact and unaltered, pre-1950s world's fair site in the United States. Recognized as a National Historic Landmark for its architecture (the only such landmark in Dallas), Fair Park is an attraction year-round, but especially so during the annual State Fair of Texas (last weekend of Sept and first 3 weeks of Oct), which just celebrated its 50th year.

The 277-acre grounds include several museums and performance and sporting facilities like the State Fair Coliseum, Cotton Bowl, Fair Park Bandshell, and Starplex Amphitheater, one of the city's top concert venues. The two major areas are the Esplanade and the Lagoon. There's much to see and do at Fair Park, so depending on your time, you may have to pick and choose. Plan on 2 or 3 hours minimum, and a full day during the State Fair of Texas. Below are the highlights:

The Women's Museum ⭐⭐, 3800 Parry Ave. (ℰ **214/915-0860;** www.thewomensmuseum.org), is a huge coup for Dallas. The pet project of a trio of Texas women and designed by Wendy Joseph, the chief designer behind the Holocaust Museum in Washington, D.C., this exciting $25 million museum is an ambitious, high-tech architectural feast, audacious enough to encompass the accomplishments of women over the past century.

The museum presents two dozen mostly interactive exhibits, with a clear predilection for engaging the visitor with technological wizardry. Audio guides (handheld cellphones) feature the voices of "mentors" Connie Chung, Gladys Knight, and the former Texas governor Ann Richards. "It's Amazing" is a glass labyrinth of female stereotypes, behind which are revealed several women who defied convention; "Mothers of Invention" showcases popular inventions by women (such as Liquid Paper, conceived by a Dallas secretary, and the brown paper bag). The museum is open Tuesday from 10am to 9pm (free admission after 5pm); Wednesday through Saturday from 10am to 5 pm; and Sunday from noon to 5pm. Admission is $5 for adults, $4 for seniors and students ages 13 to 18, and $3 for children ages 5 to 12.

The **Hall of State,** 3939 Grand Ave. (✆ **214/421-4500;** www.hallofstate. com), is the centerpiece and principal Art Deco legacy at Fair Park. Inside is a Texan's dream, the Hall of Heroes, with larger-than-life (as any Texan will tell you they were in real life) stalwarts of the Republic of Texas, including Sam Houston and Stephen F. Austin. Venture into the four-story-high Great Hall, yet more proof that bigger is always better in Texas.

Trains evoke nostalgic feelings of travel and exploration in just about everyone; the collection at the **Age of Steam Railroad Museum,** 1105 Washington St. (✆ **214/428-0101;** www.dallasrailwaymuseum.com), including 28 locomotives, steam-era Pullman passenger cars, and Dallas's oldest surviving train depot, is sure to feed such impulses in visitors of all ages. The entry in the "Bigger in Texas" sweepstakes? Big Boy, the world's largest steam locomotive. The museum is open Wednesday through Sunday from 10am to 5pm; admission is $5 for adults, $2.50 for children.

The **African-American Museum,** 3536 Grand Ave. (✆ **214/565-9026**), is the only museum in the Southwest (and one of eight in the country) that focuses on the African-American experience and culture. The standout exhibit is the fine collection of African-American folk art, supplemented by a survey of African art objects and contemporary African-American art. Admission is free; it's open Tuesday through Friday from noon to 5pm, Saturday from 10am to 5pm, and Sunday from 1 to 5pm.

The small but diverse collection of marine life at **The Dallas Aquarium at Fair Park,** 1300 Cullum Blvd. (✆ **214/670-8443**), highlights some of the weirder aquatic specimens your kids will have lain eyes on, including walking fish, four-eyed fish, upside-down jellyfish, and desert fish. And who can resist watching the piranhas and sharks being fed? The newest and largest addition is the Amazon Flooded Forest, a 10,000-gallon tank with 30 species from the Amazon River. The aquarium is open daily from 9am to 4pm; admission is $3 for adults, $1.50 for children ages 3 to 11.

The **Dallas Museum of Natural History,** 3535 Grand Ave. (✆ **214/421-3466;** www.dallasdino.org), is the place to view the kind of wildlife that roamed Texas before steers and longhorns: namely, dinosaurs. Permanent exhibits include "Paleontology Lab" and "Prehistoric Texas." The museum is open Monday through Saturday from 10am to 5pm, Sunday from noon to 5pm; admission is $6.50 for adults, $5.50 for seniors, $5 for students ages 13 to 18, and $4 for children ages 3 to 12.

The **Science Place & Planetarium/IMAX Theater,** 1313 2nd Ave. (✆ **214/428-5555;** www.scienceplace.org), is a great place to entertain the kids with more than 300 hands-on science exhibits—where they can amaze themselves by lifting a half-ton with one hand and playing with electricity—and the massive, domed IMAX theater. The Planetarium features stargazing shows Monday through Saturday.

3809 Grand Ave. (bordered by S. Fitzhugh, Washington, and Parry aves., and Cullum Blvd.). ✆ **214/670-8400,** or 214/421-9600 for museum and event information. www.bigtex.com.

Meadows Museum of Art ★★ *Finds* On the campus of Southern Methodist University is a well-kept secret: the finest collection of Spanish art outside Spain (so significant, in fact, that it spent much of 2000 on display at the top-tier Thyssen-Bornemisza museums in Madrid and Barcelona). A Dallas oil magnate, Algur Meadows, went to Spain to search for oil, entertaining himself at the Prado Museum. He came up dry, but his sojourn into Spanish art history bore fruit: Meadows began to assemble a splendid collection of works from the 15th to 20th centuries, including pieces by Spanish masters from the Golden Age of Spanish painting (such as Velázquez, Goya, Ribera, Murillo, Zurbarán—just about the only big name missing is El Greco). Having moved into a new building six times larger than the old site, Meadows Museum is one of the best small museums with a singular focus in the U.S. Of special note among the nearly 700 items on display are Ribera's *Retrato de un Caballero de Santiago* and Goya's *El Corral de los Locos* (by many accounts the finest Goya found in the United States), as well as a series of 200 works on paper by Goya. The 20th-century Spanish masters Picasso, Dalí, Miró, and Tàpies are also represented.

Owens Fine Arts Center, SMU Campus, 5900 Bishop Blvd. at Mockingbird Lane (next to the Ford stadium, west of I-75). © 214/768-2516. www.smu.edu/meadows/museum. Free admission ($3 donation suggested). Mon–Tues and Fri–Sat 10am–5pm; Thurs 10am–8pm; Sun 1–5pm. Free public tours Sept–May Sun at 2pm and occasional Sun in summer.

Old City Park ★ *Kids* Dallas's Old West heritage is on self-conscious display in this downtown 13-acre park of three dozen historic buildings. The complex re-creates a late-19th-century village, complete with a redbrick Main Street, Victorian homes, a log cabin dating from 1847, and Old West standards like a train depot, general store, one-room church, schoolhouse, bank (said to have been robbed by Bonnie and Clyde in the 1930s), and law offices. All have been transported from their original locations in and around Dallas, immaculately restored and reconstructed on the attractive grounds, which have the glittering city skyline as a backdrop. Guided tours escort visitors inside several of the buildings, including a "Living Farmstead," a re-creation of a North Texas farm (ca. 1860). On selected dates during the first 2 weeks of December, the village celebrates "Candlelight at Old City Park," a popular "Victorian Holiday Celebration." (Candlelight admission tickets are $3 more than regular prices.)

A pretty good restaurant, Brent Place, occupies an 1876 "architecture catalogue" farmhouse (ordered by mail and shipped by rail to rural areas) and serves lunch Tuesday through Saturday from 11am to 3pm; call © 212/421-3057 for reservations. Visitors are also allowed to picnic on the grounds. Plan to spend 1½ hours or so here.

1717 Gano St. (between Harwood and Ervay sts., south of I-30). © 214/421-5141. www.oldcitypark.org. Admission $7 adults, $5 seniors, $4 children ages 3–12. Tues–Sat 10am–4pm; Sun noon–4pm (buildings closed on Mon, but grounds remain open).

Swiss Avenue Historic District Toward the turn of the 20th century, the Dallas elite began to abandon the area that now comprises the Arts District and move east (near the modestly funky Lakewood neighborhood). Sprawling, grand homes from the early 1900s—English Tudor, Georgian, Spanish, you name it—line a broad avenue, about 4 blocks of which are listed in the National Register of Historic Places. The Wilson Blocks (2800 and 2900), named for Frederick Wilson, who built a number of the homes there, are especially attractive. Around the holidays, Swiss Avenue is a favorite for Christmas lights cruisers. A drive-by can be done in 15 minutes; allow a half-hour if you want to stroll.

Northeast of downtown, along Swiss Ave. between La Vista Dr. and Fitzhugh Ave. (take Fitzhugh east from I-75).

MORE TO SEE & DO

The Dallas World Aquarium *Kids* Housed in a former warehouse in the West End district, the Dallas aquarium *not* at Fair Park is a good place to hide out from the sun downtown. My niece and nephew enjoy communing with the stingrays, sea turtles, sharks, and reef fish. Their favorite, though, is "Orinoco— Secrets of the River," an immersion into the tropical rainforest of Venezuela, a cool area teeming with Peruvian squirrel monkeys, endangered Orinoco crocs, jaguars, and soft-billed toucans. Plan on about an hour's visit. A restaurant and a cafe are on the premises.

1801 N. Griffin (West End District). © **214/720-2224.** Admission $11 adults, $8.66 seniors and children ages 3–12, free for children under 3. Daily 10am–5pm. DART Light Rail: West End station.

Dallas Zoo *Kids* If you're headed west to Fort Worth, and one zoo trip will do, you'd be better off waiting (the Fort Worth Zoo, along with the one in San Antonio, are the two best in Texas and two of the best in the country). Otherwise, if the kids are clamoring for some wild animals, the recently renovated Dallas Zoo—the oldest zoo in Texas, founded in 1888—isn't likely to disappoint (one feature, "Wilds of Africa," was named the top African zoo exhibit in the country). The 85-acre park also features a habitat for rare Sumatran tigers, a chimpanzee forest, and a monorail safari ride. A couple of hours spent here should suffice for the kids.

650 S. R. L. Thornton Fwy. (in Oak Cliff, 3 miles south of downtown Dallas). © **214/670-5656.** www.dallas zoo.org. Admission $8 adults, $4 seniors, $5 children ages 3–11, free for children under 3. Daily 9am–4pm. Parking $5. DART Light Rail: Dallas Zoo station.

The Studios at Las Colinas *Kids Overrated* North Texas's major movie and TV studio—where *Walker, Texas Ranger* and *Silkwood* were filmed—offers daily tours of its grounds, including displays of movie memorabilia and hands-on demonstrations of special effects (from that memorable blockbuster *Addams Family Values*) and blue-screen technology. You'll see the Oval Office set used in Oliver Stone's *JFK,* as well as costumes from *Star Trek* and *Forrest Gump.* If you've been to studios in Hollywood or the movie museums in other parts, you've probably seen more and better; however, if you've always wanted to visit a movie set, you'll at least get a glimpse here. Tours last about an hour and 15 minutes.

6301 N. O'Connor Blvd., Irving (southeast of 35E and Royal Lane). © **972/869-FILM** or 972/869-7752. www.studiosatlascolinas.com. Admission $13 adults, $11 seniors and students, $8.95 children ages 5–12, free for children 4 and under. Guided tours Mon–Sat at 10am, noon, and 2pm (Sat also at 4pm). Closed Easter, Thanksgiving, Dec 24–25, and Jan 1.

ESPECIALLY FOR KIDS

Older children who have studied the 1960s and Kennedy should appreciate the **Sixth Floor Museum.** Younger kids are likely to have a better time at the **Dallas Zoo** or either **The Dallas Aquarium at Fair Park** or **The Dallas World Aquarium.**

Fair Park has plenty to offer families, especially if you happen to be in Dallas during the State Fair of Texas (in Oct). Even if you miss the fair, Fair Park's The Science Place/Planetarium (with its Robot Zoo) and IMAX Theater are great places to hide from the Texas sun. Girls of all ages (and open-minded boys) may find interactive inspiration at the new Women's Museum. Kids tend to like trains, so a whistle stop at the Age of Steam Railroad Museum should be diverting, as should be a visit to the Dallas Museum of Natural History (with its life-size dinosaur models).

The staging of life on the prairie at **Old City Park,** with actors re-creating the late 19th and early 20th centuries, is plenty of fun for both kids and adults. Check out family theater productions at the **Dallas Children's Theater,** Crescent Theater, 2215 Cedar Springs at Maple (© **214/978-0110**). The Dallas Museum of Art's **Gateway Gallery** has cool interactive art displays for kids, and children into movies may want to check out Hollywood sets and memorabilia at **The Studios at Las Colinas.**

The **Plano Balloon Festival,** a 3-day event held at the end of September in Oak Point Park, 2801 E. Spring Creek Pkwy., is one of the country's largest. More than 100 hot-air balloons, many of them curious shapes and recognizable figures, launch each day at 7am and 6pm. It's worth the drive (and early rise), unless it's too windy to launch; visit www.planoballoonfest.org for more information. **Sporting events,** such as games of the Cowboys, Rangers, Sidekicks, and Stars, draw huge family crowds. Finally, just getting around parts of Dallas can be fun for children; take the **DART Light Rail system** around downtown (especially direct to the Dallas Zoo) and be sure to hop aboard the historic **trolleys** that patrol McKinney Avenue.

Arlington, midway between Dallas and Fort Worth, is the big draw for families, with **Six Flags Over Texas** amusement park, **Texas Rangers baseball** (including the excellent Legends of the Game Baseball Museum), **Hurricane Harbor** water park, **The Palace of Wax & Ripley's Believe It or Not** and more. And if you're looking to combine shopping with entertainment for the kids, Texas malls are in themselves theme parks (with skating rinks and much more). See "Arlington," later in this chapter.

ORGANIZED TOURS

Gray Line/Coach USA (© **972/263-0294** or 866/767-9849; www.grayline.com) is the big daddy of bus tours. It offers at least six themed sightseeing tours in the Dallas–Fort Worth area. Choose from "JFK Historical Tour," "Rodeo Roundup," or a Western-themed daylong tour of Fort Worth that includes horseback riding and a hayride. Prices range from $30 per person for a 3-hour tour to $45 per person for a 9-hour Dallas and Fort Worth trip (half price for children). For simple, standard, dependable tours, these are an okay deal.

Dallas Surrey Services (© **214/946-9911**) offers horse-drawn carriage tours of historic Dallas 7 nights a week, weather permitting. Standard tours originate in the West End and visit Dealey Plaza and the Texas School Book Depository, Pioneer Plaza, and the Arts District, lasting about 20 minutes ($30 for up to four people). Longer, custom tours can last up to an hour ($100, four people). **Belle Starr Carriages** (© **972/734-3100**) also offers horse-drawn tours of downtown Dallas, including "Christmas Light Tours" through Highland Park during the month of December.

DFW Heli-Tours (© **972/623-3000;** www.dfwhelitours.com) takes up to six passengers out over Dallas for a bird's-eye view in a red Bell 'copter, starting from $25 per person for a short 5-minute ride.

Hour-long **Walking Arts District Strolls** ($7 per person) covering the zone's art and architecture are conducted the first Saturday of every month at 10:30am, leaving from in front of the Trammell & Margaret Crow Collection of Asian Art, 2010 Flora St. Call © **214/953-1977** for additional information and reservations.

OUTDOOR ACTIVITIES

BIKING, IN-LINE SKATING & JOGGING   White Rock Lake, 5 miles east of downtown Dallas (off Loop 12), is the most popular area for cycling, skating, and running (and of course, walking). A 12-mile loop traces the banks of the lake. The park is open from 6am to midnight, though I wouldn't advise hanging about too long after dark falls. Nearby bike and skate shops offer rentals.

GOLF   North Texas, where golf legends like Byron Nelson, Ben Hogan, and Lee Trevino hail from, has a huge number of golf courses, from challenging championship courses to comfortable courses suited to players of all stripes. **TPC at the Four Seasons Resort & Club** (© 972/717-2400; greens fees $150), home of the PGA Byron Nelson Classic, is the best and most spectacular course in the area—but you'll have to stay at the Four Seasons to play (see p. 96 for a full review). Another hotel golf course, rated among the top 50 resorts in the United States, is **Hyatt Bear Creek Golf Club,** at the Hyatt Regency DFW, 3500 W. Airfield Dr./DFW Airport (© 972/615-6800; greens fees and cart $78–$88, with twilight reduced rates available) featuring two nicely designed championship 18-hole courses.

The City of Dallas operates several courses open to the public. The newest addition is **Keeton Park Golf Course,** 2323 Jim Miller Rd. southeast of downtown Dallas off I-30 (© 214/670-8784), which has pecan tree–lined fairways and numerous ponds. Greens fees are $17. **Tenison Golf Course,** 3501 Samuell Blvd. (© 214/670-1402), just 5 miles east of downtown, has two 18-hole courses divided by White Rock Creek. Greens fees are $14 to $34, on weekends $17 to $39.

Located not so close to Dallas, but the only four-star-rated course in the DFW area to be named among the "Best Places to Play" by *Golf Digest* (and rated one of the top five public courses in Texas) is **Buffalo Creek Golf Club,** 624 Country Club Dr., Rockwall (© 972/771-4003), near Lake Ray Hubbard. Greens fees, including cart and range balls, are $69 Monday through Friday, $89 Saturday and Sunday. One of the most difficult courses is **Sleepy Hollow Country Club,** 4747 South Loop 12, just 10 minutes south of downtown (© 214/371-3433), which is private but allows the public to play as guests. Greens fees Monday through Friday are $22 before noon and $27 after noon; Saturday through Sunday, $32 before noon, $42 after noon. All rates include a cart; if you're walking, fees are $13 less.

Golf fanatics who like to imagine themselves winning the Masters or British Open may want to venture north of Dallas and Fort Worth, to Flower Mound,

---

Packin' Heat, Texas-Style

The right to own, use, and brag about firearms is a protected birthright in Texas. I'm not necessarily advocating this—I mean, I think it's a little odd that the local concealed gun law allows Texans to take their pistols to church on Sunday, and museums post signs that warn "No Firearms"— but if you want to play Texan while in Big D, what better way than to fire off a few rounds? If that's your idea of R&R (and who am I to say?), take a ride over to the **DFW Gun Club & Training Center,** 1607 Mockingbird Lane (© 214/630-4866; www.dfwgun.com), for a little indoor range shooting. They offer shooting instruction and even concealed handgun license classes!

Texas, where the **Tour 18 Dallas** course reproduces 18 of the best-known holes in golf (from courses such as Winged Foot and Augusta National). The course, 8718 Amen Corner, Flower Mound, TX (© **800/946-5310;** www.tour18golf. com), is west of 35E and 121. Greens fees are $65 to $140.

TENNIS   Even though Dallas is littered with swank (and off-limits) private tennis clubs, there are several public courts where visitors can play a few sets. The following are all city-owned but have privately run pro shops: **Fair Oaks,** 7501 Merriman Pkwy. (© **214/670-1495**), near White Rock Creek (4 miles north of White Rock Lake), has 16 lit courts; **Fretz Park,** 14700 Hillcrest (© **214/670-6622**), where I took lessons as a kid, has 15 lit courts.

SPECTATOR SPORTS

Dallas is a sports-mad city, one of the only ones in the U.S. to support teams in six professional sports. Tickets to pro sporting events are available from **Central Tickets** (© **817/335-9000**), **Star Tickets** (© **972/660-8300**), and **Ticketmaster** (© **214/373-8000**).

AUTO RACING   The **Texas Motor Speedway,** I-35W at Highway 114, north of Fort Worth (© **817/215-8500;** www.texasmotorspeedway.com), is said to be the third-largest sporting complex in the world. It's the place to see NASCAR, Indy, and motorcycle racing. Plan on joining a crowd; more than 150,000 people can attend the races here.

BASEBALL   The **Texas Rangers** play from April to October at one of the finest stadiums in the country, **The Ballpark in Arlington,** I-30 at Highway 157, Arlington (© **817/273-5100;** www.texasrangers.com), a home field that recalls the glory days of baseball. Of special interest is the fascinating **Legends of the Game Baseball Museum,** with rare pieces on loan from the Cooperstown Baseball Museum (the only stadium so fortunate). See p. 107 for additional information.

BASKETBALL   The **Dallas Mavericks** (© **214/747-MAVS** or 214/665-4797; www.nba.com/mavericks), now one of the best teams in the league, call the American Airlines Center home. The excellent arena, built by the same architect who created the critically acclaimed Ballpark in Arlington for the Texas Rangers, opened in July 2001. Single-game tickets are $10 to $225 and can be a bit hard to come by, as popular as the Mavs are at home.

FOOTBALL   The **Dallas Cowboys,** five-time Super Bowl Champions and (at least formerly) "America's Team," play from August to December at **Texas Stadium,** 2401 E. Airport Freeway, Irving (© **972/785-4800;** www.dallas cowboys.com), the arena with the famous hole in the roof. Tickets, which cost $36 to $68, used to be nearly impossible to come by, but as the team's fortunes have dipped, you have a better chance of scoring one on short notice. The Dallas Cowboy Cheerleaders, who started a professional trend of scantily clad females on the sidelines, still shimmy and cheer them on, big hairdos and all. Tours of Texas Stadium are available on a daily basis.

GOLF   The PGA **Byron Nelson Classic,** named for a local legend, has been held in Dallas for the past 3 decades every May. Check out some of the top names in professional golf at the **Four Seasons Resort & Club** (call © **972/717-1200** for tickets).

HOCKEY   Dallas may not seem like the most logical place for a professional hockey team, but Big D has one of the best, the **Dallas Stars** (the 2000 Western

Conference Champions). Dallasites are wild about them. They play at the new American Airlines Center; the season is September through April. The Stars sell out all of their home games, so plan ahead if you want to see a game (© **214/ 665-4797** or 214/GO-STARS; www.dallasstars.com). Tickets range from $25 to $150, and family packs (tickets and food) are available.

RODEO   One of the top rodeos in Texas, and a huge draw for out-of-towners and travelers from abroad, is the **Mesquite Championship Rodeo,** about 20 miles northeast of downtown at Resistol Arena, 1818 Rodeo Dr. (© **800/ 833-9339** or 972/285-8777; www.mesquiterodeo.com). You can check out some authentic professional rodeo action—bull riding, saddle and bareback riding, calf roping, and chuck wagon races—on Friday and Saturday nights at 8pm (reserved grandstand seating $14; general admission $10 adults, $7 seniors, $4 children under 12). Animal rights sympathizers might feel a bit squeamish watching some of the roping exercises, which snap calves' heads back violently. There's a petting zoo for kids and a gift shop for Western duds just like the ones the cowboys and their fans will be sporting. Rodeo season is April through October.

SOCCER   The **Dallas Sidekicks** have grown in popularity along with soccer in the United States. Catch one of their indoor games at the American Airlines Center. Games are weekends from June to October, and individual tickets range from $10 to $28. Call © **214/665-4797** or 214/653-0200, or visit www.dallas sidekicks.com for more information.

The newest professional team in the area, the **Dallas Burn,** play outdoor soccer (MLS) at the Cotton Bowl from April to October. Tickets cost $9 to $60. Call © **214/979-0303** or visit www.dallasburn.com for more information.

SHOPPING

In Big D, shopping isn't merely a mundane chore necessary to outfit yourself, your kids, and your home. Shopping is a sport and a pastime, a social activity and entertainment. Dallasites don't pull on sweats and go incognito to the mall; they get dolled up and strut their stuff. Having grown up in North Dallas, I know all too well that locals are world-class shoppers. Every time I return home, I initially have a hard time even finding my way around—retail outlets, mostly national chain stores, seem to continually reproduce like a computer virus, blanketing all four corners of every intersection in the bedroom communities that envelop Big D. The Dallas Convention and Visitor's Bureau likes to tout that there are more shopping opportunities per capita in Dallas than any other city in the United States. So if you're a shopper, and come from a place less rich in retail mania, you've got your work cut out for you.

If you need to focus your shopping attention, incline it toward Western duds (especially Texas-made cowboy boots) and upscale clothing and accessories (this is the home of world-famous Neiman Marcus, after all). Texans aren't fond of taxes (there's no state income tax, still), but there is a state sales tax, and it's one of the highest in the country: 8.25%.

Great Shopping Areas

Downtown Dallas largely has been eviscerated of shopping outlets as inhabitants flocked to the suburbs. Only Neiman Marcus, the mother of all Dallas purveyors of luxury goods, has stayed put. The **West End MarketPlace** was carved out of an old candy and cracker warehouse to draw hungry tourists and get things going downtown. The real high-volume shopping is done north of downtown, in **Uptown** as well as **Highland Park, North Dallas** (north of LBJ Fwy.), and **suburbs** like Plano and Carrollton.

In the area real-estate agents have designated **Uptown,** a vintage trolley line travels along McKinney Avenue, allowing shoppers to jump off to duck into its many antiques shops, art galleries, restaurants, and specialty shops. The streets Knox and Henderson, bisected by Central Expressway, are lined with home furnishing stores and antiques dealers, with an eclectic decoration shop or two mixed in. Routh and Fairmount streets have a large number of art galleries and antiques shops. **Greenville Avenue** is home to a dizzying array of funky shops, including antiques dealers and vintage clothing stores. The avenue gets a little funkier the farther south you travel, with Lower Greenville in particular home to plenty of bars and restaurants that make great pit stops. **Deep Ellum,** which rules the alternative night, is loaded by day with funky furnishings stores, art galleries, folk art shops, and vintage resale shops. Of course locals head straight for the malls, and if you're in Dallas doing some big-volume shopping, you might do the same; the best are listed below.

Native to Big D
Neiman Marcus (which my father-in-law loves to call "Needless Mark-ups"), established in 1907, is a local institution; its annual holiday catalog has become part of pop culture (a once-a-year opportunity to order "His & Her Mummies" or perhaps your own personal $20 million submarine). Beyond those attention-grabbing stunts, Neiman Marcus remains one of the classiest high-end retail stores around, and its downtown flagship store has a chic retro look that is suddenly very hip today. It's not to be missed, even if you can't fritter away your rent money on a pair of Manolo Blahniks. The downtown store at 1618 Main at Ervay Street (℃ **214/741-6911;** www.neimanmarcus.com) is open Monday through Saturday from 10am to 5:30pm; stores in the NorthPark and Prestonwood malls are open on Sunday.

Dallas is an especially good place to pick up Western wear—boots, hats, shirts, and belts—whether you want to look the part of a real cowboy or prefer the more adorned "drugstore cowboy" look. Boots of all leathers and exotic skins, both machine- and handmade, from Texas boot companies (Justin, Tony Lama, Nokona) are good deals in Dallas. You can even order custom-made boots if you've got a grand or so to burn. Compare pricing at any of the following, all of which have excellent selections, and be sure to ask about proper boot fit: **Boot Town,** 5909 Belt Line Rd. at Preston (℃ 972/385-3052; www.boottown.com) or 2821 LBJ Fwy. at Josey Lane (℃ 972/243-1151); **Wild Bill's,** West End MarketPlace, 3rd floor (℃ 214/954-1050); **Cavender's Boot City,** 2833 LBJ Fwy. (℃ 972/239-1375); and **Western Warehouse,** 2475 Stemmons Fwy. (℃ 214/634-2668) or 10838 N. Central Expressway at Meadows (℃ 214/891-0888). Vintage Western clothing can be a bit hard to come by. Check out **Ragwear,** 200 Greenville (℃ 214/827-4163), a vintage store that stocks collectible Western shirts at $100 and up, as well as more pedestrian models. **Ahab Bowen,** 2614 Boll St. (℃ 214/720-1874), occasionally stocks vintage Western shirts, along with a nice selection of other carefully chosen items. If you're headed to Fort Worth, there are several good Western wear stores clustered around the Stockyards; see "Shopping" in Fort Worth, later in this chapter. Fancy gift items for the upscale cowboy—sterling silver money clips, Michel Jordi wrist watches and belt buckles with longhorns and state-of-Texas and cowboy insignias and the like—can be had for a price at **Bohlin,** 5440 Harvest Hill, Suite 172 (℃ 972/960-0335; www.bohlinmade.com).

Dallas Farmers Market, 1010 S. Pearl Expressway (℃ 214/939-2808), spread over 12 acres just south of downtown Dallas, is one of the nation's largest open-air produce markets. First opened in 1941, it looks across at the glittering Dallas skyline. Farmers from around the area sell directly to the consumer. The market is open daily from 7am to 6pm.

Department Stores & Malls

It would be impossible to cover Dallas's dozens of major shopping malls here—and more difficult still to hit them all on your visit to Dallas. A few of the best are the following, both for the number and quality of stores and their general ambience:

NorthPark Center, Northwest Highway/Loop 12 at I-75 (© 214/363-7441), is the most traditional mall and, to my mind, the most elegant. North-Park has 160 shops and major anchor stores (including Neiman Marcus, Tiffany's, and Nordstrom), as well as natural lighting and best of all, a rotating display of owner Ray Nasher's fabulous sculpture collection of modern masters throughout the mall. Not a mall, but not far from NorthPark, is one of my favorite shopping stops in Dallas: the sprawling **Half Price Books Records & Magazines** store at 5915 E. Northwest Hwy., just east of Central Expressway (© 214/363-8374). The massive selection of books—including art books, coffee-table books, books on tape, and language books—blows away almost any new bookstore, and everything at half price or less. It's a place to load up.

The Galleria, LBJ Freeway and Dallas Parkway North (© 972/702-7100; www.dallasgalleria.com), is a huge mall with a light-filled atrium (said to mimic the original Galleria in Milan, Italy). It attracts some of Dallas's most sophisticated shoppers to Macy's, Nordstrom, Saks Fifth Avenue, Versace, Cartier, and Hugo Boss. You'll also find an ice-skating rink, a Westin Hotel, and a host of restaurants—but many people seem to come just to stroll.

Highland Park Village, Mockingbird Lane at Preston Road (© 214/559-2740), is as close as you'll get to Beverly Hills's Rodeo Drive in Dallas. This ultrachic corner of high-end shopping in the midst of Dallas's most exclusive neighborhood was built in the 1930s and sports an eclectic mix of today's most fashionable boutiques (such as Calvin Klein, Prada, and Hermès). Shops aren't enclosed like a traditional American mall; rather, they face inward for a more enjoyable (or shall we say, European) shopping experience.

WHERE TO STAY

If you're in Dallas for a business trip or just a brief vacation, or you simply abhor the thought of driving everywhere, you'd do well to choose your hotel according to neighborhood. Some of the city's best hotels are downtown near the central business and Arts District, and in the area called Uptown, but many more hotels (especially more affordable chains) are nestled in North Dallas and near Irving. For most people, the latter locations will involve considerably more highway time, since Dallas is so spread out.

Dallas has a bundle of excellent choices at the top end, many of them surprisingly old-world in feel. The majority of hotel offerings in the city are large and luxurious, well-run hotels aimed squarely at business travelers. The best of the cheaper options are all-suites hotels. *Note:* Reservations in Dallas are toughest to come by when conventions take over the city. Check as early as possible with the **Dallas Convention & Visitors Bureau** (www.dallascvb.com) to see if your visit coincides with major business traffic to the city.

The rates cited below are high-season rack rates—few people pay list price, and you shouldn't either. At a minimum, request the lower, corporate rate and ask about special deals. Virtually all hotels offer some deals, especially on weekends when their business clientele dries up. Check the individual hotels' websites for special online offers. The hotel occupancy tax in Dallas is 15% (the rates quoted below do not include tax). Breakfast, either continental or buffet, is offered free at several hotels, as noted below. Do not assume that breakfast is included; if it is not, it can really add to your bill.

DOWNTOWN, UPTOWN & OAK LAWN
Very Expensive

The Adolphus Hotel ★★★   Built in 1912 by the Missouri beer baron Adolphus Busch in his adopted city, this hotel is the grande dame of Dallas hotels. In the midst of the financial district, just a couple of blocks from another, more contemporary landmark—Neiman Marcus—this beaux-arts hotel exudes luxury and refinement. Behind its historic facade guests enter a world of baroque splendor and deep pampering: dark-wood parlors, beautiful art and antiques such as 17th-century Flemish tapestries and crystal chandeliers, a grand ballroom, and an opulent dining room. Rooms are quite large and tastefully appointed in English country-house style, with marble bathrooms and separate sitting and dining areas. The suites are about as large as Texas. The graceful, old-world style of the Adolphus is epitomized by the three-course English tea served in the lobby living room every afternoon from 3 to 5pm. The French Room, serving classic French cuisine, is one of Dallas's finest restaurants (see p. 97 for a full review); it is about as baroque a dining room as you'll find in town.

1321 Commerce St. (at Akard), Dallas, TX 75202. ℂ **800/221-9083** or 214/742-8200. Fax 214/651-3561. www.hoteladolphus.com. 428 units. $285–$395 double; $425–$455 junior suite. Special packages are sometimes as low as $150 double; see website for details. AE, DC, DISC, MC, V. Valet parking $15. DART Light Rail: Akard station. **Amenities:** Restaurant; bar; fitness room and athletic club; 24-hr. concierge; free airport shuttle; salon; 24-hr. room service; babysitting; same-day laundry service/dry cleaning. *In room:* A/C, TV w/pay movies, hair dryer.

Hôtel St. Germain ★★★   The St. Germain is blissfully out of place in Dallas. The tiny, intimate boutique hotel and restaurant envelop guests in old-world luxury, with a library, parlors, and sumptuous style that borders on bordello. Equal parts late-19th-century France and New Orleans, each of the seven suites is individually decorated, with pampering features like wood-burning fireplaces, tapestries, draped Napoléon sleigh beds, bidets, and Jacuzzis and soaking tubs. Indulgence is rarely cheap, and it certainly isn't here (though the two most expensive suites really skew the price range), but if price is no object, you won't object to the refined white-glove treatment. Continental breakfast is included. The romantic restaurant, which overlooks an ivy-covered garden courtyard and serves a seven-course, prix-fixe gourmet dinner (Tues–Sat, on antique Limoges china and by candlelight for $85 per person), is ideal for a special occasion (jackets required) or merely a superior meal.

2516 Maple Ave. (at Mahon St.), Dallas, TX 75201. ℂ **214/871-2516.** Fax 214/871-0740. www.hotelst germain.com. 7 units. $290–$650 double. AE, DC, DISC, MC, V. Free parking. **Amenities:** Restaurant; fitness center; concierge; 24-hr. room service; in-room massage; same-day dry cleaning/laundry service. *In room:* A/C, TV w/pay movies, dataport, minibar, hair dryer, safe.

The Mansion on Turtle Creek ★★★   Where movie stars, princes, and presidents stay, and most of the rest of us paupers merely dream about, the hilltop Mansion, usually lauded as the most desirable hotel in the city, is luxury personified. Whereas the Adolphus has an old-world moneyed feel, the Mansion has a brasher new-money atmosphere. It is perhaps the top place in the state for a blowout splurge; it consistently lands among the very top hotels in polls in national glossy travel magazines. If it feels like a home, albeit a very grand and showy one, that's because it once was the spectacular home of a Texas cotton magnate in the 1920s and 1930s. The Mansion is all marble floors, inlaid wood ceilings, and stained-glass windows. Regular rooms are gargantuan, as are the beds and bathrooms, and the suites ridiculously so. All have top-quality linens and bath products (Lady Primrose), but some visitors report that weekend rate rooms suffer in comparison with the top-flight ones. Service, though, is faultless across the board. The Mansion's restaurant (p. 101), which serves sumptuous Southwestern fare, continues to be one of Dallas's finest hotel dining experiences.

2821 Turtle Creek Blvd. (off Cedar Springs Rd.), Dallas, TX 75219. © **800/422-3408** or 214/599-2100. Fax 214/528-4187. www.mansiononturtlecreek.com. 141 units. $400–$475 double; from $675 suite. Weekend rates and other packages available. AE, DC, DISC, MC, V. Small pets allowed with surcharge. **Amenities:** Restaurant; bar; outdoor heated pool; sauna; fitness center; concierge; 24-hr. room service; in-room massage; babysitting; same-day dry cleaning/laundry service. *In room:* A/C, TV w/pay movies, dataport, minibar, hair dryer, safe.

Expensive

The Melrose Hotel ✯ This is another one of Dallas's upscale hotels with an old-world, rather than an Old West, atmosphere. It lies in the heart of the Oak Lawn neighborhood, near the nightlife of Cedar Springs and Turtle Creek, and the midsize Melrose feels like a gracious old neighbor. Built in 1924, the eight-floor hotel was completely renovated in 1999. Once a favorite of artists and entertainers like Arthur Miller, Elizabeth Taylor, and Luciano Pavarotti, today the newly revamped hotel caters mostly to execs and couples on weekend getaways. No two rooms are alike, though they are uniformly luxurious and inviting, with 10-foot ceilings, crown molding, antiques, and marble-tiled bathrooms. The renovated Landmark restaurant consistently wins accolades in the local and national press.

3015 Oak Lawn Ave. (at Cedar Springs Rd.), Dallas, TX 75219. © **800/635-7673** or 214/521-5151. Fax 214/521-2470. www.melrosehoteldallas.com. 184 units. $219–$345 double. Weekend rates available. AE, DC, DISC, MC, V. Free parking. **Amenities:** Restaurant; piano bar; fitness center; concierge; complimentary local shuttle service; 24-hr. room service; 24-hr. dry cleaning. *In room:* A/C, TV w/pay movies, dataport, minibar, hair dryer, safe.

Moderate

AmeriSuites West End If you want to be right in the thick of it—within walking distance of the restaurants and rowdy bars of the West End, the Sixth Floor Museum and Dealey Plaza, and the Arts District—but don't want to burn through your savings, AmeriSuites is a good, safe, and convenient choice. The West End location is one of nine of this national chain across the Metroplex. All

---

⟨Tips⟩ Hotel & Motel Chains

The following national chains have several hotels in the Dallas area and can serve as dependable, affordable places to stay, especially if many of those reviewed in this chapter are full: **La Quinta** (© 800/531-5900; www.laquinta.com; "Texas Specials" starting at $49); **Comfort Inn** (© 800/228-5150; www.comfortinn.com; 10% discount for booking online); **Courtyard by Marriott** (© 800/321-2211; www.courtyard.com); **Holiday Inn Select** (© 800/HOLIDAY; www.basshotels.com); **Days Inn** (© 800/325-2525; www.daysinn.com); and **Super 8** (© 800/652-7437; www.super8.com).

| Kids | Family-Friendly Hotels in DFW |

Embassy Suites Park Central (see below)   Large and airy, with glass elevators that stream up the interior of a huge central atrium, this hotel welcomes the whole family—even pets. Distractions include a nice pool, full free breakfasts, and racquetball courts. The kids will actually think they're on vacation. For the parents, there are free cocktails every evening.

Four Seasons Resort and Club at Las Colinas (p. 96)   Your kids don't have to be golfers, but if they're into any sports at all, this resort should seem like an amusement park to them, with tennis courts, three outdoor pools, and one indoor pool, as well as a host of complimentary children's programs.

Residence Inn Forth Worth (p. 130)   Perfect for families, this friendly hotel has rooms that are more like apartments, with fully equipped kitchens and comfortable sitting areas. When you tell the kids they can walk to the acclaimed Fort Worth Zoo, they're sure to think you've made the right choice.

the rooms are good-sized, comfortable suites with kitchenettes—nothing fancy, but solid accommodations. Visiting businesspeople should find the business center to their liking, while more leisurely visitors should take to the second-floor outdoor pool, which, though small, has privileged views of the Big D skyline.

1907 N. Lamar St. (at Corbin), Dallas, TX 75202. © 800/833-1516 or 214/999-0500. Fax 214/999-0501. www.amerisuites.com. 149 units. $127–$169 double. Rates include breakfast buffet. AE, DC, DISC, MC, V. Valet parking $12. **Amenities:** Outdoor pool; fitness center; laundry service. *In room:* A/C, TV, dataport, kitchenette, fridge, coffeemaker, hair dryer, iron, safe.

NORTH & EAST DALLAS
Moderate

Embassy Suites Park Central *(Kids*   In far North Dallas, on the edge of the bedroom community Richardson, this large all-suites hotel is equally comfortable for families and business travelers (especially those with Texas Instruments and the telecom businesses along the corridor just north on Central Expressway). Rooms are all suites; they're comfortable and simply outfitted with separate living areas and sleeper sofas, and are built around a large central, airy atrium. The Embassy Suites chain was recently ranked number one by J. D. Power & Associates for customer satisfaction for all-suites chains.

13131 N. Central Expressway (just north of LBJ Fwy.), Dallas, TX 75243. © 800/EMBASSY or 972/234-3300. Fax 972/437-9863. www.embassy-suites.com. 279 units. $129–$169 double. $99 special offers frequently available. AE, DC, DISC, MC, V. Free parking. Pets 25 lb. or less allowed with $25 surcharge. **Amenities:** Restaurant; bar; indoor pool; sauna; fitness center; laundry service. *In room:* A/C, TV, dataport, minibar, coffeemaker, hair dryer, iron, safe.

The Guest Lodge at Cooper Aerobic Center *(Finds*   Worried that every time you go on vacation you seem to put on a few pounds? Then I've got the place for you. This isn't one of those hard-core boot-camp spas, but an inviting retreat at one of the nation's foremost health facilities, the Cooper Clinic. Set on 30 acres of trees, trails, and duck ponds in North Dallas, the Guest Lodge is a place to relax, if not necessarily a place to relax your gut. The small hotel is a bit of a well-kept secret, a place to unwind and work off stress and pounds. The spacious, comfortable rooms have French doors that open onto private balconies. Guests have complimentary access to the Cooper Fitness Center, which is connected to the famous sports clinic named for a physician, Kenneth Cooper, the author of a dozen fitness books and one of the most influential figures in American fitness training and diagnostics. The facilities include a 40,000-square-foot health club, tennis courts, pools, and running track as well as a Mediterranean-style spa for all manner of relaxing body treatments. You can't very well stay at a place like this without eating healthfully, so most guests take full advantage of the complimentary full continental breakfast and "heart-healthy" fare at the Colonnade Room restaurant.

12230 Preston Rd. (at Churchill), Dallas, TX 75230. (*) **800/444-5187** or 972/386-0306. Fax 972/386-2942. www.cooperaerobics.com. 62 units. $175 double; from $215 suite. All-inclusive spa packages available. AE, DC, DISC, MC, V. Free parking. **Amenities:** Restaurant; outdoor pool; tennis courts; fitness center; spa; laundry service. *In room:* A/C, TV, dataport, minibar, hair dryer, safe.

Inexpensive

The Bradford at Lincoln Park *Value* This new residential-style hotel—the most upscale member of this exceptional-value small chain that operates in Texas and Colorado—may be the best deal in Dallas. It's where all of my wife's co-workers stay when they visit the Dallas home office. Popular with business visitors who stay for a week or more, the stylish and spacious suites are coolly decorated in muted tones, with fully equipped kitchens. (There are three different floor plans to choose from, but for most visitors the "Executive," the cheapest room, will be more than sufficient.) Conveniently located just off Central Expressway and near NorthPark Center and Northwest Highway, it's just 10 minutes from downtown (unless you catch rush hour, when it could take forever) and even nearer the nightlife options of Greenville and McKinney avenues.

8221 N. Central Expressway (U.S. 75 at Northwest Hwy.), Dallas, TX 75225. (*) **888/486-7829** or 214/696-1555. Fax 214/696-1550. www.bradfordsuites.com. 161 units. $105–$139 double. Weekend rates available; rate reductions for stays of more than 6 nights. AE, DISC, MC, V. Free parking. **Amenities:** Outdoor pool; fitness center; business center; laundry service. *In room:* A/C, TV, dataport, kitchen, minibar, hair dryer, iron, safe.

NEAR THE AIRPORT
Very Expensive

Four Seasons Resort and Club at Las Colinas *Kids* Plenty of visitors come to Dallas to work, but at the Four Seasons they also come to play, and seriously. With perhaps the top golf course in the area (off-limits to nonguests), this is the place to stay if you've got to play golf and any old course won't do. The pros show up to play the PGA Byron Nelson Classic here every May, and the course consistently wins accolades as one of the best in the nation. Other sports enthusiasts will also be happy: The property was a top-of-the-line sports club before it became a resort hotel, and there are tennis courts, pools, tracks, and a full-service European spa on the 400-acre grounds. Guest rooms are large, airy, and very elegant; golf villa rooms have terraces overlooking the 18th green or the handsomely landscaped pool garden. The hotel is only about 15 minutes from DFW Airport.

4150 N. MacArthur Blvd. (at Mills Lane), Irving, TX 75038. (*) **972/717-0700.** Fax 972/717-2550. www.fourseasons.com. 357 units. $295–$415 double; from $650 suite (rates include use of sports club and spa; greens fees are extra). Sports and many other packages available. AE, DC, DISC, MC, V. Valet parking $10. **Amenities:** Restaurant; bar; 3 outdoor pools and an indoor lap pool; golf course; 8 lit outdoor and 4 indoor tennis courts; fitness center; children's programs; concierge; 24-hr. business center; 24-hr. room service; babysitting; same-day dry cleaning/laundry service. *In room:* A/C, TV, dataport, hair dryer, iron, safe.

Inexpensive

Quality Suites DFW Airport   As its name makes abundantly clear, this new addition to the Quality Suites chain offers convenience to travelers on their way in or out of Dallas. What you'll find are good, standard-size rooms (with surprisingly bold bed covers and curtains) and a range of services and amenities designed to make your short stay hassle-free. One-bedroom suites feature extra sofa sleepers in the living room and large work desks, while executive rooms sport cathedral ceilings and skylights, and some come equipped with whirlpool tubs. And if you're not inclined to stay in your room and work, you can take advantage of the free full hot breakfast buffet and "Manager's Social Hour," which serves beer, wine, and hors d'oeuvres every weekday from 5 to 7pm.

4700 W. John Carpenter Fwy. (just south of I-114, between Esters and International Pkwy.), Irving, TX 75063. ✆ **800/228-5151** or 972/929-9097. Fax 972/929-9247. www.qualityinn.com. 108 units. $85–$119 double. Weekend rates available. AE, DC, DISC, MC, V. Free parking. **Amenities:** Outdoor pool; exercise room; Jacuzzi; car-rental desk; free airport shuttle; business center; laundry service. *In room:* A/C, TV, fridge, coffeemaker, hair dryer, iron, safe.

WHERE TO DINE

It wasn't long ago that the Dallas dining scene was pretty unexciting: It was mostly *pro forma* Mexican, undistinguished steakhouses, and halfhearted Southwestern themes. That has changed considerably, and today Dallas has much more than a couple of fancy places for the oil barons and bankers and bland chain restaurants for everyone else. While you can still get home cooking, Tex-Mex, chili, and barbecue in abundance, Dallas is suddenly cosmopolitan, with a host of exciting pan-Asian, Italian, and Southwestern newcomers injecting life into diners and even into the old stalwarts. The Dallas Visitors Bureau claims four times more restaurants per capita in Dallas than New York City; since I'm from the former and spend much of my time in the latter, I'm a bit dubious about such a claim, but it's certain that you won't suffer from lack of choice.

DOWNTOWN & DEEP ELLUM
Very Expensive

The French Room ★★★ FRENCH   Perhaps *the* Dallas restaurant that will make the biggest impression on your dining companions and credit card statement, the French Room, under an elaborate vaulted ceiling in the historic Adolphus Hotel (p. 93), is a standout in every way. Formal but not stuffy, with impeccable service, it is a place to feel like king and queen for a day. An interesting twist is the price structure: You simply pay according to the number of courses ($59 for two, $67 for three, or $77 for four; the vegetarian menu, however, is four courses for $67). Dinner here is the closest thing in Dallas to a state dinner at Versailles. From beef tenderloin with a black truffle-potato terrine to miso-marinated Alaskan halibut with baby shiitake and sweet potatoes in carrot ginger sauce, the menu is superb throughout. Dessert might be a crème brûlée trio or, even better, the soufflé of the day (flavors change daily). As you might expect, the wine list is museum-quality, but there are also accessible options. Coat and tie are required for men.

1321 Commerce St. (at Akard), in the Adolphus Hotel. ✆ **214/742-8200.** Reservations required. Prix-fixe dinners $59–$77 (not including wine, tips, or tax). 6-course chef's tasting menu $90 or $125 (with wine). AE, DC, DISC, MC, V. Tues–Sat 6–10pm. DART Light Rail: Akard station.

Moderate

Monica's Acá y Allá ⚡ TEX-MEX   Tex-Mex in a funky Deep Ellum setting—part restaurant, part bar, part dance floor—is the ticket at "Monica's Here and There," now in its second decade of consistent popularity. The inviting space is big on atmosphere, with deep red bordello walls, a long pale yellow banquet, and funky sconces, the perfect venue for high-volume salsa music and dressed-up margaritas (which are excellent, by the way). The creative menu offers new twists on Tex-Mex like Mexican lasagna, snapper verde (in a green tomatillo sauce), and sirloin noir. If the food makes you want to get up and dance, feel free; Friday and Saturday nights, the place heats up like a loud nightclub, but Sunday afternoons and early evenings are quieter, and there are free Latin dance lessons. Sunday brunch is popular, and weeknight specials include half-price entrees on Tuesday, 50¢ margaritas on Wednesday, and $3.99 enchiladas on Thursday. If you like Monica's, you'd be wise to check out her latest restaurant, the more upscale **Ciudad,** 3888 Oak Lawn Ave. in Turtle Creek Village (① 214/219-3141); locals have been quick to proclaim it the finest Mexican in town.

2914 Main St. ① **214/748-7140.** Reservations recommended. Main courses $7–$18. AE, DISC, MC, V. Tues–Fri 11am–2pm and 5–10pm; Fri–Sat 5pm–midnight; Sat–Sun 11am–3pm; Sun 6–11pm.

Inexpensive

Frank Tolbert's Chili Parlor *Kids* CHILI   Just as you can't very well go to Texas and not have barbecue, you can't miss out on some authentic Texan chili. One of the most famous joints is this chili parlor, begun by a *Dallas Morning News* reporter, Frank X. Tolbert, who became a statewide guru on chili. He opened his eponymous restaurant downtown in the mid-1960s. The thing to ask for is the "five alarm" chili (way hot) or the Tolbert's original. It's sacrilege, but you can also score a burger and fries (at least get some chili on it!).

350 N. Saint Paul St. (at Bryan, in One Dallas Centre office building). ① **214/953-1353.** Main courses $4–$8. AE, DISC, MC, V. Mon–Fri 11am–7pm. DART Light Rail: St. Paul station.

UPTOWN
Expensive

Il Solé ⚡⚡ MEDITERRANEAN   Il Solé calls itself both a restaurant and wine bar, which suits its fashionable, affluent clientele perfectly. The place's restrained look might not bowl you over, but the menu and wine list should. Its wine cellar will satisfy the most demanding oenophiles, while the Mediterranean menu, though it steers clear of showy inventiveness, is consistently appealing, with items like tamarind-glazed Chilean sea bass in a sweet and spicy portobello sauce, or espresso-cured venison. The succulent, thick pork chop with a balsamic vinegar glaze and served with fava bean whipped potatoes, is also a winner. A splendid appetizer is the Frico salad, greens served in an edible bowl of *montasio,* a hard Italian cheese. Il Solé, in a difficult second-story walk-up location in one of Dallas's hottest spots for restaurants, is a kitchen spin-off from the family that runs Mi Piaci, a very successful Italian eatery in North Dallas. With a new chef hired from Hôtel St. Germain, the restaurant is even more solid. Whether you come for a simple weeknight plate of puttanesca pasta or a blowout meal on a weekend, Il Solé's worth the walk up.

4514 Travis St. (Travis Walk, at Armstrong). ① **214/559-3888.** Reservations recommended. Main courses $14–$32. AE, DC, DISC, MC, V. Mon–Fri 11am–2:30pm; Sun–Thurs 5–10pm; Fri–Sat 5pm–midnight.

Moderate

Fishbowl ⚡ ASIAN/SEAFOOD   On the fashionable Knox-Henderson corridor, this hip spot has gone through a few incarnations of late. Most recently, the

(Kids) Family-Friendly Restaurants in DFW

Cattlemen's Steakhouse (p. 130)   No slick banker's steakhouse, this homey, well-worn place in the heart of the Stockyards has several separate rooms, and kids get placemats adorned with barnyard animal stickers, a kiddie menu, and a lollipop treat. And parents get what they come for: a good-value steak.

Frank Tolbert's Chili Parlor (p. 98)   Kids love chili—and if they don't, they should. Jump-start 'em with a big bowl of Texas chili, with or without beans, and they'll be fired up for a day out on the town. You can ride DART to get there, and hit the West End MarketPlace afterward.

Highland Park Pharmacy (p. 100)   This old-time soda fountain and lunch counter serves the kind of food a kid and nostalgic parent should love: grilled cheese sandwiches and chicken salad, followed by a milk shake or root-beer float.

Kinkaid's Grocery Market (p. 133)   Burger heaven in Fort Worth is an old-time 1940s grocery store that makes just about the best burgers in Texas. Kids are sure to be entertained by the protocol: You place your order at the open kitchen in back, get a white paper bag with your name scrawled on it, pay at the register, and then pick out a spot at a communal table beneath a jungle of inflatable toys hanging from the ceiling.

La Calle Doce (p. 102)   This cheery, brightly painted Mexican home is sure to delight the kids. The parents can sample affordable but well-prepared seafood dishes, while the kids pig-out on enchiladas and other familiar Tex-Mex.

Railhead Smokehouse (p. 133)   A Fort Worth barbecue fave that draws families every night of the week for its tasty barbecue and relaxed atmosphere. The place is noisy without rising to the levels of a Chuck E. Cheese's, and excellent-value children's plates will keep the kids happy.

Sonny Bryan's Smokehouse (p. 102)   Kids may wonder if they're really on vacation when they sit down to eat at a one-armed school desk at this atmospheric little shack, but the beef sandwich with barbecue sauce, a heckuva sloppy joe, should keep them from squirming.

upscale Aquaknox merged with its more informal cousin Fishbowl and assumed (for the most part) the vibe and lower-priced menu of the latter: It's now a combo noodle shop and sushi bar. The chic and dramatic room that was Aquaknox has morphed into the "zen den," and the epicenter of activity is now the more raucous bar-front area, a great spot for a light meal and a few well-chosen items from the exotic drinks list. The menu emphasizes nouveau Asian, though much of the exquisite seafood of the former incarnation remains. The menu is still creative, but top-heavy with appetizers and snack foods that go well with Singapore Slings and sake. You might try the beef tenderloin Korean-style with kimchi and wok-seared vegetables, Spanish mackerel sushi with grapefruit and cilantro, or snack foods like tangy fried calamari with chile.

3214 Knox St. (at Cole). © 214/219-2695. Reservations recommended. Main courses $11–$21. AE, DC, DISC, MC, V. Mon–Wed 5–10:30pm; Thurs 5–11pm; Fri–Sat 5pm–midnight.

Inexpensive

Highland Park Pharmacy *Kids* *Finds* LUNCHEONETTE/SODA FOUN-TAIN   It's sad that most places like this have disappeared across the country. Amazingly, this one, in Dallas since 1912, hasn't. An authentic slice of Americana, this old-time soda fountain and lunch counter (and yes, pharmacy) has stood its ground, even as everything in its midst has become an ultrachic bar, restaurant, or home furnishings store. If you've got a hankering for a grilled pimento cheese sandwich, homemade chicken salad, or a limeade, milk shake, or root-beer float, this is the place; just grab a bar stool. It's a good spot for breakfast, too. Just don't ask the soda jerk for a latte or other fancy fixins.

3229 Knox St. (at Travis). © 214/521-2126. Dishes $3–$7. AE, MC, V. Mon–Fri 7am–6pm; Sat 9am–5:30pm.

OAK LAWN
Very Expensive

Bob's Steak & Chop House ★★ STEAK   Consistently ranked one of the top steakhouses in the country, Bob's has the requisite dark, clubby look down, with mahogany booths and crisp white table linens. But its steaks set it apart. Bob Sambol serves monster portions of wet-aged (a difference steak connoisseurs will recognize), corn-fed Midwestern prime beef and sirloin filets. And they come accompanied by "smashed" potatoes, heavy on butter, bits of chopped onion, and a honey-glazed whole carrot. That adds up to a ton of food. The porterhouse weighs in at 28 ounces; the signature, though, is a 20-ounce, bone-in prime rib broiled like a steak. Other entrees also worth considering include a perfect rack of lamb, veal chop, and lobster. And the chophouse salad—mixed greens with cucumber, tomato, bell pepper, onion, bacon, and hearts of palm—is splendid. Bob's is a bit homier than other big-time steakhouses; even though it gets plenty of businessmen in suits and boots, if you're not wearing a jacket, you won't feel out of place—especially in the back room, where diners don denim. Serious cigar smokers are in luck, especially if they catch one of Bob's cigar dinners, in which every course is served with a different cigar.

4300 Lemmon (at Wycliff). © 214/528-9446. Reservations required. Main courses $20–$49. AE, DISC, MC, V. Mon–Thurs 5–10pm; Fri–Sat 5–11pm.

Citizen ★★ EURO-ASIAN   This ultrasleek, posh restaurant is inspired by the Orient, though it takes its name from that quintessential American film, *Citizen Kane*. It is one of the city's hottest and most exciting restaurants to enliven the scene, even though service and attention to detail have suffered a bit recently. The decor is spare but spectacular, with slate tiles and bold bursts of color. Main courses can be delightfully tricky, but the best are the ones that don't try too hard: scrumptious grilled and sliced Kobe beef, black cod served with blonde miso, and papaya salad with chunks of fried calamari. The signature dish is a martini tuna tartare with caviar and crème fraîche: a mound of raw, red tuna served on the bottom of an inverted martini glass. There is also, of course, a very nice sushi bar and selection of high-end sakes, which come served in wooden boxes. The wine list contains an interesting, good-value $15 sake sampler. If the buzz gets too deafening inside, head outdoors to the rock garden patio.

3858 Oak Lawn (at Blackburn St.). © **214/522-7253**. Reservations required. Main courses $17–$34. AE, DC, DISC, MC, V. Mon–Fri 11:30am–2:30pm; Fri–Sat 5:30–11pm; Sun–Thurs 5:30–10pm.

The Mansion on Turtle Creek ★★ SOUTHWESTERN   If you like to dream big, the Mansion is Dallas's biggest splurge, though for that single spectacular occasion, I'd opt for the elegant prix-fixe menu at Hôtel St. Germain (p. 93). The Mansion is high glam all the way, in the way that the old TV soap *Dallas* was (the waitstaff wears custom-made Lucchese cowboy boots). Celebrity chef Dean Faring serves wildly creative Southwestern dishes in a rich, elegant setting. Though it's suffered some hits to its reputation lately, it's still *the* place to see and be seen in Big D—though regular folks seem to get overlooked with all the star-studded clientele demanding attention. Starters include the signature tortilla soup and lobster tacos. Main courses up the ante: How about Broken Arrow ranch antelope with homemade mango Worcestershire glaze on guizo of rabbit, morels, and tomatillos? The wine list is a novella. The prix-fixe lunch is a bargain, and Sunday brunch ($38) a Texas favorite. Keep in mind that you are expected to attire yourself for a mansion: A jacket is required for men.

2821 Turtle Creek Blvd. (off Cedar Springs Rd.). © **800/422-3408** in TX, or 214/599-2100. Reservations required. Main courses $26–$55. AE, DC, DISC, MC, V. Mon–Sat 11:30am–2pm; Sun 11:30am–2:30pm; daily 6–10pm.

Expensive

Javier's Gourmet Mexicano ✦ GOURMET MEXICAN   For a quarter of a century, Javier's has been the top spot in Dallas for authentic, gourmet Mexico City cooking. Don't expect cheapo fajitas or enchilada plates here (the valet parking out front might be your first clue). Javier's serves exquisitely prepared grilled fish and meat dishes, and it's justly famous for its black-bean soup. Also well done is the *barra de Navidado,* shrimp in diablo sauce flavored with coffee and orange juice, and *pollo ahumado,* mesquite-smoked chicken. The handsome, clubby setting (Spanish colonial in feel) is all dark wood, leafy plants, copper zinc bar tops, and stuffed animal heads. There's even a full-sized stuffed bear. That may sound like a mess, but it's very inviting, with separate dining rooms and three bars, one of which is a fancy cigar bar where the young, fashionable, and affluent sip top-shelf margaritas and primo tequilas and choke on big stogies.

4912 Cole Ave. (between Monticello and Harvard; it's difficult to find, so call for directions). © **214/ 521-4211**. Reservations recommended. Main courses $17–$25. AE, DISC, MC, V. Mon–Thurs 5:30–10:30pm; Fri–Sat 5:30–11pm; Sun 5:30–10pm.

Star Canyon ★★ SOUTHWESTERN   If the Mansion and the French Room epitomize Old Money Dallas, Star Canyon is the place for flashy upstarts. Though by now it should seem like a Southwestern cliché, Star Canyon continues to impress and innovate. This Oak Lawn restaurant with a touch of Texas kitsch, including all the names of Texas towns branded on the ceiling, has been the most talked-about restaurant in Dallas for much of the past decade, and it's still a struggle to get a reservation on weekends. A good value at dinner is the recently added five-course tasting menu, with wines selected to accompany each course for just $60 ($40 without wine). One dish that fits the *nuevo Tejano* decor perfectly is the bone-in cowboy rib-eye steak with red chile onion rings and prime beef tenderloin chili. Other winners include the tamale tart with roast garlic custard and crabmeat, and grilled lamb and enchiladas stuffed with wild mushrooms and smoky-sweet tasting *cuitlacoche* (a corn fungus). I'd also suggest the shark steak, which goes well with all the exotic-skinned cowboy boots you're likely to see.

3102 Oak Lawn (in The Centrum at Cedar Springs shopping center). © 214/520-STAR (7827). Reservations required. Main courses $16–$25. AE, DC, DISC, MC, V. Mon–Fri 11:30am–2pm; Sun–Thurs 5:30–10pm; Fri–Sat 5:30–11pm.

Moderate

La Calle Doce *Kids* *Finds* MEXICAN/SEAFOOD   This cozy Mexican joint, in a modest old blue house in Oak Cliff, south of Dallas, is one of the best home-style Mexican restaurants in the area. A cult favorite, it deserves to be much better known. The extensive menu focuses on nouvelle Mexican fish dishes, such as superb ceviche (fish and shrimp marinated with lime), Mexican seafood cocktails, and main courses like *chile relleno de mariscos* (poblano pepper stuffed with shrimp, scallops, octopus, and fish). They even do respectable Spanish paella, or you can opt for the more standard Tex-Mex plates. The soups, like *sopa de pescado* (fish soup) and *caldo Xochitl* (Oaxacan-style chicken soup) make wonderful appetizers.

If you can't make it to Calle Doce's south-of-downtown Oak Cliff location, try the branch in Lakewood at 1925 Skillman Dr. (© 214/824-9900); it's much less atmospheric but serves the same menu.

415 W. 12th St. (between Zang and Tyler, west of I-35E; best to call for directions). © 214/941-4304. Reservations recommended. Main courses $6–15. AE, DC, DISC, MC, V. Mon–Fri 11am–9:30pm; Sat 11am–10:30pm; Sun 11am–9pm.

Inexpensive

Sonny Bryan's Smokehouse *Kids* *Finds* BARBECUE   Barbecue is serious business down here. Everybody's got a favorite, whose merits they'll defend like it was the Alamo, but just about all Dallasites agree that legendary Sonny Bryan's is the original, the one barbecue spot you've gotta visit before you leave Dallas. Dating from February 1910 (when it was in Oak Cliff), the ramshackle little building in a humble section of Oak Lawn is so popular that even on 100°F days you'll see businesspeople with their sleeves rolled up, leaning against their cars, trying in vain not to get barbecue sauce all over themselves. Inside the smoke shack, there are just two rows of tiny one-armed school desks, under signs that read "Reserved, Phyllis" or "Little Jerrie." Place your order for hickory-smoked

---

Tips Picnic Places

Dallas isn't really the kind of place with great public spaces ideal for mounting a picnic lunch. Mostly it's either too hot or too cold, and people stick to their offices and cars. However, picking up some food-stuffs on your way over to the **Dallas Arboretum** and **White Rock Lake** is a fine idea. One of the best places to pick up some healthful eats is **Whole Foods Market,** 2218 Greenville Ave. at Belmont (© **214/824-1744**). The market, which started in Austin, has a great selection of fruits, vegetables, cheeses, and breads, as well as a cafe serving pre-pared foods and sandwiches. A superb gourmet takeout market is **Eatzi's,** 3403 Oak Lawn Ave. (© **214/526-1515**), which has made inroads into New York City and stocks literally thousands of items, including dozens of prepared entrees and enough cheeses to make a Frenchman weep. The time to go is after 9pm, when the day's pre-pared foods that have to go get marked down to half-price.

brisket, meaty ribs, sliced beef sandwiches, and juicy "handmade" onion rings at the counter. Then grab a bottle of sauce in a mini Mexican beer bottle and a fistful of napkins, and squeeze into a desk—or grab a spot at one of the picnic tables in the parking lot (or, heck, jump on the hood of your car). Come early though; Sonny's is only open until the food runs out, which is apt to happen before the stated closing time. There are now new, more consumer-friendly branches of Sonny Bryan's serving up the same great and sloppy barbecue across Dallas, but they don't have anywhere near the appeal of the original.

2202 Inwood Rd. (near Harry Hines Blvd.). ℭ 214/357-7120. Dishes $4–$9. AE, DISC, MC, V. Mon–Fri 10am–4pm; Sat 10am–3pm.

GREENVILLE AVENUE & EAST DALLAS
Moderate

Liberty Noodles (at the Pavilion) 🛪 PAN-ASIAN/NOODLES   Annie Wong's funky little noodle palace recently moved from its boho Lower Greenville location to a much larger (but still stylish) shopping center space. Hipsters now mix with families (there's even a kid's menu), in private dining areas or at the communal table, for excellent "big noodle" and rice dishes, such as Liberty pad Thai and green Thai curry, *khao soi* (coconut milk broth with tofu, mushrooms, and noodles), or a Korean grill. Those who fear noodles might be too delicate can opt for a big mixed grill of beef and pork or a filet mignon. The multicourse chef's menu ($30, or $50 with wine) is a good place to start if you're having trouble choosing. Check out the good selection of sakes and Thai iced coffee; though a pan-Asian place might not necessarily seem like a place for oenophiles, Liberty Noodles received *Wine Spectator*'s coveted "Award of Excellence."

5600 Lover's Lane. ℭ 214/350-1133. Reservations recommended. Main courses $8–$20. AE, DISC, MC, V. Mon–Sat 11am–2pm; Mon–Thurs 5–10pm; Fri–Sat 5–11pm (bar open till 1am).

Inexpensive

Ali Baba Café *Value* MIDDLE EASTERN   Family-owned (two brothers and their mom, by way of Syria) Ali Babba draws crowds for its good, and cheap, Middle Eastern fare during limited dining hours. Don't be surprised to find a line clamoring to get in. This plain, tiny place, tucked in among the vintage shops, bars, and furniture stores of Lower Greenville, packs them in for great, rich hummus, marinated beef, grilled chicken, falafel, and Syrian and Lebanese dishes like stuffed kibe. The tabbouleh and signature rice dish, made with vermicelli and sautéed in seasoned olive oil, are standouts. If you find yourself in North Dallas rather than downtown, check out the new **Ali Baba Café & Market,** 19009 Preston Rd. (ℭ 972/248-8855), a larger and better lighted branch that contains a small market selling pastries and other foodstuffs.

1905 Greenville Ave. (at Alta). ℭ 214/823-8235. Main courses $6–$14. Tues–Sat 11:30am–1:45pm and 5:30–8:45pm.

Matt's Rancho Martinez 🛪 TEX-MEX   In the gently bohemian Lakewood neighborhood east of downtown, Matt's is a Tex-Mex favorite—the real deal. Simple and relaxed, with a nice patio dining area, it's Texan to the core, and laid-back as all get-out (though it can get pretty noisy when the margarita-drinking hordes descend). Start with great chips and salsa, of course (or the renowned Bob Armstrong queso dip—stir the ingredients), and move on to the chile rellenos topped with green sauce, raisins, and pecans. If you're not big into

Tex-Mex, try the chicken-fried steak: Matt's version of the classic Texas dish even found its way into the pages of *Gourmet* magazine. Matt's has 10 different types of fajitas, grilled specials like quail, and 14 daily lunch specials, bargains at $5.95 (available Sat and all day Tues). Next door is **Matt's No Place** (© 214/823-9077), a country cousin that skips the Mex and goes full throttle with funky Texas prairie fare like wild boar.

Lakewood Theater Plaza, 6312 La Vista Dr. (at Gaston). © 214/823-5517. Reservations recommended on weekends. Main courses $8–$17. AE, DISC, MC, V. Mon–Thurs 11am–9:30pm; Fri–Sat 11am–10:30pm.

BIG D AFTER DARK

Dallas has a lively nightlife scene, with enough in the way of performing arts and theater to entertain highbrows and more than enough bars and clubs to satisfy the young and the restless. In fact, in recent years the live music scene has outpaced that of Austin (which continues to call itself the "Live Music Capital of the World" but lost much of its cool in the dot-com makeover of the city). If you've come to North Texas to wrangle a mechanical bull, you may have to go to Fort Worth, but there are a couple of sturdy honky-tonks in Big D where you can strap on your boots and your best Stetson and do some two-steppin' and Western swing dancing.

For listings, check out the "Weekend Guide" section of the *Dallas Morning News* (www.dallasnews.com) and the *Dallas Observer* (www.dallasobserver.com). You can also check the website of the Dallas Convention & Visitors Bureau (www.dcvb.com) for events.

THE PERFORMING ARTS

The **Morton H. Meyerson Symphony Center,** 2301 Flora St. at North Pearl (© **214/871-4000;** www.dallassymphony.com), is home to the Dallas Symphony Orchestra, a very respectable outfit led by maestro Andrew Litton. The I. M. Pei–designed auditorium is equipped with excellent acoustics and a spectacular pipe organ. Tickets to events are as little as $15, and free concerts are occasionally held. (Free tours are available on selected days at 1 pm; call in advance for schedule.) The **Dallas Opera** performs at Campbell Center #1, 8350 N. Central Expressway (© **214/443-1043;** www.dallasopera.org). The **Dallas Theater Center,** Kalita Humphreys Theater, 3636 Turtle Creek Blvd. (© **214/526-8210;** www.dallastheatercenter.org), is a little gem, the only professional working theater built by the famed American architect Frank Lloyd Wright, and the best place for theater in the Dallas area. Local and touring productions, some fairly adventurous by Dallas standards (like *Angels in America*), are on the card here. Less traditional theater is performed by the acclaimed **Kitchen Dog Theater Company,** 3120 McKinney Ave. (© **214/953-1055**). Of interest to families may be the shows put on by the **Dallas Children's Theater,** 2215 Cedar Springs (© **214/978-0110;** www.dct.org).

Tips **Ticket Central**

For tickets to sporting events and performances, try **Central Tickets** (© 817/335-9000), **Star Tickets** (© 972/660-8300), **Encore Tickets** (© 800/460-4500), **Cowboy Conxtion** (© 888/397-8822), and **Ticketmaster** (© 214/373-8000). For most events, there's little need to secure tickets in advance of your trip.

LIVE MUSIC

Deep Ellum, the rowdy district east of downtown, is entering its second decade as the epicenter of live music and late-night dance clubs. It used to play almost exclusively to the alternative scene, but it has expanded its offerings to include discos, blues bars, and honky-tonks. The top live music venues include Dallas's current standard bearer for live performance, the **Gypsy Tea Room,** 2548 Elm St. (℃ **214/74-GYPSY;** www.gypsytearoom.com), which contains a vintage hall, as well as long-timers **Trees,** 2709 Elm St. (℃ **214/748-5009;** www.trees. com), with a stellar record for hosting the latest and greatest alternative bands, and **Club Dada,** 2720 Elm St. (℃ **214/744-DADA**), where you'll find rock as well as folk acts. Competing for some of the same acts as the Gypsy Tea Room are the more spacious **Sons of Hermann Hall,** 3414 Elm St. (℃ **214/747-4422**), which is equal parts pickup bar, live music venue, and honky-tonk, hosting rock, country, and occasional rockabilly acts (and swing dance classes on Wed); and old favorite **Bronco Bowl** (and the tiny bar tucked inside, **Canyon Club**), 2600 Fort Worth Ave. (℃ **214/943-1777**). For live Christian rock and pop, check out **The Door,** 3202 Elm St. (℃ **214/742-DOOR**).

    Greenville Bar & Grill, 2821 Lower Greenville Ave. (℃ **214/823-6691**), has been cool since I was sneaking in as a high school senior. The crowd, mostly folks intent on resisting the big 4-0, come for rock, country, and blues nightly. Around since 1933, it's also a good spot for a casual meal. In the district that cradled blues legend Blind Lemon Jefferson, live blues are on the card Thursday through Sunday at **Blue Cat Blues,** 2612 Commerce St. (℃ **214/744-CATS**). **Dallas Alley,** Munger Avenue at Marker Street (℃ **214/720-0170**), is a touristy mix of bars aimed at businessmen entertaining clients and visitors staying in West End hotels. From karaoke to country and oldies clubs, it's one-stop shopping for most groups looking for a night out on the town with a view of the skyline. Don't count on heaps of local flavor and authenticity, but the drinking and carousing seem contagious for most.

    For live jazz nightly, dark and ambience-heavy **Sambuca,** 2618 Elm St. (℃ **214/744-0820**), as much restaurant as jazz cafe, has the proper look. A bit of Greenwich Village and a dose of Paris, it is hands-down Dallas's best jazz club, with real rather than light jazz. It has another North Dallas branch, also a Mediterranean restaurant, at 15207 Addison Rd. at Belt Line, in Addison (℃ **972/385-8455**). **Balcony Club,** 1825 Abrams at La Vista (℃ **214/826-8104**), is a relaxed and popular place near the historic Lakewood Theater, with live jazz Thursday through Saturday. You can usually find some live jazz and blues at **Poor David's Pub,** 1924 Lower Greenville Ave. (℃ **214/821-9891**), a venerable old club that shows its age delightfully.

DANCE CLUBS

Club Clearview, 2803 Main St. (℃ **214/939-0077**), is a stalwart of the Deep Ellum scene. Now connected to three other bars (Art Bar, Blind Lemon, and Red Complex), it offers an eclectic mix of dance-oriented and live bands—everything from swing to techno to blues. **Lizard Lounge,** 2424 Swiss Ave. (℃ **214/826-4768**), is the city's best dance club; trendy and slightly seedy, but resolutely sexy, it trades in percolating dance beats and a hot crowd. Sunday night is Goth Night. At **Red Jacket,** 3606 Lower Greenville Ave. (℃ **214/823-8333**), DJs spin dizzying electronica, '70s funk and soul, and pump-it-up new wave tunes. For something out of the ordinary—dancing to Tejano music—check out **Escapade 2001,** 10707 Finnell St. (℃ **214/654-0545**).

Strip (aka "Gentleman's") Clubs

Strip clubs do monster business in Dallas, especially with out-of-town conventioneers. So if you're here with the boys, or you have to go because your boss is dragging you, here are a few contenders for your folded ones and fives: **Obsession Gentleman's Club,** I-35 and Commonwealth (© 214/634-9300); **The Million Dollar Saloon,** 6826 Greenville at Park Lane (© 214/363-4506; www.milliondollar.com), where a couple of girls from my high school, who went on to become *Playboy* centerfolds, danced; **Baby Dolls,** 3039 W. Northwest Hwy. (© 214/358-5511), with large-screen sports distractions; **Dallas Gentleman's Club,** 2117 W. Northwest Hwy. (© 972/869-3376), a glitzy place that bills itself as a "Sports Cabaret" and is packed every weekday at lunch, when they serve free grub; and **Texas Showgirls,** 10945 Composite Dr. (© 214/353-9366), which is BYOB All-Nude and gives away free ½-pound burgers from noon to 2pm. Babes and burgers—how can you beat that?

HONKY-TONK HEAVEN

Although the cavernous meat market Country 2000 went down swingin', there are other hot spots for boot-scootin' in the area, such as **Stampede,** 5818 LBJ Fwy. at Preston Road (© 214/702-8081), known as the country scene's biggest meat market. However, the best spots are outside of Dallas. Worth the drive if you're a fan is the must-see **Billy Bob's Texas** in Fort Worth. A Big D branch of Houston's famous **Gilleys** should have opened by the time you read this, at 1601 S. Lamar (© 214/888-GILLEYS); Gilleys, lest we forget, shot to fame with John Travolta on a bucking bronco in *Urban Cowboy.*

For a more intimate, down-and-dirty take on the honky-tonk scene, check out **Adair's Saloon,** 2624 Commerce St. in Deep Ellum (© 214/939-9900), which the regulars call "Aayy-dares." It gets its share of clean-scrubbed SMU students, but mostly you'll find down-to-earth patrons and infectious country and redneck rock bands that go down well with the cheap beer, shuffleboard, and tables and walls blanketed in graffiti. The perfectly greasy burgers with a whole jalapeño on top are surprisingly tasty; some say they're the best in Dallas. The only rule here is in plain English on the sign behind the bar: NO DANCIN' ON TABLES WITH SPURS.

THE BAR SCENE

Samba Room, 4514 Travis St. at Knox Street (© 214/522-4137), is a trendy, high-decibel, Latin-chic hangout for Big D's beautiful people. On one side is a surprisingly good restaurant, the other a packed watering hole with a cool serpentine bar. It's a good place to sip a *mojito,* the Cuban rum, lime, and mint favorite (but the *caipirinha,* a Brazilian drink favorite made with *cachaça,* doesn't even approach authenticity). A happening new spot, with a lot of downtown nightclub weight behind it, is **Umlaut,** 1602-B Main St. (© 214/742-2DOT; www.umlautbar.com). It calls itself a "19th-century underground lounge dressed in 21st-century design." You probably know right there if that appeals to you. Stark, sleek, and self-consciously cool, it has extensive beer and wine lists and DJs spinning mellow techno sounds.

The Old Monk, 2847 N. Henderson (© **214/821-1880**), is a dark, handsome bar 1 block east of Central Expressway with an excellent selection of Belgian beers, single malts, and great pub grub—go with the Belgian mussels with fries and spicy mayo. In Uptown, just off McKinney Avenue, **The Ginger Man,** 2718 Boll St. (© **214/754-8771**), has a great beer garden and a beer selection to die for: about 200 beers from around the world, including 70 on tap. Beware the cigar-smoking big shots. If you want to heighten the effect an expensive cocktail has on you, check out **The Dome,** 50 stories above ground in the revolving Reunion Tower ball, 300 Reunion Blvd. (© **214/712-7145**).

A step up from karaoke is **Pete's Dueling Pianos,** 4980 Belt Line Rd. #200, Addison (© **972/726-7383**), a piano bar where four accomplished players tickle the ivories on two baby grands and everybody sings along (loudly, enthusiastically) to tunes by the Stones, Beatles, and other boomer faves.

THE GAY & LESBIAN SCENE

The Crew's Inn, 3215 N. Fitzhugh Ave. (© 214/526-9510), was recently named the "Best Gay Bar" by *Dallas Observer.* It caters to the widest possible common denominator of the gay community, rather than microniches. Another long-time favorite is **J. R.'s Bar and Grill,** 3923 Cedar Springs Rd. (© 214/528-1004). **Village Station,** 3911 Cedar Springs Rd. (© 214/559-0650), is a gay dance club that features nightly drag shows in the Rose Room and Trash Disco every Sunday. **Buddies II,** 4025 Maple Ave. (© 214/526-0887), is tops for lesbians: hot music and SGWF looking for same. Gay country swing and line dancers should check out the **Texas Twisters** (www.texastwisters.org), a group that organizes two-stepping and the like for gays and lesbians around the Dallas area, frequently at the **Round-Up Saloon,** 3912 Cedar Springs (© 214/522-9611), a gay country bar that features a Monday karaoke night.

3 Arlington

Sandwiched between Dallas and Fort Worth, the medium-size city of Arlington has become known as a pro sports center and the family playground of the Metroplex. If you're a sports fan, or have kids in tow (or are a kid at heart), it makes a good day trip. If none of those applies, you're probably better off in Arlington's bigger and more important cousins. To get to Arlington, take I-30 from either Dallas or Fort Worth. Plan on it taking you about an hour if traffic's heavy from either city. Having your own car is pretty much required to get around to any of the places below.

Arlington's **Visitor Information Center** is located at 1905 E. Randol Mill Rd. (© **800/342-4305** or 817/461-3888; www.arlington.org).

THE TOP ATTRACTIONS

The Ballpark in Arlington/Legends of the Game Baseball Museum ★ *Kids*
The home of the Texas Rangers professional baseball team is one of the finest

---

Tips **Discounts**

In addition to the coupons available in the *Dallas/Fort Worth Area Visitors Guide* (available from tourist information offices), look for the brochure "The Dallas Metroplex: One Exciting Savings Place," which contains coupons worth $10 at Six Flags.

ballparks in the country. The graceful, redbrick-and-granite 50,000-seat stadium was designed (by architect David Schwarz) to echo classic American baseball parks. The flat, painted billboards in the outfield with retro graphics and the absence of glaring neon lend a yesteryear feel to the park. It's a terrific place to see a game, even for folks (like me) who aren't huge baseball fans.

Even if you can't see a Rangers game (Apr–Sept), you can take a 50-minute tour of the park, which visits the dugout, press box, clubhouse, batting cages, and owner's suite, and visit the Legends of the Game Baseball Museum. The museum traces the history of baseball in this country, with uniforms and artifacts on loan from Cooperstown, the Hall of Fame Museum. See Joe DiMaggio's glove; the jerseys of Babe Ruth, Mickey Mantle, Ted Williams, Hank Aaron, and Walter Johnson; and cool antique baseball cards. Upstairs is a neat little Learning Center of hands-on baseball exhibits for Little Leaguers.

1000 Ballpark Way, Arlington. ⓒ 817/273-5220, 817/273-5100 ticket office, or 817/273-5600 museum. www.texasrangers.com. Ballpark tour admission $6 adults, $5 seniors and students, $4 children ages 4–18. Museum admission $6 adults, $5 seniors, $4 children ages 6–13. Combination tour and museum tickets $10 adults, $8 seniors and students, $6 children ages 4–18. Ballpark tours Mon–Sat hourly 9am–4pm and 9am–1pm on game days. Museum Apr–Oct Mon–Sat 9am–5:30 pm, Sun 11am–4pm; Nov–Mar Tues–Sat 9am–4pm, Sun 11am–4pm. To get there, take I-30 from either Dallas or Fort Worth and exit at Nolan Ryan Expressway/Ballpark Way.

The Palace of Wax & Ripley's Believe It or Not *Kids*

Merged under one roof are these two oddballs of family fun. The Palace of Wax features wax dummies of movie stars and historical figures like Mother Theresa, Tom Hanks as Forrest Gump, Jesus Christ, and Dorothy and her *Wizard of Oz* pals. Ripley's is a collection of the hard-to-swallow and bizarre, like the giraffe-necked woman of Burma and the double-eyed man of China. Really small kids may get freaked, but most children over 5 are likely to find the exhibits pretty cool.

601 E. Safari Pkwy./I-30 at Belt Line, Grand Prairie. ⓒ 972/263-2391. www.palaceofwax.com. Admission to either attraction $14 adults, $11 seniors and military, $6.95 children ages 4–12, free for children under 4. Combination visit to both $17 adults, $14 seniors and military, $9.95 children ages 4–12, free for children under 4. Visit website for discount coupon. Mon–Fri 10am–5pm; Sat–Sun 10am–6pm. Parking $6.

Six Flags Hurricane Harbor *Kids*

The biggest water park in North Texas is 3 million gallons of water and 50 acres of relief from the Texas sun. The kids will go nuts at feature attractions like Hook's Lagoon (pirate ships and 12 levels of interactive features), Black Hole (a tentaclelike thrill ride that plunges through dark wet tubes), and the Bubba Tub (an inner-tube ride that begins at the top of a 70-ft. tower). There are a couple of dozen more rides, slides, and pools, including a 1-million-gallon wave pool, to entertain and douse you and your families. Professional lifeguards are on duty.

1800 E. Lamar Blvd., Arlington. ⓒ 817/265-3356. www.sixflags.com. $29 adults, $19 children under 4 ft. tall and seniors, free for children under 2. Mid-May to mid-Aug daily, mid-Sept to mid-May weekends only; check website for hours. Parking $7.

Six Flags Over Texas *Kids*

Now 40 years old, Six Flags is the place I used to dream about as a kid. The 200-acre amusement park, one of the biggest and best in the country, is the top draw in Texas (and it can be a little crowded on summer weekends). It has Texas-size roller coasters, including the Texas Giant (the world's tallest wooden coaster that hits speeds of more than 60 mph), Batman the Ride (a suspended looping coaster with six inversions and corkscrew spirals), and Mr. Freeze (the fastest and tallest roller coaster in the Southwest). There are also tons of shows, eateries, and nostalgic rides like the Parachute Drop and Log

Grapevine

One of the oldest settlements in North Texas, Grapevine—north of DFW Airport and wedged between Dallas and Fort Worth—is known for its handsomely restored historic Main Street, the Grapevine Opry, several Texas wineries, and a number of art galleries housed in turn-of-the-20th-century buildings. Downtown, there are some 75 historic buildings, including the **Torian Log Cabin** (Liberty Park, 201 S. Main St.) and **1901 Cotton Belt Train Depot.** The **Grapevine Opry,** which inhabits the 1940 Palace Theatre at 308 S. Main St. (© **817/481-8733),** holds foot-stomping hootenannies on Saturday nights and features concerts by top-name country stars throughout the year.

The **Grapevine Visitor Information Center** is located at 701 S. Main St. (© **800/457-6338** or 817/410-8136; www.ci.grapevine.tx.us). You can pick up information about **wine tours** and tastings at La Buena Vida Vineyards, La Bodega Winery, and North Star Winery.

The best way to visit old Grapevine is by train. The Tarantula Steam Train travels from Stockyards Station in Fort Worth to historic Grapevine; see p. 116 for additional information on this nostalgic locomotive. Otherwise, take Highway 114 northwest from Dallas or Highway 121 northeast from Fort Worth.

Ride, with its peculiar green water that thrilled my little girlfriends and me back in the '70s.

I-30 at Hwy. 360, Arlington. © 817/530-6000. www.sixflags.com. $30 adults, $18 children under 4 ft. tall and seniors, free for children under 2. Mid-May to late Aug daily; Mar to mid-May and Sept–Oct weekends only. Check website for hours. Parking $9.

Trader's Village A rollicking and locally famous flea market (spread out over 100 acres), Trader's Village has been trading everything under the sun since the early 1970s. It attracts a couple of thousand dealers each weekend and tens of thousands of shoppers searching through the junk for the occasional find. There are also rides and games for the kids.

2602 Mayfield Rd., off Hwy. 360 in Grand Prairie, south of Arlington. © 972/647-2331. www.tradersvillage. com. Free admission. Sat–Sun 8am–dusk. Parking $2.

4 Fort Worth

In recent years, easygoing Fort Worth has lived in the shadow of Dallas, its brash cousin to the east. Yet one gets the feeling that others' perceptions of their city as second-class don't matter much to Fort Worth natives. The city exudes a quiet confidence, reserve, and sense of comfort that are often missing in Big D.

Fort Worth, nicknamed "Cowtown," revels in its role as the gateway to the West; the mythic qualities of the American West—great unfilled spaces and even grander dreams—are still palpable here. In the mid–19th century, on the heels of the war between Texas and Mexico, Fort Worth began as a frontier army town in the Republic of Texas, assigned with protecting settlers from Native American attacks. The outpost grew into the last major stop along the Chisholm Trail, the major thoroughfare of the great Texas cattle drives that took ranchers and their livestock 500 miles north to the railheads and more lucrative markets of Dodge City and Abilene, Kansas. The trail's importance transformed little Fort Worth into a busy trading post. By 1881, more than five million head of cattle had been driven through town on their way to market. Saloons, bordellos, and gambling houses staked out the rough-hewn area of town called "Hell's Half Acre."

With the arrival of the railroad, the stampede of cattle north grew exponentially, and strategically positioned Fort Worth became a place for ranchers to keep their herds before moving them for sale. The Fort Worth Stockyards opened in 1890, followed by the arrival of major meat-packing plants, transforming Fort Worth into a major cattle shipping center and one of the country's top livestock markets. Fort Worth had become a wealthy city, a cow town to be reckoned with. The rise of the oil business in West Texas bolstered Fort Worth's commercial prospects, and oil fortunes replaced the cattle-ranching riches of the early 20th century.

If, in frontier days, Fort Worth was where the East fizzled out and the West began, today the city is a place where cowboy culture meets high culture. The city of nearly half a million is home not only to a tenacious pride in its Old West past, and plenty of modern-day cowboys and Western flavor, but also to one of the country's most celebrated cultural scenes. Local philanthropists have endowed the city with superlative collections of art and hired some of the world's most prestigious architects—Philip Johnson, Louis Kahn, and Tadao Ando—to build the Kimbell, newly expanded Amon Carter, and new Museum of Modern Art. Fort Worth is also home to a symphony orchestra, an impressive botanic garden, several theater companies, and the Van Cliburn International Piano Competition. It turns out that this cowboy town with a rough-and-tumble past has a remarkably sophisticated and arts-minded soul. Even if you come to the Dallas area with little time to spare, enjoyable Fort Worth is absolutely worth a visit.

As if by well-devised plan, Fort Worth's downtown, a charming and dignified center of business and entertainment, is almost perfectly equidistant between the Stockyards National Historic District and the Cultural District. Fort Worth natives may like to keep the essential elements of their city separate, but they seem to recognize that they add up to a cohesive whole.

ESSENTIALS
VISITOR INFORMATION
Besides the DFW Airport Visitor Information (see section 1, earlier in this chapter), the **Fort Worth Convention & Visitors Bureau** (© **800/433-5747** or 817/336-8791; www.fortworth.com) maintains tourist information centers downtown at 415 Throckmorton St. (© **817/336-8791**); in the Stockyards National Historic District at 130 East Exchange Ave. (© **817/624-4741**); and in the Cultural District at 3401 Lancaster Ave., in the Will Rogers Memorial Center (© **817/882-8588**).

The city's events hot line is © **817/332-2000.**

CITY LAYOUT
Fort Worth lies just west of I-35, which runs north-south. Fort Worth for most visitors means three distinct districts, which the city calls the "Western Triangle": the Stockyards National Historic District, 2 miles north of downtown; historic downtown, which includes Sundance Square, just north of I-30, running

east-west; and the Cultural District, 2 miles west of downtown. See "The Dallas–Fort Worth Metroplex" map on p. 70 to help orient yourself.

THE NEIGHBORHOODS IN BRIEF

Stockyards National Historic District This area was the focus of the old cattle-raising and livestock business of Fort Worth. Today the district retains its Old West feel and is where rodeos and Wild West shows take place, as well as daily cattle drives down Exchange Avenue. A handful of hotels and restaurants aimed at visitors are located here, though it's not overly touristy.

Downtown Downtown is the center of the Fort Worth business community and includes **Sundance Square,** where much of the city's restaurant, bar, and theater nightlife and most business-oriented hotels are located. Staying in this area is best if you want to get around easily between the Cultural District, the Stockyards District, and downtown's attractions.

Cultural District Fort Worth's outstanding museums, including the Kimbell, Modern, and Amon Carter, are clustered in the Cultural District. Just south are parks and gardens, including the Fort Worth Zoo and Botanic Garden. Art lovers will want to base themselves here, but the Stockyards District and downtown are better for families.

Medical District Immediately south of downtown, this is the site of major hospitals and several residential areas, and Fort Worth's major university, Texas Christian University (TCU). Many hotels and restaurants are located south of I-30 as well. There's no major benefit to basing yourself here, but it's where you'll find some of the cheaper hotel options.

GETTING AROUND
By Public Transportation

For information on getting to Fort Worth from DFW Airport, see section 1, earlier in this chapter.

Within the city, the only public transportation most visitors will need is the **Trolley,** green buses dressed up like trolleys that run every 20 minutes among the three major districts, from the Fort Worth Zoo all the way to the Stockyards, making stops downtown on the way. The trolleys run daily from 11am to 6pm between downtown's Sundance Square and the Cultural District, and from 11am to 11pm between downtown and the Stockyards National Historic District. The regular one-way fare is $2 for adults; $1 for seniors, travelers with disabilities, and students ages 6 to 16; and $5 for a Day Pass. However, virtually every museum and attraction in Fort Worth gives out free gold trolley tokens, which allow visitors to ride the Longhorn Trolley for free. Pick up a schedule at any of the visitor information centers or obtain information on schedules by calling ✆ **817/215-8600** or 817/334-0092, or by visiting the website at www.the-t.com. Weekdays, the free "Lunchtime Trolley" is a perfect way to get to a restaurant for lunch; it runs from 10:55am to 2:15pm, leaving from the Intermodal Transportation Center (ITC) along 9th Street, Commerce, Belknap, Houston, and back to 12th Street.

The **Trinity Railway Express (TRE)** is the most convenient and hassle-free way to travel to Dallas without having to worry about traffic. It's an express commuter train connecting the two cities, traveling to DFW Airport, Irving, Dallas' American Airlines Center (for Mavericks and Stars games), and Dallas Union Station ($4 round-trip). Pickup and drop-off points are the Texas & Pacific Station and the Intermodal Transportation Center downtown. Call ⓒ **877/215-8600** or visit www.the-t.com for route and schedule information.

By Car

You can quite easily manage to get around Fort Worth without a car. However, if you want to spend time in Dallas or Arlington, you will be better off with an automobile. Car-rental agencies in Fort Worth include **Avis,** 801 W. Weatherford (ⓒ **817/335-3211**); **Budget,** 1001 Henderson (ⓒ **817/329-2277**); **Enterprise,** 2832 W. 7th St. (ⓒ **817/560-3600**); and **Hertz,** 917 Taylor St. (ⓒ **817/654-3131**).

By Taxi

You'll have to call a cab unless you're lucky enough to catch one outside a hotel. The two major companies operating in Fort Worth are **Checker Cab** (ⓒ **817/469-1111**) and **Yellow Cab** (ⓒ **817/534-5555**). Fares are $2 (initial drop) and 40¢ for each additional ¼ mile. Extras include $2 extra passenger charge, $2.60 airport exit fee, and 50¢ airport drop-off fee.

 FAST FACTS: **Fort Worth**

Babysitters If your hotel does not offer babysitting services, **Sitters Unlimited** (ⓒ **817/535-4449**) arranges babysitting at hotels throughout Fort Worth.

Dentists Call ⓒ **800/577-7320** for a dentist referral service.

Doctors Call the **Tarrant County Medical Society** (ⓒ **817/732-3997**) for a doctor referral.

Drugstores Area locations for **Eckerd Drugs** include 3208 N. Main St., near the Stockyards (ⓒ **817/625-6179**), and 611 Houston St. at Sundance Square (ⓒ **817/336-7105**). The Eckerd store at 6389 Camp Bowie Blvd. in the Cultural District (ⓒ **817/737-3125**) is open 24 hours.

Hospitals Two large, full-service hospitals located in the Medical District, south of downtown, are **Columbia Plaza Medical Center,** 900 Eighth Ave. (ⓒ **817/336-2100**), and **All Saints Episcopal Hospital–Fort Worth,** 1400 8th Ave. (ⓒ **817/926-2544**).

Internet Access One centrally located cybercafe is **Cyber Rodeo,** 1309 Calhoun St., within the Rodeo Steakhouse (ⓒ **817/332-1288**).

Maps Any of the Fort Worth tourist information centers can provide you with free maps of all of Fort Worth or of individual districts.

Newspapers & Magazines Both *The Fort Worth Star-Telegram* and the *Dallas Morning News* "Weekend Guide" have plenty of arts, entertainment, and dining information for Fort Worth and the Metroplex.

Police For an emergency, dial ⓒ **911.** For nonemergencies, call ⓒ **817/871-6458.** The main police station in downtown Fort Worth is located at 350 W. Belknap (at Taylor).

Post Office The main downtown post office, 251 W. Lancaster (ⓒ **817/348-0565**), is open Monday through Friday from 7:30am to 7pm.

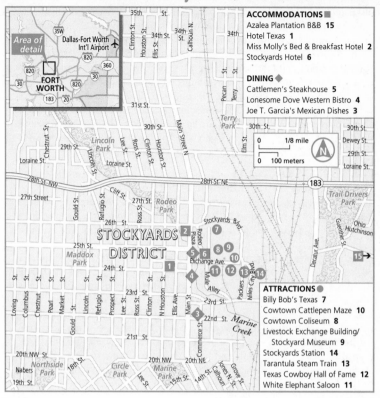

ACCOMMODATIONS ■
Azalea Plantation B&B **15**
Hotel Texas **1**
Miss Molly's Bed & Breakfast Hotel **2**
Stockyards Hotel **6**

DINING ◆
Cattlemen's Steakhouse **5**
Lonesome Dove Western Bistro **4**
Joe T. Garcia's Mexican Dishes **3**

ATTRACTIONS ●
Billy Bob's Texas **7**
Cowtown Cattlepen Maze **10**
Cowtown Coliseum **8**
Livestock Exchange Building/
  Stockyard Museum **9**
Stockyards Station **14**
Tarantula Steam Train **13**
Texas Cowboy Hall of Fame **12**
White Elephant Saloon **11**

Safety For a city of nearly 500,000, Fort Worth is a relaxed and, from most appearances, a safe city. Still, as in any large city, visitors should exercise caution and keep an eye on their handbags, especially at night, in major tourist destinations like the Stockyards and Cultural District, and downtown around Sundance Square. Beyond Sundance Square, which is lively at night, much of downtown Fort Worth is virtually deserted after 9pm. Drive or take a taxi late at night.

Taxes The general sales tax is 8.25%, hotel tax is 15%, and restaurant tax is 7%.

Transit Info For general public transportation questions, call the **Fort Worth Transportation Authority** at ✆ **817/871-6200.** For "the T" bus schedule and Trolley information, call ✆ **817/215-8600** or 817/334-0092 or visit the website, www.the-t.com.

Weather For the latest weather information, call ✆ **817/787-1111.**

EXPLORING FORT WORTH

Despite its laid-back image and small size, Fort Worth abounds with sights, sounds, and things to do. Whether you're a cowboy, aesthete, or historian—or just plain folk—Fort Worth, an enjoyable and relaxed city that's also remarkably well organized for visitors, should prove entertaining. There are three distinct parts, each a couple of miles from one another: the Stockyards National Historic District, the focus of the city's cattle-raising and livestock auction legacy as the cow town of the cattle drives north in the 19th century; newly revitalized historic downtown Fort Worth, a beautifully laid-out, clean, and renovated core; and the Cultural District, a world-class museum, arts, and architecture center with the superlative Kimbell Museum (Texas's finest art museum), the Amon Carter Museum of Western Art, and the fantastic new Modern Art Museum. We'll take them in that order, though where you start should be in accord with your interests in either art or a living museum of the Old West.

THE TOP ATTRACTIONS
The Stockyards National Historic District ★★
Two miles north of downtown Fort Worth, off North Main Street, is the still-beating heart of Fort Worth's Old West heritage. The Stockyards National Historic District is part theme park and part living history museum. The livestock industry's 1880s roots are here, and it became the biggest and busiest cattle, horse, mule, hog, and sheep marketing center in the Southwest (and quite a pocket of wealth). The 125-acre district encompasses the **Livestock Exchange Building,** the focus of old livestock business; **Cowtown Coliseum,** the world's first indoor rodeo arena; **Stockyards Station,** the former hog and sheep pens, now overrun with Western shops and restaurants; **Billy Bob's Texas,** known as the world's largest honky-tonk; Western shops and authentic saloons, such as the **White Elephant;** and the historic **Stockyards Hotel,** where bar stools are topped by saddles and Bonnie and Clyde once camped out while on the lam. Western heroes like Gene Autry, Dale Evans, Roy Rogers, and Bob Wills are honored in bronze along Exchange Avenue's **Trail of Fame.**

Cowtown Cattlepen Maze *(Kids* A "Texas-size human maze," constructed to resemble the cattle pens of the Old West, is a fun diversion for kids (and older folks eager to test their skills against the labyrinth). Parents can watch from the observation deck to track how the kids are doing.

E. Exchange Ave. (across from Stockyards Station). © **817/624-6666.** www.cowtowncattlepenmaze.com. $4.25 adults, $3.25 children ages 5–12 (additional trips to score a faster time, $2.25). Special group rates and unlimited 45-min. runs for birthday parties available. Daily 10am–dusk (5pm in winter, 8–9pm in summer). Closed Thanksgiving, Dec 25, and Jan 1.

Tips **Longhorn Express: Fort Worth Herd**

Amazingly, the Fort Worth Stockyards still look the part of the Old West. To enhance the atmosphere even more, a twice-daily "cattle drive" takes place on the main drag, Exchange Avenue (at N. Main St.), at 11:30am and again at 4pm. About 15 head of 1-ton longhorn steers, led by cowhands dressed the part in 19th-century duds, rumble down the red-brick street past the Stockyards, on their way to grazing near the West Fork of the Trinity River and back again to the Stockyards. Claimed to be the world's only daily longhorn cattle drive, it's perfect for photo ops. The best places to view the longhorns are the front lawn of the Livestock Exchange building and from the catwalk above the cattle pens. For more information, call © **817/336-4373.**

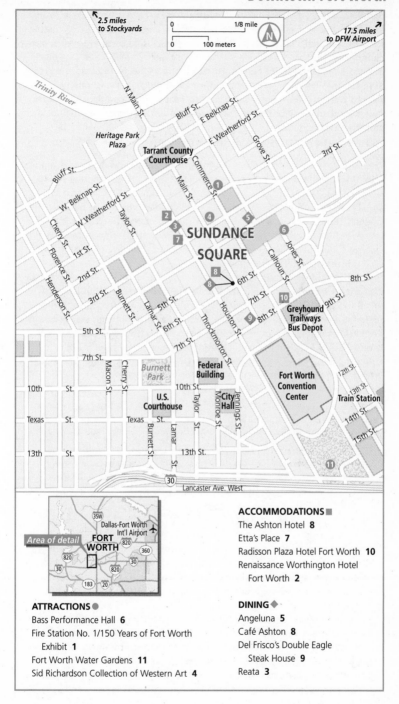

2.5 miles to Stockyards

0 | 1/8 mile
0 | 100 meters

17.5 miles to DFW Airport

Trinity River

N Main St.

Bluff St.

E Belknap St.

E Weatherford St.

Grove St.

3rd St.

Heritage Park Plaza

Tarrant County Courthouse

Commerce St.

Main St.

Bluff St.

W. Belknap St.

W Weatherford St.

Taylor St.

Cherry St.

1st St.

Florence St.

2nd St.

Henderson St.

3rd St.

Burnett St.

Lamar St.

5th St.

6th St.

Calhoun St.

Jones St.

❶

❷ ❸ ❹ ❺ ❻

❼

SUNDANCE SQUARE

❽ ❽ 6th St.

7th St.

8th St.

8th St.

❿

Greyhound Trailways Bus Depot

9th St.

Throckmorton St.

Houston St.

❾ 8th St.

5th St.

7th St.

Macon St.

Cherry St.

Burnett Park

7th St.

Federal Building

10th St.

10th St.

St.

Texas St.

13th St.

St.

U.S. Courthouse

Texas St.

Burnett St.

Lamar St.

13th St.

Taylor

Monroe St.

City Hall

Jennings St.

Fort Worth Convention Center

12th St.

13th St.

Train Station

14th St.

15th St.

30

Lancaster Ave. West

⓫

Area of detail

35W

Dallas-Fort Worth Int'l Airport

FORT WORTH

820

360

820

30

30

820

183

20

Stockyard Museum This small museum, part of the North Fort Worth Historical Society, is located inside the historic Livestock Exchange building that dates from 1893. It displays artifacts—guns, barbed wire, furniture, and clothing—from Fort Worth's glory days. Have a look, in the section on women, at the exhibit of the 1920s Fort Worth Stock Show Queen's coronation and the 19th-century "bad luck" wedding dress, which "brought personal misery or disaster to everyone who wore it or planned to wear it." There's a livestock auction center inside the building, where you can see a few cowboys checking out the animals on the monitors.

131 E. Exchange Ave. ℂ 817/625-5087. Free admission (donation requested). Mon–Sat 10am–5pm.

Texas Cowboy Hall of Fame Fans of rodeo and the cowboy life will appreciate this small museum, in restored horse and mule barns, honoring the stalwarts of Texas rodeo, including such (Texas) household names as Larry Mahan and Ty Murray. On display are the honorees' saddles, chaps, belt buckles, and trophies collected over the course of their careers. Also of interest are the fully restored 60 Sterquell Wagons dating from the 18th and 19th centuries. About an hour should be sufficient to take in the cowboys, though some visitors could do a run-through in half that time.

For those who want to broaden their knowledge of the Old West, the **National Cowboys of Color Museum Hall of Fame,** 2100 Evans Ave. (ℂ 817/922-999; www.cowboysofcolor.org), pays much-needed tribute to a group of cowboys whose contributions were critical to opening the American West and are sadly often overlooked. The museum is open Wednesday through Saturday from 11:30am to 6pm and by appointment; admission is free.

128 E. Exchange Ave., Barn A. ℂ 817/626-7131. www.texascowboyhalloffame.com. Admission $4 adults, $3 seniors, $2 children 3–12. Mon–Thurs 10am–6pm; Fri–Sat 10am–7pm; Sun noon–6pm.

(Kids The Tarantula Steam Train

To jump into the turn-of-the-20th-century Old West character of the Stockyards, don your best Western duds and hop aboard Steam Engine #2248 of the Tarantula Railroad (also called the Grapevine Steam Train). The train makes the Trinity River Run, a 1-hour trip from Stockyards Station to 8th Avenue in Fort Worth, and another travels along the Chisholm Trail to the Cotton Belt Depot in historic Grapevine, Texas. Both trains operate Wednesday through Sunday. The train trip to Grapevine is more involved and interesting (as well as more expensive) than the one that ends in Forth Worth. The name Tarantula stems from a tale in the late 19th century, when a local newspaperman's plans for rail lines were derided as looking like "the legs of a hairy tarantula."

Call ℂ 800/457-6338 or 817/625-RAIL or visit www.tarantulatrain. com for exact schedules. To 8th Avenue, the train leaves the Stockyards on Saturday at noon and Sunday at 3pm (round-trip $10 adults, $9 seniors, $6 children ages 3–12). To Grapevine, trains leave the Stockyards Saturdays at 2pm and Sundays at 4:45pm, arriving in Grapevine an hour and 15 minutes later (round-trip $20 adults, $18 seniors, and $10 children ages 3–12).

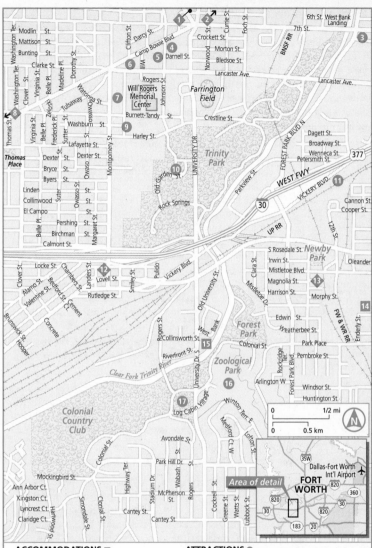

ACCOMMODATIONS ■
Residence Inn Fort Worth **15**
The Texas White House Bed
  & Breakfast **14**

DINING ◆
Angelo's **2**
Kinkaid's **8**
Paris Coffee Shop **13**
Railhead Smokehouse **12**
Sardines Ristorante Italiano **1**

ATTRACTIONS ●
Amon Carter Museum of Western Art **6**
Cattle Raisers Museum **3**
Fort Worth Botanic Garden **10**
Fort Worth Museum of Science and History **7**
Fort Worth Zoo **16**
Kimball Art Museum **5**
Log Cabin Village **17**
Modern Art Museum of Fort Worth **4**
National Cowgirl Museum and Hall of Fame **9**
Thistle Hill House Museum **11**

Historic Downtown & Sundance Square ⊛

Charming, unassuming, and remarkably unhurried, downtown's centerpiece, Sundance Square (named for the Sundance Kid, who hid out here with the Hole-in-the-Wall Gang and a prime stop along the Chisholm Trail during the cattle drives of the 1800s), is 14 blocks of redbrick streets, late-19th-century buildings, and attractions that include the Bass Performance Hall, a couple of museums, and a pair of Art Deco movie theaters. Downtown Fort Worth is lit up like a Christmas tree at night, and Sundance Square's bars and restaurants are the heart of downtown nightlife.

Bass Performance Hall ⊛   Fort Worth's magnificent music hall, inaugurated in 1998 and funded entirely by private donations, is a spectacular addition to the city's already thriving cultural life. Touted as one of the top 10 opera houses in the world, Bass Hall is a handsome showpiece, constructed in a tiered horseshoe shape with excellent acoustics and great sight lines. The work of the architect David Schwarz (the man who built The Ballpark at Arlington and the American Airlines arena), Bass Hall is a 10-story, 2,000-seat jewel. Gracing the exterior are two huge limestone angels, trumpets to lips, heralding patrons to the evening's performance. Inside, the entrance hall is paved with cut Italian marble and the dome is painted with a Texas noonday sky, ringed by silvery laurel leaves. The bathrooms are charmingly decorated with notes from Dvorak's "Going Home." Guided tours—best for those with a keen interest in architecture—last about 45 minutes. Bass Hall hosts the Fort Worth opera, symphony, theater, and dance companies; see "Fort Worth After Dark," later in this chapter, for more details.

4th and Calhoun sts. ℭ **877/212-4280** or 817/212-4325 information hot line. www.basshall.com. Free guided public tours given Sat 10:30am (performance schedule permitting); meet in East Portal at the corner of Calhoun and Commerce.

Fire Station No. 1/150 Years of Fort Worth Exhibit   Tucked away in historic Fire Station No. 1 (which dates from 1907), this annex of the Fort Worth Museum of Science and History tells the history of Cowtown from its frontier days and the Chisholm Trail cattle drives to present day. Good for a quick and painless overview of Old West history.

Corner of 2nd and Commerce sts. ℭ **817/255-9408.** Free admission. Daily 9am–8pm.

Sid Richardson Collection of Western Art   Admirers of art depicting the Old West should tack a visit to the Sid Richardson onto a visit at the more important Amon Carter Museum (p. 119). This small collection, which belonged to a Fort Worth oilman, comprises just 60 paintings by Frederic Remington and Charles M. Russell, two late-19th- and early-20th-century biggies of Western art. If you're not a fan of colorful renderings of wagon trails and Native Americans on horseback, this may not be your glass of whiskey, but the museum does have a couple of great saddles with silver ornamentation. Allow about a half-hour.

309 Main St. ℭ **817/332-6554.** www.sidrmuseum.org. Free admission. Tues–Wed 10am–5pm; Thurs–Fri 10am–8pm; Sat 11am–8pm; Sun 1–5pm. Free tours Sat at 2pm.

The Cultural District ⊛⊛⊛

Fort Worth is the cultural capital of the Southwest, with the finest art museums in Texas and the most impressive small art museum in the country. The city ropes off the Cultural District, making it an elite island by placing it safely apart from downtown business interests, a couple of miles west. Arts philanthropy has

Book your air, hotel, and transportation all in one place.

Hotel or hostel? Cruise or canoe? Car? Plane? Camel? Wherever you're going, visit Yahoo! Travel and get total control over your arrangements. Even choose your seat assignment. So. One hump or two? travel.yahoo.com

powered by
COMPAQ

YAHOO!
Travel

Tips A Water Break

Take a breather at the refreshing **Fort Worth Water Gardens,** designed by the famed architect Philip Johnson—4 acres of water (19,000 gal. per min.) cascading over cement and into five pools. At Commerce and 15th streets, downtown, call © **817/871-7699** for more information.

---

thrived in Fort Worth to a degree unmatched in Texas and many parts of the United States. Wealthy patrons and an enthusiastic city have welcomed some of the world's most celebrated architects, including Louis Kahn, Philip Johnson, and Tadao Ando, to create museums that make much larger and more cosmopolitan cities salivate with envy. The presence of the new Modern Art Museum across the street from the Kimbell and down the block from Philip Johnson's expanded Amon Carter has entrenched Fort Worth as perhaps the top art and architecture city between the two coasts. South of downtown is an area of parks, gardens, historic homes, and the Fort Worth Zoo, considered one of the top five in the country.

Amon Carter Museum of Western Art ★★ Reopened in 2001 after a 2-year, $39 million expansion by the original architect, Philip Johnson, which tripled the size of its galleries, the Amon Carter is now an even more splendid showcase for its wide-ranging collection of American art. The museum possesses the finest and most complete collection of works by Frederic Remington and Charles M. Russell, two giants of Western art, as well as a major photography collection (works by Ansel Adams, Man Ray, Elliot Porter, and many others); early scenes of the West by John Mix Stanley and Albert Bierstadt; and important paintings by Marsden Hartley, Georgia O'Keeffe, and Stuart Davis. The publisher of the *Fort Worth Star-Telegram,* Amon G. Carter's original collection of 400 paintings, drawings, and works of sculpture by Remington and Russell has grown to over 300,000 works. I'd suggest allowing about 2 hours here, though fans of Americana may need even more time.

3501 Camp Bowie Blvd. (at Montgomery and W. Lancaster). © **817/738-1933.** www.cartermuseum.org. Free admission. Tues–Wed and Fri–Sat 10am–5pm; Thurs 10am–8pm; Sun noon–5pm.

Cattle Raisers Museum *Kids* A minor museum dedicated to the history of cattle ranching as a lifestyle, this small collection makes good use of talking dummies—ranchers and longhorn cattle—to give you a picture of life on the range. There's a theater presentation on rustlers, ropers, and mavericks, and lots of cowboy artifacts, including what is reputed to be the world's largest documented collection of branding irons, including some of those owned by famous Texans (LBJ, Stephen F. Austin, Nolan Ryan). A half-hour or so should be sufficient here, unless the kids are entranced by the talking cowboys.

1301 W. 7th St. © **817/332-8551.** $3 adults, $2 seniors and students ages 13–18, $1 children ages 4–12. Mon–Sat 10am–5pm; Sun 1–5pm.

Fort Worth Botanic Garden ★ Created during the Great Depression, this spacious showcase of more than 2,500 native and exotic species of plants in 109 acres of attractive gardens and natural settings is the oldest botanical garden in Texas. Its highlights include the Texas Rose Garden, 3,500 roses that bloom in late April and October; a serene, 7-acre Japanese Garden, which features waterfalls and a tea house and meditation space; and a 10,000-square-foot conservatory of exotic plants and tropical trees from around the world. You can drive through roads in the gardens and park at several of the individual sites.

3220 Botanic Dr. ℂ 817/871-7689. www.fwbg.org. Free admission to gardens. Enclosed conservatory $1 adults, 50¢ seniors and children ages 4–12, free for children under 4. Japanese Garden $3 adults ($3.50 weekends and holidays), $3 for seniors, $2 children ages 4–12, free for children under 4. Botanic garden daily 8am–dusk; conservatory Mon–Fri 10am–9pm, Sat 10am–6pm, Sun 1–6pm.

Fort Worth Museum of Science and History *Kids*   One of the largest of its kind in the country, with a domed Omni (IMAX) theater, planetarium, eight exhibition galleries, and hands-on science displays, this museum offers tons of fun and adventure for families. Kids should eat up the life-size Lone Star dinosaurs (at "Dinodig" they can even hunt for fossils and dig for dinosaur bones), while younger ones can hang out at Kidspace, which has a puppet theater and materials for building a house. When the tots and parents get hungry, there's a courtyard cafe on the premises. Allow a couple of hours here unless the kids get cranky.

1501 Montgomery St. ℂ 888/255-9300 or 817/255-9300. www.fortworthmuseum.org. Exhibit admission $6.50 adults, $5.50 seniors, $4.50 children ages 3–12. Omni admission $6.50 adults, $5.50 seniors, $4.50 children ages 3–12. Planetarium admission $3.50. Sept–Feb Mon–Thurs 9am–5:30pm, Fri–Sat 9am–8pm, Sun noon–5:30pm; Mar–Aug Mon–Sat 9am–9pm, Sun noon–9pm.

Fort Worth Zoo ★★ *Kids*   One of the top zoos in the country, the Fort Worth Zoo has a great layout of natural habitats and fantastic animals from around the world. I took my nephew here for his fifth birthday, and we had a blast. The zoo has an African Savannah with endangered rhinos and giraffes; a Koala Outback with kangaroos, wallabies, and lazy koalas; and Komodo dragons, lots of apes, orangutans and rainforest monkeys, and white tigers. "Texas Wild!," an 8-acre expansion showcasing native Texan animals and a late-19th-century town, opened in 2001. Allow 2 or 3 hours here, though your kids are unlikely to want to leave.

1989 Colonial Pkwy. ℂ 817/759-7555. www.fortworthzoo.org. Admission $9 adults, $5.50 seniors, $6.50 children ages 3–12, free for children under 2. Half-price tickets on Wed. Daily 10am–5pm. Parking $5.

Kimbell Art Museum ★★★   One of the country's (if not the world's) top small museums is this remarkable and gracious place, the jewel in Cowtown's crown. In 1972, the great American architect Louis Kahn created perhaps his finest building to house the art collection of local philanthropist Kay Kimbell. His modern, natural concrete structure, a masterpiece of light, symmetry, and geometry, is a reference work in worldwide architectural studies. Its cycloid-shaped vaults are suffused with natural light entering quietly through slatted skylights. The building is essentially a shell; it has no real interior walls, which allows curators total creativity to use movable walls to design exhibits. The TV art evangelist, Sister Wendy Beckett, calls the Kimbell "probably the nearest such an institution can come to perfection . . . one of the greatest achievements in the world." It is widely held to be the greatest museum building of the late 20th century.

The permanent collection matches the grace and drama of the building. Though small, it contains several superlative works, ranging from prehistoric Asian and pre-Columbian pieces to European old masters (Velázquez, El Greco, Rubens, Rembrandt) and the Impressionist and modern masters (van Gogh, Monet, Cézanne, and Picasso). Outdoors is a Zen-like, sunken sculpture garden by Isamu Noguchi. With its reputation as such an outstanding place to display and view art, the Kimbell receives some of the finest national and international shows. Major exhibits have included "Mondrian: The Path to Abstraction" and, in 2003, "Treasures of Ancient Egypt." Depending upon your interest in and the popularity of the current itinerant special exhibit, you might plan to spend a good 3 to 4 hours here.

3333 Camp Bowie Blvd. (© 817/332-8451. www.kimbellart.org. Free admission to general collection; special exhibitions, $10 adults, $8 seniors and students, $6 children ages 6–11 (Tues half-price). Tues–Thurs and Sat 10am–5pm; Fri noon–8pm; Sun noon–5pm. Tours of the collection Wed 2pm and Sun 3pm.

Log Cabin Village *(Kids)*   Six mid-19th-century log cabins, presented as a living history museum, were transplanted to Forest Park southwest of downtown in the 1950s. The village includes a gristmill and actors decked out in pioneer costumes, who re-create the Old West of early Cowtown posing as spinners, candle makers, and blacksmiths. Pay a visit primarily if you need an inexpensive way to entertain your kids.

2100 Log Cabin Village Lane. (© 817/926-5881. www.logcabinvillage.org. Admission $2 adults, $1.50 seniors and children ages 4–17, free for children under 4. Tues–Fri 9am–5pm; Sat 10am–5pm; Sun 1–5pm (gates close at 4:30pm).

Modern Art Museum of Fort Worth ★★★   The most noteworthy development in Fort Worth—and one of the most important on the national culture scene—is the brand-new Modern, a landmark design by the celebrated modernist Japanese architect Tadao Ando and a true notch on the city's belt. Opened in December 2002, the museum, already being hailed as a masterpiece, contains over 50,000 square feet of gallery space, making it second in size only to the Museum of Modern Art in New York among museums dedicated to contemporary and modern art. The galleries, with 20-foot-high ceilings and suffused with spectacular natural light, are housed in three rectangular, flat-roofed pavilions built around a large pond. In fact the oldest art museum in Texas (chartered in 1892), the Modern possesses an impressive permanent collection of modern and contemporary paintings, sculpture, and works on paper by Picasso, Rothko, Warhol, Stella, Rauschenberg, and Pollock. It also hosts itinerant exhibitions by modern artists such as Wayne Thiebaud and others. The outdoor sculpture collection includes large-scale works by Tony Cragg, George Segal, and Antony Gormly. Plan to spend at least a couple of hours here.

3200 Darnell St. (across the street from the Kimbell Museum). (© **866/824-5566** or 817/738-9215. www.themodern.org. $8 adults, $6 students and seniors, free for children under 13. Tues–Sat 10am–8pm; Sun

---

Moments **Fort Worth Stock Show and Rodeo**

If you're in Fort Worth at the end of January and first few days of February, you can't miss attending the Fort Worth Stock Show (officially known as the Southwestern Exposition and Livestock Show), which harkens back to its earliest days at the end of the 19th century. At the Will Rogers Memorial Center near the art museums (on Amon Carter Sq.), you'll see horse shows and auctions, and be able to check out all sorts of livestock, from beef cattle to llamas and swine. There's plenty of entertainment during the show and also an all-western parade on the first Saturday. The rodeo is especially lively during the Stock Show; tickets are $16 to $18. For more information and an exact schedule of events, call (© **817/877-2400** or visit www.fwstockshowrodeo.com.

noon–5pm. Free public tours Sat–Sun 2pm (no prior arrangement necessary). Call for information about artist-led tours (3rd Sun of the month) and lectures.

National Cowgirl Museum & Hall of Fame ✭   Opened in June 2002, the newest addition to Fort Worth's Cultural District recognizes the importance of women who shaped the American West, and is the only museum in the world honoring their pioneering spirit. It's a fun and educational visit for the entire family; interactive exhibits in three gallery spaces and a state-of-the-art theater depict cowgirls working their ranches, the role of cowgirls in the media and fashion, and cutting horse and barrel racing displays. A rotunda honors more than 150 notable Western women (from Dale Evans and the first woman to cross the Rockies to Annie Oakley and the artist Georgia O'Keeffe). The museum was designed by David Schwarz, who also built Bass Performance Hall and The Ballpark in Arlington. Don't miss the gift shop, a great place to score things like vintage suitcases, antique Western goodies, and rhinestone duds. Allow an hour or two.

1720 Gendy St. (west of intersection of Montgomery and Burnett-Tandy, next to Will Rogers Memorial Center). ⓒ 817/336-4475. www.cowgirl.net. $6 adults, $4 children ages 6–18, free for children under 6. Tues 10am–8pm; Wed–Sat 10am–5pm; Sun noon–5pm.

Thistle Hill House Museum   This historic 1903 Georgian Revival mansion, the former residence of two prominent Fort Worth families, has been lovingly restored with period furnishings. The residence, rumored to be ghost-ridden, has an elegant oak grand staircase and a wealth of interesting details, including eight fireplaces, five full bathrooms, and, unusual for the period, electric and gas lighting and built-in closets. The 45-minute guided tour relates the curious anecdotes of the mansion's history. The cattle baron W. T. Waggoner built the home for his eccentric daughter Electra (who took milk baths and is said to have been the first to spend $20,000 in a single day at Neiman Marcus); it then passed to Winfield Scott, who made many changes in the home, adding its limestone columns; and it finally became a girl's school, later abandoned.

1509 Pennsylvania Ave. ⓒ 817/336-1212. www.thistlehill.org. Admission $4 adults, $2 seniors and children ages 7–12. Mon–Fri 11am–3pm; Sun 1–4pm.

ESPECIALLY FOR KIDS

Fort Worth is loaded with activities for children. The top choice among the options is the **Fort Worth Zoo,** one of the very finest in the country and a splendid array of exotic animals in natural habitats. Kids can play and learn at the **Fort Worth Museum of Science and History,** which has an Omni (IMAX) theater and hands-on science displays, including "Dinodig," where they can play amateur paleontologist. If the kids are restless and just need to get outside, take them to the **Fort Worth Botanic Garden,** with acres and acres of gardens, exotic plants, and tropical trees.

The Stockyards National Historic District should entertain little cowboys and cowgirls. Twice a day, a herd of longhorn cattle rumble down brick-paved Exchange Avenue. **Texas Town** in Stockyards Station is a theme park of sorts: an Old West hotel, bar, outhouse, and jail, as well as a vintage ride park, with an antique merry-go-round. Actors in chaps and vests enact *High Noon* gun duels. Nearby, kids can try to find their way through the **Cowtown Cattlepen Maze,** designed to resemble the cattle pens of the Old West. An enjoyable excursion for families is the **Tarantula Steam Train,** a steam locomotive that travels from Stockyards Station to 8th Avenue in Fort Worth and to historic Grapevine.

Young cowboys and cowgirls will enjoy **horseback trail rides** at the Stockyard Station Livery (chuckwagon dinners available for groups of 10 or more; call ℂ 817/624-3446 for more information), and, if you're here in January, the **Fort Worth Stock Show and Rodeo.** The gals may feel empowered by a visit to the **National Cowgirl Museum and Hall of Fame.** If the kids are hungry for more Old West adventures, trot them over to the **Cattle Raisers Museum,** which depicts life on the range as seen through talking ranchers and cattle and a theater presentation.

See additional family activities in "Arlington," earlier in this chapter.

ORGANIZED TOURS

Hourly guided **Walking Tours of the Stockyards,** with visits to the major sights, leave from the Visitor Information Center at 130 E. Exchange Ave. (ℂ 817/624-4741). Tours cost $8 for adults and $6 for seniors and children, and they are given Monday through Saturday from 10am to 4pm and Sunday from noon to 4pm.

Cowtown Walking Tours (ℂ 800/817-2676) provides guided tours of downtown Fort Worth, from "Hell's Half Acre" to the historic courthouse. Tours last 90 minutes and begin at 10am from Monday to Friday, leaving from General Worth Square near the Convention Center. Tickets, available at the Amtrak Station lobby, cost $8 for adults, $6 for seniors, and $2.50 for children ages 5 to 13.

See additional Fort Worth and Dallas tours in "Organized Tours" in the "Dallas" section of this chapter.

OUTDOOR ACTIVITIES

BIKING, IN-LINE SKATING & JOGGING   Excellent for all outdoor activities are **Trinity Park** (near the Cultural District just north of I-30) and **Forest Park,** south of I-30. Depression-era Trinity Park encompasses the Botanic Garden and 8 miles of cycling and jogging trails. Forest Park is the site of another well-known Fort Worth landmark, the Fort Worth Zoo. The scenic **Trinity River Trails,** which run 35 miles along the Trinity River, are my pick for biking, hiking, and in-line skating. Pick up a map at a tourist information center.

Serious runners may want to come prepared to participate in (or watch) the **Cowtown Marathon** (and 10K), which draws runners from around the world to the Stockyards National Historic District. Call ℂ 817/735-2033 for dates and other information. You can also obtain a monthly runners' calendar at ℂ 800/433-5747.

GOLF   Fort Worth has five public courses. **Meadowbrooks Golf Course,** 1815 Jenson Rd. (ℂ 817/457-4616), just east of downtown, is one of the top 25 municipal golf courses in Texas. The popular par-71 course is set amid rolling terrain. Also at the top of the list is **Pecan Valley Golf Course,** 6400 Pecan Dr. (ℂ 817/249-1845); it has two 18-hole golf courses: the "River" and the "Hills." **Rockwood Golf Course,** 1851 Jacksboro Hwy. (ℂ 817/624-1771), has a short 18-hole course and an additional, fairly difficult 9 holes called the Blue Nine. **Sycamore Creek Golf Course,** Martin Luther King, Jr. Freeway (ℂ 817/535-7241), is a 9-hole layout with narrow tree-lined fairways. And **Z. Boaz Golf Course,** 3200 Lackland Rd. (ℂ 817/738-6287), west of downtown, is a pretty straightforward 18-hole course. Greens fees for all five public courses range from $4 to $20, depending on the day and time. For general information, visit www.fortworthgolf.org.

HORSEBACK RIDING **Stockyards Station Livery,** 130 E. Exchange Ave. (© 817/624-3446), offers horseback trail riding for riders of all skill levels (as well as wagon rides and chuckwagon dinners). Trail riding costs $22 for the first hour and $15 for each additional hour.

TENNIS The swank **Renaissance Worthington Hotel** (p. 128) has two rooftop courts available for $10 per day to nonguests; call © **817/882-1000** to reserve. The public can get on an indoor or outdoor court at the **Don McLeland Tennis Center,** 1600 W. Seminary (© **817/921-3134**), or the **TCU Tennis Center,** 3609 Bellaire North on the campus south of downtown (© **817/ 921-7960**), which has two dozen lit outdoor courts and five indoor courts. There are **public clay courts** at 7100 S. Hulen (© **817/292-9787**).

SPECTATOR SPORTS

See "Spectator Sports" in the "Dallas" section of this chapter for professional football, baseball, soccer, basketball, and more hockey and golf.

AUTO RACING The **Texas Motor Speedway,** I-35W at Highway 114, north of Fort Worth (© **817/215-8500;** www.texasmotorspeedway.com), is said to be the third-largest sporting complex in the world. It's the place to see NASCAR, Indy, and motorcycle racing. Plan on joining a crowd; more than 150,000 people can attend the races here.

GOLF Fort Worth's stop on the PGA tour is the **MasterCard Colonial Golf Tournament,** which takes place every May at Fort Worth's prestigious Colonial Country Club (© **817/927-4278** or 817/927-4280).

HOCKEY The **Fort Worth Brahmas** play from January to March at the Fort Worth Convention Center. Call © **888/597STAR** or visit www.brahmas.com for schedule and ticket information.

RODEO/LIVESTOCK SHOWS Fort Worth's famous **Cowtown Coliseum,** 121 E. Exchange Ave. (© **817/625-1025**), is the top place to see professional rodeo. Rodeos are usually every Friday and Saturday night (tickets $7.50–$13). Popping up frequently on the Coliseum schedule is **Pawnee Bill's Wild West Show,** a reenactment of the original, which was once the largest Wild West show anywhere. Events range from trick roping to trick shooting, and are accompanied by Western music and an arena full of buffalo, longhorns, and horses. For information and tickets, call © **888/COWTOWN** or 817/625-1025 or visit www.cowtowncoliseum.com. Look for $2 coupons in the *Fort Worth Key Magazine,* available at tourist information offices.

The **Kowbell Rodeo,** about 15 minutes from downtown, has rodeos yearround on Saturday and Sunday nights, as well as bull riding Monday, Wednesday, and Friday evenings. Call © **817/477-3092** for more information.

The big event in Fort Worth is the annual **Southwestern Exposition and Livestock Show & Rodeo,** which is staged from the end of January to early February. The nation's oldest livestock show features a Western parade, auctions, and cowboys and cowgirls at the nightly rodeo at **Will Rogers Memorial Center,** located in the Cultural District at 3301 W. Lancaster (© **817/877-2400**).

SHOPPING
Great Shopping Areas

Fort Worth can't compare to Dallas as a shopping mecca, but, especially if you're looking for Western clothing and souvenirs of the city's cow town history, you're in luck. The top tourist area, the **Stockyards National Historic District** (and particularly **Stockyards Station,** a mall of pure Texan shops converted from the old sheep and hog pens), has plenty of authentic Western fashions, antiques, art, and souvenirs, many found in shops inhabiting historic quarters. **Sundance Square** in the downtown historic district is populated with art galleries, museum gift shops, and fashionable clothing and furnishing stores, most in turn-of-the-20th-century buildings. Along Camp Bowie Boulevard in the **Cultural District,** there are a number of art galleries and design-oriented shops. The **Downtown Fort Worth Rail Market,** a European-style market that bills itself as "Texas's First True Public Market," is located in the historic Santa Fe Warehouse, 1401 Jones St. (© **817/335-6758;** www.fortworthrailmarket.org). It has a good farmer's market and a couple dozen permanent merchants.

Western Gear

Two of the best Western shops, for real ropers, urban cowboys, and rodeo queens, are on the Stockyards' classic Exchange Avenue. **M. L. Leddy's,** 2455 N. Main at Exchange (© **817/624-3149**), with the big boot sign out front, is one of the city's oldest Western wear shops. It has fine cowboy duds like hand-made belts, formalwear, custom-made boots, and the best-selling top-of-the-line cowboy hat, the pure Beaver. Across the street from the Stockyards Hotel, **Maverick,** 100 E. Exchange Ave. (© **817/626-1129**), has high-end Western wear like hand-embroidered shirts, saloon-ready 19th-century–style suits, and other swank cowboy duds. It even has a bar inside, so you can grab a longneck while shopping.

    Peters Brothers Hats, 909 Houston St. at 9th Street (© **800/TXS-HATS;** www.petersbros.com), stocks Stetsons and hats of all kinds, including Western fedoras and custom-made cowboy hats. If the duds at these stores are a bit too dear for your cowboy wallet, check out **Western Wear Exchange,** 2809 Alta Mere, 183S at I-30 (© **817/738-4048**), a rare resale shop dealing exclusively in Western wear. If it's already broken in, you'll be closer to looking and feeling the part of a real roper.

    Once you've got the duds, you need the tunes. **Ernest Tubb's Record Shop,** 140 E. Exchange Ave. in Stockyards Station (© **800/229-4288** or 817/624-8449), has a great stock of honky-tonk, cowboy, and country-and-western recordings, including old vinyl and hard-to-find stuff.

Antiques

The Antique Colony, 7200 Camp Bowie Blvd. (© **817/731-7252**), has some 120 dealers of antiques and collectibles. **Cowtown Antiques,** 2400 N. Main St. (© **817/626-4565**), gathers 25 dealers in one space just a block from the Stockyards' main drag. You'll find Western antiques, vintage clothing, chaps and saddles, mounts and hides, and those loveable antler chandeliers. Just up the street is **Cross-Eyed Moose,** 2340 N. Main St. (© **817/624-4311**), run by the same folks and stocking slightly more affordable Western goods. I picked up a great pair of $10 boots here for my nephew.

Department Stores & Malls

Stockyards Station, 140 E. Exchange Ave. (© **817/625-9715**), once the Southwest's largest hog and sheep marketing center, has been converted into a cute center of nearly two dozen restaurants and shops featuring Western apparel, Lone Star wines, country-and-western music, leather goods, Texas products, and arts and crafts. There's even a **Stockyards Wedding Chapel** (© **817/624-1570**) for cowboys and girls dying for a true Old West ceremony.

University Park Village, located 2 blocks south of I-30 on S. University Drive near Texas Christian University (℃ **817/654-0521**), is an upscale shopping center with Talbot's, Williams-Sonoma, Ann Taylor, Voyagers—The Travel Store, and Wolf Camera.

WHERE TO STAY

Fort Worth may not be loaded with super-deluxe places with all the amenities, but it does have a nice mix of affordable hotels, including an attractive roster of Western-flavored small hotels and bed-and-breakfasts. Accommodations are spread pretty evenly among the major districts of interest, so you can stay on the main drag of the Stockyards, downtown on Sundance Square, or south of town near the Cultural District. Everything in Fort Worth is pretty close and easily accessible, though, so you needn't choose your hotel strictly according to your primary sightseeing interests.

At Stockyards District hotels, unlike in most places, weekends are higher than weekday rates. The rates quoted below do not include 15% hotel occupancy tax. Breakfast, either continental or buffet, is offered free at several hotels, as noted below. Do not assume that breakfast is included; if it is not, it can really add to your bill.

The rates cited below, it bears repeating, are high-season rack rates. At a minimum, request the lower corporate rate, and ask about special deals. Virtually all hotels offer some deals, especially on weekends when their business clientele dries up. Check individual hotels' websites for special online offers.

STOCKYARDS NATIONAL HISTORIC DISTRICT
Expensive

Stockyards Hotel ✸✸   A true taste of the Old West, the Stockyards Hotel has, since 1907, been the heart of Fort Worth's illustrious cowboy and railroad past (the original hotel was destroyed by fire in 1915). Bonnie and Clyde hid out here, Wild West poker games and gunslinging fights went down here, and country music stars have come to perform at nearby Billy Bob's. Behind the historic brick facade, each of the rooms works a different aspect of an Old West theme. You can stay in the Davy Crockett, Geronimo, or Victorian Parlor room, or sleep where Bonnie and Clyde did in the early '30s (that's cool enough to make it my favorite). The Stockyards Hotel gets the look and feel right: It's not a stretch to imagine cowboys riding up in a cloud of dust and tying their horses up to the posts out front. The connected restaurant and bar is the H3 Ranch Steakhouse, just a notch below the Cattlemen's Steakhouse around the corner, but a good place for wood-fired steaks, ribs, and spit-roasted pork and chicken. Appetizers and desserts are as colorful as the barstools (which are horse saddles).

109 W. Exchange Ave., Fort Worth, TX 76106. ℃ **800/423-8471** or 817/625-6427. Fax 817/624-2571. www.stockyardshotel.com. 52 units. Weekends $169 double, $225–$375 suite; weekdays $139–$150 double, $179–$279 suite. AE, DC, DISC, MC, V. Valet parking $8. **Amenities:** Restaurant; bar; concierge; 24-hr. room service; laundry service. *In room:* A/C, TV, dataport, minibar, hair dryer, safe.

Moderate

Azalea Plantation B&B ✸   Near the Stockyards, but secluded on a couple of acres of oaks, magnolias, and azaleas, this 1948 plantation-style home is a peaceful place that invites relaxation: It has a gazebo and wooden yard swing, a fireplace in the parlor, crystal and china, and a Victorian dining room. There are two upstairs rooms and two cottages, all with comfortable beds. The Lily of

Tips **Hotel Chains in a Pinch**

If you can't get a room in any of the suites hotels reviewed in this section, three chain hotels especially worth looking into in Fort Worth are **La Quinta Inn**, 4900 Bryant Irvin Rd. (© **800/531-5900**), which has attractive two-room suites with kitchenettes, pool, and gazebo; **Courtyard by Marriott/University**, 3150 Riverfront Dr. (© **817/335-1300**); and **Courtyard by Marriott Downtown**, 601 Main St. (© **817/885-8700**).

the Valley Room has a whirlpool tub, king-size poster-bed, and veranda; the Bluebonnet Bungalow is a cottage with a cow-town theme; and the Rose of Sharon room has a king-size canopy bed, marble-floored bathroom, and opening to a veranda. The Magnolia cottage features a private parlor and giant Jacuzzi. Some guests might find the furnishings and decor to be a bit frilly for their tastes, though others will eat it up. Early-morning coffee and a "hearty plantation" breakfast will start you out on the right foot.

1400 Robinwood Dr., Fort Worth, TX 76111. © **800/687-3529** or 817/838-5882. www.azaleaplantation. com. 4 units. $125 double; $159 cottage. Rates include full breakfast. AE, DC, DISC, MC, V. Free parking. *In room:* A/C, TV, CD player.

Miss Molly's Bed & Breakfast Hotel ⭐   For real late-19th-century Texas style, this home on the second floor above what is now the Star Café can't be beat. Miss Molly's is an elegant and slightly bawdy little place (it was a former bordello, after all) that's seen all manner of folks come through: cattle barons, outlaws, railroaders, and cowboys. Today, it's much more likely to host couples looking to indulge in a little Old West romanticism. The Victorian house, a second story wedged in among the saloons and Western shops on the main drag of the Stockyards, is plushly decorated, with Western quilts, handsome period pieces, and Victorian lamps. The seven rooms are arranged around the lobby/ living room, at the top of a staircase. Rooms are named for their decorative theme; for example, the Cattlemen's room has a carved oak bed beneath mounted longhorns, and Miss Amelia's has lace curtains, a white iron bed, and handmade linens. Miss Josie's, the Victorian bedroom of the former madam and my favorite, is twice as large as the other rooms. Guests share three bathrooms with claw-foot tubs.

109½ W. Exchange Ave., Fort Worth, TX 76106. © **800/99-MOLLY** or 817/626-1522. Fax 817/625-2723. www.missmollys.com. 7 units. $125–$200 double. Rates include breakfast. AE, MC, V. Free parking. *In room:* A/C.

Inexpensive

Hotel Texas *Value*   A charmingly simple, small hotel right on the main drag of the Stockyards, this 1939 hotel is big on Texas hospitality. The former Exchange Hotel, reopened in 1995, retains the airs of a place where cattlemen might have stayed when venturing into the big city for auction. The 21 renovated rooms, including a couple of spacious suites, are understated, though the Honeymoon Room has a Jacuzzi and the second-story Bob Wills Suite comprises four separate guest rooms and has great views of the Stockyards. Within easy walking distance of all the major attractions, restaurants, and nightlife in the Stockyards district, Hotel Texas is a nice and comfortable place to camp out in Cowtown, whether you're here for a romantic weekend or to build a stable.

2415 Ellis Ave. (at W. Exchange Ave.), Fort Worth, TX 76106. © **800/866-6660** or 817/624-2224. Fax 817/
624-7177. 21 units. Weekends $79–$89 double, $149 honeymoon suite; weeknights $55 double, $99 honey-
moon suite. Rates include continental breakfast. AE, DC, DISC, MC, V. Free parking Thurs–Sat (other days free
street parking available). *In room:* A/C, TV.

DOWNTOWN
Expensive

The Ashton Hotel ★★★   Incorporating restored historic buildings on Main
Street, just a few slow paces from Bass Performance Hall and Sundance Square,
the city's only small luxury hotel—a member of Small Luxury Hotels of the
World—is a welcome addition to the Fort Worth scene. It features richly
appointed, elegant rooms with custom-designed mahogany furnishings, invit-
ingly plush king-size beds and Italian linens, an art collection featuring Texas-
born artists, and very attentive service. Some rooms have romantic two-person
claw-foot Jacuzzi tubs. The hotel's elegant restaurant, Café Ashton, one of the
most notable new eateries to open in the Dallas–Fort Worth area in the past
year, serves breakfast, lunch, and dinner (p. 131).

610 Main St., Fort Worth, TX 76102. © **800/327-4866** or 817/332-0100. Fax 817/477-8274. www.the
ashtonhotel.com. 39 units. $250–$340 double. Weekend and executive packages available; see website.
AE, DC, DISC, MC, V. Valet parking $12, self-parking $8 per day. Small pets welcome. **Amenities:** Restaurant;
piano bar; concierge; 24-hr. room service; same-day dry cleaning/laundry service. *In room:* A/C, TV, minibar,
hair dryer, iron.

Renaissance Worthington Hotel Fort Worth ★   Downtown's largest and
swankiest hotel, the massive Worthington is the place where modern-day cattle
barons—oilmen and other execs—like to cool their heels in Fort Worth. A block
from the courthouse and only steps away from Bass Performance Hall and the
array of restaurants and bars clustered around Sundance Square, the hotel dominates one part of downtown like a huge, docked cruise ship. The large and elegant, understated lobby is a hint of the spacious rooms, which are sedate and
very handsomely appointed, with very comfortable beds, large writing desks,
neutral color schemes, and large bathrooms. The Star Grill serves Southwestern
cuisine and is open for breakfast, lunch, and dinner. The Star Bar is a casual
restaurant for light meals and snacks.

200 Main St., Fort Worth, TX 76102. © **800/468-3571** or 817/870-1000. Fax 817/338-9176. www.
renaissancehotels.com. 534 units. $169–$219 double; $425–$1,000 suite. Moonlight and weekend packages
available. AE, DC, DISC, MC, V. Valet parking $12, self-parking $8 per day. **Amenities:** 2 restaurants; bar;
indoor pool; sauna; fitness center; concierge; business center; 24-hr. room service; babysitting; same-day dry
cleaning/laundry service. *In room:* A/C, TV, dataport, minibar, coffeemaker, hair dryer, iron.

Moderate

Etta's Place ★★   In the heart of historic downtown, Etta's is more like a
small, cozy hotel than a mom-and-pop B&B. Occupying the second floor of a
landmark building that houses Fort Worth's venerable jazz club, Caravan of
Dreams, the inn is within easy walking distance of all the downtown shops and
restaurants, and just a short drive or trolley ride from the Cultural District and
Stockyards. Named for Etta Place, the girlfriend of the Sundance Kid (and said
to be the most comely of Wild West women), the 5-year-old inn has spacious
rooms with lots of light and well-chosen Texas touches, including antiques,
horseshoe lamps, and Americana quilts. The handsome library and music
rooms, with clubby leather chairs, are great places to relax with a book or chat
with other guests. There are five good-size Queen rooms, a corner King room
with a view of Sundance Square, three roomy luxury suites with a king-size bed

and kitchen, and a very cool third-floor split-level loft, "Etta's Room" (room no. 302), that looks out onto the rooftop terrace. A full home-cooked breakfast is included.

200 W. 3rd St., Fort Worth, TX 76102. © **817/654-0267.** Fax 817/878-2560. www.ettas-place.com. 10 units. $125–$145 double; $150–$165 suite. Rates include full breakfast. AE, DC, DISC, MC, V. **Amenities:** Restaurant; game room; laundry service. *In room:* A/C, TV, fax, dataport, kitchenette in suites.

Radisson Plaza Hotel Fort Worth   Formerly the historic Texas Hotel (where JFK was memorably photographed the morning of his assassination), this large and centrally located hotel, just 1 block from the Fort Worth Convention Center, is popular with groups, conventioneers, and other visiting businesspeople. A respectable place and decent deal, it has rooms in the old hotel and newer ones in an adjacent annex. The older Southwestern-style rooms are decent size and comfortably outfitted with standard furnishings, but have smallish bathrooms. The newer rooms are the choice of most travelers, though the original rooms have all been renovated. For a $20 upgrade (well worth it), you can get a room on the concierge floor and complementary breakfast, hors d'oeuvres, and cookies and milk. Yee-haw!

815 Main St., Fort Worth, TX 76102. © **800/333-333** or 817/870-2100. Fax 817/882-1300. www.radisson. com. 517 units. $159–$179 double. Weekend rates available. AE, DC, DISC, MC, V. Valet parking $10, self-parking $7. **Amenities:** 2 restaurants; outdoor pool; fitness center; spa; concierge; 24-hr. room service; laundry service. *In room:* A/C, TV, dataport, coffeemaker, hair dryer, iron.

CULTURAL DISTRICT
Moderate

The Texas White House Bed & Breakfast *Value*   A big, handsome, and yes, white house with a wraparound porch and backyard with gazebo, this elegant country home is a fine place to kick up your boots. In the Medical District, near All Saints Episcopal Hospital, the house has hardwood floors, a spacious parlor, a living room with fireplace, formal dining room, and well-maintained, attractive accommodations with plush beds. There's no Lincoln Bedroom, but The Lone Star Room has nice antiques like a triple armoire and a parson's bench sitting area and claw-foot tub. The Land of Contrast Room is done in black and white and has a large bathroom and queen-size brass bed; it may be a little frilly for some cowboys. And the Tejas Room has light oak furniture, his-and-hers rocking chairs, and a large platform tub. The Mustang and Longhorn suites have special amenities like a balcony porch and fireplace (the Mustang even has a two-person, in-room sauna). The friendly owners are happy to give out all sorts of dining and activities recommendations.

1417 8th Ave., Fort Worth, TX 76104. © **800/279-6491** or 817/923-3597. Fax 817/923-0410. www.texas whitehouse.com. 5 units. $125 double; $185 suite. Rates include full breakfast. Reduced rates for more than 1-night stays; special packages for honeymoons and anniversaries. AE, DC, DISC, MC, V. *In room:* A/C, TV, dataport, hair dryer, iron.

Value One-Stop Shopping

Dan Dipert Vacations (© **800/433-5335;** www.traveltotexas.com) has a "Fort Worth Getaway" package deal that gives you 3 days accommodations and tickets to major museums, shows, and attractions, all starting at $79 per person. You have a choice of hotels, sights, and shows, and they'll have the tickets waiting for you when you check in.

Inexpensive

Residence Inn Fort Worth *Kids* *Value*   Formerly an apartment complex, Residence Inn still feels that way—much more like a residence than a chain motel. The spacious layouts, on two floors, have fully equipped kitchens and sitting areas. Most suites even have fireplaces. The penthouse suites are lofts. Many visitors are relocating businesspeople and families, and the inn does its best to foster a community; every evening there's a happy hour with free beer and wine and enough snacks to amount to a light evening meal. This place is great for families, as it's within walking distance of the Fort Worth Zoo and near the Cultural District.

1701 S. University Dr., Fort Worth, TX 76107. ℂ **800/331-3131** or 817/870-1011. Fax 817/732-2114. 120 units. $129 double; $139–$159 suite. 4 nights or more, $10 discount per night. Rates include full breakfast buffet. AE, DC, DISC, MC, V. Free parking. Pets welcome. **Amenities:** Outdoor pool; Jacuzzi; fitness center privileges; limited room service; laundry facilities; same-day dry cleaning. *In room:* A/C, TV, dataport, kitchenette.

WHERE TO DINE
STOCKYARDS NATIONAL HISTORIC DISTRICT
Expensive

Cattlemen's Steakhouse ⭐ *Kids* STEAK   Cattlemen's has been serving the good people of Fort Worth for more 50 years now. It's a relaxed (if frequently boisterous), affordable, and nicely worn place for a thick steak in the heart of cattle country, just around the corner from the Stockyards' main drag. It's great for families: There are separate rooms, like pens, and the server will bring place mats with barnyard animal stickers, a kiddie menu, and a lollipop at the end of the meal. The thick, juicy, charcoal-broiled cuts of beef include a 13-ounce Kansas City sirloin, three cuts of rib-eye, a 16-ounce Texas T-bone, and a pretty good and juicy version of chicken-fried steak. The service is very friendly and low-key, and the crowd is a mix of families and, as my nephew observed, "lotsa men drinkin' wine and tellin' jokes." Those are the same guys who know that Cattlemen's is a good place to bust your aorta without breaking the bank.

2458 N. Main St. ℂ **817/624-3945.** www.cattlemenssteakhouse.com. Reservations recommended. Main courses $5.45–$11 lunch, $9.95–$31 dinner. AE, DC, DISC, MC, V. Mon–Thurs 11am–10:30pm; Fri–Sat 11am–11pm; Sun 1–9pm.

Moderate

Lonesome Dove Western Bistro ⭐⭐ SOUTHWESTERN   A wildly successful little restaurant, this cozy venture is decorated in the style of an old saloon, with a long bar, high-backed Mexican iron barstools, copper-toned tin ceiling, and bold paintings with Western themes. The eclectic menu is rather adventurous for the Old West neighborhood. Appetizers include barbecued duck spring rolls and seared sweet lobster cakes with corn/black-bean salsa and cilantro-orange butter sauce. The terrific main courses opt for unique touches, like the sesame-crusted king salmon, served with jalapeño-honey stir-fried vegetables. For lunch, go with a fresh buffalo burger or the daily Stockyards lunch special, a steal at $5. For dessert, the cappuccino flan is creamy and delicious. Tim and Emilie Love, the delightful first-time restaurant owners, are determined that visitors become regulars; he can often be seen in the back, doing prep work in a cowboy hat and she serving patrons at the bar. The restaurant's wine list now includes two bottles from its private label.

2406 N. Main St. ℂ **817/740-8810.** Reservations recommended. Main courses lunch $5–$10, dinner $16–$26. AE, MC, V. Tues–Sat 11am–2:30pm; Thurs–Sat 5pm–11pm.

Inexpensive

Joe T. Garcia's Mexican Dishes *Value* TEX-MEX   At this institution just south of the Stockyards, almost everyone already knows that they don't have menus, only do two dinner dishes, and only take cash. That's because they've been here many times before and will be back again and again. This 60-year-old restaurant, in a home that looks like a pretty Mexican hacienda, has a great, lush outdoor patio sitting area (large enough to seat 1,000 hungry eaters) set around a pool. Indoors is comfortably relaxed, but outdoors is the place to be—unless the heat is suffocating. Ordering couldn't be simpler: Choose between a heaping plate of succulently grilled chicken or beef fajitas or a combination enchilada plate. Joe T.'s is a margarita factory, spitting out thousands of margaritas on the rocks and frozen. Service can be a little erratic, though it's frequently lightning fast. A Mexican-style brunch is served on Saturdays and Sundays from 11am to 2pm.

2201 N. Commerce St. © 817/626-4356. Reservations not accepted. Main courses $9.25–$11. No credit cards. Mon–Thurs 11am–2:30pm and 5–10pm; Fri–Sat 11am–11pm; Sun 11am–10pm.

DOWNTOWN
Expensive

Angeluna ★ ECLECTIC/FUSION   Facing the huge angels of Bass Performance Hall, this chic, minimalist place draws hep cats and Fort Worth's beautiful people before and after theater and music performances. Under a celestial-painted ceiling of clouds and angels, Clark McDaniel's eclectic fusion menu is hard to pin down—dishes are New American, Asian, and Mediterranean, or bits of all three. Daring appetizers (some more successful than others) include yummy lobster dumplings and flash-fried calamari with "burnt chile" sweet-and-sour sauce. My pick for a main course is the sesame ahi tuna, served with boiled soybeans and jasmine rice. Gourmet pizzas (such as jerk chicken and spinach and mushroom), baked in a wood-fired oven, are also excellent. The volume in Angeluna's trendy main dining room can rise to the levels of a concert hall; quieter tables can be had in the side dining room or the cozy and leafy patio, where smoking is allowed.

215 E. 4th St. © 817/334-0080. Reservations recommended. Main courses lunch $10–$14, dinner $13–$29. AE, MC, V. Mon–Fri 11:30am–2pm; Mon–Thurs 5–9:30pm; Fri 5–11pm; Sat 11am–11pm; Sun 11am–9:30pm.

Café Ashton ★★ NEW AMERICAN   Fort Worth natives aren't usually too impressed by anything too slick or haute, but this fine new addition to the dining scene, in the elegant Ashton Hotel (p. 128), may change the way diners think about this cow town. The menu at Café Ashton, a small and sleek restaurant decorated in soothing colors, is stellar. The young chef is keen on presentation, and his efforts nicely show off creative dishes like beef stroganoff with morels in brandy-laced cream sauce; and Chilean sea bass with a fresh crab and potato puree, tomato, and mandarin orange chutney. For an appetizer, the warm shrimp beignets, served on greens with mango salsa and crème fraîche, are not to be missed. The small but select wine list will surely grow as the restaurant solidifies its place at the top of the Fort Worth dining scene. Even if you're not staying at this fine hotel, make an effort to eat here, even if it's only for a rewarding breakfast.

610 Main St. © 817/332-0100. Reservations recommended. Main courses $14–$30. AE, MC, V. Daily 6:30–10am and 11am–2pm; Sun–Fri 6–9pm; Sat 6–10pm.

Del Frisco's Double Eagle Steak House ★★ STEAK Fort Worth's top steakhouse is a clubby two-level place for cattle barons, power brokers, jet-setters, and mere steak lovers. In a redbrick corner building (ca. 1890s), huge top-notch steaks are the story. The filet mignon (in 8- and 12-oz. versions) is butter-soft; other cuts of prime beef include a marbled rib-eye, prime porterhouse, and Santa Fe peppercorn steak. Pinstripe and new economy types will love the cigar lounge, which has a nice selection of Robustos, and the deep wine cellar. Desserts are every bit as artery-clogging and overwhelming as the main courses. For some Fort Worth natives, though, this bit of Big D swagger and priceyness is a bit much for their laid-back downtown. Cattlemen's Steakhouse is a little more low-key, though a step down in quality for beef lovers.

812 Main St. at 8th St. (℅ **817/877-3999**. Reservations recommended. Main courses $18–$32. AE, DC, DISC, MC, V. Mon–Thurs 5–10pm; Fri–Sat 5–11pm.

Reata ★ SOUTHWESTERN Reata is newly risen, having moved to a new location after the great Fort Worth tornado of 2000 condemned its former home, the Bank One tower. Named for the ranch in the movie *Giant,* Reata now sports a huge rooftop bar and dining area inside the glass dome on the roof. Chef Grady Spears, who bet the ranch on "Texas cowboy" Southwestern cuisine (initially innovative and then so widely imitated that it became a cliché), is no longer in the kitchen, but the boldness and swagger live on. The basic fare, like chicken-fried steak and chicken chile rellenos, and more creative interpretations such as carne asada with cacciota cheese enchiladas and the grilled pork chop stuffed with Mexican cheeses and pears, is consistently well prepared enough to keep more adventurous diners interested. Portions are still huge. The waitstaff are appropriately outfitted in jeans and cowboy vests; they efficiently herd the crowds of casual and big-night-out diners.

310 Houston St. (℅ **817/336-1009**. Reservations recommended. Main courses $13–$27. AE, MC, V. Daily 11am–2:30pm and 5–10:30pm.

CULTURAL DISTRICT
Moderate

Sardines Ristorante Italiano *(Finds* ITALIAN After a protracted, heated battle, this Fort Worth landmark, formerly across from the museums, finally succumbed to the big bad development monster (the old digs are being flattened and transformed into a parking lot). The longtime popular favorite has now moved to West Fort Worth and, amazingly, succeeded in transplanting its unique look and ambience—a cross between a smoky jazz dive and a neighborhood Italian joint in Brooklyn—to the new spot. All the antique pieces, metal signs, and photographs have been relocated, and the dark and intimate feel perfectly replicated. Sardines is perfect for dependable, generous helpings of Italian grub, inexpensive wine, and an abundance of good vibes and good nightly jazz

---

Finds **Sweets for the Sweet**

The best spot for dessert in Fort Worth has to be **Randall's Gourmet Cheesecake Co. & European Market,** 907 Houston St. ((℅ **817/336-2253)**. The cozy little spot serves Euro bistro fare, but is best known for its homemade desserts, which include a spectacular array of scrumptious cheesecakes—5 by the slice, 60 if you order a whole—for dining in or taking back to the hotel.

---

tunes. Some veal dishes can be mediocre; your best bet is to stick to the list of good pastas like *linguine alla rosa* (with artichokes, capers, and olive oil) and seafood. The weekday lunch specials are a good deal, and there's a popular happy hour Monday through Friday from 2 to 5pm.

509 S. University (✆ 817/332-9937. www.itsanice.com. Reservations recommended. Main courses $10–$17. AE, DISC, MC, V. Mon–Fri 11–2pm; Mon–Thurs 5–11:30pm; Fri–Sat 5pm–12:30am; Sun 3–11:30pm.

Inexpensive

Angelo's *(Finds* BARBECUE   Fort Worth's classic Texas barbecue joint, in this spot since 1958, is the real deal. A few blocks north of the Cultural District and west of downtown, it looks kind of like a large Texas Jaycees convention hall, with wood paneling, mounted deer and buffalo heads, metal ceiling fans, and Formica tables. It's nearly as full of flavor as the hickory-smoked barbecue. The sliced beef sandwich and beef brisket plates are the standard, though you can also detour toward salami, ham, turkey, and Polish sausage. The side dishes, such as coleslaw, pinto beans, and potato salad, are all excellent. Chicken and pork ribs are served all day "while they last," though hickory-smoked beef ribs don't make an appearance until after 3:30pm, and cold Bud comes in frosted steins. This place is so low-key that there's not even "waitress service" until mid-afternoon.

2533 White Settlement Rd. (✆ 817/332-0357. Reservations not accepted. Main courses $2.25–$9.50. No credit cards. Mon–Sat 11am–10pm.

Kinkaid's Grocery Market *(Kids* *(Value* BURGERS   A 1940s grocery store that one day started making burgers, Kinkaid's is now a beloved institution in Fort Worth and the perennial winner of "Best Burger in Texas" polls. The standard order is a thick, juicy burger and fries or onion rings. There are a few other items, like grilled chicken, hot dogs, and grilled cheese sandwiches, but few people move beyond the time-tested basics. The large space, with pistachio ice cream–colored green cinder block walls, has a few communal picnic tables in front, long rows of stand-up counters, and an open kitchen in back. Place your order at the kitchen, pick up a white paper bag with your name scrawled on it, pay at the register, and find a spot under the inflatable toys hanging from the ceiling.

4901 Camp Bowie Blvd. (at Eldridge). (✆ 817/732-2881. Reservations not accepted. Main courses $3.50–$7. No credit cards. Mon–Sat 10am–6pm.

Paris Coffee Shop *(Value* DINER   Around since the Great Depression, this big, wood-paneled dining room heaving with hungry Texans for breakfast and lunch is a longtime down-home favorite. There's not an ounce of Paris in it save the name. (Or maybe it's referring to Paris, Texas.) Service is classic southern hospitality. Breakfast is the star: Choose from awesome pancakes, omelets, grits, and biscuits and gravy (on weekdays you can get "red-eye gravy," made with coffee, cinnamon, and bacon grease). Lunch is standard fare like sandwiches, plate lunches (with a choice of meats and vegetables for $6.99), and chili, though there are lunch specials like enchiladas and ham steak—and that famous red-eye gravy. Try the pies; in a place like this, you know they're good.

700 W. Magnolia Ave. (at Hemphill). (✆ 817/335-2041. Reservations not accepted. Main courses $6–$9. AE, DISC, MC, V. Mon–Fri 6am–3pm; Sat 6–11am.

Railhead Smokehouse *⭐* *(Kids* BARBECUE   No Old West town can sit on its barbecue laurels, and Fort Worth has several new Texas barbecue joints to go along with the old-time favorites. Railhead is one of the best. It's spiffy, but it still attracts the hats-and-boots crowd in their pickups, as well as soccer moms and families pulling up in Lexus SUVs for takeout. The smoky barbecue with tangy sauce gets rave reviews; the plates are heaping; and the ribs, sliced beef, fries, and cheddar peppers (cheese-stuffed jalapeños) are excellent. Come for absurdly cheap weekday plate specials and have a beer or margarita out on the patio, which is something of a happy-hour hot spot. Cheap and filling children's plates are served, and you can also load up on barbecue by the pound, though I can't vouch for how well the stuff travels.

2900 Montgomery St. (at Vickery). (② 817/738-9808. Reservations not accepted. Main courses $6.75–$9.35. AE, DISC, MC, V. Mon–Thurs 11am–9pm; Fri–Sat 11am–10pm.

FORT WORTH AFTER DARK

Despite its decent size, Fort Worth still feels like a small town, and plenty of young people looking for a bigger scene split for Big D on weekends. Still, Cowtown has a few good nightlife options, especially at the two extremes of the scale: high culture and cowboy culture. Whether you're inclined toward opera, symphony, and theater, or up for some boot scootin', Fort Worth has some fine venues. Exchange Avenue in the Stockyards is where you want to be on weekends for some hot Western swing, Texas shuffle, and honky-tonk tunes. The street becomes a cruising strip of souped-up trucks, guys and dolls in cowboy and cowgirl finery strutting their stuff, and dancers ducking into honky-tonks and cowboy discos.

For listings, check out the "Startime" section of the *Fort Worth Star-Telegram* or check the weekly listings posted on its website, www.star-telegram.com/justgo. For tickets, try Arts Line at **Ticketmaster** (② **817/467-ARTS** or 214/631-ARTS; www.ticketmaster.com) or **Texas Tickets** (② **817/277-3333**).

THE PERFORMING ARTS

Bass Performance Hall (p. 118) is one of the top places in the country to see a musical or theater performance. Home to the distinguished Fort Worth Symphony Orchestra, its stage has welcomed productions such as *The Nutcracker* and Handel's *Messiah,* Broadway shows (like *Bring in 'Da Noise, Bring in 'Da Funk*), and pop, jazz, and country big-name concerts by the likes of Tony Bennett, k.d. lang, and Ibrahim Ferrer (of the Buena Vista Social Club).

Casa Mañana Theater, 3101 W. Lancaster at University Drive (② **817/332-2272;** www.casamanana.org), the country's first permanent theater designed for the musicals-in-the-round, is an aluminum geodesic dome with an oval stage. It recently underwent a $3 million renovation. Casa, as it's known locally, puts on a wide range of dramas, comedies, and musicals, and is home to one of the top children's theater operations in the United States, mounting productions such as *Aladdin.*

The **Jubilee Theatre,** 506 Main St. (② **817/338-4411;** www.jubileetheatre.org) is home to intimate African-American theater, staging dramas like *Brother Mac* (adapted from Shakespeare's *Macbeth*) and *A Raisin in the Sun* as well as musicals like *Lysistrata Please* (a rock version of the Aristophanes classic) and *Road Show,* an original production.

THE BAR SCENE

The oldest bar in Fort Worth and the site of the city's most famous gunfight in 1897, **White Elephant Saloon,** 106 E. Exchange Ave. (② **817/624-1887**), is an authentic Cowtown saloon, a great place to knock back a Lone Star longneck in the afternoon or check out some live Western music nightly on the small stage. The atmospheric bar is decorated with donated hats (from the likes of Ray Wylie Hubbard and Jimmie Dale Gilmore) and cases of porcelain and ceramic white elephants. There's also a nice beer garden, with live bands under the trees.

Flying Saucer Draught Emporium, 111 E. 4th St. (© **817/336-7468**), is a beer snob's dream, boasting 75 beers on tap and 125 bottles, including a slew of American microbrews and exotics like Belgian *guerze* and German seasonals. For the novice looking for something new, there are "flights," sampler trays from around the world. The place can get rowdy on weekends with cigar-smokers and TCU students, but it's still one of the best places in Fort Worth to wet your whistle. Food tends toward beer-complementary items like bratwurst and beer cheese soup.

A great spot for a few glasses of wine before dinner or a show at Bass Performance Hall is **The Grape Escape,** 500 Commerce St. (© **817/336-9463**). The agreeable little spot specializes in wines from around the world, served by the glass, half-glass, and in sampling flights. Lots of snack foods, including mini pizzas and fries, are also served.

HONKY-TONK HEAVEN

The one place that's practically a required stop in Fort Worth is **Billy Bob's Texas,** 2520 Rodeo Plaza (© **817/624-1711**; www.billybobstexas.com). A cavernous barn for prize cattle in a former life, this absurdly large honky-tonk has it all. With 40 bar stations, a monster dance floor for hardcore boot scootin', a rodeo arena, video games, pool tables, mechanical bulls, and pro bull riding, it's 125,000 square feet of country-and-western heaven. Open for over 20 years, Billy Bob's continues to draw the biggest names in country music, including George Jones, LeAnn Rimes, Willie Nelson, and Jerry Jeff Walker. Its fame is such that you'll see real ropers in their best hats and tight jeans, drugstore cowboys, and a swell of German and Japanese tourists, all soakin' up the flavor. Located in the heart of the Stockyards, Billy Bob's does business Monday through Saturday from 11am to 2am, and Sunday from noon to 2am. The cover charge varies according to the musical act; day visits cost $1. Don't miss the pro live bull riding on Friday and Saturday at 9 and 10pm; admission is $2.

A real contender for hottest honky-tonk in Texas, **Big Balls of Cowtown,** 302 W. Exchange Ave. (© **817/624-2800**; www.bigballsincowtown.com), is surely the best dance spot in Fort Worth. Big Balls really swings on Friday, Saturday, and Sunday nights, when real cowboys and their rodeo queens crowd the dance floor and launch into Western swing to a live band. In 1997, owners Joyce "Bubbles" Miller and Gary "Beav" Beaver, Okies transplanted to Fort Worth, enlivened this spot on the main drag of the Stockyards, and it's now one of the most popular joints in the city. The dance floor is on one side, a long bar with cowhide-covered barstools on the other. The cover is generally $5.

Tips **Everybody, Get in Line**

If you want to learn to line dance, shuffle, and two-step like a Texan, why not do it in one of the most famous honky-tonks in the world, Billy Bob's Texas? Wendell Nelson is the dance man who will lead you—and even the whole family—through the basics. Classes are Thursdays at 7pm for the family (free) and Sundays from 4 to 8pm for couples ($5 per person). Call © 817/923-9215 for additional information.

Also in the Stockyards District, there's live country music at **Rodeo Exchange,** 221 W. Exchange Ave. (© **817/626-0181**) and **Ernest Tubbs Record Shop,** 140 E. Exchange Ave. (© **817/624-8449**), the latter only on Saturday afternoons.

LIVE MUSIC

The Black Dog Tavern, 903 Throckmorton St. (© **817/332-8190**), has nightly jazz, rockabilly, and blues jams, as well as open-mic comedy sessions on Sunday evenings and occasional poetry open-mic nights. **Ridglea Theater,** 6025 Camp Bowie Blvd. (© **817/738-9500**), is a hip, restored 1940s Art Deco theater that plays host to touring rock bands, including alternative flavors of the month. **Aardvark,** 2905 W. Berry St. (© **817/926-7814**), is a legendary hole-in-the-wall that has a wide-ranging roster of pop, rock, and folk acts Wednesday through Saturday.

The top blues joint in town is **J&J Blues Bar,** 937 Woodward St. (© **817/ 870-2337**), just north of the Cultural District. A little rough around the edges—how else would you want your blues bar?—it hosts both national and local acts Wednesday through Sunday nights. The crowd is a mix of blues traditionalists and college kids from TCU.

For traditional live C&W, also check out the bands scheduled at two of the most famous spots in Fort Worth, **Billy Bob's Texas** and **White Elephant Saloon,** as well as **Big Balls of Cowtown.**

5

Houston & East Texas

by David Baird

Situated on a flat, near featureless Gulf Coast plain, Houston sprawls from its center in vast tracts of subdivisions, freeways, office parks, and shopping malls. In undisturbed areas you'll find marshy grasslands in the south and woods in the north. Meandering across this plain are several bayous on whose banks cypress and southern magnolia trees chance to grow. Many visitors, imagining the Texas landscape as it is usually drawn—barren and treeless—are surprised by such green surroundings, but, in fact, the city is at the tail end of a large belt of natural forest coming down through East Texas, and the climate is much the same as coastal Louisiana and Mississippi—warm and humid with ample rainfall.

Houston is the fourth-most populated city in the United States. If we compare the populations of greater metro areas rather than cities, then it ranks only 10th. Yet in geographical expanse Houston ranks second. The city is more than half as large as the state of Rhode Island and continues to expand outward. But in the past few years there has been a strong shift in residential construction toward downtown and the inner city. Town houses in the central part of town are going up at a furious rate, and lofts, condos, and apartments are now a major part of downtown construction.

Houston is not usually considered a tourist destination; most visitors come here for business or family reasons and are lured into playing tourists only after getting here. It is a business town, and the oil and gas industry remains the big enchilada, but other sectors have added so much to the local economy that oil and gas's contribution is only about 50%. The Texas Medical Center is the largest concentration of medical institutions in the world. It is virtually a city within a city, with 14 hospitals and many clinics, medical schools, and research facilities. Construction and engineering companies also contribute much to the economy, and the newest big player is the high-tech industry.

Houston's society is socially and economically wide open. Houstonians inherently dislike being told what to do, and this dislike cuts across the political spectrum: opinion surveys show that gun control is highly unpopular but so is government control over reproductive rights. Among urban planners Houston is famous (or infamous) as the only major U.S. city that doesn't have zoning, allowing the market to determine land-use instead. On the plus side, this love for individual freedoms gives Houston a dynamism that is palpable and has brought a flood of newcomers from around the world, who have found here a welcoming city. Houston seems to be growing more cosmopolitan every day, as ethnic restaurants and specialty shops spring up throughout the city along with exotic temples and churches—Taoist, Buddhist, Hindu, Islamic, Russian Orthodox—built much like they would be back in the mother country. On the minus side, this is the land of Enron, the go-go company that preached to state and federal governments to deregulate the energy markets and then profited illegally from it. This is also a city that is struggling with an air pollution problem that has the local government painfully considering unpopular regulations to keep the city habitable.

The arts give proof to the city's dynamism. In the performing arts, Houston excels: an excellent symphony orchestra, its highly respected ballet and opera companies, and a dynamic theater scene that few cities can equal in quantity or quality. There are some excellent museums, too, and, if art isn't your bag, there's the world-famous NASA Space Center, which is unlike anything else on this planet. While you're enjoying the attractions, keep your eyes open and you can appreciate another thing Houston is known for, its architecture, which stands out for its bold, even brash character. This is, after all, home to the first dome stadium—the Astrodome—which was billed at the time as "the eighth wonder of the world." Several buildings are striking not only for their dramatic appearance but for their irreverence—one skyscraper is crowned with a Mayan pyramid, another wryly uses the architectural features of Gothic churches for a bank

building, and a pair of towers in the Medical Center unmistakably represent two giant syringes. There is little that is staid about this city, and the more time one spends here, the more this is appreciated.

Galveston is the opposite of Houston—far from being a boomtown, its population of 60,000 isn't even double that of 1900. Once Texas's commercial capital, two events changed everything: the Great Storm of 1900, which remains the deadliest natural disaster ever to strike the U.S.; and the dredging of the Houston Ship Channel in 1914. Today, Galveston is a good destination for families who want to visit small-town Texas, combining small-town easiness with a good mix of museums and activities that children can enjoy. Its old commercial district has more historical buildings than all of Houston, and is popular with visitors. But the main draw for visitors (mostly Houstonians) are the beaches.

East Texas is something else again. It borders Louisiana from the coastal cities of Beaumont, Port Arthur, and Houston all the way north to where the state meets Arkansas. The biggest attractions are large national forests, state parks, and the many rivers and lakes. This is why the area is visited more by campers and fishermen than any other species of traveler.

1 Orientation

ARRIVING
BY PLANE
Houston has two major airports: the George Bush Intercontinental Airport (IAH), 22 miles north of downtown, and the smaller William P. Hobby Airport, 9 miles southeast of downtown.

GEORGE BUSH INTERCONTINENTAL AIRPORT Houston's primary airport (© 281/233-1730; www.houstonairportsystem.org) functions as a hub for Continental Airlines, though it's serviced by all of the major national and international carriers. The airport has all the facilities of major international airports, including ATMs and currency exchange desk.

Getting to & from the Airport Taxi service from IAH to downtown costs about $45 and the ride takes 40 minutes; getting to the Galleria-area hotel

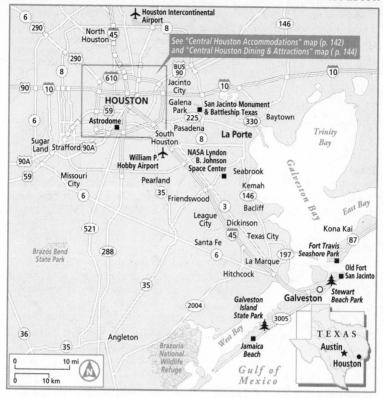

See "Central Houston Accommodations" map (p. 142) and "Central Houston Dining & Attractions" map (p. 144)

district costs a few dollars more. **Express Shuttle USA** (✆ 713/523-8888) ferries passengers from the airport to the major hotels downtown, in the Galleria area, in the Medical Center, and in Greenway Plaza. Service is from 7:30am to 11:30pm. To or from downtown costs $19 ($34 round-trip) per person; one-way and round-trip fares for the other three locations are $20 and $36. Shuttle ticket counters are at airport terminals A and C. The shuttles run frequently and usually get you out of the airport in 15 minutes. Another option is the **city's bus service** (✆ 713/635-4000), which operates bus route nos. 101 and 102 Monday through Friday from 6:30am to 7pm between Terminal C and downtown. The fare is $1 or $1.50, depending on the time. Exact change is required, but the machines accept $1 bills. Buses run about every 30 minutes, and travel time to downtown is a little less than an hour.

All of the major car-rental companies are represented at each of the terminals. John F. Kennedy Boulevard is the main artery into the airport. When leaving the airport, you'll see signs pointing the way either toward the North Freeway (I-45) or the Eastex Freeway (Tex. 59) to the left. The Eastex is shorter and generally quicker for downtown.

WILLIAM P. HOBBY AIRPORT Hobby Airport (www.houstonairportsystem.org) is used mostly by Southwest Airlines. All the major car-rental agencies have counters here with either staff or a service phone. Taxis from Hobby to the downtown area cost about $30, and to the Galleria area $40. **Express Shuttle**

USA buses (© **713/523-8888**) cost $15 to downtown, the Galleria area, the Medical Center, and Greenway Plaza, and can take passengers to Houston Intercontinental for $20. Operating hours are the same as for the Houston Intercontinental Airport, except for the shuttle service between the airports, which stops at 9pm.

BY CAR

Houston is connected to Dallas and Fort Worth by I-45; to San Antonio, New Orleans, and Beaumont by I-10. From Austin, you can take either Tex. 71 through Bastrop to Columbus, where it joins I-10, or you can take Tex. 290 east through Brenham.

BY TRAIN

Amtrak (© **800/872-7245;** www.amtrak.com) trains from New Orleans, Chicago, and Los Angeles (and points in between) arrive and depart from the **Southern Pacific Station** at 902 Washington Ave. (© **713/224-1577**), close to downtown.

VISITOR INFORMATION

The **Greater Houston Convention and Visitor's Bureau** has an elaborate visitor center located in the City Hall Building at 901 Bagby St. between Walker and McKinney (© **713/227-3100**). Here you can get brochures for just about anything, a range of city maps, architectural and historical guides, and answers from the center's staff. Make sure to pick up a copy of the *Official Guide to Houston* magazine. They publish it quarterly and include a helpful calendar of events. At the visitor center you can also play with the interactive computer stations and see a short introductory film of the city. The center is open daily from 9am to 4pm. If you're driving, park your car at the underground lot that is 1 block north of city hall. To get there, turn onto Walker, drive past City Hall, and immediately turn right on Bagby, then right again on Rusk; you'll see a sign that says THEATER DISTRICT PARKING 2. It's free for visitors; just get your parking ticket stamped at the visitor center.

For advance information, try © **800/4-HOUSTON** or www.houston-space cityusa.com. Other websites you might find helpful are **www.houston chronicle.com** and **www.houstonpress.com**. The *Houston Chronicle* is the daily newspaper; the *Houston Press* is a weekly tabloid freebie, which has a large entertainment section.

CITY LAYOUT

Houston is a difficult city to know in depth; it was built with no master plan, and most of its streets are jumbled together with little continuity. The suburban areas look alike and have indistinctive street names, usually ending in things like "crest," "wood," and "dale." To make matters worse, the terrain is so flat the only visible points of reference are tall buildings. But most of the main attractions are not far off the freeways or other main arteries. With a basic knowledge of these, you can keep your bearings and get from one place to another.

To understand the layout of Houston's freeways, it's best to picture an irregularly shaped spider web. The lines that radiate out from the center are in the following clockwise order: At 1 o'clock is the Eastex Freeway (Tex. 59 north), which usually has signs saying CLEVELAND, a town in East Texas; at 3 o'clock is the East Freeway (I-10 east to Beaumont and New Orleans); between 4 and 5 o'clock is the Gulf Freeway (I-45 south to Galveston); at 6 o'clock is the South Freeway (Tex. 228 to Lake Jackson and Freeport); between 7 and 8 o'clock is the

Southwest Freeway (Tex. 59 to Laredo, look for signs that read VICTORIA); at 9 o'clock is the Katy Freeway (I-10 west to San Antonio); at 10 o'clock is the Northwest Freeway (Tex. 290 to Austin); and at 11 o'clock is the North Freeway (I-45 north to Dallas). As the freeways approach the downtown area they form a tight loop that has actually come to define the geographical borders of downtown. Also, there are two circular freeways that connect these highways to each other in the same manner as the concentric circular strands of a spider web. The first is Loop 610 (known as "the Loop"), which has a 4- to 5-mile radius from downtown. The second is known alternately as Sam Houston Parkway or Beltway 8. It has a 10- to 15-mile radius from downtown and is mostly a toll road except for the section near the Bush Intercontinental Airport.

In addition to the freeways, there are certain arteries that most newcomers would do well to know. Here are brief descriptions of the main thoroughfares:

Main Street heads south-southwest from the city's center. It intersects Montrose Boulevard a couple of miles from downtown at a traffic circle called the Mecom Fountain; this is the heart of the Museum District. Beyond the fountain, Main Street passes Hermann Park and the Rice University campus. This stretch of South Main has lots of green space and is lined with oak trees. Past Hermann Park is the Medical Center and then Reliant Park, with the new football stadium, the old Astrodome, and the Astroworld/Waterworld amusement parks.

Montrose Boulevard runs due north from the Mecom Fountain crossing Westheimer Road and Buffalo Bayou. It gives its name to the Montrose area and is lined by several bistros around the Museum District. After it crosses the bayou, Montrose becomes Studemont and then Studewood when it enters a historic neighborhood known as the Heights.

Westheimer Road is the east-west axis around which most of western Houston turns. It begins in the Montrose area and continues for many miles through various urban and suburban landscapes without ever coming to an end. Past the Montrose area, Westheimer crosses Kirby Drive. To your right will be River Oaks, home to Houston's rich folk. Farther along is Highland Village Shopping Center, then Loop 610, where it enters the popular commercial district known as the Galleria Area or Uptown. Farther west Westheimer passes through an endless series of fast-food restaurants, strip malls, and chain retail stores as it runs through suburbia.

Kirby Drive in an important north-south artery. It intersects Westheimer Road by River Oaks and runs due south skirting the Greenway Plaza and passing under the Southwest Freeway. Once south of the freeway, Kirby enters University Place, which stretches around the western borders of the Rice University campus and is the favorite residential area for Houston's doctors, lawyers, and other professionals. Kirby eventually intersects South Main Street in the vicinity of the Reliant Astrodome.

THE NEIGHBORHOODS IN BRIEF

Downtown Once a ghost town in the evenings and weekends, downtown Houston is now the place to be. Restaurants and bars are opening (and in some cases closing) in quick succession; hotels are enjoying boom times, and several new hotels have gone up in the last 2 years. Much of the revitalization is taking place on the northwest side of downtown, in and around Old Market Square and the theater district, where Houston's symphony orchestra, ballet, opera, and its principal theater company all reside. To the east, within walking

Central Houston Accommodations

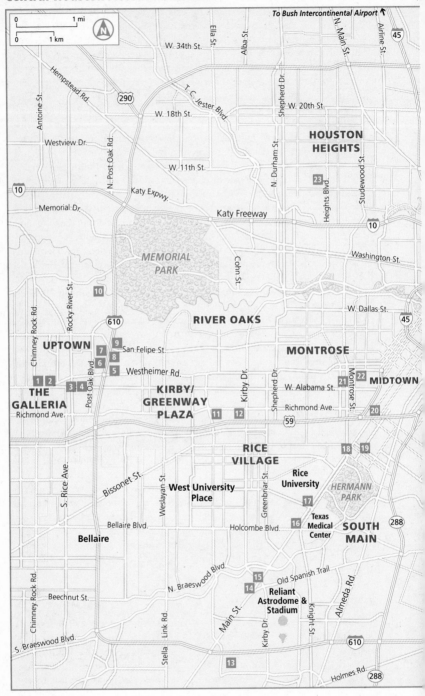

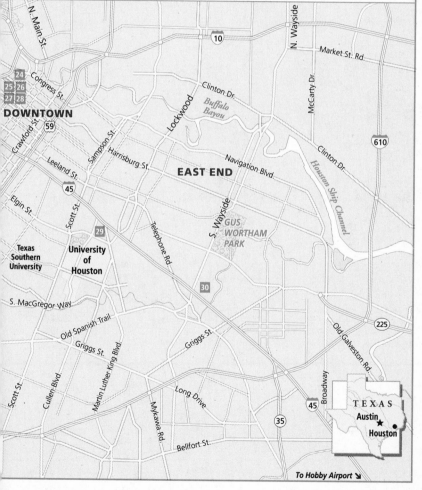

Central Houston Dining & Attractions

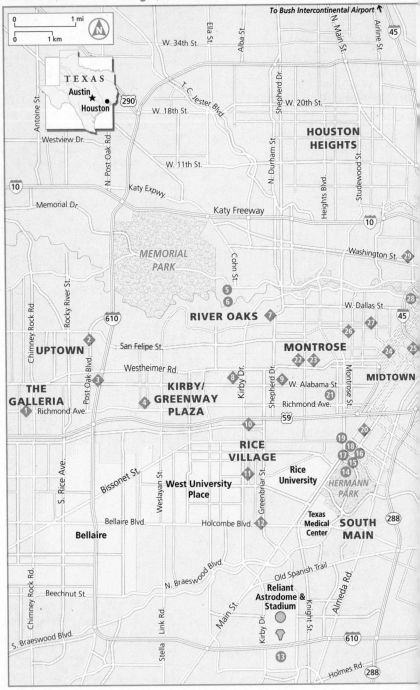

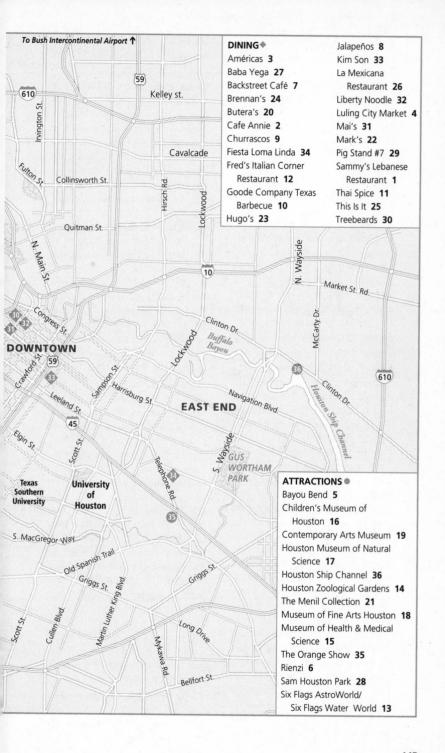

To Bush Intercontinental Airport ↑

Kelley st.

Cavalcade

Irvington St.

Fulton St.

Collinsworth St.

Quitman St.

N. Main St.

Congress St.

DOWNTOWN

Crawford St.

Leeland St.

Elgin St.

Texas Southern University

University of Houston

S. MacGregor Way

Old Spanish Trail

Griggs St.

Scott St.

Cullen Blvd.

Martin Luther King Blvd.

Hirsch Rd.

Lockwood

Sampson St.

Harrisburg St.

Telephone Rd.

EAST END

GUS WORTHAM PARK

Clinton Dr.

Buffalo Bayou

Lockwood

Navigation Blvd.

N. Wayside

Market St. Rd.

McCarty Dr.

S. Wayside

Clinton Dr.

Houston Ship Channel

Griggs St.

Long Drive

Mykawa Rd.

Bellfort St.

DINING ◆

Américas **3**
Baba Yega **27**
Backstreet Café **7**
Brennan's **24**
Butera's **20**
Cafe Annie **2**
Churrascos **9**
Fiesta Loma Linda **34**
Fred's Italian Corner
  Restaurant **12**
Goode Company Texas
  Barbecue **10**
Hugo's **23**

Jalapeños **8**
Kim Son **33**
La Mexicana
  Restaurant **26**
Liberty Noodle **32**
Luling City Market **4**
Mai's **31**
Mark's **22**
Pig Stand #7 **29**
Sammy's Lebanese
  Restaurant **1**
Thai Spice **11**
This Is It **25**
Treebeards **30**

ATTRACTIONS ●

Bayou Bend **5**
Children's Museum of
  Houston **16**
Contemporary Arts Museum **19**
Houston Museum of Natural
  Science **17**
Houston Ship Channel **36**
Houston Zoological Gardens **14**
The Menil Collection **21**
Museum of Fine Arts Houston **18**
Museum of Health & Medical
  Science **15**
The Orange Show **35**
Rienzi **6**
Sam Houston Park **28**
Six Flags AstroWorld/
  Six Flags Water World **13**

distance, are the George Brown Convention Center and the new baseball park, Minute Maid Field (formerly called Enron Field).

Most of downtown is connected by a network of tunnels and elevated walkways that total more than 6 miles. Shops and restaurants line these tunnels, forming an underground city. As is typical of Houston, almost all of these pedestrian tunnels are private, not public, developments. South of downtown is **Midtown,** an area in transition, with town houses and shops gradually replacing vacant lots and small office buildings. Vietnamese shopkeepers and restaurateurs have settled into the western side, especially along Milam Street, where you can find an array of excellent Vietnamese restaurants with reasonable prices.

East End Before Houston was established on the banks of Buffalo Bayou, the town of Harrisburg already existed 2 miles downstream. As Houston grew eastward it incorporated Harrisburg, leaving behind little of the old town. There is a small commercial Chinatown a couple of blocks east of the convention center; beyond that, the area becomes residential. The inner East End is an up-and-coming neighborhood of mixed ethnicity. As you move farther east, the residences mix with small-scale manufacturing, auto mechanic and body shops, and service industries for the ship channel. In the far southern part is NASA's Space Center Houston; Kemah, which is Houston's version of Fisherman's Wharf; and Galveston Island. Most of the hotels located in this area are along the Gulf Freeway. The main reason for staying here is that the hotel rates are for the most part moderate, and the location between downtown,

Hobby Airport, and the above-mentioned attractions makes the East End convenient.

South Main South of downtown and midtown is the **Museum District** and Hermann Park. This is a lovely part of town with lots of green space. Most of the museums are set closely together within a few blocks of each other. Here also are the Houston Zoological Gardens and the Rice University campus. On the south side of the park begins the Texas Medical Center. A bit further south is a complex of buildings holding the new Reliant Stadium, the old Astrodome, and the AstroWorld and WaterWorld amusement parks. There are many hotels in this part of town to suit all budgets. The location is quite convenient. It's close to downtown, to Uptown, and to the restaurants and shops of the Kirby District.

Montrose Directly west of downtown is this hip, artsy, and colorful part of town known for its clubs, galleries, and shops. The Museum District extends into the southern part of the Montrose to include the famous Menil Collection and its satellite galleries, which are a must-see for any visitor interested in the arts. Upscale in certain sections, downscale in others, the Montrose contains a broad cross-section of Houston society. It's also the de facto center of Houston's large and active gay community. With downtown to the east, the South Main area to the south, and the Kirby District to the west (with Uptown just beyond that) and the Heights to the north, it is nothing if not centrally located, and it has some of the best restaurants in the city.

Kirby District & Greenway Plaza The area bordering Kirby Drive from River Oaks to University

Place offers the most restaurants of any district in Houston. Near Kirby Drive's midway point, where it crosses the Southwest Freeway is the Greenway Plaza, an integrated development of office buildings, movie theaters, a sports arena, and shops. Farther south is the Rice Village, a retail development consisting of 16 square blocks of smart shops and restaurants. It is phenomenally popular with Houstonians and visitors and attracts all kinds of shoppers and diners.

Uptown Farther west, all the way to Loop 610, is where Uptown begins. It is still informally called the **Galleria area,** after the large indoor shopping mall, entertainment, and hotel complex. But the district's business owners had to devise another name for it because the developer of the Galleria protected the use of its name so closely that it became problematic to use the word in any commercial context. Thus, we have "Uptown."

This area has the greatest concentration of hotels in the city. Aside from the Galleria, most of the shopping malls and stores front Post Oak Boulevard from Westheimer Road north for a half-mile to a mall called Uptown Park. You'll know you're in Uptown when you see the futuristic traffic lights, arches, and street signs at the intersections.

North Houston & The Heights All the neighborhoods described above are south of I-10, which cuts Houston into northern and southern halves. North Houston is largely a mix of working- and middle-class neighborhoods and commercial centers and, with the exception of the Heights, has little to offer visitors. Over the years, developers tried to establish upscale communities here, but an inherent quality of suburbanism is that you can always build farther out, and, with each successive subdivision, the inner suburbs lose a little more of their luster. Ultimately, the developers took this to its logical extreme, skipping over vast tracts of land to build so far north that the city will never touch them. Thus we have The Woodlands and Kingwood, two upscale residential developments that are so far out one can't consider them as part of Houston.

The Heights, interestingly enough, could have served as the original model for the subdivisions that came later; it was conceived as an independent, planned residential community in the 1890s and remained so until 1918 when it was annexed by Houston. Many of the houses one finds in the area are lovely Texas Victorians. The Heights is a peaceful neighborhood close to downtown and the Montrose area, but note: The Heights is "dry" (no alcohol) and, as a consequence, there are no good restaurants here, but some great shopping can be found, especially for antiques and folk art.

2 Getting Around

BY CAR

Houston is organized around the personal automobile. A car is almost a necessity unless you confine your explorations to the downtown area and the Museum District. Buses linking these two areas are frequent and easy to use so that it is possible to stay in a downtown or South Main hotel and get around by bus and, if available, the hotel shuttle and perhaps the occasional taxi. Otherwise, you'll probably need a car.

Traffic can be a problem and Houston's freeways are no place for the meek: Many drivers don't obey speed limits, bob and weave through the lanes, and make their turnoffs at the last possible moment. The best thing to do is make sure you have a clear idea of where you're headed and what exit you'll need to take before you get on the freeway. As freeway systems go, Houston's is logical and has good directional signs. Traffic in Houston can be heavy throughout the day, especially during rush hour or when there's freeway or other construction. The Public Works Department in Houston is answerable only to God and has managed to make a mess of the downtown area for the greater part of 2 years. You can use the **Texas Department of Transportation Info Hot Line** (*C* **713/ 802-5074**) to check for lane closures on local freeways. The *Houston Chronicle* also provides this information as well as info on street closures.

RENTALS   The prices for rental cars in Houston are lower than those for many tourist destinations, but there are several taxes that raise the price by as much as 27%. Keep this in mind when the sales person tries to bump you up to a higher-priced model. As is the case when renting cars anywhere, you probably don't need to buy extra insurance if you're already covered by your personal auto insurance. The major car-rental companies with locations around the city include: **Alamo** (*C* 800/462-5266), **Avis** (*C* 800/230-4898), **Budget** (*C* 800/ 527-7000), **Dollar** (*C* 800/800-3665), **Enterprise** (*C* 800/736-8222), **Hertz** (*C* 800/654-3131), **National** (*C* 800/227-7368), and **Thrifty** (*C* 800/847- 4389).

BY PUBLIC TRANSPORTATION

The **Metropolitan Transportation Authority (MTA)** (*C* **713/635-4000** or www.ridemetro.org) operates citywide bus service with stops indicated by red, white, or blue signs. Customer service staff can tell you over the phone what bus to take (and where to pick it up) to any specific destination you give them. There are five free Metro Trolley routes that circle through the downtown area and are handy for visitors. You can pick up a map of these routes at the Houston visitor center in City Hall (see "Visitor Information," above). The standard bus fare is $1; $1.50 for express buses (seniors pay 40¢ and children under 4 ride free); exact change is required, and the machines accept dollar bills. On average, buses run every 30 minutes but become less frequent in the late hours of the evening.

BY TAXI

Taxis are plentiful in the city, but trying to hail one on the street can be an exercise in frustration. Call ahead or use hotel taxi stands. The principal companies are **Yellow Cab** (*C* 713/236-1111), **Fiesta Cab** (*C* 713/225-2666), **Liberty Cab** (*C* 713/695-6700), and **United Cab** (*C* 713/699-0000). Rates are set by the city: $3 for the first mile; $1.65 for each additional mile.

 FAST FACTS: Houston

American Express There is an office at 5085 Westheimer, Suite 4600, on the third floor of the Galleria Mall II (*C* **713/626-5740**). It's open Monday through Friday from 9am to 6pm, and Saturday from 10am to 5pm.

Area Codes Houston has 10-digit dialing for local calls. All numbers must begin with one of Houston's three area codes: 713, 281, or 832.

Dentists For a referral, call ℂ **800/922-6588.**

Doctors For minor emergencies or to see a doctor without an appointment, call **Texas Urgent Care** at ℂ **800/417-2347.**

Drugstores **Walgreens,** 3317 Montrose Blvd. at Hawthorne Street (ℂ **713/520-7777**), is open 24 hours a day. In the vicinity of the Medical Center, there is a 24-hour **Eckerd Drug Store** at 7900 S. Main St. (ℂ **713/660-8934**).

Hospitals The **Ben Taub General Hospital,** 1502 Taub Loop at the Texas Medical Center (ℂ **713/873-2600**), has a fully equipped emergency room.

Internet Access **Copy.com,** 1201-F Westheimer in the Montrose area (ℂ **713/528-1201**), has several computers and is open from 7am to midnight on weekdays, 11am to 7pm on Saturdays, and noon to 9pm Sundays.

Maps Salespeople, repairmen, and others who must travel about rely on something called a "Key Map," a binder of detailed maps that divides Houston into a grid system. This homegrown Houston creation became so popular here that it has been copied by map companies in other cities. It may offer more information than most visitors want. You can buy standard street maps at any drugstore and at many convenience stores, and you'll find some helpful maps of downtown, the Museum District, and other parts of the city at the visitor center in City Hall.

Newspapers & Magazines The local daily is the *Houston Chronicle.* The *Houston Press,* a weekly freebie that covers local politics and culture, can be found around town at restaurants, stores, and just about anywhere people congregate.

Police Dial ℂ **911** in a emergency; for nonemergencies, dial ℂ **311.**

Post Office The downtown branch, 401 Franklin St. (ℂ **713/226-3066**), is open Monday through Friday from 9am to 5pm, and Saturday from 9am to noon.

Safety Houston is a safe town for visitors. Exercise caution at night in the downtown areas that lie outside the theater district.

Taxes The local hotel tax is 17%; the local sales tax 8.25%.

Transit Information Call ℂ **713/802-5074.**

Weather Call ℂ **713/228-8703.**

3 Where to Stay

The downtown area continues to gain popularity with several new hotels opening their doors, but the Uptown/Galleria area, with all the shopping and dining options, still remains hotel central and has a couple of recent openings, too. Both of these are the obvious options for where to stay but don't make them your automatic choice without first giving some thought to where you'll be spending your time in Houston. See the "Neighborhoods in Brief" section above for more suggestions about where to stay.

The hotel listings that follow include "rack rates" (the base retail price for a room with no discount) for double occupancy. You should use this as a basis for comparison and not think of these prices as etched in stone. Always ask about promotional rates, particularly at large chain hotels. Houston is a business town, and you can usually find deep discounts for weekend stays. Keep in mind that there is a 17% hotel tax, which is not included in the rates shown here and is rarely included in hotel price quotes.

DOWNTOWN
VERY EXPENSIVE

Four Seasons Hotel Houston Center ★★★   This member of the luxury hotel chain does everything right. It stands out especially in the areas of service (reliable concierge, attentive staff, and a European spa) and spaciousness (everything about the hotel is large—guest rooms, suites, and all common areas). The best views are to be had in rooms facing west and north. What impresses me the most about this hotel is the ease with which services are provided. Need a fridge, a fax machine, or a VCR delivered to your room? No problem. Need your suit dry cleaned at 2 in the morning for use later that day? No problem. The hotel is located near the city's convention center and within easy walking distance of the baseball park, Minute Maid Field. Connected to the hotel are The Park Shops, a shopping center, and the Houston Center Athletic Club, whose facilities are available to guests free of charge. (The hotel has a large, well-equipped health club of its own and offers guests access to a nearby racquet club, too.) Chef Tim Keating's cooking has made the hotel restaurant, Quattro, the favorite spot for fine dining downtown.

1300 Lamar St., Houston, TX 77010. ⓒ **800/332-3442** or 713/650-1300. Fax 713/276-4787. www.four seasons.com. 399 units. $310 standard; $360–$400 executive suite; $650 and up specialty suite. Children under 18 stay free in parent's room. Weekend rates and packages available. AE, DC, DISC, MC, V. Valet parking $21. Pets allowed. **Amenities:** Restaurant; 2 bars; large outdoor heated pool; health club; spa; Jacuzzi; sauna; concierge; courtesy car; business center; 24-hr. room service; in-room massage; babysitting; 24-hr. laundry service/dry cleaning. In room: A/C, TV w/pay movies, dataport, minibar, hair dryer, iron, safe.

Lancaster Hotel ★★★   For those who enjoy the performing arts and nightlife, there is no better place to stay in Houston. Within 1 block of the hotel are the symphony, the ballet, the opera, and the Alley Theatre (see "Houston After Dark," later in this chapter), and when reserving a room you can have the concierge buy tickets for performances at any of these venues as well as the Hobby Center for the Performing Arts. Also a block away is Bayou Place, where you can catch a movie or a live blues or rock act, and within a few blocks are many restaurants and clubs. The hotel occupies a small 12-story building that dates from the 1920s and looks all the smaller for being near the Chase Tower (the tallest skyscraper west of the Mississippi). Rooms are a little smaller than their counterparts at other downtown hotels but better furnished, and with more of the character of an old hotel. Bathrooms are ample and have lots of counter space. Service is excellent and includes lots of personal touches such as fresh-cut flowers in the rooms.

701 Texas Ave., Houston, TX 77002. ⓒ **800/231-0336** or 713/228-9500. Fax 713/223-4528. www.lancaster. com. 93 units. $275–$315 standard; $325–$550 suite. Children under 18 stay free in parent's room. Promotional rates and weekend packages available. AE, DC, DISC, MC, V. Valet parking $20. **Amenities:** Restaurant; bar; fitness room; concierge; courtesy car; 24-hr. room service; in-room massage; babysitting; overnight laundry service/dry cleaning. *In room:* A/C, TV/VCR w/pay movies, fax, dataport, minibar, hair dryer, iron, safe, CD player.

EXPENSIVE

Doubletree Allen Center ★   There's a coziness and a European feel to this hotel that the designers were clever to create. It doesn't feel like a 300-room establishment. The common areas are designed to evoke a residential feel. In this it is the opposite of the Hyatt, which is just a block away. The midsize rooms are furnished attractively in modern style with more flair than most hotel rooms. They are more attractive than those in the Hyatt. The beds are comfortable, and bathrooms are large and well lit with plenty of counter space. The hotel is situated in the middle of the business district. In amenities and service it compares with the Hyatt, but not with the Four Seasons or the Lancaster.

400 Dallas, Houston, TX 77002. (C) **800/222-TREE** or 713/759-0202. Fax 713/752-2734. www.doubletree hotels.com. 350 units. $119–$249 standard; $219–$279 ambassador; $269–$419 suite. AE, DC, DISC, MC, V. Valet parking $10 weekends, $20 weekdays. **Amenities:** Restaurant; bar; fitness center; concierge; car-rental desk; courtesy car; business center; limited room service; same-day laundry service/dry cleaning. *In room:* A/C, TV w/pay movies, dataport, coffeemaker, hair dryer, iron.

Hyatt Regency Houston   A classic Hyatt with the towering atrium lobby, glass elevators, and ivy draping from the walls, this hotel remained popular and busy while several other downtown hotels closed in the 1980s. Now, with downtown's revival, it's more popular than ever. From its 30 floors you can see much of the boldest portion of Houston's skyline. The rooms with the best views are along the north side; a still better view can be had from a table in Spindletop, the hotel's revolving restaurant. Rooms are not as big as those in the Doubletree next door, but are comfortably furnished. The Hyatt is connected to the tunnel system and is in proximity to most of the major downtown office buildings and City Hall.

1200 Louisiana St., Houston, TX 77002. (C) **800/233-1234** or 713/654-1234. Fax 713/646-6953. www. hyatt.com. 984 units. $165–$320 standard; $350–$550 regency suite; $400–$600 imperial suite. Children under 18 stay free in parent's room. Internet specials sometimes available. AE, DC, DISC, MC, V. Valet parking $21; self-parking $15. **Amenities:** 3 restaurants; bar; outdoor heated pool; fitness center; concierge; car-rental desk; courtesy limo; business center; salon; limited room service; in-room massage; overnight laundry service/dry cleaning; executive floor. *In room:* A/C, TV, dataport, coffeemaker, hair dryer, iron.

The Magnolia Hotel ⭐   Opened in 2003 in what was the Houston Post Dispatch Building (1920s), the Magnolia has a contemporary feel with a few anachronistic touches thrown in as references to the building's past, which keep things interesting. The common rooms, especially the club area, include the old-style wood paneling and club chairs, while the guest rooms make use of textured fabrics and surface treatments to contrast with their modern furnishings. Rooms are large and quite comfortable. The focal point of the hotel is the mezzanine club that holds a free continental breakfast in the morning and cocktails and snacks in the afternoon and evening (the hotel doesn't have a full service restaurant but it does have a full kitchen for room service). The club is meant to be an area where guests can relax outside the four walls of their guest rooms, perhaps play a little billiards in the game room, read the paper in the library, or surf the Web over a drink (the entire club is set up for high-speed wireless access).

1100 Texas Ave., Houston, TX 77002. (C) **888/915-1110** or 713/221-0011. Fax 713/221-0022. www. magnoliahotels.com. 314 units. $149–$310 standard; $249–$425 studio suite; $349–$525 1-bedroom suite. Rates include continental breakfast and evening cocktails. AE, DC, DISC, MC, V. Valet parking $20. **Amenities:** Bar; heated rooftop pool; fitness center; Jacuzzi; children's programs; game room; concierge; courtesy car; secretarial services; limited room service; in-room massage; babysitting; coin-op laundry; same-day laundry service/dry cleaning; executive level. *In room:* A/C, TV w/pay movies, dataport, minibar, coffeemaker, hair dryer, iron, safe.

INEXPENSIVE

Days Inn Downtown/Medical Center   The best features of this hotel are its proximity to downtown and its price. In fact, this is the cheapest place to stay near downtown. Years ago, it was a 280-room Holiday Inn that closed down when this part of Main Street started to decay. Reopened a few years ago, the owners have refurbished 194 of the rooms. The common areas tend toward ugliness, but the large guest rooms are simply but attractively furnished and comfortable. They all have split bathrooms (the vanity area in the bedroom) with plenty of counter space. One of the inconveniences here is that there is no restaurant, though there are a few coffee shops and fast-food joints within a couple of blocks, and the area isn't dangerous. There is a complimentary shuttle to downtown and the Medical Center that leaves on demand from 6:30am to 10pm.

4640 S. Main St., Houston, TX 77002. (C) **800/799-9964** or 713/523-3777. Fax 713/523-7501. www.daysinn. com. 194 units. $59 double. Rates include continental breakfast. AE, DC, DISC, MC, V. Free secured parking. **Amenities:** Large outdoor pool (open in season); courtesy shuttle; coin-op laundry. In room: A/C, TV, hair dryers some rooms.

EAST END
MODERATE

Drury Inn & Suites Houston Hobby *Value* This hotel is virtually identical (except in price) to the Drury Inn & Suites Near the Galleria (p. 159). It's worth your while to check prices here because the rooms and amenities are competitively priced and often discounted, and the property is well managed. Deluxe rooms and suites are large and come with fridge and microwave. Complimentary cocktails are served in the afternoon from Monday to Thursday.

7902 Mosely Rd., Houston, TX 77061. (C) **800/DRURYINN** or (C) and fax 713/941-4300. www.drury-inn.com. 134 units. $88 double; $98 deluxe; $108 suite. Rates include breakfast buffet. Weekend and Internet specials available. AE, DC, DISC, MC, V. Free parking. **Amenities:** Heated indoor/outdoor pool; exercise room; Jacuzzi; coin-op laundry; same-day laundry service/dry cleaning. In room: A/C, TV, dataport, coffeemaker, hair dryer, iron.

Hilton University of Houston ⭐ This is unlike any other Hilton Hotel in that it is part of the Conrad Hilton College of Hotel and Restaurant Management and is staffed not only by professional full-timers, but also by students performing their lab work. It deserves consideration because of its rates, which often drop significantly when there are no academic conferences or parents' weekends; its location on the University of Houston campus between downtown and the attractions in Houston's southeast side; and its service, which is often excellent. Rooms throughout the hotel's eight floors are large L-shaped layouts with modern furnishings that include a sleeper sofa. Eric's, the hotel's restaurant, is far better than most hotel restaurants and offers a menu with a Latin flair. The University Center next door has a health club, a large pool, game room, and beauty salon, all of which the guests have access to. Note that the parking garage has a low ceiling and cannot accommodate vehicles such as large SUVs and pick-up trucks.

4800 Calhoun Rd., Houston, TX 77004. (C) **800/HOTELUH** or 713/741-2447. Fax 713/743-2472. www.hilton. com. 86 units. $130 double. AE, DC, DISC, MC, V. Parking $4. **Amenities:** Restaurant; bar; limited room service; same-day dry cleaning. In room: A/C, TV w/pay movies, dataport, coffeemaker, hair dryer, iron.

INEXPENSIVE

Red Carpet Inn Hobby Regency Motor Lodge Nice and cheap and with its own peculiar character, this hotel offers the most inexpensive lodging of any place on this side of town. The rooms are midsize with 1970s-style furniture, but they're clean and comfortable. The real character of the place comes from the Restaurant and the Pu San Lounge. The former is a sterling example of a roadside Tex-Mex joint; the latter is the archetypal Houston neighborhood blue-collar bar with red carpet that smells slightly of stale beer. The bar has a friendly staff, a pool table, dartboards, and a TV always tuned to sports.

6161 Gulf Fwy., Houston, TX 77023. © **800/928-2871** or 713/928-2871. Fax. 713/928-3050. 150 units. $37–$45 double. Weekly rates available. AE, DC, DISC, MC, V. Free off-street parking. **Amenities:** Restaurant; bar; outdoor pool (open in season); coin-op laundry. *In room:* A/C, TV.

SOUTH MAIN
EXPENSIVE

Hilton Houston Plaza ★★ In terms of amenities, service, and location, this is the best of the hotels around the Medical Center. Consequently, it enjoys a high occupancy rate, especially with people attending medical conferences. As the occupancy rate increases so do the prices (well above those quoted here). Try to book early and, if you have any flexibility, get rates for different dates. Making matters worse for travelers on a budget is the small number of standard rooms, only 40 out of 181.

The hotel's facilities set this hotel apart from neighboring hotels. The large rooms are comfortable and well furnished. The building is 19 stories tall, with views toward either the Medical Center or Rice University; it's a toss-up as to which is prettier. The hotel's location on the rim of the Medical Center is actually an advantage over its principal Medical Center rivals (a Marriott and a Crowne Plaza) because it makes getting to and from the hotel much easier, avoiding the Medical Center traffic jams and the tight parking garages.

6833 Travis St., Houston, TX 77030. © **800/HILTONS** or 713/313-4000. Fax 713/313-4660. www.houston plaza.hilton.com. 181 units. $145 double; $165 suite. Weekend rates available. AE, DC, DISC, MC, V. Valet parking $14; self-parking $8. **Amenities:** Restaurant; bar; large outdoor heated pool; health club; Jacuzzi; sauna; courtesy shuttle; business center; limited room service; same-day laundry service/dry cleaning. *In room:* A/C, TV w/pay movies, dataport, minibar, fridge, coffeemaker, hair dryer, iron.

The Warwick Hotel ★★ At one time the Warwick was at the top of the list of luxury hotels in Houston. Over the years, it has lost its high ranking but not its charm or its enviable location on the greenest, most attractive part of South Main, in the middle of the Museum District and near the Montrose Area. Rooms throughout its 12 stories have lots of windows and offer good views in any direction. Most of the rooms are large; all come furnished in period-style, predominantly French pieces. The bathrooms are midsize and come with ample counter space. Service is good.

5701 S. Main St., Houston, TX 77005. © **800/298-6199** or 713/526-1991. Fax 713/526-0359. 308 units. $159–$199 double; $189–$450 suite. Promotional rates and weekend packages available. AE, DC, DISC, MC, V. Valet parking $15; self-parking $8. **Amenities:** Restaurant; bar; heated outdoor pool; exercise room; sauna; concierge; courtesy shuttle; business center; 24-hr. room service; in-room massage; babysitting; overnight laundry service/dry cleaning. *In room:* A/C, TV w/pay movies, coffeemaker, hair dryer, iron.

MODERATE

Holiday Inn Hotel and Suites Houston Medical Center This hotel can be a bargain. Spot checks on prices turned up a number of instances when standard rates were floating well below the published rack rates. The hotel has an excellent location across from the Medical Center, at the intersection with Holcombe Boulevard. Rooms are comfortable but furnished with little effort to hide their hotel-like character. Some suites have full kitchens. What's not to like is the shortage of staff at the front desk and in guest services that makes getting attended an exercise in patience. The same is true for the service at the hotel restaurant.

6800 S. Main St., Houston, TX 77035. © **800/HOLIDAY** or 713/528-7744. Fax 713/528-6983. www.holiday-inn.com. 284 units. $120–$150 double; $150–$175 suite. Medical rates for hospital outpatients available. AE, DC, DISC, MC, V. Free parking. **Amenities:** Restaurant; bar; small pool; fitness room; courtesy shuttle; salon;

limited room service; overnight laundry service/dry cleaning. *In room:* A/C, TV, dataport, coffeemaker, hair dryer, iron.

La Quinta Inn Astrodome   This two-story motel is just down the road from AstroWorld and WaterWorld. The rooms include extras like free local calls and 25-inch TVs that are larger than what you usually find in hotels in this price range. Bathrooms are spacious and well lit. The furniture and decoration are the result of a recent renovation that succeeded in making the rooms comfortable and attractive, albeit unmistakably motel-like. More important is the fact that they shield out the noise from the freeway.

9911 Buffalo Speedway (at Loop 610), Houston, TX 77054. ✆ 800/531-5900 or 713/668-8082. Fax 713/668-0821. www.laquinta.com. 115 units. $79–$92 double. Rates include continental breakfast. Children under 18 stay free in parent's room. AE, DC, DISC, MC, V. Free parking. **Amenities:** Outdoor pool (open in season). *In room:* A/C, TV, coffeemaker, hair dryer, iron.

Patrician Bed & Breakfast Inn ★★ *Finds*   This is a smart choice for those who want a location near the Museum District that's also a straight shot into downtown. Lovely wood floors, lots of area rugs, a few period pieces, old-fashioned wallpaper—you'll definitely get the B&B experience, but not in its most gussied-up aspect. Patricia Thomas, the owner, gives equal emphasis to comfort and convenience. All rooms come with queen-size beds, cable TV, and terry-cloth robes. The doubles are quite spacious with ample bathrooms that sport claw-foot tubs with shower fixtures; the one on the first floor also offers a large desk, which makes it attractive to the business traveler. With its proximity to downtown and convenient parking, this B&B gets a number of businesspeople on the weekdays. For the weekenders there are rooms sporting two-person whirlpool tubs and walk-in showers. Prices vary according to room size and location. The common areas are attractive and comfortable, and, for the convenience of guests, Ms. Thomas provides a microwave and a fridge stocked with complimentary bottled water and soft drinks.

1200 Southmore Blvd., Houston, TX 77004. ✆ 800/553-5797 or 713/523-1114. Fax 713/523-0790. www.texasbnb.com. 7 units. $100–$165 double. Rates include full breakfast. AE, DC, DISC, MC, V. Free parking. *In room:* A/C, TV (VCR in some units), hair dryer, iron.

INEXPENSIVE

Grant Palm Court Inn ★ *Kids* *Value*   This is the best lodgings bargain in Houston: attractive, immaculate rooms on well-kept grounds at astonishingly low rates. All rooms are quiet and are comparable to rooms costing twice as much at many other hotels. The higher rate is for rooms with two full beds that can accommodate up to four people at no extra charge. The rooms occupy a couple of two-story buildings separated by lovely grounds that hold a pool, a Jacuzzi, a wading pool, and a swing set. The hotel is close to both the Medical Center and the Astrodome/AstroWorld complex. As with all hotels in this part of Houston, prices go up in February, when the rodeo comes to town.

8200 S. Main St., Houston, TX 77025. ✆ 800/255-8904 or 713/668-8000. Fax 713/668-7777. 64 units. $39–$49 double. Rates include continental breakfast. AE, DISC, MC, V. Free parking. **Amenities:** Outdoor pool; Jacuzzi; coin-op laundry. *In room:* A/C, TV/VCR, hair dryer, iron available upon request.

Parkview Inn and Suites   This is a simple motel with two stories of rooms lining a large parking lot. The quietest rooms are the ones at the back of the property; the front ones can be noisy. The rooms have simple painted-wood furniture and two full-size beds; most come with a small fridge and a microwave, which makes them a value for people wanting to save money on dining. Suites are twice the size of the standard rooms and come with kitchenettes, dining table and chairs, and a sleeper sofa. Bathrooms are clean but a little small. There is a complimentary shuttle to the major hospitals in the Medical Center that leaves every hour.

9000 S. Main St., Houston, TX 77025. © and fax **713/666-4151**. 93 units. $45 double; $59 suite. Rates include continental breakfast. AE, MC, V. Free parking. **Amenities:** Courtesy shuttle; coin-op laundry. *In room:* A/C, TV.

MONTROSE
VERY EXPENSIVE

La Colombe d'Or ★★★   If you enjoy the smallness of scale of a B&B and the fact that the rooms don't look like hotel rooms, but you want more space, in-room dining, and more privacy, this is the hotel for you. The five suites are extremely large, with hardwood floors, area rugs, antiques, king-size beds, and large bathrooms. Some suites come with separate dining rooms, and the in-room service, from either the bar or the restaurant, is one of the things this hotel is known for. The penthouse is more than twice as large as any of the suites and offers a lot of open space, a bar, a study, and a parlor. The original mansion that the hotel occupies was built in the 1920s for oilman Walter Fondren. The interior has some beautiful architectural features, and its location puts you close to museums, restaurants, and the downtown area.

3410 Montrose Blvd., Houston, TX 77006. © **713/524-7999**. Fax 713/524-8923. www.lacolombedor.com. 6 units. $195–$275 suite; $575 penthouse. AE, DC, DISC, MC, V. Free valet parking. **Amenities:** Restaurant; bar; limited room service; limited laundry service. *In room:* A/C, TV; hair dryer and iron available upon request.

MODERATE

Lovett Inn ★   One block off Westheimer and 3 blocks from Montrose Boulevard, the Lovett Inn offers plenty of quiet, without being far from the busy restaurant and club district of the Montrose Area. The house dates from the early 1900s and was built by one of Houston's mayors. Rooms in the main house are spacious and well furnished with period furniture, wood floors, area rugs, and none of the cutesyness that so many B&Bs feel obliged to deliver. Larger and more modern rooms are in buildings in back of the main house; they have separate entrances that offer greater privacy and additional amenities such as a microwave, wet bar, and whirlpool tubs. Guests have access to a patio, the library, and the dining room, and the use of a washer and dryer.

501 Lovett Blvd., Houston, TX 77006. © **800/779-5224** or 713/522-5224. Fax 713/528-6708. www.lovett inn.com. 13 units, 11 with private bathroom. $75–$85 double with shared bathroom; $115–$175 double with private bathroom. Rates include continental breakfast. AE, DC, DISC, MC, V. Limited off-street parking. **Amenities:** Outdoor pool; in-room massage. *In room:* Fridge in some units, coffeemaker, hair dryer, iron.

KIRBY DISTRICT
EXPENSIVE

Renaissance Houston Hotel ★★   The only hotel in the Greenway Plaza (though there are a few nearby), this 20-story hotel enjoys access to Greenway's office buildings through its concourse level of shops, food court, a post office, and a movie theater. It is also connected to the Houston City Club by another walkway, and hotel guests can enjoy the use of its facilities including indoor tennis courts, racquetball, and jogging track. Also next door is the Compaq Center, Houston's sports arena for basketball and hockey. The hotel's location off the Southwest Freeway means quick access to either downtown or Uptown.

All standard rooms are spacious and decorated in an eclectic style, which makes them a bit more interesting than your standard hotel room. Rooms on the concierge floors offer extra services such as complimentary continental breakfast and evening cocktails.

6 Greenway Plaza East, Houston, TX 77046. (C) 800/HOTELS-1 or 713/629-1200. www.renaissancehotels. com. 388 units. $189–$199 double; $350–$1200 suite. Weekend rates available. AE, DC, DISC, MC, V. Valet parking $14; self-parking $8. **Amenities:** 2 restaurants; bar; outdoor heated pool; health club; sauna; concierge; complimentary shuttle; business center; salon; 24-hr. room service; same-day laundry service/dry cleaning; nonsmoking rooms; concierge level. *In room:* A/C, TV, dataport, coffeemaker, hair dryer, iron.

MODERATE

Ramada Plaza Hotel *Value*   This is a businessperson's hotel that's comfortable and well situated. It has easy access to the freeway, which leads either downtown or toward the Galleria, both just a few minutes away. Rates are very competitive. Rooms are spacious and nicer than the usual Ramadas because the property was not long ago a Doubletree Club Hotel. The rooms have plenty of light, and the furnishings are modern and functional without looking cheap; some rooms have sofa sleepers.

2828 Southwest Fwy., Houston, TX 77098. (C) 800/272-6232 or 713/942-2111. Fax 713/526-8709. www. ramada.com. 216 units. $99 double. Weekend rates available. AE, DC, DISC, MC, V. Free parking. **Amenities:** Deli; bar; outdoor pool (open in season); fitness room; car-rental desk; business center; limited room service; same-day dry cleaning. *In room:* A/C, TV w/pay movies, dataport, coffeemaker, hair dryer, iron.

UPTOWN
VERY EXPENSIVE

Doubletree Guest Suites   This 26-story hotel, located 1 block west of the Galleria shopping complex, offers large, plainly furnished suites, each with a fully equipped kitchen (with microwave and dishwasher) and a dining area for four people. The bedroom includes two full-size beds and a medium-sized TV; the sitting room includes a sofa or two and armchairs, and a large TV. Bathrooms are large with plenty of counter space. The hotel is well priced, gets a lot of repeat business, and is a favorite for extended stays. The service is good.

5353 Westheimer Rd., Houston, TX 77056. (C) 800/222-TREE or 713/961-9000. Fax 713/877-8835. www. doubletreehotels.com. 335 suites. $210 1-bedroom suite; $310 2-bedroom suite. AE, DC, DISC, MC, V. Valet parking $17; self-parking $8. **Amenities:** Restaurant; bar; outdoor heated pool; fitness room; Jacuzzi; concierge; courtesy shuttle; business center; 24-hr. room service (limited menu after 11pm); coin-op laundry; same-day laundry service/dry cleaning. *In room:* A/C, TV w/pay movies, dataport, coffeemaker, hair dryer, iron, safe.

Hotel Derek ★★★   The creators of this hotel have gone to great lengths to separate it from the pack. They've even given it a persona—its namesake, Derek, a fictitious aging rock star and owner of the hotel. Given the premise, it would have been easy to lapse into cliché and stereotype, but no such thing happens. Yes, there are some nods to the 1960s, but these are cleverly mixed with unexpected touches and the playful use of materials new and old to express a light vision of the counterculture. With the guest rooms, the designers have succeeded in creating a space that is functional for the business traveler while having the feel of a "pad" with all the accompanying informality. The decor is modern: The desk, side tables, and bathroom counter are thick glass with metal supports; the mattresses (mostly king-size) are on platform beds; and the sitting area is a wonderful mohair velvet built-in sofa stretching the width of the room. There are details that show thoughtfulness: Instead of drawers, there are baskets (which make a lot more sense in a hotel room); a full-spectrum light for applying makeup; and the safes are big enough to accommodate a briefcase.

2525 W. Loop South, Houston, TX 77027. (C) 866/292-4100 or 713/961-3000. Fax 713/297-4393. www.hotel derek.com. 314 units. $280 standard; $310 studio; $375 and up suite. Weekend and promotional rates sometimes available. AE, DC, DISC, MC, V. Valet parking $18. **Amenities:** Restaurant; bar; fitness center with spa treatments; concierge; courtesy car; business center; 24-hr. room service; in-room massage; same-day laundry service/dry cleaning. *In room:* A/C, TV w/pay movies, dataport, minibar, hair dryer, iron, safe.

InterContinental Houston ★★★ Walking into the busy lobby of this new hotel, I was astonished at how quickly people were being attended to. I was most impressed by the number of staff on duty, their efficiency, the concierge's abilities, and with the attention I received before anyone knew my business there. The rooms also impress. They are remarkably quiet owing to space-age insulated windows. Room design inserts high-tech amenities into warm, comforting surroundings that steer clear of trendiness. They are informal but make use of expensive materials, including marble, granite, leather, and textured fabrics. Highlights include an oversize safe with outlets for recharging cellphones or computers, comfortable pillow-top beds, and well thought-out desks with lots of workspace and multiple dataport options.

2222 W. Loop South, Houston, TX 77027. ✆ **800/327-0200** or 713/627-7600. Fax 713/961-3327. www. intercontinental.com. 485 units. $319–$329 standard; $359 deluxe; $399 and up suite. Promotional rates and packages available. AE, DC, DISC, MC, V. Valet parking $20. Pets allowed with $75 fee. **Amenities:** 2 restaurants; 2 bars; heated outdoor pool; 24-hr. state-of-the-art health club; spa treatments; outdoor Jacuzzi; children's program; concierge; courtesy car; business center with 24-hr. secretarial services; 24-hr. room service; 24-hr. express laundry service/dry cleaning; nonsmoking rooms; club level. *In room:* A/C, TV w/pay movies, dataport, minibar, coffeemaker, hair dryer, iron, safe, CD player.

JW Marriott Hotel by the Galleria On Westheimer facing the Galleria, this luxury high-rise hotel offers lots of amenities and a central location. Rooms are smaller than at the Westin hotels but are more attractive, come with more features, and the Marriott has more amenities. Bathrooms are well lit and come with make-up mirrors and terry-cloth robes. The decor is nothing spectacular, but at least it isn't ugly. Avoid reserving a room on the fifth floor, where the health club is located. The hotel's room service offers Pizza Hut pizzas from its kitchen.

5150 Westheimer Rd., Houston, TX 77056. ✆ **800/228-9290** or 713/961-1500. Fax 713/961-5045. www. marriott.com. 514 units. $249 double; $269–$800 suite. Promotional rates and packages available. AE, DC, DISC, MC, V. Valet parking $19; self-parking $11 in garage; limited free parking in open lot. **Amenities:** Restaurant; 2 bars; heated indoor/outdoor pool; health club; Jacuzzi; sauna; children's program; concierge; business center; salon; limited room service; massage; babysitting; same-day laundry service/dry cleaning; nonsmoking rooms; concierge level. *In room:* A/C, TV w/pay movies, dataport, coffeemaker, hair dryer, iron.

Omni Houston Hotel ★ *Kids* This hotel is an island of tranquillity in Uptown's sea of commotion. Flanking it on one side is a broad expanse of lawn with a decorative pool fed by cascading water and adorned with a small troop of black swans; on the other side is the heavily wooded Memorial Park. You'd think that you're miles from the busy Uptown malls, but you're not. In contrast to the modern exterior of this 11-story building—angular lines, bold colors, stark surfaces—the guest rooms are pictures of traditionalism, with 18th-century-style furniture, damask and brocade upholstery, and bedspreads with flounces in neoclassical patterns. The rooms are large and come with a view either of Memorial Park with downtown in the background or of the pools, the lawn, and the black swans.

4 Riverway, Houston, TX 77056. ✆ **800/THE-OMNI** or 713/871-8181. Fax 713/871-8116. www.omnihotels. com. 373 units. $229–$350 double; $259–$809 suite. Promotional rates available. AE, DC, DISC, MC, V. Valet parking $16; free outdoor self-parking. **Amenities:** Restaurant; 2 bars; 2 large outdoor pools (1 heated); 4 lit tennis courts; health club; Jacuzzi; sauna; children's programs; game room; concierge; courtesy limo; 24-hr. room service; massage; babysitting; same-day laundry service/dry cleaning. *In room:* A/C, TV/VCR w/pay movies, dataport, minibar, coffeemaker, hair dryer, iron, CD player.

Kids Family-Friendly Hotels

Grant Palm Court Inn (p. 154)   This little economy motel allows children to stay at no extra cost and has a wading pool and small playscape area. It's also situated close to AstroWorld and WaterWorld, of interest to older kids.

Omni Houston Hotel (p. 157)   With its Omni Kids Program, this hotel makes a special effort to keep smaller children amused. Kids receive a packet of goodies at check in, and parents can even request a small, pretend suitcase that holds more games and such. As part of the program, the concierge can organize activities and trips for children to such places as the Zoo.

Sheraton Suites Houston Near the Galleria   The rooms at this all-suite hotel are attractive and show more character than most hotel rooms in the Galleria area. The headboards and accents are postmodern, and the granite countertops are snazzy. These suites aren't as big as those at the Doubletree Guest Suites, but they are in many ways more comfortable and more attractive. An easy-to-use retractable door makes the living room and bedroom usable as one large space or as two separate rooms with the ample bathroom accessible from either. The best rooms face westward away from Loop 610. There are 18 "smart suites" that include more business features such as fax machines and copiers. The service here is attentive and personal. One caveat: If you like to read in bed, this hotel is not for you; the bedside lights are much too dim.

2400 W. Loop South, Houston, TX 77027. ℂ **800/325-3535** or 713/586-2444. Fax 713/586-2445. www. sheraton.com/suiteshouston. 281 suites. $229 suite. AE, DC, DISC, MC, V. Valet parking $15; self-parking $10. **Amenities:** Restaurant; bar; outdoor pool; fitness center; Jacuzzi; concierge; courtesy shuttle; business center; limited room service; babysitting; overnight laundry service/dry cleaning. *In room:* A/C, TV w/pay movies, dataport, fridge, coffeemaker, hair dryer, iron, safe.

Westin Galleria and Westin Oaks *(Overrated*   Similar in size, name, and appearance, these two hotels are often confused by travelers who arrive believing the destination has been reached only to find that they must yet again negotiate the mall parking lot. The Westin Oaks is on the east side of the Galleria mall (the side closest to Loop 610) and faces Westheimer Road. It is a family hotel, with no alcohol in the minibars. The Westin Galleria is attached to the west side of the Galleria and faces West Alabama Street. It targets business travelers, offering a business center and more formal dining than the Westin Oaks.

In other aspects the hotels are much alike. I find them a mix of good and bad. On the good side, they have the great location that allows you to walk from your hotel room into the mall without ever having to leave the great indoors. The rooms are extra large, the beds are comfortable, and the balconies—an uncommon feature in urban hotels—offer the best way to enjoy the view of perpetual motion below and the serene skyline above (get a north-facing room at the W. Oaks; a south-facing room at the W. Galleria). On the bad side, the recent remodeling of the W. Galleria (and which will soon be carried out at the W. Oaks) has not been money well spent. The floor, ceiling, and walls of the guest rooms are a dull grayish green, as is even the artwork. I find the overwhelming monochromatic effect unattractive and even a little depressing. The wood furniture, finished in a cherry wood stain, fails to enliven the scene. And the two small easy chairs, cheaply upholstered in gray fabric, just make matters worse. Another problem is the service: There weren't enough staff present on my visits, and the concierge, once located, didn't inspire confidence.

5060 W. Alabama St. and 5011 Westeimer Rd. Houston, TX 77056. (✆ **800/WESTIN-1** or 713/960-8100. Fax 713/960-6553 (Westin Galleria) or 713/960-6554 (Westin Oaks). www.westin.com. 487 units in Westin Galleria, 406 units in Westin Oaks. $299 double; $519 suite. AE, DC, DISC, MC, V. Valet parking $22; free self-parking. **Amenities:** 1 restaurant in each hotel; 1 bar in each hotel; heated outdoor swimming pool; health club access ($11/day fee); children's program; concierge; car-rental desk; business center; 24-hr. room service; babysitting; same-day laundry service/dry cleaning. *In room:* A/C, TV w/pay movies, dataport, minibar, coffeemaker, hair dryer, iron, safe.

MODERATE

Drury Inn & Suites Near the Galleria *Value* If you cross to the other side of Loop 610, room prices fall considerably even though the hotels are only a couple of blocks farther from the Galleria. One of the best lodging values in this area is this Drury Inn. Rooms are midsize and comfortable, with extra-long double beds, perfect for tall folk. Instead of the usual easy chair and ottoman, there is a recliner; the TV is larger than normal. King rooms are slightly larger and come with microwave and fridge. While the bathrooms are of okay size, they offer limited counter space. The hotel doesn't have a restaurant, but it offers free evening cocktails Monday through Thursday and a continental breakfast. Hotel guests have the use of a nearby health club.

Post Oak Park at W. Loop South, Houston, TX 77027. (✆ **800/DRURY-INN** or (✆ and fax 713/963-0700. www.drury-inn.com. 126 units. $90–$105 standard; $99–$114 king room. Rates include continental breakfast. Promotional and weekend rates sometimes available. AE, DC, DISC, MC, V. Free parking. Pets accepted with $25 deposit. **Amenities:** Indoor/outdoor heated pool; fitness room; Jacuzzi; coin-op laundry; same-day laundry service/dry cleaning. *In room:* A/C, TV, dataport, coffeemaker, hair dryer, iron.

La Quinta Inn & Suites Galleria You can tell at first glance that this immaculately clean inn, constructed in 1998, is a new breed of La Quinta, with a gurgling fountain in the lobby, a fitness room, and a fairly large outdoor heated pool with separate hot tub. Proximity to the shopping along Post Oak and in the Galleria seals the deal. Standard rooms come with two double beds; the "King Plus" room comes with king-size bed and a recliner. The rooms are unmistakably motel-like in their furnishings and a couple smelled of cleaning solution.

1625 W. Loop South, Houston, TX 77027. (✆ **800/687-6667** or 713/355-3440. Fax 713/355-2990. www.laquinta.com. 173 units. $112–$124 double; $147 suite. Weekend rates available. Rates include complimentary breakfast. AE, DC, DISC, MC, V. Free parking. **Amenities:** Outdoor heated pool; Jacuzzi; coin-op laundry; same-day dry cleaning. *In room:* A/C, TV w/pay movies, dataport, coffeemaker, hair dryer, iron.

THE HEIGHTS
MODERATE

Sara's Bed and Breakfast Inn For the traditional B&B experience—period decor, themed rooms, beautifully furnished common rooms—this is the place to stay. Sara's occupies a large Texas Victorian house in the Heights. It is immaculately kept and brightly decorated. Most rooms come with a queen-size or a king-size bed; some come with a full or a king and a full. Several of the rooms are inspired by other cities of Texas, including Fort Worth, San Antonio, and Galveston. The hosts serve a full breakfast, and a stay here is delightful.

941 Heights Blvd., Houston, TX 77008. (✆ **800/593-1130** or 713/868-1130. Fax 713/868-3284. www.saras.com. 13 units, 11 with private bathroom. $70–$125 double; $105–$150 suite. AE, DC, DISC, MC, V. Limited off-street parking. No children under age 12. *In room:* A/C, TV.

NEAR BUSH INTERCONTINENTAL AIRPORT
EXPENSIVE

Houston Airport Marriott ★　Don't let the address fool you—this hotel is not on "Hotel Row." It's located smack dab in the middle of the airport itself between terminals B and C, and it's on the airport tram line, which means no messing with taxis, shuttle buses, or rental cars. With this enviable location, the hotel gets a lot of business conferences. The revolving rooftop restaurant adds to the hotel's popularity—you'll see planes landing and taking off with a view that is pretty much the same as that of the airport's control tower. Guest rooms at the hotel are large and attractively furnished. The bathrooms are not particularly big, but the beds are comfortable, and everything else about the rooms is great. The revolving rooftop restaurant is a lovely place for dinner, which is served from 5:30 to 10pm (open for lunch to groups only).

18700 JFK Blvd., Houston, TX 77032. © 800/228-9290 or 281/443-2310. Fax 281/443-5294. www.marriott. com. 566 units. $180–$220 standard; $350 suite. AE, DC, DISC, MC, V. Free self-parking. **Amenities:** 2 restaurants; 2 bars; heated outdoor pool; large exercise room; Jacuzzi; limited room service (includes Pizza Hut pizzas); same-day laundry service; nonsmoking rooms. *In room:* A/C, TV w/pay movies, dataport, coffeemaker, hair dryer, iron.

MODERATE

Wingate Inn *Value*　As far as airport hotels go, this one has the most extras for the buck. Rooms are large, comfortable, and well equipped, including two phone lines (including a cordless phone) with free local calls, microwave, and in-room safe. Most come with two full beds. Services include free airport shuttle and continental breakfast (even though there's no restaurant).

15615 JFK Blvd., Houston, TX 77032. © 800/228-1000 or 281/987-8777. Fax 281/987-9317. www.wingate inns.com. 101 units. $89 double. Weekend rates available. Rates include continental breakfast. Children under 18 stay free in parent's room. AE, DC, DISC, MC, V. Free parking. **Amenities:** Small outdoor pool; exercise room; Jacuzzi; complimentary shuttle; same-day laundry service. *In room:* A/C, TV, dataport, fridge, coffeemaker, hair dryer, iron, safe.

4 Where to Dine

The Houston restaurant scene, like the city itself, is cosmopolitan. The primary influences come from Louisiana, Mexico, and Southeast Asia, but you can find restaurants serving just about any cuisine you can think of. There are several that serve Continental cuisine, including Tony's, an institution among Houston's wealthy and perhaps known more for the people who go there than for the food served. What constitutes Houston's native cooking is well represented by barbecue, soul food, Tex-Mex joints, and steakhouses. But try to make it to a Vietnamese restaurant at least once: Houston's Vietnamese population is large and has made an indelible imprint on the city's dining scene.

DOWNTOWN/MIDTOWN
VERY EXPENSIVE

Brennan's ★★★　SOUTHERN/CREOLE　Fine dining a la New Orleans: Brennan's opened in 1967 as a sister restaurant to the famous New Orleans original, and it's a perennial favorite on most local "Top Restaurant" lists. It's now independent and offers some great dishes that the original doesn't. The various dining rooms are strikingly elegant. (I don't think you'll find a lovelier table in all of Houston.) The service is superb, and the menu will be new territory to all but those coming from Louisiana. The selection of dishes varies daily but usually has a few classic Creole specialties such as roux-less seafood gumbo or its well-known turtle soup. Brennan's is also known for its chef's table, which is located in the restaurant's kitchen. The table must be reserved far in advance and can accommodate between 4 and 10 people at $75 per person. For that price, guests are treated to several of the chef's special creations right as they come off the stove.

3300 Smith (at Stuart). © **713/522-9711.** Reservations recommended. Main courses $27–$32. AE, DC, DISC, MC, V. Mon–Fri 11:30am–2pm and 5:45–10pm; Sat 11am–2pm and 5:45–10pm; Sun 10am–2pm and 5:45–10pm. Take Smith St. (one-way headed south from downtown); when it crosses Elgin/Westheimer, look for the restaurant on your right. Be careful not to pass it or you will get fed onto the Southwest Fwy.

EXPENSIVE

Liberty Noodle ★ PAN-ASIAN   At night this is clearly the feeding ground for Houston's young smart set. The restaurant is located on the ground floor of the old Rice Hotel, now one of the hottest addresses in the city, and many diners show up from the nearby theater district. You can dine outdoors under the old hotel's original cast-iron canopy, or in the slightly cramped dining room, decorated with Asian and modern sparseness. Asian noodle dishes are finding a warm reception by those who want quick food that's not fried or too fatty but still has flavor. The most popular dishes here are the spicy noodles with beef or chicken or tofu, the spicy coconut soup (delicious), and duck noodles. The restaurant uses mostly rice noodles for its dishes, but at times will use a few varieties of Japanese noodles. Vegetarian substitutions can be made for any dish. At lunch the prices are substantially lower and the crowd is more office workers.

909-E Texas Ave. © **713/222-2695.** Reservations accepted for parties of 5 or more. Main courses $8–$24; lunch $8–$13. AE, DC, DISC, MC, V. Mon–Fri 11am–2:30pm and 5–10pm (until 11pm Wed–Thurs, midnight Fri); Sat 11am–midnight.

MODERATE

Mai's ★★ VIETNAMESE   Occupying a two-story brick building with green awnings on Milam just south of downtown, Mai's is the last of a half-dozen Vietnamese restaurants you'll pass in the preceding 6 blocks. In several ways it is the best choice, but it should not be thought of as having a lock on good Vietnamese food. I do, however, appreciate its dependability and the long hours it keeps because you never know when you might get a yen for a bowl of Vietnamese noodles (and they are all good). This would be a good place to try *pho,* the national dish, a soup to which you add vegetables and aromatic herbs and lime juice. Sample the ever-popular spring and summer rolls served with *nam pla* and/or peanut sauce, and try a chicken stir-fry with chile and lemon grass. The last time I was there I enjoyed the *Nam Noung* (ground pork and shrimp with thin vermicelli) and the Mekong sweet and sour soup (try the catfish version).

3403 Milam. © **713/520-7684.** Reservations recommended on weekends. Main courses $6–$16. AE, DC, DISC, MC, V. Mon–Thurs 10am–3am; Fri–Sat 10am–4am.

INEXPENSIVE

Pig Stand #7 (Kids (Moments TEXAN/AMERICAN   What indeed can be said of a place that defines itself as the "Home of the Pig Sandwich"? A place where totemic pig art in all its many genres (more than you can imagine) festoons the walls and windows from floor to ceiling? And then consider that the entire collection of "pigaphenalia" was acquired over the years exclusively through donations by the restaurant's many loyal if misguided patrons. But is it art? You decide.

A few things must be cleared up. Firstly, the "#7" is misleading; there are a couple of Pig Stands surviving still in Beaumont and a couple in San Antonio,

Fast Food a la Houston

When it's necessary to find a meal that can be had quickly, conveniently, and cheaply, you don't have to suffer at the hands of the national fast food chains, where the fare tastes the same whether you're in Houston or Honolulu. There are a number of local chains that do a good job of cooking up fast food with character and local flavor. Here are four worth considering:

James Coney Island Hot Dogs started up in Houston in the 1930s at its present downtown location. It's famous for its bowls of dark, meaty chili and its original chili dogs. (Most Houstonians consider hot dogs without chili as either unfulfilled potential or foreign novelty.) You can order the chili with or without beans or as a chili pie. For hot dogs I recommend the original Coney or the Texas chili dog *without* cheese. There are 23 locations around Houston, including downtown (815 Dallas St.), in the Kirby District (3607 Shepherd at the corner of Richmond), in the Galleria area (1600 S. Post Oak), and out along the Gulf Freeway (6955 Gulf Fwy. and 10600 Gulf Fwy.).

In 1962 the Antone family, originally from Lebanon, opened an exotic import grocery store on Taft Street near Allen Parkway called **Antone's.** There they introduced Houston to their now famous po'boy (sub) sandwiches, which caught on in a big way. For lunch, you can't go wrong with one of these, which come already prepared. Get the original green label or the super red label, both of which are a combination of ham, salami, cheese, pickles, and special chow-chow on fresh baked bread. Antone's locations include 807 Taft (close to downtown), 2424 Dunstan (in the Village), 8110 Kirby (across from the Astrodome complex), 1440 S. Voss (at San Felipe, about a mile from the Galleria), and 3823 Bellaire (at Stella Link, just west of the Medical Center).

Beck's Prime is a local chain of upscale burger joints that are known for big juicy burgers and great shakes. Locations include 2902 Kirby Dr. (at Westheimer), inside the Galleria, and at 910 Travis (in the downtown tunnel system below Bank One Center).

Café Express operates under the guiding principle that fast food can be nutritious, fresh, and cooked with at least some artistry. The owner of the chain is the chef at Cafe Annie's, a very expensive and popular restaurant in the Uptown area that often tops the list of Houston's fine dining spots. Specialties at Café Express include a variety of salads, lively pasta dishes, juicy roast chicken, and a large bar of condiments that includes olives, olive oil, peppers, mustards, and vinegars. They also have a small children's menu. One location is in the basement of the Fine Arts Museum (the new building); other locations include 3200 Kirby Dr. (near the Village), 1422 W. Gray (in the River Oaks Shopping Center), and 1101 Uptown Park (just off Post Oak in the Galleria area).

but those are far different in character from #7. Secondly, the "pig sandwich" is not what brings people here. Mostly they come for classic Texas roadhouse fare such as chicken-fried steak, any of the breakfasts, the burgers and the shakes, and of course, to be transported by the "porcine revival" decor set off by flourishes of Formica, vinyl, and imitation wood paneling.

2412 Washington Ave., a bit northwest of downtown. ℰ 713/864-4041. Reservations not accepted. Main courses $5–$10. AE, DISC, MC, V. Mon–Thurs 6am–7:30pm; Fri–Sat 6am–10pm; Sun 7am–8pm.

This Is It SOUL FOOD   If you yearn for soul food plain and simple, make your way over to this little place just southwest of downtown. Chitlins, clove-scented yams, meat loaf, braised oxtails, and lots of greens are served cafeteria-style to all comers. Owner Craig Joseph's wall of fame, photos of celebrities who have visited the restaurant, and the work of African-American artists adorn the walls of this popular establishment. Recently this neighborhood was blanketed with town houses. It's part of the Fourth Ward, which includes Freedmen's town, where the newly liberated slaves built their houses shortly after the Civil War. According to local historians, it was one of the most prosperous black communities in the South.

207 W. Gray. ℰ 713/659-1608. Reservations not accepted. Main courses $7. AE, DISC, MC, V. Mon–Sat 11am–8pm; Sun 11am–6pm. Breakfast daily 6:30–10am. West Gray is a continuation of Gray, which crosses Main St. 1 block south of the freeway overpass. The restaurant is near the intersection with Bagby.

Treebeards ⭐ *Value* CREOLE   This place gets my vote for best food for your money. Others see it the same way, and this is why Treebeards restaurant on Old Market Square gets such a crowd of office workers for lunch. Beat the crowd by going late or early and you won't have to wait in line. You can enjoy red beans and rice, chicken and shrimp gumbo, jambalaya, good corn bread, and all the rest. Food is served cafeteria-style. Look for three more downtown locations: 1117 Texas Ave. (next to Christ Church Cathedral), 1100 Louisiana (in the tunnel), and at 700 Rusk, at the corner of Louisiana Street.

315 Travis St. (between Preston and Congress). ℰ 713/228-2622. Reservations not accepted. Main courses $5.50–$8. AE, DC, MC, V. Mon–Fri 11am–2pm; Fri 5–9pm.

EAST END
MODERATE

Kim Son VIETNAMESE/CHINESE   The menu is the most imposing part of this casual, highly regarded Vietnamese restaurant. Don't worry, though, because there are no poor choices among the 100 or so options. Enjoy finely prepared delicacies as well as the expected fare, like terrific spring rolls and lovely noodle dishes. (The pan-seared shrimp with jalapeños and onions proves a delightful combination.) The menu includes several vegetarian dishes. Look for the exotic fish pool at the entrance. The restaurant has another location at 300 Milam near the theater district (ℰ 713/222-2790).

2001 Jefferson. ℰ 713/222-2461. Reservations accepted for parties of 8 or more. Main courses $6–$15. AE, DC, DISC, MC, V. Daily 11am–midnight. Located in the small Chinese commercial center 1 block east of the Brown Convention Center and the elevated Tex. 59 Fwy.

INEXPENSIVE

Fiesta Loma Linda ⭐⭐ TEX-MEX   I like my Tex-Mex restaurants to be homey, unpretentious places where you're not likely to run into the see-and-be-seen crowd. Of course, that was true of all Tex-Mex restaurants before the rise of the fajita, which became so popular that it eventually pulled Tex-Mex into the orbit of the truly trendy. Fiesta Loma Linda brings to mind those simpler times with its unselfconscious decoration and furniture and its utter lack of anything approaching trendiness. It also has an old-time 1930s tortilla maker specially designed to make the old-fashioned puffy tortillas that you always used to get when ordering chile con queso. The things to order here are of course the "puffy chile con queso" for an appetizer and the "puffy beef tacos," the beef or cheese enchiladas with chile gravy, and the combination dinners.

2111 Telephone Rd. ℂ **713/924-6074.** Reservations not accepted. Main courses $5–$10; lunch specials $5.50–$6.50. AE, DC, DISC, MC, V. Daily 10am–10pm (until 11pm on weekends). Located 6 blocks off the Gulf Fwy. (I-45). Exit Telephone Rd. and turn north; it will be on your right.

SOUTH MAIN
MODERATE

Fred's Italian Corner Restaurant SOUTHERN ITALIAN This is a rarity in Houston—a true neighborhood Italian restaurant. The seating is tightly packed into the dining room, but that's the nature of these neighborhood institutions. You can get a good thin-crust pizza (an uncommon variety is the Sicilian pizza with shrimp, parsley, and eggs), pasta in many sauces, and a great selection of entrees, such as eggplant rollatini, and the spinach tortellini clam Alfredo. The lunch specials are a good bargain; you order at the counter. The wine is not overpriced.

2278 W. Holcombe. ℂ **713/665-7506.** Reservations not accepted. Main courses $7–$12. AE, DC, DISC, MC, V. Mon–Thurs 11am–3pm and 5–9:30pm; Fri 11am–3pm and 5–10:30pm; Sat 5–10:30pm. From S. Main drive west on Holcombe. Fred's is in a shopping center on your right, facing Greenbriar St.

INEXPENSIVE

Butera's DELI A favorite haunt for museum-goers located in the Chelsea Market shopping center, this deli offers healthful fare in an airy and cheerful setting. Popular favorites include the Reuben sandwich, the Cobb salad, and the fettuccine Alfredo. Among the soups, the seafood gumbo is awfully good.

4621 Montrose Blvd. (between Bissonnet and the freeway overpass). ℂ **713/523-0722.** Salads $2.25–$8; soups $2–$6; sandwiches $6. AE, DC, DISC, MC, V. Daily 11am–9pm.

MONTROSE
VERY EXPENSIVE

Mark's ★★★ NEW AMERICAN Many in Houston hold this to be the city's best restaurant, and they won't get any quarrel from this reviewer. Mark Cox, the former chef at Tony's, has a good idea of the direction in which American cooking should be headed—fresh ingredients prepared in a manner that's new and creative while being hearty and satisfying. There is a set menu that changes seasonally and a menu of daily specials, but a representative sampling of dishes would include grilled shrimp on a bed of fennel, basil, and tomato with a crab risotto, bourbon-glazed pork with yams and an apple compote, roasted breast of chicken with Mississippi-style grits scented with white truffles, or lamb in a basil sauce with white cheddar potatoes. The restaurant occupies an abandoned church on Westheimer. The main dining room is in the nave and the choir loft. Alongside the nave, the owners have built an eye-catching smaller dining room with Gothic rib vaulting.

1658 Westheimer. ℂ **713/523-3800.** Reservations recommended. Main courses $15–$26. AE, DC, DISC, MC, V. Mon–Fri 11am–2pm; Mon–Thurs 6–11pm; Fri–Sat 5:30pm–midnight; Sun 5–10pm.

EXPENSIVE

Backstreet Café ★★★ CONTEMPORARY AMERICAN Wonderful cooking, a good selection of wines, and excellent service make this place perennially popular especially in good weather when diners flock to the tree-shaded patio. The starters are delicious creations, especially the portobello mushrooms stuffed with shrimp and crawfish and the smoked corn crab cakes (don't miss these).

Among the main courses I like the grilled pork chops with a Creole mustard wine reduction, served with sweet potatoes au gratin and a poached pear. The meatloaf tower with mushroom gravy and garlic mashed potatoes warms my heart like nothing else and is a work of architectural splendor. Something new on the menu is the braised duck with a zinfandel flavored au jus on top of a wild rice/shitake cake. Side dishes can be anything from corn pudding to fried green tomatoes. Dining areas include two upstairs rooms, one downstairs, and the patio. For dessert try the bread pudding, with macadamia nut brittle and vanilla ice cream (if you dare). Don't even try to park your car; let the valet do it.

1103 S. Shepherd. © 713/521-2239. Reservations recommended. Main courses $13–$19. AE, DC, DISC, MC, V. Sun–Thurs 11am–10pm; Fri–Sat 11am–11pm. Despite the address, the restaurant is located 1 block east of Shepherd and 2 blocks north of W. Gray and the River Oaks Shopping Center, off McDuffie St.

Hugo's ★★★ MEXICAN   Serving the best interior Mexican food in Houston, this new restaurant is quickly attracting a following with the locals. For an appetizer try the tostadas or the *sopecitos* (small, thick handmade tortillas with toppings). Main courses include duck in a *mole poblano* (the classic dark red, bittersweet sauce of the Mexican highlands) and a chile relleno with roasted chicken smothered in a *pipián* (a spicy sauce in a base of ground roasted pumpkin seeds). Keep an eye out for daily specials; the chef/owner, Hugo Ortega, enjoys seasonal cooking. In cold weather, he'll often make a delicious seafood soup Zihuatanejo-style, flavored with a little *chile guajillo,* a black sauce made from *chile morita,* and a rich, fresh-tasting fish stock. For dessert, the specialty is the homemade Mexican hot chocolate, accompanied by small *churros* (the Spanish equivalent of donuts). These were delicious, but so were the margaritas, which for me also make an excellent dessert. The dining room is large and airy, owing to a very high ceiling—the building dates from 1935 and was once a drugstore. Sometimes the noise reverberates a bit.

1602 Westheimer Rd. (at Mandell St.). © 713/524-7744. Reservations recommended. Main courses $13–$25. AE, DC, DISC, MC, V. Sun–Thurs 11am–10pm; Fri–Sat 11am–midnight.

MODERATE

Baba Yega *Finds* SANDWICHES/PASTA/VEGETARIAN   Set in a small bungalow on a side street off Westheimer, Baba Yega is one of the hippest places in the Montrose. The restaurant offers several small dining areas, all of which are agreeable, particularly the garden veranda in back. Next door is an herb shop that belongs to the owner, and, whenever possible, he cooks with his own herbs. The most popular lunch items are the sandwiches, of which there are several vegetarian choices. For dinner the daily specials are what most people order, and these usually include at least one chicken and one fish dish. Tuesday is the "Italian Special," a plate of pasta and glass of wine. A particularly good entree is the chicken *pomodoro.*

2607 Grant St. © 713/522-0042. Reservations not accepted. Main courses $10–$14; sandwiches $6–$9. AE, DC, DISC, MC, V. Sun–Thurs 11am–10pm; Fri–Sat 11am–11pm.

La Mexicana Restaurant ★★ MEXICAN   Once a little Mexican grocery store, La Mexicana started serving tacos and gradually turned exclusively to the restaurant business. It's well known for delicious Mexican breakfasts such as *huevos a la mexicana* (eggs scrambled with onions, tomatoes, and Serrano chiles) or *migas* (eggs cooked with fried tortilla strips)—both particularly good as are their frijoles and the green *salsa de mesa*—and classic enchilada plates (red or green are good choices). Some dishes are *"muy auténtico,"* such as the *nopalitos* *en salsa chipotle* (cactus leaves cooked in chipotle chile sauce) or the tacos *de guisado de puerco* (pork stewed in dried chile sauce) or *de chicharrón en salsa verde* (pork cracklings in tomatillo sauce; one of my favorites but not for everyone). Other dishes are Tex-Mex standbys, such as the fajitas and the combination plates. Service is good, and there's a choice of dining outside or inside.

1018 Fairview. © **713/521-0963.** Reservations not accepted. Main courses $7–$13. AE, DC, DISC, MC, V. Daily 7am–11pm.

KIRBY DISTRICT
EXPENSIVE

Churrascos ★★ SOUTH AMERICAN/STEAKS When this restaurant opened about 10 years ago, it caught on like a house on fire. The owners have since opened another restaurant, Américas (p. 167). This has thinned the crowds somewhat, and fans of this place couldn't be happier. Churrascos is simpler and more elegant than Américas, and a good bit less noisy. It is modeled after a simple Argentinean estancia in colors of white, red, and black. The signature dish is the beef tenderloin butterflied and served with *chimichurri* sauce, the Argentine condiment that always accompanies steak. Also very different for the Houston dining scene are the fried plantain chips served at every table, the Argentinean empanadas, the Cuban-style black bean soup, and the Peruvian-style ceviche. Grilled vegetables come "family style" with every entree. All in all, the menu is less "out there" and less trendy than Américas, but it can't be considered humdrum. For dessert, the restaurant is famous for its *tres leches* cake, and justifiably so.

2055 Westheimer. © **713/527-8300.** Reservations recommended. Main courses $14–$24; lunch $7.50–$9.50. AE, DC, DISC, MC, V. Mon–Thurs 11am–10pm; Fri 11am–11pm; Sat 5–11pm.

MODERATE

Goode Company Texas Barbecue ★★★ BARBECUE Jim Goode, a name in the local restaurant business, cooks up some great barbecue at this rickety joint on Kirby, 4 blocks south of the Southwest Freeway. Beer signs and country music on the jukebox set the scene. To get great smoked flavor, Mr. Goode cooks with the greenest wood he can find. Especially tasty are the pork ribs and the brisket, but you can also get duck, chicken, and links. Order by the pound, the plate, or the sandwich. For dessert, the pecan pie is a must. An additional location is in west Houston at 8911 Katy Fwy. (© 713/464-1901).

5109 Kirby Dr. © **713/522-2530.** Barbecue plates $7–$10. AE, DC, DISC, MC, V. Daily 11am–10pm.

Jalapeños MEXICAN/TEX-MEX In Houston, Mexican food restaurants run the gamut from basic fajitas to classic *alta cocina* to new wave *nueva cocina;* this restaurant does a good job of crossing genres to create a menu with plenty of variety. You can get fajitas for sure (prepared with a lovely marinade and grilled over an honest wood fire), but you can also get spinach enchiladas, or fish cooked in the most popular Mexican versions—*al mojo de ajo* (in butter and garlic) and *a la veracruzana* (in a tomato-based sauce with capers, olives, chiles, and onions). The menu has several vegetarian options; the appetizers are good here and so is the black bean soup. Also, they have a long list of brand-name margaritas to try, though the house margarita isn't too shabby (order them on the rocks). The dining area isn't terribly large, but the big windows make it seem roomier and the bright colors make it a cheerful place. At times it can be a little noisy.

2702 Kirby Dr. © **713/524-1668.** Main courses $9–$17. AE, DC, DISC, MC, V. Mon–Sat 11am–10pm (to 11pm Fri–Sat); Sun 10:30am–10pm (Sun brunch until 2:30pm).

Family-Friendly Restaurants

James Coney Island (see "Fast Food a la Houston," p. 162)   What hot dog place isn't popular with kids? But most of these restaurants are decorated in bright colors that make them especially attractive to the young, and they offer kid specials.

Pig Stand #7 (p. 161)   Children enjoy all the various and sundry representations of pigs here, as well as the menu of burgers and shakes. The jukebox, with its repertoire of country-and-western classics, also grabs their attention.

Thai Spice ★★★ *(Value)* THAI   Houston is particularly rich in Thai restaurants and in the Rice Village there are three highly recommended ones, each with its own loyal following. Of these, Thai Spice gets the nod, mostly because the service is friendlier and the dining area is roomier, more attractive, and better furnished, but also because the food is a particularly appealing interpretation of Thai that doesn't burn out your taste buds. The lunch buffet is worthy of special note for being more complete than in most places. The dinner menu is well laid out and doesn't try to confuse you with options by listing the same basic dish four times. The spicy shrimp soup is good, and the "summer palace" is a great spicy option for a stir-fry. There are also several mild dishes, including a wonderfully simple grilled lemon grass chicken breast. All of the curries are worth ordering, and the pad Thai is excellent.

5117 Kelvin (at Dunstan). ✆ 713/522-5100. Main courses $8.50–$11; lunch buffet $7.95. AE, DC, DISC, MC, V. Mon–Sat 11am–2:30pm (lunch buffet) and 5–10pm; Sun 11:30am–3pm and 5–9pm.

INEXPENSIVE

Luling City Market BARBECUE   This is great barbecue served in a traditional setting, which for Texas barbecue joints means that any effort spent decorating appears, at least, as purely an afterthought and, at most, as the owner's misguided attempt to find a place for all the objets d'art that have been cluttering up his attic. This place follows the minimalist approach. Service is lunch counter style. I heartily recommend the ribs and the sausage. At night the quiet little bar fills up with regulars with whom you can have some good-natured conversation, mostly about sports.

4726 Richmond Ave. ✆ 713/871-1903. Reservations not accepted. Barbecue plates $7.50–$9. AE, DC, DISC, MC, V. Mon–Sat 11am–9pm; Sun noon–7pm.

UPTOWN
VERY EXPENSIVE

Américas ✦ PAN-AMERICAN   Stuck in a gastronomical rut? This restaurant is an admirable choice for busting loose. From the way-out decor that combines realistic representations of Incan stonework, blown-up images of Indian basketry, and a polychromatic rainforest canopy, to the highly inventive menu of dishes loosely inspired by the national cuisines of the New World, there is nothing ho-hum about dining here. Corn-crusted gulf red snapper with a Mexican cream sauce, the yucca polenta, and a refined version of *anticuchos* (chunks of beefheart cooked over a fire en brochette, a favorite street food in Peru) are indicative of what you can order. Wildly popular with Houston natives, the restaurant is packed most nights; make sure to get reservations for dining, or perhaps stop by for drinks and a glance at the brave new surroundings. My biggest complaint about the restaurant is the noise level.

1800 Post Oak Blvd. ⓒ **713/961-1492.** Reservations recommended. Main courses $15–$30. AE, DC, DISC, MC, V. Mon–Thurs 11am–10pm; Fri 11am–11pm; Sat 5–11pm.

Cafe Annie ★★★ SOUTHWESTERN   Singing the praises of this restaurant makes me feel like nothing more than a member of the choir. Over the last 20 years, no restaurant in Houston has received more coverage, more acclaim, and more awards from the national press than Cafe Annie. The same can be said of chef/owner Robert Del Grande. If you're looking for *the* restaurant in Houston, and especially if you're on a fat expense account, this should be your choice. Those of us who aren't so fortunate can save money by going for lunch or for the *botanitas* (tapas), served at the bar. One of the restaurant's signature dishes is the crabmeat tostadas, available on the dinner, lunch, and *botanitas* menus. These are wonderful compositions of fresh lump crabmeat, avocado, a little finely shredded cabbage, and a touch of piquancy. Also, notable is the risotto of Maine lobster and Gulf shrimp in a broth lightly flavored with *chile cascabel* and cream. The tortilla soup is another option and is one of the perennial favorites on the menu. Everything I sampled was delicious and different. The dining room is perfectly in character with the restaurant—nice and quiet, softly lit, with lots of dark woodwork.

1728 Post Oak Blvd. (just south of San Felipe). ⓒ **713/840-1111.** Reservations recommended. Main courses $26–$38. AE, DC, DISC, MC, V. Mon–Fri 11:30am–2pm and 6:30–10pm; Sat 6:30–10:30pm.

MODERATE

Sammy's Lebanese Restaurant LEBANESE   While there are more elaborate and upscale Middle Eastern options in town, this very casual and friendly restaurant remains a longtime favorite for its mouth-watering, inexpensive food and a surprising wine list. It's popular for its appetizer platters, and offers a large selection of seafood and vegetarian dishes. Baked kibbe, sure, but check out the chicken wings and garlic-laced mashed-potato dip. Sammy's is on a stretch of Richmond Avenue just a few blocks west of the Uptown area, known as the "Richmond Strip" for its many clubs and restaurants.

5825 Richmond. ⓒ **713/780-0065.** Reservations accepted for parties of 6 or more. Main courses $9–$14. AE, DC, DISC, MC, V. Mon–Thurs 11am–10:30pm; Fri–Sat 11am–11pm; Sun noon–10pm.

FAR WEST HOUSTON
VERY EXPENSIVE

Lynn's Steakhouse ★★★ STEAKS   This restaurant in far west Houston is a favorite steakhouse for those who can afford it and who like a bottle of wine to accompany their steak. It is especially known for its melt-in-your-mouth filets and chateaubriand, and for its extensive wine list that wins high praise from grape enthusiasts. Salads come with every steak, and vegetables are a la carte. The bread is homemade. The dining rooms are comfortable and quiet with ample space between tables, and reservations truly mean something here. The dress code precludes shorts or T-shirts.

955 Dairy Ashford. ⓒ **281/870-0807.** Reservations recommended. Steaks $28–$37. AE, DC, MC, V. Mon–Fri 10am–2pm and 5–10pm; Sat 5–10pm. From downtown take the Katy Fwy (I-10 west). Look for Dairy Ashford, which is the second exit after the Sam Houston Pkwy.

5 Seeing the Sights

Since Houston isn't generally considered a major tourist destination, there isn't much in the way of tourism infrastructure except for the downtown visitor center. Most of the available resources are geared toward conventions and large groups, not independent travelers. This means that you'll have to work harder to find information about the city's attractions. A case in point is downtown Houston, which has fascinating and important architecture by internationally prominent architects, and a lot of important public sculpture, yet there is no regularly scheduled tour of downtown. If you're interested in finding a tour of downtown, see "Organized Tours," later in this section; the following listings, organized geographically, will guide you to Houston's many points of interest.

THE TOP ATTRACTIONS
DOWNTOWN

Downtown tunnel system   There are 6 miles of tunnels below Houston's downtown; most of the system is private property. Along those corridors are restaurants, shops, and businesses of all varieties. You can get a map of the tunnels from the city's visitor center or you can take a guided tour if you schedule it in advance. See "Organized Tours," later in this section.

Accessible from the visitor center in City Hall and all neighboring buildings, as well as most downtown hotels. Free admission. Mon–Fri 7am–6pm.

Heritage Society at Sam Houston Park   Just a couple of blocks from Houston's visitor center is this park that serves as a repository for eight of Houston's oldest houses and buildings, which were moved here from their original locations. The oldest building dates from before Texas's Independence; it is a small and simple cabin originally built close to where NASA is today. Another house was built by a freed slave in 1870, and there's a church dating from 1892. The Heritage Society has worked hard to restore them to their original state and furnish them with pieces from the appropriate eras. The only way to see these buildings is by guided tour, which leaves every hour on the hour from the tour office at 1100 Bagby; it takes about 45 minutes. The guides are well informed and add a lot to a visit here. The Heritage Museum can be visited without taking the tour. It features permanent exhibits on Texas history.

1100 Bagby. © 713/655-1912. Tours $6 adults, $4 seniors and children ages 13–17, $2 children 6–12. Mon–Sat 10am–3pm; Sun 1–3pm.

EAST END & BEYOND

Battleship Texas and San Jacinto Monument & Museum ★ (Kids)   On the San Jacinto Battleground in 1836, Texas won its independence from Mexico with a crushing surprise attack by the Texan forces, whose battle cry was "Remember the Alamo!" To commemorate that victory, civic leaders in 1936 built a towering obelisk as tall as the Washington Monument but topped with a Texas Lone Star. In the base of the monument is a small museum of Texas history with some interesting exhibits, such as one about the relatively unsung Texas hero, "Deaf" Smith, and a collection of watercolors of the Mexican War painted by Sam Chamberlain. There is also a small auditorium where you can watch a 35-minute documentary of the battle. If you would like to view some of the Port of Houston as well as the rest of the land for miles around, you can take the elevator up to the observation room in the top floor of the tower, which is more than 500 feet above the ground.

Across from the monument, in roughly the same place from where the Texans began their advance, is the USS *Texas*. Built in 1914, before improvements in warplane technology made these large dreadnought battleships vulnerable, she is the last of her kind. Between the wars the navy modernized the ship with antiaircraft and torpedo defenses, but it is still surprising that it survived World War II, having fought in both the Atlantic and the Pacific theaters. When you visit you can clamber up to its small-caliber guns or onto the navigation bridge, inspect the crew's quarters and check out the engine room. Life on board was no picnic—the quarters were cramped and facilities were minimal—so it is interesting to learn that this ship was considered a lucky assignment. Plan on at least an hour to see the *Texas*, and as much again for the monument.

3527 Battleground Rd. ℭ **281/479-2431.** Battleship admission $5 adults, $4 seniors, $3 children ages 6–18; free admission to the monument and museum; observation room $3 adults, $2 children; movie $3.50 adults, $2.50 children. Daily 10am–5pm. Take the La Porte Fwy. (Tex. 225) east from Loop 610 east. For 15 miles you will pass large refineries and tank farms. (If tears well up in your eyes and your throat muscles begin to constrict involuntarily, you'll know you're headed in the right direction.) Exit Battleground Rd. (Tex.134) and turn left.

Houston Ship Channel ⊛   For those fortunate enough not to live among the industrial areas along the Texas Gulf Coast, the landscape of refineries and their intricate tangle of pipes, their forests of cooling towers and stacks, and their fields of tanks are as exotic as the Zanzibar coast. If you find this sort of thing intriguing you can take a free boat ride on the Sam Houston Inspection Ship, which tours the upper 7 miles of the deep water channel. The boat dates from the 1950s and has a lovely cabin trimmed in mahogany as well as fore and aft observation decks. I hail from Houston but rarely have the opportunity to see the ship channel up close, and I enjoyed this trip. You should probably make reservations well in advance during the summer months when it is quite popular, but I'm told that the ship channel is best seen in cooler weather, when there is no risk of bad smells. The trip takes a total of 90 minutes, during which you will most likely see large container ships, tall grain elevators, tugs, and barges. If after the trip, you want to see more of the channel, you can drive to the San Jacinto Battlefield, where the Battleship *Texas* is on display (see review above).

7300 Clinton Dr. at Gate 8. ℭ **713/670-2416.** Free admission. Tues–Sun 10am and 2:30pm; no morning trips Sun or Thurs. Call for reservations. Closed Sept and holidays. Take the Gulf Fwy. south; get on Loop 610 east, which takes you over the ship channel; exit Clinton Dr. Turn right on Clinton (look for small green signs pointing the way); after a mile, you'll come to a traffic light and a sign reading PORT GATE 8. Turn left.

Kemah Boardwalk   Many visitors to Space Center Houston (see review below) will afterward go out for seafood at nearby Kemah, which is as touristy as the Houston area gets. It used to be a rustic shrimping port on Galveston Bay where you could buy some shrimp and a beer and sit by the dock on an afternoon to watch the shrimp boats come in. Most of the pier was washed away in 1984 by a hurricane, and in the 1990s it was bought by a developer who built the boardwalk, several restaurants, a hotel, and some touristy stores and attractions. The restaurants overlook the water; if you stroll down the boardwalk you'll pass every one. Pick the one that appeals most to you. Among the attractions is a 50,000-gallon, floor-to-ceiling aquarium housing more than 100 species of tropical fish in the Aquarium Restaurant.

Tex. 146, Kemah. ℭ **877/285-3624.**

The Orange Show ⊛⊛ (*Kids*) (*Finds*)   This may not be the "greatest show on earth" but it must be the quirkiest. In truth it's not a show at all, at least not as we commonly understand the word. Rather, it's the life work of one man, former postman Jeff McKissack, who spent his last 25 years assembling a collection of found objects and building materials into an architectural collage that students of folk art call a "folk art environment." It stands in a quiet working-class neighborhood just off the Gulf Freeway, where it dares to be different. With the many flagpoles, spindles, wagon wheels, and wrought-iron birds rising up from behind its walls, it seems like an outpost for spontaneity in a wilderness of cookie-cutter ranch-style houses.

Inside, the viewer is presented with all kinds of curiosities: two small arenas, observation decks, a small museum, and lots of cheerful wrought-iron decoration and tile work. Inscriptions adorn the walls; many of these honor that best of all fruits, "The orange: a great gift to mankind." Seeing the whole thing takes less than an hour. Upon the death of Mr. McKissack, The Orange Show fell into decay until it was rescued by the Orange Show Foundation, located in the house across the street and a center for Houston's folk art world. It is the organizer of the Art Car Parade and the Art Car Ball (see "Texas Calendar of Events" in chapter 2). It is also the organizer of Eyeopener Tours (see "Organized Tours," later in this section). If you like folk art, consider purchasing their driving tour audiocassette of Houston's other folk art treasures. (The tape comes with a map.)

2401 Munger St. ℂ 713/926-6368. www.orangeshow.org. Admission $1 adults, free for children under 12. Memorial Day to Labor Day Wed–Fri 9am–1pm, Sat–Sun noon–5pm; mid-Mar to mid-Dec Sat–Sun noon–5pm. From downtown, take Gulf Fwy. Exit Telephone Rd. and make the 3rd right off the feeder road on to Munger (before you get to the Telephone Rd. intersection).

Space Center Houston ★★★ *Kids*   Space Center Houston is the visitor center for NASA's Johnson Space Center. It's the product of the joint efforts of NASA and Disney Imagineering. Easily the most popular attraction in the Houston area, there's nothing like it anywhere else in the world. You'll find plenty of exhibits and activities to interest both adults and children, and they do a great job of introducing the visitor to different aspects of space exploration. The center banks heavily on interactive displays and simulations on the one hand and actual access to the real thing on the other. For instance, the Feel of Space gallery simulates working in the frictionless environment of space by using an air-bearing floor (something like a giant air hockey table). Another simulator shows what it's like to land the lunar orbiter. For a direct experience of NASA you can take the 1½-hour tram tour that takes you to, among other places, the International Space Station Assembly Building and NASA control center. You get to see things as they happen, especially interesting if there's a shuttle mission in progress. You might also see astronauts in training. And, on top of all this, Space Center Houston has the largest IMAX in Texas. Plan on staying here at least 4 hours.

1601 NASA Rd. 1, Clear Lake. ℂ 281/244-2100. Admission (including tours and IMAX theater) $17 adults, $15 seniors, $12 children ages 4–11. Daily 9am–7pm in summer; otherwise Mon–Fri 10am–5pm, Sat–Sun 10am–6pm. Parking $4. The Space Center is about 25 miles from downtown Houston. Take the Gulf Fwy. to NASA Rd. 1, turn left, and go 3 miles.

SOUTH MAIN/MUSEUM DISTRICT

Children's Museum of Houston ★★ *Kids*   The goal behind the Children's Museum was to create a place where children can engage the world around them on their own terms, a place that will spark their imaginations, and a place where they will learn the joy of discovery. It is for children up to 12 years old, but even if you're without kids in tow, you might like to take a glance at the museum's fun exterior designed by Robert Venturi in association with Jackson & Ryan Architects of Houston. It's a playful send-up of the classical museum facade and is apt clothing for this institution that blurs the distinction between museum and playhouse.

The museum's staff seems to be very much in touch with the inner child. They have developed such fun interactive exhibits as Bubble Lab and Kid-TV, which gives kids the opportunity to imitate what they see on the tube while giving them a behind-the-scenes understanding of television production. Another exhibit re-creates the Mexican Indian village of Yalalag; another, called Tot Spot, focuses on the 6-month to 3-year-old crowd, helping build motor skills through ingenious forms of play. The museum managers bring in many visitors and special shows; inquire about what they might be planning to do during your visit. The best time to go is in the afternoons when there is less probability of school trip crowds.

1500 Binz. ℂ 713/522-1138. www.cmhouston.org. $5 per person, free for children under 2, free family night Thurs 5–8pm. Tues–Sat 9am–5pm; Sun noon–5pm; Mon 9am–5pm Memorial Day to Labor Day only. The Children's Museum is on the same street as the Museum of Fine Arts, Houston (the street name changes from Bissonnet to Binz), 4 blocks to the east.

Contemporary Arts Museum   This silver-aluminum parallelogram, located on the corner of Montrose and Bissonnet cater-cornered to the Fine Arts Museum, presents temporary exhibitions of modern art and design. It has no permanent collection; what you might find here is purely the luck of the draw. When I go to the Fine Arts Museum, I always stick my head into the CAM to see what's going on because it's right across the street and it's free.

5216 Montrose Blvd. ℂ 713/284-8250. www.camh.org. Free admission. Tues–Sat 10am–5pm (Thurs until 9pm); Sun noon–5pm.

Hermann Park   This park has 545 acres of land and lies just beyond the Museum District, on the west side of South Main Street. The parkland is well wooded and has an 18-hole public golf course, picnic areas, and playscapes. Near the Houston Museum of Natural Science, which borders the park, is a Garden Center with beautiful rose gardens and a garden of aromatic herbs. Also in that vicinity is a Japanese garden and Miller Outdoor Theater, which often holds free plays and musical performances.

Fannin St. at Hermann Park Dr.

Houston Museum of Natural Science ★★ *Kids*   This is all a natural science museum should be and then some. In the museum proper you can find dinosaur skeletons, displays of Texas wildlife, a stunning gem and mineral collection, a Foucault pendulum, and exhibits on early cultures of the Americas, climatology, chemistry, and oil and gas exploration. But what gets most of the buzz is the miniature rainforest environment created in the Butterfly Center. You can walk among hundreds of living butterflies as they dance about in the steamy air amidst a small waterfall. As you enter, you pass through the insect zoo, which holds some fascinating and bizarre living specimens of beetles, spiders, and other bugs that you wouldn't necessarily want running around freely with you.

Also in the museum are an IMAX theater and a planetarium. The museum recently reequipped the planetarium with new computer animation projectors that enhance the visual quality of its programs about stars, galaxies, nebulas, and other astral bodies. In years past, the directors have assembled some great temporary exhibits, so ask about any temporary shows that might be open during your visit. The museum occupies a corner of the Hermann Park about 3 blocks from the Museum of Fine Arts next to the equestrian statue of Sam Houston.

1 Hermann Circle Dr. ✆ 713/639-4629. www.hmns.org. Museum $6 adults, $3.50 seniors and children ages 3–11; planetarium and Butterfly Center each are $5 adults, $3.50 seniors and children; IMAX tickets $7 adults, $4.50 seniors and children. Multivenue ticket packages available. General hours Mon–Sat 9am–6pm, Sun 11am–6pm; hours for Butterfly Center and IMAX can differ. Parking $3 (garage entrance on Caroline St.).

Houston Zoological Gardens *Kids*   Located within Hermann Park is this 50-acre zoo featuring a gorilla habitat, rare albino reptiles, cat facility, huge aquarium, and vampire bats that eat lunch every day at 2:30pm (and yes, you can watch them feed). The zoo is a mixed bag—it's an old zoo that every few years builds a new facility for part of its occupants, but it still has some old-fashioned cages. The Brown Education Center, open daily from 10am to 6pm, allows visitors to interact with the animals.

1513 N. MacGregor. ✆ 713/523-5888. $3 adults, $2 seniors, $1 children ages 3–12. Daily 10am–6pm.

Museum of Fine Arts, Houston (MFAH) ★★★   This is by far the best and biggest public art museum in Texas. It's a wonderful testament to what a lot of oil money can do, and the manner in which it evolved tells something about the development of the city's sense of aesthetics. The original museum, built in the 1920s, was pure neoclassical—the attitude was that if Houston was to have a museum, it was to look like a museum. In the '50s, the MFAH directors hired Mies van der Rohe, the grand architect of the International Style to build an addition. In the '70s that addition received an addition, also designed by Mies. Both of these were bold statements of modern architecture—lots of glass and steel forming a light and airy space—but, unfortunately, not the kind of space that lends itself well for the exhibition of much of the museum's collection. Because the additions were so large, the museum found itself with a dispropor-tionate amount of open exhibition space.

In the '90s, the museum's directors hired Spanish architect Rafael Moneo to design a building that would be a return to traditional galleries. It, the Audrey Jones Beck Building, is across South Main Street from the main building. (A tun-nel connects the two; make a point of visiting it.) The new building aims at rec-onciling the boldness of modernism with the staid character of traditional design. Constructed with rich materials and designed on grand proportions, the build-ing feels monumental. All the galleries on the second floor take advantage of interesting "roof lanterns," which allow Houston's plentiful natural light to enter in regulated amounts. The Beck building doubles MFAH's gallery space and allows the directors to attract first-rate traveling exhibitions. The museum's col-lection of more than 40,000 pieces is wide and varied, but it is perhaps strongest in the area of Impressionist and post-Impressionist works, baroque and Renais-sance art, and 19th- and 20th-century American art. There is also a fine collec-tion of African tribal art, as well as ancient artwork from several civilizations.

Aside from the two gallery buildings, there is a large sculpture garden designed by Isamu Noguchi located across Bissonnet from the main building, and the Glassell School of Art, which can be seen just to the north of the sculp-ture garden. Look for a building made of a strangely reflective glass brick (another architectural pun). The museum also owns two collections of the dec-orative arts that are displayed in two mansions in the River Oaks area; see Bayou Bend (p. 176) and Rienzi (p. 176).

1001 Bissonnet St. ✆ 713/639-7300. www.mfah.org. $7 adults, $3.50 seniors and children ages 6–18; free general admission every Thurs. Tues–Wed 10am–5pm; Thurs 10am–9pm; Fri–Sat 10am–7pm; Sun 12:15–7pm.

Museum of Health & Medical Science ★★★ *Kids*   We have all heard about just what an amazing thing the human body is, but just how well are most of us really acquainted with its workings? This family museum will surprise most visitors with its extensive use of audio, video, holograms, and medical technology to provide a graphic view of human physiology.

Because of the Texas Medical Center, Houston has a large medical community, which has been the driving force behind the creation of this museum. With additional contributions from corporations and individual doctors, it has constructed an eye-catching interactive exhibition called the **Amazing Body Pavilion.** The exhibit is itself a metaphor for the body. Visitors enter through the mouth and proceed down the digestive tract learning about all the organs that process our food. (Children seem to think this is pretty cool.) The exhibit covers all the major organs in ways that provide lots of interaction for children, and explanatory text and monologues by little holographic figures are well written and manage to provide info that most adults will find interesting. Of course, with so many doctors involved, you can be sure that there will be some preaching about the need for a good diet and to avoid smoking, and don't expect the museum's snack bar to offer any junk food. But do check out the gift shop; it has an assortment of curious and intriguing items that you won't easily find elsewhere.

Seeing the exhibit takes a little more than an hour. One other note: You might want to ask at the front desk about the next scheduled organ dissection. When I was there, the organ of the month was the sheep brain; I opted to forego the performance.

1515 Hermann Dr. © 713/521-1515. www.mhms.org. Admission $5 adults, $3 seniors and children ages 4–11; free admission on family-night Thurs 4–7pm. Tues–Sat 9am–5pm (Mon in summer); Sun noon–5pm. The museum is 1 block south of the Children's Museum.

Six Flags AstroWorld & Six Flags WaterWorld *Kids*   Farther south of Hermann Park and the Texas Medical Center is the Astrodome, and just south of it across the Loop 610 Freeway are these two large amusement parks. AstroWorld is a 75-acre park with several high-tech roller coasters, other thrill rides, performance venues, and theme areas. Highlights include the Serial Thriller, a roller coaster that has you suspended in a seat while it twirls you through seven inversions. In Dungeon Drop you can experience free fall, and the Texas Tornado steel roller coaster does four loops at breakneck speed. Almost all of these rides are for children 48 inches or taller. For smaller children there are themed areas such as the one based on Warner Bros. Looney Tunes characters.

Tips **It's in the Air**

Houston has earned the unofficial nickname of "Air Conditioning Capital of the World." In the summer the air can be hot and uncommonly humid. If you are unaccustomed to high humidity, allow a day to let your body adjust, drink plenty of water, and plan indoor activities. Many visitors experience languor and sluggishness at first, but this will dissipate with time.

In the summertime the only place to cool off is indoors. But if you're in the Museum District and it's not too dreadfully hot, you could hang out at the sculpture garden in front of the Fine Arts Museum, or by the reflection pool of the broken obelisk in front of the Rothko Chapel.

WaterWorld is one of those aquatic amusement parks that requires a sturdy bathing suit. It's full of water rides and games with a mixture of chutes and slides that you ride with or without a raft or other device. Again, many require that children be 48 inches or taller. The entrance to WaterWorld is next to that of AstroWorld. Six Flags owns another, larger water park called SplashTown (p. 177).

9001 Kirby Dr. ℂ 713/799-1234. www.sixflags.com. AstroWorld $36 adults, $25 seniors 55 and older, $18 children under 48 in., free for children under 3. WaterWorld $20 adults, $15 children under 48 in., $14 seniors 55 and older. Prices do not include tax. AstroWorld is generally open daily late May to late Aug; Fri–Sun Mar–May and Sept–Nov; closed Nov–Feb. Hours generally 11am–10pm, depending on the season. Water-World is open only during the summer months. Call ahead or check the website, since times often vary. Parking $5.

MONTROSE

Menil Collection ★★★ *Value*   Here, on display in an unremarkable neighborhood near the University of St. Thomas, is one of the world's great private collections. Jean and Dominique de Menil arrived in Houston in the 1940s after fleeing the war in Europe. For more than 4 decades, they purchased and commissioned works of art; brought artists, architects, and academics to the city; organized groundbreaking exhibitions; and did much for Houston's art museums and for the art departments of Rice University and St. Thomas University. Their collection, especially the modern art, is vast, so much so that only a fifth of it can be exhibited in the museum at one time. The structure housing the collection was designed by Renzo Piano, who worked closely with Mrs. de Menil. It is graceful and personable and doesn't seek to impress the visitor or impose itself on the collection. In these qualities it is the physical embodiment of Mrs. de Menil's ideas about experiencing art. When you walk into the museum there is nothing between you and the art—no grand lobby with marble stairway, no large banners or gift shop vying for attention, no tickets to buy, no tape-recorded tours. Viewing the art becomes a direct and personal experience.

The Menil Collection is concentrated in four areas: antiquity, Byzantine and medieval, tribal art, and 20th century. This may seem an incongruous mix, but, strangely enough, it holds together. The collectors never intended to gather up the best or most representative of a period; they simply followed their own tastes, which were modern. And one interesting consequence of this fact (intended or not) is that, in walking through these galleries one right after another, the viewer gradually discerns a universality in some modern art that connects it all the way back to antiquity and across the boundaries of western culture to the tribal peoples of other continents.

In addition to the main museum, there are four satellite buildings to visit that form a museum campus. One of these satellite buildings is the much-talked-about **Rothko Chapel,** with its 14 brooding paintings by Mark Rothko, created specifically for this installation and the last works by the artist before his death. In front of the chapel stands Barnett Newman's *Broken Obelisk.* A block south of the Rothko Chapel is the **Byzantine Fresco Chapel Museum,** which is worth the viewing, as much for the building that houses them (designed by François de Menil, son of Jean and Dominique) as for the frescoes themselves, which were ransomed from international art thieves. Across the street from the main museum, in a building also designed by Renzo Piano, is a permanent exhibition of the works of Cy Twombly, which, though perhaps difficult to approach, are easy to view owing to the gallery's exquisite light. It lends a luminous quality to the large artworks, and somehow just being in the place livens one's spirits.

Finally, there is **Richmond Hall,** 2 blocks south of the campus, which holds an installation by neon light artist Don Flavin.

1515 Sul Ross St. ℰ **713/525-9400.** www.menil.org. Free admission. Wed–Sun 11am–7pm.

KIRBY DISTRICT

Bayou Bend ★★   Ima Hogg was the daughter of Gov. Jim Hogg, a man who obviously had a cruel sense of humor. Miss Hogg, however, did not grow up shy and self-effacing. Long after the governor was dead, she was a power to be reckoned with in local affairs and did much to keep the chicanery in city hall to a minimum. Her mansion, Bayou Bend, was built in the 1920s by Houston's most prominent architect, John F. Staub. It holds in its 28 rooms a treasure trove of American furniture, paintings, and decorative objects dating from colonial times to about 1870, and is set amid 14 acres of beautifully tended gardens in a variety of styles. This is a must-see for antiques collectors and gardeners.

Part of the Museum of Fine Arts, the collection can be seen by self-guided audio tour or by guided tour, for which you must make reservations. I prefer the guided tour, mostly, because I like to ask questions. It takes 90 minutes and costs the same as the audio tour. Guided tours leave every 15 minutes. You can see the gardens on your own. Bayou Bend is on the backside of River Oaks, but is unapproachable from the main entrance to the neighborhood. The only way to get there is to go down Memorial Drive, which follows the north shore of Buffalo Bayou, then turn left onto Westcott to enter the grounds.

1 Westcott St. ℰ **713/639-7750.** www.mfah.org/bayoubend. Admission (includes audio tour) $10 adults, $8.50 seniors, $5 youths ages 10–18, $1.50 under 10. Tues–Fri 10am–5pm; Sat–Sun 1–5pm. Reservations required for guided tour.

Rienzi   In a 1950s River Oaks mansion designed by John F. Staub, the Museum of Fine Arts displays its collection of European decorative arts. Most of the collection predates 1800. Both the house and the collection were donated by the family that lived here. This museum will be of most interest to collectors of English porcelain and of no interest to children. Call for a tour. On Sundays you can now visit without taking a tour, from 1 to 4pm.

1406 Kirby Dr. ℰ **713/639-7800.** Admission $6 adults, $4 seniors. Mon and Thurs–Sat 10am–4pm; Sun 1-4pm. Reservations required.

FARTHER AFIELD

George Ranch Historical Park (Kids)   You can experience the life of four generations of a Texas family on this 400-acre outdoor museum, a working cattle ranch. Wander through a restored 1820s pioneer farm, an 1880s Victorian mansion, an 1890s cowboy encampment, and a 1930s ranch house. Savor Victorian-style tea on the porch of an 1890s mansion, or sit around the campfire with cowboys during a roundup and watch crafts demonstrations such as rope twisting. Picnic areas are provided. Plan to spend a half-day here.

10215 FM 762, Richmond. ℰ **281/343-0218.** www.georgeranch.org. Admission $8.50 adults, $7.50 seniors 55 and over, $5 children ages 3–12. Daily 10am–5pm. Take the Southwest Fwy. (Tex. 59 south); before getting to the town of Richmond, exit FM Hwy. 762 and go 6 miles south.

National Museum of Funeral History   Do you give much thought to how you would like to be remembered once you've shuffled off this mortal coil? Or perhaps your thoughts just naturally drift toward things funereal? If so, then this private museum is the thing for you. Its owner, Service Corporation International, is the largest funeral company in the United States, and it has obviously been at pains to assemble the nation's largest collection of funeral memorabilia.

The exhibits include a restored horse-drawn hearse, antique automobile hearses, and a 1916 Packard funeral bus. You can see memorabilia and trivia from the funerals of many famous people including Martin Luther King, Jr., John Wayne, Elvis, Abraham Lincoln, JFK, Nixon, and many more. Other attractions include a full-size replica of King Tut's sarcophagus.

415 Barren Springs (north Houston, near airport). ⓒ 281/876-3063. www.nmfh.org. Admission $6 adults, $5 seniors and veterans, $3 children under 12, free for children under 3. Mon–Sat 10am–4pm; Sun noon–4pm.

SplashTown *Kids*   A 45-minute drive from downtown, SplashTown is larger and has a few more rides than WaterWorld. Special events are held and live entertainment is on offer throughout the season. It gets really crowded here, mainly with kids from north Houston suburbs and The Woodlands. Unless you're staying in north Houston, this park is more out of the way than WaterWorld.

Northbound I-45 at Louetts Rd., Spring. ⓒ 281/355-3300. www.sixflags.com. $24 adults, $18 children under 48 in. and seniors over 55. Daily 11am–10pm during summer months. Hours vary—call or check website. Follow I-45 north toward Dallas; take Exit 69-A, before The Woodlands.

ESPECIALLY FOR KIDS

As a parent can quickly grasp, Houston is kid-friendly. Easily half of the above-mentioned attractions are geared for kids or have a large component especially suitable for them.

A tour of southeast Houston will take you to **The Orange Show,** with which young kids display an almost instinctual connection; the boat trip on the **Ship Channel;** a visit to the **Battleship *Texas;*** and the wonders of **Space Center Houston.** After that there's a visit to the boardwalk in **Kemah,** or a trip to the **beach** or to **Moody Gardens** in Galveston (see "A Side Trip to Galveston," later in this chapter).

South of downtown you have the Museum District, which includes the **Children's Museum,** the **Houston Museum of Natural Science,** and the **Museum of Health & Medical Science.** And of course there's **Houston Zoological Gardens,** which has a special children's zoo that explores the different ecological zones of Texas. Further south are the theme parks **AstroWorld** and **Water-World,** which are very popular. To the north is **SplashTown,** another water park, and to the southwest is the **George Ranch Historical Park** for kids interested in cowboys and the Old West.

ORGANIZED TOURS

If you'd like a bus tour of the city to help you get your bearings, you're out of luck. There are companies such as Gray Line, but they offer tours only to conventions and visiting groups, not the general public. There is, however, a different kind of tour that can introduce you to what makes Houston unique. If you're planning to be in Houston during the second weekend of the month, you might be able to sign up for one of the offbeat tours offered by **Eyeopener Tours.** Part of the Orange Show Foundation, they put together a tour on some months that focuses on a particularly interesting aspect of the city. Transportation by charter bus, snacks, and drinks are included in the price (usually around $35). Past tours have included folk art sites of the city, places of worship, architectural highlights, architectural lowlights, blues centers, and ethnic markets. Most of those who participate are resident Houstonians who want to learn about an unknown part of the city. Eyeopener Tours also sells an audiocassette and map for a self-guided tour of Houston's folk art environments. This is a good offering if you're pretty good at following directions and working with a map. For information, call ☎ **713/926-6368** or check www.orangeshow.org/eyeopener.

The other option is walking tours (yes, walking tours in Houston) by **Houston Walks and the Houston Tunnel Association.** These walking tours are run by Sandra Lord, known locally as the Tunnel Lady. One of the most popular is that of the Houston tunnel system, which includes several downtown sights. Other possible walking tours include the Museum District, and a tour of the public sculpture and art of downtown. The tours are by appointment, and prices vary. Ms. Lord occasionally offers scheduled seasonal walks that anyone can sign up for. You can contact her by e-mail at tunnellady@aol.com or call ☎ **713/222-9255.**

6 Sports & Outdoor Activities

OUTDOOR FUN

BIKING, JOGGING & WALKING   By far the most popular jogging and walking track is in **Memorial Park.** This is a large and beautiful park clothed in pine trees along Buffalo Bayou west of downtown, just inside the Loop. It's easy to reach; take Memorial Drive, which follows the north bank of Buffalo Bayou, from downtown to the park. It can be very crowded and doesn't work for biking, for which there are other trails. Another biking option is to ride through **the Heights,** a quiet neighborhood of old houses and antiques shops not far from Memorial. Many visitors will prefer the hike and bike trail along the banks of **Buffalo Bayou** from North Shepherd to downtown. It runs along both banks of the bayou for 1½ miles, so you can run a 3-mile loop. It offers lovely vistas of the downtown skyline and is decorated with numerous sculptures that can be both fun and interesting (and it takes you right into the Theater District). During the day it's fine, but I wouldn't advise venturing along the bayou at night. To rent a bike in this area, see **West End Cycles** at 5427 Blossom (☎ **713/225-6372**), which is in the neighborhood next to Memorial Park. They can set you up and give you information about good rides.

A 10-mile hike and bike trail runs along the banks of **Brays Bayou** from Hermann Park through the Medical Center, where it goes under South Main Street then heads southwest almost all the way to Beltway 8.

GOLF   Houston proper has public golf courses at most of the city's biggest parks, but with the exception of the Memorial Park Golf Course, the best public courses are outside the city. Probably the best public course (and one of the most difficult) in the area is the **Tournament Players Course at the Woodlands,** located 25 miles north of Houston in The Woodlands (☎ **281/364-6440**) and home to Shell Houston Open. Greens fees range from $95 to $125; tee times must be made at least 3 days in advance. One of the loveliest and best-regarded courses in the area is the **Longwood Golf Club** (☎ **281/373-4100**), 13300 Longwood Trace in Cypress, at the northwest edge of Houston; to get there, take Tex. 290 (45 min. from downtown). Fees are $55 to $65 and include cart; tee times should be reserved at least 3 days in advance. Another course that a lot of people talk about is **Tour 18 Houston** (☎ **281/540-1818**), which copies 18 of the greatest holes in golf. The course is at 3102 FM 1960 East in Humble, about 12 miles north of Houston and about 35 minutes from downtown. Greens fees are $60 to $105 (cart included); reserve a tee time at least a week in advance.

In town, there's **Memorial Park Golf Course** (☎ **713/862-4033**), one of the top courses in the area. Greens fees are $23 to $32, and you can reserve a tee time 3 days in advance. **Hermann Park's golf course** is centrally located (© **713/526-0077**), with greens fees ranging from $32 to $41. You can reserve a tee time 3 days in advance. At both the Memorial Park and Hermann Park courses, there is an extra $10 to $15 fee for reservations more than 3 days in advance.

TENNIS Of course, the best strategy to get some tennis in is to stay at a hotel with courts. **Memorial Park** has some of the best of the public courses; make reservations well in advance by calling © **713/867-0440.**

SPECTATOR SPORTS

If you're in Houston and decide on the spur of the moment to try to get tickets to a game, you can call **Ticket Stop,** 5925 Kirby Dr. #D (© **713/526-8889**), a private ticket agency. They charge extra for the tickets, so if possible, it's best to buy direct or in advance.

AUTO RACING Every year in September, Houston hosts the **Texaco Havoline Grand Prix,** a race through the city's downtown streets that's part of the CART circuit. For information and tickets, call © **713/739-7272.**

BASEBALL **Houston Astros** fans are enjoying the indoor/outdoor downtown stadium, Minute Maid Field, with its retractable roof that's open mostly in the early part of the season before the weather gets too hot. With a little planning, tickets aren't hard to come by; call © **877/9-ASTROS** or visit www.astros.com.

BASKETBALL The **Houston Rockets** play at the Compaq Center in Greenway Plaza, located off of the Southwest Freeway between downtown and the Loop. This is a popular team and tickets must be purchased well in advance to get anything approaching good seats (© **713/627-3865;** www.nba.com/rockets). The women's team, the **Comets,** has won several WNBA championships and is popular with local sports fans. The Comets play at the Compaq Center, too. For ticket info, call © **713/627-9622** or look them up online at www.wnba.com/comets. Construction on a new basketball arena downtown is slated for completion by the end of 2003.

FOOTBALL The Houston Texans, the NFL's newest team, plays host to opponents in the new Reliant Stadium, with a retractable roof. It's located off South Main, close by the Medical Center. For information and/or tickets, call © **713/336-7700,** or check out www.houstontexans.com.

GOLF TOURNAMENTS The **Shell Houston Open** happens in The Woodlands in late April. For information and tickets, call © **281/367-7999.**

GREYHOUND RACING **Gulf Greyhound Park,** located off the Gulf Freeway between Houston and Galveston via Exit 15 (© **800/275-2946;** www.gulfgreyhound.com), offers racing year-round six times a week. General admission $1.

HOCKEY The **Houston Aeros,** of the International Hockey League, play at the Compaq Center; tickets are usually not difficult to obtain. Call © **713/627-8767** or visit www.aeros.com.

HORSE RACING **Sam Houston Race Park,** 7575 N. Sam Houston Pkwy. (© **800/807-7223** or 281/807-7223; www.shrp.com), is in northwest Houston on the Beltway 8 between where it crosses Tex. 290 and I-45. Quarter horse racing is from June to September; thoroughbred racing is from October to March. General admission is $3 for adults, $1 for seniors. Races are most weekends (Thurs–Sun).

MARATHONS   The **Houston Methodist Marathon** occurs in January and attracts more than 6,000 entrants from around the world. Call ✆ **713/957-3453** for more information.

RODEO   Houstonians go all out "Western" for a couple of weeks every February, when the **Houston Livestock Show and Rodeo** takes place. Billed as the largest event of its kind, the rodeo includes the usual events like bull riding and calf roping as well as performances by famous country artists. Call ✆ **713/791-9000** for more information; for tickets, call **Ticketmaster** at ✆ **713/629-3700.**

7 Shopping

If you're anywhere in Houston, you probably aren't far from a mall, of which there are many more than can be mentioned here. They're usually located at or near an intersection of a freeway with the Loop or Beltway 8 or other major artery. These are good for general shopping, but hold little of interest for most visitors. A different story is the outlet malls, the principal one being **Katy Mills** out at the far western boundary of Houston, in the town of Katy. Take the Katy Freeway (I-10 west) until you spot the signs; the drive is about 25 miles. This mall is a mammoth collection of about 200 factory outlet stores that offer a large selection of merchandise at discount prices. The size of the discounts varies; some are good deals. There are also restaurants and a large movie theater present.

GREAT SHOPPING AREAS

Whether you're a purposeful shopper or a last-minute accidental one, you'll need to know something about the shopping terrain of Houston. Of course, the main shopping area in Houston is Uptown, but other areas have a diversity of offerings that might prove to be just what you're looking for.

DOWNTOWN

The oldest of Houston's department stores, **Foley's,** still has its original store on Main Street at Lamar (✆ 713/405-7035). It's a large five-story building that occupies an entire block. It carries several lines of expensive clothing and perfumes as well as some moderately priced ones. The other happy shopping ground downtown is **The Park Shops,** 1200 McKinney, across the street from the Four Seasons Hotel (✆ 713/759-1442). It's a group of about 40 small stores, mostly boutiques and specialty shops.

EAST END

Just the other side of the freeway from the George Brown Convention Center is a commercial **Chinatown,** where you can find all kinds of goods imported from across Asia. Furniture, foods, curios—you can browse your way through a number of little import stores, all within a 4-block area, between Dowling on the east, Chartreuse on the west, Rusk on the north, and Dallas on the south.

MONTROSE

Along Westheimer from Woodhead to Mandell you'll find several antiques and junk shops that are perfect for the leisurely shopper who's out to find a diamond in the rough. If after browsing through these you haven't had your fill, there is a grouping of similar stores on 19th Street in the Heights. (For the more discriminating antiques stores, go to the Kirby District.) Don't ever accept the first price you're offered at these places—they almost always will lower the price. Also along Westheimer are a number of vintage clothing stores that offer some entertaining shopping. North of Westheimer, on West Gray where it intersects with

Shepherd, a whole different sort of shopping awaits at the **River Oaks Shopping Center.** This is Houston's oldest shopping center. It's 2 blocks long and extends down both sides of West Gray in white-and-black Art Deco. It's a chic collection of galleries, boutiques, antiques shops, and specialty stores as well as some fine restaurants and an art cinema.

KIRBY DISTRICT

Kirby is more uniformly upscale than the Montrose. Where it begins by Westheimer there are a couple of strip malls, the largest of which is **Highland Village,** 4000 Westheimer (✆ **713/850-3100**). Highland Village, like so much of the retail business in this part of town, is aimed at the upper-middle-class shopper with such stores as Williams-Sonoma and Pottery Barn and a few one-of-a-kind boutiques. From this part of Kirby Drive to where it passes the Rice Village is a section known informally as Gallery Row, with a mix of galleries, designer showrooms, and shops of antiques and special furnishings. And finally there's **the Village,** a 16-block neighborhood of small shops now mixed with outlets from high-dollar national retailers. A few of the small shops are survivors from simpler times that are now a bit at odds with their new environment of day spas, expensive shoe stores, and famous designer boutiques. There is also a wide variety of restaurants to choose from in the Village when it's time to take a break from browsing.

UPTOWN

To start with there's the **Galleria,** 5075 Westheimer (✆ **713/622-0663**), which occupies a long stretch of land along Westheimer and Post Oak. It has 320 stores that include big department stores such as Saks Fifth Avenue, Lord & Taylor, and Neiman Marcus, and small designer retailers such as Gucci, Emporio Armani, and Dolce & Gabbana. Across Westheimer from the Galleria is another shopping center called **Centre at Post Oak,** with stores such as FAO Schwarz and Barnes & Noble. If you're in Uptown and are looking for the finest in Western wear, go to **Stelzig of Texas,** 3123 Post Oak (✆ **281/629-7779**). This store has been selling clothing, saddles, and other Western goods to Houstonians for generations. It sells some of the high-dollar apparel—handmade boots, ranger belts with silver buckles, and so forth.

THE HEIGHTS

On 19th Street in the Heights is some fun shopping if you're interested in antiques or Latin American folk art. The antiques shops, of which there are a dozen or so, are inexpensive. The merchandise is set down just about anywhere the owners can find a place for it, and dusting is a once in awhile practice. This is for bargain hunters.

One notable shop is **Casa Ramírez,** 239 W. 19th St. (✆ **713/880-2420**). It displays a panoramic collection of Mexican folk art from across the country.

SOUTHWEST

In southwest Houston just beyond the Loop is where the Asian bazaar meets American suburb. I find the area fascinating. This is simultaneously adventure shopping and an exploration into the brave new world of postmodern America. First, drive down **Harwin Drive** between Fondren and Gessner. You will see store after store and strip mall after strip mall selling jewelry, designer clothes, sunglasses, perfumes, furniture, luggage, and handbags. Most of the stores are run by Indian, Pakistani, Chinese, and Thai shopkeepers, but other cultures are represented, too. Occasionally one will get raided for selling designer knock-offs. Everything is said to be at bargain-basement rates, but buyer beware. What I like the best are the import stores where you're never sure what you'll find. Every store is a different experience. Farther out, on **Bellaire Boulevard** in the middle of a large commercial Chinatown is an all-Chinese mall, where you can get just about anything Chinese, including tapes and CDs, books, food and cooking items, of course, and wonderful knickknacks.

8 Houston After Dark

THE PERFORMING ARTS

For fans of the performing arts, Houston is fertile ground. Few cities in the country can equal it in the quality of its resident orchestra, opera, ballet, and theater companies. In addition, there are several organizations that bring talented artists and companies here from around the country and the world, presenting everything from Broadway shows to Argentine tango groups to string quartets. Tickets aren't usually discounted for the opera, ballet, or symphony, but you should ask anyway. For information about performances, visit **www.houston-guide.com** or the websites of the various organizations listed below.

The symphony, the ballet, the opera, and the Alley Theatre (the city's largest and oldest theater company), all hold their performances in the theater district downtown. The opera and the ballet share the **Wortham Center,** 500 Texas Ave. (© 713/237-1439); the symphony plays a block away at **Jones Hall,** 615 Louisiana St. (© 713/227-3974); and the **Alley Theatre** is one of those rare companies that actually owns its own theater, located at 615 Texas Ave. (© 713/228-8421), cater-cornered from the symphony. Also in the theater district are the **Aerial Theater** (in Bayou Place), which hosts a wide variety of musical and dramatic acts, and the new **Hobby Center for the Performing Arts,** 800 Bagby (© 713/227-2001), which will be shared by the Society for Performing Arts and Theater Under the Stars.

The Society for the Performing Arts (SPA), 615 Louisiana St. (box office © 713/227-4772), is a nonprofit organization that brings to Houston distinguished dance companies, jazz bands, theater productions, and soloists. Within SPA, there's a program called the Broadway Series, which brings popular productions from Broadway and London's West End. The organization uses Jones Hall, the Wortham Center, and the Hobby Center. For information, visit www.spahouston.org. Tickets for the Broadway Series must be purchased through **Ticketmaster** (© 713/629-3700; www.ticketmaster.com). You can purchase tickets to other SPA events from Ticketmaster, but you'll save money by buying them directly from the SPA.

Following are brief descriptions of the principal organizations; there are many more, especially independent theater companies that present several plays a year.

CLASSICAL MUSIC, OPERA & BALLET

The **Houston Symphony** (© 713/224-7575; www.houstonsymphony.org) is the city's oldest performing arts organization. Its season is from September to May, during which it holds about 100 concerts in Jones Hall. The classical series usually contains a number of newer compositions with visits by several guest conductors and soloists from around the world. There is also a pops series and a chamber music series, which often holds its performances at Rice University.

Da Camera of Houston (© 713/524-5050; www.dacamera.com) brings classical and jazz chamber music orchestras to the city and holds concerts either at the Wortham or in the lobby of the Menil Collection. You can buy tickets from the box office at 1427 Branard St. in the Montrose area.

The nationally acclaimed **Houston Grand Opera** is the fifth-largest opera company in the United States. Known for being innovative and premiering new operas such as *Nixon in China,* its productions of classical works are brilliant visual affairs. The opera season is from October to May. For tickets and information, visit www.houstongrandopera.org or call © **713/228-6737** at the Wortham Center.

The **Houston Ballet** (© **713/227-ARTS;** www.houstonballet.org) has garnered enormous critical acclaim from across the country. A lot of the credit belongs to director Ben Stevenson, who came to Houston more than 25 years ago under the condition that the company create its own school to teach dance as Stevenson believed it should be taught. This school, the Houston Ballet Academy, now supplies the company with 90% of its dancers, and its graduates dance in many other top ballet companies. The company tours a great deal but manages around 80 performances a year in Houston.

THEATER

The **Alley Theatre,** 615 Texas Ave. (© **713/228-8421;** www.alleytheatre.org), has won many awards for its productions. Its home holds a large theater and an arena theater, and during the year the company uses both to stage about 10 different productions, ranging from Shakespeare to Stoppard and even a musical or two. Ask about half-price tickets for sale the day of the show for weekday and Sunday performances. Pay-what-you-can-days are sometimes offered, but you have to show up in person to buy the tickets. Box office hours are Monday through Saturday from 10am to 6:30pm and Sunday from noon to 6:30pm.

Theatre Under The Stars, 800 Bagby (© **713/558-8887;** www.tuts.com), specializes in musicals that it either brings to town or produces itself, averaging 200 performances annually. The organization got its name from having first worked at Miller Outdoor Theater in Hermann Park. It uses the new Hobby Center for the Performing Arts.

The **Ensemble Theatre,** 3335 Main St. (© **713/520-0055**), is the city's largest black theater company. Founded in 1976, the Ensemble has grown from a band of strolling players into a resident professional company of 40 actors and 8 directors. Their specialty is African-American and experimental theater.

THE CLUB & MUSIC SCENE

Having a night on the town in Houston doesn't require a lot of planning, but pick up a copy of the *Houston Press,* the free weekly that you can find at many restaurants and shops. It provides a good rundown of what musical and comedy acts are in town, and it includes a lot of advertising from the clubs. There's also the daily paper, the *Chronicle,* which has a well-organized entertainment section, and a pullout published on Thursdays. If you want to know what's going on in the clubs before you get to Houston, try their websites, **www.houstonpress.com** and **www.houstonchronicle.com.**

In general, the most popular locations for nightspots are the following: downtown, around the theater district and Old Market Square; in the Montrose area; and south of the Galleria along Richmond Avenue (called the Richmond Strip). There are enough clubs in these places that you can move from one to another quickly and easily until you find something you like.

MEGACLUBS

In the theater district in downtown Houston, a developer has converted the old convention center into a complex of restaurants, clubs, bars, and a movie theater. It's called **Bayou Place** (© 713/230-1666) and is located at 500 Texas Ave. It houses the **Aerial Theater,** which usually has live music or comedy (call the number above); the **Hard Rock Cafe** (© 281/479-7025), with some live acts on the weekends; **Harlon's Bayou Blues** (© 713/230-0111), with live blues Thursday through Saturday; and **Slick Willie's** (© 713/230-1277), a billiards club. Also, there are a few video and dance bars with canned music that are very popular with a younger crowd. The movie theater is called **Angelika Film Center and Café** (© 713/225-5232), a popular place to hang out in the evening before going clubbing or to a concert.

City Streets, 5078 Richmond Ave. (© **713/840-8555**), is one of those large complexes holding six clubs under one roof: the Rose, a large country-and-western dance hall with recorded music and a full-size replica of the Alamo; the Blue Monkey, a karaoke bar; Stray Cats, where dueling pianists play sing-alongs, perform skits, exchange barbs with each other, and get members of the audience involved, too; Atlantis, a dance club with '70s and '80s music; Cages, a '90s music dance club; and Midway, a large billiards club with televised sporting events. It draws a crowd of all ages and is open from Wednesday to Saturday. Cover charges vary, usually $3 for weeknights and $5 or more for weekends.

ROCK

One of the best venues for catching live rock acts is the old Houston institution known as **Fitzgerald's,** 2706 White Oak (© **713/862-3838**). It occupies an old Polish dance hall near the Heights neighborhood and gets talented local and touring bands. Look for their advertisement in the *Houston Press* to see who's playing while you're in town and to check ticket prices.

For alternative rock acts in a suitably grungy place, go to the **Engine Room** (© **713/654-7846**). It's in the southeast part of downtown at 1515 Pease near the intersection with La Branch. This club gets a mostly 20-something clientele, which comes to hear bands that are as far away from pop as they can get.

JAZZ

To hear some jazz, your best bet is one of two clubs downtown that are fairly similar and close by each other. If you're not wild about the band at one, you can walk over to the other. The more formal and expensive one is called **Sambucca Jazz Café,** 909 Texas Ave. (© **713/224-5299**). It gets a dressed-up crowd and lines up some talented bands. The **Red Cat Jazz Café** is at 924 Congress (© **713/227-2200**), 3 blocks away. I heard a great band here playing interesting arrangements of bebop standards. Both cafes require a minimum consumption depending on the night of the week and what band is playing.

Another option is to check out some swing band music at **Scott Gernter's Skybar** (© 713/520-9688) in the Montrose area. It's on the top floor of a 10-story building at the corner of Montrose and Hawthorne at 3400 Montrose Blvd. There are often guest bands playing other varieties of jazz. The club has a dance floor and a rooftop terrace.

BLUES

Houston has several blues clubs. One to investigate in particular is **Billy Blues** at 6025 Richmond Ave. (© **713/523-9999**). One of the many clubs along the Richmond Strip, this one sets itself apart by signing up very good blues acts from around the country. Monday and Tuesday is open-mic night with some good local talent and no cover charge. The clientele tends to be 30- to 50-somethings. Another club to try is the **Big Easy Social and Pleasure Club,** 5731 Kirby Dr. (© **713/523-9999**), out near South Main. This club lines up a lot of local blues talent that is uncommonly good, as well as touring acts. The clientele is a real mix of everything from yuppies to bikers. Both places charge admission, which can be anywhere between $5 and $15, depending upon the act.

FOLK & ACOUSTIC
Anderson Fair, 2007 Grant (© **713/528-8576**), is the place to play if you're a folk singer. The club is a survival from the 1960s, and looks every bit the product of its age. In its many years it has nurtured several folk artists who went on to become big names in folk, including Nancy Griffith. That it opens only Fridays and Saturdays only adds to its aura of counterculture. People of all ages hang out here, though there are a lot of former hippies. It's located 1 block off Montrose, behind the Montrose Art Supply building.

Another folk and bluegrass institution in Houston is **McGonigel's Mucky Duck** (© **713/528-5999**). It offers pub grub and burgers, wine and beer, and live music every night (except Sun, when it's closed). Wednesday Irish jam sessions are free, as are Mondays. The club is at 2425 Norfolk, near Kirby Drive where it intersects the Southwest Freeway.

COUNTRY & WESTERN
Blanco's (© **713/439-0072**) is a Texas-style honky-tonk that packs 'em in Mondays through Fridays, attracting all sorts, from River Oaks types to tool pushers. Lots of good Texas bands like to play here, so it's a good opportunity to see a well-known band in a small venue. There's a midsize dance floor. Monday through Wednesday is open-mic night, usually with one or another local band. Thursday and Friday offer live music, and the club is closed on Saturdays for private parties. It's located at 3406 W. Alabama, between Kirby Drive and Buffalo Speedway. When there's live music, the cover ranges from $5 to $15.

DANCE CLUBS
One of the first clubs to set up downtown was **Spy,** 112 Travis (© **713/225-2229**), near the theater district in downtown. It's still very popular with a 20- and 30-something crowd, and there are a lot of singles. Music varies depending on the night and the DJ, but it's mostly Euro and techno, with a little hip-hop. If you want to go back in time to the 1970s and 1980s, try **Poly Esther's Culture Club,** 6111 Richmond Ave. (© **713/279-1977**). This club, popular with singles and a wide range of ages, is full of the icons from that era, and you can expect to dance to a lot of disco and pop music along the lines of early Madonna.

A COMEDY CLUB
By far the best place for stand-up in Houston is the **Laff Stop,** 1952-A W. Gray (© **713/524-2333**), by the River Oaks Shopping Center. Many of the acts have a biting edge and are not appropriate for kids; call before you go. There are usually three to four acts a night. You can expect to pay between $10 and $20 per night.

THE BAR SCENE
La Carafe, 813 Congress (© **713/229-9399**), has been around for ages, and the small two-story brick building it occupies even longer. In fact, it is the oldest commercial building in the city and sits slightly askew on a tiny lot facing Old

Market Square. The jukebox is something of a relic, too, with the most eclectic mix possible and some obscure choices. The clientele is mostly older downtowners who were here before the resurgence, mostly office types, in-line skaters, and reporters from the *Chronicle*. For sheer character, no place can beat it.

Another bar with a unique flavor is **Marfreless,** 2006 Peden (© **713/528-0083**). This is the darkest bar I've ever been in. The background music is always classical, and the ambience is understated. Little alcoves here and there are considered romantic. The only trouble is finding the bar. It's in the River Oaks Shopping Center on West Gray. If you stand facing the River Oaks Theater, walk left then make a right into the parking lot. Look for an unmarked door under a metal stairway.

SPORTS BARS

The best sports bar in Houston has to be **Grif's,** 3416 Roseland (© **713/528-9912**), in the Montrose area. This is the archetypal sports bar before they became super large, high-tech, multi-screen palaces. It has been in business since the '60s and has the worn-in look to show for it. The friendly crowd includes many regulars, giving the bar that comforting feel of an honest neighborhood gathering place. Be prepared to talk sports. The bar is 1 block east of Montrose and 2 blocks south of Westheimer.

For the large multi-screen version of a sports bar, with lots of pool tables, go to **Dave And Buster's,** 6010 Richmond Ave. (© **713/952-2233**). It can handle a large crowd that enjoys a game of pool with a background of several sporting events—unless there's a particularly big game on, when the crowd becomes focused and drops their pool cues.

GAY & LESBIAN NIGHTLIFE

Most of Houston's gay nightlife centers around the Montrose area, where there are more than a dozen gay bars and clubs mostly along lower Westheimer Road and Pacific Street. For current news, pick up a copy of *Houston Voice.*

For a large and popular dance club, go to **Rich's,** 2401 San Jacinto (© **713/759-9606**), in the downtown area. Rich's gets a mixed crowd that's mostly gay men and women. It's noted for its lights and decorations and a large dance floor with a mezzanine level. It's very popular on Saturdays. For something more low-key, try **EJ's,** 2517 Ralph (© **713/527-9071**), in the Montrose area. It's just north of the 2500 block of Westheimer. Gay men of all ages come for drinks and perhaps a game of pool. There's also a dance floor, and a small stage for the occasional drag show. A friendly lesbian bar frequented by couples and singles from all walks of life is **Club Rainbow,** 1417-B Westheimer (© **713/522-5166**). It has a popular dance floor and plays a variety of music.

9 A Side Trip to Galveston

50 miles E of Houston

Galveston is a port city and beach resort on a barrier island just off the mainland coast of Texas. Its main attractions are the downtown historic district with its Victorian commercial buildings and houses, and the beaches, which draw crowds of Houstonians and other Texans during the summer. The city is only an hour's drive from Houston and is a good destination for families; it's a quiet town with many points of interest including Moody Gardens and the tall ship *Elissa,* and it's not far from NASA and Kemah.

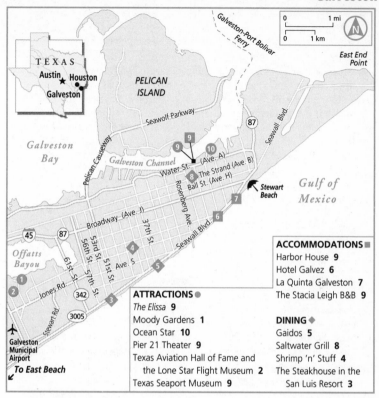

ATTRACTIONS ●
The Elissa **9**
Moody Gardens **1**
Ocean Star **10**
Pier 21 Theater **9**
Texas Aviation Hall of Fame and
   the Lone Star Flight Museum **2**
Texas Seaport Museum **9**

ACCOMMODATIONS ■
Harbor House **9**
Hotel Galvez **6**
La Quinta Galveston **7**
The Stacia Leigh B&B **9**

DINING ◆
Gaidos **5**
Saltwater Grill **8**
Shrimp 'n' Stuff **4**
The Steakhouse in the
   San Luis Resort **3**

ESSENTIALS

GETTING THERE   The best way to reach Galveston is by car. Take the Gulf Freeway (I-45 south). After crossing over to Galveston Island, the highway becomes a wide boulevard called Broadway.

ORIENTATION   Broadway, Galveston's main street, doesn't cut directly across the island to the seashore; instead it slants eastward and arrives at the seashore on the east end of the island, in front of Stewart Beach. Streets crossing Broadway are numbered; those parallel to Broadway have letters or names.

The East End Historic District and the old **Strand District** are north of Broadway. The Historic District is the old silk-stocking neighborhood that runs from 9th to 19th streets between Broadway and Church Street. It has many lovely houses that have been completely restored. Three large mansions-turned-museums have regular tours (see "Exploring Galveston," below), and the city's historical preservation society holds tours of several private houses in May (inquire at the visitor center). The Strand District is the restored commercial district that runs between 19th and 25th streets between Church Street and the harbor piers. When cotton was king, Galveston was a booming port and commercial center, and the Strand was dubbed the "Wall Street of the Southwest." What you see now are three- and four-story buildings along 6 blocks of the Strand and along some of the side streets; many of these are Victorian iron-fronts, so called because the facades included structural and decorative ironwork. This was a common

The Storm

At the end of the 19th century, Galveston was a thriving port and a fast-growing city with a bright future. In fact, it was the largest city in Texas and had the third busiest port in the country. Of course, being on the Gulf meant the risk of a hurricane, but the prevailing thought held that the shallow bottom on the western shore of the Gulf of Mexico would prevent the formation of large waves and blunt the force of any approaching storm. This assumption held sway despite the fact that a storm completely wiped out the Texas port town of Indianola in 1886. But more evidence to the contrary came in the form of a massive storm that hit Galveston in September 1900.

It came ashore at night with a 20-foot surge that washed completely over the island. Houses were smashed into matchwood and their dwellers spilled out into the dark waters. By morning more than 6,000 islanders—one out of every six—were drowned. It remains the worst natural disaster ever to strike the United States. The city's population dropped even further when many of the survivors moved elsewhere to rebuild their lives on safer shores. Those who remained went to work to prevent a reoccurrence of the disaster. Galveston erected a stout seawall that now stretches out along 10 miles of shoreline with several jetties of large granite blocks projecting out into the sea. It also filled in land under the entire city, raising it 17 feet in some places and jacking up all the surviving houses to the new level. Despite all the effort, Galveston would never regain its momentum. The memory of "the storm" proved too compelling for many of Galveston's merchants, who preferred the safety of an inland port and provided much impetus for the dredging of the Houston Ship Channel, which was completed in 1914. And, it was in this way that "the storm" rewrote the destinies of these two Texas cities.

building practice before the turn of the 20th century, but you won't find a better-preserved collection of these buildings anywhere else in the United States. Nowadays the Strand is a shopping and dining area that offers a wide variety of stores.

VISITOR INFORMATION If you're planning a trip, check the Galveston Convention & Visitors Bureau's website at www.galvestoncvb.com or call ℂ **888/GAL-ISLE.** If you're in town already, visit their information center at 2428 Seawall Blvd., close to 25th Street (ℂ **409/763-4311**). It's open daily from 9am to 5pm.

GETTING AROUND Most of Galveston's hotels, motels, and restaurants are located along the seawall from where Broadway meets the shore all the way west past 60th Street. If you're on the seawall around 25th Street (near the visitor center), you can take the **Galveston Island Rail Trolley** to the Strand District. The fare is $1 from the seawall to the Strand, but to ride just around the Strand is free.

EXPLORING GALVESTON

The beaches are always Galveston's most popular attraction. They may not measure up to those of the most popular beach destinations; the sand is a light tan color instead of white but it's all sand and no rocks, and while the water isn't turquoise, it's at a wonderful temperature for much of the year. **East Beach** and **Stewart Beach,** operated by the city, have pavilions with dressing rooms, showers, and restrooms, ideal for day-trippers. Stewart Beach is located at the end of Broadway, and East Beach is about a mile east of Stewart Beach. There's a $5 per vehicle entrance fee. Most other beaches are free; many of the nicest are on the west side of the island. Another activity popular with visitors and locals alike is to walk, skate, or ride a bike atop the seawall, which extends 10 miles along the shoreline.

Unlike Houston, there are many tours offered here: **Galveston Harbour Tours** (© 409/765-1700) offers a Saturday morning dolphin watch tour and a more frequent harbor tour; **Duck Tours** (© 409/621-4771) offers bus tours of the island; and **Ghost Tours** (© 409/949-2027) offers a walking tour of the Strand District. On Broadway there are a few massive 19th-century mansions that offer tours: **Ashton Villa,** 2328 Broadway (© 409/762-3933); the **Bishop's Palace,** 1402 Broadway (© 409/762-2475), the most interesting of the bunch because there's more to see; and the **Moody Mansion,** 2618 Broadway (© 409/762-7668). Call for rates and additional information.

MUSEUMS

Except for Moody Gardens and its neighbor, the Lone Star Flight Museum (see review below), all of Galveston's museums are in and around the Strand, the old commercial center. I enjoyed the museums here; they offer a variety of entertainment and they aren't stuffy in the way you might thing of museums. Highlights include **Pier 21 Theater** (© **409/763-8808**), which shows a short documentary about the 1900 storm that devastated the town, and another about a one-time Galveston resident, the pirate Jean Laffite. On the same pier is the **Texas Seaport Museum** (© **409/763-1877**) and the *Elissa,* a restored tall ship. Admission is $6 for adults, $4 for children 7 to 17, and a family rate of $16 for 2 adults and 3 children.

Next door, at Pier 19, is a one-of-a-kind museum about offshore drilling rigs. You will probably already have noticed that around the harborside area next to the Strand, the most eye-catching objects in view are the massive offshore rigs that are often parked on the other side of Galveston's ship channel. These mammoth constructions often come to the Port of Galveston to be reconditioned. Since they spend most of their time far offshore, one doesn't see them often, but here in Galveston you have an opportunity to view one, the **Ocean Star** (© **409/766-STAR**), a rig converted into a museum. Through a short film, scale models, actual drilling equipment, and interactive displays, every aspect of the drilling process is explored, including the many rather daunting engineering challenges. Those with a grasp of technical and engineering issues will enjoy this museum the most, but others will appreciate the broader aspects and the sheer size of these constructions. Hours for this and the other museums around the Strand are roughly the same, daily from 10am to 4pm (until 5pm in summer).

Moody Gardens (Kids) Moody Gardens, an education/entertainment museum, is easily recognizable for its three large glass pyramids. The first one built was the rainforest pyramid, which holds trees, plants, birds, fish, and butterflies from several different rainforest habitats. A stroll through the building will fascinate anyone who has never been in a rainforest environment, and the unusual species of Amazonian fish, birds, and butterflies are not often seen in zoos. The aquarium pyramid displays life from four of the world's oceans: penguins from Antarctica, harbor seals from the northern Pacific, and Caribbean and South Pacific reef dwellers. There is also a petting aquarium for those who feel compelled to touch the little darlings. The discovery pyramid displays space exploration but doesn't come close to the nearby Space Center Houston. Also of note are the two IMAX theaters: one is 3-D and the other is a Ridefilm. On top of all this there is a pool and white-sand beach for children and parents, and an old paddlewheel boat that journeys out into the bay. There is also a large hotel and spa on the grounds.

Just down the road at 2002 Terminal Dr. is the **Texas Aviation Hall of Fame and the Lone Star Flight Museum** (✆ 409/740-7106). It has two hangars filled with aircraft in varying states of reconstruction. Many of the planes are from World War II. Admission is $6 for adults, $4 to children ages 4 to 13.

1 Hope Blvd. ✆ 800/582-4673. www.moodygardens.org. Admission prices vary depending upon the season. You can buy a ticket to just one exhibit or IMAX theater, or buy a full-day pass for all exhibits and theaters that costs $30 but is sometimes cheaper during the off-season. See the website for details. Daily 10am–9pm in summer; Sun–Thurs 10am–6pm and Fri–Sat 10am–8pm rest of year.

FESTIVALS

The three most popular festivals on the island are **Mardi Gras** (Feb/Mar), the **American Institute of Architects (AIA) Sandcastle Competition** (June), and **Dickens on the Strand** (first weekend in Dec). For Mardi Gras, book a hotel room well in advance; it is a tremendously popular celebration with parades, masked balls, and a live-entertainment district around the Strand. Mardi Gras here has some advantages over New Orleans—there are fewer tourists, and it's very lively without all the public displays of drunkenness. For info, call ✆ **888/ 425-4753** or visit www.mardigrasgalveston.com.

The most unusual event is the annual AIA Sandcastle Competition. More than 70 architectural and engineering firms from around the state show up on East Beach and get serious about the building of sandcastles and sand sculptures and take this pastime to new heights. It all happens in 1 day, and the results are phenomenal. Call ✆ **713/520-0155.**

For its Christmas celebration Galveston hosts "Dickens on The Strand," a street party for which revelers dress up in Victorian costume. The entire affair is a testament to just how much we associate traditional Christmas with the Victorian era (perhaps largely due to Dickens himself). The Strand—with its Victorian architecture and the association with its namesake—is a natural venue for such a celebration. The party includes performers, street vendors, readings of Dickens, and music. Admission is charged. Houstonians often come down for it, but for me, it's one of those things you might go to if you're already in the area. Call ✆ **409/765-7834** for more information.

WHERE TO STAY

All the economical hotel/motel chains have properties in Galveston, with higher prices for lodgings along the seawall. Of the big chains, **La Quinta Galveston,** 1402 Seawall Blvd. (✆ 800/531-5900), ranks highly. Galveston also has a dozen B&Bs, most of which are in Victorian-era houses. The most unusual of these is actually a boat tied to Pier 22, **The Stacia Leigh B&B** aboard the *Chryseis* (✆ **409/750-8858;** www.stacia-leigh.com). The owners renovated and modified a large yacht built in 1906 for the European industrialist Louis Renault.

I recommend it for those who are bored of the standard B&B experience. Most of the rooms are midsize, and they have so many interesting details that it's quite outside the ordinary.

Harbor House ⭐ *(Finds)*   A very different kind of hotel for Galveston, the Harbor House is built on a pier overlooking the harbor instead of a beach. It's actually an excellent location, near the Strand District and next to a few restaurants and museums that have taken over the neighboring piers. The architecture and exterior design are quite different as well. Rooms are large and well appointed in modern style without a lot of clutter. Bleached wood floors, Berber carpets, and exposed wood and steel superstructure are design highlights. The hotel offers nine marina slips but no restaurant; however, with so many restaurants within 2 blocks, it isn't missed. The high rate listed below is for special weekends such as Mardi Gras; usually the lower rate applies, and weekday rates are usually less than $100.

No. 28, Pier 21, Galveston, TX 77550. ℂ **800/874-3721** or 409/763-3321. Fax 409/765-6421. www.harbor housepier21.com. 42 units. $135–$205 double. Weekday rates available. Rates include continental breakfast. AE, DC, DISC, MC, V. Parking $8. **Amenities:** Overnight laundry service/dry cleaning. *In room:* A/C, TV, dataport, coffeemaker, hair dryer, iron.

Hotel Galvez ⭐   Galveston's historic grand hotel, the Galvez has been thoroughly renovated to make the guest rooms more comfortable and to correct the mistakes of previous renovations. Rooms are spacious, well furnished (most with two double beds), and conservatively decorated. The hotel is located on the shore facing the seawall and one of the municipal beaches. It is also on the trolley line leading to the Strand district. Again, rates often run less expensive than what is listed below.

2024 Seawall Blvd., Galveston, TX 77550. ℂ **800/WYNDHAM** or 409/765-7721. Fax 409/765-5780. www. wyndham.com. 231 units. $115–$270 double. Extra person $20. Packages available. AE, DC, DISC, MC, V. Valet parking $9; free self-parking. **Amenities:** Restaurant; bar; large outdoor pool; fitness center; Jacuzzi; limited concierge; business center; limited room service; same-day laundry service/dry cleaning. *In room:* A/C, TV, dataport, coffeemaker, hair dryer, iron.

WHERE TO DINE

Seafood is what people come to Galveston for, and there's quite a variety. There are local representatives of chain restaurants such as Landry's and Joe's Crab Shack, which do a credible job, but for the best of Galveston's seafood try one of the places listed below. If you're craving steak, the best in town is **The Steakhouse in the San Luis Resort,** 5222 Seawall Blvd. (ℂ **409/744-1500**).

Gaidos ⭐⭐⭐ SEAFOOD   This restaurant is a Galveston tradition that has been owned and operated by the Gaido family for four generations. The Gaidos have maintained quality by staying personally involved in all the aspects of the restaurant—thus the seafood is fresh and the service attentive. The soups and side dishes are mostly traditional Southern and Gulf Coast recipes that are comfort food for the longtime customers. Main dishes include a few chicken, pork, and beef items but are mainly seafood. The stuffed snapper is the best I've had. If pompano is on the menu, it's worth considering. The steaks and pork chops are high quality and done justice in the kitchen. The menu varies seasonally. The dining room is large, with tables well spread out. There is a large bar area for people waiting for a table.

3800 Seawall Blvd. ℂ **409/762-9625.** Reservations not accepted. Main courses $14–$33; complete dinners $19–$29. AE, DISC, MC, V. Daily 11:45am–10:30pm. Closes an hour or 2 earlier during low season.

Saltwater Grill ★★★ SEAFOOD   This restaurant prints up a menu daily that usually includes some inventive seafood pasta dishes, perhaps a gulf red snapper pan-sautéed and topped with lump crabmeat, a fish dish with an Asian bent, gumbo and/or bouillabaisse, and a few nonseafood options. The preparation shows a light touch. The starters are excellent. I had asparagus spears fried in a tempura-style batter so thin as to be translucent—and they were cooked perfectly. Situated in an old building near the Strand, the dining room has a pleasant mix of past and present, formal and informal.

2017 Post Office St. ⓒ **409/762-FISH.** Reservations recommended. Main courses $12–$27. AE, DC, MC, V. Mon–Fri 11am–2pm; Mon–Thurs 5–10pm; Fri–Sat 5–11pm; Sun 5–9pm. Free parking in rear.

Shrimp 'n' Stuff (*Value*) SEAFOOD   This small unassuming restaurant where you order at the counter is thought by many locals to serve the best seafood for the money. The seafood is mostly fried Southern-style and served with hush puppies. I love the fried fish and the oysters most of all. Especially popular are the oyster and the shrimp po'boys, the fried shrimp, and the seafood platter.

3901 Ave. O. ⓒ **409/763-2805.** Reservations not accepted. Main courses $7–$10. AE, DC, MC, V. Sun–Thurs 10:30am–8pm; Fri–Sat 10:30am–9pm.

10 Side Trips to East Texas

BEAUMONT & PORT ARTHUR

By taking I-10 east towards New Orleans, you'll arrive in **Beaumont** in 1½ hours. Beaumont is an inland port, a refinery town and manufacturing center, with a population of 120,000. Twenty minutes beyond Beaumont, on the Louisiana border is **Orange** (pop. 20,000), another refinery town, and southeast, to the coast is **Port Arthur** (pop. 60,000), another refinery town. This area isn't the prettiest part of East Texas, but it is the most urban and economically active. Boosters of these three cities dubbed it the "Golden Triangle," for which they caught plenty of abuse from other Texans because of the gaping chasm between reality and propaganda. They have since toned it down to the "Cajun Triangle," underlining the fact that much of the population is Cajun, having moved here from southwest Louisiana during the oil boom years.

It was just outside of Beaumont, on a rise of land called Spindletop, where drillers struck the world's first true gusher in 1901, thereby initiating the long association of Texas with oil. A large granite monument to the well lies south of town just off the highway to Port Arthur. Other attractions include a small fire-fighting museum and a museum dedicated to Babe Didrikson Zaharias, a native of Beaumont and considered by many to be the most amazing woman athlete of the century. (She dominated the women's golf tour, was all-American in basketball, and held world records in several track and field events.) For information on these and other area attractions, contact the **Beaumont Convention & Visitors Bureau,** 801 Main St., Beaumont (ⓒ **409/880-3749** or 800/392-4401), open weekdays from 8am to 5pm. If time is not on your side, you will probably want to drive right on through Beaumont, but should you need a place to spend the night, the national chains are represented mostly along I-10, including a **Hilton,** 2355 I-10 (ⓒ **800/HILTONS**), and an upscale **Holiday Inn,** 3950 I-10 (ⓒ **800/HOLIDAY**). If you should want to stop for lunch or an early dinner, try **Richard's Café,** 2510 College St. (ⓒ **409/835-7063**). You can get any of the classics of Beaumont-style home cookin', such as oxtails and gravy, meatloaf, or smothered pork chops, and all of the sides. Gumbo and a couple of other Creole specialties are also on the menu. For dessert, sample a piece of their assorted homemade pies.

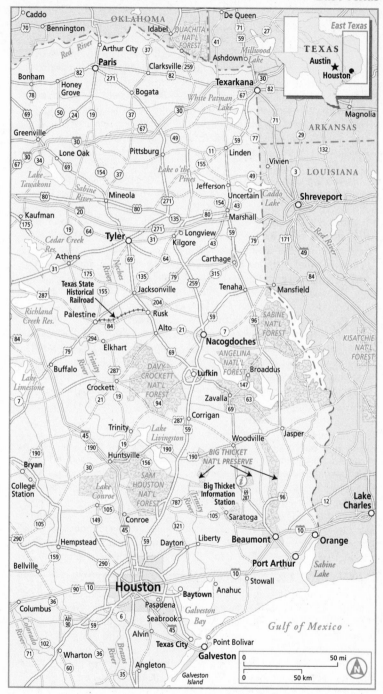

Race Relations in East Texas

Travelers to East Texas might well wonder about visiting here. In the last 10 years there have been several news stories about racially motivated hate crimes. These stories provoke—but leave unanswered—questions like "Will visitors feel safe here? Will they feel welcome?" And because the news coverage focuses on the crime first and the community second, it can invoke in the reader's mind the prevailing image of the old Southern town—closed, repressive, and ready to explode, where outsiders are viewed as either meddlers or provocateurs. This isn't the case, but one can't deny that racial prejudice still exists in East Texas, that there are groups of the Klan here, and that hate crimes have occurred. Given these facts, you might be surprised by what I say next—that race relations in East Texas, as they play out day to day, are far from seething; that they are actually open, respectful, and even cordial. I've spent time in these places and I've looked into this issue. The Klan may be out there, but they are isolated and marginalized. Their rallies are usually better attended by the press than by their own members. In short, civil society in East Texas is not broken and divided.

A case in point is the town of Jasper (pop. 9,000), where James Byrd, an African-American man, was brutally murdered by three whites in 1998. I was there 8 months ago on an assignment to interview people from all sectors of society. I went there expecting to find a polarized community, but what I heard and saw convinced me that Jasper was no powder keg. Roughly half of the town's population is black, and blacks occupy several of the most powerful positions in the community, including the office of mayor. Their personal safety was a nonissue for them.

Port Arthur is much like Beaumont only smaller and not on the way to anywhere. Like Beaumont, it has a famous daughter—the '60s blues and rock icon, Janis Joplin. She doesn't have her own museum, but the **Museum of the Gulf Coast,** 700 Proctor St. (© **409/982-7000**), has a groovy exhibit honoring her, including a replica of her psychedelic Porsche, her album covers, and several personal possessions. The museum also displays a collection of artwork by Port Arthur native Robert Rauschenberg, the painter; it's a general survey featuring a lot of his prints. The museum is open Monday through Saturday from 9am to 5pm, Sunday from 1pm to 5pm; admission is $3.50 for adults, $1.50 for children.

PINEY WOODS & BIG THICKET NATIONAL PRESERVE

If from Beaumont you drive north on Tex. 69, you immediately enter the forestland known in Texas as the **Piney Woods.** This is a lovely part of the state that stretches all the way north to Arkansas. Tex. 69 runs through the heart of it and is one of the most enjoyable drives in the state, especially in the fall or the early spring, which are my favorite times for visiting East Texas. Several of the following attractions can be reached by this road. The first of these is the **Big Thicket National Preserve.** The new information station for the preserve (© **409/246-2337;** www.nps.gov/bith) is 30 miles from Beaumont, 8 miles past the town of Kountze. It will be on the right, just off the highway at the

Yes, some people were thought to be prejudiced, but they didn't consider these people dangerous, even though one of the killers did, in fact, come from the community. The black and white communities in Jasper do tend to congregate amongst themselves, but they also interact and share a sense of community.

In other towns of East Texas I've encountered a greater or lesser degree of separation, but always with an easy interaction. The exception to this is the all-white town of Vidor (pop. 11,000), which lies about 10 miles east of Beaumont. Vidor is infamous as a stronghold of the Klan. It has been labeled by *Texas Monthly Magazine* as the most hate-filled town in Texas. In 1994 the Department of Housing and Urban Development persuaded four black families to integrate Vidor's public housing, but after being harassed, snubbed, and threatened, these families chose to move.

Integration still hasn't made it to Vidor, but it has to the rest of East Texas. Its progress, to be sure, has been uneven. Vestiges of segregation remain, especially with housing: A recent study found Beaumont and Port Arthur to have the most segregated neighborhoods of any large city in Texas (with Houston and Dallas next on the list and decreasing as you moved west, with the least segregated city being El Paso). Progress has been quicker in fields such as education, employment opportunities, and access to services. Nowadays racial discrimination has retreated to more subtle manifestations (the same sort of thing you'll find elsewhere) and the infrequent but chilling acts of a small throwback group filled with hate.

intersection of Highway 69 and Farm Road 420. The station is open daily from 9am to 5pm, except for Christmas and New Year's Day.

The Big Thicket is a lowland forest that occupies a land of swamps, bayous, and creeks. It is dotted with the occasional meadow, but for the most part grows so dense as to become impassable. In earlier times, it extended over 3 million acres and was an impenetrable and hostile place for early settlers. Stories abound of people getting lost in these woods and of outlaws using the place for their hideouts. With lumbering, oil exploration, roads, and settlement, the Big Thicket has been reduced to a tenth of its original size. Of what's left, almost 100,000 acres have been preserved by acts of Congress. The preserved area is not one large expanse of land but 12 separate units, most of which follow the courses of rivers, creeks, and bayous.

The most remarkable thing about the Big Thicket is its diversity of life: The land is checkered with different ecological niches that bring together species coexisting nowhere else. It has been called the American Ark. Hickory trees and blue birds from the eastern forests dwell close by cacti and roadrunners from the American Southwest and southern cypress trees and alligators from the southern coastal marshes. The variety is astonishing. Of the five species of North American insect-eating plants, four live inside the Big Thicket.

For the visitor, the area offers opportunities for hiking, canoeing, and primitive camping. Some of the units are closed during hunting season (mid-Sept to mid-Jan) and some might be closed by flooding. You can get maps and detailed information on the hiking trails, free permits for primitive camping, and books about this fascinating area at the information station. The choice of trails offers walks anywhere from half a mile to 20 miles. Although leaving the designated hiking trails is permitted, you must be careful not to get lost; trailblazing in this dense brush can be slow-going and painful. Canoeing in some ways has an advantage over hiking, though it limits your travel to those waterways with easy access for dropping off and picking up the canoes. At the station, you can get information about canoe outfitters who operate from the towns of Kountze and Silsbee, mostly just from late spring to early fall. For lodging and food, you'll have to rely on the establishments in one of the nearby towns; there are no such facilities in the preserve. If you're in Kountze during lunchtime on any weekday, the most interesting place to eat is at the county courthouse, where most of the locals like to show up.

NATIONAL FORESTS

North and west of the Big Thicket, the ecological complexity gives way to pine forest habitat. Inside this large belt of pine forest are four national forests that provide opportunities for hiking, camping, boating, and fishing. These areas are a nice getaway, especially in the nonsummer months when the weather is more agreeable. They are much less visited than national parks and forests elsewhere. You can easily get to them from either Beaumont or Houston. Highway 69 leads directly into **Angelina National Forest** about 50 miles north of Kountze. And the **Sam Houston National Forest** is only 55 miles north of Houston (take I-45). The other two are **Davy Crockett National Forest,** north of Sam Houston National Forest, and the **Sabine National Forest,** east of Angelina National Forest, on the Louisiana border. Each of these forests is roughly 150,000 acres, and each offers more or less the same activities: hiking, camping, boating, and fishing with such facilities as boat ramps, camping grounds, and hiking trails. For canoeing, there are a few interesting places in these forests, but it's mostly large expanses of open water, which aren't as fun as what you'll find in the Big Thicket or Lake Caddo (described below).

When the weather is agreeable, they are lovely places for hiking, especially in Sam Houston National Forest or Davy Crockett, which have the majority of trails. One hiking trail in Sam Houston is 126 miles long and crosses private property in three or four places; this is a real standout for Texas, which despite its image isn't such a wide-open state. Landowners here are firm believers in barbed-wire fences and the rights of private property, but this trail makes use of the goodwill of local landowners. Fishing draws many visitors, and a lot of places rent boats and equipment and can sell a temporary fishing licenses ($20) in the towns that lie in or next to these national forests. Your best bet for fishing is the Angelina or Sabine forests.

For general information about a specific national forest, visit www.southern region.fs.fed.us/texas or call one of the following numbers. The Sam Houston National Forest ranger offices are in the town of New Waverly (© 936/344-6205); Davy Crockett National Forest ranger offices are in Crockett (© 936/655-2299); Angelina National Forest ranger offices are in Zavalla (© 936/897-1068); and the Sabine National Forest ranger offices are in Hemphill (© 409/787-3870).

Kids Texas State Railroad State Park

After passing through the Angelina National Forest, Highway 69 continues through Lufkin before reaching the town of Rusk, a drive of about 60 miles. Here, you can ride an old steam locomotive train 25 miles through pine forest to the town of Palestine and back again. Many railroad enthusiasts consider this to be one of the best steam train rides in the country. On the days when the railroad is in operation, trains leave each terminus at the same time and pass each other at the mid-point. Passengers travel in vintage railway cars, either in first class (which has air-conditioning in summer only) or regular. The tracks and right of way and the land surrounding both terminuses belong to Texas's state parks. The train runs on a limited schedule (usually weekends) from March to October. The round-trip journey through pine forest takes 4 hours and costs $15 regular and $20 first class for an adult, $9 and $12 for children 3 to 12 years old. For general information and reservations, call © 903/683-2561 (or 800/442-8951 toll-free in Texas).

CADDO LAKE & JEFFERSON

Caddo Lake and the town of **Jefferson** (pop. 2,600) share a curious history. The former owes its origin, and the latter its glory days to an immense, naturally occurring logjam on the Red River, which was known as the "Great Raft." This logjam existed for centuries and stretched from 80 to 150 miles along the river, raising the water level upstream enough to form Caddo Lake and to make Big Cypress Bayou navigable by steamboat as far as Jefferson. The town became the biggest river port in Texas and the sixth-largest city. In fact, commerce was so good during the mid–19th century that of the Texas ports, only Galveston shipped more tonnage. But this prosperity came to an abrupt end when the Army Corps of Engineers dynamited the raft in 1873, shrinking the lake and isolating the town. The lake is back, owing to an earthen damn built by the Corps in 1914.

The town is back, too, but now its livelihood depends in large part on B&Bs and antiques stores. The return of good times to Jefferson dates from about 1961 with the restoration of the old Excelsior Hotel (now called Excelsior House) by the town's garden club. This sparked a restoration frenzy that has made Jefferson the best-restored town in East Texas. In fact, the entire central part of town is listed in the National Register of Historic Places, with a number of antebellum houses (several turned into B&Bs), churches, and commercial buildings listed. It is a pleasant place to visit and stroll about. Weekends are when the town is most lively, with several tours offered; weekdays are when you get the best lodging rates. One of the best attractions is robber baron Jay Gould's personal railroad car, the **Atalanta** ($2 guided tour): It is in great condition, has a fascinating history, and gives the visitor a wonderful idea of luxury travel in the late 19th century.

Jefferson offers better lodging than what you'll find at Caddo Lake, and when in Jefferson, the place to stay for me is the **Excelsior House** (© 903/665-2513;

http://theexcelsiorhouse.com), which has been in continuous operation, more or less, since 1850. The 15 rooms are all furnished with antiques, many of which were here before the hotel was purchased by the garden club. Guests are invited to take a fun little tour of the hotel (nonguests $4). You can also stay at one of the many B&Bs in town. For a list of these as well as information on tours, contact the **Marion County Chamber of Commerce** at © **888/GO-RELAX** or 903/665-2672, or visit www.jefferson-texas.com. There are several dining options, including **Matt's,** 109 N. Polk St. (© **903/665-9237**), a Tex-Mex joint, and the **Bakery Restaurant,** 201 W. Austin St. (© **903/665-2253**) for home cooking, both of which I recommend.

Jefferson is situated between two lakes. To the west is Lake O' the Pines, which is good for swimming and general recreation, but the real point of interest is Caddo Lake, some 10 miles to the east. It is a large lake of 26,800 acres, half of which is in Louisiana, but the more interesting half is in Texas, where the lake breaks up into smaller channels removed from most of the boat traffic. The small town of **Uncertain** (pop. 300) is on the southern shore of the lake. Here you can get a tour and find lodging. Also on the southern shore is **Caddo Lake State Park** (© **903/679-3351**). Like several state parks, it has cabins for rent, which are popular and must be reserved well in advance by calling the central reservation number at © **512/389-8900.** It also has campsites, which you can reserve by calling the park.

Caddo Lake is for boating or canoeing, not swimming. Instead of being an open expanse of water, it's more like a watery forest broken up into several smaller areas. Cypress trees draped in Spanish moss crowd the lake's broken shore, their roots rising from the murky water in deformed shapes. The lake also harbors abundant wildlife, including alligators, otters, water snakes, and many types of waterfowl.

For a tour, you have several options. You can get a seat on an old-fashioned steamboat that runs from spring to fall. **Caddo Lake Steamboat Co.** (© **903/789-3978**) offers a 1-hour trip along the main water channels that costs $15 per person. It's fun, especially for kids, but for a closer look at the lake and its wildlife, try a tour on a pontoon boat (1½ hr.) that takes you beyond the main channel of the lake; contact **Caddo Grocery** in Uncertain (© **903/789-3495;** www.caddogrocery.com). An even closer look can be had by contacting **Mystique Tours** (© **903/679-3690**), run by David J. Applebaum, a highly recommended guide. The tour takes 2 to 3 hours on a smaller boat. Your final option is to rent a canoe and paddle into the quiet parts of the lake that see few motorboats because they're too shallow and have too many roots below the surface. Try a couple of places called Carter's Lake and Clinton Lake. Talk to the rangers at the state park. They can point out on a map the canoe routes and put you in touch with the concessionaire.

6

The Texas Gulf Coast

by Don & Barb Laine

Warm year-round temperatures and the blue-green waters of the Gulf of Mexico make this region the vacationland of Texas. This is where Texans come to escape the crowds and stress of Houston and Dallas and the icy winter cold of Amarillo.

The Texas Gulf Coast gives us wonderful beaches like Padre Island National Seashore and South Padre Island, with deep-sea fishing, boating, swimming, and even surfing. In addition, this region is one of the premier bird-watching areas in America, with a number of wildlife refuges and other sites where you might spy species of birds seen nowhere else in the United States. One warning, though: The conditions that bring numerous birds here also attract another smaller but extremely annoying species of wildlife, so those planning trips to the coast need to carry plenty of mosquito repellent.

Corpus Christi, the area's largest city, remains a comfortable and inviting community while offering practically all the big-city amenities; and the fishing boats that head into the Gulf of Mexico each day bring back some of the best seafood you've ever tasted. Gulf Coast towns such as Rockport are evolving as art centers, with fine art galleries and a growing number of resident artists; and a growing interest in the region's rich history and natural resources has helped produce some fascinating museums. In short, the Gulf Coast offers an escape from the serious side of Texas—the cities with their traffic jams and business suits—and there is plenty more here than just a beach.

1 Corpus Christi

207 miles SW of Houston; 377 miles S of Dallas; 143 miles S of San Antonio; 691 miles SE of El Paso

This major deepwater seaport is a fun place to visit and a good base for exploring Padre Island and other attractions. With a population of just under 300,000 people, Corpus Christi is the eighth largest city in Texas, but it doesn't feel like a city. Possibly because of its waterfront and mild weather, Corpus Christi has an appealing small-town atmosphere. Visitors will want to check out the museums, aquarium, and our favorite stop here, the USS *Lexington* aircraft carrier. Then hit the beach for some serious R&R.

ESSENTIALS

GETTING THERE

BY PLANE The **Corpus Christi International Airport,** located within the city limits on the south side of Tex. 44, west of Padre Island Drive/Tex. 358 (© 361/289-0171), is served by **American Eagle** (© 800/433-7300); **Atlantic Southeast/Delta** (© 800/221-1212); **Continental/Continental Express**

(© 800/523-3273); and **Southwest** (© 800/435-9792). All the major car-rental agencies can be found here.

BY CAR Tex. 35 follows the Gulf Coast—albeit slightly inland—from the Houston and Galveston area to Corpus Christi. From San Antonio follow I-37 southeast to Corpus Christi.

GETTING AROUND

Most visitors to Corpus Christi will use a car to get around. Mostly free parking is fairly easy to find, and traffic isn't all that bad, considering that this is a small city. A bus service operates in summer; check with the Convention & Visitors Bureau or call © **361/289-2600** for the current schedule.

Downtown embraces the intersection of I-37 and Tex. 286, known as the Crosstown Expressway, and continues east to the bay. Shoreline Boulevard runs along the bay, and major downtown arteries leading westward are Main, Leop-ard, Lipan, Laredo, and Agnes streets.

VISITOR INFORMATION

Contact the **Corpus Christi Convention & Visitors Bureau,** 1201 N. Shore-line Blvd. (© **800/678-6232** or 361/881-1888; www.corpuschristicvb.com). Visitor centers are located at 1823 N. Chaparral, 1433 I-37, and 14252 S. Padre Island Dr.

FAST FACTS The **Corpus Christi Medical Center** (www.ccmedicalcenter. com), has three locations: Doctors Regional, 3315 S. Alameda (© **361/761-1400**); Bay Area, 7101 S. Padre Island Dr. (© **361/761-1200**); and The Heart Hospital, 7002 Williams Dr. (© **361/761-6800**). The main **post office,** 809 Nueces Bay Blvd., is open Monday through Friday from 7:30am to 5:30pm and Saturday from 8am to 1pm.

WHAT TO SEE & DO
THE TOP ATTRACTIONS

Art Museum of South Texas This huge modern art museum is bound to have something you like on display. It offers changing exhibits from a variety of mediums, and frequently exhibits works from the museum's permanent collec-tion—art of the Americas, mostly Texas and the surrounding states including northern Mexico. In addition, a small gallery contains local artists' works for sale. Lectures, workshops, and musical performances are scheduled regularly; call or check the website for the current schedule. Allow 1 to 2 hours for your museum visit.

1902 N. Shoreline Blvd. © **361/825-3500.** Fax 361/825-3520. www.stia.org. Admission $3 adults; $2 stu-dents, active military personnel, and seniors over 60; free for children 12 and under and for everyone on Thurs. Tues–Sat 10am–5pm; Sun 1–5pm; first Thurs each month 10am–9pm. Closed major holidays.

Asian Cultures Museum & Educational Center ★ The place to come to explore Asian and Far Eastern cultures, this gem of a museum contains more than 10,000 square feet of exhibits. You'll see a 5-foot-tall bronze Buddha statue, a Singapore taxicab (bicycle-powered), some fascinating Kabuki theater dolls (our favorite exhibits here), Noh theater masks, and Japanese kimonos, as well as clay circle figures (buried with the remains of the dead). The museum also hosts special events. Allow 1 hour.

1809 N. Chaparral St. © **361/882-2641.** www.geocities.com/asiancm. Admission $5 adults, $2 children 12 and under. Tues–Sat 9am–5pm. Closed major holidays.

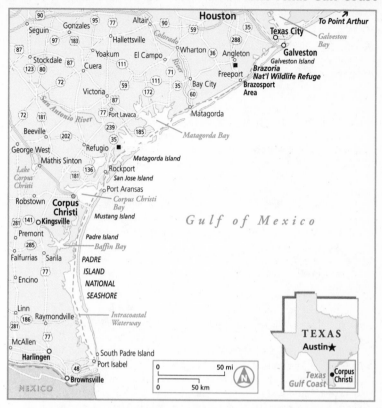

Corpus Christi Botanical Gardens ★★ Kids

These delightful gardens along Oso Creek offer a refreshing escape from the museums and other city attractions of Corpus Christi. Here you can wander among gardens and wetlands and see dozens of tropical hibiscus, exotic bromeliads, cacti, stunning plumeria, and a wide variety of desert and tropical plants. The rose garden contains some 300 roses in a tranquil setting of arbors, trellises, and benches; and there are some 2,000 orchids in a specially constructed orchid greenhouse. The shady Bird & Butterfly Trail—a favorite of kids—meanders through a native south Texas habitat, taking you to an observation tower over Gator Lake, where you'll likely see white pelicans, ducks, egrets, roseate spoonbills, and maybe even the seldom seen but often talked about alligator (if it really does exist). There's also an art gallery with works by local artists, a playground, and a shaded picnic area. Allow 2 hours.

8545 S. Staples St. ☎ 361/852-2100. www.ccbotanicalgardens.org. Admission $3 adults, $2.50 seniors 65 and over, $1.50 children ages 5–12, free for children under 5. Tues–Sun 9am–5pm; call for holiday hours. Leashed pets allowed.

Corpus Christi Museum of Science & History Kids

This well-executed collection includes exhibits on everything from seashells to early American Indians to the numerous plants and animals that call this area home. We especially like the hands-on exhibit depicting shipwrecks—a Spanish ship in 1554 and a

French one in 1686. There are replicas of the Spanish ships *Santa Maria* and *Pinta*, an interesting exhibit on the human impact of Columbus's explorations, and an authentic 16th-century carved dome ceiling from Castile, Spain. Kids enjoy the interactive Children's Wharf. Allow 1½ hours.

1900 N. Chaparral St. (℗ 361/883-2862. Admission $9 adults, $7 seniors 60 and over, $6 military with ID, $5 ages 5–12. Tues–Sat 10am–5pm; Sun noon–5pm. Closed some major holidays.

Texas State Aquarium *Kids*   This is the place to come to explore the under-sea world of the Gulf of Mexico, and you don't even have to get your feet wet! This state-of-the-art facility offers a wide variety of exhibits, ranging from the Flower Gardens Coral Reef to a sea turtle tank and the swamp exhibit, complete with alligator. You'll see a sand tiger shark, barracuda, and other ocean-dwelling creatures of all varieties, and you can touch a stingray or bamboo shark if that's what you really want to do. The latest addition to the aquarium is Dolphin Bay, a protected environment for Atlantic bottle-nosed dolphins that are unable to survive in the wild. Children enjoy the Kids' Port Playground, and there's also a gift shop and food court. Allow 1 to 2 hours.

2710 N. Shoreline Blvd. (℗ 800/477-4853 or 361/881-1200. www.texasstateaquarium.org. Admission $12 adults, $9.95 seniors 60 and older, $6.95 youths ages 4–17, free for children under 4. Mon–Sat 9am–5pm; Sun 10–5pm; open until 6pm Memorial Day to Labor Day. Closed Thanksgiving and Dec 25. Parking $3.

USS Lexington Museum on the Bay *★★*   This floating naval museum was the highlight of our trip to Corpus Christi, in large part because being turned loose in and on a huge World War II–era aircraft carrier is something we had never experienced before, and we found it fascinating. During World War II the *Lexington* was in almost every major operation in the Pacific Theater, and planes from her decks destroyed 372 enemy aircraft in flight and an additional 475 on the ground. She was dubbed "The Blue Ghost" because of the ship's blue-gray color, and because Japanese propaganda radio broadcaster Tokyo Rose repeatedly and mistakenly announced that the Lexington had been sunk. The *Lexington* was modernized in the 1950s and served in the U.S. Seventh Fleet, including duty during the Vietnam War.

Tours of the "Lady Lex" are self-guided. A big screen theater shows IMAX movies, and a video details the history of the ship with historic film footage. There are a number of exhibits, such as a Navy Seal submarine and interpretive displays of ship engines, plus a flight simulator that, for $3.50 per person, provides a wild 5-minute ride simulating the experience of flying. However, it is the experience of climbing up and down ladders between decks, seeing the ship's hospital and mess hall, exploring its narrow passages, and imagining what it would be like to live in the claustrophobic conditions of the crew's sleeping quarters that captivated us. On the flight deck are more than a dozen aircraft from the 1930s to the 1960s, including an F-14A Tomcat and a Cobra helicopter. You'll also get a close-up look at the ship's 40-millimeter antiaircraft guns and peer out from the pilothouse and imagine you're at sea. The *Lexington* has a large gift shop and a snack bar. Allow at least 2 hours.

Note: Although some parts of the USS *Lexington* are easily accessible by anyone, seeing many of the best parts, such as the flight deck, bridge, and engine room involves climbing a lot of steep, old metal stairs and ladders, stepping over metal barricades, and maneuvering through tight passageways. Those with mobility problems will most likely not be able to get to everything.

2914 N. Shoreline Blvd., in Corpus Christi Bay. (℗ 800/523-9539 or 361/888-4873. www.usslexington.com. Admission $10 adults, $5 children ages 4–12, $8 seniors 60 and older and active military. Theater admission

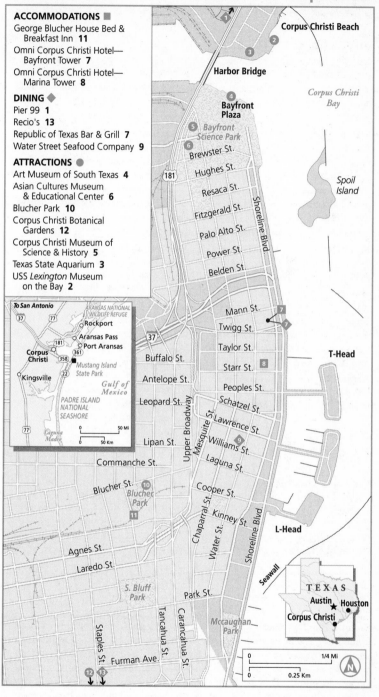

Corpus Christi

ACCOMMODATIONS ■
George Blucher House Bed &
Breakfast Inn **11**
Omni Corpus Christi Hotel—
Bayfront Tower **7**
Omni Corpus Christi Hotel—
Marina Tower **8**

DINING ◆
Pier 99 **1**
Recio's **13**
Republic of Texas Bar & Grill **7**
Water Street Seafood Company **9**

ATTRACTIONS ●
Art Museum of South Texas **4**
Asian Cultures Museum
& Educational Center **6**
Blucher Park **10**
Corpus Christi Botanical
Gardens **12**
Corpus Christi Museum of
Science & History **5**
Texas State Aquarium **3**
USS *Lexington* Museum
on the Bay **2**

Corpus Christi Beach

Harbor Bridge

Bayfront
Plaza

*Corpus Christi
Bay*

Bayfront
Science Park

Brewster St.

Hughes St.

181

Resaca St.

Fitzgerald St.

Palo Alto St.

*Spoil
Island*

Power St.

Belden St.

Shoreline Blvd.

Mann St.

Twigg St.

Taylor St.

T-Head

Buffalo St.

Starr St.

Antelope St.

Peoples St.

Leopard St.

Schatzel St.

Lawrence St.

Upper Broadway

Mesquite St.

Lipan St.

Williams St.

Commanche St.

Laguna St.

Blucher St.

Cooper St.

*Blucher
Park*

Chaparral St.

Kinney St.

Shoreline Blvd.

L-Head

Agnes St.

Water St.

Laredo St.

*S. Bluff
Park*

Park St.

Seawall

Tancahua St.

Carancahua St.

*Mccaughan
Park*

Staples St.

Furman Ave.

To San Antonio
37   77

ARANSAS NATIONAL
WILDLIFE REFUGE

Rockport

181

Aransas Pass

37

Port Aransas

**Corpus
Christi**

361

358

*Mustang Island
State Park*

22

Kingsville

*Gulf of
Mexico*

PADRE ISLAND
NATIONAL
SEASHORE

77

*Laguna
Madre*

0   50 Mi
0   50 Km

TEXAS
Austin ★ Houston
Corpus Christi

0   1/4 Mi
0   0.25 Km

203

$3. Free admission to the Hanger Deck for those with disabilities. Daily 9am–5pm; open until 6pm Memorial Day to Labor Day. Last entry ½ hr. before closing. Parking $2.50.

OUTDOOR ACTIVITIES

Bird-watching, fishing, and watersports are the key outdoor activities here, and some of the best beaches are on nearby Padre Island, which is discussed later in this chapter. Among local parks is the city-maintained **Corpus Christi Beach,** north of Harbor Bridge (© **361/884-7275**), with a playground, showers, and picnicking.

BIRD-WATCHING   Like most of the Texas Gulf Coast, the Corpus Christi area has great birding opportunities. Among the more than 500 species that have been sighted here are brown pelicans, masked ducks, black-bellied whistling ducks, roseate spoonbills, black-necked stilts, ruby-throated hummingbirds, tri-colored herons, and red-shouldered hawks. Good birding spots include the **Corpus Christi Botanical Gardens** (p. 201) as well as **Blucher Park** (downtown at the intersection of Blucher and Carrizo sts.), which is known for attracting songbirds during their spring and fall migrations.

FISHING   This is a wonderful area for both deep-sea and bay fishing. You can cast your line from numerous piers, jetties, and beaches, or head out to sea on a charter or party boat. Charter services are generally similar but might vary in boat size, areas visited, and the captain's personality. Those planning a fishing trip should contact several charter boat companies and discuss the trip to decide which is best for them. Charter boats usually cost from $300 to $400 for a full-day trip for one or two people, while party boats are about $70 per person for a full day. There are numerous guides available, including charter boat services from **Don Hand** (© 361/993-2024), **Salty Aggie Guide Service** (© 800/322-3346 or 361/991-6045), **Ingram's Guide Service** (© 800/368-6032), and **Warren Alan's Fishing Guide Service** (© 877/322-7448 or 361/992-2972; www.texasfishingguides.org/hart). For party boats, try **Copeland's Marine** (© 800/567-5132 or 361/854-1135) or **Captain Clark Fishing** (© 361/884-4369).

WHERE TO STAY

Among the numerous national chain motels in Corpus Christi are **Best Western Garden Inn,** 11217 I-37, Exit 11B (© 800/937-8376 or 361/241-6675); **Comfort Suites,** 3925 S. Padre Island Dr. (© 800/228-5150 or 361/225-2500); **Days Inn,** 4302 Surfside Blvd. (© 800/325-2525 or 361/882-3297); **Embassy Suites Hotel,** 4337 S. Padre Island Dr. (© 800/362-2779 or 361/853-7899); **La Quinta,** 5155 I-37, Exit 3A (© 800/687-6667 or 361/888-5721); **Motel 6,** 845 Lantana St., I-37 Exit 4B (© 800/466-8356 or 361/289-9397); and **Travelodge,** 910 Corn Products Rd., I-37, Exit 5 (© 800/578-7878 or 361/289-5666). A reasonably priced independent motel is the **Sea Shell Inn,** 202 Kleberg Place (© 361/888-5291), with rates for two of $50 to $125. Room tax adds 15% to rates, and the highest rates in the Corpus Christi area are in the summer.

George Blucher House Bed & Breakfast Inn ★★★   This wonderful B&B combines the ambience of an elegant historic home with modern amenities including private bathrooms and plush robes. Built in 1904 for well-to-do Corpus Christi residents George and Alice Von Blucher, this 5,000-square-foot home was purchased in 1999 by history buff Tracey Smith, who thoroughly researched the home's past to guarantee that the restoration be as accurate as possible. After about a year of work the B&B opened with six uniquely decorated units, each named for one of the Von Blucher's children. For instance, the ultra-feminine Pearl's Room is pink, with American and French antiques, a queen-size bed, and a private balcony with views of downtown; and Nellie's Room is decorated in a floral motif, with American and French country furnishings and two twin beds. Most rooms are on the second floor, but one ground-level unit, Jasper's Room, is wheelchair accessible.

Breakfasts here are a splendid event, served by candlelight, and might include entrees such as chicken pecan quiche or eggs Benedict with artichokes, spinach, and cream cheese; and a fruit dish such as baked apple with maple syrup and pecans and wrapped in a puff pastry. There's a library, with a comfortable sitting area and chess, dominos, backgammon, and other games. In addition, the inn is across the street from Blucher Park, a prime bird-watching area. Smoking is not permitted inside.

211 N. Carrizo, Corpus Christi, TX 78401. ℂ 866/884-4884 or 361/884-4884. Fax 361/884-4885. www. georgeblucherhouse.com. 6 units. $100–$175 double. Rates include full breakfast. Holiday and special event weekends require a minimum 2-night stay. MC, V. Children over 12 accepted with prior approval. *In room:* A/C, TV/VCR.

Omni Corpus Christi Hotel ★★ *Value* The best choice in Corpus Christi for those seeking a full-service hotel, the Omni consists of two towers, Bayfront and Marina, overlooking Corpus Christi Bay. The spacious rooms are simply but very tastefully appointed in a classic modern America hotel style, and all have private balconies. Standard rooms have two doubles or one king-size bed, large working desks, plush chairs, large closets, and several telephones. We especially like the basic king rooms, which have floor-to-ceiling windows that offer spectacular views of the Gulf, particularly from the upper floors of the 20-story Bayfront Tower. One of the three on-site restaurants is the highly rated Republic of Texas Bar & Grill (p. 206). Because this hotel gets a lot of weekday business travelers, you'll get especially good rates on weekends.

900 and 707 N. Shoreline Blvd., Corpus Christi, TX 78401. ℂ 800/843-6664 or 361/887-1600. Fax 361/887-6715. www.omnihotels.com. 821 units. $99–$154 double; suites from $200. Golf packages available. AE, DC, DISC, MC, V. Free covered parking. **Amenities:** 3 restaurants; 2 heated indoor/outdoor pools; nearby golf course; nearby lit tennis courts; fully-equipped health club; Jacuzzi; dry sauna; bike rental; airport shuttle; salon; limited room service; massage; laundry service. *In room:* A/C, TV, dataport, hair dryer, iron.

CAMPING

RVers have plenty of camping choices in the Corpus Christi area, and although many of the RV parks will accept tenters, the rates are often the same as for sites with RV hook-ups, and those in tents will be surrounded by RVs. We suggest that tenters head to nearby Padre Island National Seashore or other public lands in the area, which are listed elsewhere in this chapter.

Among RV parks here, the best is **Colonia del Rey,** 1717 Waldron Rd., near the entrance to Padre Island (ℂ 800/580-2435 for reservations, or 361/937-2435; www.gocampingamerica.com/coloniadelrey), which has a swimming pool, Jacuzzi, and all the other usual amenities, and can accommodate rigs up to 85 feet long. Some sites have telephones, and rates are $21 to $23 for full hook-ups, including cable TV.

WHERE TO DINE

The favorite local fast-food burger chain is **Whataburger,** which began and remains headquartered in Corpus Christi. It has more then 20 locations in the city and over 500 more throughout Texas and the surrounding states.

Whataburgers are open around the clock with similar prices but slightly better food (at least in our opinion) than the better-known national chains. And they must be doing something right—the company celebrated its 53rd anniversary in 2003.

Pier 99 SEAFOOD/STEAKS *Value*   For good food at reasonable prices and a definitely upbeat atmosphere, leave your suit and tie in the car and head to Pier 99. This is a fun beach hangout, where the noisy dining room has way too many neon beer signs and other items adorning the walls and even the ceiling, from which a large replica of a shark peers down at you. We like the back deck, which offers a good view of the USS *Lexington* aircraft carrier in the harbor. The menu features fresh seafood (what else?) like the fried shrimp, fish, or oyster plates for under $8; an all-you-can-eat fish special; and more elaborate entrees such as shrimp scampi, Cajun shrimp, boiled shrimp, and Alaska snow crab. You can also get chicken, good rib-eye steaks, and burgers. You won't leave Pier 99 hungry. There's often music on the back deck (no cover charge), which brings up one of the house rules: Don't feed the birds or band members, regardless of how hungry or cute you think they look.

2822 N. Shoreline Blvd. ℂ **361/887-0764.** Main courses $4.95–$17. AE, DISC, MC, V. Sun–Thurs 11am–9pm; Fri–Sat 11am–10pm.

Recio's ★★ *Finds* MEXICAN   South Texas is littered with *taquerias*—restaurants that specialize in *taquitos* (similar to a burrito but folded), tacos, enchiladas, and other Tex-Mex and Mexican favorites—and Recio's is among the best. Locally owned and operated by Robert and Minerva Recio, this justly popular restaurant serves homemade cooked-to-order food in a pleasant, casual atmosphere. Decor is simple, with an open dining room of white walls, light wood tables, and colorful paintings by local artists. Try Rob's Parillada for Two, a platter of beef and chicken fajitas, topped with bell peppers and onions and served with ranchero beans, rice, guacamole, pico de gallo, and salad; or a barbecue platter of mesquite-smoked brisket or ribs. Breakfast is served all day on weekends.

3150 S. Alameda St. ℂ **361/888-4040.** Main courses $3.75–$8.95. AE, DC, DISC, MC, V. Mon–Sat 7am–8pm; Sun 7am–2pm.

Republic of Texas Bar & Grill ★★ *Moments* STEAK   This is the spot to celebrate a special occasion. Located on the 20th floor of the Omni Bayfront hotel, the Republic of Texas Bar & Grill is expensive, and worth every penny. There are four levels to the dining room, all with breathtaking views of the bay and a refined, subdued atmosphere. Appetizers include the delightful giant portobello mushroom, stuffed with sweet sausage and garlic herb cheese. This is primarily a steakhouse, and all beef is top USDA premium choice corn-fed that is hand cut and grilled over a fire of oak and mesquite. You won't be disappointed with any of the beef, but we particularly recommend the 16-ounce New York strip or the 24-ounce porterhouse. The menu usually also offers several game dishes, such as mesquite-grilled quail, and seafood such as the wonderfully moist and flaky mesquite-grilled Pacific Northwest salmon. Sides include huge baked Idaho potatoes and garlic mashed potatoes, which are fine, but the house specialty hash browns are exquisite. There is also an extensive wine list. Service is excellent.

At the Omni Bayfront Hotel, 900 N. Shoreline Blvd. ℂ **361/886-3515.** www.omnihotels.com/republic. Reservations strongly recommended. Main courses $14–$35. AE, DISC, MC, V. Mon–Sat 5:30–10:30pm; Sun 5:30–9pm.

Water Street Seafood Company ★★★ SEAFOOD Our vote for the best seafood restaurant in Corpus Christi goes to the Water Street Seafood Company and its attached sister restaurant, the Water Street Oyster Bar, which has the same menu. Naturally, the restaurants are decorated in a nautical motif. The extensive menu includes specialties such as shrimp enchiladas—red corn tortillas stuffed with shrimp, Monterey and hot pepper jack cheeses, and topped with a spicy homemade sauce—and a mesquite-grilled 8-ounce Angus tenderloin filet. But before even looking at the menu those in the know check the blackboard for the daily fish specials, which can be prepared blackened, mesquite-grilled, sautéed, broiled, or fried, and are served with a salad, seasonal vegetables, and the restaurant's wonderful rice pilaf. Everything at Water Street is prepared fresh, and the staff is very accommodating about making substitutions, meeting individuals' dietary needs, or providing smaller portions (at a lower price!).

309 N. Water St. © **361/882-8683.** Reservations accepted for large parties only. Main courses $5.95–$18. AE, DISC, MC, V. Sun–Thurs 11am–10pm; Fri–Sat 11am–11pm. Closed Thanksgiving and Dec 25.

2 Padre Island National Seashore ⓕ

37 miles SE of Corpus Christi; 180 miles S of San Antonio; 414 miles S of Dallas

Some 70 miles of delightful white-sand beach, picturesque sand dunes, and warm ocean waters make Padre Island National Seashore a favorite year-round playground along the Texas Gulf Coast. One of the longest stretches of undeveloped coastline in America, this is an ideal spot for swimming, sunbathing, fishing, beachcombing, windsurfing, camping, and four-wheeling, and also offers excellent bird-watching opportunities and a chance to see several species of rare sea turtles. The island was named for Padre José Nicolás Balli, a Mexican priest who in 1804 founded a mission, settlement, and ranch about 26 miles north of the island's southernmost tip.

Padre Island is a barrier island, essentially a sand bar that helps protect the mainland from the full force of ocean storms. Like other barrier islands, one of the constants of Padre Island is change; wind and waves relentlessly shape and re-create the island, as grasses and other hardy plants strive to get a foothold in the shifting sands. Padre Island's Gulf side, with miles of beach accessible only to those with four-wheel-drive vehicles, offers wonderful surf fishing; while the channel between the island and mainland—the Laguna Madre—offers excellent windsurfing and a protected area for small power and sailboats.

ESSENTIALS

GETTING THERE From Corpus Christi take Tex. 358 (South Padre Island Dr.) southeast across the JFK Causeway to Padre Island, and follow Park Road 22 south to the national seashore. The drive takes 45 minutes to an hour.

VISITOR INFORMATION For information contact **Padre Island National Seashore,** P.O. Box 181300, Corpus Christi, TX 78480-1300 (© **361/949-8068;** www.nps.gov/pais). The Park Service also maintains a recorded beach and road condition information line (© **361/949-8175**). The park is open 24 hours a day.

The **visitor center complex,** along Park Road 22 at Malaquite Beach, has an observation deck, a bookstore, and a variety of exhibits, including the endangered Kemp's ridley sea turtle. In the same complex are a snack bar and **Padre Island Park Company** (© **361/949-9368;** www.foreverresorts.com), a store that sells camping and fishing supplies and gift items, and rents chairs, umbrellas, body boards, and other beach toys. The visitor center is open from 8:30am to 6pm Memorial Day through Labor Day weekend, and from 8:30am to 4:30pm the rest of the year (closed Dec 25 and Jan 1), and the snack bar and store are usually open similar hours.

FEES & REGULATIONS   Entry for up to 7 days costs $10 per vehicle, or $5 per individual on foot or bike. There is also a $5 day-use fee at Bird Island Basin. Regulations here are much like those at other National Park Service properties, which essentially require that visitors not disturb wildlife or damage the site's natural features and facilities. Pets must be leashed and are not permitted on the swimming beach in front of the visitor center. Although driving off road is permitted on some sections of beach, the dunes, grasslands, and tidal flats are closed to all vehicles.

WHEN TO GO   Summer is the busiest time here, although it is generally hot (highs in the 90s) and very humid. Sea breezes in late afternoon and evening help moderate the heat. Winters are generally mild, with highs from the 50s to the 70s, and lows in the 40s and 50s. Only occasionally does the temperature drop below 40°F (4°C), and a freeze is extremely rare. Hurricane season (June–Oct) is the rainiest time of the year and also has the highest surf. Our favorite months to visit Padre Island are November and December, when it is still usually warm enough for swimming but not nearly as hot or crowded as summer.

SAFETY   Swimmers and those walking barefoot on the beach should watch out for the Portuguese man-of-war, a blue jellyfish that can cause a painful sting. There are also poisonous rattlesnakes in the dunes, grasslands, and mud flats; and hazardous materials, such as medical waste, occasionally wash up on the beach.

RANGER PROGRAMS   Various **interpretive programs** are held year-round, ranging from guided beach or birding walks to talks outside the visitor center and evening campground campfire programs. These programs usually last from 30 to 45 minutes and cover subjects such as migrating or resident birds, seashells, the island's plant life or animals, or things that wash up on the beach. There's also a **Junior Ranger Program** for kids 5 to 13, who answer questions in a free booklet and talk with rangers about the national seashore to earn certificates, badges, and sea-turtle stickers.

WHAT TO SEE & DO
EXPLORING THE HIGHLIGHTS BY CAR
Padre Island National Seashore has an 8½-mile paved road, with good views of the Gulf and dunes, that leads to the visitor center complex. In addition, most of the beaches are open to licensed street-legal motor vehicles; some sections have hard-packed sand that makes an adequate roadbed for two-wheel-drive vehicles while most of the beach requires four-wheel-drive. See "Four-Wheeling," below.

OUTDOOR ADVENTURES
BEACHCOMBING   The best times for beachcombing are usually early mornings, and especially immediately after a storm when you're apt to find a variety of seashells, seaweed, driftwood, and the like. These types of items can be collected, but live animals and historical or archaeological objects should be left. Among shells sometimes found at Padre Island are lightning whelks, moon snails, Scotch bonnets, Atlantic cockles, bay scallops, and sand dollars. The best shell hunting is often in winter, when storms disturb the water and thrust shells ashore; and many of the best shells are often found on Little Shell and Big Shell

beaches, accessible only to those with four-wheel-drive vehicles. Metal detectors are not permitted on the beach.

BIRD-WATCHING & WILDLIFE VIEWING   More than 350 species of birds frequent Padre Island, and every visitor is bound to see and hear at least some of them. The island is a key stopping point for a variety of migratory species traveling between North and Central America, making spring and fall especially good times for bird-watching. And, since a number of species don't get any further south than Padre Island, winter also provides ample birding opportunities. Additionally, this is the northern boundary of some Central American species, such as green jays and jacanas.

Birding here is very easy, especially for those with four-wheel-drive vehicles who can drive slowly down the more remote stretches of beach. Experienced bird-watchers say it is best to remain in your vehicle because humans on foot

The Race to Save the Sea Turtles

The Gulf of Mexico is home to five species of sea turtles, all of which are either endangered or threatened, including the Kemp's ridley, considered to be the most endangered sea turtle in the world with only about 3,000 in existence. Kemp's ridleys have almost circular shells, grow to about 2 feet long, and weigh about 100 pounds. Adults are olive green on top and yellow below, and their main food source is crabs. Their main nesting area historically is along a 16-mile stretch of beach at Playa de Rancho Nuevo in Tamaulipas, Mexico, and although females lay about 100 eggs at a time, only about 1% of the hatchlings survive to adulthood.

In the 1970s, an international effort was begun to establish a second nesting area at Padre Island National Seashore, using the theory that sea turtles always return to the beach where they were hatched to lay their eggs. More than 22,000 eggs were gathered from Playa de Rancho Nuevo between 1978 and 1988, placed in boxes containing Padre Island sand, and shipped to Texas where they were placed in incubators. After hatching, about 13,500 baby turtles were released on the beach at Padre Island National Seashore and allowed to crawl into the water for a quick swim. Fearing that the young turtles would become lunch for predators, National Park Service biologists captured them and sent them to a marine fisheries lab in Galveston, where they spent up to a year growing big enough to have a better chance of survival in the wild. They were then tagged and released into the Gulf of Mexico.

Since then some of the turtles have returned to Padre Island and other sections of the Texas Gulf Coast to nest, and Park Service workers have collected a number of eggs for incubation and eventual release. The eggs are collected in late spring and summer, and anyone seeing a nesting sea turtle is asked to not disturb it but to report its location to national seashore personnel. The public can attend releases of the hatchlings, which usually occur in June and August; for information on release dates call the **Hatchling Hotline** at ✆ **361/949-7163.**

scare off birds sooner than approaching vehicles. As would be expected by its name, Bird Island Basin is also a good choice for birders as long as the marshes have water. The most commonly observed bird is the laughing gull, which is a year-round resident. Other species to watch for include rare brown pelicans plus the more common American white pelicans, long-billed curlews, great blue herons, sandhill cranes, ruddy turnstones, Caspian and Royal terns, willets, Harris' hawks, reddish egrets, northern bobwhites, mourning doves, horned larks, great-tailed grackles, and red-winged blackbirds.

In addition to birds, the island is home to the spotted ground squirrel, which is often seen in the dunes near the visitor center, white-tailed deer, coyotes, black-tailed jackrabbits, lizards, and a number of poisonous and nonpoisonous snakes.

BOATING A boat ramp is located at Bird Island Basin, which provides access to Laguna Madre, a protected bay that is ideal for small power- and sailboats. Boat launching is not permitted on the gulf side of the island, except for sailboats and soft-sided inflatables. To rent a sailboard, contact **Worldwinds Windsurfing** (© **361/949-7472;** www.worldwinds.net) Personal watercraft are not permitted in Laguna Madre (except to get from the boat ramp to open water outside the park boundaries) but are allowed on the Gulf side beyond the 5-mile marker.

FISHING Fishing is great year-round. Surf fishing is permitted everywhere along the Gulf side except at Malaquite Beach, and yields whiting, redfish, black drum, and speckled sea trout; while anglers in Laguna Madre catch flounder, sheepshead, and croaker. A Texas fishing license with a saltwater stamp is required. Licenses, along with current fishing regulations and some fishing supplies, are available at **Padre Island Park Company** (© **361/949-9368;** www.foreverresorts.com).

FOUR-WHEELING Licensed and street-legal motor vehicles (but not ATVs) are permitted on most of the beach at Padre Island National Seashore (but not Malaquite Beach or the fragile dunes, grasslands, and tidal flats). Most standard passenger vehicles can make it down the first 5 miles of South Beach, but those planning to drive farther south down the island (another 55 miles are open to motor vehicles) will need four-wheel-drive vehicles. Markers are located every 5 miles, and those driving down the beach are advised to watch for soft sand and high water, and to carry a shovel, jack, boards, and other emergency equipment. Unless otherwise posted, the speed limit on the beach is 15 mph. Northbound vehicles have the right of way.

HIKING We love walking along the beach, and the national seashore has miles and miles of beach that are ideal for walking and hiking. There's also the paved and fairly easy **Grasslands Nature Trail,** a ¾-mile self-guided loop trail that meanders through grass-covered areas of sand dunes. Numbered posts correspond with descriptions of plants and other aspects of the natural landscape in

---

Tips **For Travelers with Disabilities**

Specially designed fat-tire wheelchairs for use in the sand, and even in the water, are available at no charge at the visitor center. They do require someone to push.

> **Fun Fact** What in the World Is Red Tide?
>
> Up and down the Gulf Coast you'll hear about and sometimes see what is called "red tide," which sounds a lot scarier than the phenomenon really is. Red tide appears to be one of the few environmental problems that we probably can't blame on human beings. It's a naturally occurring situation in which a higher than usual concentration of a type of algae called *Gymnodinium breve* occurs, resulting in discoloration of the ocean water that usually produces red patches on the water surface. The bad part is that this alga produces a toxin that paralyzes fish, including their ability to breathe, so the fish die and often wash up on Gulf Coast beaches such as at Padre Island.
>
> The Texas Department of Health says that it is usually safe to eat fish, crabs, and shrimp during a red tide infestation (although not ones found sick or dead since you wouldn't know what affected them); but you should not eat oysters, clams, or other bivalve mollusks from red tide water because you could get neurotoxic shellfish poisoning, which is not fatal but can cause severe nausea and dizziness. In addition, the red tide alga in the ocean water and even in ocean spray has been known to irritate the lungs, nose, and throat of some people. The good news is that red tides are usually isolated patches that don't affect an entire beach, and usually do not remain in any location very long.

a free brochure available at the trail head or the visitor center. You'll need insect repellent to combat mosquitoes, and because western diamondback rattlesnakes also inhabit the area, stay on the trail and watch where you put your feet and hands.

SWIMMING & SURFING   Warm air and water temperatures make swimming practically a year-round activity here—January through March are really the only time it's too chilly—and swimming is permitted along the entire beach. The most popular swimming area is 4½-mile-long Malaquite Beach, also called Closed Beach, which is closed to motor vehicles. You have to jostle for a spot only at spring break and on summer weekends. Note that there are no lifeguards on duty here. Although waves here are not of the Hawaii or California size, they're often sufficient for surfing, which is permitted in most areas, but not at Malaquite Beach.

WINDSURFING   The Bird Island Basin area on Laguna Madre is considered one of America's best spots for windsurfing because of its warm water, shallow depth, and consistent, steady winds. **Worldwinds Windsurfing (© 361/949-7472;** www.worldwinds.net) sells and rents windsurfing equipment and wetsuits here, and offers windsurfing lessons during the summer. Call for current fees and schedule.

WHERE TO STAY & DINE

The closest hotels and restaurants are in Corpus Christi; see section 1 in this chapter. If you want to stay in the park, you'll have to camp.

Padre Island National Seashore's developed **Malaquite Campground** ✮, about ½ mile north of the visitor center, is a great spot to bed down, with 50 sites ($8 per night) that are available on a first-come first-served basis year-round. Sites, within 100 feet of the beach, have good views of the Gulf, and the campground has cold showers, restrooms, and picnic tables. There are no RV hook-ups, but there is a dump station. For those who don't mind its limitations, it's definitely the best place to camp; it gets crowded only during spring break and on summer weekends.

The primitive **Yarborough Pass Campground,** located on the Laguna Madre 16 miles south of the visitor center, is accessible only with a four-wheel-drive vehicle. It's open all year but has no facilities, and no fee is charged. Get directions from the visitor center before setting out. In addition, free primitive camping is permitted on the **Gulf beaches** and at **Bird Island Basin.**

3 South Padre Island

286 miles S of San Antonio; 366 miles SW of Houston; 531 miles S of Dallas; 815 miles SE of El Paso

South Padre Island is a true resort town, with about 3,000 year-round residents, and an influx of several thousand more when the winter chill sends northerners south in search of sunshine and warmth. Watersports are a major draw, from powerboating, sailing, and windsurfing to bay, surf, and deep-sea fishing. And some of us simply want to relax on the beach, allowing the gentle murmur of the water to soothe our senses and wash away the stress of this hectic modern world. More energetic visitors can also bicycle, play tennis and golf, and go horseback riding. Birding is as popular here as in other areas of south Texas, with more than 300 species.

The sunsets are grand, reflecting in the water of the Laguna Madre, and many restaurants capitalize on their location with outdoor seating. Set your taste buds to enjoy fresh seafood of all kinds prepared in a variety of seasonings— Continental to Mexican, broiled to deep-fried. And if you catch your own, some restaurants will be happy to cook it for you (the ones that do advertise it)!

The town of South Padre Island stretches along 25 miles of sand on the southern tip of Padre Island just across the Laguna Madre from the mainland, and the small town of Port Isabel. Easily accessible by plane into nearby cities, it has become a favored place for conventions. But don't bring your business suits— South Padre Island takes its role of laid-back vacation spot seriously, and ties are expressly forbidden.

ESSENTIALS
GETTING THERE
BY PLANE   The closest airport is the **Brownsville/South Padre Island International Airport** (✆ **956/542-4373;** www.flybrownsville.com) at Brownsville (about 28 miles southwest), which is served by Continental Express (✆ **800/525-0280**). All of the major car-rental companies have desks here.

BY CAR   From U.S. 77/83, which connects to Harlingen, McAllen, and Corpus Christi, take Tex. 100 east to Port Isabel and then across the Queen Isabella Causeway to the south end of South Padre Island. From Brownsville, take Tex. 48 northeast to Tex. 100.

GETTING AROUND
A car is handy on South Padre Island, and parking and traffic congestion are not usually a problem, except possibly during spring break and on summer weekends.

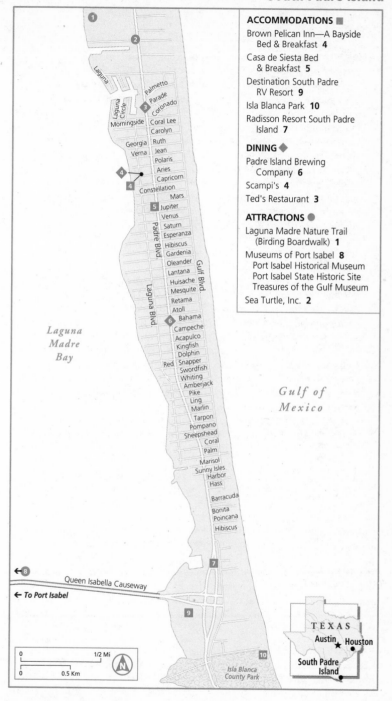

ACCOMMODATIONS ■

Brown Pelican Inn—A Bayside
Bed & Breakfast **4**

Casa de Siesta Bed
& Breakfast **5**

Destination South Padre
RV Resort **9**

Isla Blanca Park **10**

Radisson Resort South Padre
Island **7**

DINING ◆

Padre Island Brewing
Company **6**

Scampi's **4**

Ted's Restaurant **3**

ATTRACTIONS ●

Laguna Madre Nature Trail
(Birding Boardwalk) **1**

Museums of Port Isabel **8**
Port Isabel Historical Museum
Port Isabel State Historic Site
Treasures of the Gulf Museum

Sea Turtle, Inc. **2**

South Padre Island Proclamation

WHEREAS, South Padre Island is a subtropical vacation and meeting destination for hundreds of thousands of people each year; and

WHEREAS, Visitors come across the Laguna Madre bay to the island to escape the workday world, refocusing their priorities on our beautiful white sandy beaches along the Gulf of Mexico, the unequaled recreational opportunities, fresh-caught seafood, game fishing, birding and nature trails, and all of the informal ambience anyone could ever desire for a vacation or for the site of an island convention; and

WHEREAS, Because this pristine atmosphere is sometimes shattered by the appearance of the most blatant symbol of conformity and business throughout the world—the "tie"—it has become necessary to further protect our visitors and citizens. Ties have been spotted in hotel lobbies, along Padre Boulevard, and even poolside at some of our most exotic resorts. The very appearance of a tie causes a discordant note for our visitors, sometimes causing serious regression back to their humdrum and ordinary business lives.

NOW, THEREFORE, be it proclaimed by the Board of Aldermen of the Town of South Padre Island, Texas, the "tie" is detrimental to the welfare of South Padre Island and its visitors and is hereby banished from our land and waters forever. A written warning notice will be issued to first offenders by the South Padre Island Police Department. This warning notice will be accompanied by a complimentary South Padre Island T-Shirt to assist such offenders in adjusting to the correct attire and lifestyles of the island. Second offenders will be fined the amount of a fine silk tie and the offending tie will be confiscated and destroyed.

IN WITNESS THEREOF, I have set my hand and caused the seal of the Town of South Padre Island, Texas, to be affixed this the 4th day of June, 1997.

Edmund K. Cyganiewicz, Mayor
Attested by Joyce Adams, City Secretary

However, it's quite possible that you won't be using your car much, since many of the major hotels, restaurants, and beaches are within easy walking distance of each other. Also, there is a free year-round bus service called The Wave (© **956/ 761-1025**) that operates daily from 7am to 7pm. It runs the length of the island and to Port Isabel, with runs about very 25 minutes. Padre Boulevard is the main drag along the island and runs north-south. Parallel to it are Laguna Boulevard 1 block west and Gulf Boulevard on the east side of the island, facing the Gulf of Mexico.

VISITOR INFORMATION

Contact the **South Padre Island Convention and Visitors Bureau,** 600 Padre Blvd., South Padre Island, TX 78597 (© **800/767-2373** or 956/761-6433; www.sopadre.com), which operates a visitor center. You can pick up maps or talk to the staff for suggestions and advice.

FAST FACTS   Health services are available at **Balley Regional Island Clinic,** 3000 Padre Blvd. The **post office,** 4701 Padre Blvd., is open Monday through Friday from 8am to 4pm, Saturday from 10am to noon.

WHAT TO SEE & DO
DISCOVERING THE AREA'S PAST

Shipwrecks, war, plus some of the happier aspects of this area's history come alive at the facilities of the **Museums of Port Isabel** ✯ with headquarters at the Port Isabel Historical Museum, 317 E. Railroad Ave., Port Isabel (✆ **956/943-7602;** www.portisabelmuseums.com). The two museums and historic lighthouse are within easy walking distance of each other. Allow a half-hour to 1 hour to visit each one.

The excellent **Port Isabel Historical Museum** ✯, located in a restored 1899 Victorian commercial building, houses exhibits that describe the history of the area from the time it was a supply depot during the Mexican-American War, through the Civil War, and the area's development as a shrimping and fishing capital. There are interactive exhibits, a large display of Mexican-American War artifacts, and a fascinating 1906 Victor Morales "Fish Mural," plus a theater. The displays about shipwrecks will interest kids and adults alike. Nearby, the **Treasures of the Gulf Museum** focuses on three Spanish shipwrecks, which occurred in 1554 just off the coast. Exhibits include murals, artifacts, and various hands-on activities, including a children's discovery lab. There is also a theater and gift shop.

The **Port Isabel Lighthouse State Historic Site,** at the west end of the Queen Isabella Causeway, is hard to miss. This 72-foot-high lighthouse, which helped guide ships through Brazos Santiago Pass to Point Isabel from 1852 until 1905, now affords panoramic views of Port Isabel, South Padre Island, and as far as the eye can see out over the Gulf of Mexico. Also on the property is a replica of the lighthouse keeper's cottage made from the 1850 blueprints for the original. The cottage contains exhibits on the history of the lighthouse, and there's a picnic area.

Both museums are open Tuesday through Saturday from 10am to 4pm (last entry at 3:30pm), and the lighthouse and cottage are open daily from 9am to 5pm (last entry at 4pm). Admission to each site is $3 adults, $2 for seniors 55 and older, $1 for students with ID, and free for children under 5. Combination tickets for all three sites cost $7 for adults, $5 for seniors, and $2 for students.

OUTDOOR ACTIVITES

BIRD-WATCHING   More than 300 species of birds make South Padre Island their home during part or most of every year. The **Laguna Madre Nature Trail** ✯, adjacent to the South Padre Island Convention Centre at the north end of town, is a boardwalk that meanders out over the wetlands of the Laguna Madre and around a freshwater pond. There are a few blinds where you can set up a scope and sit for hours unseen by the birds. Some of the birds you might watch for are egrets, herons, oyster-catchers, rails, soras, kingfishers, moorhens, terns, and the white-phase reddish egret. The boardwalk is wheelchair accessible and open 24 hours, free of charge. Plan to spend at least a half-hour here.

FISHING   There have been record-setting catches made in the waters around South Padre Island: The state record blue marlin, at 876½ pounds, was taken offshore.

The beach and jetties are easily accessible and very popular with "winter Texans," retired residents of the northern United States and Canada who spend at least part of the winter in the south Texas warmth. There are numerous local charter captains specializing in offshore big game fishing, where anglers try for blue marlin, white marlin, sailfish, swordfish, wahoo, tuna, and mako shark. Offshore fishing also includes red drum, spotted sea trout, snapper, grouper, tarpon, and king mackerel.

The Laguna Madre, on average only 2 feet deep, is perfect for world-class light-tackle sport fishing. The lush carpet of sea grasses on its bottom provides good habitat and food for red drum, spotted sea trout, flounder, black drum, and snook, and locals brag that there are more of these fish per acre than in any other bay on the Texas Gulf.

The **Texas International Fishing Tournament** has been going strong for more than 60 years and attracts more than 1,000 participants each July. The 5-day event includes bay, offshore, and tarpon fishing divisions, and is open to anglers of all ages. Visit www.tift.org or contact the **South Padre Island CVB** (© **800/767-2373** or 956/761-6433; www.sopadre.com) for details.

SUNBATHING & SWIMMING   The beaches of South Padre Island are some of the best on the Gulf: The sand is fine and white, and the water is warm and shallow. In town there are 23 access points with free parking, plus the county has a park at each end of town, with a $4 all-day parking fee, good at both parks. Our favorite stretch of beach is between the Radisson and Holiday Inn. Incidentally, although lined with hotels and condos, the shoreline and adjacent beaches are public and open to everyone.

WINDSURFING   With winds about 15 mph year-round, these waters are ideal for windsurfing. Spring and fall is best, usually with beautiful weather. Hurricane season runs from August to early November, but is not often a serious problem.

Tips **Face to Face with a Sea Turtle**

Each of the seven worldwide species of sea turtles are either threatened or endangered, and five species are found in the Gulf of Mexico. Ila Loetscher, affectionately dubbed the "Turtle Lady," founded Sea Turtle, Inc., in 1977 to help protect the most endangered species of sea turtles, Kemp's ridley. The organization supports conservation and rehabilitation of all marine turtles, and operates a rehabilitation center where you can see four of the five Gulf of Mexico sea turtle species. Volunteers give presentations with live sea turtles Tuesday through Sunday at 10am, which help you identify the different species and explain how each of us can help protect them, and self-guided and guided tours of the facility, including the turtle tanks, are available at other times. **Sea Turtle, Inc.,** is located at 6617 Padre Blvd. (© **956/761-4511**; www.seaturtleinc.com), and admission costs $2 for adults and $1 for children. It's open Tuesday through Sunday from 10am to 4pm. Allow at least 45 minutes, and please buy something in the gift shop—all proceeds go to saving the sea turtles!

WHERE TO STAY

Room rates vary widely in South Padre Island over the course of the year, with the lowest rates usually in winter. Among the national chain motels in South Padre Island are **Days Inn,** 3913 Padre Blvd. (© **800/329-7466** or 956/761-7831); **Comfort Suites,** 912 Padre Blvd. (© **800/424-6423** or 956/772-9020); and **Super 8,** 4205 Padre Blvd. (© **800/800-8000** or 956/761-6300). Room tax adds about 13%.

Brown Pelican Inn—A Bayside Bed & Breakfast ☆   This deceptively simple two-story beach house with wraparound porches on both floors is an elegant and sumptuously peaceful inn. Each room is individually decorated with American and English antiques and collectibles. Two rooms are downstairs: Our personal favorite, the Big Thicket room faces the bay and has a king-size bed and private entrance from the porch, and the Hill Country room is fully accessible for travelers with disabilities and has a queen-size bed. The upstairs rooms all have queen-size beds, and two face the bay, affording front seat views of stunning sunsets over the Laguna Madre. Seven rooms have showers only, one has a tub/shower combo. There are rocking chairs on the porches to entice you to sit back and relax, allowing the gentle Gulf breezes to gently caress your face. Enjoy the homemade breakfast on the bayside porch or in the great room—the plat de jour, freshly baked pastries, homemade granola, fresh fruit and juices, and gourmet coffee and tea. Smoking outside only.

207 W. Aries Dr. (P.O. Box 2667), South Padre Island, TX 78597. © 956/761-2722. Fax 956/761-8683. www.brownpelican.com. 8 units. $95–$135 double. Rates include full breakfast. AE, DISC, MC, V. Children under 12 not allowed. Reservations required. *In room:* A/C, TV.

Casa de Siesta Bed & Breakfast ☆   Although located right on the main drag, the hacienda-style design of this B&B provides privacy and quiet, all within a half-block walk of the beach. All the rooms open onto a portal lined with large planters that surrounds the attractive central patio with a fountain and swimming pool. The rooms are huge, with a dressing room and private bathroom with step-in showers. There are large stained-glass windows, colorful Mexican tile, rustic solid wood furniture from Mexico, saltillo tile floors, high ceilings, and ceiling fans. The doors are magnificent: 8 feet high, custom-made wood with rounded tops. Smoking outside only.

4610 Padre Blvd., South Padre Island, TX 78597. © 956/761-5656. Fax 956/761-1313. www.casadesiesta.com. 12 units. Oct–Jan $99 double; Mar and June–Aug $150 double; rest of year $125 double. Extra person $20. Holiday rates higher. Rates include continental breakfast. AE, DISC, MC, V. Pets accepted with $20 one-time fee. Children under 12 not allowed. *In room:* A/C, TV, fridge.

Radisson Resort South Padre Island ☆   For a top-notch full-service hotel and the nicest beach in town, our vote goes to this Radisson. Two Catalina macaws—Rad and General—greet you as you enter the high-ceilinged lobby, and the birds seem quite at home, surrounded by tropical plants. The landscaping around the pools is lovely, with plenty of palm trees and flowers, and the popular public beach just outside the hotel is great. The cabanas—the "standard" rooms!—are colorfully decorated with floral bedspreads and artwork with a fish motif. Those with beach views are the best, and those with ocean fronts are the most expensive. The suites, which are actually two-bedroom condos, are large, handsomely appointed units with sleeping for up to six, two full bathrooms, a full kitchen, and a spacious living/dining room.

500 Padre Blvd., South Padre Island, TX 78597. © 800/333-3333 or 956/761-6511. Fax 956/761-1602. www.radissonspi.com. 188 units. $100–$200 double; $205–$380 suite. AE, DC, DISC, MC, V. **Amenities:**

Restaurant; 2 outdoor pools; 4 outdoor lit tennis courts; 3 Jacuzzis; limited room service. *In room:* A/C, TV, kitchen in suites, coffeemaker, hair dryer, iron.

CAMPING

Isla Blanca Park ★★ (© **956/761-5493**), on the southern tip of South Padre Island, is our choice for a developed campground on the island, with easy beach access. Part of the Cameron County Park System (P.O. Box 2106, South Padre Island, TX 78597), this well-maintained facility has 600 paved sites, many of which are pull-through, and more than half have full RV hook-ups. The park also offers restrooms with showers, dump station, a sandy beach, fishing jetty, boat ramp and marina, playground, a bike trail, and beach pavilions with concessions. There is a primitive tent area right on the Laguna Madre. Rates are $12 to $22.

Those looking for a developed resort should head to **Destination South Padre RV Resort** (© **800/867-2373** or 956/761-5665; www.destinationsouth padre.com), just south of the Queen Isabella Causeway on Padre Boulevard. It offers 190 gravel sites with full hook-ups, restrooms with showers, guest laundry, and security. There's a large heated pool, spa, boat dock, rec hall and game room, and numerous planned activities. Rates are $28 to $37. There are pet restrictions, and tents are not allowed.

WHERE TO DINE

Padre Island Brewing Company ★ BREWPUB/PIZZA   Hearty brewpub fare (and some pretty good beer, too) makes Padre Island Brewing Company a must-stop for us whenever we're in the area. We especially like the cooked-to-order burgers and sandwiches such as the chicken fajita served on a French roll. Entrees include steaks, baby back ribs, Texas quail, stuffed chicken breast, crab-stuffed flounder, and really tasty breaded beer batter shrimp. Eat outside on the second story deck for terrific views, or stay out of the sun inside where decor is simple—a few chile ristras and bright posterlike paintings of different beers. As in most brewpubs, the brewing vats are ranged behind the bar, and visible from the front parking lot through tall windows.

3400 Padre Blvd., at Bahama St. © 956/761-9585. Main courses $5.50–$19. AE, DISC, MC, V. Tues–Sun 11:30am–10:30pm; Mon 5–10:30pm.

Scampi's ★★ *(Moments* SEAFOOD   Scampi's is one of the most elegant restaurants on the island, with white linen tablecloths, teal-and-white chairs, and floral photographs on the walls. The food is upscale also, with some unique offerings. Try the Peanut Butter Shrimp, prepared with garlic, ginger, soy sauce, sugar, peanut butter, and a touch of jalapeño, served with a rice pilaf; Shrimp Italiano, jumbo Gulf shrimp in olive oil, white wine, butter, garlic, and capers; or the simpler broiled, blackened, or grilled Gulf red snapper. The menu also offers filet mignon, rib-eye steak, veal, lamb, an Oriental stir-fry, Chinese vegetable salad, and several pasta dishes. There's patio dining overlooking the Laguna Madre Bay and a fine wine list.

206 W. Aries. © 956/761-1755. www.scampisspi.com. Main courses $14–$25. AE, DC, DISC, MC, V. Apr–Oct Sun–Thurs 6–10pm, Fri–Sat 6–11pm; Nov–Mar Sun–Thurs 5–9pm, Fri–Sat 5–11pm; bar year-round Sun–Thurs 4:30pm–12am, Fri–Sat 4:30pm–1am. From Padre Blvd., turn west onto Aries and drive to the end. Scampi's is on your right.

Ted's Restaurant ★ *(Value* AMERICAN   This small, casual restaurant offers good food at reasonable prices, and the entire menu is available at all times.

There are about a dozen Formica-topped tables, Roman shades on the windows, and hanging plants scattered about. Although small, the room is light and airy, and the service is prompt. (Food is cooked to order though, so don't be impatient.) Breakfast includes the usual eggs, pancakes, and waffles, plus a breakfast taco, *migas* (two eggs scrambled with onions, tomato, and corn tortilla, garnished with cheese and served with refried beans, salsa, and tortillas), and huevos rancheros. Our choice for lunch is beef or chicken fajitas with flour tortillas, picante sauce, refried beans, and several optional toppings like jalapeños, guacamole, or sour cream. Also offered are burgers, sandwiches, and salads.

5717 Padre Blvd. ⓒ 956/761-5327. Main courses $3.25–$5.95. MC, V. Daily 7am–3pm.

4 Brazosport

65 miles SE of Galveston; 50 miles S of Houston; 185 miles NW of Corpus Christi

There's actually no such place as a city or town, or even a community called "Brazosport." The name refers to close to a dozen small communities in Brazoria County, and primarily southern Brazoria County near the mouth of the Brazos River along the Gulf of Mexico. These towns, which have a combined population of about 90,000, include Clute, Freeport, Surfside Beach, Lake Jackson, Angleton, Quintana Beach, West Columbia, and Brazoria. There's a pleasant small-town atmosphere here that combined with the docks, fishing boats, and beaches remind us of the south shore of Long Island in the 1950s. Some critics put down the area for its admittedly somewhat ugly chemical plants and other manufacturing and refinery facilities—Dow Chemical, Phillips 66, and BASF Corporation have major divisions here—but the jobs these industries have created, plus outright donations from the companies, have made possible many of the recreation and cultural attractions here.

While fishing and enjoying the area's 21 miles of beach are certainly major attractions, the area is world famous for its bird-watching—the annual Christmas bird count in the town of Freeport often reports more species of birds seen in 1 day than at any other location in the United States. There are several wildlife refuges in the area, and practically anywhere along the shore will provide opportunities to see dozens if not hundreds of bird species. In addition, the Brazosport area has the distinction of being the birthplace of Texas, the spot where the first Anglo settlement was established in 1821. The winter climate is delightful, with daytime temperatures often in the 70s and even 80s. Summers, however, are hot, with highs of about 100°F (38°C), and the coastal areas are subject to hurricanes from late summer through fall.

ESSENTIALS
GETTING THERE
BY PLANE The nearest commercial airports are in Houston (see chapter 5).

BY CAR From Houston take Tex. 288 south about 45 miles to Angleton, the Brazoria County seat. Lake Jackson is another 10 miles south on Tex. 288, and Bus. 288 leads from Angleton to Clute (10 miles south). Tex. highways 332 and 288 intersect in Lake Jackson, heading southeast around it and Clute and then divide, 332 continuing southeast to Surfside Beach and 288 heading south to Freeport and Quintana. Brazoria is just west of Lake Jackson on Tex. 332. West Columbia is about 15 miles west of Angleton on Tex. 35, and 8 miles north of Brazoria via Tex. 36, which also connects Freeport to Brazoria.

GETTING AROUND

The only practical way to explore this area is by car; the attractions discussed below are all within a 45-minute drive. Traffic and parking are seldom an issue. The major roads are Tex. highways 288, 332, 35, and 36. Tex. 288/332 wraps around the west and south sides of Lake Jackson and Clute, where many motels are located.

VISITOR INFORMATION

Although most of the towns in the Brazosport area have their own chambers of commerce, and some have visitor centers, you can get area-wide information from the **Southern Brazoria County Visitors Convention Bureau,** 1239 W. Tex. 332, Clute, TX 77531 (© **800/938-4853** or 979/265-2508; www.tourist-info.org); and the **Brazosport Convention & Visitors Council,** 420 Tex. 332 West, Brazosport (Clute), TX 77531 (© **888/477-2505** or 979/265-2505; www.tourtexas.com/brazosport). Both organizations operate visitor centers.

FAST FACTS The **Brazosport Memorial Hospital,** 100 Medical Dr. (just off Tex. 288), Lake Jackson (© **979/297-4411**), has a 24-hour emergency room. **Clute's post office,** located at 530 E. Main St., is open Monday through Friday from 8:30am to 4:30pm, Saturday from 10am to noon. The **Lake Jackson post office,** located at 210 Oak Dr. South, is open Monday through Friday from 8:30am to 5pm, Saturday from 10am to 2pm.

WHAT TO SEE & DO
THE TOP ATTRACTIONS

Brazoria County Historical Museum ⭐ A must-stop for anyone interested in the real Old West and the beginnings of Texas, this museum is located in the 1897 Brazoria County Courthouse, a restored structure that was built in the Italian Renaissance–style popular in the late 1800s, and then "modernized" between 1913 and 1927. The Anglo influence that dominates Texas today began in Brazoria County in 1821, when Stephen F. Austin established a colony of 300 families at the mouth of the Brazos River. This museum's prime permanent exhibit does an excellent job of describing not only the colony, but also all the events since the arrival of the first Anglo settlers. The large exhibit, which contains 68 panels, replicas of the era's weapons and tools, and a variety of artifacts and documents, is located in the historic courtroom on the second floor (access for visitors with disabilities is available).

Most of the rest of the museum is devoted to changing exhibits that include historic subjects such as the courthouses of Texas and the Civil War's impact on the area. During our visit we were especially impressed with an exhibit on the hurricanes that struck the Texas Gulf Coast in the early 1900s. The museum also has a well-stocked gift and bookshop, and a research center that is an excellent source for those doing genealogical or other research on Brazoria County. Allow at least 1 hour.

100 E. Cedar St., just off Bus. 288, Angleton. © **979/864-1208.** www.bchm.org. Free admission (donations welcome). Mon–Fri 9am–5pm; Sat 9am–3pm; research center closed Mon. Closed major holidays.

The Center for the Arts & Sciences ⭐⭐⭐ *(Finds* One of those rare entities that does a whole lot of things very well, The Center for the Arts & Sciences is just what its name implies: a large center that includes a fine natural history museum, a small planetarium, an attractive art gallery, two theaters for a variety of performing arts events, and a nature trail. You'll need at least 2 hours here to even begin seeing it. Under the wing of the Brazosport Fine Arts Council, the center is also home to a theater group, symphony orchestra, and the Brazosport Art League.

The **Museum of Natural Science** has a collection of more than 14,000 seashells, and is credited with instigating the movement to make the lightning whelk the official State Shell of Texas. Also in its 12,000 square feet of floor space are exhibits on archaeology, fossils, dinosaurs, rocks, and minerals (including a fluorescent mineral room), and a collection of jade and ivory carvings. The **Planetarium** has a 30-foot dome and lots of high-tech projection equipment to produce a variety of night sky experiences. A ¾-mile self-guided **nature trail** meanders through bottomland along Oyster Creek adjacent to the center.

The center's **art gallery** presents nine exhibits each year, ranging from local artists to national shows. The exhibits change every 4 to 6 weeks, and the works are often for sale. There are also music recitals in the gallery, and art classes and workshops are periodically offered in the adjacent studio. Contact the center offices for the current schedule.

There are two modern, well-designed theaters in the center: a proscenium theater and an arena theater, which sometimes presents theater-in-the-round. **Center Stages,** the longest running continuously operating theater group in Texas (it began in 1943), presents about a half dozen productions each year. The **Symphony Orchestra** presents a variety of concerts ranging from classical to pop during its September-to-May season, with a combination of local musicians and guest artists. In addition, every other year (in even numbered years) the center stages as a fundraiser an elaborate and wonderfully fun **Elizabethan Madrigal Feast** ✸✸, in full costume, on the first 2 weekends in December.

400 College Dr., Clute. ℂ **979/265-7661.** www.bcfas.org. Free admission to the museum, art gallery, and nature trail; planetarium $3 adults, $2 students. Theater and orchestra performances $8–$12. Museum and art gallery Tues–Sat 10am–5pm, Sun 2–5pm; closed major holidays. Planetarium shows Tues 7pm. Nature trail open daily dawn to dusk. From the intersection of Tex. highways 332 and 288 in Lake Jackson head east on

 ### The Great Texas Mosquito Festival

What do you do in a popular tourist destination when the mosquitoes come out in full force? Follow the lead of the fun-loving folks in Clute, Texas, and throw a party, dedicated to this delightful little bloodsucker. The **Great Texas Mosquito Festival** ✸, which began in 1981, takes place the last Thursday, Friday, and Saturday of each July, offering carnival rides, games, races, way too much food, arts and crafts sales, and generally a good time for all. There's dancing to live music by top country, rock, Tejano, and R&B groups, plus barbecue and fajitas cook-offs, a horseshoe-pitching tournament, haystack dives, bike and skate tours, and a disc golf tournament. Specialty contests— perhaps the highlights of the festival—include the Mosquito Legs competition, the Mosquito Calling contest, the Senior Citizen Mosquito Swatter contest, and the ever-popular Ms. Quito Beauty Pageant. For more information, contact the **Clute Parks and Recreation Department** (ℂ **800/371-2971** or 979/265-8392), or the **Southern Brazoria County Visitors Convention Bureau** (ℂ **800/938-4853** or 979/265-2508; www. tourist-info.org). And don't forget your insect repellent.

Oyster Creek Dr., through Lake Jackson and into Clute; Oyster Creek Dr. becomes College Dr. after it crosses the railroad tracks in Clute. The Center is just ahead on the left, adjoining the campus of Brazosport College. In Clute, you can take Dixie Dr. north from Tex. 332/288 and turn right onto Oyster Creek Dr. From Bus. 288 turn west (right) directly onto College Dr. and the Center will be on your right after crossing the bridge over Oyster Creek.

Sea Center Texas   You want to see a really big fish? Sea Center Texas has a 50,000-gallon aquarium where you'll see marine life of the Texas Gulf Coast, including Gordon, a 250-pound grouper, and sharks up to 12 feet long. There are also tanks with exhibits on other types of marine environments, including salt marshes, reefs, and a coastal bay. A shallow Touch Pool contains blue crabs, hermit crabs, snails, urchins, and other marine creatures that can be handled, and just outside the visitor center is a 5-acre wetlands with elevated boardwalks and signs discussing the numerous birds and other wildlife you might encounter. A free nature checklist is available. Allow 1 hour.

300 Medical Dr., Lake Jackson. ✆ **979/299-1808.** Free admission (donations welcome). Tues–Fri 9am–4pm; Sat 10am–5pm; Sun 1–4pm. Closed major holidays. From Tex. 332/288 turn west onto Plantation Dr. to Medical Dr. and turn north (right), then follow the signs.

OUTDOOR ACTIVITIES

Birding, fishing, and hanging out on the beach are the top outdoor pursuits here.

BIRD-WATCHING   The Texas Gulf Coast is renowned for its bird-watching, and birders come from around the world to catch a glimpse of roseate spoonbills, black-necked stilts, crested caracaras, and several hundred other species. Binoculars or cameras with telephoto lenses are especially helpful, and insect repellent is practically mandatory year-round.

There are several wildlife refuges in the Brazosport area. The most developed is the **Brazoria National Wildlife Refuge,** which covers 43,388 acres and was established to protect coastal wetlands for migratory birds and other wildlife. The Information Center, located near the entrance to the refuge, has interpretive panels on what you want to watch for, and a boardwalk outside the Information Center leads across wetlands, where you may spot an alligator. The boardwalk provides access to the ⅝-mile Big Slough Birding Trail, which loops through a stand of trees where you might see songbirds such as warblers and vireos, as well as sandhill cranes, snow geese, pintails, and mottled ducks. The refuge also has a 2-mile hiking and biking trail that follows an abandoned railway line and provides views across a terrain of prairie, where you might see more than a dozen species of sparrows, white-tailed hawks, and white-tailed kites. In addition, a 7-mile driving tour offers excellent opportunities to see a wide variety of birds and other wildlife, and also provides access to several observation decks. The refuge, which also allows fishing and hunting, is open September through May daily from 8am to 4pm, and during the summer it's open the same hours the first weekend of each month and intermittently during the week. Admission is free. To get to the refuge, take FM 523 north from Freeport or south from Angleton to CR 227, which you follow 1¾ miles northeast to the refuge entrance. For additional information, contact the refuge at ✆ **409/849-7771** or visit http://southwest.fws.gov.

In the community of Quintana Beach the **Neo-Tropical Bird Sanctuary** is located on Lamar Street across from the Quintana Beach Town Hall (✆ **979/233-0848**), where you can get a bird checklist and other information. The small wooded preserve is open 24 hours a day with free admission. It attracts numerous migrating birds, as well as butterflies, small animals, and a few too many mosquitoes. It has a short loop trail (dirt) with strategically located benches. Nearby is a separate xeriscape garden.

FISHING   This area offers excellent fishing for grouper, ling, amberjack, and red snapper—the state record 36.1-pound red snapper was caught in 1995 off the Freeport coast. Anglers can choose from among about a dozen charter fishing boats, most based in Freeport Harbor, such as **Captain Elliott's Party Boats** (© **979/233-1811;** www.deep-sea-fishing.com), which offers 12-hour deep-sea fishing trips at $75 per adult weekends, $70 weekdays, and $45 for children 12 and under. There are numerous places for shore, beach, pier, and jetty fishing, including Quintana and Surfside beaches, and a number of public boat ramps—check with one of the visitor bureaus (see "Visitor Information," above) for locations.

FUN ON THE BEACH   Although the beaches here are far from pristine—they tend to be rocky and the sand is more brown than white—it's still fun to dig your toes into the cool sand, walk along the shore, build a sand castle, watch the freighters and shorebirds, and look for seashells among the stones. Driving is permitted on most beaches here, although we especially like the pedestrian-only beach at **Quintana Beach County Park,** 5th Street, in the community of Quintana (© **800/872-7578** or 979/233-1461), which has a campground (see "Camping," below), good bird-watching, a playground, horseshoe pits, and a picnic area, and charges a $4 per vehicle day-use fee.

WHERE TO STAY

Among the national chain motels in the Brazosport area is our favorite, **La Quinta Inn,** 1126 Tex. 332 West, Clute (© 800/531-5900 or 979/265-7461), with spacious, very attractive rooms. Other reliable chains include the **Days Inn,** 805 Tex. 332 West, Clute (© 800/329-7466 or 979/265-3301); **Ramada Inn,** 925 Tex. 332, Lake Jackson (© 800/272-6232 or 979/297-1161); and **Super 8,** 915 Tex. 332, Lake Jackson (© 800/800-8000 or 979/297-3031). Also see the section on **Quintana Beach County Park** under "Camping," below. Tax adds about 13% to lodging bills unless otherwise noted.

Roses & the River ★★   A delightful Texas farmhouse–style home in an idyllic setting is what you'll find at Roses & the River. Sitting on almost 3½ acres along the San Bernard River, this B&B has an abundance of beautiful rose bushes. Because of the warm Gulf Coast climate, the roses bloom year-round, although they're usually best in October and November. There are sitting areas along the river (plus a dock for those who brought boats), plus a long veranda offering a peaceful and protected sitting area. Inside, the lobby/living room has a fireplace with comfortable seating, and a separate dining room where the homemade breakfasts are served. There are three guest rooms, all on the second floor (no elevator), that are rose themed—somewhat elegant yet cheerful and inviting. Each of the spacious rooms has a full private bathroom (one with a fantastic claw-footed spa tub), and one queen-size bed. Guest rooms contain a few antiques, but mostly contemporary furnishings. Two rooms have views of the river; the third overlooks the rose garden. Smoking is not permitted.

2434 County Rd. 506, Brazoria, TX 77422. © **800/610-1070** or 979/798-1070. Fax 979/798-1070. www. roses-and-the-river.com. 3 units. $125–$150 double (tax included). Rates include full breakfast. AE, DISC, MC, V. Children 12 and older allowed. From Brazoria, go southwest on Tex. 521, cross the San Bernard River and take the first right turn, onto County Rd. 506. After about 1½ miles, you'll find Roses & the River on the right. *In room:* A/C, TV/VCR (free movies available).

CAMPING

Our choice for camping in this area is the Brazoria County–run **Quintana Beach County Park,** 5th Street, in the community of Quintana. Practically on the water, this campground has fairly close sites, but there are some low palm trees and lots of grass, and it's a very short walk to the beach. There are 56 sites (including 19 pull-through RV sites), and a small group of grassy "tent only" sites. The campground has paved roads, showers, a self-serve laundry, an RV dump station, picnic tables, grills, a playground, and horseshoe pits. Boardwalks lead from the campground among several weathered wood buildings to the beach. Camping rates from May to September are $18 to $20 for water, sewer, and electric hook-ups; $18 for water and electric; and $15 for no hook-ups. From October to April, rates are $17 to $18 for full hook-ups, $16 for water and electric, and $12 for no hook-ups. Day use costs $4 per vehicle. There are also several cabins, with sleeping areas, bathrooms, and kitchen, but no linens or kitchen utensils, which rent for $70 to $100 from May to September and $55 to $85 from October to April. Information is available by calling © **800/872-7578** or 979/233-1461. From Tex. 36/288 in Freeport, turn right onto FM 1495, and after crossing the Intercoastal Waterway on a swing bridge, turn left onto Quintana Road, which becomes Lamar Street in Quintana. Turn right on 8th Street, then left on Burnett Street to 5th Street.

Those who don't mind roughing it can also drive onto and camp for free on most parts of Quintana Beach (ask for details at the RV park or at area visitor centers).

WHERE TO DINE

Café Annice ⍟ CONTINENTAL   There's a decidedly uptown feel to this casual modern restaurant that is a favorite of local businesspeople, and, in our estimation, borders on fine dining for both lunch and dinner. Modern art decorates the light-colored brick walls, and the high ceiling makes the dining room appear larger than it really is. Lunch choices include a variety of innovative sandwiches, such as the Caesar wrap—chicken breast, romaine lettuce, carrots, red onions, plum tomatoes, and a homemade Caesar spread, wrapped in a roasted garlic and herb tortilla. Dinner entrees feature tempting selections of seafood, Angus beef, and chicken, including the excellent chicken Annice—breaded chicken topped with mushrooms, artichokes, tomatoes, and capers, sautéed with Marsala wine and served with grilled vegetable ragout and garlic mashed potatoes. Among the more than a dozen fresh-baked desserts, we heartily recommend the Italian cream cake.

24 Circle Way, Lake Jackson. © **979/292-0060.** Reservations accepted for large parties only. Main courses lunch $5.95–$8.95, dinner $9.95–$25. AE, DISC, MC, V. Mon–Fri 11am–2pm; Sat 11am–2:30pm; Mon–Thurs 5–9pm; Fri–Sat 5–10pm. Closed major holidays. From Tex. 332/288, turn northeast onto This Way, take the first left onto Circle Way and follow it around to downtown.

The Jetties AMERICAN   We kept expecting to see singer Jimmy Buffett and a bunch of noisy beach bums burst into The Jetties during our visit. Well, Jimmy didn't make it, but at least the beach bums did, sandy feet and all. This is an ultracasual, friendly, funky beach hangout, with a small dining room with great views of the Gulf, where you can watch the fishing boats and freighters chug by. There's also an outside deck and additional seating in the sand along the jetty. The food is really good, from the half-pound burgers served with hand-cut french fries to the beer-batter-dipped shrimp, a favorite of the locals. Sandwiches, burgers, and baskets (such as fresh battered catfish served with hush puppies and tarter sauce) are served all the time, but dinners, such as grilled shrimp or a charcoal-grilled rib-eye steak, are served only after 5pm. Service is a bit slow here, mostly because everything is prepared fresh as it's ordered, but The Jetties has such a friendly, happy atmosphere that nobody seems to care.

104 2nd St., Quintana Beach. (C) **979/373-9730.** Main courses lunch $3.95–$9.95, dinner $3.95–$17. No credit cards. Sun–Thurs 10am–9pm; Fri–Sat 10am–10pm. From Tex. 36/288 in Freeport, turn right onto FM 1495, then left onto Quintana Rd., which becomes Lamar St. Turn right on 8th St., then left on Burnett St., right on 2nd. The Jetties is at the end of the road.

Red Snapper Inn ★★ SEAFOOD   What's the point in going to the Gulf if you're not going to indulge in fresh seafood? And it doesn't get any fresher and better than at the Red Snapper. Not surprisingly, the decor is nautical, with a large aquarium, beach flotsam, and a surfboard highlighting the somewhat upscale but still very casual dining room. Although the menu is primarily classic seafood such as shrimp sautéed with garlic and mushrooms, or grilled boneless flounder stuffed with crabmeat dressing, you'll also find some exciting Greek and Cajun touches. We especially recommend the baked shrimp, with feta cheese and fresh tomatoes, and served with buttered spaghetti; and the sautéed fillet of snapper in a sauce of pulverized onions, oregano, lemon juice, and olive oil. Also a good bet are the oysters brochette, grilled bacon-wrapped oysters (not breaded) with meunière butter and served on rice pilaf. Nonseafood items include a charbroiled choice 14-ounce rib-eye steak, the very popular charbroiled Greek meatballs with spaghetti, and that Texas standard, chicken-fried steak with cream gravy.

402 Bluewater Hwy., Surfside Beach. (C) **979/239-3226.** Reservations accepted for large parties only. Main courses $4.95–$17. No credit cards. Mon–Fri 11am–2pm and 5–9pm; Sat–Sun 11am–9pm. As you enter Surfside Beach on Tex. 332, you come to a traffic light, turn northeast (left) onto Bluewater Hwy. The restaurant will be on your right a few blocks down.

5 Rockport ★★

35 miles NE of Corpus Christi; 182 miles SW of Houston; 161 miles SE of San Antonio

If we were going to live on the Gulf Coast, it would be in picturesque Rockport, Texas. This is a delightful little town, with a good (although not great) public beach, wonderful opportunities for bird-watching, boating, fishing, and other outdoor activities, and the best art scene of any of the small towns we've seen in southern and western Texas.

Rockport and its neighbor Fulton have a combined population of about 9,000, but are home to about 150 resident artists and a half dozen or so commercial art galleries, in addition to the excellent Rockport Center for the Arts. Tiny Fulton was established in 1866 by rancher George Ware Fulton, and the much larger Rockport emerged the following year as a seaport. Today the Rockport-Fulton area, along with Aransas Pass (12 miles south), are a major port for commercial and sport fishing, and famous as the winter home for North America's largest flock of whooping cranes.

ESSENTIALS
GETTING THERE & AROUND
You'll need a car to get here and to explore the area. Both Rockport and Fulton are along Tex. 35, which connects with U.S. 87 to the north and U.S. 181 to the south.

VISITOR INFORMATION

If you need maps of the area or advice, contact the **Rockport-Fulton Area Chamber of Commerce,** 404 Broadway, Rockport, TX 78382 (© **800/826-6441** or 361/729-6445; www.rockport-fulton.org).

FAST FACTS   The nearest full-service hospital, with a 24-hour emergency room, is **North Bay Hospital,** 11 miles south of Rockport at 1711 W. Wheeler Ave., Aransas Pass (© **361/758-8585**). The **post office,** located at 1550 FM 2165 in Rockport, is open Monday through Friday from 9am to 4:30pm, Saturday from 9am to noon.

WHAT TO SEE & DO
THE TOP OUTDOOR ATTRACTION

This region is among the nation's premier bird-watching destinations, and the best spot for birding here is the **Aransas National Wildlife Refuge** ★★. Although almost 400 species of birds have been seen at the refuge, its primary claim to fame is that this is the main winter home for the near-extinct whooping crane, America's tallest bird, at 5 feet high, and with a 7-foot wingspan. In the 1930s there were only 15 whooping cranes known to exist in North America, but they are making a comeback and now there are an estimated 400, more than half of which spend their winters (usually Nov–Apr) at Aransas National Wildlife Refuge. The whoopers spend the warmer months in Canada's Northwest Territories at Wood Buffalo National Park, about 2,400 miles north.

Other birds you're likely to see at the refuge include American white pelicans, great blue herons, great and snowy egrets, roseate spoonbills, mottled ducks, black and turkey vultures, American kestrels, northern bobwhites, western and least sandpipers, laughing gulls, Caspian terns, scissor-tailed flycatchers, cliff swallows, northern mockingbirds, white-eyed vireos, northern cardinals, red-winged blackbirds, and eastern meadowlarks. Although from late fall to spring is the best time to see birds, some, such as northern bobwhites, killdeer, herons and egrets, mottled ducks, vultures, mourning doves, Carolina wrens, and vireos are year-round residents. April and May usually see large numbers of colorful songbirds.

In addition to birds, the refuge is home to about 30 species of snakes (about a half dozen are poisonous), turtles, lizards, and the refuge's largest reptile, the American alligator. Mammals commonly seen include white-tailed deer, javelina, wild boars, raccoons, eastern cottontail rabbits, and nine-banded armadillos. Also present but only occasionally seen are bobcats and opossums.

A 16-mile paved auto tour loop meanders through a variety of habitats, offering access to a 40-foot observation tower, a boardwalk that leads through a salt marsh to the coastline, and other viewing areas. The refuge has nine walking trails, ranging from 0.1 to 1.4 miles, a picnic area, and an impressive Wildlife Interpretive Center with information, exhibits, a bookstore, and administration offices. There are also seasons for hunting and saltwater fishing access. Camping is not permitted.

For more information, contact the Aransas National Wildlife Refuge at © **361/286-3559** or visit http://southwest.fws.gov. It's located about 36 road miles northeast of Rockport via Tex. 35, FM 774, and FM 2040. The refuge is open daily from just before sunrise to just after sunset, and the Wildlife Interpretive Center is open daily from 8:30am to 4:30pm. Admission to the refuge costs $5 per vehicle ($3 if there's only one person). Binoculars are available to borrow at the Wildlife Interpretive Center. Insect repellent is recommended year-round.

MORE OUTDOOR FUN

BIRD-WATCHING   As one of the best birding areas in North America, you'll generally find that whatever you're doing outdoors will be interrupted to look at birds, ranging from rare whooping cranes to colorful songbirds and rare neotropical species seldom seen in the United States. Among areas to go to see birds and other wildlife is the **Connie Hagar Cottage Sanctuary,** at First and Church streets in Rockport, which has trails and a self-guided tour on the property where well-known bird-watcher Connie Hagar (1886–1973) and her husband lived. The grounds are open daily from sunrise to sunset, and admission is free. Local birding clubs have produced a booklet with a bird checklist and driving tours, available for $2 from the Rockport-Fulton Area Chamber of Commerce (see "Visitor Information," above).

A number of companies offer **birding tours,** generally November through March, and either on land or by boat. Boat tours are in shallow draft boats and usually are 3 to 4 hours long. Cost is about $30 per person, with discounts for children and seniors, but several companies will take small groups at a flat rate of $150 to $200. Some guarantee that you'll see whooping cranes. Among those that charge per person are **Captain Billy Gaskins** (✆ 866/729-2997 or 361/729-2997); **Captain Dan Grosse or Captain Marvin Horner** (✆ 800/782-2473 or 361/729-4855); and **Captain Eddy Polhemus Pisces** (✆ 361/729-7525). Those offering the flat rate option for up to four people include **Captain Sally's Reel Fun Charters** (✆ 361/729-9095; www.captainsally.com). **Aransas Bay Birding Charters** (✆ 361/727-2689) offers 6-hour tours for up to 6 people for $300. Check with the Rockport-Fulton Area Chamber of Commerce (see "Visitor Information," above) for information on land-based birding tours.

FISHING   Along with birding, fishing is extremely popular here, and with very good reason—fishing's great for a variety of species including trout, croaker, flounder, sheepshead, and redfish in the bay and sailfish, marlin, tarpon, ling, king mackerel, grouper, and red snapper offshore. There are public fishing piers in Fulton Harbor and at Rockport Beach Park, as well as numerous other areas. Fishing guides offer bay and deep-sea fishing trips, and rates vary considerably. Contact **Gold Spoon Charters** (✆ 361/727-9178; www.goldspooncharters. com), **Green Hornet Fishing Guide Service** (✆ 361/749-5904; www.green hornetguideservice.com), and **Hook Line & Sinker** (✆ 866/993-3131 or 361/727-0910).

PARKS & BEACHES   Anglers and birders especially like **Goose Island State Park** (✆ 361/729-2858; www.tpwd.state.tx.us/park/goose), which not only is a good spot to see the endangered whooping crane but also is home to The Big Tree, a giant live oak with seemingly countless twisting branches that is estimated to be more than 1,000 years old. It's more than 35 feet in circumference, 44 feet high, and has a crown spread of 90 feet. The park has a short paved hiking and biking path, two playgrounds, picnic tables and grills, a boat ramp, and a lighted fishing pier. Fish caught here include speckled trout, redfish, flounder, and sheepshead, and crabbing and oystering are also popular. There are 102 campsites with water and electric hook-ups and 25 sites with water only, and the park also has restrooms with showers and an RV dump station. Entrance to the park costs $2 per person age 13 and older per day, and camping costs an

Finds   **Texas's Most Deserted Beach**

Those seeking an escape from civilization will find a long, picturesque beach with an abundance of birds and other wildlife, excellent fishing, but little else at **Matagorda Island State Park** (© **361/983-2215;** www.tpwd.state.tx.us/park/matagisl/matagisl.htm). Located about 7 water miles south of the community of Port O'Connor, Matagorda Island is accessible only by boat—your own, a charter, or the park-operated passenger ferry that runs between the island and Port O'Connor. Private motor vehicles are not permitted on the island, but the park operates a shuttle service from the boat docks to the beaches. Visitors also can take mountain bikes to the island.

Once there, you'll find a narrow 38-mile-long island covering almost 44,000 acres that has practically no development. A variety of guided tours are offered, in which you'll get to see whooping cranes and other birds, go beachcombing, examine the marine ecosystem, or see some of the island's historic sites, such as an 1852 lighthouse. Tours are usually from 6 to 9 hours. Most tours cost $8 for adults and $4 for children age 12 and under; whooping crane boat tours cost $20 for adults and $15 for children 12 and under and include transportation from Port O'Connor to Matagorda Island.

Anglers catch southern flounder, mackerel, redfish, and spotted sea trout, among other species. In addition to the numerous birds to be seen on the island, those interested in wildlife should also watch for alligators, white-tailed deer, raccoons, coyotes, and jackrabbits. In all, there is about 80 miles of beach, dirt roads, and paths available for hiking and mountain biking.

Primitive campsites on the beach cost $4 per night (up to four people), and a rustic bunkhouse has 22 beds with linens, plus restrooms and a common kitchen ($15 per person per night). An outdoor cold-water rinse is available near the docks. The passenger ferry runs a limited schedule from Thursday to Sunday plus holidays, and charges $10 for adults and $5 for children age 12 and younger. Use of the island shuttle is free for those who arrive by ferry; for those who travel to the island by private or charter boat the shuttle costs $2 for adults and $1 for children 6 to 12, and free for children under 6. For ferry times and reservations call the park office (see above).

additional $8 to $15 per night, with reservations available (© **512/389-8900**). The park is about 12 miles from Rockport. Follow Tex. 35 north 10 miles to Park Road 13, which you follow 2 miles east to the park entrance.

Among our favorite beaches along the Gulf is at **Mustang Island State Park** 🏖🏖 (© **361/749-5246;** www.tpwd.state.tx.us/park/mustang), which has more than 5 miles of wide, sandy beach, with fine sand, few rocks and broken shells, and almost enough waves for surfing. A barrier island, Mustang Island offers excellent fishing from jetties, a swimming beach with a bathhouse, picnic tables with sun shelters, and good bird-watching for pelicans, terns, gulls, and other permanent residents plus migratory species in spring and fall. A campground that unfortunately looks too much like a parking lot has 48 sites with water and electric hook-ups ($15 per night, with reservations ℂ **512/389-8900**), showers, and an RV dump station. A better bet, if you can stand to forego hookups, is the almost unlimited beach camping at $7 per night. Campers and day users age 13 and older must also pay the $3 per person day-use fee. Day-use hours are 7am to 10pm. The park is especially busy on summer weekends. Mustang Island is connected to Corpus Christi by a bridge and causeway at the south end and to Aransas Pass via a free ferry on the north end.

You'll find a pleasant beach, with picnic tables, restrooms, and a pavilion at **Rockport Beach Park** (ℂ **361/729-2213, ext. 134**). The thin mile-long strip of beach is sandy, although a little rough with stones and broken shells, and during a November visit there were quite a few jellyfish. Beach parking costs $3 per day.

INDOOR ATTRACTIONS

Rockport Center for the Arts 🌟 Several attractive art galleries and a delightful outdoor sculpture garden make the Rockport Center for the Arts one of the area's top attractions, where you can easily spend an hour or two. The Main Gallery presents about 10 changing exhibits each year that range from local to international artists, with a variety of themes. There are often displays of students' work, and sometimes hands-on exhibits, in the Garden Gallery; and the Members Gallery presents an eclectic selection of works by members of the Rockport Art Association, which manages the center. Although subject matter varies considerably, there are often a number of sea and harbor scenes—we especially enjoyed some of the watercolors of docks, boats, and pelicans in the Members Gallery during our visit. Each of the gallery shows opens with a public reception, at which many of the artists are present, and works are often for sale. The Rockport Art Association sponsors the Rockport Art Festival each summer, in late June and/or early July; and also sponsors a series of art classes, workshops, and concerts (call for the current schedule).

902 Navigation Circle, Rockport. ℂ **361/729-5519**. www.rockportartcenter.org. Free admission. Tues–Sat 10am–4pm; Sun 1–4pm.

Texas Maritime Museum 🌟 From pirates to shipbuilding to offshore oil drilling, this excellent small museum brings to life the story of the Texas Gulf Coast, with lots of hands-on exhibits, historic fishing gear, and old strange-looking outboard motors. Among its changing and permanent exhibits you'll see artwork, such as the "Lighthouses of Texas" watercolors by Harold Phenix, and a life-size ship's bridge where you can imagine yourself on the high seas. On the museum grounds are a survival capsule (used to escape offshore oil rigs in emergencies), a 26-foot-long lifeboat, and a replica of a scow sloop fishing boat. Allow at least 1 hour.

1202 Navigation Circle, Rockport. ℂ **361/729-1271**. www.texasmaritimemuseum.org. Admission $5 adults, $4 seniors 60 and older, $2 children ages 5–12, free for children 4 and under. Tues–Sat 10am–4pm; Sun 1–4pm. Closed major holidays.

WHERE TO STAY & DINE

Among the national chain motels in the Rockport and Fulton areas are the **Best Western Inn by the Bay**, 3902 N. Tex. 35, Fulton (ℂ **800/235-6076** or 361/729-8351); and **Days Inn**, 1212 E. Laurel St. (at Tex. 35), Rockport (ℂ **800/329-7466** or 361/729-6379).

Village Inn Motel ★ *Finds*   This extremely well-maintained two-story older motel—some parts are pre-1930—is an excellent choice for those seeking economical, comfortable lodging within walking distance of Rockport's beach, piers, attractions, and restaurants. Inside the bright yellow wood exterior are a wide variety of simply but attractively decorated units. The rooms are larger than average, with modern furnishings and from one to four beds. Several standard rooms have small refrigerators and microwaves; there are also kitchenette units and several two-bedroom apartments with full kitchens. Twelve units have shower only; the rest have shower/tub combos.

503 N. Austin St., Rockport, TX 78382. © 800/338-7539 for reservations, or 361/729-6370. 26 units. Summer $55–$65 double, $60–$75 kitchenette units, $100–$110 2-bedroom apartments; winter $52–$55 double, $55–$65 kitchenette units, $95 2-bedroom apartments. AE, DC, DISC, MC, V. Pets accepted ($10 per pet per day). **Amenities:** Outdoor pool; coin-op laundry. *In room:* A/C, TV, kitchen and fridge in some units.

WHERE TO DINE

Hungry bargain hunters love **The Big Fisherman,** on Tex. 188 between Rockport and Aransas Pass (© **361/729-1997**), open daily from 11am until 9pm or later. It offers a wide variety of basic seafood, beef, and chicken items, including a number of all-you-can-eat specials, with most main courses from $3.95 to $15. Another good choice is **Panjo's,** in the Harbor Oaks Village Shopping Center at 2744 N. Tex. 35, Rockport (© **361/729-1411**), which serves an excellent crispy-crust pizza plus burgers and pasta dishes, with main courses from $4.95 to $9.95 and pizzas from $3.25 to $15. Panjo's is open daily from 11am until 9pm (until 10pm Fri–Sat).

For a somewhat more upscale dining experience we recommend **The Duck Inn,** 701 N. Tex. 35 (© **361/729-6663**), open Tuesday through Sunday from 5:30am to 2:30pm and 5 to 9pm. The seafood platter is especially good, as are the shrimp gumbo and oyster stew. Prices for dinner main courses range from $7.25 to $17, except market price for the fish of the day, which could be grouper, ling, tuna, swordfish, or whatever.

7

San Antonio

by Edie Jarolim

San Antonio is Texas's top tourist destination for a good reason: It's got something for everyone. I love the city for its museums, missions, and restored historic buildings; I could wander downtown's meandering streets for days without getting bored. But people who like playing golf and just kicking back on the River Walk, sipping cactus margaritas, will be happy here too, as will families; the city has two major theme parks and loads of other kid-friendly activities. I'd be hard pressed to think of anyone who wouldn't want to spend at least 3 days here.

The ninth-largest city in the United States and one of the oldest, San Antonio wasn't always as visitor-oriented as it is today. For a good part of the last century, it was a military town that happened to have a nice river promenade running through its decaying downtown area. Now, with the downsizing and privatizing of Kelly Air Force Base and the continuing development of the River Walk, the city has come to be considered a tourist destination, and locals have begun to reap the economic benefits that come with large numbers of visitors. The North American Free Trade Agreement (NAFTA), signed in 1994, was also a boon for the city, which hosts the North American Development Bank, the financial arm of NAFTA. With a Hispanic population of nearly 60%, regular flights to Mexico City, cultural attractions such as the prestigious Latin American wing

of the San Antonio Museum of Art, and a history of strong business relations with Mexico, San Antonio is ideally positioned to take advantage of the increasing economic reciprocity between the two nations.

Historically speaking, relations with Mexico weren't always quite so sanguine. Remember the Alamo? Its original name was Mission San Antonio de Valero, and it was established in 1719 as the first of five missions built along the banks of the San Antonio River. The city that came to be known as San Antonio—comprising the mission complex, the military garrison designed to protect it, and a civilian town known as Bexar (pronounced *Bear*)—belonged to Spain until 1821, when Mexico won its independence. The mission became far more famous when, refashioned as a fortress, it became the site of the battle for Texas's own battle for freedom in 1836. Some 180 volunteers—among them Davy Crockett and Jim Bowie—serving under the command of William Travis died trying to defend it against a vastly greater number of General Santa Anna's men.

San Antonio almost lost the Alamo again—it was slated to be turned into a hotel in 1905—and it almost lost the San Antonio River: When a storm caused it to overflow its banks in 1921, killing 50 people and destroying many downtown businesses, there was serious talk of cementing it over. It was rescued by the San Antonio Conservation Society and architect

Robert H. H. Hugman, who devised a plan for lining it with shops, restaurants, and entertainment areas buttressed by floodgates. It didn't really become a tourist attraction, however, until 1968, when the HemisFair Exposition was held in downtown San Antonio and visitors thronged to the River Walk. Commercial development took off after that and it just keeps accelerating. Instead of falling victim to the city's suburban spread, the place where San Antonio began was revitalized by its river—just as the Conservation Society had predicted.

Of course, San Antonio's tourism growth can be a mixed blessing. A battle is currently being fought by developers, who want to build PGA City, a vast residential/hotel golf complex, and locals and environmentalists, who are worried that the project will taint the city's water supply (it's slated to sit on the recharge zone for the Edwards Aquifer, San Antonio's main water source). The litigation, which started in 2000, was still ongoing at press time—and there's no reason to assume that the glut of court cases on the docket will be resolved any time soon.

1 Orientation

For visitors, San Antonio is really two cities. Downtown, site of the original Spanish settlements, is the compact, eminently strollable hub. The other city, where most locals live and work, is spread out, generally low rise, and connected by freeways.

ARRIVING
BY PLANE
The two-terminal **San Antonio International Airport** (℃ 210/207-3411; www.sanantonio.gov/airport), about 13 miles north of downtown, is compact, clean, well marked—even cheerful.

GETTING TO & FROM THE AIRPORT   Loop 410 and U.S. 281 south intersect just outside the airport. If you're renting a car here (all of the major agencies are represented), it should take about 15 to 20 minutes to drive downtown via U.S. 281 south.

VIA Metropolitan Transit's bus no. 2 is the cheapest (80¢) way to get downtown but also the slowest; it'll take from 40 to 45 minutes.

SA Trans (℃ **800/868-7707** or 210/281-9900; www.saairportshuttle.com), with a booth outside each of the terminals, offers shared van service from the airport to the downtown hotels for $9 per person one-way, $16 round-trip. Vans run from about 6am until 1am; call 24 hours in advance for van pickup from your hotel.

There's also a **taxi** queue in front of each terminal. It should cost you about $14 to $16 to get downtown.

BY CAR
As has been said of Rome, all roads lead to San Antonio. The city is fed by four interstates (I-35, I-10, I-37, and I-410), five U.S. highways (U.S. 281, U.S. 90, U.S. 87, U.S. 181, and U.S. 81), and five state highways (Tex. 16, Tex. 13, Tex. 211, Tex. 151, and Tex. 1604). The distance between San Antonio and Dallas is 282 miles, Houston 199 miles, and Austin 80 miles.

BY TRAIN
Amtrak provides service three times a week between the coasts and daily service between San Antonio and Chicago. The depot, at 350 Hoefden (℃ **210/223-3226**), is on the east side of downtown. Trains arrive at ungodly hours and the

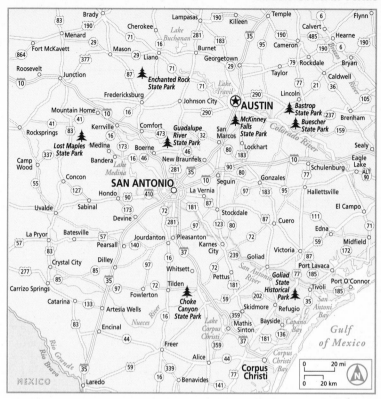

station isn't within walking distance of most hotels, but it's a quick, inexpensive cab ride to them.

BY BUS

San Antonio's bustling **Greyhound** station, 500 N. St. Mary's St. (© **210/270-5824**), is located downtown about 2 blocks from the River Walk. The station, open 24 hours, is within walking distance of a number of hotels, and many public streetcar and bus lines run nearby.

VISITOR INFORMATION

The main office of the **City of San Antonio Visitor Information Center,** open daily from 8:30am to 6pm, is across the street from the Alamo, at 317 Alamo Plaza (© **210/207-6748**).

Publications such as the free *Fiesta,* a glossy magazine with interesting articles about the city, and *Rio,* a tabloid focusing on the River Walk, are available at the Visitor Information Center, as well as at most downtown hotels and many shops and tourist sights. Both of these ad-based tourist publications list sights, restaurants, shops, cultural events, and some nightlife. Also free but less obviously ad-driven is San Antonio's alternative paper, the *Current.* It's pretty skimpy, but it's a good source for nightlife listings. The *San Antonio Express-News,* the city's only real newspaper, has a good arts/entertainment section called "The Weekender," which comes out on Friday and is available for free around town.

Tips **Shameless Plug**

For more in-depth coverage of San Antonio and the Hill Country, pick up
a copy of *Frommer's San Antonio & Austin,* 5th edition.

CITY LAYOUT

Although it lies at the southern edge of the Texas Hill Country, San Antonio
itself is basically flat. Neither the city's compact central downtown nor its West-
ern-style, freeway-laced sprawl is laid out in a neat grid system; many of downtown's streets trace the meandering course of the San Antonio River, while a
number of the thoroughfares in the rest of town follow old conquistador routes
or 19th-century wagon trails.

MAIN ARTERIES & STREETS   Welcome to loop land. Most of the major
roads in Texas meet in San Antonio, where they form a rough wheel-and-spoke
pattern: I-410 traces a 53-mile circumference around the city, and Tex. 1604
forms an even larger circle around them both. I-35, I-10, I-37, U.S. 281,
U.S. 90, and U.S. 87, along with many smaller thoroughfares, run diagonally,
but not always separately, across these two loops to form its main spokes. You
may hear locals referring to something as being "in the loop." That doesn't mean
it's privy to key information but, rather, that it lies within the circumference of
I-410, and is therefore in central San Antonio.

Downtown is bounded by I-37 on the east, I-35 on the north and west, and
U.S. 90 (which merges with I-10) on the south. Within these parameters,
Durango, Commerce, Market, and Houston are important east-west thoroughfares. Alamo and Santa Rosa are major north-south streets, the former on the
east side, the latter on the west side.

THE NEIGHBORHOODS IN BRIEF

A sure sign of urban sprawl is when areas stop acquiring names and begin getting geo-
graphical designations. The older areas described here, from downtown through Alamo
Heights, are all "in the loop" (I-410). The Medical Center area lies just outside of it. The city's
two resorts are in outlying, developing areas—Westin La Cantera is in the Northwest, near
Six Flags Fiesta Texas, and the Hyatt Regency Hill Country Resort is in the West, near Sea-
World—but most visitors are likely to want to stay in or around downtown.

Hotels, restaurants, and attractions in Downtown, King William Historic District, and
Southtown can be located on the "Central San Antonio" map; all other areas are shown on
the "Greater San Antonio" map.

Central San Antonio

Downtown Site of San Antonio's
three oldest Spanish settlements,
this area includes the Alamo and
other historic sites, along with
the River Walk, the Alamodome,
SBC Center, the convention center, the Rivercenter Mall, and
many high-rise hotels, restaurants,
shops, and, increasingly, entertainment complexes. This is the most
convenient—and generally most
expensive—area for travelers to stay.

King William Historic District
The city's first suburb, this historic
district directly south of downtown
was settled in the mid- to late 1800s
by wealthy German merchants who
built some of the most beautiful
mansions in town. If you like bed-
and-breakfasts, and don't mind

being a bit distant from restaurants and nightlife, this is a good place to spend the night.

Southtown Alamo Street marks a rough border between King William and Southtown, the adjoining commercial district. Long a depressed area, it's now becoming trendy, thanks to a Main Street refurbishing project and the opening of the Blue Star arts complex. You'll find a nice mix of Hispanic neighborhood shops and funky coffeehouses and galleries here, but no lodgings.

Greater San Antonio

South Side The old, largely Hispanic southeast section of town that begins where Southtown ends is home to four of the five historic missions. Thus far, it hasn't been experiencing the same gentrification and redevelopment as much of the rest of the city, but that may change as the hike and bike trail along the stretch of the San Antonio River that runs through this area is completed.

Monte Vista Historic District Immediately northwest of downtown, Monte Vista was established soon after King William by a conglomeration of wealthy cattlemen, politicos, and generals who moved "on to the hill" at the turn of the 20th century. It hasn't reached King William status yet, but this is already a highly desirable (read: pricey) place to live—and to stay, as it has several good B&Bs.

Fort Sam Houston Built in 1876 to the northeast of downtown, Fort Sam Houston hosts a number of stunning officers' homes. Much of the working-class neighborhood surrounding Fort Sam is now run-down, but renewed interest in restoring San Antonio's older areas is beginning to have some impact

here, too. It's loaded with inexpensive motel chains, but it's still too seedy to make it a good overnight stop.

Alamo Heights Area One of the city's most exclusive neighborhoods, Alamo Heights is home to wealthy families, expensive shops, and trendy restaurants. **Terrell Hills** to the east, **Olmos Park** to the west, and **Lincoln Heights** to the north are all offshoots of this moneyed area; the latter is home to the Quarry, once just that, but now a ritzy golf course and shopping mall. The Witte Museum, the San Antonio Botanical Gardens, and Brackenridge Park are all in this part of town. Oddly, you won't find good lodgings in this area, but it's worth the drive to dine where the locals do.

Northwest The mostly characterless neighborhood surrounding the South Texas Medical Center (always just referred to as **Medical Center**) is one of the city's more recently established areas. Much of the shopping and dining is in strip malls, and chain motels proliferate. The farther north you go, the nicer the housing and shopping complexes get. The high-end Westin La Cantera resort and several tony new golf courses mark the direction that development is taking in the far northwest part of town, just beyond Six Flags Fiesta Texas and near the public Friedrich Park.

North Central San Antonio is inching towards Bulverde and other Hill Country towns via this major corridor of development clustered from Loop 410 north to Loop 1604, east of I-10 and west of I-35, and bisected by U.S. 281. The **airport** and many developed industrial strips line U.S. 281 in the southern section, but the farther

Greater San Antonio Accommodations, Dining & Attractions

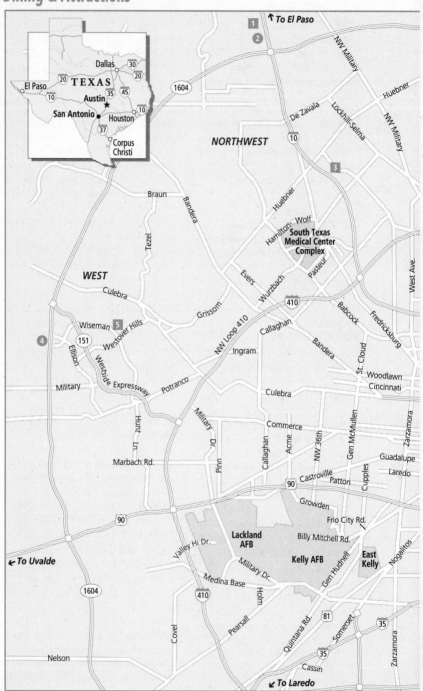

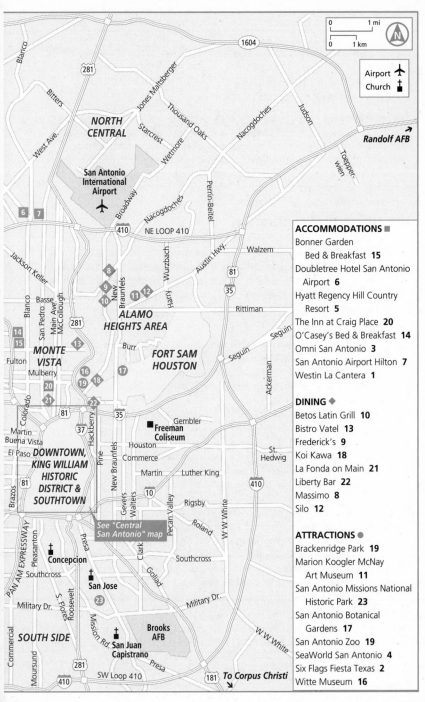

ACCOMMODATIONS ■
Bonner Garden
  Bed & Breakfast **15**
Doubletree Hotel San Antonio
  Airport **6**
Hyatt Regency Hill Country
  Resort **5**
The Inn at Craig Place **20**
O'Casey's Bed & Breakfast **14**
Omni San Antonio **3**
San Antonio Airport Hilton **7**
Westin La Cantera **1**

DINING ◆
Betos Latin Grill **10**
Bistro Vatel **13**
Frederick's **9**
Koi Kawa **18**
La Fonda on Main **21**
Liberty Bar **22**
Massimo **8**
Silo **12**

ATTRACTIONS ●
Brackenridge Park **19**
Marion Koogler McNay
  Art Museum **11**
San Antonio Missions National
  Historic Park **23**
San Antonio Botanical
  Gardens **17**
San Antonio Zoo **19**
SeaWorld San Antonio **4**
Six Flags Fiesta Texas **2**
Witte Museum **16**

north you go, the more you see the natural beauty of this area, hilly and dotted with small canyons.

West Although SeaWorld has been out here since the late 1980s, and the Hyatt Regency Hill Country Resort settled in during the early 1990s, other development was comparatively slow in coming. Now, the West is booming with new mid-price housing developments, strip malls, schools, and businesses. Road building hasn't kept pace with growth, however, so traffic can be a bear.

2 Getting Around

If you're staying in downtown, a car is more of a hindrance than an asset: Traffic and parking are a pain, and public transportation is good. If you're bunking anywhere else in San Antonio, however, you'll definitely want wheels—and you might as well rent them at the airport, where all the major car-rental companies are represented at each of the terminals.

BY PUBLIC TRANSPORTATION

In addition to its 104 bus lines, which run throughout the city, **VIA Metropolitan Transit Service** (© 210/362-2020; www.viainfo.net), offers four convenient downtown streetcar routes that cover all the most popular tourist stops. The streetcar fare is 50¢. The regular bus routes cost 80¢ for regular lines, with an additional 15¢ charge for transfers, and $1.60 for express buses (15¢ for transfers). In all cases, you'll need exact change.

BY CAR

If you can avoid driving downtown, by all means do so. The pattern of one-way streets is confusing and parking is extremely limited. It's not that the streets in downtown San Antonio are narrower or more crowded than those in most old city centers; it's just that there's no need to bother when public transportation is so convenient.

As for highway driving, because of the many convergences of major freeways here—described in the "Main Arteries & Streets" section, above—if you're not constantly vigilant, you'll find yourself in the express lane to somewhere you really don't want to go. Don't let your mind wander; watch the signs carefully and be prepared to make lots of quick lane changes.

Rush hour lasts from about 7:45am to 9am and 4:30pm to 6pm Monday through Friday. The crush may not be bad compared with those of Houston or Dallas, but it's getting worse all the time. Because of San Antonio's rapid growth, you can also expect to find major highway construction or repairs going on somewhere in the city at any given time. Areas that will be particularly hard hit in the next few years are the Loop 410/I-10 and Loop 410/U.S. 281 links, where four-level interchanges, with ramps directly connecting the respective freeways with one another, are in the works. Construction is not scheduled to be completed until 2005 or '06.

PARKING Parking meters are not plentiful in the heart of downtown, but you can find some on the streets near the River Walk and on Broadway. The cost is $1 per hour (which is also the time limit) in San Fernando Plaza and near the courthouse, 75¢ in other locations. Though too few signs inform you of this, parking next to meters is free after 6pm Monday through Saturday and all day Sunday, except during Alamodome events, at which time meters are enforced. If

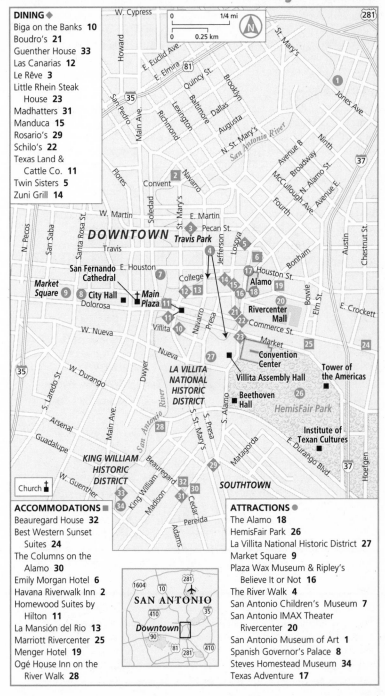

DINING ◆
Biga on the Banks **10**
Boudro's **21**
Guenther House **33**
Las Canarias **12**
Le Rêve **3**
Little Rhein Steak House **23**
Madhatters **31**
Manduca **15**
Rosario's **29**
Schilo's **22**
Texas Land & Cattle Co. **11**
Twin Sisters **5**
Zuni Grill **14**

ACCOMMODATIONS ■
Beauregard House **32**
Best Western Sunset Suites **24**
The Columns on the Alamo **30**
Emily Morgan Hotel **6**
Havana Riverwalk Inn **2**
Homewood Suites by Hilton **11**
La Mansión del Rio **13**
Marriott Rivercenter **25**
Menger Hotel **19**
Ogé House Inn on the River Walk **28**

ATTRACTIONS ●
The Alamo **18**
HemisFair Park **26**
La Villita National Historic District **27**
Market Square **9**
Plaza Wax Museum & Ripley's Believe It or Not **16**
The River Walk **4**
San Antonio Children's Museum **7**
San Antonio IMAX Theater Rivercenter **20**
San Antonio Museum of Art **1**
Spanish Governor's Palace **8**
Steves Homestead Museum **34**
Texas Adventure **17**

you don't observe the laws, you'll be ticketed pretty quickly. Except during Fiesta or other major events, you shouldn't have a problem finding a parking lot or garage for your car; rates run from $5 to $7 per day. Prices tend to go up during special events and summer weekends. If you're only staying for a short time, consider leaving your car in the Rivercenter Mall garage and getting your ticket validated at one of the shops; you don't have to buy anything and you'll have 2 hours of free parking.

BY RIVER TAXI

Why walk or ride when you can motor down the river? The **Rio Trans River Shuttle** (② 210/244-5700; www.sarivercruise.com) has several ticket locations on the River Walk; call to find the one nearest you. Shuttle stops on the River Walk are marked by Rio Trans signs, but you have to get your ticket before you board. At $3.50 one-way, $10 for an all-day pass, or $25 for a 3-day pass, it's more expensive than ground transport, but it's a treat.

BY TAXI

Cabs are available outside the airport, near the Greyhound and Amtrak terminals, and at most major downtown hotels, but they're next to impossible to hail on the street; most of the time, you'll need to phone for one in advance. The best of the major taxi companies in town is **Yellow-Checker** (② 210/222-2222), which has an excellent record of turning up when promised.

 FAST FACTS: San Antonio

American Express There are no Amex offices in San Antonio. If you need to exchange currency, there's an exchange counter at the airport, and **Frost Bank,** 100 W. Houston St. at Main Street (② 210/220-4711).

Babysitters Your hotel should be able to recommend a reliable service.

Dentist Contact the **San Antonio District Dental Society,** 3355 Cherry Ridge, Suite 214 (② 210/732-1264).

Doctor For a referral, phone the **Bexar County Medical Society** at 202 W. French Place (② 210/301-4368).

Drugstores Most branches of **Eckerd** and **Walgreens,** the major chain pharmacies in San Antonio, are open late Monday through Saturday. There's an Eckerd downtown at 211 Losoya/River Walk (② 210/224-9293). Call ② 800/925-4733 to find the Walgreens nearest you.

Hospitals The main downtown hospital is **Baptist Medical Center,** 111 Dallas St. (② 210/297-7000). **Christus Santa Rosa Health Care Corp.,** 519 W. Houston (② 210/704-2011), is also downtown. Contact the **San Antonio Medical Foundation** (② 210/614-3724) for information on other facilities.

Newspaper The *San Antonio Express-News,* owned by the Hearst Corporation, is the only mainstream source of news in town.

Police The **Sheriff's Department** number is ② 210/270-6000, and the **Texas Highway Patrol** can be reached at ② 210/533-9171. In an emergency, dial ② 911.

Post Office The main post office is at the far northeast part of town at 10410 Perrin-Beitel, but the most convenient location is downtown at

615 E. Houston St., just across from the Alamo. It's open Monday through Friday from 8:30am to 5:30pm. Call © **800/275-8777** to find other branches.

Safety The crime rate in San Antonio has gone down along with that of the rest of the country, and there are frequent police patrols downtown at night; as a result, muggings, pickpocketings, or purse snatchings in the area are rare. It's not generally a good idea to stroll south of Durango after dark.

Taxes Sales tax is 7.875%; the city surcharge on hotel rooms comes to a whopping 16.75%.

Transit Information Call VIA Metropolitan Transit Service at © **210/362-2020.**

Weather For weather information, call © **210/226-3232.**

3 Where to Stay

You don't have to leave your lodgings to sightsee in San Antonio: The city has the highest concentration of historic hotels in Texas. Even low-end hotel chains are reclaiming old buildings—some are covered in this chapter—so don't judge a place on the basis of its name. Most of these, as well as other, more recently built luxury accommodations, are in the downtown area. Prices in this prime location can be high, especially for hotels on the river, but you'll generally get your money's worth. You'll also economize by eliminating the need to rent a car.

In recent years, a number of the old mansions in the King William and Monte Vista Historic Districts have been converted into bed-and-breakfasts; several are listed in this section, too. For information about additional B&Bs in these areas and in other neighborhoods around the city, check out the website of the **San Antonio Bed & Breakfast Association,** www.sanantoniobb.org.

See "The Neighborhoods in Brief" section, above, for a sketch of various lodging area pros and cons. Wherever you decide to stay, but especially if it's downtown, try to book as far in advance as possible. And don't even think about coming to town during Fiesta (the 3rd week in Apr) if you haven't reserved a room 6 months in advance.

The **San Antonio Convention and Visitors Bureau**'s annual SAVE (San Antonio Vacation Experience) promotion features discounts on hotel rooms as well as on dining and entertainment. Call © **800/447-3372** for more information. The "Accommodations" section of www.sanantoniovisit.com is a good resource, too. Some B&Bs and hotels offer better rates to those who book for at least 4 days, though a week is usually the minimum. Even though most leisure travelers visit in summer, rooms tend to be less expensive then; in general, rates are highest November through April, when conventions converge on the town.

DOWNTOWN
VERY EXPENSIVE

La Mansión del Rio ★★ This lushly landscaped Spanish hacienda–style hotel—converted from a 19th-century seminary—not only oozes character, but it also sits right on the River Walk. Moorish arches, Mexican tile, a central patio, wrought-iron balconies, and antique pieces in every nook and cranny combine to create a low-glitz, high-tone Mediterranean atmosphere. The layout is a bit mazelike, but staff discretion and a willingness to cater to special requests makes this hotel the pick for many of San Antonio's high-profile visitors (their entourages no doubt steer them in the right direction). Guest rooms recently underwent a massive revamp and are now better than ever, with rich green, gold and burgundy draperies and bedspreads complementing the rough-hewn beamed ceilings, and brick walls. The more expensive quarters boast balconies overlooking the River Walk, but the interior courtyard views are fine, too.

112 College St. (between St. Mary's and Navarro), San Antonio, TX 78205. ✆ **800/292-7300** or 210/518-1000. Fax 210/226-0389. www.lamansion.com. 337 units. $249–$329 double; $575–$1,949 suite. AE, DC, DISC, MC, V. Valet parking $15. Pets accepted, subject to room availability and manager's approval. **Amenities:** Restaurant; bar; heated outdoor pool; exercise room; concierge; business center; 24-hr. room service; babysitting; same-day dry cleaning. *In room:* A/C, TV w/pay movies, dataport, minibar, coffeemaker, hair dryer, iron.

Marriott Rivercenter ✰   Serious retail hounds will find heaven in this glitzy conventioneer high-rise; they can shop more than 100 Rivercenter emporiums until they're ready to drop, and then collapse back into their hotel rooms without ever leaving the mall. Sightseers will be happy here, too: A cruise along the River Walk departs from the mall's downstairs "dock," and the Alamo and HemisFair Park are just a few blocks away. Convenience is definitely the goal here— free washers and dryers on the same floor as the health club let you bicycle while your clothes cycle. Guest rooms have an earth-toned, simple elegance. Many afford spectacular River Walk or city views.

101 Bowie St. (at Commerce), San Antonio, TX 78205. ✆ **800/228-9290** or 210/223-1000. Fax 210/223-4092. www.marriotthotels.com. 1,001 units. $279 double; suites from $450. River barge packages available. AE, DC, DISC, MC, V. Self-parking $12; valet parking $17. Pets under 20 lbs. permitted w/ $25 deposit. **Amenities:** 2 restaurants; coffee shop; bar; indoor pool; heated outdoor pool; excellent health club; Jacuzzi; sauna; concierge; car-rental desk; business center; 24-hr. room service; babysitting; coin-op laundry; same-day dry cleaning; executive and business equipped rooms. *In room:* A/C, TV w/pay movies, dataport, coffeemaker, hair dryer, iron.

EXPENSIVE

Emily Morgan Hotel ✰✰ *Value*   Emily, we hardly knew you. The Emily Morgan Hotel was long a moderately priced Ramada in a historic building. The location, a musket shot from the Alamo and the River Walk, is as good as ever, and the facade of the 1926 Gothic revival medical arts center was undisturbed, but the dowdy public areas and guest rooms were seriously glamorized in 2002. Now the rooms have a light, contemporary feel, designed to appeal to the young affluent crowd who go for the pared-down "I don't have time for fuss" look popularized by the W hotels. But here any industrial chic coldness is offset by lots of dark, burnished wood and such touches as a lit votive candle at turndown. Of course, you aren't going to get 250-count sheets, Aveda bath products, 27-inch TVs, and, in 115 of the rooms, jetted tubs at Ramada prices. But this place is still considerably less expensive than many comparable ones that sit right on the river, and its combination of hipness, luxury, and history is hard to beat.

705 E. Houston St. (at Ave. E), San Antonio, TX 78205. ✆ **800/824-6674** or 210/225-8486. Fax 210/225-7227. www.emilymorganhotel.com. 177 units. $189–$229 double; suites $259–$289. Corporate and promotional rates available. AE, DC, DISC, MC, V. Valet parking $16. **Amenities:** Restaurant; bar; heated outdoor pool; decent exercise room; Jacuzzi; sauna; concierge; 24-hr. room service; same-day dry cleaning. *In room:* A/C, TV w/pay movies, dataport, coffeemaker, hair dryer, iron, CD player.

Menger Hotel ✿   In the late 19th century, no one who was anyone would consider staying anywhere but the Menger, which opened its doors in 1859 and never closed them. Ulysses S. Grant, Sarah Bernhardt, and Oscar Wilde were among those who walked—or, rumor has it, in the case of Robert E. Lee, rode a horse—through the halls, ballrooms, and gardens. Successfully combining the original, restored building with myriad additions, the Menger now takes up an entire city block. The hotel's location is terrific—smack between the Alamo and the Rivercenter Mall, a block from the River Walk, with the tourist information office on the ground floor—and its public areas, particularly the Victorian Lobby, are gorgeous. The Menger also has a small spa, still a rarity in San Antonio hotels. The rooms, however, are somewhat tired, and no longer the bargain they've been in the past. Decor ranges from ornate 19th-century to modern. If you want one of the antiques-filled Victorian rooms, be sure to request it when you book.

204 Alamo Plaza (at Houston), San Antonio, TX 78205. ✆ **800/345-9285** or 210/223-4361. Fax 210/228-0022. www.historicmenger.com. 316 units. $195–$215 rooms; $250–$495 suite. AE, DC, DISC, MC, V. Self-parking $13; valet parking $17. **Amenities:** Restaurant; bar; heated outdoor pool; exercise room; spa; Jacuzzi; shopping arcade; limited room service; same-day dry cleaning. *In room:* A/C, TV w/pay movies, dataport, mini-bar in suites, fridge rentals for $25, hair dryer, iron, safe.

MODERATE

Havana Riverwalk Inn ✿   This is the hippest place to stay on the river. Decked out to suggest travelers' lodgings from around the 1920s, this intimate inn, built in 1914 in Mediterranean Revival style, is a blast. All the rooms are delightfully different, with a safari hat covering a temperature control gauge here, an old photograph perched over a toilet paper roll there, gauzy curtains draped on a canopy bed, wooden louvres on the windows, brick walls, and so on. Touches like fresh flowers and bottled water add to the charm. Not all rooms have closets, however, so be prepared to have your clothes hanging in public view if you plan to invite anyone to your room—a good thing to remember if you're thinking of hitting the hotel's super-hot cigar bar, Club Cohiba.

1015 Navarro (between St. Mary's and Augusta), San Antonio, TX 78205. ✆ **888/224-2008** or 210/222-2008. Fax 210/222-2717. www.havanariverwalkinn.com. 27 units. $109–$209 double; $249–$599 suite. Special packages available. AE, DC, DISC, MC, V. Self-parking $10. Children under 15 not accepted. **Amenities:** Restaurant; bar; concierge; secretarial services; limited room service; same-day dry cleaning. *In room:* A/C, TV w/pay movies, dataport, hair dryer, iron.

Homewood Suites by Hilton *(Kids (Value*   Opened in the mid-1990s in the former San Antonio Drug Company building (built in 1919), this all-suites hotel is a good downtown deal. Located on a quiet stretch of the river, it's convenient to attractions such as Market Square and only a few extra blocks from the Alamo. In-room amenities such as microwaves, refrigerators with icemakers, and dishwashers appeal to business travelers and families alike; the dining area can double as a workspace, and there's a sleeper sofa in each suite as well as two TVs with VCRs—so fewer squabbles over TV shows and movies. The decor is a cut above that of most chains, with Lone Star–design headboards, light wood desks and bureaus, and attractive Southwestern bedspreads and drapes. Two suites have river views.

432 Market St. (at St. Mary's), San Antonio, TX 78205. ✆ **800/CALL-HOME** or 210/222-1515. Fax 210/222-1575. www.homewood-riverwalk.com.146 units. $139–$249 suite. Rates lower during the week. AE, DC, DISC, MC, V. Valet parking $16. Rates include continental breakfast and afternoon drinks and snacks. **Amenities:** Heated rooftop pool; small exercise room; Jacuzzi; concierge; 24-hr. business center; self-service laundry;

same-day dry cleaning. *In room:* A/C, TV/VCR w/pay movies, dataport, kitchenette, coffeemaker, hair dryer, iron.

INEXPENSIVE

Best Western Sunset Suites ★★ *(Kids)* *(Value)*   Don't be put off by the fact that this all-suites hotel is on the wrong side of the tracks, uh, highway. In a converted turn-of-the-20th-century building you'll find some of the nicest rooms in downtown San Antonio—large, with custom-made Arts and Crafts–style furnishings, including comfy, clean-lined lounge chairs and faux Tiffany lamps. They're also some of the best equipped: All offer sleeper sofas, microwaves, minifridges, and 27-inch TVs. And talk about deals. You get a free hot buffet breakfast, free afternoon cocktails, free local calls, and free trolley passes. With all the money you've saved, you can afford to have dinner at Ruth's Chris Steakhouse, just a few blocks away in the Sunset Station entertainment complex.

1103 E. Commerce St. (at Hwy. 281), San Antonio, TX 78205. © **866/560-6000** or 210/223-4400. Fax 210/223-4402. www.bestwesternsunsetsuites.com. 64 units. $89–$119 double. Rates include breakfast. Free parking. **Amenities:** Exercise room; business center. *In room:* A/C, TV w/pay movies, dataport, kitchenette, coffeemaker, hair dryer, iron.

KING WILLIAM HISTORIC DISTRICT
EXPENSIVE

Ogé House Inn on the River Walk ★★   One of the most glorious of the mansions that grace the King William district, the 1867 Greek revival–style Ogé House is more boutique inn than bed-and-breakfast. You'll still get the personalized attention you would expect from a host home, but it's combined here with the luxury of a sophisticated small hotel. All rooms are impeccably decorated in high Victorian style, but feature modern conveniences; many have fireplaces and views of the manicured, pecan-shaded grounds, and one looks out on the river

---

(*Kids* **Family-Friendly Hotels**

Hyatt Regency Hill Country Resort (p. 247)   In addition to its many great places for kids to play (including a beach with a shallow swimming area), this hotel has Camp Hyatt, a special program of excursions, sports, and social activities for children ages 3 to 12. This program fills up fast during school breaks and other holidays, when reservations are mandatory.

Homewood Suites by Hilton (p. 243)   This reasonably priced all-suites hotel, with in-room kitchen facilities and two TVs (each with its own VCR), not to mention a guest laundry, is a good bet for families who want to stay downtown.

O'Casey's Bed & Breakfast (p. 246)   Usually B&Bs and family vacations are a contradiction in terms, but O'Casey's is happy to host well-behaved kids (they accept the other kind too, but you can't expect happiness). Best bet: Stay in the separate guest house with the foldout bed, and join the main house guests for breakfast in the morning.

Westin La Cantera (p. 246)   It's close to Six Flags Fiesta Texas, it's got two pools just for children, and it's got the Enchanted Rock Kids Club from May to September, an activities program for ages 4 through 12.

from its own wrought-iron balcony. The units downstairs aren't as light as those on the upper two floors but they're less expensive and offer private entrances. A bountiful gourmet breakfast is served on individual white-clothed tables set with the finest of crystal and china.

209 Washington St. (at Turner), San Antonio, TX 78204. © 800/242-2770 or 210/223-2353. Fax 210/226-5812. www.ogeinn.com. 10 units. $155 double; $185–$225 suite. Rates include breakfast. Corporate rates available for single business travelers (Sun–Thurs). AE, DC, DISC, MC, V. Free off-street parking. 2-night minimum stay on weekends, 3-night minimum during holidays and special events. In room: A/C, TV, dataport, fridge, hair dryer, iron.

MODERATE

Beauregard House ★ *Finds*   You can tell that an artist runs this appealing B&B as soon as you walk through the door. Owner Lisa Fittipaldi, who painted most of the vibrant pictures that hang on the walls (and after she lost 90% of her vision), decorated the 1908 house with creative flair. Fittipaldi is also somewhat of a historian: She gathered clean-lined antiques contemporary with the period for the rooms, which she named for authors (Faulkner, Hemingway) who were writing during this era. Accommodations are gorgeous without being fussy and come with extras, such as sewing kits, usually only found in the larger hotels. Cellphones are available with a deposit, and they also provide complimentary trolley tickets. Yet another bonus: Lisa's husband, Al, is a trained chef who had a successful restaurant on Long Island. His 40 morning recipes incorporate organic ingredients whenever possible.

215 Beauregard St. (at Madison), San Antonio, TX 78204. © 888/667-0555 or 210/222-1198. www.beauregardhouse.com. 6 units. $109–$114 double; $129–$139 suite. Rates include breakfast. Extended stay plans available. AE, DISC, MC, V. Free off-street parking. 2-night minimum stay on weekends; 3- to 4-night minimum during holidays and special events. **Amenities:** Bike rental. In room: A/C, TV (VCR in some units, one w/ DVD), dataport in some units, fridge, coffeemaker, hair dryer.

The Columns on Alamo ★   Guests at this B&B, which straddles the boundary between King William and the livelier Southtown, can stay in the 1892 Greek revival mansion from which the inn derives its name; the adjacent guesthouse, built 9 years later; or a separate limestone cottage that's new but built in rustic early 1880s style. The mansion, where the innkeepers live, is the most opulent and offers unusual walk-through windows leading to a veranda, but the guesthouse, which houses most of the lodgings, affords more privacy if you're uncomfortable with the idea of staying in someone else's home. All the rooms are light, airy, and very pretty, although this is not the place for those allergic to pastels and frills; pink dominates many of the accommodations, and even the darker-toned Imari Room has lace curtains. (The Rock House, done in more casual country style, is the exception.) Several of the units boast two-person Jacuzzis and gas-log fireplaces.

1037 S. Alamo (at Sheridan), San Antonio, TX 78210. © 800/233-3364 or 210/271-3245. www.columnssanantonio.com. 13 units. $92–$162 double; $162–$255 cottage. Rates include breakfast. Extended-stay discounts available. AE, DC, DISC, MC, V. Free off-street parking. In room: A/C, TV, dataport, fridge, hair dryer, iron.

MONTE VISTA HISTORIC DISTRICT
MODERATE

The Inn at Craig Place ★   This 1891 mansion turned B&B will appeal to history, art, and architecture buffs alike. It was built by one of Texas's preeminent architects, Alfred Giles, for H. H. Hildebrand, one of San Antonio's movers and shakers, and the living room boasts a mural by Julian Onderbronk, an influential Texas landscape artist. But that's all academic. More to the point, this place is gorgeous, with forests of gleaming wood and clean Arts-and-Crafts lines, as well as cushy couches and a wraparound porch. Rooms are at once luxurious—all have working fireplaces, hardwood floors, and come with robes, slippers, feather pillows, and down comforters—and equipped for modern needs. To gild the lily, one of the innkeepers, Tamra Black, worked as a professional chef, so you can expect the three-course breakfasts to be outstanding.

117 W. Craig Place (off N. Main), San Antonio, TX 78212. ⓒ **877/427-2447** or 210/736-1017. Fax 210/737-1562. www.craigplace.com. 4 units. $115–$200. Corporate rates available. Rates include breakfast. AE, DC, MC, V. Street parking. *In room:* A/C, TV, dataport, iron, CD player.

INEXPENSIVE

Bonner Garden Bed & Breakfast ★ *Value* Those who like the intimacy of the bed-and-breakfast experience but aren't keen on Victorian froufrou should consider staying at this large Italianate villa, built in 1910 for Louisiana artist Mary Bonner. It has a beautiful, classical simplicity and lots of gorgeous antiques—not to mention a 45-foot sunken swimming pool. The Portico Room, in which guests can gaze up at a painted blue sky with billowing clouds, offers a private poolside entrance. Most of the rooms feature European-style decor, but Mary Bonner's former studio, separate from the main house, is done in tasteful Santa Fe style. A rooftop deck with a wet bar affords a sparkling nighttime view of downtown—or, if you prefer your views virtual, you can take advantage of the desktop computer with DSL access in the living room.

145 E. Agarita (at McCullough), San Antonio, TX 78212. ⓒ **800/396-4222** or 210/733-4222. Fax 210/733-6129. www.bonnergarden.com. 6 units. $85–$105 double; $115–$125 suite. Rates include full breakfast. Extended stay (minimum 3 nights) and corporate rates (Sun–Thurs) available. AE, DISC, MC, V. Free off-street parking. **Amenities:** Outdoor pool; small exercise room; Jacuzzi; bike rental. *In room:* A/C, TV/VCR (film library in house), dataport in some units, iron.

O'Casey's Bed & Breakfast *Kids* *Value* If there's a twinkle in John Casey's eye when he puts on a brogue, it's because he was born on U.S. soil, not the auld sod. But his and his wife Linda Fay's down-home friendliness is no blarney. This Irish-themed B&B is one of the few around that welcomes families, and it's well equipped to handle them. One suite in the main house has a sitting area with a futon large enough for a couple of youngsters; another has a trundle bed for two kids in a separate bedroom. And the studio apartments in the carriage house both offer full kitchens. Which is not to suggest that accommodations are utilitarian—far from it. Rooms in the main house—a gracious structure built in 1904—feature hardwood floors and fine antiques, and many bathrooms have claw-foot tubs. There's also a wraparound balcony upstairs.

225 W. Craig Place (between San Pedro and Main), San Antonio, TX 78212. ⓒ **800/738-1378** or 210/738-1378. www.ocaseybnb.com. 7 units. $79–$99 double; $89–$99 suite; $109 apt. Rates include breakfast. Lower weekday rates; discounts on stays of 5 nights or more. AE, DISC, MC, V. Street parking. Pets allowed in apartments ($10 fee per night). *In room:* A/C, TV, kitchen in some units, no phone.

NORTHWEST
VERY EXPENSIVE

Westin La Cantera ★★★ *Kids* With its knockout facilities, gorgeous grounds, and abundance of Texas character, the Westin is an all-around winner. Its proximity to Six Flags Fiesta Texas and excellent children's programs make it family friendly; its two championship courses appeal to duffers; and drop-dead views from one of the highest points in San Antonio make this a romantic retreat, too. Casual elegant rooms, beautifully decorated in muted earth tones and subtle florals, are likely to be abandoned for the resort's myriad recreation areas. The indigenous plant life and animal life—deer, rabbits, and wild turkeys come out at dusk—should have you oohing and aahing. So will the Southwest cuisine (speaking of game . . .) and the sundown vistas of Francesca's at Sunset, the resort's excellent fine dining room.

16641 La Cantera Pkwy. (¾ miles west of the La Cantera exit of I-10), San Antonio, TX 78256. Ⓒ **800/ WESTIN-1** or 210/558-6500. Fax 210/641-0721. www.westin.com/lacantera. 508 units. $200–$500 double; $380–$1,800 suite; $350–$1,200 casitas. AE, DC, DISC, MC, V. Free self-parking; valet parking $10. **Amenities:** 3 restaurants; coffee shop; 2 bars (including cigar bar); 5 outdoor pools (2 heated); 2 18-hole golf courses; 2 tennis courts (1 lit); health club; spa; 2 Jacuzzis; children's programs; game room; concierge; car-rental desk; business center; 24-hr. room service; in-room massage; same-day dry cleaning. *In room:* A/C, TV w/pay movies, dataport, minibar, coffeemaker, hair dryer, iron, safe.

EXPENSIVE

Omni San Antonio ★ *Kids* This polished granite high-rise off I-10 West is convenient to SeaWorld, Six Flags Fiesta Texas, the airport, and the Hill Country, and the shops and restaurants of the 66-acre Colonnade complex are within easy walking distance. The lobby is soaring and luxurious, and guest rooms, updated in 2001, are well appointed in a traditional European style. The proximity to the theme parks as well as in-room Nintendo and various other Omni Kids features makes this hotel as appealing to families as it is to business travelers, who appreciate its exercise facilities, better than most in San Antonio and definitely the best in this part of town, dominated by inexpensive chains. Although the hotel sees a lot of tourist and Medical Center traffic, service here is always prompt and courteous.

9821 Colonnade Blvd. (at Wurzbach), San Antonio, TX 78230. Ⓒ **800/843-6664** or 210/691-8888. Fax 210/ 691-1128. www.omnihotels.com. 326 units. $169 double; $300–$600 suite. Special packages available. AE, DC, DISC, MC, V. Free self-parking; valet parking $7. Pets 25 lb. or under permitted with $50 deposit. **Amenities:** Restaurant; bar; indoor pool and heated outdoor lap pool; excellent exercise room; 2 Jacuzzis; sauna; game room; concierge; complimentary airport shuttle; business center; limited room service; babysitting; same-day dry cleaning; executive rooms. *In room:* TV w/pay movies and Nintendo, dataport, minibar, coffeemaker, hair dryer, iron.

WEST
VERY EXPENSIVE

Hyatt Regency Hill Country Resort ★★★ *Kids* You'll find something at the Hyatt to fulfill your every need—except the one to make money to pay for all this and the one never to leave. Guest quarters are done in updated (read unfussy) country style—carved maple beds topped with quilt-style covers, walls with stenciled borders. Recreation facilities are as top-notch as you'd expect, especially the 950-foot-long Ramblin' River, a lushly landscaped 4-acre park where you can grab an inner tube and float your cares away. The setting, on 200 acres of former ranchland, is idyllic, and SeaWorld of Texas sits at your doorstep. And, not one to rest on its laurels—or in this case, its live oaks—the resort added a fantastic new spa in 2002, definitely the best pampering palace in this part of Texas but super low-key and relaxing.

9800 Hyatt Resort Dr. (off Tex. 151, between Westover Hills Blvd. and Petranco Rd.), San Antonio, TX 78251. Ⓒ **800/233-1234** or 210/647-1234. Fax 210/681-9681. http://hillcountry.hyatt.com. 500 units. $275–$380 double; $450–$1,550 suite. Rates lower late Nov to early Mar; golf, spa, and other packages available (rates may drop as low as $99 per night). AE, DC, DISC, MC, V. Free self-parking; valet parking $8. **Amenities:** 4 restaurants; coffee shop; snack bar; 2 bars; heated outdoor pool; 18-hole golf course; 3 tennis courts (2 lit); health club; spa; 2 outdoor Jacuzzis; bike rental; children's program; game room; concierge; car-rental desk;

business center; limited room service; self-serve laundry; same-day dry cleaning; executive rooms. *In room:* A/C, TV w/pay movies, dataport, fridge, hair dryer, iron.

NORTH CENTRAL (AIRPORT)
EXPENSIVE

San Antonio Airport Hilton   You'll go straight from the airport to the heart of Texas if you stay at this friendly hotel, where the cheerful lobby has a bull-rider mural and the guest quarters feature Lone Star–pattern chairs and cowboy lamps. The decor may be fun, but the rooms, loaded with up-to-date amenities, also get down to business. Jocks will like Tex's sports bar, with Texas sports memorabilia and enough TVs to let patrons tune in to their favorite home games. One caveat: Despite the 24-hour security guards, the Hilton is locally notorious for its parking lot break-ins. Don't leave any valuables in your car if you stay here.

611 NW Loop 410 (San Pedro exit), San Antonio, TX 78216. *C* **800/HILTONS** or 210/340-6060. Fax 210/377-4674. www.hilton.com. 386 units. $165–$175 double; $425–$550 suite. Romance and weekend packages available. AE, DC, DISC, MC, V. Free covered parking. Pets up to 20 lb. accepted. **Amenities:** Restaurant; bar; outdoor heated pool; putting green; exercise room; Jacuzzi; sauna; game room; business center; complimentary shuttle to airport and other places within 2-mile radius; limited room service; same-day dry cleaning; executive-level rooms. *In room:* TV w/pay movies, dataport, coffeemaker, hair dryer, iron.

MODERATE

Doubletree Hotel San Antonio Airport ✦   For an airport hotel, the Doubletree is surprisingly serene. The same developer who converted a downtown seminary into the posh La Mansión del Rio (p. 241) was responsible for this hotel's design. Moorish arches, potted plants, stone fountains, and colorful Mexican tile create a Mediterranean mood in the public areas; intricate wrought-iron elevators descend from the guest floors to the lushly landscaped pool patio, eliminating the need to tromp through the lobby in a swimsuit. Guest rooms are equally appealing, with brick walls painted in peach or beige, wood-beamed ceilings, draped French doors, and colorful contemporary art. The hotel has a large business clientele, much of it from Mexico.

37 NE Loop 410 (McCullough exit), San Antonio, TX 78216. *C* **800/535-1980** or 210/366-2424. Fax 210/341-0410. www.sanantonio.doubletreehotels.com. 291 units. $130–$170 double; $230–$300 suite. Various packages and discounts available. AE, DC, DISC, MC, V. Free self-parking. **Amenities:** Restaurant; 2 bars; outdoor pool; exercise room; Jacuzzi; sauna; concierge (on executive level); 24-hr. complimentary shuttle service to airport and other places within 2-mile radius; business center; limited room service; same-day dry cleaning; executive-level rooms. *In room:* A/C, TV w/pay movies, dataport, coffeemaker, hair dryer, iron.

4 Where to Dine

It's easy to eat well in San Antonio; there's something to satisfy every taste and wallet. The downtown dining scene is burgeoning, but although eating on the river is a unique, not-to-be-missed experience, many of the restaurants that overlook the water are overpriced and overcrowded. I've noted several exceptions here.

The two closest concentrations of places near downtown to eat are the Monte Vista area, north of I-35 and west of Tex. 281, and the section around North St. Mary's (the Strip), where you can get live entertainment dished up with your food on the weekends; a dining scene is also beginning to evolve at Southtown, just below downtown. By far the best eating area in San Antonio, however, is on and around Broadway, starting a few blocks south of Hildebrand, extending north to Loop 410, and comprising much of the posh area known as Alamo

Heights. Brackenridge Park, the zoo, the Botanical Gardens, and the Witte and McNay museums are in this part of town, so you can combine your sightseeing with some serious eating.

DOWNTOWN
VERY EXPENSIVE

Biga on the Banks ✪ NEW AMERICAN   With its new millennium move to the River Walk, one of San Antonio's earliest culinary innovators got a venue to match its menu: elegant, bold, and contemporary. Clean lines, high ceilings, gleaming wood floors, and lots of seraglio-sexy white draperies—plus a balcony with dramatic river views—set the scene for chef/owner Bruce Auden's consistently interesting cuisine. The game packet starters, for example, cross a few continents, combining Texas and Asia in spring-style rolls filled with minced venison, buffalo, ostrich, and pheasant accompanied by two spicy dipping sauces. The T-bone steak with garlic "mashers" and beer-battered onion rings raises comfort-cum-bar cuisine to new heights. That's the good news. The bad news is that Auden seems to be spending less time in the kitchen, and the food is not nearly as dazzling as it was when the setting was more low-key. Still, it's way above average, and if you're willing to eat early (5:30–6:30pm), you can sample a three-course meal for a bargain $29 per person.

International Center, 203 S. St. Mary's St./River Walk. ✆ 210/225-0722. Reservations recommended. Main courses $17–$35. AE, DC, DISC, MC, V. Mon–Thurs 5:30–10pm; Fri–Sat 5:30–11pm; Sun 11am–2:30pm and 5:30–10pm.

Las Canarias ✪ NEW AMERICAN   The fine dining room at La Mansión del Rio (p. 241) has a couple of things going for it: The setting and the food. You have a choice of dining on inventive and beautifully presented cuisine on a lovely riverside veranda; a palm-decked, Mexican-tiled patio; or inside in one of several cozy, antiques-filled interior rooms where you can listen to the soft music of a grand piano or a classical guitarist.

Menus change seasonally, but such dishes as seared yellowfin tuna with saffron grits and grilled venison loin with roasted corn flan demonstrate the chef's ability to balance unusual textures and flavors. Appetizers are equally exciting, but you'll want to share to leave room for dazzling desserts like the phyllo-crusted banana cream pie with chocolate pecan ice cream on the side. One caveat: All types of (legal) smoking are permitted in the outdoor areas; if someone is stoking a stogie at the next table, your al fresco dining experience can be ruined.

In La Mansión del Rio, 112 College St./River Walk. ✆ 210/518-1063. Reservations recommended. Main courses $19–$36; 6-course tasting menu $50 ($65 paired with wine); champagne brunch $30. AE, DC, DISC, MC, V. Sun–Thurs 6:30am–10:30pm; Fri–Sat 6:30am–11pm; Sun brunch 10:30am–2:30pm.

Le Rêve ✪✪ FRENCH   Chef/owner Andrew Weissman, a local boy who studied in France and did a stint at New York's famed Le Cirque, is very serious about his food—and it shows. Presentations are gorgeous, and everything's made from scratch with the freshest of ingredients, so such dishes as the caramelized onion tart appetizer, duck breast with foie gras and calvados apples, and the light but rich sour cream cheesecake are sensual delights.

But Weissman expects patrons to take food as seriously as he does. The staff has been known to give tables away when diners don't show up and this is the only place in town that requires men to wear jackets. I don't think the food quite justifies the attitude. Still this tiny, chic dining room with a peek-a-boo view of the river is one of the prime see-and-be-seen spots in town. And if you want to experience Weissman's cooking in the Alamo City (as opposed to Houston, where the chef is planning to move by 2004), now's your chance.

152 E. Pecan St. at St. Mary's. ℰ 210/212-2221. Reservations required. Jacket required for men. 3 courses $65; 4 courses $75; $5 courses $85. AE, DC, DISC, MC, V. Tues–Sat 5:30–11pm (last reservation taken for 8:30pm seating).

Little Rhein Steak House AMERICAN/STEAKS Built in 1847 in what was then the Rhein district, the oldest two-story structure in San Antonio has hosted an elegant steakhouse abutting the river and La Villita since 1967. Antique memorabilia decks the indoor main dining room, and a miniature train surrounded by historic replicas runs overhead. Leafy branches overhanging the River Walk patio are draped in little sparkling lights. The choice USDA Prime steaks from the restaurant's own meat plant are tasty, but competition from chains such as The Palm and Morton's, nearby, have resulted in a price hike. Now everything here is a la carte: You'll shell out $4.75 for a baked potato, another $6.95 for creamed spinach (you do still get a loaf of fresh wheat bread, gratis). The restaurant can also get quite noisy. That said, this is still one of the few family-owned steakhouses around, and it offers a unique River Walk dining experience.

231 S. Alamo at Market. ℰ 210/225-2111. Reservations recommended. Main courses $20–$35. AE, DC, DISC, MC, V. Daily 5–10pm.

EXPENSIVE

Boudro's ✹✹ NEW AMERICAN Locals tend to look down their noses at River Walk restaurants—that is, with the long-running exception of Boudro's. And with good reason. The kitchen uses fresh local ingredients and the preparations and presentations do them justice. The setting is also out of the ordinary: a turn-of-the-20th-century limestone building with hardwood floors and a handmade mesquite bar.

You might start with the guacamole, prepared tableside and served with tostadas, or the pan-fried Texas crab cakes. The prime rib, blackened on a pecan-wood grill, is deservedly popular, as are the lamb chops with peach chutney and garlic mashed potatoes. The food may be innovative, but the portions are not nouvelle. Lighter alternatives include the coconut shrimp with orange horseradish and the grilled yellowfin tuna. For dessert, the whisky-soaked bread pudding is fine, but the lime chess pie with a butter pastry crust . . . divine. Service is very good, especially considering the volume of business and the time the servers spend mixing up guacamole.

421 E. Commerce St./River Walk. ℰ 210/224-8484. Reservations strongly recommended. Main courses $15–$32. AE, DC, DISC, MC, V. Sun–Thurs 11am–11pm; Fri–Sat 11am–midnight.

Manduca ✹ REGIONAL MEXICAN It's not easy to find genuine Mexican food—as opposed to Tex-Mex—everywhere in San Antonio, so it's especially surprising to find a well executed, wide-ranging south-of-the-border menu on the tourist-driven River Walk. Thank Jorge Cosio, a young chef from Mexico City, who's betting that gringos will like his adventurous fare if they just give it a chance. I hope he's right. I was certainly pleased with the *sopa azteca*, a variation on the traditional soup that uses black beans instead of clear broth; the Veracruz-style fish, as tasty as any I've had in Mexico; and the Friday regional special, *puntas rancheras*, tender beef tips grilled in a tangy tomato-based sauce. *Manduca* means "to have a large feast"; come prepared to do just that.

215 Losoya St./Riverwalk. ✆ **210/475-9099.** Reservations recommended on weekends. Main courses $13–$25. AE, DC, DISC, MC, V. Sun–Thurs 11am–10pm; Fri–Sat 11am–11pm.

Zuni Grill ⭐ SOUTHWESTERN   With its chile strings, stylized steers, and chic Southwestern menu, this popular River Walk cafe is a little bit of Santa Fe-on-the-San Antonio. If you've never had a prickly pear margarita, this is the place to try one: Pureed cactus fruit, marinated overnight in tequila and cactus-juice schnapps, turns the potent, delicious drink a shade ranging from pink to startling purple, depending on the ripeness of the fruit.

This is a good place to come from morning till dark. Kick-start your day with a breakfast taco, or take a mid-afternoon break with a grilled salmon sandwich with black bean and corn relish. At night, vegetarians will appreciate the gardener and gatherer platter (grilled vegetables accompanied by roasted garlic mashed potatoes and wilted spinach). For something more substantial, try the honey-coriander pork loin with adobo sauce or seared ahi with polenta. You might want to finish with another culinary dazzler, a pecan crème brûlée that tastes every bit as good as it sounds.

223 Losoya St./River Walk. ✆ **210/227-0864.** Reservations accepted only for parties of 6 or more. Main courses $14–$25. AE, DC, DISC, MC, V. Daily 8am–10pm.

MODERATE

Texas Land & Cattle Co. _Value_ AMERICAN/STEAKS   If you're hankering for a big meat fix, slip into some jeans and mosey on down to this dining room that shouts "Texas" from its branding irons to its wagon-wheel chandeliers—and its huge mesquite-grilled steaks. Located on a quiet stretch of the river, this is a kicked-back downtown bargain—not as fancy as the likes of Morton's and Ruth's Chris, but not nearly as pricey, either. Here you'll find Mexican charro-style steaks served with guacamole, pico de gallo, and warm flour tortillas; great baby back ribs; sides such as salads and soup included with the meal; and desserts like the outrageous brownie/ice cream sundae. Come to think of it, better make that a pair of your reserve "fat" jeans that you slip into.

201 N. St. Mary's St. ✆ **210/222-2263.** Main courses $11–$22. AE, DC, DISC, MC, V. Sun–Thurs 11am–10pm; Fri–Sat 11am–11pm.

INEXPENSIVE

Schilo's _Kids_ _Value_ GERMAN/DELI   You can't leave town without stopping in at this San Antonio institution, if only for a hearty bowl of split-pea soup or a piece of the signature cherry cheesecake. The large, open room with its worn wooden booths is a door into the city's German past. It's a great refueling station near Alamo Plaza for the entire family, with a large kid-friendly selection and retro low prices. For around $5, a good, greasy Reuben or a kielbasa plate should keep you going for the rest of the day.

424 E. Commerce St. ✆ **210/223-6692.** Reservations for large groups for breakfast and dinner only. Sandwiches $2.90–$4.75; hot or cold plates $4.75–$5.45; main dishes (served after 5pm) $6.85–$8.95. AE, DC, DISC, MC, V. Mon–Sat 7am–8:30pm.

Twin Sisters _Finds_ HEALTH FOOD/DELI   If you want to avoid overpriced sandwiches and junk food while sightseeing, join the downtown working crowd at this bakery and health food cafe just a few blocks from the Alamo. Eggless and meatless doesn't mean tasteless here—you can get great Greek salads, spicy tofu scrambles, and salsa-topped veggie burgers—but carnivores can also indulge in the likes of ham, pastrami, and salami sandwiches on the excellent bread made

> ### ⏺ *Kids* Family-Friendly Restaurants
>
> **Betos Latin Grill** (p. 255) and **La Fonda on Main** (p. 253) Both are great places to introduce your kids to Mexican food. La Fonda has inexpensive children's plates, and Betos has plenty of child-friendly choices—not to mention a sandbox.
>
> **EZ's** Personal pizzas and calzones fresh from a brick oven, spit-roasted chicken, tasty burgers, good Caesar salads, and thick, creamy shakes, all served up in a colorful retro diner make EZ's a great quick break for the entire family. Of the five locations of this San Antonio–based chain, the most popular is at the Quarry shopping center, 255 E. Basse Rd. (② **210/804-1199**).
>
> **Madhatters** (p. 253) Even if your kids aren't up for an entire children's tea, they'll be happy to find their faves on the menu, from PB&J to plain turkey or cheese sandwiches. The chocolate chip cookies and brownies won't be sneezed at, either.
>
> **Schilo's** (p. 251) A high noise level, a convenient location near the River Walk (but with prices far lower than anything you'll find there), and a wide selection of familiar food make this German deli a good choice.

on the premises. This popular place fills up by 11:30am but empties after 12:45pm, so gauge your visit accordingly.

124 Broadway at Travis. ② **210/354-1559**. Reservations not accepted. $1.80–$6 breakfast; $3.80–$8.80 lunch. MC, V. Mon–Fri 8am–3pm.

KING WILLIAM HISTORIC DISTRICT & SOUTHTOWN
MODERATE

Rosario's ✦ MEXICAN/REGIONAL MEXICAN This long-time Southtown favorite, recently relocated, is hipper and more colorful than ever, with its witty Frida Kahlo and Botero knock-offs, its abundant use of neon—and its knockout margaritas. Come here to sample versions of such adventurous regional dishes as *nopalito* (cactus pad) tacos along with Tex-Mex standards, all freshly prepared and all tasty. Unfortunately, the noise level has risen to the point where it's tough to have a conversation here; fortunately, the food and drink are worth focusing on.

910 S. Alamo. ② **210/223-1806**. Reservations not accepted. Main courses $7.25–$13. AE, DC, DISC, MC, V. Mon 11am–3pm; Tues–Thurs 11am–10pm; Fri–Sat 11am–11pm (Fri bar till 2am).

INEXPENSIVE

Guenther House ✦ *Value* AMERICAN Not only is the food good at the Guenther House, but dining here is also a great way to spend some time inside one of King William's historic homes. Hearty breakfasts and light lunches are served indoors in a pretty art nouveau–style dining room added on to the 1860 Guenther family residence or outdoors on a trellised patio. The biscuits and gravy are a morning specialty and the chicken salad at lunch is excellent, but you can't go wrong with anything that involves the wonderful baked goods made on the premises. The house fronts a lovely stretch of the San Antonio River; in the back, you can still see the Pioneer Flour Mill that earned the family its fortune.

205 E. Guenther St. ✆ **210/227-1061.** Reservations not accepted. Breakfast $3.25–$6.25; lunch $4.75–$6.95. AE, DC, DISC, MC, V. Daily 7am–3pm (the house and mill store are open Mon–Sat 8am–4pm, Sun 8am–3pm).

Madhatters *(Kids* *(Finds* DELI/ECLECTIC   This colorful, sprawling storefront attracts everyone from nouveau hippies to buttoned-down refugees from the convention center, only 5 minutes away. They come for the Age of Aquarius meets south-of-the-border food: granola bowls or breakfast burritos in the a.m., veggie sandwiches or pork tamales in the p.m. For after work (or protests), there are cold cases full of reasonably priced wines and beers. Among the various tea parties offered, the one for kids includes PB&J sandwiches (crusts cut off, naturally).

320 Beauregard St. ✆ **210/212-4832.** Reservations not accepted. Breakfasts $3.30–$11; sandwiches and salad plates $5.95–$7.95. AE, MC, V. Mon 7am–6pm; Tues–Thurs 7am–10pm; Sat 9am–11pm; Sun 9am–6pm.

MONTE VISTA HISTORIC DISTRICT
MODERATE

La Fonda on Main ⭐ *(Kids* *(Value* MEXICAN   One of San Antonio's oldest continually operating restaurants, established in 1932, has revamped both its premises and menu. The lovely red-tile-roof residence was spiffed up, rendering the dining rooms cheerful and bright—almost as inviting as the garden-fringed outdoor patio. Classic Tex-Mex combination plates such as the La Fonda Special (one cheese enchilada, one beef or chicken taco with rice and refried beans) mingle on the menu with a "Cuisines of Mexico" section, including such traditional dishes as *mojo de ajo,* Gulf shrimp with garlic butter served with squash.

2415 N. Main. ✆ **210/733-0621.** Reservations recommended for 6 or more. Main courses $6.95–$12. AE, DC, MC, V. Mon–Thurs 11am–3pm and 5–9:30pm; Fri–Sat 11am–3pm and 5–10:30pm; Sun brunch 11am–3pm.

Liberty Bar ⭐ *(Finds* NEW AMERICAN   You'd be hard-pressed to guess that this ramshackle former brothel (opened 1890) near the Highway 281 underpass hosts one of the hippest haunts in San Antonio. But as every foodie in town can tell you, it's bright and inviting inside, and you'll find everything here from comfort food (pot roast, say, or a ham-and-Swiss sandwich) to regional Mexican cuisine (the chiles rellenos *en nogada* are super). The toasted English bread with

 South-of-the-Border Savvy

Some of the best and most popular places to eat Mexican have been reviewed in this section, but you can be sure you'll run into San Antonians who are passionate about their personal favorite *tacquerias.* Three high-ranking ones near downtown include **Estela's,** 2200 W. Martin St. (✆ **210/226-2979**), which has mariachi breakfasts on Saturday and Sunday from 9:30 to 11:30am, as well as a great conjunto/Tejano jukebox to fill in the musical void; and **Taco Haven,** 1032 S. Presa St. (✆ **210/533-2171**), where the breakfast *migas* or *chilaquiles* will kick-start your day. In Olmos Park, **Panchito's,** 4100 McCullough (✆ **210/821-5338**), has 'em lining up on weekend mornings for *barbacoa* plates, heaped with two eggs, potatoes, beans, and two homemade tortillas along with the Mexican-style barbecue.

roast garlic spread or eggplant puree goes great with many of the fine—and generally affordable—wines available by the glass; there's a good beer selection, too. And don't worry—even if you've had a few too many, you're not imagining it: The house really is leaning.

328 E. Josephine St. © 210/227-1187. Reservations recommended. Main courses $6.95–$19. AE, MC, V. Sun–Thurs 11:30am–10:30pm; Fri–Sat 11:30am–midnight; Sun brunch 10:30am–2pm. Bar Sun–Thurs till midnight; Fri–Sat till 2am.

ALAMO HEIGHTS AREA
EXPENSIVE

Bistro Vatel ★★ *Value* FRENCH   Talk about a pressure cooker. In 1671, the great French chef Vatel killed himself out of shame because the fish for a banquet he was preparing for Louis XIV wasn't delivered on time. Fortunately his descendent, Damian Watel, has less stress to contend with in San Antonio, where diners are very appreciative of the chef's efforts to bring them classic French cooking at comparatively reasonable prices. The restaurant is in a strip mall and the dining room has a low, acoustic-tile ceiling, but copper pots, wine racks, and white tablecloths help create a charming, intimate atmosphere. You can't go wrong with the rich escalope of veal with foie gras, and fans of sweetbreads will be pleased to find them here beautifully prepared in truffle crème fraîche sauce. Your best bet is the bargain prix-fixe dinner, where you can choose one each from a trio of appetizers, entrees, and desserts of the day.

218 E. Olmos Ave. at McCullough. © 210/828-3141. Reservations recommended on weekends. Main courses $15–$22; prix-fixe dinner $27. AE, MC, V. Tues–Fri 11:30am–1:30pm; Tues–Sat 5:30–9:30pm.

Frederick's ★★ *Finds* FRENCH/ASIAN FUSION   Of all the recently opened restaurants I've tried, this one, in the back of a Broadway strip mall, is my hands-down favorite. The setting is nothing special, although the low-ceiling, darkish room has been prettified by white draperies and sunny antiqued walls. But once the food started arriving at the table, I wouldn't have noticed if I'd been dining inside a concrete bunker.

For starters, I sampled tempura-battered sushi, strange in the abstract but wonderful in fact; an oh-so-crispy spring roll with shrimp, pork, and mushrooms; and a delicate crab salad with avocado. These were followed by an entree of seabass with bok choy and shiitake over a sesame galette. (Yes, the restaurant's specialty is seafood.) Call the cuisine Indochine—it's a mix of French and Vietnamese—or call it French fusion, as the menu does. I just call it delicious.

771 Broadway, Suite 20 (in the back of Dijon Plaza). © 210/828-9050. Reservations recommended on weekends. Main courses $17–$29. AE, MC, V. Mon–Thurs 11:30am–2pm and 5:30–10pm; Fri 11:30am–2pm and 5:30–11pm; Sat 5:30–11pm.

Massimo ★★ ITALIAN   There's lots of good Americanized Italian fare in San Antonio, but for authentic *cucina italiana,* prepared by a chef from Rome (by way of New York), this is the place. The kitchen is particularly strong in pastas and risottos, all made fresh on the premises; the potato gnocchi are a special treat. If you want to economize, share a generous salad—I'd recommend the primavera, with artichokes, asparagus, and hearts of palm—followed by one of those carbs. Of course, then you'd miss such excellent *secondi* as duck breast in a delicate balsamic sauce or the saltimbocca, a Roman specialty. The Tuscan yellow dining rooms are airy (though some of the tables are a bit too close together) and the romantic Red Room Bar has become a popular place to listen to live music on the weekends.

1896 Nacogdoches Rd. © **210/342-8556.** Reservations recommended on weekends. Main courses $18–$26; pastas $13–$18. AE, DC, DISC, MC, V. Mon–Fri 11am–2:30pm and 5:30–10:30pm; Sat 5:30–10:30pm; bar Mon–Sat 5pm–2am.

Silo ★★★ NEW AMERICAN   Silo is consistently top-listed by San Antonio foodies, and deservedly so. Chef Mark Bliss has poured his considerable talents into a small but well-balanced menu that uses fresh ingredients in fresh combinations. Starters such as the seared sea scallop on a roasted garlic potato blini get the mix of textures and tastes just right, as do entrees like pork tenderloin on a bacon, corn, and potato hash. Desserts are divine too, and change nightly. Although the chic, industrial-design perch makes for a somewhat cold setting, service is warm, and super efficient to boot.

1133 Austin Hwy. © **210/824-8686.** Reservations not accepted except for large private parties. Main courses $16–$24. AE, DC, DISC, MC, V. Sun–Thurs 5:30–9:30pm; Fri–Sat 5:30–10:30pm.

MODERATE

Koi Kawa ★ JAPANESE   Sushi rules at Koi Kawa, which has won diehard fans because of its high-quality ingredients, such as real crabmeat and hothouse-grown cucumbers. But if you're not in a raw fish mood (today or ever), you've got plenty of other options. The crispy vegetable, seafood, and shrimp tempuras get a lot of attention, as do the various udon (wheat noodle) and soba (cold buckwheat noodle) soups, meals in themselves. In the back of the Boardwalk complex, with a view of the tree-shaded banks of the San Antonio River (admittedly, a generally stagnant section), Koi Kawa is a bit hard to locate, but by all means persevere if you're a Japanese food fan.

4051 Broadway (in the back corner of the Boardwalk Complex, closest to the Witte Museum). © **210/805-8111.** Reservations recommended on weekends. Main courses $10–$22. AE, DC, DISC, MC, V. Mon–Fri 11:30am–2pm and 5:30–10pm; Sat 5:30–10pm.

INEXPENSIVE

Betos Latin Grill (Kids) (Value) LATIN AMERICAN/MEXICAN   The colorful, tropical shack–style Betos is a hot, hot, hot Alamo Heights spot to listen to live Latin music and drink sangria while munching tacos *al pastor*—slow-roasted pork basted with a spicy adobado pineapple sauce. But it's also a great place to bring kids, who can be as messy as they like on the picnic tables on the covered back deck. You'll find all the usual Tex-Mex suspects—nachos, quesadillas, fajitas—along with some Mexican regional specialties and South American–influenced dishes. Especially popular: The Sunday all-you-can-eat breakfast bar ($6.95), featuring chilaquiles, posole, soups, fruit, desserts, and more.

7325 Broadway. © **210/930-9393.** Reservations not accepted. Empanadas, tacos, and sandwiches $2.40–$6.95, combination plates $7.95–$14. AE, DISC, MC, V. Mon–Wed 11am–9pm; Thurs–Sat 11am–10pm; Sun 10am–2pm.

5 Seeing the Sights

San Antonio's dogged preservation of its past and avid development of its future guarantee that there's something in town to suit every interest. It's easy to get to wherever you want to go, too: San Antonio has excellent and inexpensive tourist transportation lines, extending to such far-flung sights as SeaWorld and Six Flags Fiesta Texas, and walkers will love being able to hoof it from one downtown attraction to another.

THE TOP ATTRACTIONS
DOWNTOWN AREA

The Alamo   Visiting San Antonio without going to the Alamo is like visiting New York and not going to the Statue of Liberty. You can do it, but it would be wrong. Don't expect anything dramatic, however. Texas's most visited site and the symbol of its turmoil-filled history is not only rather small, but sits smack in the heart of downtown San Antonio. Still, you'll immediately recognize the graceful mission church, where 188 Texas volunteers defied the much larger army of Mexican dictator Santa Anna for 13 days in March 1836. Although all the men, including pioneers Davy Crockett and Jim Bowie, were killed, their deaths were used by Sam Houston in the cry "Remember the Alamo!" to rally his troops and defeat the Mexican army at the Battle of San Jacinto a month later, securing Texas's independence.

But there's more to the Alamo than a single battle. It was founded on a nearby site in 1718 as the Mission San Antonio de Valero, and many converted Indians from a variety of tribes lived and died there. The complex was secularized by the end of the 18th century and leased out to a Spanish cavalry unit; by the time the famous battle took place, it had been abandoned. Little remains of the original mission today; only the **Long Barrack** (formerly the *convento,* or living quarters for the missionaries) and the **mission church** are still here. The former houses a museum detailing the history of Texas in general and the battle in particular; the latter includes artifacts of the Alamo fighters, along with an information desk and small gift shop. A larger museum and gift shop are at the back of the complex. There's also a peaceful garden and an excellent research library (closed Sun)

The Alamo: The Movie(s)

Volumes—well, at least one, Frank Thompson's *Alamo Movies*—have been devoted to the plethora of films featuring the events that occurred at San Antonio's most famous site. Some outtakes:

Most famous movie about the Alamo not actually shot at the Alamo: *The Alamo* (1959), starring John Wayne as Davy Crockett. Although it has no San Antonio presence, it *was* shot in Texas. Wayne had considered shooting the film in Mexico, but was told it wouldn't be distributed in Texas if he did.

Latest controversy-ridden attempt to tell the story of the Alamo: A 2003 Disney version with a script by John Sayles which may or may not be directed by Ron Howard. It's being filmed near Austin.

Most accurate celluloid depiction of the Alamo story (and also the largest): *Alamo—The Price of Freedom,* showing in the San Antonio IMAX Theater Rivercenter. According to writer and historian Stephen Harrigan *(The Gates of the Alamo)* in an interview on National Public Radio, it's "90% accurate."

Least controversial film featuring the Alamo: *Miss Congeniality,* starring Sandra Bullock and Benjamin Bratt. A beauty pageant moderated by William Shatner takes place in front of the shrine to the Texas martyrs.

Value **Discounts, Discounts, Discounts**

Before you visit any of the paid attractions, stop in at the **San Antonio Visitor Information Center,** 317 Alamo Plaza (© **210/207-6748**), and ask for their free SAVE San Antonio discount book, including everything from the large theme parks to some city tours and museums. Many hotels also have discount coupons for their guests.

on the grounds. All in all, though, the complex is fairly small. You won't need to spend more than an hour here.

300 Alamo Plaza. © **210/225-1391.** www.thealamo.org. Free admission (donations welcome). Mon–Sat 9am–5:30pm; Sun 10am–5:30pm. Closed Dec 24–25. Streetcar: Red and Blue lines.

King William Historic District ⭐ San Antonio's first suburb was settled in the late 19th century by prosperous German merchants who displayed their wealth through extravagant homes and named the 25-block area after Kaiser Wilhelm of Prussia. The area has gotten so popular that tour buses have been restricted after certain hours. But it's much more pleasant to stroll up and down tree-shaded King William Street, gawking at the beautifully landscaped, magnificent mansions. Stop at the headquarters of the San Antonio Conservation Society, 107 King William St. (© 210/224-6163; www.saconservation.org), and pick up a self-guided walking tour booklet outside the gate. If you go at a leisurely pace, the stroll should take about an hour. Only the Guenther House (p. 252) and the Steves Homestead Museum, 509 King William St. (© 210/225-5924 or 210/227-9160), built in 1876 for a lumber magnate, are open to the public. Tours of the Steves house are available daily from 10am to 4:15 pm; admission is $3 adults, children under 12 free.

East bank of the river just south of downtown (within walking distance of the Convention Center). Streetcar: Blue Line.

La Villita National Historic District ⭐ Developed by European settlers along the higher east bank of the San Antonio River in the late 18th and early 19th centuries, La Villita was revitalized in the late 1930s by artists and craftspeople and by the San Antonio Conservation Society. Now boutiques, crafts shops, and restaurants occupy this historic district, which resembles a Spanish/Mexican village, replete with shaded patios, plazas, brick-and-tile streets, and some of the settlement's original adobe structures, including the house of General Cós, the Mexican military leader who surrendered to the Texas revolutionary army in 1835. It should only take you about 20 minutes to do a brisk walk-through, unless you're an inveterate shopper, in which case all bets are off. One of my favorite jewelry stores, Chamade, is here, and, though you have to search a bit, there are some other high quality crafts shops.

Bounded by Durango, Navarro, and Alamo sts. and the River Walk. © **210/207-8610.** www.lavillita.com. Free admission. Shops daily 10am–6pm. Closed Thanksgiving, Dec 25, Jan 1. Bus: 40. Streetcar: Red, Purple, and Blue lines.

Market Square ⭐ It may not be quite as colorful as it was when live chickens squawked around overflowing, makeshift vegetable stands, but Market Square will still transport you south of the border. Stalls in the indoor El Mercado sell everything from onyx paperweights and manufactured serapes to high-quality crafts from the interior of Mexico. Across the street, the Farmer's Market, which formerly housed the produce market, has carts with more modern goods. The best time to pay a visit to the square is during a festival.

Bring your appetite along with your wallet: In addition to several sit-down Mexican restaurants (one open 24 hr. a day), almost every weekend sees the emergence of food stalls selling specialties such as *gorditas* (chubby corn cakes topped with a variety of goodies) or funnel cakes (fried dough sprinkled with powdered sugar). Most of the city's Hispanic festivals are held here, and mariachis usually stroll the square. The Alameda National Center for Latino Arts and Culture, a Smithsonian Institution affiliate scheduled to open in the Centro des Artes building in 2004, should provide a historic context to an area that can seem pretty touristy—though no more so than any Mexican border town.

Bounded by Commerce, Santa Rosa, Dolorosa, and I-35. ⓒ 210/207-8600. Free admission. El Mercado and Farmer's Market Plaza, June–Aug daily 10am–8pm; Sept–May daily 10am–6pm; restaurants and some of the shops open later. Closed Thanksgiving, Dec 25, Jan 1, and Easter. Streetcar: Red, Purple, and Yellow lines.

The River Walk (Paseo del Rio) ★★★ Just a few steps below the streets of downtown San Antonio lies another world, alternately soothing and exhilarating, depending on where you venture. The quieter areas of the 2½ paved miles of winding riverbank, shaded by cypresses, oaks, and willows, exude a tropical, exotic aura; the River Square and South Bank sections have a festive, sometimes frenetic feel. Tour boats, water taxis, and floating picnic barges regularly ply the river, and local parades and festivals fill its banks with revelers.

It wasn't until the late 1960s, when the River Walk proved to be one of the most popular attractions of the HemisFair exposition, that its commercial development began in earnest. There's a real danger of the River Walk becoming overdeveloped, but plenty of quieter spots still exist. And if you're caught up in the sparkling lights reflected on the water on a breeze-swept night, you might forget there was ever anyone else around.

Downtown from the Municipal Auditorium on the north end to the King William Historic District on the south end. Streetcar: All lines.

San Antonio Museum of Art This attraction may not be top-listed by everyone, but I like doable (read: not overwhelmingly large) museums with interesting architecture and collections related to the city in which they're located, and this one definitely fits the bill. Several castlelike buildings of the 1904 Lone Star Brewery were gutted, connected, and turned into a visually exciting exhibition space in 1981. Holdings range from early Egyptian, Greek, Oceanic, and Asian (a new wing devoted to the genre will debut in spring 2004) to 19th- and 20th-century American, but the prime reason to come is the $11 million **Nelson A. Rockefeller Center for Latin American Art,** a 30,000-square-foot wing with the most comprehensive collection of Latin American art in the United States. You'll see everything here from magnificently ornate Spanish Colonial altarpieces to a whimsical contemporary Day of the Dead tableau. If any of this sounds appealing to you, allow at least 2 hours for your visit.

200 W. Jones Ave. ⓒ 210/978-8100. www.sa-museum.org. Admission $6 adults, $5 seniors, $4 students with ID, $1.75 children 4–11, free for children 3 and under. General admission free on Tues 3–9pm (fee for some special exhibits). Tues 10am–9pm; Wed–Sat 10am–5pm; Sun noon–5pm. Bus: 9, 11, or 14.

SOUTH SIDE

San Antonio Missions National Historic Park ★★ Remember the Alamo? Well, it was originally just the first of five missions established by the Franciscans along the San Antonio River to Christianize the native population.

The four missions that now fall under the aegis of the National Parks Department are still active parishes, run in cooperation with the Archdiocese of San Antonio. But the missions were more than churches; they were complex communities. The Parks Department has assigned each of them an interpretive theme to educate visitors about the roles they played in early San Antonio society. You can visit them separately, but if you have time, see them all; they were built uncharacteristically close together and—now that you don't have to walk there or ride a horse—it shouldn't take you more than 2 or 3 hours, total. If your time is limited, definitely visit San José and try to make it to San Francisco, even though it's the farthest from downtown.

Concepción, 807 Mission Rd. at Felisa, is the oldest unrestored Texas mission, and looks much as it did 200 years ago. **San José** ★★, 6539 San José Dr. at Mission Road, established in 1720, was the largest, best known, and most beautiful of the Texas missions. It was reconstructed to give visitors a complete picture of life in a mission community. Popular mariachi masses are held here every Sunday at noon (come early if you want a seat). Moved from an earlier site in east Texas to its present location in 1731, **San Juan Capistrano,** 9102 Graf at Ashley, doesn't have the grandeur of the missions to the north, but the original simple chapel and the wilder setting give it a peaceful, spiritual aura. The southernmost mission in the San Antonio chain, **San Francisco de la Espada** ★, 10040 Espada Rd., also has an ancient, isolated feel, although the beautifully maintained church shows just how vital it still is to the local community.

Headquarters: 2202 Roosevelt Ave. ℂ **210/534-8833.** Visitors Center: 6701 San José Dr. at Mission Rd. ℂ **210/932-1001.** www.nps.gov/saan. Free admission (donations accepted). Missions daily 9am–5pm. Closed Thanksgiving, Dec 25, Jan 1. National Park Ranger tours daily. Bus: 42 stops at Mission San José and near Mission Concepión.

ALAMO HEIGHTS AREA

Marion Koogler McNay Art Museum ★★   Well worth a detour from downtown, this is one of my favorite places to visit. It's got a knockout setting on a hill north of Brackenridge Park with a forever view of the city, and it's in a sprawling Spanish Mediterranean–style mansion (built 1929) so picturesque that it's constantly used as a backdrop for weddings and photo shoots. The McNay doesn't have a world-class art collection, but it has a good one, with at least one work by most American and European masters of the last 2 centuries. And the Tobin Collection of Theatre Arts, including costumes, set designs, and rare books, is outstanding. The NcNay also hosts major traveling shows. It'll take you at least an hour to go through this place at a leisurely pace, longer if its cool enough for you to stroll around the beautiful 23-acre grounds, dotted with sculpture and stunning landscaping.

6000 N. New Braunfels Ave. ℂ **210/824-5368.** www.mcnayart.org. Free admission ($5 suggested donation; fee for special exhibits). Tues–Sat 10am–5pm; Sun noon–5pm. Docent tours Sun at 2pm Oct–May. Closed Jan 1, July 4, Thanksgiving, and Dec 25. Bus: 11.

Witte Museum ★ *Kids*   A family museum that adults will enjoy as much as kids, the Witte focuses on Texas history, natural science, and anthropology, but often ranges as far afield as the Berlin Wall or the history of bridal gowns in the United States. Your senses will be engaged along with your intellect: You might hear animal cries as you crouch through south Texas thorn brush, or feel rough-hewn stone carved with Native American pictographs under your feet. Children especially like the exhibits devoted to mummies and dinosaurs, as well as the EcoLab, where the live Texas critters range from tarantulas to tortoises. But the biggest draw for kids is the terrific HEB Science Treehouse, a four-level, 15,000-square-foot science center, with hands-on activities geared to all ages. Also on the grounds are a butterfly and hummingbird garden and three restored historic homes.

3801 Broadway (adjacent to Brackenridge Park). (©) 210/357-1900. www.wittemuseum.org. Admission $5.95 adults, $4.95 seniors, $3.95 children 4–11, children 3 and under free. Free on Tues 3–9pm. Mon and Wed–Sat 10am–5pm (June–Aug till 6pm); Tues 10am–9pm; Sun noon–5pm (June to early Aug till 7pm). Closed Thanksgiving, Dec 25. Bus: 9.

NORTHWEST

Six Flags Fiesta Texas ★ *Kids*   Every year seems to bring another major thrill ride or two to this 200-acre amusement park, set in an abandoned limestone quarry and surrounded by 100-foot cliffs on the northwest side of town. In 2002, the Scooby Doo Ghostblasters scarefest joined the Superman Krypton Coaster, nearly a mile of twisted steel with six inversions; the Rattler, the world's highest and fastest wooden roller coaster; the 60-mph-plus Poltergeist roller coaster; and Scream!, a-20-story space shot and turbo drop—to name just a few. Wet 'n' wild attractions include the Lone Star Lagoon, the state's largest wave pool, and the Texas Treehouse, a five-story drenchfest, with a 1,000-gallon cowboy hat that tips over periodically to soak the unsuspecting.

If you want to avoid both sogginess and adrenaline overload, you can visit a vast variety of food booths, shops, crafts demonstrations, and live shows—everything from 1950s musical revues to big-name live concerts in summer. This place still has some local flavor, dating back to the days when it was plain old Fiesta Texas: Themed areas include a Hispanic village, a western town, and a German town. But when it came under the aegis of Six Flags—a Time Warner company—such Looney Tunes cartoon characters as Tweety Bird became ubiquitous, especially in the endless souvenir shops.

17000 I-10 West (corner of I-10 West and Loop 1604). (©) 800/473-4378 or 210/697-5050. www.sixflags. com. Admission $37 adults, $25 seniors, $23 children under 48 in., free for children under 3. Discounted 2-day and season passes available. The park is generally open late May to mid–Aug daily, Mar–May and Sept–Oct Sat–Sun only; call ahead or visit the website for hours and latest information. Take exit 555 on I-10 West. Parking $7 per day. Bus: 94.

WEST

SeaWorld San Antonio ★ *Kids*   Leave it to Texas to provide Shamu, the performing killer whale, with his most spacious digs: At 250 acres, this SeaWorld is the largest of the Anheuser Busch–owned parks, which also makes it the largest marine theme park in the world. If you're a theme park fan (I'm not), you're likely to find the walk-through habitats where you can watch penguins, sea lions, sharks, tropical fish, and flamingos do their thing fascinating, but the aquatic acrobatics at such stadium shows as Shamu Visions, combining live action and video closeups, might be even more fun. The humans hold their own with an impressive water-skiing exhibition on a 12½-acre lake.

You needn't get frustrated by just looking at all that water: There are loads of places here to get wet. The Lost Lagoon has a huge wave pool and water slides aplenty, and the Texas Splashdown flume ride and the Rio Loco river-rapids ride also offer splashy fun; younger children can cavort in Shamu's Happy Harbor and the "L'il Gators" section of the Lost Lagoon. Nonaquatic activities—hey, there's Fiesta Texas to compete with—include the Steel Eel, a huge "hyper-coaster," and The Great White, the Southwest's first inverted coaster—which means riders will go head-over-heels during 2,500 feet of loops (don't eat before either of them).

10500 SeaWorld Dr., 16 miles northwest of downtown San Antonio at Ellison Dr. and Westover Hills Blvd. ℂ **210/523-3611.** www.seaworld.com. 1-day pass $38 adults, $35 seniors, $28 children 3–11, free for children under 3. Discounted 2-day and season passes available. Generally open weekends and some weekdays in spring and fall, daily during summer. Closed late Nov to early Mar. Call ahead or check website for hours and latest information. From Loop 410 or from Hwy. 90 West, exit Hwy. 151 West to the park. Parking $7 per day. Bus: 64.

MORE ATTRACTIONS
DOWNTOWN

HemisFair Park *(Kids)*   Built for the 1968 HemisFair, an exposition celebrating the 250th anniversary of the founding of San Antonio, this urban oasis boasts water gardens and a wood-and-sand playground constructed by children (near the Alamo Street entrance). Among its indoor diversions is the **Institute of Texan Cultures** ✮, 801 S. Bowie St. (ℂ **210/458-2300;** www.texancultures. utsa.edu), an educational center with hands-on displays highlighting the 28 ethnic and cultural groups that contributed to Texas (admission $5 adults, $2 seniors and children 3–12; open Tues–Sun 9am–5pm). Another attraction is the **Tower of the Americas** ✮, 600 HemisFair Park (ℂ **210/207-8616**), a 750-foot-high structure with an observation deck; it's a great place to get a fix on the city (admission $3 adults, $2 seniors, $1 children 4–11, children 3 and under free; open Sun–Thurs 9am–10pm, Fri–Sat till 11pm). The **Schultze House Cottage Garden** ✮, created and maintained by Master Gardeners of Bexar County, is also worth checking out for its heirloom plants, varietals, tropicals, and xeriscape area; it's located at 514 HemisFair Park, behind the Federal Building.

Bounded by Alamo, Bowie, Market, and Durango sts. Streetcar: Yellow and Purple lines.

Spanish Governor's Palace ✮ *(Finds)*   Never actually a palace, this 1749 adobe structure formerly served as the residence and headquarters for the captain of the Spanish presidio. It became the seat of Texas government in 1772, when San Antonio was made capital of the Spanish province of Texas and, by the time it was purchased by the city in 1928, it had served as a tailor's shop, barroom, and schoolhouse. The building, with high ceilings crossed by protruding viga beams, is beautiful in its simplicity, and the 10 rooms crowded with period furnishings paint a vivid portrait of upper-class life in a rough-hewn society. I love to sit out on the tree-shaded, cobblestoned patio, listening to the burbling of the stone fountain.

105 Plaza de Armas. ℂ **210/224-0601.** Admission $1.50 adults, 75¢ children 7–13, free for children under 7. Mon–Sat 9am–5pm; Sun 10am–5pm. Closed Thanksgiving, Dec 25, Jan 1, San Jacinto Day (during Fiesta week in late Apr). Streetcar: Purple Line.

ALAMO HEIGHTS AREA

Brackenridge Park   With its rustic stone bridges and winding walkways, the city's main park, opened in 1899, has a charming, old-fashioned feel. It serves as a popular center for recreational activities including golf, polo, biking, and picnicking. A particularly appealing section is the **Japanese Tea Garden**—also called the Japanese Sunken Garden—created in 1917 by prison labor to beautify an abandoned cement quarry. You can still glimpse a brick smokestack and a number of the old lime kilns among the beautiful flower arrangement. Next door, the **San Antonio Zoo,** 3903 N. St. Mary's St. (ℂ **210/734-7183;** www.sazoo-aq.org), hosts more than 700 species. It's considered one of the country's top zoos because of its conservation efforts and breeding programs, but the cages are small and the animals look depressed to me (admission $7 adults, $5 children ages 3–11 and seniors 62 and over, children 2 and under free; open Labor Day to Memorial Day, daily 9am–5pm, until 6pm in summer).

Main entrance 2800 block of N. Broadway. ☏ 210/207-3000. Daily dawn–dusk. Bus: 8.

San Antonio Botanical Gardens Take a horticultural tour of Texas at this gracious 38-acre garden, encompassing everything from south Texas scrub to Hill Country wildflowers. The formal gardens section includes a garden for the blind, a Japanese garden, an herb garden, a biblical garden, and a children's garden. Perhaps most outstanding is the Lucile Halsell Conservatory complex, a below-ground greenhouse replicating a variety of tropical and desert environments. The 1896 Sullivan Carriage House, built by Alfred Giles and moved stone-by-stone from its original downtown site, serves as the entryway to the gardens. It hosts a gift shop and restaurant offering salads, quiches, sandwiches, and outrageously rich desserts (open Tues–Sun 11am–2pm).

555 Funston. ☏ 210/207-3255. www.sabot.org. Admission $4 adults, $2 seniors and military, $1 children 3–13, free for children under 3. Daily 9am–5pm. Closed Dec 25 and Jan 1. Bus: 11.

ESPECIALLY FOR KIDS

Without a doubt, the prime spots for kids in San Antonio are SeaWorld and Six Flags Fiesta Texas. They'll also like the hands-on, interactive Witte Museum and the various ethnic pride kids' programs at the Institute of Texas Cultures. In addition to these sights, detailed in "The Top Attractions" and "More Attractions" sections above, there's the **San Antonio IMAX Theater Rivercenter** ⋆, 849 E. Commerce St., in the Rivercenter Mall (☏ **800/354-4629** for recorded schedule information, or 210/247-4629; www.imax-sa.com). Having kids view "Alamo: The Price of Freedom" on a 6-story-high screen with a stereo sound system is a surefire way of getting them psyched for the historical battle site just across the street. Your ticket also buys you entry into the nearby **Texas Adventure,** 307 Alamo Plaza (☏ **210/227-8224;** www.texas-adventure.com), yet another retelling of the Alamo story, this one with special effects that include life-size holographic images of the Alamo heroes. It's not terribly exciting but it takes only 30 minutes and if you've already paid for the IMAX theater, you might as well give it a go.

Adults may get the bigger charge out of the waxy stars and some of the oddities collected by the globetrotting Mr. Ripley at the **Plaza Wax Museum & Ripley's Believe It Or Not,** 301 Alamo Plaza (☏ **210/224-9299;** www.plaza waxmuseum.com), just down the block, but there's plenty for kids to enjoy at this twofer attraction. The walk-through wax Theater of Horrors usually elicits some shudders and at Believe It Or Not, youngsters generally get a kick out of learning about people around the world whose habits are even weirder than their own. Also downtown, the **San Antonio Children's Museum** ⋆⋆, 305 E. Houston St. (☏ **210/21-CHILD;** www.sakids.org), provides a wonderful introduction to the city for the pint-sized and grown-up alike. San Antonio history, population, and geography are all explored through such features as a miniature River Walk, a multicultural grocery store—even a teddy bear hospital. See also "San Antonio After Dark," below, for the **Magik Theatre.**

ORGANIZED TOURS

San Antonio's organized tours basically provide you with an efficient way to get around and pick up some local lore. **San Antonio City Tours,** 1331 N. Pine (☏ **800/868-7707** or 210/281-9900; www.sacitytours.net), serves up a large menu of guided bus excursions, covering everything from San Antonio's missions and museums to shopping forays south of the border. **Alamo Trolley Tours,** 216 Alamo Plaza (© 210/247-0238; www.sacitytours.net) offers two routes: One touches on all the downtown highlights, plus two of the missions in the south; the second, uptown tour goes north to the San Antonio Museum of Art, the botanical gardens, the zoo, and the McNay and Witte museums. If you want to get off at any of these sights, you can pick up another trolley (they run every 45 min.) after you're finished.

You'll really know you're in San Antonio if you take one of the **Yanaguana Cruises** (© 210/244-5700; www.sarivercruise.com). These amusing, informative tours, lasting from 35 to 40 minutes, take you more than 2 miles down the most built-up sections of the Paseo del Rio, with interesting sights pointed out along the way. Buy tickets either at the Rivercenter Mall or across the street from the Hilton Palacio del Rio Hotel on the River Walk.

6 Sports & Outdoor Activities

OUTDOOR FUN

Most San Antonians head for the hills—that is, nearby Hill Country—for outdoor recreation. Some suggestions of sports in or around town follow; see the "Hill Country Side Trips from San Antonio" section, later in this chapter, for more.

BIKING There aren't many scenic cycling trails within San Antonio proper—locals tend to ride in **Brackenridge Park,** in **McAllister Park** on the city's north side at 13102 Jones-Maltsberger (© 210/207-PARK or 210/207-3120), and around the area near **SeaWorld of Texas**—but there are a number of appealing places to bike in the vicinity. If you didn't bring your own two-wheeler, **Britton's Bicycles,** 4230 Thousand Oaks (© 210/656-1655; www.brittonbikes.com), can deliver one to your hotel. The store is a good resource, too, for cycling events around town. You might also log on to the **San Antonio Wheelmen**'s website (www.sawheelmen.com) for details on organized rides in the area.

GOLF Golf has become a big deal in San Antonio, with more and more visitors coming to town expressly to tee off. Of the city's six municipal golf courses, two of the most notable are **Brackenridge,** 2315 Ave. B (© 210/226-5612), featuring oak- and pecan-shaded fairways; and northwest San Antonio's $4.3 million **Cedar Creek,** 8250 Vista Colina (© 210/695-5050), repeatedly ranked as south Texas's best municipal course in golfing surveys. Other options for unaffiliated golfers include the 200-acre **Pecan Valley,** 4700 Pecan Valley Dr. (© 210/333-9018; www.thetexasgolftrail.com), which crosses the Salado Creek seven times and has an 800-year-old oak near its 13th hole; the high-end **Quarry,** 444 E. Basse Rd. (© 210/824-4500; www.quarrygolf.com), on the site of a former quarry and one of San Antonio's newest public courses; and **Canyon Springs,** 24400 Canyon Golf Rd. (© 888/800-1511 or 210/497-1770; www. canyonspringscc.com), at the north edge of town in the Texas Hill Country, lush with live oaks and dotted with historic rock formations.

There aren't too many resort courses in San Antonio because there aren't too many resorts, but the two at **La Cantera,** 16401 La Cantera Pkwy. (© 800/ 446-5387 or 210/558-4653), have knockout designs and dramatic hill-and-rock outcropping settings to recommend them. To get a copy of the free *San Antonio Golfing Guide,* call © 800/447-3372 or log on to www.santonio visit.com.

HIKING Friedrich Wilderness Park, 21480 Milsa (© 210/698-1057), operated by the city of San Antonio as a nature preserve, is crisscrossed by 5½ miles of trails that attract bird-watchers as well as hikers; a 2-mile stretch is accessible to visitor with disabilities. The park offers free guided hikes, lasting about 2 hours, the first Saturday of every month at 9am.

WATERSPORTS For tubing, rafting, or canoeing along a cypress-lined river, San Antonio river rats head 35 miles northwest of downtown to the 2,000-acre Guadalupe River State Park, 3350 Park Rd. 31 (© 830/438-2656; www. tpwd.state.tx.us). On Tex. 46, just outside the park, you can rent tubes, rafts, and canoes at the Bergheim Campground, FM 3351 in Bergheim (© 830/336-2235). Standard tubes run $6 per person (but the ones with a bottom for your cooler, at $7, are better), rafts are $15 per person (half-price for children ages 12 and under), and canoes go for $25.

SPECTATOR SPORTS

BASKETBALL From mid-October to May, the city's only major-league franchise, the San Antonio Spurs, shoots hoops at the SBC Center, opened October 2002. For most games, tickets are sold only for the dome's lower level, where prices range from $25 to $69. Nosebleed-level seats, running from $9 to $15, open up for the most popular contests. Tickets are available at the Spurs Ticket Office in the SBC Center (© 210/444-5819) or via Ticketmaster San Antonio (© 210/224-9600; www.ticketmaster.com). Get schedules, players' stats, promotional news and directions to the Spurs' new stadium online at www.nba.com/spurs.

GOLF The SBC Championship, an Official Senior PGA Tour Event, is held each October at the Oak Hills Country Club, 5403 Fredericksburg Rd. (© 210/698-3582; www.pgatour.com). One of the oldest professional golf tournaments, now known as the Westin Texas Open at La Cantera, showcases the sport in September at 16401 La Cantera Pkwy. (© 201/558-4653). Call the San Antonio Golf Association (© 800/TEX-OPEN or 210/341-0823) for additional information.

RODEO If you're in town in early February, don't miss the chance to see two weeks of Wild West events like calf roping, steer wrestling, and bull riding at the annual San Antonio Stock Show and Rodeo. You can also hear major live country music talent and you're likely to find something to add to your luggage at an exposition hall, packed with Texas handcrafts. Contact the San Antonio Livestock Exposition Inc. (© 210/225-5851; www.sarodeo.com) for additional advance information.

7 Shopping

San Antonio offers the retail-bound a nice balance of large malls and little enclaves of specialized shops. You'll find everything here from the utilitarian to the unusual: huge Sears and Kmart department stores, a Saks Fifth Avenue fronted by a 40-foot pair of cowboy boots, a mall with a river running through it, and some lively Mexican markets.

You can count on most shops around town being open from 9 or 10am until 5:30 or 6pm Monday through Saturday, with shorter hours on Sunday. Malls are generally open Monday through Saturday from 10am to 9pm and Sunday from noon to 6pm.

GREAT SHOPPING AREAS

Most out-of-town shoppers will find all they need **downtown,** between the large Rivercenter Mall, the boutiques and crafts shops of La Villita, the colorful Mexican wares of Market Square, and assorted retailers and galleries on and around Alamo Plaza. More avant-garde boutiques and galleries, including Blue Star, can be found in the adjacent area known as Southtown.

San Antonians tend to shop the Loop 410 malls—especially **North Star** and the **Alamo Quarry Market** near the airport—and cruise the upscale strip centers along Broadway in **Alamo Heights** (the posh **Collection** and **Lincoln Heights** are particularly noteworthy). Weekends might see locals poking around a number of terrific flea markets; one to check out is **Eisenhauer Road Flea Market,** 3903 Eisenhauer Rd. (© 210/653-7592). For bargains on brand labels, they head out to **New Braunfels** and **San Marcos,** home to two large factory outlet malls (see "Hill Country Side Trips from Austin" in chapter 8 for details).

MALLS & SHOPPING CENTERS

Although it's officially **Alamo Quarry Market,** 255 E. Basse Rd. (© **210/225-1000**), no one ever calls San Antonio's hottest newcomer to the mall scene anything but "The Quarry"—in large part because from the early 1900s until 1985 the property was in fact a cement quarry. This unenclosed mall has a series of large emporiums (such as Borders and Old Navy) and smaller upscale boutiques (Laura Ashley and Aveda). Starring Saks Fifth Avenue and upscale boutiques like Abercrombie & Fitch and Williams-Sonoma, **North Star Mall,** Loop 410, between McCullough and San Pedro (© **210/340-6627**), is the crème de la crème of the San Antonio indoor malls. But there are many sensible shops here, too, including a Mervyn's department store. The mall is fronted by a very Texan sculpture: a huge pair of cowboy boots. Both the Quarry and North Star Mall are about 15 minutes from downtown. At the light-filled, bustling **Rivercenter Mall,** 849 E. Commerce (© **210/225-0000**), you can pick up a ferry from a downstairs dock, listen to bands play on a stage surrounded by water, or visit the IMAX theater and a comedy club. The 130-plus shops, anchored by Dillard's and Foleys, run the price gamut, but tend toward upscale casual.

ART

In Southtown, the **Blue Star Arts Complex,** a huge converted warehouse filled with individual galleries, 1400 S. Alamo St. (© 210/227-6960), is the best place to buy the work of up-and-coming artists, but **Sala Diaz,** not far away at 517 Stieren St. (© **210/325-5923**), is a good alternative. At the northwest edge of downtown, the cutting-edge **Art Pace,** 445 N. Main Ave. (© **210/212-4900**), features rotating shows displaying the work of artists selected by a prestigious international panel for 3-month residencies at the facility. Three of the top downtown galleries that show more established (and more expensive) artists are **Galería Ortíz,** 102 Concho in Market Square (© 210/225-0731), San Antonio's premier place to buy Southwestern art; **Nanette Richardson Fine Art,** 513 E. Houston St. (© **210/224-1550**), with a wide array of oils, watercolors, bronzes, ceramics, and handcrafted wood furnishings; and **Parchman Stremmel,** 203 N. Presa (© **210/266-8752**), featuring the work of contemporary artists who've made it big (or come close).

For more details on these and other galleries, pick up a copy of the **San Antonio Gallery Guide** at the San Antonio Convention and Visitors Bureau,

317 Alamo Plaza (② **210/207-6700**). You can also check out the art scene online at the Office of Cultural Affairs' website, **www.sanantonio.gov/art/ website**, with links to several local galleries.

WESTERN WEAR

A one-stop shopping center for all duds Western, **Boot Hill** at Rivercenter Mall, 849 E. Commerce, Suite 213 (② **210/223-6634**), is one of the few left in town that's locally owned. At **Lucchese Gallery,** 255 E. Basse, Suite 800 (② **210/ 828-9419**), footwear is raised to the level of art. If it ever crawled, ran, hopped, or swam, these folks can probably put it on your feet. Lucchese is far better known than **Little's Boots,** 110 Division Ave. (② **210/923-2221**) but this place—established in 1915—uses as many esoteric leathers and creates fancier footwear designs. If you're willing to wait a while, you can get anything you like hand-customed for you. Pope John Paul II, Prince Charles, and Dwight Yoakam have all had headgear made for them by **Paris Hatters,** 119 Broadway (② **210/ 223-3453**), in business since 1917 and still owned by the same family. About half of the sales are special order, but the shelves are stocked with high-quality ready-to-wear hats.

HANDICRAFTS/FOLK ART

Mexican folk art and handicrafts make wonderful take-homes from San Antonio, and several of the best places to find them are in Southtown. They include the **Red Iguana,** 918 South Alamo St. (② **210/281-9667**), where you'll find everything from intricately wrought silver jewelry (vintage and new) to Spanish colonial–style paintings; **San Angel Folk Art,** 1404 South Alamo, Suite 410, in the Blue Star Arts Complex (② **210/226-6688**), chock-a-block with colorful, whimsical, and well-made wares; and **Tienda Guadalupe Folk Art & Gifts,** 1001 S. Alamo (② **210/226-5873**), where you can pick up a Day of the Dead T-shirt, or anything else you can think of relating to the early November holiday celebrated with great fanfare in San Antonio.

Just north of downtown, near Monte Vista, the two-level **Alamo Fiesta,** 2025 North Main at Ashby (② **210/738-1188**), catering to local Hispanic families, has a huge selection of crafts at extremely reasonable prices. In the same area, **Uriarte Talavera** 204 West Olmos (② **210/930-5595**), is a magnet for pottery aficionados, who know that the ceramics sold in the Uriarte Talavera workshop in Puebla, Mexico, are renowned for their artistry and high quality. This San Antonio wholesaler owns the factory in Mexico and is the U.S. distributor, so it has the country's largest selection—and also the lowest prices.

8 San Antonio After Dark

San Antonio has its symphony and its Broadway shows, and you can see both at one of the most beautiful old movie palaces in the country. But much of what the city has to offer is less mainstream. A Latin flavor lends spice to some of the best local nightlife: San Antonio is America's capital for Tejano music, a unique blend of German polka and northern Mexico ranchero sounds, with a dose of pop for good measure. You can sit on one side of the San Antonio River and watch colorful dance troupes like Ballet Folklórico perform on the other. And Southtown, with its many Hispanic-oriented shops and galleries, celebrates its art scene with the monthly First Friday, a kind of extended block party.

For the most complete listings of what's on while you're visiting, pick up a free copy of the weekly alternative newspaper, the *Current,* or the Friday "Weekender"

section of the *San Antonio Express-News*. You can also check out the **San Antonio Arts & Cultural Affairs Hotline** at (*C* 210/222-ARTS or www.sanantonio.
gov/art. There's no central office in town for tickets, discounted or otherwise.
Reserve seats directly through the theaters or clubs, or, for large events, through
Ticketmaster ((*C* 210/224-9600; www.ticketmaster.com).

THE PERFORMING ARTS

The San Antonio Symphony is the city's only resident performing arts company
of national stature, but smaller, less professional groups keep the local arts scene
lively, and cultural organizations draw world-renowned artists. The city provides
them with some unique venues for their work. Because, in some cases, the theater is the show—or at least an interesting component thereof—and because
such showcases offer an eclectic array of performances, I've included a category
called "Major Arts Venues" here.

MAJOR ARTS VENUES

If you're visiting San Antonio from May to August, be sure to see something at
the **Arneson River Theatre,** La Villita ((*C* 210/207-8610; www.lavillita.com),
built by the Works Projects Administration (WPA) in 1939 as part of architect
Robert Hugman's design for the River Walk. This unique theater stages shows—
mostly with a south-of-the-border flair—on one side of the river while the audience watches from an amphitheater on the other.

The baroque Moorish/Spanish revival–style **Majestic Theatre,** 230 E. Houston ((*C* 210/226-3333; www.majesticempire.com), hosts some of the best
entertainment in town—the symphony, major Broadway productions, big-
name solo performers.

There's always something happening at the **Guadalupe Cultural Arts Center,** 1300 Guadalupe ((*C* 210/271-3151; www.guadalupeculturalarts.org), the
main locus for Latino cultural activity in San Antonio. Visiting or local directors
put on six or seven plays a year; the Xicano Music Program celebrates the popular local conjunto and Tejano sounds; and the CineFestival, running since
1977, is one of the town's major film events.

Occupying a natural acoustic bowl in Brackenridge Park, the **Sunken Garden Theater,** North St. Mary's Street (Mulberry Ave. entrance; (*C* 210/207-
3076), boasts an open-air stage set against a wooded hillside. Built by the WPA
in 1936, this theater offers a little bit of everything—rock, country, hip-hop,
Tejano, sometimes even the San Antonio Symphony.

(Fun Fact   A Theater that Lives Up to Its Name

Everyone from Jack Benny to Mae West played the Majestic, one of the
last "atmospheric" theaters to be built in America: The stock market
crashed 4 months after its June 1929 debut and no one could afford such
expensive showplaces again. Designed by John Eberson, this former
vaudeville and film palace features an elaborate village above the sides
of the stage and, overhead, a magnificent night sky dome, replete with
twinkling stars and scudding clouds. Designated a National Historic Landmark, the Majestic affords a rare glimpse at a literally gilded era: We're
talking genuine gold leaf detailing.

CLASSICAL MUSIC

The **San Antonio Symphony,** 222 E. Houston St. (© **210/554-1000** or 210/554-1010 box office; www.sasymphony.org), is one of the finest in the United States. Founded in 1939, the orchestra celebrated its 50th anniversary by moving into the Majestic Theatre, the reopening of which was planned to coincide with the event. The classical series showcases the talents of music director emeritus Christopher Wilkens and a variety of guest performers, while for the pops series, the orchestra plays second fiddle to the likes of Al Jarreau and Burt Bacharach. Tickets range from $18 to $55.

THEATER

The big-production, Broadway shows turn up at the Majestic Theatre, but several smaller local troupes are worth checking out. The community-based **Josephine Street Theater,** 339 W. Josephine St. (© **210/734-4646**), near downtown, puts on an average of five productions a year. The award-winning group does mostly musicals, but has also performed dramatic classics. Whether it's an original piece by a member of the company or a work by a guest artist, anything you see at **Jump-Start Performance Company,** 108 Blue Star Arts Complex at 1400 S. Alamo (© **210/227-JUMP**), is likely to push the social and political envelope. This is the place to find the big-name performance artists like Karen Finley, and also to discover who's cutting it on the local cutting edge. The only professional family theater in town, the popular **Magik Theatre,** Beethoven Hall, 420 S. Alamo in HemisFair Park (© **210/227-2751;** www.magiktheatre.org), features a daytime series with light fare for ages 3 and up, and evening performances, recommended for those 6 and older, that may include weightier plays. About half the plays are adaptations of published scripts, while the other half are originals, created especially for the theater. For information on other small theaters in San Antonio and links to many of those listed in this section, log on to the website of the **San Antonio Theater Coalition** at www.satheatre.com.

THE CLUB & MUSIC SCENE

The closest San Antonio comes to having a club district is the stretch of North St. Mary's between Josephine and Magnolia—just north of downtown and south of Brackenridge Park—known as **the Strip.** This area was hotter about a decade ago, but it still draws young locals to its restaurants and lounges on the weekend. The **River Walk** clubs tend to be touristy and many of them close early because of noise restrictions. Downtown's **Sunset Station,** 1174 E. Commerce (© **210/222-9481;** www.sunset-station.com), a multi-venue entertainment complex in the city's original train station, has yet to take off when there are no events in the nearby Alamadome. When there are, you can get down at **Studio 794,** a high energy dance club with a 1916 steam engine in it, and **Club Agave,** where the movement has a Latin flavor.

COUNTRY & WESTERN

John T. Floore, the first manager of the Majestic Theatre, opened up **Floore's Country Store,** 14664 Old Bandera Rd., 2 miles north of Loop 1604 (© **210/695-8827**), in 1942. A couple of years later, he added a cafe and a dance floor—at half an acre, the largest in south Texas—and since then, it's hosted country greats such as Willie Nelson, Hank Williams, Sr., and more recently, Lyle Lovett and Dwight Yoakam. The lively 1880s-style **Leon Springs Dancehall,** 24135

I-10, Boerne Stage Road exit (© 210/698-7072), can pack some 1,200 people into its 18,000 square feet. Lots of folks come with their kids when the place opens at 7pm. Some of the best local country-and-western talent is showcased here on Friday and Saturday nights, the only 2 nights the dance hall is open.

JAZZ & BLUES

If you like big bands and Dixieland, there's no better place to listen to music downtown than **The Landing,** Hyatt Regency Hotel, River Walk (© **210/223-7266**), one of the best traditional jazz clubs in the country. You might have heard cornetist Jim Cullum on the airwaves: His American Public Radio program, *Riverwalk, Live from the Landing,* is now broadcast on more than 225 stations nationwide. The live jazz at tiny **Salute!,** 2801 N. St. Mary's (© **210/732-5307**), tends to have a Latin base, but you never know what you're going to find

---

 Conjunto: An American Classic

Although conjunto is one of America's original contributions to world music, for a long time few people outside of Texas knew much about it. It evolved at the end of the 19th century, when south Texas was swept by a wave of German immigrants who brought with them popular polkas and waltzes. These sounds were easily incorporated into—and transformed by—Mexican folk music; the newcomer accordion, cheap and able to mimic several instruments, was happily adopted, too. With the addition at the turn of the century of the *bajo sexto,* a 12-string guitarlike instrument for rhythmic bass accompaniment, conjunto was born.

San Antonio is to conjunto music what Nashville is to country. The most famous bajo sextos were created in San Antonio by the Macías family—the late Martín and now his son, Alberto. The undisputed king of conjunto, Flaco Jimenez—a mild-mannered triple-Grammy winner who has recorded with the Rolling Stones, Bob Dylan, and Willie Nelson, among others—lives in the city. And San Antonio's Tejano Conjunto Festival, held every May, is the largest of its kind, drawing aficionados from around the world—there's even a conjunto band from Japan.

Most of the places to hear conjunto are off the beaten tourist path, and they come and go fairly quickly. Those that have been around for a while—and are visitor friendly—include **Arturo's Sports Bar & Grill,** 3310 S. Zarzamora St. (© **210/923-0177**); **Cattleman's At Woodlake,** 3711 Roland Rd. (© **210/337-3880**); and **Cool Arrows,** 1025 Nogalitos St. (© **210/227-5130**). For live music schedules, check the Tejano/Conjunto section under "Entertainment" and "Music" of **MySanAntonio.com** (www.expressnews.com), the website of the *San Antonio Express-News.* You can also phone **Salute!** (© **210/732-5307**) to find out which night of the week they're featuring a Tejano or conjunto band. Best yet, just attend one of San Antonio's many festivals—you're bound to hear these rousing sounds.

here—anything from synthesized '70s sounds to conjunto. A friendly music garden, **Tycoon Flats,** 2926 N. St. Mary's St. (© 210/737-1929), is a fun place to kick back and listen to blues, rock, acoustic, or jazz. The burgers are good, too. Bring the kids—an outdoor sandbox is larger than the dance floor.

ROCK

Loud and not much to look at—low ceilings, red vinyl booths, garage pin-up calendars stapled to the ceiling—tiny **Taco Land,** 103 W. Grayson St. (© 210/223-8406), is the hottest alternative music club in San Antonio, showcasing everything from mainstream rock to surf punk. Nirvana played here before they hit the big time. One of the few alternative rock venues on the Strip, **White Rabbit,** 2410 N. St. Mary's St. (© 210/737-2221), attracts a mostly younger crowd to its black-lit recesses.

THE BAR SCENE

MICROBREWERIES   Preppie and gallery types don't often mingle, but the popularity with college kids of the **Blue Star Brewing Company,** 1414 S. Alamo, no. 105 (© 210/212-5506), in the Blue Star Arts Complex demonstrates the transcendent power of good beer (the pale ale is especially fine). Stress tests were once conducted in the room where the beer is now brewed at **The Laboratory,** 7310 Jones-Maltsberger (© 210/824-1997), formerly the lab for the old Alamo Quarry cement factory. Enjoy the "authentic" Bavarian hefeweizen in the huge, two-level main room or on a leafy outdoor patio.

A HISTORIC BAR   More than 100 years ago, Teddy Roosevelt recruited men for his Rough Riders unit at the dark, wooded **Menger Bar,** Menger Hotel, 204 Alamo Plaza (© 210/223-4361); they were outfitted for the Spanish-American War at nearby Fort Sam Houston. Constructed in 1859 on the site of William Menger's earlier successful brewery and saloon, the bar was moved from its original location in the Victorian hotel lobby in 1956, but 90% of its historic furnishings remain intact. You can still see an "X" on the bar put there by prohibitionist Carrie Nation, and Spanish Civil War uniforms hang on the walls.

LOCAL FAVORITES   During the week, lawyers and judges come to unwind at the **Cadillac Bar & Restaurant,** 212 S. Flores (© 210/223-5533), in a historic stucco building near the Bexar County Courthouse and City Hall; on weekends, singles take the stand. Gallery groupies tend to gather at **La Tuna,** 100 Probant (© 210/224-8862), in Southtown's Blue Star Arts district—look for the brightly colored sign on a tiny concrete-and-corrugated aluminum building—but lots of nonartsy types drop by for a beer, too.

A BAR WITH A VIEW   No matter what, or how much, you have to drink, you'll get higher at the bar of the **Tower of the Americas** restaurant, 222 HemisFair Park (© 210/223-3101), than anywhere else in San Antonio—more than 700 feet high, in fact. Sample a Top of the Tower—light rum, vodka, apricot brandy, and fruit juices—and you might never want to come down.

A SPORTS BAR   If you want to hang with the Spurs, come to **Tex's,** San Antonio Airport Hilton and Conference Center, 611 NW Loop 410 (© 210/340-6060), regularly voted San Antonio's best sports bar in the *Current* readers' polls. Among Tex's major array of exclusively Texas sports memorabilia are a signed Nolan Ryan jersey and one of George Gervin's basketball shoes—the other is at the newer Tex's on the River, at the Hilton Palacio del Rio.

GAY & LESBIAN NIGHTLIFE

For a calendar of events, log on to the website of the **Gay & Lesbian Community Center of San Antonio,** 611 E. Myrtle Ave. (© **210/223-6106;** www.glccsa.org).

Tina Turner, Debbie Harry, and LaToya Jackson—not female impersonators—have all played the **Bonham Exchange,** 411 Bonham (© **210/271-3811**), a high-tech dance club in a restored 1880s building near the Alamo. You'll find an occasional cross-dressing show here, but the mixed crowd of gays and straights, young and old, come mainly to move to the beat under wildly flashing lights. Main Street just north of downtown—nicknamed the "gay bar mall"—has three gay clubs in proximity: **Pegasus,** 1402 N. Main (© **210/299-4222**), is your basic cruise bar; **The Silver Dollar,** 1418 N. Main (© **210/227-2623**), does the country-and-western thing; and **The Saint,** 1430 N. Main (© **210/225-7330**), caters to dancing fools.

9 Hill Country Side Trips from San Antonio

A rising and falling dreamscape of lakes and rivers, springs and caverns, the Hill Country is one of Texas's prettiest regions, especially in early spring when wildflowers daub it with every pigment in nature's palette. Dotted with old dance halls, country stores, and quaint Teutonic towns—more than 30,000 Germans emigrated to Texas during the great land-grant years of the Republic—the region also lays out an appealing tableau of the state's history. Although you can visit the following towns on day trips from San Antonio, staying overnight is recommended. You can make a loop from San Antonio to Comfort, Bandera, and Castroville (which is how these towns are arranged in the following listings), or pick and choose between these and the Hill Country towns detailed in the "Hill Country Side Trips from Austin" section in chapter 8; New Braunfels and San Marcos are especially close to San Antonio. See the "South Central Texas" map on p. 233 to locate these towns.

COMFORT ★★

True to its name, Comfort, founded by freethinking German immigrants in 1852, is one of the most pleasant of the Hill Country towns. The rough-hewn limestone buildings in the center of Comfort may comprise the most complete 19th-century business district in Texas. Some of the offices were designed by architect Alfred Giles, who also left his distinctive mark on the streets of San Antonio (about 40 miles to the southeast via I-10). The earliest church in town was built some 40 years after the first settlers arrived because during the initial period, the founders' antireligious beliefs, for which they had been persecuted in the old country, prevailed. Most of the settlers were also opposed to the Confederacy during the Civil War. The **Treue der Union (True to the Union) Monument,** on High Street between Third and Fourth Streets, was erected in 1866 to commemorate 36 antislavery settlers killed by Confederate soldiers when they tried to defect to Mexico.

A majority of the town's high-quality and high-priced antiques shops are in the limestone buildings along High Street; more than 30 dealers gather at the **Comfort Antique Mall,** 734 High St. (© **830/995-4678**). But make your first stop the **Ingenhuett Store,** 830–34 High St. (© **830/995-2149**), owned and operated by the same German American family since 1867. Along with groceries, outdoor gear, and sundries, the store carries maps and other sources of tourist information. It's open far more frequently than the **Comfort Chamber** of Commerce (℘ 830/995-3131), on Seventh and High streets, which has very limited hours.

WHERE TO STAY

One of the largest and most interesting antiques shops in town, **Comfort Common,** 818 High St. (℘ 830/995-3030; www.comfortcommon.com), doubles as a bed-and-breakfast. Two reasonably priced ($80) rooms, in what was once the 19th-century Faust-Ingenhuett Hotel, built by Alfred Giles, are imaginatively decorated and look out onto a peaceful garden. Nearby, two separate cottages and a log cabin go for $110 to $175.

WHERE TO DINE

The chef/owner of **Arlene's,** 426 Seventh St., just off High Street (℘ 830/995-3330), used to be a food columnist for the *San Antonio Express-News,* and her freshly made soups, quiches, sandwiches, and desserts prove she knew whereof she wrote. **Mimi's Cafe,** 814 High St. (℘ 830/995-3470), also specializes in light repasts prepared daily on the premises. The chocolate French silk pie and apple cherry crisp are particularly popular. Both are primarily lunch only.

BANDERA ★★★

About 30 miles northwest on Tex. 16 from its intersection with loop 1604 in San Antonio, Bandera is a slice of life out of the Old West. Practically everything and everybody here seems to have come straight off a John Ford film set. Established as a lumber camp in 1853, this popular guest-ranch center still has the feel of the frontier: Not only are many of its historic buildings intact—including **St. Stanislaus** (1855), the second-oldest Polish church in the country—but people are as genuinely friendly as any you might imagine from America's small-town past.

You can explore Bandera's distant past by picking up a self-guided tour brochure of historic sites at the **Bandera County Convention and Visitors Bureau,** 1134A Main St. (℘ 800/364-3833 or 830/796-3045; www.bandera cowboycapital.com). But most people take advantage of the town's living traditions by strolling along Main Street, where a variety of crafters work in the careful, hand-hewn style of yesteryear.

Area activities include horseback riding, rodeo watching, and kayaking, canoeing, and tubing on the Medina River. The Convention and Visitors Bureau can direct you to the best outfitters, and can also let you know about rodeos or roping exhibitions in the area—they occur often in summer and, less regularly, in fall. Canter through the **Hill Country State Natural Area,** 10 miles southwest of Bandera (℘ 830/796-4413), the largest state park in Texas allowing horseback riding. About 20 miles southeast of town (take Tex. 16 to R.R. 1283), **Medina Lake** is the place to hook crappie, white or black bass, and, especially, huge yellow catfish.

STAYING AT A GUEST RANCH

For the full flavor of this region, plan to stay at one of Bandera's many guest ranches; you'll find a full listing on the Bandera website. Most have a 2-night (or more) minimum stay. Two of the most established ones include the **Dixie Dude Ranch** (℘ 800/375-Y'ALL or 830/796-4481; www.dixieduderanch.com), a long-time favorite retreat with a 725-acre spread ($95–$120 per adult per night); and the **Mayan Ranch** (℘ 830/796-3312 or 830/460-3036; www. mayanranch.com), another well-established family-run place ($130 per adult). Rates are based on double occupancy and include three home-cooked meals, two trail rides, and most other activities.

WHERE TO DINE

Main Street's **O.S.T.** (© **830/796-3636**), named for the Old Spanish Trail that used to run through Bandera, has been serving down-home Texas and Tex-Mex victuals since 1921. An open deck overlooking the Medina River is one of the draws at **Billy Gene's,** 1105 Main St. (© **830/460-3200**), which features huge platters of down-home country standards at retro prices, as well as less health-defying food. The **Cabaret Dance Hall** (see below) has a cafe known for its good prime rib and Gulf Coast seafood.

AFTER DARK: A COUPLE OF HONKY-TONKS

Don't miss **Arkey Blue & The Silver Dollar Bar** (© **830/796-8826**), a gen-uine spit-and-sawdust cowboy honky-tonk on Main Street. When there's no live music, plug a quarter in the old jukebox and play a country ballad by owner Arkey. Just down the road a piece, the old **Cabaret Dance Hall** (© **830/796-8166**), established in 1936, was recently resuscitated. Larger than Arkey's, it can accommodate bigger-draw names like Don Walser and Chris Ledoux.

CASTROVILLE ⭐

Even though Castroville is very close to San Antonio—20 miles via U.S. 90 west—it has maintained a pristine, rural atmosphere, perhaps because the town doesn't encourage growth. It was founded on a scenic bend of the Medina River in 1844 by Henri Castro, a Portuguese-born Jewish Frenchman, who recruited most of his 2,134 émigrés from the Rhine Valley, and especially from the French province of Alsace. You can still hear Alsatian, an unwritten dialect of German, spoken by some of the older members of town. *Note:* Castroville closes down on Monday and Tuesday, and some places are shuttered on Wednesday and Sunday as well. If you want to find everything open, come on Thursday, Friday, or Saturday.

You can pick up a booklet that contains a walking tour of the town's histori-cal buildings, as well as a map that details the location of the various boutiques and antiques shops (they're not concentrated in a single area) from the **Castro-ville Chamber of Commerce,** 802 London St. (© **800/778-6775** or 830/538-3142; www.castroville.com).

Almost 100 of the original settlers' unevenly slope-roofed houses remain in Castroville, some still occupied by the builders' descendants. The oldest stand-ing structure, the **First St. Louis Catholic Church,** went up in 1846 on the corner of Angelo and Madrid. Many of the European-style headstones in the **cemetery** at the western edge of town, where Henri Castro's wife, Amelia, is buried, date from the 1840s.

Get some insight into the town's history at the **Landmark Inn State Histor-ical Park,** 402 E. Florence St. (© **830/931-2133;** www.tpwd.state.tx.us/park/landmark/landmark.htm), which also counts among its attractions a nature trail, an old gristmill, and a stone dam. The inn that serves as the park's centerpiece offers eight simple rooms (no TVs or phones) decorated with early Texas pieces dating to the 1940s (doubles with private bathroom $61; shared bathroom, $55).

WHERE TO DINE

Get a delicious taste of the past at **Haby's Alsatian Bakery,** 207 U.S. 90 East (© **830/931-2118**), featuring apple fritters, strudels, stollens, breads, and cof-feecakes. A gourmet surprise in this rural region, **La Normandie Restaurant,** 1302 Fiorella St. (© **800/261-1731** or 830/538-3070), has a classic French menu, including the excellent house special veal *à la normande.*

8

Austin

by Edie Jarolim

Aaah, Austin, that laid-back city in the lake-laced hills, home to cyberpunks and environmentalists, high culture and haute cuisine. A leafy intellectual enclave lying well outside the realm of Lone Star stereotypes, Austin has been compared to Berkeley and Seattle, but it is at once its own place and entirely of Texas. With its gigantic health food emporia, privately owned bookstores, and homegrown chain of running stores, the city indulges its yuppie-dom with pure Texas excess. But, although it's passed the half-million population mark within its city limits alone, Austin still has a quirky small-town atmosphere.

Born on the frontier out of the grandiose dreams of a man whose middle name was Buonaparte (Mirabeau Lamar), Austin spent its formative years fighting to maintain its status as capital. Texan hubris and feistiness remain key to Austin's character today—from state legislators who descend, squabbling, on the grand state capitol building every other year, to the locals fighting to save the golden-cheeked warbler from the developer's bulldozer.

During the 1990s, Austin rode the wave of the country's digital boom. The population increased by a whopping 41% as lucrative high tech jobs lured out-of-staters, quite a few of them Californians with lots of disposable cash. And although the majority of Austin's newer residents moved to the suburbs, the economic expansion aided in downtown's resurgence. The debut of the Austin-Bergstrom International Airport on the southside at the end of the decade helped with the nascent development of South Congress Street (dubbed SoCo, of course), just beyond downtown; it's now lined with hip boutiques and galleries. And in an ultimate Austin act of recycling, the abandoned hangers of the old Robert Mueller airport were turned into a film production studio, which added jobs and activity to a once-decaying north-central neighborhood.

By the beginning of the new millennium, many people feared that Austin was losing its unique character. The upscaling of rents meant that many of the struggling musicians who gave Austin's music scene its vitality could no longer afford to live in town, and construction began blocking traffic on already choked downtown streets.

But the question of whether Austin was becoming a victim of its own success was put on hold when the tech balloon burst in 2001. Unemployment has been on the rise and several buildings were abandoned, mid-construction. Of course, Austin's ability to make amazing comebacks—it completely recovered from the oil bust of the 1980s—tends to vie with its strong counterculture urges. The city's ambivalence about material success of the traditional sort is perhaps epitomized by the current dispute over the question of who owns the copyright to the slogan "Keep Austin Weird."

If you're interested in soaking in history, playing outdoors, and listening to live music in terrifically low-key, intimate venues, you'll want to linger here for a minimum of 3 days and nights, perhaps staying on the west side near one of the Highland Lakes for an additional day of kicking back. But if you're looking for the major art museums of Fort Worth or the mega-malls of Dallas, you might just want to tour the capitol and other down-town sights in a day and move on.

1 Orientation

Thousands of acres of parks, preserves, and lakes have been set aside for public enjoyment in Austin, making it an unusually people-friendly city. It's easy to miss all that, however, when you're busy negotiating the city's freeways. As soon as possible, get out of your car and smell the flowers: Just a few blocks south of downtown's office towers lie the green shores of Town Lake, where you'll begin to see what Austin is really all about.

ARRIVING
BY PLANE

The $581 million **Austin-Bergstrom International Airport** (© 512/495-7550), opened in 1999 on the site of the former Bergstrom Air Force Base, just off Highway 71/Ben White Boulevard and some 8 miles southwest of the capi-tol, is the town's transportation darling. Its geek's dream of a website, **www.ci.austin.tx.us/austinairport**, features a virtual reality tour of the terminal, flight schedules, links to the airlines and car-rental companies, and more.

Taxis from the major companies in town (usually) form a queue outside the terminal; they're not always in sight. To ensure off-hour pickup in advance, phone **American Yellow Checker Cab** (© 512/542-9999) before you leave home. The ride between the airport and downtown generally costs around $25. The flag-drop charge is $1.50, and it's $1.75 for every mile after that.

If you're not in a huge rush to get to your hotel, **SuperShuttle** (© 800/BLUE-VAN or 512/258-3826; www.supershuttle.com) is a less expensive alter-native to cabbing it, offering comfortable minivan service to hotels and resi-dences. Prices range from $10 one-way ($18 round-trip) to a downtown hotel, $12 ($20 round-trip) to a central hotel, and $15 ($26 round-trip) to a hotel in the northwest part of town. You don't have to book in advance for arrival, but you do need to phone 24 hours ahead of time to arrange for a pickup when you're ready to return.

Most of the major car-rental companies—Advantage, Alamo, Avis, Budget, Dollar, Hertz, and Thrifty—have outlets at the airport, and you can now just walk across the road from the terminal building to pick up (and drop off) your car. The trip from the airport to downtown by car or taxi could take anywhere from 25 minutes to an hour, depending on the time of day and the current state of highway repairs. *Tip:* If you're heading downtown from the airport, it's best to take Riverside Drive and then Congress Avenue north rather than staying on Tex. 71 and using I-35. If you want to get to the northwest, take Tex. 183 all the way, again avoiding the often-congested I-35.

BY CAR

I-35 is the north-south approach to Austin; it intersects with Tex. 290, a major east-west thoroughfare, and Tex. 183, which also runs roughly north-south through town. If you're staying on the west side of Austin, hook up with Loop 1, almost always called Mo-Pac by locals.

> **Tips** Shameless Plug
>
> For more in-depth coverage of Austin and the Hill Country, pick up a copy of *Frommer's San Antonio & Austin,* 5th Edition.

BY TRAIN

The **Amtrak** station, 250 N. Lamar Blvd. at West First St. (© **512/476-5684**), is in the southwest part of downtown. There are generally a few cabs around to meet the trains, but if you don't see one, a list of phone numbers of taxi companies is posted near the pay phones. Some of the downtown hotels offer courtesy pickup from the train station. A cab ride shouldn't run more than $4 or $5 (there's a $3 minimum charge).

BY BUS

The **Greyhound** bus terminal, 916 E. Koenig Lane (© **512/458-3823**), is near Highland Mall, about 10 minutes north of downtown and just south of the I-35 motel zone. Some hotels are within walking distance, and many others are a short cab ride away; a few taxis usually wait outside the station. Bus no. 7 (Duval) or no. 15 (Red River), which stop across the street, can get you downtown.

VISITOR INFORMATION

The **Austin Convention & Visitors Bureau,** 201 E. Second St. (© **800/926-2282;** www.austintexas.org), down the street from the convention center in southeast downtown, is open Monday through Friday from 8:30am to 5pm, Saturday from 9am to 5pm, and Sunday from noon to 5pm (extended hours Memorial Day to Labor Day; closed Thanksgiving and Dec 25).

Inside Line (© **512/416-5700**) can clue you in on Austin information from the essential to the esoteric—everything from weather forecasts and restaurant reviews to financial news and bat facts. Punch extension 4636 for instructions on how to use the system. The free alternative newspaper, the *Chronicle,* distributed to stores, hotels, and restaurants around town every Thursday, is the best source of information about Austin events. It's got a close rival in *XLent,* the weekend entertainment guide put out by the *Austin-American Statesman,* which is also free and also turns up on Thursday at most of the same places that carry the *Chronicle.*

CITY LAYOUT

In 1839, Austin was laid out in a grid on the northern shore of the Colorado River, bounded by Shoal Creek to the west and Waller Creek to the east. The section of the river abutting the original settlement is now known as Town Lake, and the city has spread far beyond its original borders in all directions. The land to the east is flat Texas plain; the rolling Hill Country begins on the west side of town. Central Austin is, very roughly, bounded by Oltdorf to the south, Tex. 290 to the north, I-35 to the east, and Mo-Pac (Loop 1) to the west.

MAIN ARTERIES & STREETS   I-35, comprising the border between central and east Austin, is the main north-south thoroughfare; Mo-Pac (formally, Loop 1), is its west side equivalent. Tex. 290, running east and west, merges with I-35 when it comes in on the north, briefly reestablishing its separate identity on the south side of town before it merges with Tex. 71 (called Ben White Blvd.

between Tex. 183 and Lamar Blvd.). Tex. 290 and Tex. 171 split up again in Oak Hill, on the west side. Not confused enough yet? Tex. 2222 changes its name from Koenig to Northland and, west of Loop 360, to Bullcreek, while, in the north, Tex. 183 is called Research Boulevard. Important north-south city streets include Lamar, Guadalupe, and Burnet. If you want to get across town north of the river, use Cesar Chavez (once known as First St.), 15th Street (which turns into Enfield west of Lamar), Martin Luther King Jr. Boulevard (the equivalent of 19th St., and usually just called MLK).

THE NEIGHBORHOODS IN BRIEF

Although Austin, designed to be the capital of the independent Republic of Texas, has a planned, grand city center similar to that of Washington, D.C., the city has spread out far beyond those original boundaries. These days, with a few exceptions, detailed below, locals tend to speak in terms of landmarks (the University of Texas) or geographical areas (east Austin) rather than neighborhoods.

Hotels, restaurants, and attractions in the Downtown, University of Texas, and Hyde Park areas can be located on the "Central Austin" map; all other areas are shown on the "Greater Austin" map.

Central Austin

Consisting roughly of the area north of Barton Springs Road/East Riverside Drive up until 45th Street, bordered by I-35 on the east and Mo-Pac on the west, Central Austin includes Downtown as well as several neighborhoods on its fringes.

Downtown The original city, laid out by Edwin Waller in 1839, runs roughly north-south from the river (Cesar Chavez) to MLK (around 20th St.) and east-west between I-35 and Lamar. This is the town's prime sightseeing and hotel district. Music clubs, restaurants, shops, and galleries thrive on and around **Sixth Street,** and new businesses now fill the beautiful old office buildings on and around **Congress Avenue.** The latest subsection of downtown to take off is the **Warehouse District,** a restaurant/bar mecca centered on Third and Fourth streets just west of Congress. Although downtown technically ends at Town Lake, most people would consider the lake's south shore and its hike-and-bike trail to be part of it.

University of Texas Just north of the capitol, the original 40 acres allotted for the building of the University of Texas have expanded to 357, and Guadalupe Street, along the west side of the campus, is now a popular shopping strip known as the Drag.

Hyde Park North of the university between 38th and 45th streets, Hyde Park got its start in 1891 as one of Austin's first planned suburbs; renovation of its Victorian and early Craftsman houses began in the 1970s, and now there's a real neighborhood feel to this pretty, tree-lined area.

Greater Austin

South Austin For a long time, not a lot was happening south of Barton Springs Road/East Riverside Drive. Then in the 1990s, **South Congress,** the once-derelict stretch of Congress Avenue that extends (presently) to Oltorf Street, started becoming gentrified—or at least trendified. It's now lined with cutting-edge art galleries, antiques boutiques, and retro clothing shops, and has, naturally, been nicknamed "SoCo." And since the 1999 debut of the **airport** at Ben White Boulevard, just east of Tex. 183, hotels and services have started cropping

Greater Austin Accommodations, Dining & Attractions

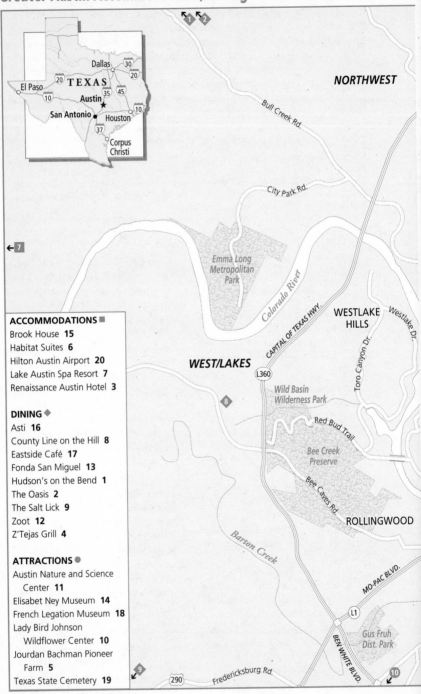

NORTHWEST

Bull Creek Rd.

Dallas

TEXAS

El Paso

Austin

San Antonio

Houston

Corpus Christi

City Park Rd.

Emma Long Metropolitan Park

Colorado River

WESTLAKE HILLS

Westlake Dr.

WEST/LAKES

Capital of Texas Hwy.

L360

Toro Canyon Dr.

Wild Basin Wilderness Park

Red Bud Trail

Bee Creek Preserve

Bee Caves Rd.

ROLLINGWOOD

Barton Creek

MO-PAC BLVD.

L1

Gus Fruh Dist. Park

Ben White Blvd.

290

Fredericksburg Rd.

ACCOMMODATIONS ■
Brook House **15**
Habitat Suites **6**
Hilton Austin Airport **20**
Lake Austin Spa Resort **7**
Renaissance Austin Hotel **3**

DINING ◆
Asti **16**
County Line on the Hill **8**
Eastside Café **17**
Fonda San Miguel **13**
Hudson's on the Bend **1**
The Oasis **2**
The Salt Lick **9**
Zoot **12**
Z'Tejas Grill **4**

ATTRACTIONS ●
Austin Nature and Science Center **11**
Elisabet Ney Museum **14**
French Legation Museum **18**
Lady Bird Johnson Wildflower Center **10**
Jourdan Bachman Pioneer Farm **5**
Texas State Cemetery **19**

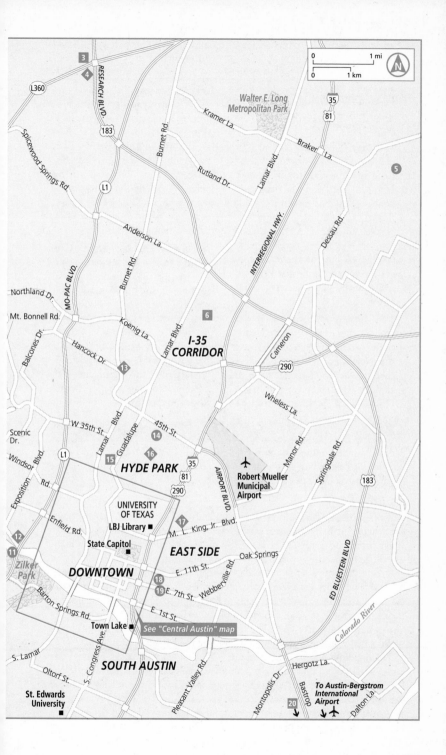

up in an area once dominated by faceless residential developments. It's not until you head farther south and west, towards the Lady Bird Johnson Wildflower Center, that south Austin begins to reassert its rural roots.

East Side The section east of I-35 between Cesar Chavez and Manor Road is home to many of Austin's Latino and African-American residents. Mexican restaurants and markets dot the area, which also hosts a number of African-American heritage sites, including the George Washington Carver Library and Museum; the French Legation Museum and state cemetery are also in this area.

I-35 Corridor Austin has grown around the heavily traveled connector area between Central and the Northwest, where the airport used to be located. Lined with chain hotels and restaurants, it's as charmless as it sounds, but it's convenient to both downtown and the north.

West/Lakes As you head along Lake Austin and Lake Travis into Hill Country, you'll encounter such affluent residential developments as **Westlake Hills** (where Michael Dell lives) and **Lakeway,** as well as the more charming, low-key **Bee Cave.** But you don't have to live here to play here: This is also where those who live in Central Austin come to splash around and kick back on nice weekends.

Northwest This high-growth area, Austin's version of the suburbs, consists largely of upscale business, shopping, and residential complexes; The Arboretum is this area's retail heart. The northwest has been described as extending north from Tex. 2222 to Dallas, but Parmer Lane is probably the real northern boundary. Farther north are such bedroom communities as Round Rock and Cedar Park.

2 Getting Around

Although public transportation is good, especially in the downtown area, a car is by far the best way to get around. If you need to rent wheels, getting them at the airport makes the most sense.

BY CAR

Between its long-standing traffic oddities and the more recent, but rampant, construction, driving in Austin can be a bear. Don't fall into a driver's daze anywhere in town; you need to be as vigilant on the city streets as you are on highways. The former are rife with signs that suddenly insist LEFT LANE MUST TURN LEFT or RIGHT LANE MUST TURN RIGHT—generally positioned so they're only noticeable when it's too late to switch. A number of major downtown streets are one-way; many don't have street signs or have signs so covered with foliage that they're impossible to read. Driving is particularly confusing in the university area, where streets like "32½" suddenly turn up. Multiply the difficulties at night, when you need X-ray vision to read the ill-lit street indicators.

The highways are no more pleasant. I-35 is mined with tricky on- and off-ramps and, around downtown, a confusing complex of upper and lower levels; it's easy to miss your exit. The rapidly developing area to the northwest, where Tex. 183 connects I-35 with Mo-Pac and the Capital of Texas Highway, requires particular vigilance, as the connections occur very rapidly. There are regular lane mergings and sudden, precipitous turnoffs. Nervous? Good. Better a bit edgy

Central Austin Accommodations, Dining & Attractions

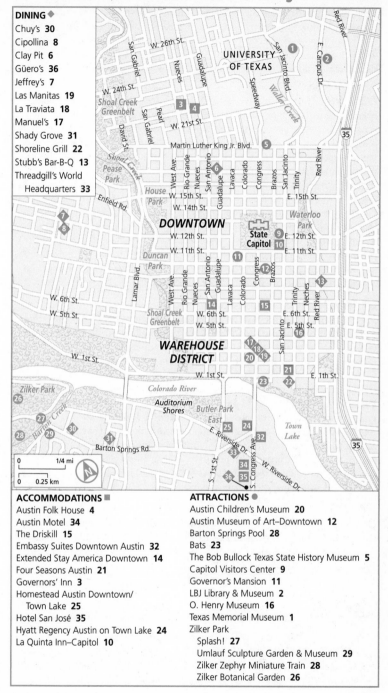

DINING ◆
Chuy's **30**
Cipollina **8**
Clay Pit **6**
Güero's **36**
Jeffrey's **7**
Las Manitas **19**
La Traviata **18**
Manuel's **17**
Shady Grove **31**
Shoreline Grill **22**
Stubb's Bar-B-Q **13**
Threadgill's World
  Headquarters **33**

ACCOMMODATIONS ■
Austin Folk House **4**
Austin Motel **34**
The Driskill **15**
Embassy Suites Downtown Austin **32**
Extended Stay America Downtown **14**
Four Seasons Austin **21**
Governors' Inn **3**
Homestead Austin Downtown/
  Town Lake **25**
Hotel San José **35**
Hyatt Regency Austin on Town Lake **24**
La Quinta Inn–Capitol **10**

ATTRACTIONS ●
Austin Children's Museum **20**
Austin Museum of Art–Downtown **12**
Barton Springs Pool **28**
Bats **23**
The Bob Bullock Texas State History Museum **5**
Capitol Visitors Center **9**
Governor's Mansion **11**
LBJ Library & Museum **2**
O. Henry Museum **16**
Texas Memorial Museum **1**
Zilker Park
  Splash! **27**
  Umlauf Sculpture Garden & Museum **29**
  Zilker Zephyr Miniature Train **28**
  Zilker Botanical Garden **26**

than lost or injured. Consult maps in advance and, when driving around the university or downtown, try to gauge the number of blocks before turns so you won't have to be completely dependent on street signs. You might also check the Texas Department of Transportation's (TXDot) website, www.dot.state.tx.us, for the latest information on road conditions, including highway diversions, construction, and closures.

PARKING   Unless you have congressional plates, you're likely to find the selection of parking spots downtown extremely limited during the week. There are a number of lots around the area, costing anywhere from $5 to $7, but the most convenient ones tend to fill up quickly. If you're lucky enough to find a metered spot, it'll run you 75¢ per hour, with a 2-hour limit, so bring change. Although there's virtually no street parking available near the capitol before 5pm during the week, there is a free visitor garage on 15th and San Jacinto (2-hr. time limit).

The university area is similarly congested during the week; trying to find a spot near the shopping strip known as the Drag can be just that; even the parking lots along Guadalupe Street fill up quickly. Cruise the side streets; you're eventually bound to find a lot that's not filled. Log on to www.utexas.edu/business/parking/resources for details on additional places to put your car on campus, and for parking maps.

BY PUBLIC TRANSPORTATION
Austin's public transportation system, **Capital Metropolitan Transportation Authority,** includes more than 50 bus lines and it's a bargain: The regular adult one-way fare on Metro routes is 50¢; express service from various Park & Ride lots costs $1; and the five downtown/UT 'Dillo routes—Red, Yellow, Orange, Blue, and Silver—are free. Getting around on the buses is really only an option if you're staying downtown. You'll need exact change or fare tickets to board the bus; free transfers are good for 3 hours on weekdays, 4 hours on weekends. Log on to www.capmetro.austin.tx.us or call © **800/474-1201** or 512/474-1200 for routing information. You can also pickup a schedule booklet at any HEB, Fiesta, or Albertson's grocery store or at the Capital Metro Information Center, 106 E. Eighth St., just off Congress. Buy a Ticket Book at any of these centers and you can get 20, 50¢ tickets for only $5—a 50% savings. Children ages 5 years or younger ride free when accompanied by adults.

BY TAXI
Don't expect to be able to hail a cab on the street. If you want to phone for one, try **Austin Cab** (© 512/478-2222), **Roy's Taxi** (© 512/482-0000), or **American Yellow Checker Cab** (© 512/452-9999). Rates are regulated by the city: It's $1.50 for the flag-drop fee, $1.75 for each additional mile.

FAST FACTS: Austin

American Express There's an office at 2943 W. Anderson Lane (© 512/452-8166), open Monday through Friday from 9am to 6pm.

Babysitters **Grandparents Unlimited** (© 512/280-5108) is a licensed and bonded childcare provider that employs seniors or other older reliable people.

Dentists Call the **Dental Referral Service** at $\mathcal{C}$ **800/917-6453.**

Doctors The **Medical Exchange** ($\mathcal{C}$ **512/458-1121**) and **Seton Hospital** ($\mathcal{C}$ **512/324-4450**) both have physician referral services.

Drugstores You'll find many **Walgreens, Eckerd,** and **Randalls** drugstores around the city; most HEB grocery stores also have pharmacies. Several Walgreens are open 24 hours. Have your zip code ready and call $\mathcal{C}$ **800/ 925-4733** to find the Walgreens branch nearest you.

Hospitals **Brackenridge,** 601 E. 15th St. ($\mathcal{C}$ **512/324-7000**), **St. David's,** 919 E. 32nd St. at I-35 ($\mathcal{C}$ **512/397-4240**), and **Seton Medical Center,** 1201 W. 38th St. ($\mathcal{C}$ **512/324-1000**) have good and convenient emergency-care facilities.

Internet Access Most **Schlotzky's Delis,** a chain that originated in Austin, offer free Internet access via computer stations; you're limited to 20 minutes but that should give you enough time to check your e-mail. Of the 17 Schlotzky's in Austin, the two locations most convenient to the majority of visitors are 106 E. Sixth St. in downtown ($\mathcal{C}$ **512/473-2867**), and 1915 Guadalupe near the University of Texas ($\mathcal{C}$ **512/457-1129**). Log on to www.cooldeli.com for other locations.

Newspapers & Magazines The daily *Austin American-Statesman* (www.statesman.com) is the only large-circulation, mainstream newspaper in town. The *Austin Chronicle* (www.auschron.com), a free alternative weekly, focuses on the arts, entertainment, and politics. From Monday to Thursday, the University of Texas publishes the surprisingly sophisticated *Daily Texan* (www.dailytexanonline.com) newspaper, covering everything from on-campus to international events.

Police The nonemergency number for the Austin Police Department is $\mathcal{C}$ **512/974-5000;** in an emergency, call $\mathcal{C}$ **911.**

Post Office The city's main post office is at 8225 Cross Park Dr. ($\mathcal{C}$ **512/ 342-1252**); more convenient to tourist sights are the Capitol Station, 111 E. 17th St., in the LBJ Building, and the Downtown Station, 510 Guadalupe St. For information on other locations, call $\mathcal{C}$ **800/275-8777.**

Safety Austin has been ranked one of the top five safest cities in the United States, but that doesn't mean you can throw common sense to the wind. It's never a good idea to walk down dark streets alone at night, and major tourist areas always attract pickpockets; keep your purse or wallet in a safe place.

Taxes The tax on hotel rooms is 15%. Sales tax, added to restaurant bills as well as to other purchases, is 8.25%.

Transit Information Call $\mathcal{C}$ **800/474-1201** or 512/474-1200 from local pay phones (TTY 512/385-5872).

Weather Call $\mathcal{C}$ **512/451-2424.**

3 Where to Stay

The room shortage that long plagued Austin has finally abated: Motels have cropped up like mushrooms near Bergstrom International Airport, some excellent historic restorations have been completed in the downtown area, and several new hotels designed to serve the expanded convention center should all be open by 2004. Still, finding a room isn't always easy.

You can make some sense out of what might seem like random runs on hotel space by keeping in mind that lawmakers and lobbyists converge on the capital for 140-day sessions at the start of odd-numbered years. Also, the beginning of fall term, graduation week, and important home games of the Longhorns football team draw parents and sports fans into town en masse. And during the third week in March, record-label execs and aspiring artists attending the huge annual SxSW music conference take up all the town's rooms. It's always a good idea to book as far in advance as possible, but it's essential if you're planning to come in around these times.

Low rates and quick freeway access to both downtown and the northwest help fill the motels that line I-35 north of the old airport. But you'll get a far better feel for what makes Austin special if you stay in the verdant Town Lake area, which includes both the historic downtown area near the capitol and the newly resurgent South Congress area; closer than any others to the major sights, the hotels here are also on or near a 10-mile hike-and-bike trail. The leafy enclaves near the University of Texas, especially the Hyde Park neighborhood, are ideal for those willing to trade some chain motel or luxury motel perks for hominess and character. Convenient to various high-tech complexes and to the new airport are, respectively, the expanding accommodation clusters in the northwest and southern sections of town. It takes anywhere from 15 to 45 minutes to reach downtown's main attractions from the outlying areas.

Austin has some glitzy high-rises but only a few historic hotels and motels; if it's character you're after, you might opt for one of the town's many bed-and-breakfasts. For Austin inns that belong to **Historic Accommodations of Texas,** check the website at **www.hat.org** or call ℂ **800/HAT-0368.**

DOWNTOWN
VERY EXPENSIVE

The Driskill 🐾🐾 Talk about historic cachet. Lyndon Johnson holed up here during the final days of his presidential campaign; Ann Richards held her inaugural ball here when she became governor; and Texas lawmen met here to set an ambush for Bonnie and Clyde. Still, opening in 1886 has its down side: It's hard to stay gorgeous and up-to-date when you're over 100 years old. But a $35 million renovation, celebrated with the new millennium, restored the Driskill's former sheen—and then some. Although you're near all the prime tourist spots (the hotel is one of them), you've got plenty of reasons to hang around: the 1886 Café, with good breakfast selections; the Driskill Grill for dinner; a cushy piano bar; and a small but well equipped spa.

The guest rooms—100 of them in a 1929 addition, the rest in the original structure—feature beautiful reproductions of the original 19th-century furnishings, plus all the Austin modcons. Some of the king rooms are quite small, though, and dominated by the large bed so there's little room to move about (at least the sink and mirror are outside the tiny bathroom). It's a good idea to check the size before settling in.

604 Brazos St. (at E. 6th St.), Austin, TX 78701. ℂ **800/252-9367** or 512/474-5911. Fax 512/474-2214. www.driskillhotel.com. 188 units. $270–$290 double; suites from $450. AE, DC, DISC, MC, V. Valet parking $17. Pets 20 lb. and under accepted for $50 fee, per pet per stay. **Amenities:** 2 restaurants; bar; exercise room; spa; 24-hr. concierge; business center; 24-hr. room service; same-day dry cleaning/laundry service. *In room:* A/C, TV, dataport, hair dryer, safe.

Four Seasons Austin ★★★ *Kids*   If someone else was footing the bill, this is where I'd most want to stay in Austin. It's got a great location on Town Lake, near all the downtown attractions; large, comfortable rooms; an excellent restaurant; and the best health club and spa downtown. And the service is superb. Polished sandstone floors, a cowhide sofa, horn lamps, and an elk head hanging over the fireplace in the lobby remind you you're in Texas, but the guest rooms are European country manse elegant, with light florals and wood and live plants. The city views are fine, but the ones of the lake are prime.

98 San Jacinto Blvd. (at 1st/Cesar Chavez St.), Austin, TX 78701. ✆ **800/332-3442** or 512/478-4500. Fax 512/478-3117. www.fourseasons.com. 291 units. $250–$360 double; $395–$1,400 suite. Lower rates on weekends; bed-and-breakfast and romance packages available. AE, DC, MC, V. Self-parking $10; valet parking $15. Small pets accepted at no extra cost; advance notice to reservations required. **Amenities:** Restaurant; bar; heated outdoor pool; excellent health club and spa; bike rental; 24-hr. multilinguial concierge; car-rental desk; secretarial services; 24-hr. room service; same-day laundry service/dry cleaning (1 hr. pressing); physician on call. In room: A/C, TV w/pay movies, dataport, minibar, hair dryer, iron, safe, CD player.

Hyatt Regency Austin on Town Lake ★★   Austin's Hyatt Regency brings the outdoors in, with its signature atrium lobby anchored by a Hill Country–type tableau of a limestone-banked flowing stream, waterfalls, and oak trees. The genuine item outside is more striking still: Because the hotel sits on Town Lake's south shore, its watery vistas have stunning city backdrops.

Although the Hyatt is just minutes from downtown, outdoor recreation, such as Town Lake excursions and mountain biking on the nearby hike-and-bike trail, makes the hotel tick. All the rooms are decorated in vibrant Southwest tones and rich woods; the ones on the higher floors facing Town Lake are the most coveted.

208 Barton Springs Rd. (at S. Congress), Austin, TX 78704. ✆ **800/233-1234** or 512/477-1234. Fax 512/480-2069. www.hyatt.com. 447 units. $260–$300 double; $345–$650 suite. Weekend specials, corporate, and state-government rates available. AE, DC, DISC, MC, V. Self-parking $8; valet parking $12. **Amenities:** Restaurant; bar; heated outdoor pool; good exercise room; Jacuzzi; bike rental; business center; limited room service; same-day laundry/dry cleaning; complimentary laundry facilities; executive floors. In room: A/C, TV, hair dryer, iron.

EXPENSIVE

Embassy Suites Downtown Austin *Kids* *Value*   Embassy Suites are generally a good deal for those traveling on business or with families, and this link in the national chain also has a great location: It's convenient to the airport, the state capitol, and the row of restaurants on Barton Springs Road. And when you step outside the hotel's door, you're only a few minutes on foot from the Town Lake hike-and-bike trail. All the attractive, modern suites have two TVs, two 2-line phones, microwave, refrigerator, and a living room with a queen-size sleeper sofa, the better to bunk and feed the family and preserve the peace should there be telecommunication conflicts. The large breakfasts and afternoon snacks, both gratis, help cut costs.

300 S. Congress Ave. (at Barton Springs Rd.) Austin, TX 78704. ✆ **800/EMBASSY** or 512/469-9000. Fax 512/480-9164. www.embassysuites.com. 262 units. $159–$209 double. Rates include full breakfast and complimentary afternoon cocktails and snacks. Children 18 and under stay free in parent's room. AE, DC, DISC, MC, V. Free indoor parking garage; valet parking $10. **Amenities:** Restaurant; heated indoor pool; exercise room; Jacuzzi; sauna; game room; complimentary transfers to airport and downtown; limited room service; same-day dry cleaning; coin-op laundry; executive-level rooms. In room: A/C, TV w/pay movies, dataport, kitchen, fridge, coffeemaker, hair dryer, iron.

MODERATE

Hotel San José ★   This revamped 1930s motor court in trendy SoCo is the darling of hip travelers. It's got retro appeal, with its little porches and small

---

> (*Value* It Pays to Stay Awhile
>
> If you're planning to settle in for a spell, two downtown accommodations at prime locations will save you major bucks. You'll pay $409 a week to bunk at the **Extended Stay America Downtown,** 600 Guadalupe (© **800/ EXT-STAY** or 512/457-9994; www.extstay.com), located within easy walking distance of both the Warehouse District and the Lamar and 6th shops. Seven days at **Homestead Austin Downtown/Town Lake,** 507 S. 1st St. (© **888/782-9473** or 512/476-1818; www.homesteadhotel.com), near the Barton Springs restaurant row, the hike-and-bike trail, and the new Long Performing Arts Center, will run you $385 (less if you book online). Full kitchens and coin-op laundries at both bring your costs down even more.

---

pool, and the staff has the requisite semi-haughty attitude (except to the musicians and their handlers who bed down here). There are nods to local design—red Spanish tile roofs and Texas pine beds—but the dominant atmosphere is Zen, with Japanese-style outdoor landscaping and rooms so stripped down that they border on stark. Of course, being in the moment in Austin requires the high-tech basics like high-speed Internet access, plus such entertainment requisites as VCRs and CD players. Book a room in the back to avoid the Congress Avenue traffic noise.

1316 S. Congress Ave. (south of Nelly, about ½ mile south of Riverside), Austin, TX 78704. © **800/574-8897** or 512/444-7322. Fax 512/444-7362. www.sanjosehotel.com. 40 units. $75–$145 double (lower price with shared bathroom); $165–$200 suite. Corporate/entertainment discounts available. AE, DC, MC, V. Free parking. Dogs permitted for $10 per day with $100 deposit. **Amenities:** Bar; coffee shop; small heated outdoor pool; bike rental; same-day dry cleaning; limited room service. *In room:* A/C, TV/VCR, dataport, CD player.

La Quinta Inn–Capitol *(Finds*   Practically on the grounds of the state capitol, this is a great bargain for both business and leisure travelers. Rooms are more attractive than your typical motel—TVs are large and the rich-toned furnishings look far from cheesy—and perks such as free local phone calls and free continental breakfast keep those annoying extras off your bill. The sole drawback is that there's no restaurant on the premises, and there aren't that many places to eat in the area on weekends.

300 E. 11th St. (at San Jacinto), Austin, TX 78701. © **800/NU-ROOMS** or 512/476-1166. Fax 512/476-6044. www.laquinta.com. 145 units. $89–$119 double; $150 suite. Rates include continental breakfast. Children under 18 stay free in parent's room. AE, DC, DISC, MC, V. Valet parking $10. **Amenities:** Heated outdoor swimming pool; secretarial services; same-day laundry service/dry cleaning (Mon–Fri). *In room:* A/C, TV w/pay movies, dataport, coffeemaker, hair dryer, iron.

INEXPENSIVE

Austin Motel ★ *(Value*   It's not only nostalgia that draws repeat guests to this Austin institution, established in 1938 on what used to be the old San Antonio Highway. A convenient (but not quiet) location on nouveau chic South Congress Avenue and reasonable rates help, too. Other assets are a classic kidney-shaped pool, free HBO, and El Sol y La Luna, a good Latin restaurant that's popular with Town Lake athletes on weekend mornings. Ask to see the room—all are different and some are more recently renovated—before settling in.

1220 S. Congress St. (south of Nelly, about ½ miles south of Riverside), Austin, TX 78704. © and fax **512/ 441-1157.** www.austinmotel.com. 41 units. $70–$99 double; $140 suite. AE, DC, DISC, MC, V. Free parking. Limited number of rooms for pets; $10 fee. **Amenities:** Heated outdoor pool; coin-op laundry. *In room:* A/C, TV, fridge in some units, coffeemaker, hair dryer, iron, safe.

UNIVERSITY OF TEXAS
MODERATE

Austin Folk House ★★ Value   You get the best of both worlds at this appealing B&B in an 1880s house near the University of Texas: old time charm and new plumbing. The sunny rooms have newly painted walls and the wiring to accommodate mega-channel cable TVs, private phone lines, and radio/alarms with white noise machines, not typical of B&Bs. At the same time, nice antiques and such amenities as fancy bedding and towels make you feel like you're in a small luxury inn. The lavish breakfast buffet does nothing to dispel that sense, either. Come to think of it, maybe you'd better book a room before the young owner realizes what a bargain this place is and raises her rates to the level they warrant.

506 W. 22nd St., Austin, TX 78705. ℂ 866/472-6700 or 512/472-6700. 9 units. $85–$125 double. Rates include breakfast. AE, DISC, MC, V. Free off-street parking. Pets that don't have fleas, shed excessively, or bark when left alone permitted. *In room:* TV/VCR, dataport, hair dryer, iron.

INEXPENSIVE

Brook House ★ Value   This 1922 colonial revival–style on a quiet block just north of the University of Texas used to be a crash pad; chances are that Janis Joplin, who lived in the area in the 1960s, dropped in now and then. Although it's been a respectable bed-and-breakfast since 1985, the Brook House has still got good vibes. The main house contains three lovely but unfussy rooms, two with their own screened porches, and all with antique furnishings. A romantic private cottage has its own kitchen and sitting deck, as does the lower of the two bedrooms in the separate carriage house. Convenience, extensive in-room features, and generous breakfasts add up to excellent value for your money. (To locate this hotel, see the "Greater Austin" map.)

609 W. 33rd St., Austin, TX 78705. ℂ 800/871-8908 or 512/459-0534. www.austinbedandbreakfast.com. 6 units. $79–$119 double. Rates include breakfast. AE, DC, DISC, MC, V. Free parking. Pets on flea preventatives accepted (walking service offered). **Amenities:** Same-day dry cleaning. *In room:* A/C, TV/VCR, dataport, fridge in some units, coffeemaker, hair dryer, iron.

I-35 CORRIDOR
MODERATE

Habitat Suites ★★ Kids Finds   Don't be put off by the generic name and nondescript location on the outskirts of Highland Mall. This "ecotel" offers Kukicha twig tea, at least one vegan and macrobiotic entree at breakfast, and a swimming pool that uses ionized water; lush gardens (tended without chemical fertilizers, natch) and little front porches or decks, are among the many details that make this lodging far from cookie cutter. The rooms themselves don't have much character, but they're extremely large and offer full kitchens, as well as real fireplaces and—that rarity—windows that open. Suites for chemically sensitive people are available at no extra charge.

Value I-35 Corridor

The I-35 corridor north of downtown isn't especially scenic, but if you're willing to forgo a room with a view, there's a good chance you'll get an excellent deal in this area. It's less in demand than it was when Robert Mueller International Airport served the city and, since it draws mainly business travelers, you're likely to get great weekend rates.

500 E. Highland Mall Blvd., Austin, TX 78752. © 800/535-4663 or © and fax 512/467-6000. www.
habitatsuites.com. 97 units. $127 1-bedroom suite; $187 2-bedroom suite. Lower weekend rates and
extended-stay rates available. Rates include full breakfast and (Mon–Sat) afternoon wine and snacks. AE, DC,
DISC, MC, V. Free parking. Take Exit 2222 off I-35 to Airport Blvd., then take a right to Highland Mall Blvd.
Dogs and cats over 2 yr. accepted with $50 fee. **Amenities:** Heated outdoor pool; Jacuzzi; coin-operated laun-
dry; limited dry cleaning. *In room:* A/C, TV, dataport, kitchen, fridge, coffeemaker, hair dryer, iron.

NORTHWEST
EXPENSIVE
Renaissance Austin Hotel ★★ *Value*   Anchoring the upscale Arboretum
mall on Austin's northwest side, the tony Renaissance caters to executives visiting nearby computer firms. But on weekends, when rates are slashed, even
underlings can afford to take advantage of the hotel's many amenities, including
an excellent health club, a nightclub, and direct access to the myriad allures
of the mall (movie theaters among them). Silk wallpaper, lacquer chests, and
Japanese-design draperies and bedspreads, in muted tones, add an Asian flavor
to the oversize guest rooms, all with comfortable sitting areas.

9721 Arboretum Blvd. (off Loop 360, near Research Blvd.), Austin, TX 78759. © 800/HOTELS-1 or
512/343-2626. Fax 512/346-7945. www.renaissancehotels.com. 478 units. $199–$239 double; suites from
$249. Weekend packages available. AE, DC, DISC, MC, V. Free self-parking; valet parking $10. Pets under 20
lb. allowed. **Amenities:** 2 restaurants; deli; nightclub; indoor/outdoor heated pool; exercise room; Jacuzzi;
sauna; concierge; business center; secretarial services; 24-hr. room service; babysitting; same-day dry clean-
ing/laundry service; executive-level rooms. *In room:* A/C, TV w/pay movies, dataport, fridge in suites, coffeemaker, hair dryer, iron.

WEST/LAKES
VERY EXPENSIVE
Lake Austin Spa Resort ★★★   If you had to create the quintessential Austin
spa, it would be laid-back, located on a serene body of water, offer lots of outdoor activities, and feature super-healthy food that lives up to the locals' high
culinary standards. You'll sign off on every item of that wish list here. The property takes advantage of its proximity to the lovely Hill Country by offering such
activities as combination canoe/hiking trips or excursions to view the wildflowers. Guest rooms, many in cottages with private gardens, fireplaces, and hot
tubs, are casual elegant, with all natural fabrics and locally crafted furniture. The
only thing that's not quite up to snuff is the spa, which is fairly small. That
should be remedied by early 2004, when a large new facility is slated to open.

⟨Kids⟩ Family-Friendly Hotels

Four Seasons Austin (p. 285)   Tell the reservations clerk that you're
traveling with kids when you book a room here and you'll be automatically enrolled in the free amenities program: Age-appropriate
snacks—cookies and milk for children under 10, popcorn and soda for
those older than 10—along with various toys and games will be waiting for you when you arrive.

Embassy Suites Downtown Austin (p. 285) and **Habitat Suites** (p. 287)
That "suites" in the name of these properties says it all. These guest
quarters all offer spacious, *not* in-your-face quarters, plus the convenience (and economy) of kitchen facilities, so you don't have to eat out
all the time. Habitat Suites also has an ecologically correct playground.

1705 S. Quinlan Park Rd. (5 miles south of Hwy. 620), Austin, TX 78732. ℂ 800/847-5637 or 512/372-7300. Fax 512/266-1572. www.lakeaustin.com. 40 units. $390 per person for 1 night, standard double; $450 per person luxury double. Rates include all meals, classes, and activities. 3-, 4-, and 7-night packages, seasonal specials, and a variety of theme packages available. No children under 14 allowed. AE, DISC, MC, V. Free parking. Pets under 30 lb. accepted in Garden Cottage rooms with $250 fee. **Amenities:** Restaurant; snack bar; heated indoor and outdoor pool; 2 lit tennis courts; health club; spa; watersports equipment; bikes; limited room service; complimentary laundry service and laundry facilities. In room: A/C, TV/VCR, dataport, hair dryer.

SOUTH AUSTIN
EXPENSIVE

Hilton Austin Airport   Beam me up, Scotty. Austin's only full-service airport hotel, located in the former administrative center of Bergstrom Air Force base, has a distinctively space-y look. It's completely round and, although the underground tunnels and fallout shelters of the secure facility were capped off when Hilton took over, the building remains rock-solid and blissfully soundproof. But there's nothing remote about this place. Centered under a sky-lit dome, the lobby is light and airy, with lots of limestone, wood, and live plants. Large, comfortable rooms are equipped with all the amenities.

9515 New Airport Dr. (½ mile from the airport, 2 miles east of the intersection of Hwy. 183 and 71), Austin, TX 78719. ℂ 800/445-8667 or 512/385-6767. Fax 512/385-6763. www.hilton.com. 262 units. $189 double. Weekend discounts. AE, DC, DISC, MC, V. Self-parking $8; valet parking $12. **Amenities:** Restaurant; bar; heated outdoor pool; exercise room; business center; complimentary airport transfers; 24-hr. room service; same-day laundry service/dry cleaning; executive-level rooms. In room: A/C, TV w/pay movies, dataport, minibar, coffeemaker, hair dryer, iron.

4 Where to Dine

You would expect to eat well in a town where lawmakers schmooze with power brokers, high-tech firms try to lure outside talent, and academics can be tough culinary graders. Austin doesn't disappoint. Chic industrial spaces vie for diners' dollars with gracious 100-year-old houses and plant-filled hippie shacks.

The hottest areas to eat are downtown's West End/Warehouse district, near Fourth and Colorado streets, and South Congress Avenue, less than a mile away, but if you prefer a view of Town Lake to a view of black-clad young people, several more established restaurants in the same general vicinity—one conveniently near most tourist attractions—should appeal. Many popular downtown eateries have branches in the northwest, near the Arboretum mall. Fast-food joints tend to be concentrated to the north, off I-35. If you're looking for authentic Mexican eateries, East Austin is the place. Barton Springs Road, near Zilker Park; Lake Austin, near the Tom Miller Dam; and the tiny town of Bee Cave to the far west are also popular dining enclaves, but there's good food to be found in almost every part of town.

It's a good idea to eat at off-hours, either early or late, if the restaurant you're interested in doesn't take reservations (and an irritatingly large number of places don't). If you arrive at a popular place at prime time—around 7:30pm—you may find yourself waiting an hour or more for a table. Make reservations as far in advance as possible—dining out can be a competitive sport in Austin.

DOWNTOWN
VERY EXPENSIVE

Jeffrey's ★★ NEW AMERICAN   Although chef David Garrido creates some of the most dazzlingly innovative fare in town, the setting for his performance is low-key. People walk into this three-room former storefront in the artsy Clarksville neighborhood wearing anything from a T-shirt to a tux. You can't tell what'll turn up on the ever-changing menu, but you can depend on flavors and textures to dance wildly together without tripping. The crispy oysters topped with five-alarm honey garlic butter are deservedly famous, desserts such as Chocolate Intemperance live up to their diet-destroying promise, and the wine list is outstanding.

1204 W. Lynn. © 512/477-5584. Reservations strongly recommended. Main courses $25–$39. AE, DC, DISC, MC, V. Mon–Thurs 6–10pm; Fri–Sat 5:30–10:30pm; Sun 5:30–9:30pm.

EXPENSIVE

La Traviata ★★ ITALIAN   I love the Euro-chic atmosphere of this Italian bistro, the way the textured limestone walls of the 1890s building complements the hardwood floors, sleek bar, and sunny yellow walls. And everything I tried, from the simple seared salmon salad, the chicken Parmesan, and a wonderfully light tiramisu dessert, was delicious. The crispy polenta with gorgonzola sauce and the divers scallops with couscous and smoked bacon get raves too.

314 Congress Ave. © 512/479-8131. Reservations accepted (and recommended for dinner). Main courses $15–$25; pasta $9.50–$16. AE, MC, V. Mon–Thurs 11am–2pm and 5:30–9pm; Fri 11am–2pm and 5–10pm; Sat 5–10:30pm.

Shoreline Grill ★ SEAFOOD/NEW AMERICAN   Fish is the prime bait at this tony grill, which looks out over Town Lake and the Congress Avenue Bridge, but in late spring through early fall, when thousands of Mexican free-tailed bats emerge in unison from under the bridge at dusk, patio tables for viewing the phenomenon are at a premium. When they're not going batty, diners focus on such starters as semolina-crusted oysters and the cinnamon-glazed salmon entree. Nonaquatic dishes include Parmesan-crusted chicken with penne pasta and prime rib with goat cheese potatoes. A nice cocktail menu complements a wine list with a good by-the-glass selection.

98 San Jacinto Blvd. © 512/477-3300. Reservations recommended (patio is first-come, first-served). Main courses $16–$29. AE, DC, DISC, MC, V. Mon–Fri 11am–10pm; Sat 5–10pm; Sun 5–9pm.

Zoot ★★ NEW AMERICAN   Texas chauvinism and eco-consciousness come together at Zoot to produce a cuisine that's creative, fresh, and delicious. This cozy Enfield restaurant, set in a 1920s cottage, uses only organic vegetables, and designs its dishes around ingredients grown in the area. Appetizers such as the orange sesame marinated beef satay show an Asian influence, but the backbone of the seasonally changing menu is revisited American standards. Vegetarians will be thrilled to find something to eat besides pasta—perhaps cabbage stuffed

---

Tips Musical Brunches

For a religious experience on Sunday morning that doesn't require entering a church or temple, check out the gospel brunch at **Stubb's Bar-B-Q**, 801 Red River St. (© **512/480-8341**). The singing is heavenly and the pork ribs are divine. If you worship at the altar of the likes of Miles Davis, the Sunday jazz brunch at **Manuel's Downtown**, 310 Congress Ave. (© **512/ 472-7555**), lets you enjoy eggs with venison chorizo or corn gorditas with garlic and cilantro while listening to hot live jazz or Latin sounds. At **Threadgill's World Headquarters**, 301 W. Riverside (© **512/472-9304**), you can graze at a Southern-style buffet while enjoying inspirational sounds.

with quinoa, pine nuts, and raisins. The presentations are always gorgeous. (To locate this restaurant, see the "Greater Austin" map.)

509 Hearn. (C) **512/477-6535.** Reservations recommended, especially on weekends. Main courses $18–$36; 6-course tasting menu $50. AE, DC, DISC, MC, V. Daily 5:30–10pm.

MODERATE

Clay Pit ⭐ *Value* INDIAN   An elegant setting—a historic building with wood floors and exposed limestone walls, softly lit—and sumptuous recipes, including creative curries, raise this brainchild of a husband-and-wife team and a New Delhi–trained chef to gourmet status. For an entree, consider *khuroos-e-tursh,* baked chicken breast stuffed with nuts, mushrooms, and onions and smothered in a cashew-almond cream sauce. A bargain buffet and a series of wraps made with naan make this a great lunch stop for those touring the nearby capitol.

1601 Guadalupe St. (C) **512/322-5131.** Reservations recommended. Main courses $8.95–$16; $6.50 lunch buffet. AE, DC, DISC, MC, V. Mon–Fri 11am–2pm; Sun–Thurs 5–10pm; Fri–Sat 5–11pm.

INEXPENSIVE

Chuy's *Kids* MEXICAN   One of the row of low-priced, friendly restaurants that line Barton Springs Road just east of Zilker Park, Chuy's stands out for its determinedly wacky decor and its sauce-smothered Tex-Mex food. You're not likely to leave hungry after specials like Southwest enchiladas, piled high with smoked chicken. And this has been a local landmark since 2001, when Jenna Bush got busted here for underage drinking.

1728 Barton Springs Rd. (C) **512/474-4452.** Reservations not accepted. Main courses $6–$9. AE, DC, DISC, MC, V. Sun–Thurs 11am–10pm; Fri–Sat 11am–11pm.

Cipollina ⭐ *Finds* ITALIAN/DELI   It's worth the short drive from downtown to have lunch or a light dinner at this casual chic neighborhood favorite, a large, open room with a deli case that could as easily be in Italy as Clarksville. The thin-crust pizzas, creative grilled sandwiches, and salads are all delicious. Good coffee, a nice selection of wines by the glass, and excellent pastries round out the menu. Come on your own with a good book or a newspaper; this is the kind of place where you'll immediately feel comfortable.

1213 West Lynn. (C) **512/477-5211** Reservations not accepted. Pizzas $7–$13; sandwiches $4.75–$6.50; salads $3.25–$4.95. AE, DC, DISC, MC, V. Sun–Thurs 7am–9:30pm; Fri–Sat 7am–10pm.

Las Manitas ⭐ MEXICAN   Don't leave town without checking out this colorful family-owned Mexican diner, decked out with local artwork. A rack of alternative newspapers at the door sets the political tone, but businesspeople and slackers alike pile into this small place for breakfasts of *migas con queso* (eggs scrambled with corn tortillas, cheddar cheese, and ranchero sauce) or *chilaquiles verdes* (tortilla strips topped with green tomatillo sauce, Jack cheese, and onions). This being Austin, most of the rest of the food is cooked in canola or olive oil and vegetarian items are highlighted.

211 Congress Ave. (C) **512/472-9357.** Reservations not accepted. Breakfast $2.95–$5.95; lunch $2.95–$7.95. AE, DISC, MC, V. Mon–Fri 7am–4pm; Sat–Sun 7am–2:30pm.

Shady Grove ⭐ *Kids* AMERICAN   If your idea of comfort food involves chiles, don't pass up Shady Grove. The inside dining area, with its Texas kitsch roadhouse decor and cushy booths, is plenty comfortable, but most people head for the large, tree-shaded patio when the weather permits. After a day of fresh air at nearby Zilker Park, a hearty bowl of Freddie's Airstream chili might be just the thing. Large salads or the hippie sandwich (grilled eggplant, veggies, and cheese with pesto mayonnaise) will satisfy the less carnivorous.

1624 Barton Springs Rd. ℭ 512/474-9991. Reservations not accepted. Main courses $7.25–$11. AE, DC, DISC, MC, V. Sun–Thurs 11am–10pm; Fri–Sat 11am–11pm.

NEAR UNIVERSITY OF TEXAS & HYDE PARK
To locate these restaurants, see the "Greater Austin" map on p. 278.

EXPENSIVE
Fonda San Miguel ✪ REGIONAL MEXICAN   Like American Southwest chefs who look to Native American staples such as blue corn for inspiration, Mexico City chefs have had their own back-to-the-roots movement, which might involve including ancient Aztec ingredients in their dishes. Such trends are carefully tracked and artfully translated by Fonda San Miguel, the top fine dining venue for Mexican regional cuisine. Appetizers include Veracruz-style ceviche or quesadillas with *huitlacoche,* a corn fungus as rare as French truffles. *Conchinita pibil,* pork baked in banana leaves, is one of the Yucatán offerings. Familiar northern Mexican fare, extremely well prepared, is also an option.

2330 W. North Loop. ℭ 512/459-4121. Reservations recommended. Main courses $13–$20. AE, DC, DISC, MC, V. Mon–Thurs 5:30–9:30pm; Fri–Sat 5:30–10:30pm (bar opens 30 min. earlier); Sun brunch 11am–2pm.

MODERATE
Asti ✪ (Value ITALIAN   This is the Italian place everyone wants in their neighborhood: casual, consistently good, and reasonably priced. An open kitchen and retro Formica-topped tables create a hip, upbeat atmosphere. The designer pizzas make a nice light meal, and northern Italian specialties such as the Calabrese-style trout and the pan-seared halibut with green beans are winners. Skip the unexciting risottos, though, and save room for such desserts as the creamy espresso sorbet or the amazing chocolate mousse cannoli.

408C E. 43rd St. ℭ 512/451-1218. Reservations recommended on weekends. Main courses $15–$16; pizzas and pastas $8–$16. AE, DC, DISC, MC, V. Mon–Thurs 11am–10pm; Fri 11am–11pm; Sat 5–11pm.

(Kids Family-Friendly Restaurants

Chuy's (p. 291)   Teens and aspiring teens will enjoy this colorful, inexpensive restaurant, with its cool T-shirts, Elvis kitsch, and green iguanas crawling up the walls.

County Line on the Hill (p. 294) and **The Salt Lick (p. 293)**   The Salt Lick and County Line on the Hill are great for their homey mix-and-match menus, laid-back atmosphere, and good quantity-to-price ratios. The Salt Lick also offers a discounted under-12 plate.

Güero's (p. 293)   As family friendly as it is hip, this is a great place to introduce kids to really good Mexican food; you're sure to find something on the huge menu to please even picky eaters. Special plates are available for kids under 12.

Shady Grove (p. 291)   Not only are there plenty of things for the pickiest eaters to chow down on here, but this place is sufficiently laid back and lively that no one will notice if your offspring sounds off.

EAST SIDE
MODERATE

Eastside Cafe ✦ NEW AMERICAN   Located in a nondescript neighborhood near the university and the capitol that's turning trendy, this place is hugely popular with vegetarians and nonvegetarians alike. The main courses tend toward light meats and fish—sesame-breaded catfish, say, or Szechuan chicken. You can get half orders of all the pasta dishes, including an excellent artichoke manicotti, and of some salads, such as the mixed field greens topped with warm goat cheese. A large organic garden out back is the source of said greens and other produce.

2113 Manor Rd. ✆ **512/476-5858.** Reservations recommended. Main courses $12–$20; pastas $13–$17. AE, DC, DISC, MC, V. Mon–Thurs 11am–10pm; Fri 11am–11pm; Sat 10am–11pm; Sun 10am–10pm (brunch Sat–Sun 10am–3pm).

SOUTH AUSTIN
MODERATE

Güero's ✦ *Kids* *Value* TEX-MEX   Although it's the center of the newly hip South Austin scene, this sprawling converted feed store is fine for families, and the food is seriously good. Many plates come topped with cheese, guacamole, and sour cream, but you can enjoy health-conscious versions of Tex-Mex standards as well as of some dishes from the interior of Mexico, such as the delicious grilled chicken al carbon served with whole-wheat tortillas and nonrefried beans. There's live music on Sunday afternoon. (See the "Central Austin" map to locate this restaurant.)

1412 S. Congress. ✆ **512/447-7688.** Reservations not accepted. Main courses $7–$13. AE, DC, DISC, MC, V. Mon–Fri 11am–11pm; Sat–Sun 8am–11pm.

The Salt Lick ✦ *Kids* BARBECUE   It's 12 miles from the junction of 290 West and FM 1826 (turn right) to The Salt Lick, but you'll start smelling the smoke during the last 5 miles of your trip. Moist chicken, beef, and pork, as well as terrific homemade pickles—not to mention the pretty, verdant setting—more than justify the drive. In warm weather, seating is outside at picnic tables under oak trees; in winter, fireplaces blaze in a series of large, rustic rooms.

18300 FM 1826, Driftwood. ✆ **512/858-4959** or 888/SALT-LICK (mail order). Reservations for large parties only. Sandwiches $5.95–$7.95; plates $7–$14. No credit cards. Daily 11am–10pm.

NORTHWEST
EXPENSIVE

Z'Tejas Grill ✦ *Value* SOUTHWEST   An offshoot of a popular downtown eatery, 1110 W. Sixth St. (✆ 512/478-5355), which has also branched off into other states, this northwest location improves a bit on the original. Both share a terrifically zippy Southwest menu, but this dining room is a lot more open, with floor-to-ceiling windows and sophisticated decor. Gorgonzola ravioli in a sun-dried tomato pesto makes a great starter, and if you see it on a specials menu, go for the smoked chiles rellenos, made with apricots and goat cheese. Entrees include a tender rib-eye livened up by smoked jalapeño cream sauce. For dessert, order a peanut butter pie with chocolate graham cracker crust for the table.

9400-A Arboretum Blvd. ✆ **512/346-3506.** Reservations recommended. Main courses $8.95–$18. AE, DISC, MC, V. Mon–Thurs 11am–10pm; Fri 11am–11pm; Sat 10am–11pm; Sun 10am–10pm.

WEST/LAKES
VERY EXPENSIVE

Hudson's on the Bend ✦✦ NEW AMERICAN   If you're game for game served in a very civilized setting, come to Hudson's. The chipotle cream sauce was sufficiently spicy so that it was hard to tell whether or not Omar's rattlesnake cakes tasted like chicken. But they were very good, as were the black-bean ravioli and duck and liver paté appetizers. Pecan smoked prime rib; a mixed grill of venison, rabbit, quail, and pheasant sausage; and trout served with mango habañero butter are among the excellent entrees. *One caveat:* Its popularity and its charming but acoustically poor setting can make the indoor dining rooms noisy on the weekends. Opt for the terrace when the weather is nice enough.

3509 Hwy. 620 North. (C) 512/266-1369. Reservations recommended, essential on weekends. Main courses $28–$35. AE, DC, MC, V. Sun–Mon 6–9pm; Tues–Thurs 6–10pm; Fri–Sat 5:30–10pm (closing times may be earlier in winter; call ahead).

MODERATE

County Line on the Hill *Kids* BARBECUE   Some critics deride the County Line chain for its "suburban" barbecue, but Austinites have voted with their feet (or, rather, their cars). If you don't get here before 6pm, you can expect to wait as long as an hour and a half to eat. Should this happen, sit out on the deck and soak in the views of the Hill Country, or look at the old advertising signs on the knotty-pine planks of this 1920s roadhouse, formerly a speakeasy and a brothel. In addition to the oh-so-slowly-smoked ribs, brisket, chicken, or sausage, skewered meat and vegetable plates are available. County Line on the Lake, near Lake Austin, 5204 FM 2222 ((C) 512/346-3664), offers the same menu.

6500 W. Bee Cave Rd. (C) 512/327-1742. Reservations not accepted. Plates $9–$18. AE, DC, DISC, MC, V. Mon–Fri 11:30am–2pm and 5–9pm; Sat–Sun 11:30am–10pm; closes 30 min. earlier in winter.

The Oasis AMERICAN/MEXICAN   This is where Austinites take out-of-town guests at sunset: From the 40 multilevel decks nestled into the hillside hundreds of feet above Lake Travis, everyone cheers as the fiery orb descends behind the hills on the opposite bank. No one ever leaves unimpressed. But that's by nature, not by the food. Keep it simple—nachos, burgers, and the like—and you'll be okay. Then add a margarita, and kick back. It doesn't get much mellower than this.

6550 Comanche Trail, near Lake Travis. (C) 512/266-2441. Reservations not accepted. Main courses (but don't even think about it) $10–$25. AE, DISC, MC, V. Mon–Thurs 11:30am–10pm; Fri 11:30am–11pm; Sat 11am–11pm; Sun 11am–10pm (brunch 11am–2pm).

5 Seeing the Sights

Stroll up Congress Avenue and you'll see much the same sight as visitors to Austin did more than 100 years ago: a broad thoroughfare gently rising to the grandest of all state capitols. Obsessed from early on with its place in history, the city is not neglecting it now, either: The capitol underwent a complete overhaul in the 1990s and presents a better face than ever to the public; a grand new state history museum opened its doors near the capitol in 2001; and downtown's historic Sixth Street is continually turning back the clock with ongoing restorations. The town is on a cultural tear, too, as dual multimillion-dollar complexes are being built to house the city's two top art collections, and new galleries are opening all around town.

But it's Austin's myriad natural attractions that put the city on all the "most livable" lists. From bats and birds to Barton Springs, from the Highland Lakes to the hike-and-bike trails, Austin lays out the green carpet for its visitors. You'd be hard-pressed to find a city that has more to offer fresh-air enthusiasts.

Bargain alert: There's no charge for transportation on the city's five 'Dillo lines, which cover most of the downtown tourist sites and the University of Texas. Other freebies include the Convention & Visitors Bureau's excellent guided walks and the state-sponsored tours of the governor's mansion and the state capitol.

THE TOP ATTRACTIONS
DOWNTOWN

Barton Springs Pool ★★ *Kids*   If the University of Texas is the seat of Austin's intellect, and the state capitol is its political pulse, Barton Springs is the city's soul. The Native Americans who settled near here believed these waters had spiritual powers, and today's residents still place their faith in the abilities of the spring-fed pool to soothe as well as cool them. Each day approximately 32 million gallons of amazingly clear water from the underground Edwards Aquifer bubble to the surface here; it maintains a constant 68°F (20°C) temperature year-round. The pool is huge, and there's a wide variety of people here, though they're almost exclusively locals. Lifeguards are on duty for most of the day, and a large bathhouse operated by the parks and recreation department offers changing facilities.

Zilker Park, 2201 Barton Springs Rd. © 512/476-9044. www.ci.austin.tx.us/parks. Admission $2.50 Mon–Fri, $2.75 Sat–Sun adults; $1 ages 12–17; 50¢ children 11 and under. Daily 5am–10pm except during pool maintenance (Thurs 8am–7pm). Lifeguard on duty Apr–Sept 8am–10pm, Oct to early Nov 8am–8pm, mid-Nov to Mar 9am–6pm. Gift shop and Splash! Tues–Fri noon–6pm, Sat–Sun 10am–6pm. Bus: 30 (Barton Creek Sq.).

The Bob Bullock Texas State History Museum ★ *Kids*   You'll get a quick course in Texas 101 at this museum, located near the capitol and designed to echo some of its elements: Three floors of exhibits are arrayed around a huge rotunda centered by a 50-foot polished granite map of Texas. The permanent displays—everything from Stephen F. Austin's diary to Neil Armstrong's space suit—and rotating exhibits are interesting enough, but the real treat is the multimedia, special-effects Spirit Theater, the only one of its kind in Texas, where you can experience the high-speed whoosh of the great Galveston hurricane and feel your seats rattle as an East Texas oil well hits a gusher. Austin's only IMAX theater, with 3-D capabilities, is also pretty dazzling too, though the films don't necessarily have a direct relation to the Texas history theme. If you do everything (and at a bargain $6 for a combination ticket for ages 18 and under, you really should), plan to spend at least 2½ to 3 hours here.

1800 N. Congress Ave. © 512/936-8746. www.TheStoryofTexas.com. Exhibit areas $5 adults, $4.25 seniors 65 and over, free for ages 18 and under. IMAX theater $6.50 adults, $5.50 seniors, $4.50 youth. Texas Spirit

---

Fun Fact **Going Batty**

Austin has the largest urban bat population in North America—much to the delight of Austinites. Some visitors are a bit dubious at first, but it's impossible not to be impressed by the sight of 1.5 million of the creatures emerging en masse from under the Congress Avenue Bridge. **Bat Conservation International** (© 512/327-9721; www.batcon.org), based in Austin, has lots of information about bats, and you can call the *Austin American-Statesman* **Bat Hotline** (© 512/416-5700, category 3636) to find out when the bats are going to emerge from the bridge.

Theater $5 adult, $4 seniors, $3.50 youth. Combination tickets: Exhibits and IMAX $9/$7.50/$4.50; exhibits and Spirit Theater $8/$6.50/$3.50; exhibits and both theaters $13/$10/$6 (under 3 free to theaters if they sit in a parent's lap). Parking $3 with $5 minimum museum purchase, $8 otherwise (free IMAX parking after 6pm). Mon–Sat 9am–6pm; Sun noon–6pm. Phone or check website for additional IMAX evening hours. Closed New Year's Day, Easter Sun, Thanksgiving, Christmas Eve, and Christmas Day. Bus: Orange and Blue 'Dillo.

State Capitol ★★ The largest state capitol in the country, second only in size to the U.S. Capitol—but measuring 7 feet taller—this 1888 building covers 3 acres of ground. A $187.6 million revamp restored the capitol building and grounds to their former glory and added a striking new underground annex, which connects the capitol and four other state buildings by tunnels. The legislative sessions are open to the public; go up to the third-floor visitors' balcony if you want see how politics are conducted Texas-style. Include the Capitol Visitors Center (p. 297), and figure on spending 2 hours, minimum, here. *Tip:* Wear comfortable shoes; you'll be doing a lot of walking.

11th and Congress sts. © 512/463-0063. www.tspb.state.tx.us. Free admission. Mon–Fri 7am–10pm; Sat–Sun 9am–8pm; 24 hr. a day during legislative sessions (held in odd years, starting in Jan, for 140 straight days; 30-day special sessions are also sometimes called). Free guided tours Mon–Fri 8:30am–4:30pm, Sat–Sun 9:30am–4:30pm. Bus: Orange, Red, Gold, and Blue 'Dillos, or multiple bus lines.

UNIVERSITY OF TEXAS

LBJ Library & Museum ★ Set on a hilltop commanding an impressive campus view, the LBJ Library contains some 45 million documents relating to the colorful 36th president, along with gifts, memorabilia, and other historical objects. Johnson loved political cartoons, even when he was their target; examples from his large collection are among the museum's most interesting rotating exhibits. Adults and kids alike are riveted by the animatronic version of LBJ, an eerily lifelike gesticulating figure dressed in his clothes and speaking with a tape recording of his voice.

University of Texas, 2313 Red River. © 512/721-0200. www.lbjlib.utexas.edu. Free admission. Daily 9am–5pm. Closed Christmas. Bus: 15, Blue and Orange 'Dillos, or UT Shuttle.

SOUTH AUSTIN

Lady Bird Johnson Wildflower Center ★★★ Talk about fieldwork: The researchers at this lovely complex, founded by Lady Bird Johnson in 1982 for the study and preservation of native plants, have 178 acres of wildflowers for their personal laboratory. The main attractions are the display gardens and the wildflower-filled meadow, but the native stone architecture of the visitor center and observation tower is attention grabbing, too. Free lectures and guided walks are usually given on the weekends; phone or check the website for current programs. It'll take you at least half an hour to drive here from central Austin, so plan to eat lunch here and spend a leisurely half day.

4801 La Crosse Ave. © 512/292-4200. www.wildflower.org. Admission $5 adults, $4 students and seniors 60 and older, free for 4 and younger. Tues–Sun 9am–5:30pm (Mar–Apr rates go up to $7/$5 and grounds are open Mon). Take Loop 1 (Mo-Pac) south to Slaughter Lane; drive ¾ mile to La Crosse Ave.

MORE ATTRACTIONS
DOWNTOWN

Austin Museum of Art–Downtown Plans for a major downtown museum of art have been in the works for 2 decades. This high-ceiling one-story space isn't it (architect Richard Gluckman is designing the multimillion-dollar facility that's slated to open a few blocks away sometime in this decade), but it will do nicely for the time being. Major name shows—for example, the small paintings of Alex Katz in early 2003—are complemented by exhibits of lesser known local artists, of consistently high quality.

823 Congress Ave. (at 9th St.) ⓒ 512/495-9224. www.amoa.org. Admission $5 adults, $4 seniors and students, $1 for everyone on Thurs, free for children under 12. Tues–Wed and Fri–Sat 10am–6pm; Thurs 10am–8pm; Sun noon–5pm. Bus: Red, Gold, and Orange 'Dillos.

Capitol Visitors Center ⭐

The capitol wasn't the only important member of the state complex to undergo a face-lift: Texas also spent $4 million to gussy up its oldest surviving office building, the 1857 General Land Office. If the imposing German Romanesque structure looks a bit grand for the headquarters of an administrative agency, keep in mind that land has long been the state's most important resource. Among the employees of this important—and very political—office was the writer O. Henry, who worked as a draftsman from 1887 to 1891; he based two short stories on his experiences here.

112 E. 11th St. (southeast corner of Capitol grounds). ⓒ 512/305-8400. www.texascapitolvisitorscenter. com. Free admission. Daily 9am–5pm. Bus: Gold, Orange, Red, and Blue 'Dillos.

Governor's Mansion ⭐

Although it's one of the oldest buildings in the city (1856), this opulent house is far from a mere symbol or museum piece: State law requires that the governor live here whenever he or she is in Austin. That isn't exactly a hardship, although the mansion was originally built by Abner Cook without any indoor toilets (there are now seven). Among the many historical artifacts on display are a desk belonging to Stephen F. Austin and portraits of Davy Crockett and Sam Houston. Come as close to opening time as you can; only a limited number of people are allowed to tour the mansion during the few hours when it's open to the public.

1010 Colorado St. ⓒ 512/463-5516 (recording). www.txfgm.org. Free admission. Tours offered every 20 min. Mon–Thurs 10am–noon (last tour starts 11:40am). Closed Fridays, weekends, some holidays, and at the discretion of the governor; call the 24-hr. information line to see if tours are offered the day you want to visit. Bus: Red, Blue, Gold, and Orange 'Dillos.

O. Henry Museum

When William Sidney Porter, better known as O. Henry, lived in Austin (1884–98), he published a popular satirical newspaper called the *Rolling Stone*. He also held down an odd string of jobs, including a stint as a teller at the First National Bank of Austin, where he was later accused of embezzling funds. It was while he was serving time for this crime that he wrote the 13 short stories that established his literary reputation. The modest Victorian cottage in which O. Henry lived with his wife and daughter from 1893 to 1895 showcases the family's furniture, silverware, and china. The museum is very conveniently located for visitors, and it's interesting to see how a writer lived in the 19th century.

409 E. Fifth St. ⓒ 512/472-1903. www.ci.austin.tx.us/parks/ohenry.htm. Free admission. Wed–Sun noon–5pm. Closed Thanksgiving, Dec 25, and Jan 1. Bus: Blue 'Dillo.

UNIVERSITY OF TEXAS & HYDE PARK

Elisabet Ney Museum ⭐

Strong-willed and eccentric, German-born sculptor Elisabet Ney nevertheless charmed Austin society in the late 19th century. When she died, her admirers turned her Hyde Park studio into a museum. In the former loft and working area, visitors can view plaster replicas of many of her pieces. Drawn toward the larger-than-life figures of her age, Ney had created busts of Schopenhauer, Garibaldi, and Bismarck by the time she was commissioned to make models of Texas heroes Stephen F. Austin and Sam Houston for an 1893 Chicago Exposition. (To locate this museum, see the "Greater Austin" map.)

304 E. 44th St. ℂ **512/458-2255.** www.ci.austin.tx.us/elisabetney. Free admission. Wed–Sat 10am–5pm; Sun noon–5pm. Bus: 1 or 5.

Texas Memorial Museum 🄺ids   Until recently, history vied with science for visitors' attention at this museum, opened in 1936, but now the natural sciences will rule alone. Throughout 2003, only two of the museum's four floors will remain open. Exhibits on the second floor will highlight never-before displayed specimens from the permanent collection, such as rare fossils of saber tooth tiger kittens. The third floor will continue to be devoted to Texas wildlife, past and present, including bugs and reptiles. The Hall of Geology, complete with dinosaur displays and an on-site paleontologist, won't open until 2004, but kids can still check out the dinosaur footsteps right outside the building.

University of Texas, 2400 Trinity St. ℂ **512/471-1604.** www.texasmemorialmuseum.org. Free admission (donations appreciated). Mon–Fri 9am–5pm; Sat 10am–5pm; Sun 1–5pm. Closed major holidays. Bus: Orange 'Dillo or Bus 7.

EAST SIDE

French Legation Museum   The oldest residence still standing in Austin was built in 1841 for Count Alphonse Dubois de Saligny, France's representative to the fledgling Republic of Texas. In the back of the house, considered the best example of French colonial–style architecture outside Louisiana, is a re-creation of the only known authentic Creole kitchen in the United States. A great stop if you like historic museums.

802 San Marcos. ℂ **512/472-8180.** www.frenchlegationmuseum.org. Admission $4 adults, $3 seniors, $2 students and teachers, free for 5 and under. Tours Tues–Sun 1–5pm. Go east on Seventh St., then turn left on San Marcos St.; the parking lot is behind the museum on Embassy and Ninth sts. Bus: Silver 'Dillo and Bus 4/18 stop nearby (at San Marcos and 7th sts.).

Texas State Cemetery ⭐   The city's namesake, Stephen F. Austin, is the best-known resident of this East Side cemetery, established by the state in 1851. Judge Edwin Waller, who laid out the grid plan for Austin's streets and later served as the city's mayor, also rests here, as do eight former Texas governors, and Barbara Jordan, the first black woman from the South elected to the U.S. Congress (in 1996, she became the first African American to gain admittance to these grounds). A multimillion-dollar revamp in the mid-1990s added much-needed pedestrian walkways and a visitor center, designed to suggest the long barracks at the Alamo.

909 Navasota St. ℂ **512/463-0605.** www.cemetery.state.tx.us. Free admission. Grounds daily 8am–5pm; visitors center Mon–Fri 8am–5pm. Bus: 4 and 18 stop nearby.

GREEN SPACES & LAKES

Highland Lakes   The six dams built by the Lower Colorado River Authority from the late 1930s to the early 1950s not only controlled the flooding that had plagued the areas surrounding Texas's Colorado River (not to be confused with the more famous river of the same name to the north), but also transformed the waterway into a sparkling chain of lakes, stretching some 150 miles northwest of Austin. The narrowest of them (and my personal favorite), **Town Lake,** is also the closest to downtown. The heart of urban recreation in Austin, it boasts a shoreline park and adjacent hike-and-bike trail. **Lake Austin,** the next in line, is more residential, but offers Emma Long Park as a public shore. Watersports enthusiasts go all the way to **Lake Travis,** the longest lake in the chain, which offers the most possibilities for boating, fishing, and swimming. Together with the other Highland Lakes—**Marble Falls, LBJ, Inks,** and **Buchanan**—these comprise the largest concentration of freshwater lakes in Texas. See also "Outdoor Activities," below, for activity and equipment rental suggestions.

Zilker Park   Comprising 347 acres, the first 40 of which were donated to the city by the wealthy German immigrant for whom the park is named, this is Austin's favorite public playground. Its centerpiece is **Barton Springs Pool** (p. 295), but visitors and locals also flock to the **Zilker Botanical Garden,** 2220 Barton Springs Rd. (© **512/477-8672;** www.zilkergarden.org), a peaceful Asian-style garden that's especially gorgeous from March to October, when something's always in bloom (free; garden center open Mon–Fri 8:30am–4pm, Sat 10am–5pm, Sun 1–5pm); and the **Umlauf Sculpture Garden & Museum,** 605 Robert E. Lee Rd. (© **512/445-5582;** www.umlaufsculpture.org), the former home and studio of University of Texas art instructor Charles Umlauf; most of the 250 sculptures are displayed in a lovely native garden ($3.50 adults, $2.50 seniors, $1 students, free for children 6 and under; open Wed–Fri 10am–4:30pm; Sat–Sun 1–4:30pm). See "Especially for Kids," below, and the "Outdoor Activities" section for details about the **Austin Nature and Science Center,** the **Zilker Zephyr Miniature Train,** and Town Lake canoe rentals. In addition to its athletic fields (eight for soccer, two for softball, and one for rugby), the park also hosts a 9-hole disk (Frisbee) golf course.

2201 Barton Springs Rd. © 512/476-9044. www.ci.austin.tx.us/zilker. Free admission. Daily 5am–10pm. Bus: 30.

ESPECIALLY FOR KIDS

The **Bob Bullock Texas State History Museum** and the **Texas Memorial Museum,** both described in earlier sections, are child-friendly, but outdoor attractions are still Austin's biggest kiddie draw. There's lots of room for children to splash around at **Barton Springs,** and even youngsters who thought **bats** were creepy are likely to be converted on further acquaintance with the critters.

In addition, kids enjoy the **Austin Children's Museum** ✮✮, Dell Discovery Center, 201 Colorado St. (© **512/472-2499;** www.austinkids.org), a rambling state-of-the-art facility that's got everything from low-key but creative playscapes for tots to studio sound stage replicas for teens. Bats, bees, and crystal caverns are among the subjects of the Discovery Boxes at the 80-acre **Austin Nature and Science Center** ✮, Zilker Park, 301 Nature Center Dr. (© **512/327-8181;** www.ci.austin.tx.us/nature-science), which also abounds with interactive exhibits involving rescued animals. The Dino Pit, slated to open early 2003, is sure to lure budding paleontologists. Visitors to the **Jourdan Bachman Pioneer Farm** ✮, 11418 Sprinkle Cut Off Rd. (© **512/837-1215;** www.pioneerfarm. org), enter into the worlds of three typical late-19th-century Texas families: wealthy cotton farmers, homesteaders from Appalachia, and freed slaves turned tenant farmers. The costumed interpreters clearly relish playing their historic roles, and their enthusiasm is contagious. You'll feel as though you're entering one of the sinkholes in Austin's vast underground ecosystem when you visit the dimly lit **Splash! Into the Edwards Aquifer Exhibit,** Zilker Park, 2201 Barton Springs Rd. (© **512/481-1466;** www.ci.austin.tx.us/splash), formerly the bathhouse at Barton Springs pool. Here kids can make it rain on the city, identify water bugs, or peer through a periscope at swimmers. The scenic 25-minute ride on the narrow-gauge **Zilker Zephyr Miniature Train,** 2100 Barton Springs Rd. (just across from the Barton Springs Pool; © **512/478-8286)** goes at a leisurely pace through Zilker Park along Barton Creek and Town Lake. All except Splash! and the Austin Nature and Science Center charge admission.

ORGANIZED TOURS

The aquatically inclined might consider taking one of the electric powered **Capital Cruises** (© 512/480-9264; www.capitalcruises.com), which ply Town Lake March through October. Options include bat-viewing cruises, fajita dinner cruises, and afternoon sightseeing excursions. Similar itineraries are offered by **Lone Star River Boat** (© 512/327-1388; www.lonestar.austin.citysearch.com), but they go farther upstream and add narration. Both companies depart from the dock near the Hyatt Regency Hotel. Can't decide between sea and land? Board one of the six-wheel-drive amphibious vehicles operated by **Austin Duck Adventures** (© 512/4-SPLASH; www.austinducks.com). After exploring Austin's historic downtown and scenic west side, you'll splash into Lake Travis. A comedic script and duck whistles distributed to everyone add to the fun. Tours board in front of the Austin Convention & Visitors Bureau, 201 E. 2nd St.

See "Austin After Dark," later in this chapter, for details on touring the Austin City Limits studio.

WALKING TOURS

Whatever price you pay, you won't find better guided walks than the informative and entertaining ones offered free of charge by the **Austin Convention & Visitors Bureau (ACVB),** 201 E. Second St. (© 800/926-2282 or 512/454-1545), March through November. Ninety-minute tours of the historic Bremond Block leave every Saturday and Sunday at 11am; Congress Avenue/East Sixth Street is explored for 1½ hours on Thursday, Friday, and Saturday starting at 9am, Sunday at 2pm. The hour-long Capitol Complex tour is conducted on Saturday at 2pm and Sunday at 9am. All tours depart promptly from the south entrance of the capitol, weather permitting; come even a few minutes late, and you'll miss out. The ACVB also publishes five excellent self-guided tour booklets, including one on Hyde Park and another on the state cemetery.

6 Outdoor Activities

OUTDOOR FUN

BICYCLING A city that has a "bicycle coordinator" on its payroll, Austin is a cyclist's dream. Contact **Austin Parks and Recreation,** 200 S. Lamar Blvd. (© 512/499-6700; www.ci.austin.tx.us/parks), for information on the city's more than 25 miles of scenic paths, the most popular and crowded of which are the Barton Creek Greenbelt (8 miles) and the Town Lake Greenbelt (10 miles). The **Veloway,** a 3-mile paved loop in Slaughter Creek Metropolitan Park, is devoted exclusively to bicyclists and in-line skaters. You can rent bikes and get maps and other information from **University Cyclery,** 2901 N. Lamar Blvd. (© 512/474-6696; www.ucycleaustin.com); a number of downtown hotels also rent or provide free bicycles to their guests. For information on weekly road rides, contact the **Austin Cycling Association,** P.O. Box 5993, Austin, TX 78763 (© 512/282-7413; www.austincycling.org), which also publishes a monthly newsletter, *Southwest Cycling News;* only local calls or e-mails are returned. For rougher mountain-bike routes, try the **Austin Ridge Riders;** their website, **www.austinridgeriders.com**, will have the latest contact information.

BIRD-WATCHING Endangered golden-cheeked warblers and black-capped vireos are among the many species you might spot around Austin. The **Travis Audubon Society** (✆ **512/926-8751;** www.travisaudubon.org) organizes regular birding trips and even has a rare-bird hot line. Texas Parks and Wildlife publishes *The Guide to Austin-Area Birding Sites,* which points you to the best urban perches; you should be able to pickup a copy at the Austin Convention & Visitors Bureau or at the offices of any of Austin's parks and preserves (see "Seeing the Sights: More Attractions," above).

CANOEING You can rent canoes at **Zilker Park,** 2000 Barton Springs Rd. (✆ **512/478-3852**), for $8.50 an hour, $29 all day (Sat, Sun, and holidays only Oct–Mar). **Capital Cruises,** Hyatt Regency boat dock (✆ **512/480-9264;** www.capitalcruises.com), also offers hourly rentals on Town Lake. If your paddling skills are a bit rusty, check out the instructional courses of UT's **Recreational Sports Outdoor Program** (✆ **512/471-3116**).

FISHING Go on the fly with downtown's **Austin Angler,** 312½ Congress Ave. (✆ **512/472-4553;** www.austinangler.com), an excellent place to pickup a license, tackle, and information on where to find the big ones. **Git Bit** (✆ **512/ 280-2861;** www.gitbitfishing.com) provides guide service for half- or full-day bass-fishing trips on Lake Travis.

GOLF For information about Austin's **six municipal golf courses,** call ✆ **512/480-3020;** all of the courses offer pro shops and equipment rental, and their greens fees are very reasonable. Among them are the 9-hole **Hancock,** which was built in 1899 and is the oldest course in Texas; and the 18-hole **Lions,** where Tom Kite and Ben Crenshaw played college golf for the University of Texas.

SWIMMING The best known of Austin's natural swimming holes is **Barton Springs Pool** (p. 295), but it's by no means the only one. Other scenic outdoor spots to take the plunge include **Deep Eddy Pool,** 401 Deep Eddy Ave. at Lake Austin Boulevard (✆ **512/472-8546**), and **Hamilton Pool Preserve,** 27 miles west of Austin, off Tex. 71 on R.M. 3238 (✆ **512/264-2740**). For lakeshore swimming, consider **Hippie Hollow** on Lake Travis, 2½ miles off R.M. 620 (✆ **512/473-9437**), where you can let it all hang out in a series of clothing-optional coves; or **Emma Long Metropolitan Park** on Lake Austin, 1706 City Park Rd. (✆ **512/346-1831** or 512/346-3807), which has a protected swimming area, guarded by lifeguards on summer weekends.

SPECTATOR SPORTS

There are no professional teams in Austin, but a recently established minor league baseball team has captured local attention. In addition, college sports are very big, particularly when the University of Texas Longhorns football team is playing. The most comprehensive source of information on the various teams is **www.TexasSports.com**, but you can phone the **UT Athletics Ticket Office** (✆ **512/471-3333**) to find out about schedules, and **UTTM Charge-A-Ticket** (✆ **512/477-6060**) to order tickets.

BASEBALL The **Longhorn** baseball team goes to bat February through May at Disch-Falk Field (just east of I-35, at the corner of Martin Luther King Jr. Blvd. and Comal). See Nolan Ryan's **Round Rock Express** Baseball Clubat the **Dell Diamond,** 3400 E. Palm Valley Rd. in Round Rock (✆ **512/255-BALL** for information, or 512/244-4209 for tickets; www.roundrockexpress.com), a

7,800-seat stadium where you can choose from box seats, stadium seating, or even a grassy berm in the outfield.

BASKETBALL The **Lady Longhorn** basketball and **Longhorn** basketball teams, both Southwest Conference champions, play in the **Frank C. Erwin Jr. Special Events Center** (just west of I-35 on Red River between Martin Luther King Jr. Blvd. and 15th St.) November through March.

FOOTBALL It's hard to tell which is more central to the success of an Austin Thanksgiving: the turkey or the UT–Texas A&M game. Part of the Big 12 Conference, the **Longhorn** football team often fills the huge **Darrell K. Royal/Texas Memorial Stadium** (just west of I-35 between 23rd and 21st sts., E. Campus Dr. and San Jacinto Blvd.) during home games, played August through November.

SOCCER August through December you can find the **women's UT Soccer Team** working to defend their stellar record. In 2002 they garnered all the Big 12 soccer honors, including Player of the Year, Julie Gailey. Home games are played either Fridays or Sundays at the Mike A. Myers Stadium and Soccer Field, just northeast of the UT football stadium at Robert Dedman Drive and Mike Myers Drive.

7 Shopping

When it comes to items intellectual, musical, or ingestible, Austin is a match for cities twice its size. Shopping here may not quite have evolved into an art as it has in glitzier Texas towns like Houston or Dallas, but Austin has a more than satisfying range of ways to spend your money, plus several unique retail niches.

Specialty shops in Austin tend to open around 9 or 10am, Monday through Saturday, and close at about 5:30 or 6pm; many have Sunday hours from noon until 6pm. Malls tend to keep the same Sunday schedule, but Monday through Saturday they don't close their doors until 9pm. Sales tax in Austin is 8.25%.

GREAT SHOPPING AREAS

Downtown, specialty shops, and art galleries are filtering back to the renovated 19th-century buildings along **Sixth Street** and **Congress Avenue.** Below Town Lake, **South Congress Avenue,** from Riverside south to Annie Street, is especially trendy, with art galleries and boutiques joining its rows of second-hand clothing stores. It's my preferred shopping area because it's closest to downtown and the most representative of the "real" Austin. Other rich shopping enclaves to mine include the **West End** on Sixth Street west of Lamar and, nearby, north of 12th Street and West Lynn. In the vicinity of Central Market, between West 35th and 40th Streets and Lamar and Mo-Pac, such small shopping centers as Jefferson Square are similarly charming. Many stores on **the Drag**—the stretch of Guadalupe Street between Martin Luther King Jr. Boulevard and 26th Street, across from the University of Texas campus—are student oriented, but a wide range of clothing, gifts, toys, and, of course, books can also be found here.

Still, much of Austin's shopping has moved out to the malls. The newest growth area is in the northwest, where three upscale shopping centers, **The Arboretum, The Arboretum Market,** and the **Gateway Complex** (consisting of the Gateway Courtyard, the Gateway Market, and Gateway Square), have earned the area the nickname "South Dallas." Bargain hunters go farther afield to the huge collections of factory outlet stores in San Marcos; see "Hill Country Side Trips from Austin" later in this chapter for details.

THE GOODS A TO Z
ART

It's not exactly SoHo, but the area just northwest of the capitol and south of the University of Texas—specifically, the block bounded by Guadalupe and Lavaca to the west and east and 17th and 18th streets to the south and north—has a large concentration of galleries. They include the group clustered in the **Guadalupe Arts Building,** 1705 Guadalupe, as well as Women & Their Work (see below).

Austin's commitment to music makes it a perfect location for **Wild About Music,** 721 Congress Ave. (© **512/708-1700;** www.wildaboutmusic.com), a gallery and shop strictly devoted to arts and crafts with a musical theme. Come see the multimedia prints by Texas musician Joe Ely, the instrument-shaped furniture, and the unique Texas music T-shirt collection. Winning the nod for "Best Gallery" from the *Austin Chronicle* every year from 2000 to 2002, **Women & Their Work,** 1710 Lavaca St. (© **512/477-1064;** www.womenandtheir work.org), highlights more than visual art—it also promotes and showcases women in dance, music, theater, film, and literature. "Outsider" art, created in the deep, rural South, usually by the poor and sometimes by the incarcerated, is not for everyone, but for those interested in contemporary American folk art, **Yard Dog Folk Art,** 1510 South Congress Ave. (© **512/912-1613;** www.yard dog.com), is not to be missed.

For additional information about other galleries and art events in Austin, call City Art Link at © **512/452-7773** or log on to **www.cityartlink.com.**

ECO-WARES

It's hard to typecast a shop that sells everything from greeting cards, natural insect repellent, and handwoven purses to building materials and home decorating supplies, but the common denominater at **Eco-wise,** 110 W. Elizabeth (© **512/326-4474;** www.ecowise.com) is that everything you'll find here is recycled or made from natural fabrics, and chemical free. The store offers baby and wedding shower registries for earth-friendly brides and grooms or moms and dads.

MUSIC

Carrying a huge selection of sounds, **Waterloo Records and Video,** 600A N. Lamar Blvd. (© 512/474-2500; www.waterloorecords.com), is always the first in town to get the new releases.

RUNNING GEAR

Owned by the footwear editor for *Runner's World* magazine and serving as the official wear-test center for that publication, **Run-Tex,** 422 W. Riverside Dr. (© **512/472-3254;** www.runtex.com), not only has a huge inventory of shoes and other running gear, but also does everything it can to promote healthful jogging practices, even offering free running classes and a free injury-evaluation clinic. There's also a larger Run-Tex in Gateway Market, 9901 Capital of Texas Hwy. (© 512/343-1164), a location at 2201 Lake Austin Blvd. (© 512/477-9464), and the related **WalkTex,** 4001 N. Lamar (© 512/454-WALK), but the downtown store is right near the Austin runner's mecca, Town Lake.

TEXAS SOUVENIRS

Over the years, visitors have admired—sometimes excessively—the intricately designed door hinges of the capitol. The gift shop at the **Capitol Visitors Center,** 112 E. 11th St. (© **512/305-8400;** www.texascapitolvisitorscenter.com), sells brass bookends made from the original model used, during the capitol's renovation, to cast replacements for hinges that were cadged over the years. Other Texana includes paperweights made from reproductions of the capitol's Texas seal doorknobs, local food products, and historical books. See also **Wild About Music,** listed under "Art" above.

WESTERN WEAR

Name notwithstanding, **Allen's Boots,** 522 S. Congress (© **512/447-1413**) sells a lot more than footwear. Come here too for hats, belts, jewelry, and other boot scootin' accoutrements (bring the young 'uns too). The custom-made boots of the **Capitol Saddlery,** 1614 Lavaca St. (© **512/478-9309**), were immortalized in a song by Jerry Jeff Walker. This three-level store, in the same family for 7 decades, is a bit chaotic, but you can't beat it for authentic cowboy gear. The huge Austin branch of **Sheplers,** 6001 Middle Fiskville Rd. (© **800/ 835-4004** for mail order, or 512/454-3000; www.sheplers.com), a growing chain of Western-wear department stores, has everything the well-dressed urban cowpoke might require.

8 Austin After Dark

It's hard to imagine an itch for entertainment, high or low, that Austin couldn't scratch. The city's live music scene rivals those of Seattle and Nashville, and the performing arts run the gamut from classic lyric opera to high-tech modern dance. Ironically, the source of much of the city's high culture is literally crude: When an oil well on land belonging to the University of Texas system blew in a gusher in 1923, money for the arts was assured.

The best sources for what's on around town are the *Austin Chronicle* and *XLent,* the entertainment supplement of the *Austin-American Statesman;* both are free and available in hundreds of outlets every Thursday. For a quick take on the local club action, call the **KLBJ** hot line at © **512/832-4094.** The **Austin Circle of Theaters Hotline** (© **512/416-5700, ext 1603;** www.acotonline.org) can tell you what's on the boards each week. If you want to know who's kicking around, phone **Danceline** (© **512/416-5700, ext. 3262**).

The **Ticketmaster** (www.ticketmaster.com) telephone number for the University of Texas, the locus for many of the city's performing-arts events, is © **512/477-6060;** for other major venues, phone © **512/494-1800.** Concerts at La Zona Rosa, the Backyard, and Austin Music Hall, and shows at the Paramount Theatre can be booked through **Star Tickets** (© **888/597-STAR** or 512/469-SHOW; www.startickets.com), with outlets in most Albertson's grocery stores.

The **Austix Box Office,** 3423 Guadalupe (© **512/454-8497** or 512/416-5700, ext.1603; www.austix.com), handles phone charges for many of the smaller theaters in Austin as well as half-price ticket sales (© **512/416-5700, ext. 1602**). Call for a recorded listing of what's currently being discounted, then pickup tickets at the Austix Box Office or at the **Austin Visitors Center,** 201 E. Second St., Wednesday through Saturday from noon to 6pm. Half-price tickets are also on sale at **Bookpeople,** 603 N. Lamar Blvd. (© **512/472-5050**), Thursday from 4 to 7pm.

THE PERFORMING ARTS
CLASSICAL MUSIC

A resident in Austin since 1911, the **Austin Symphony,** 1101 Red River St. © **888/4-MAESTRO** or 512/476-6064; www.austinsymphony.org), performs most of its classical works at Bass Concert Hall, though a new hall, which will also host Ballet Austin and the Austin Lyric Opera, is under construction. The informal pops shows play to a picnic table–seated crowd at the Palmer Auditorium, and a Casual Classics and Family series round out a very full, very creative musical program. The city's first professional opera company, **Austin Lyric Opera,** 901 Barton Springs Rd. (© **800/31-OPERA** or 512/472-5992 for box office; www.austinlyricopera.org), presents three or four productions annually. **The Austin Chamber Music Center,** 4930 Burnet Rd., Suite 203 (© **512/454-7562** or 512/454-0026; www.austinchambermusic.org), features an Intimate Concert series, open to the public but held at elegant private homes, and hosts visiting national and international artists.

THEATER

You never know what you'll see at the intimate **Hyde Park Theatre,** 511 W. 43rd St. (© **512/479-PLAY** for box office or 512/479-7530; www.hydepark theatre.org), but you can count on it to be intellectually engaging and focused on Austin writers, actors, and designers. The annual 5-week-long FronteraFest, the largest fringe theater/performance art festival in the Southwest, showcases local and national talent of all kinds. The **State Theater Company,** 719 Congress Ave. (© **512/472-5143** for box office or 512/472-7134; www.austin theatrealliance.org), which performs at the beautiful old theater for which it is named, is Austin's most professional troupe; their recent repertoire ran the gamut from *The Little Prince: The Musical,* to *Proof.* The Vortex theater, a converted warehouse with an outdoor courtyard and cafe, complements the avant-garde program of the **Vortex Repertory Company,** 2307 Manor Rd. (© **512/478-LAVA;** www.jollylox.com/vortex), just east of UT and I-35. You can tell by the titles alone—*Ratgirl's Holy Rockin' Christmas,* say, or *Conversations at a Bathhouse Can Be Tricky*—that you're way, way off-Broadway. Austin's oldest theater, incorporated in 1933, the **Zachary Scott Theatre Center** (© **512/476-0541** for box office or 512/476-0594; www.zachscott.com), makes use of two adjacent venues at the edge of Zilker Park: the three-sided thrust John E. Whisenhut Arena at 1510 Toomey Rd., and the theater-in-the-round Kleburg at 1421 W. Riverside Dr. Its rich and varied offerings include a Mainstage series and an Off-Broadway series, supplemented by holiday productions.

DANCE

The two-dozen professional dancers of **Ballet Austin,** 3004 Guadalupe St. (© **512/476-2163** for box office or 512/476-9051; www.balletaustin.org), leap and bound in such classics as *The Nutcracker* and *Giselle,* or more modern pieces like *Touch,* a non-narrative, multimedia work choreographed by the company's acclaimed long-time director Stephen Mills. An aptly high-tech ensemble for plugged-in Austin, **Sharir + Bustamante Dance Works,** 3724 Jefferson St., Suite 201 (© **512/458-8158** or 512/477-6060 for box office), stretches the boundaries of dance toward virtual reality by including video projections and computer-generated images in its choreography.

THE CLUB & MUSIC SCENE

The appearance of country-and-western "outlaw" Willie Nelson at the Armadillo World Headquarters in 1972 united hippies and rednecks in a common musical cause, and is often credited with the birth of the live-music scene on Austin's Sixth Street. The city has since become an incubator for a wonderfully vital, crossbred alternative sound that mixes rock, country, folk, and blues.

Although the Armadillo is defunct and Sixth Street is past its creative prime, live music in Austin is very much alive, just more geographically diffuse.

If you're here during the huge **S×SW Music, Film and Interactive Conference,** held during UT's spring break (usually the third week of Mar), you'll see the town turn into one huge, music-mad party. For current schedules and speakers/performers, check the website at **www.sxsw.com** or contact S×SW Headquarters at P.O. Box 4999, Austin, TX 78765 (© **512/467-7979**).

Note: Categories of clubs in a city known for crossover are often very rough approximations; those that completely defy typecasting are dubbed "eclectic." Cover charges range from $5 to $15 for well-liked local bands.

FOLK & COUNTRY

The Broken Spoke, 3201 S. Lamar Blvd. (© **512/442-6189;** www.lone-star. net/bspoke), is the genuine item, a Western honky-tonk dating from 1964 with a wood-plank floor and a cowboy-hatted, two-steppin' crowd. Still, it's in Austin, so don't be surprised if the band wears Hawaiian shirts, or if tongues are firmly in cheek for some of the songs. Although it also showcases rock, rockabilly, and new wave sounds, the **Continental Club,** 1315 S. Congress Ave. (© **512/441-2444;** www.continentalclub.com), holds on to its roots in traditional country, celebrating events such as Hank Williams's birthday. A small, smoky club with high stools and a pool table in the back room, this is a not-to-be-missed Austin classic.

JAZZ & BLUES

Although Willie Nelson and crossover country-and-western bands like the Austin Lounge Lizards have been known to turn up at **Antone's,** 213 W. Fifth St. (© **512/474-5314;** www.antones.net), the club has always been synonymous with the blues. Stevie Ray Vaughan used to be a regular and when major blues artists like Buddy Guy or Etta James venture down this way you can be sure they'll either be playing Antone's or stopping by for a surprise set. Stars on location in Austin mingle with T-shirted students and well-dressed older aficionados at the **Elephant Room,** 315 Congress Ave. (© **512/473-2279;** www.arthiveonline.com/elephant), an intimate club that's as dark and smoky as a jazz bar should be.

ROCK

Austin's last word in alternative music, **Emo's,** 603 Red River St. (© **512/477-EMOS;** www.emosaustin.com), draws acts of all sizes and flavors, from Johnny Cash to Green Day. It primarily attracts college kids, but you won't really feel out of place at any age. Good rock cover bands, a great selection of beers, and plenty of space set **Maggie Mae's,** 512 Trinity St. (© **512/478-8541**), apart from the collegiate-crowded clubs lining Sixth Street.

SINGER/SONGWRITER

A small, dark cavern with great acoustics and a fully stocked bar, the **Cactus Café,** Texas Union, University of Texas campus (24th and Guadalupe) (© **512/475-6515;** www.utexas.edu/student/txunion/ae/cactus), is singer/songwriter heaven. The attentive listening vibes attract the likes of Jimmy LaFave and Shawn Colvin, along with well-known acoustic combos. The adjacent **Texas Union Ballroom** (© **512/475-6645**) draws larger crowds with big names like Billy Bragg. Located in the parking garage of an apartment building, **Ego's,** 510 S. Congress Ave. (© **512/474-7091**), is dark, smoky, seedy, and loads of fun. Locals throng here for the strong drinks and live nightly music, from piano to

But There Are No Limits on the Music

PBS's longest-running show (it first aired in 1975), **Austin City Limits** has showcased such major talent as Lyle Lovett, the Dixie Chicks, and Phish; originally pure country, it has evolved to include blues, zydeco, Cajun, and Tejano. The show is taped live August through February at the KLRU-TV studio, 2504B Whitis St. (near Dean Keeton, 1 block in from Guadalupe), but the schedule is very fluid, so you have to be vigilant in order to nab the free tickets, which are distributed on a first-come, first-served basis, on the day of the taping. For details on how to get tickets, call the show's hot line at ⓒ **512/475-9077.**

You don't have to plan in advance to get a free tour of the recording studio, where you can watch an interesting video clip of the show's highlights, stroll through the control room, and get up on the stage that the stars trod and play air guitar; they're held at the KLRU studio at 10:30 every Friday except holidays (call ⓒ **800/926-2282** or 512/478-0098 to verify schedule around holidays).

You do, however, have to plan ahead if you want to attend the **Austin City Limits Music Festival,** which debuted in late September 2002; performers at this hugely successful premiere event included Emmylou Harris, Los Lobos, Shawn Colvin, Jimmie Vaughan, and Patty Griffin. For information on future festivals, log on to **www.aclfestival. com** or call ⓒ **512/478-7211;** for tickets, call ⓒ **888/597-7827.**

honky-tonk country. You'll recognize the **Saxon Pub,** 1320 S. Lamar Blvd. (ⓒ **512/448-2552;** www.thesaxonpub.com), a long-standing home to South Austin's large community of singer/songwriters, by the giant knight in shining armor in the parking lot. The walk down a dark alley in the Warehouse District to reach the multilevel **Speakeasy,** 412 Congress Ave. (ⓒ **512/476-8017;** www. speakeasyaustin.com), is all part of the 1920s Prohibition theme, which, mercifully, is not taken to an obnoxious extreme. Rather, a swanky atmosphere is created by lots of dark wood and red velvet drapes on the side of the stage. The romantic Evergreen terrace affords a nice view of downtown.

ECLECTIC
A terrific sound system and a casual country atmosphere have helped make **The Backyard,** Tex. 71 west at R.R. 620, Bee Cave (ⓒ **512/263-4146** or 512/469-SHOW for tickets; www.thebackyard.net), one of Austin's hottest venues. Since it opened in the early 1990s, the Allman Brothers, Elvis Costello, kd lang, and Bonnie Raitt have all played the terraced outdoor amphitheater. Join the martini and cigar crowd in the sophisticated **Cedar Street Courtyard,** 208 W. Fourth St. (ⓒ **512/495-9669**), where the nightly live sounds range from jazz to tango. Single gals take note: This place got the *Austin Chronicle*'s nod as the "Best Place to Watch Too Many Men Compete for Too Few Women." An Austin classic, **La Zona Rosa,** 612 W. Fourth St. (ⓒ **512/263-4146;** www. lazonarosa.com), has departed from its funky roots a bit to feature bigger names and bigger covers than in the past. But this renovated garage filled with kitschy memorabilia is still a prime spot to listen to good bands. Within the rough

limestone walls of **Stubb's,** 801 Red River St. (© **512/480-8341;** www.stubbs austin.com), you'll find great barbecue, three friendly bars, and terrific music ranging from singer/songwriter solos to hip-hop open mics to all-out country jams. Out back, the Waller Amphitheatre hosts some of the bigger acts, both road shows rolling through town and popular local bands.

THE BAR SCENE

The intimate **Bitter End B-Side Lounge & Tap Room,** 311 Colorado St. (© **512/478-5890**), serves up (canned) swing, jazz, and blues with its excellent home brews. Other draws: a cask-conditioned beer tap and a separate cigar room.

Within the confines of the thick limestone walls of the **Copper Tank Brewing Company,** 504 Trinity St. (© **512/478-8444**), sports fans, couples, and singles mingle with beer aficionados, who come to savor the light Whitetail Ale or the Big Dog Stout.

GAY & LESBIAN NIGHTLIFE

Its name notwithstanding, **Oilcan Harry's,** 211 W. Fourth St. (© **512/320-8823**), attracts a clean-cut, upscale Warehouse District crowd, while **The Rainbow Cattle Co.,** 305 W. Fifth St. (© **512/472-5288**), is Austin's prime gay country western dance hall; there's no lesbian bar or club in town, but women frequent both of these. For more venues, log on to **http://austin.about.com/cs/ gaynightlife**.

9 Hill Country Side Trips from Austin

The following towns in Texas's Hill Country, one of the state's prettiest regions, can be visited on day trips from Austin, but you'll get more of the region's leisurely flavor with a sleepover. Visits to these towns can easily be combined with those detailed in the "Hill Country Side Trips from San Antonio" section in chapter 7. To locate these towns, see the "South Central Texas" map on p. 233.

FREDERICKSBURG ✪✪✪

Although Fredericksburg is getting a bit trendy, the town also remains devoted to its European past. In 1846, Baron Ottfried Hans von Meusebach brought 120 émigrés in ox-drawn carts from New Braunfels to this site, which he named for Prince Frederick of Prussia. The town's mile-long main street is still wide enough for a team of oxen to turn around in. The permanent peace treaty Meusebach negotiated with the Comanches in 1847, claimed to be the only one in the United States that was ever honored, and the gold rush of 1849—Fredericksburg was the last place California-bound prospectors could get supplies—both helped the town thrive. Although Hollywood types have moved in, the area is still countryish enough to make it a pleasant drive.

SEEING THE SIGHTS

The new **Visitor Information Center,** 302 E. Austin St., Fredericksburg, TX 78624 (© **888/997-3600** or 830/997-6523; www.fredericksburg-texas.com), can direct you to points of interest in the town's historic district. These include a number of little **Sunday Houses,** built by German settlers in distant rural areas because they needed a place to stay overnight when they came to town to trade or attend church. The unusual octagonal **Vereins Kirche (Society Church)** in Market Square once functioned as a town hall, school, and storehouse; a 1935 replica now holds the archives of the Gillespie County Historical Society (© **830/997-2835**). The society also maintains the **Pioneer Museum Complex,** 309 W. Main St., anchored by the 1849 Kammlah House, once a family residence and general store. Other historical structures include a one-room schoolhouse and a blacksmith's forge.

The 1852 Steamboat Hotel, originally owned by the grandfather of World War II naval hero Chester A. Nimitz, is now part of the excellent **National Museum of the Pacific War** ★★, 340 E. Main St. (© **830/997-4379;** www.nimitz-museum.org), a 9-acre Texas State Historical Park and the world's only museum focusing solely on this aspect of the World War II. Other areas include the Japanese Garden of Peace, the Memorial Wall, the Pacific Combat Zone, and the George Bush Gallery.

SHOPPING

Ladies and gentleman, start your acquisition engines. If you're pressed for time, concentrate on **Main Street** between Elk and Milam, though other sections are worth exploring, too. More than 100 specialty shops, many of them in mid-19th-century houses, feature work by Hill Country artisans—everything from lace coverlets to dulcimers. Yuppies come from all over Texas to grab up the ultra-fashionable home furnishings sold at the three-story **Homestead,** 230 E. Main (© **830/997-5551**), where European rural retro meets contemporary natural fabrics. Check out **Texas Jack,** 117 Adams St. (© **914/997-3213**), which has outfitted actors for Western films and TV shows, including *Lonesome Dove, Tombstone,* and *Gunsmoke.* Becoming increasingly well known via its mail-order business is the **Fredericksburg Herb Farm,** 405 Whitney St. (© **800/259-HERB** or 830/997-8615; www.fredericksburgherbfarm.com), just a bit south of town. You can visit the flower beds that produce salad dressings, teas, fragrances, and air fresheners, and then sample some of them in the on-site restaurant (lunch only; moderate), B&B, and day spa.

WHERE TO STAY

Perhaps even more than for its shopping, Fredericksburg is known for its appealing accommodations. In addition to the usual rural motels, the town boasts more than 250 bed-and-breakfasts and *gastehauses* (individual guest cottages). The latter, which cost from about $100 to $150 per night, might be anything from an 1865 homestead to a limestone Sunday House; unlike the typical B&B, these places ensure privacy, because breakfast is provided the night before (perishables are left in a refrigerator). The main reservation services are: **Be My Guest,** 110 N. Milam (© **866/997-7227** or 830/997-7227, www.bemyguest fredericksburgtexas.com); **Bed & Breakfast of Fredericksburg,** 619 W. Main St. (© **877/396-9240** or 830/997-4712); **First Class Bed & Breakfast Reservation Service,** 909 E. Main St.(© **888/991-6749** or 830/997-0443; www.fredericksburg-lodging.com); **Gastehaus Schmidt,** 231 W. Main St. (© **866/427-8374** or 830/997-5612; www.fbglodging.com); and **Hill Country Lodging & Reservation Service,** 215 W. Main St. (© **800/745-3591** or 830/990-8455; www.fredericksburgbedbreakfast.com).

WHERE TO DINE

Fredericksburg's dining scene is very diverse, catering to the traditional and the trendy alike. The former tend to frequent the **Altdorf Biergarten,** 301 W. Main St. (© **830/997-7865**), featuring hearty German schnitzels, dumplings, and sauerbraten, and large selections of beer. The **Fredericksburg Brewing Co.,**

245 E. Main St. (② **830/997-1646**), harks back to the past with its home brews and friendly atmosphere, but the menu includes lots of lighter selections. The contemporary-chic **Navajo Grill,** 209 E. Main St. (② **830/990-8289**), features cutting edge cuisine, with dishes inspired by New Orleans, the Southwest, and occasionally the Caribbean. About 11 miles north of Fredericksburg on I-87, the **Hill Top Cafe** (② **830/997-8922**) serves excellent Cajun and Greek food. You might find the owner, a former member of the band Asleep at the Wheel, very much awake at the piano.

LYNDON B. JOHNSON COUNTRY ⊛
Welcome to Johnson territory, where the forebears of the 36th president settled almost 150 years ago. Here you'll find LBJ's boyhood home and the sprawling ranch that became known as the Texas White House.

From Fredericksburg, take U.S. 290 east for 16 miles to the entrance of the **Lyndon B. Johnson State and National Historical Parks at LBJ Ranch** ⊛, near Stonewall (② **830/868-7128** or 830/644-2252), co-run by the Texas Parks and Wildlife Department (www.tpwd.state.tx.us/park/lbj) and the National Park Service (www.nps.gov/lyjo). Tour buses depart regularly from the visitor center to the still-operating Johnson Ranch. On the other side of the Pedernales River, a reconstructed version of the former president's modest birthplace lies close to his final resting place. Also part of the state park is the **Sauer-Beckmann Living History Farm,** where costumed interpreters give visitors a look at typical Texas-German farm life at the turn of the 20th century. As interesting as Colonial Williamsburg, this is a terrific place to come with kids. Nearby are nature trails, a swimming pool (open only in summer), and lots of picnic spots. Admission is $3 per person for bus tours; all other areas are free.

It's 14 miles farther east along U.S. 290 to **Johnson City,** a pleasant agricultural town named for founder James Polk Johnson, LBJ's first cousin once removed. The modest white clapboard **Boyhood Home** ⊛, where Lyndon was raised after age 5, is the centerpiece of this unit of the national historical park. Before exploring, stop at the **visitor center**—take F Street to Lady Bird Lane and you'll see the signs. The Boyhood Home and visitor center are open from 8:45am to 5pm daily; admission is free.

The **Johnson City Visitor and Tourism Bureau,** P.O. Box 485, Johnson City, TX 78636 (② **830/868-7684;** www.johnsoncity-texas.com), can provide information about dining, lodging, and shopping in town. Those interested in staying at a local B&B should call ② **830/868-4548.**

SAN MARCOS
Some 26 miles south of Austin via I-35, the town of San Marcos was first settled by a tribe of nomadic Indians around 12,000 years ago. Some scholars claim it is the oldest continuously inhabited site in the Western Hemisphere. Now host to Southwest Texas State University, the alma mater of LBJ, San Marcos has the laid-back feel of a college town.

In the center of town—and, clearly, the reason for its existence—more than 1,000 springs well up from the Balcones Fault to form Spring Lake; its astonishingly clear waters maintain a constant temperature of 72°F (22°C). On the lake's shore sits the **Aquarena Center** ⊛⊛, 1 Aquarena Springs Dr. (② **512/ 245-7575,** www.continuing-ed.swt.edu/aquarena), an environmental research center that offers a glass bottom–boat tour, an endangered species exhibit, a natural aquarium, hikes, and a boardwalk over the wetlands, where more than 100 species of birds have been spotted.

Truth be told, however, lots of people bypass San Marcos altogether and head straight for the two factory outlet malls a few miles south of downtown—the biggest discount shopfest in Texas. Take Exit 200 from I-35 for both the **Tanger Factory Outlet Center** (© 800/408-8424 for the San Marcos office, or 800-4-TANGER for the national office; www.tangeroutlet.com) and the larger and tonier **Prime Outlets** (© 800/628-9465 or 512/396-7183; www.primeoutlets. com), right next door. Among the almost 150 stores, you'll find everything from Donna Karan, Anne Klein, Calvin Klein, and Brooks Brothers to Samsonite and Waterford/Wedgwood.

The **San Marcos Convention and Visitors Bureau,** 202 N. C. M. Allen Pkwy., San Marcos, TX 78666 (© 888/200-5620 or 512/393-5900 www.san marcostexas.com/tourism), can provide you with information on mall bus transportation, as well as a complete list of attractions, lodgings, and dining spots in town.

NEW BRAUNFELS ⚜

Some 16 miles south of San Marcos on I-35, New Braunfels sits at the junction of the Comal and Guadalupe rivers. German settlers were brought here in 1845 by Prince Carl of Solms-Braunfels, head of the Society for the Protection of German Immigrants in Texas, which also founded Fredericksburg. Although Prince Carl returned to Germany within a year to marry his fiancée, who refused to join him in the wilderness, his colony prospered. By the 1850s, New Braunfels was the fourth-largest city in Texas after Houston, San Antonio, and Galveston. New Braunfels doesn't rank nearly as high in population today, but it's not one of the Hill Country's quieter, quainter towns, either. Come here for the interesting historical attractions and a great river scene—which Fredericksburg doesn't have.

EXPLORING NEW BRAUNFELS

At the **New Braunfels Chamber of Commerce,** 390 S. Seguin, New Braunfels, TX 78130 (© 800/572-2626 or 830/625-2385; www.nbcham.org), you can pickup the *Prosit Visitor's Guide,* which can help you take an antiques-lovers' crawl. You can also get a brochure for a self-guided historic walking tour of midtown, where buildings of note include the Jacob Schmidt Building (193 W. San Antonio), built on the site where William Gebhardt, of canned chili fame, perfected his formula for chili powder in 1896; and the 1928 Faust Hotel (240 S. Seguin), believed by some to be haunted by its owner.

Several small museums are worth a visit. Prince Carl never did build a planned castle for his sweetheart, Sophia, on the elevated spot where the **Sophienburg Museum** ⚜, 401 W. Coll St. (© 830/629-1572; www.nbtx.com/ sophienburg), now stands, but it's nevertheless an excellent place to learn about the history of New Braunfels and other Hill Country settlements. The 11-acre **Heritage Village** complex includes the **Museum of Texas Handmade Furniture,** 1370 Church Hill Dr. (© 830/629-6504; www.nbheritagevillage.com), with beautiful examples of Texas Biedermeier by master craftsman Johan Michael Jahn; an 1848 log cabin; and a reproduction cabinetmaker's workshop. You can tour other historic structures, including an 1870 schoolhouse and a tiny music studio, at the nearby **Conservation Plaza,** 1300 Church Hill Dr. (© 830/629-2943). Guided tours are offered every day except Monday. The 1852 **Lindheimer Home** ⚜, 491 Comal Ave. (© 830/608-1512), is probably the best example of an early *fachwerk* house still standing in New Braunfels. Ferdinand J. Lindheimer, one of the town's first settlers, was an internationally recognized botanist. Museum hours are limited, but you can wander the lovely grounds planted with Texas native plants.

HISTORIC GRUENE ★★

You can get a more concentrated glimpse of the past at Gruene (pronounced *Green*), 4 miles northwest of downtown New Braunfels. First settled by German farmers in the 1840s, Gruene was virtually abandoned during the Depression in the 1930s. It remained a ghost town until the mid-1970s, when two investors realized the value of its intact historic buildings and sold them to businesses rather than raze them. Now tiny Gruene is crowded with day-trippers browsing the specialty shops—everything from antiques to smoked meat—in the wonderfully restored structures. In 2001, Gruene also became home to the **New Braunfels Museum of Art & Music** 1259 Gruene Rd. (© **800/456-4866** or 830/625-5636; www.nbmuseum.org). Subjects of recent exhibits, which change quarterly, have included Texas accordion music, central Texas dance halls, and cowboy art and poetry.

A brochure detailing the town's retailers, restaurants, and accommodations is available from the New Braunfels Chamber of Commerce (see above) or at most of Gruene's shops. You can also get information on the town's website, **www. gruene.net**.

WATERSPORTS

Gruene also figures among the area's impressive array of places to get wet, most of them open only in summer. Outfitters who can help you ride the Guadalupe River rapids on raft, tube, canoe, or inflatable kayak include **Rockin "R" River Rides** (© **800/553-5628** or 830/629-9999) and **Gruene River Raft Company** (© **830/625-2800** or 830/625-2873), both on Gruene Road just south of the Gruene Bridge. You can go tubing, too, at **Schlitterbahn,** 305 W. Austin St. in New Braunfels (© **830/625-2351;** www.schlitterbahn.com), Texas's largest (65 acres) water park and rated tops in the country. Those who like their water play a bit more low key might try downtown New Braunfels' **Landa Park** (© **830/608-2160**), where you can either swim in the largest spring-fed pool in Texas or calmly float in an inner tube down the Comal River.

WHERE TO STAY IN NEW BRAUNFELS & GRUENE

A prime downtown location, tree-shaded courtyard, and gorgeously florid, high-Victorian–style sleeping quarters have put accommodations at the **Prince Solmes Inn,** 295 E. San Antonio St., New Braunfels (© **800/625-9169** or 830/625-9169), in great demand. Three Western-themed rooms in a converted 1860 feed store next door are ideal for families. Rates range from $125 to $150.

For a river view, consider the **Gruene Mansion Inn,** 1275 Gruene Rd., New Braunfels (© **830/629-2641;** www.gruenemansioninn.com). The barns that once belonged to the opulent 1875 plantation house were converted to rustic elegant cottages with decks; some also offer cozy lofts. Accommodations cost from $115 to $210 per night.

The **Bed & Breakfast & Getaways Reservation Service,** 295 E. San Antonio St., New Braunfels, TX 78130 (© **800/239-8282** or 830/625-8194; www. bedbreakfastgetaways.com), lists many other similarly gemütlich places in the area. *Note:* If you're planning to come to town during *wurstfest* (late Oct to early Nov), be sure to book well in advance.

WHERE TO DINE IN NEW BRAUNFELS & GREUNE

The **New Braunfels Smokehouse,** 140 Tex. 46 S, at I-35 (© **830/625-2416**), opened in 1951 as a tasting room for the meats it started hickory smoking in 1945. Although it's a full-service restaurant today, it still offers samples of its smoked meats. The far newer **Huisache Grille,** 303 W. San Antonio St. (© **830/620-9001**), has an updated American menu that draws foodies from as far away as San Antonio. Another recent arrival on downtown's fine dining scene, pretty **Giovani's,** 367 Main Plaza (© **830/626-2235**), serves sophisticated Italian specialties at very reasonable prices.

In Gruene, the **Gristmill River Restaurant & Bar,** 1287 Gruene Rd. (© **830/625-0684**), a converted 100-year-old cotton gin, includes burgers and chicken-fried steak as well as salads on its Texas casual menu. Kick back on one of its multiple decks and gaze out at the Guadalupe River. The somewhat more upscale **Restaurant at Gruene Mansion,** 1275 Gruene Rd. (© **830/620-0760**), serving German and Continental cuisine, is a recent construction, but it looks like an old European hall. It also has an outside deck with a river view.

9

West Texas

by Eric Peterson & Don & Barb Laine

This is the real Texas: vast open spaces, longhorn cattle, pickup trucks lined up in front of roadside honky-tonks, and deeply-tanned cowboys with sweat-stained hats, slim-cut jeans, and muddy boots. While most of Texas has become quite metropolitan—the vast majority of the state's residents live in cities—the plains of West Texas retain much of the Old West flavor. Towns here are generally small and far apart, residents seldom lock their doors, and even the region's biggest city, El Paso, is in many ways just an overgrown dusty little town. But for those willing to take the time and effort, this area can be fun to explore, with a wide range of friendly people, attractions, and activities that take us back to a time when America was less sophisticated.

The region's history comes alive at numerous museums and historic sites, such as Spanish missions from the 17th and 18th centuries, several restored frontier forts, and the combination courtroom and saloon used in the late 1800s by Judge Roy Bean, the self-styled "Law West of the Pecos." West Texas also offers some surprises, including one of America's most beautiful caves; several airfields where you'll see fully operational historic aircraft; the state's oldest winery; a replica of William Shakespeare's famed Globe Theatre; an avant garde installation art complex in the sleepy town of Marfa; and numerous lakes, including 67,000-acre Lake Amistad, a national recreation area along the U.S.–Mexico border that is a joint project of both countries.

1 El Paso

43 miles SE of Las Cruces, New Mexico; 564 miles NW of San Antonio; 617 miles W of Dallas

Here, in the sun-swept, mountainous desert of Texas's westernmost corner, is El Paso, the state's fourth-largest city. Built between two mountain ranges on the shores of the Rio Grande, the city is an urban history book, with chapters dedicated to Spanish conquistadors, ancient highways, gunfighters, border disputes, and modern sprawl.

El Paso's rich history is a result of its geography. The Franklin Mountains, which now border the downtown area and occupy the city's heart, offered natural defense for the American Indians who inhabited the area for more than 10 millennia; the Rio Grande offered water. As the mountains slope into a vast canyon, the Spanish explorers who first crossed the Rio Grande in the 16th century saw it as an ideal north-south route, one that soon became known as the "Camino Real" (or "King's Highway") and served as a principal trade route for nearly 300 years.

With the 17th century came an influx of Catholic missionaries, a group that established numerous missions that survive today. But Spain saw its grip weaken,

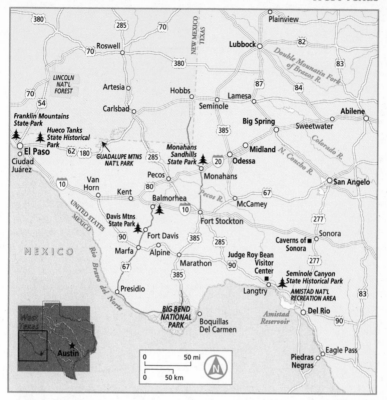

and a Mexican flag flew over El Paso when independence was established in 1821. This era was short-lived, as Mexico ceded the land north of the Rio Grande to the United States following the Mexican-American War (1846–48). After the railroad arrived in 1881, El Paso earned the nickname "Sin City," thanks to the saloons, brothels, and casinos that lined every major street. Many notorious gunfighters—including Billy the Kid and John Wesley Hardin—called the city home.

El Paso boomed in the early 20th century and again following World War II, entrenching itself as a center for agriculture, manufacturing, and international trade. The city's relationship with Ciudad Juárez has been symbiotic for centuries, even more so since the resolution of a century-old border dispute in the 1960s and the signing of the North American Free Trade Agreement in 1994.

In comparison with the wealth and glitz of Santa Fe or Tucson, El Paso is in many ways the authentic Southwest—unpolished, undiluted, and honest. Separated by a swath of the Rio Grande, El Paso and Ciudad Juárez each represent their country's largest border city, and the local culture, a fusion of Mexican and American traditions, is distinct and unique in comparison to the way of life in eastern Texas. A day or two of exploration is worthwhile; take the time to wander downtown, enjoy a Tex-Mex meal, and gain a better understanding of what a border town is all about.

El Paso

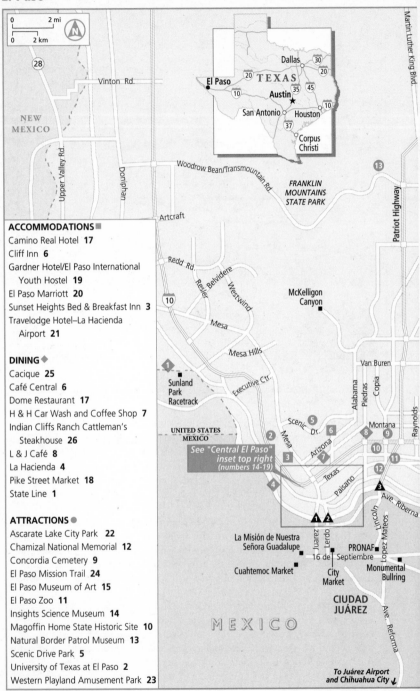

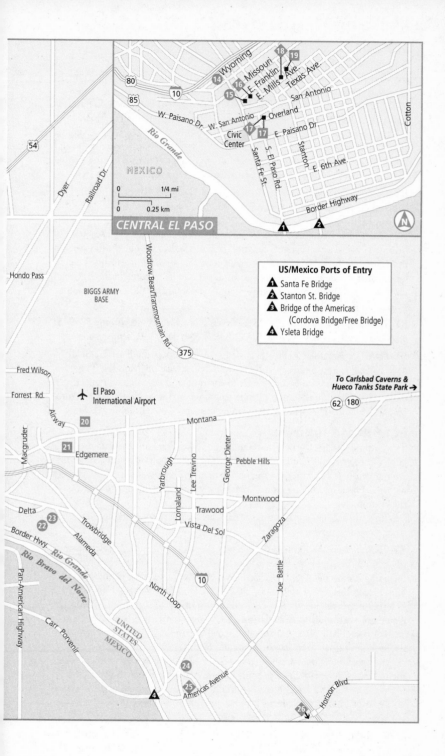

CENTRAL EL PASO

MEXICO

Rio Grande

Wyoming

Missouri
E. Franklin
E. Mills Ave.
Texas Ave.
San Antonio

W. Paisano Dr.   W. San Antonio   Overland
Civic Center   E. Paisano Dr.

Santa Fe St.
S. El Paso Rd.
Stanton
E. 6th Ave.
Cotton

80
10
85
54

0   1/4 mi
0   0.25 km

US/Mexico Ports of Entry

1 Santa Fe Bridge
2 Stanton St. Bridge
3 Bridge of the Americas
   (Cordova Bridge/Free Bridge)
4 Ysleta Bridge

Hondo Pass

BIGGS ARMY BASE

Woodrow Bean/Transmountain Rd.

375

Fred Wilson
Forrest Rd.

El Paso International Airport

To Carlsbad Caverns & Hueco Tanks State Park →

62 180

Dyer
Railroad Dr.

Alnway
Macgruder

Montana

20
21 Edgemere

Yarbrough
Lomaland
Lee Trevino
George Dieter
Pebble Hills
Montwood

Delta
23
22
Trowbridge
Alameda

Trawood
Vista Del Sol

Zaragoza
Joe Battle

Border Hwy.   Rio Grande

Rio Bravo del Norte

Pan-American Highway

Carr Porvenir

North Loop

10

UNITED STATES
MEXICO

24
25 Americas Avenue

4

26   Horizon Blvd.

317

ESSENTIALS
GETTING THERE

BY PLANE Some 200 commercial flights arrive and depart daily from **El Paso International Airport,** located a mile north of I-10 via Airway Boulevard on the city's east side (© **915/772-4271**). Most major airlines, including **Aerólitoral** (© **800/237-6639**) and **Frontier** (© **800/432-1359**), serve El Paso.

The major car-rental agencies are represented here; see "Getting Around," below. **RG Transportation** (© **915/562-8868**) offers shuttle service to and from the airport (a 15-min. trip each way); a one-way trip downtown costs $15. The service operates daily 24 hours with a reservation.

BY CAR The main artery to the east and west is I-10, bisecting El Paso between downtown and the Franklin Mountains.

From Carlsbad Caverns (160 miles from El Paso) and Guadalupe Mountains National Parks to the east (about 130 miles), visitors arrive via U.S. 62/180 (Montana Ave.), which eventually skirts the north side of downtown El Paso. For those arriving from Alamogordo, New Mexico (80 miles to the north), U.S. 54 (also known as the Patriot Fwy.) runs through El Paso's east side to the Bridge of the Americas, which crosses the Rio Grande and connects El Paso with Ciudad Juárez, Mexico.

BY BUS Interstate and intrastate bus service is provided by **Greyhound** (© **915/532-2365**) and **TNM&O** (© **915/532-3404**) both at 200 W. San Antonio Dr.

BY TRAIN Amtrak (© **800/872-7245**) offers westward rail service on Tuesday, Thursday, and Saturday and eastward rail service on Monday, Thursday, and Saturday. Trains go east and west to Orlando and Los Angeles respectively; other major cities on the route include Jacksonville, Biloxi, Houston, San Antonio, and Tucson. The depot is located downtown at 700 San Francisco St.

GETTING AROUND

Two natural features—the Rio Grande and the Franklin Mountains—have guided the urban development of El Paso for more than 400 years, so getting around can be a bit tricky for the newcomer. The city is essentially U-shaped, with the Franklin Mountains occupying the center and the downtown area at the bottom.

While El Paso has a public bus system, cars are the norm. Parking is rarely an issue, even downtown.

BY CAR There are numerous car-rental agencies in El Paso, clustered primarily around the airport in the east, and North Mesa Street on the city's west side, including **Alamo** (© 915/775-9933); **Avis** (© 915/779-2700); **Budget** (© 915/533-3435); **Enterprise** (© 800/736-8222); **Godinez Rent-A-Car** (© 915/778-4195); **Hertz** (© 915/772-4255); and **Thrifty** (© 915/778-9236). The **American Automobile Association (AAA)** maintains an office in El Paso at 1201 Airway Blvd., Suite A-1 (© 800/765-0766 or 915/778-9521), open Monday through Friday from 9am to 6pm and Saturday from 9am to 1pm.

Street parking is free almost everywhere in El Paso except downtown, where the meters must be fed 25¢ per hour. The covered garages downtown charge $3 to $6 per day. There are also many outdoor lots that are geared toward tourists on day trips to Ciudad Juárez. These usually run $2 to $5 per day.

BY BUS El Paso's bus system, **Sun Metro** (© **915/533-3333**), operates one of the world's largest fleets of natural gas–powered buses. The main transfer station is downtown on San Jacinto Plaza at Mesa and Main streets. There are also trolleys that run between the UTEP campus and downtown. Buses run from 4:30am to 8:15pm on weekdays, with slightly shorter hours on weekends and holidays; fare is $1 for adults and 50¢ for children, students, and those with disabilities, and 30¢ for seniors.

BY TAXI   Both **Yellow Cab** (© 915/533-3433) and **Sun City Cab** (© 915/544-2211) offer 24-hour service in El Paso and the surrounding area.

BY FOOT   Downtown El Paso is well suited for a walking tour, and it is popular to park downtown and walk across the Santa Fe Bridge into Ciudad Juárez.

VISITOR INFORMATION

The **El Paso Convention & Visitors Bureau** is located at One Civic Center Plaza, in the El Paso Convention and Performing Arts Center (© **800/351-6024** or 915/534-0696; www.visitelpaso.com). The CVB's biannual *El Paso: The Official Visitor's Guide* is a good publication to pick up while you're there.

There is also a **Texas Travel Information Center,** with an excellent selection of brochures, maps, and other visitor resources located 20 miles northwest of El Paso in Anthony (I-10, Exit 0), at the Texas–New Mexico border.

For information on Ciudad Juárez contact **Fiprotur Chihuahua,** Ave. de las Americas No. 2551, Ciudad Juárez, Chihuahua, Mexico (© **888/654-0394**).

 FAST FACTS: **El Paso**

American Express   Sun Travel American Express, 3100 N. Mesa St., Suite B (© **915/532-8900**), offers American Express services Monday through Friday from 8am to 5pm.

Babysitters   Front desks at major hotels often can make arrangements on your behalf.

Dentists   Contact **Four-Star Health and Referral** (© 800/828-6600).

Doctors   Call **El Paso County Medical Society** (© 915/533-0981).

Drugstores   **Walgreens Drug Stores** has a 24-hour prescription service at 1840 Lee Trevino Dr. (© **915/594-1129**).

Emergencies   For police, fire, and medical emergencies, call © **911.** To reach the **Poison Center,** dial © **800/764-7661** or 915/544-1200.

Hospitals   Full-service hospitals, with 24-hour emergency rooms, include **Sierra Medical Center,** 1625 Medical Center Dr. (© **915/747-4000**), just northwest of downtown, and **Del Sol Medical Center,** 10301 Gateway West (© **915/595-9000**), on the east side of the city.

Newspapers & Magazines   The *El Paso Times* is the city's only daily newspaper for readers of English, and an El Paso edition of *El Diario de Juárez* is published in Spanish daily. *El Paso Scene* is the city's free monthly arts-and-entertainment paper.

Post Office   The main post office, located downtown at 219 E. Mills St., is open Monday through Friday from 8:30am to 5pm, Saturday from 8:30am to noon.

Safety   While El Paso has among the lowest crime rates of any major U.S. city, it is far from crime-free, with drugs and auto theft being the two preeminent problems. It's important to keep aware of your surroundings at all times and ask at your hotel or a visitor center about the safety of a given neighborhood, especially after dark. *Note:* When visiting Mexico, it is important to remember that Ciudad Juárez is one of the world's most active drug-smuggling centers. Gangs have also grown in numbers in Juárez in recent years.

Taxes In the city of El Paso, the total sales tax is 8.25% and 14% for lodging.

Time Zone El Paso is in the Mountain Standard Time zone, like nearby New Mexico but unlike the rest of Texas, which is in the Central Standard Time zone. Set your clock back 1 hour if you enter El Paso from the east.

WHAT TO SEE & DO
THE TOP ATTRACTIONS

Chamizal National Memorial ✿ When the Mexican-American War ended in 1848, the two countries agreed upon a border: the center of the deepest channel of the Rio Grande. However, as historian Leon C. Metz once wrote, "Rivers are never *absolutely* permanent. They evaporate, flood, change channels, shrink, expand and even disappear. Rivers are, by nature, capricious." After the war, the Rio Grande gradually shifted southward, resulting in a diplomatic stalemate between Mexico and the United States over the boundary's location. This impasse lasted until 1967, finally ending when Presidents Lyndon B. Johnson and Adolfo López Mateos signed the Chamizal Treaty. Parcels of land were exchanged, residents and businesses uprooted, and a permanent, concrete channel was constructed to signify a more predictable boundary.

The 55-acre park at the Chamizal National Memorial commemorates the dispute's settlement with a bevy of facilities: 2 miles of foot trails, an outdoor amphitheater that hosts many free (and popular) concerts, and a visitor center/ museum (expect to spend 30 min. touring the museum). It's a nice open space that's more accessible and greener than the Franklin Mountains, and larger than the other municipal parks. There is also a walkway to the adjacent Bridge of the Americas leading to the memorial's Mexican counterpart, **Parque Chamizal,** with an anthropology museum and an amusement park in Ciudad Juárez.

800 S. San Marcial Dr., at Paisano Dr. and U.S. 54 (Patriot Fwy.). © **915/532-7273**. www.nps.gov/cham/ index.htm. Free admission, although there are fees for some events in the amphitheater. Park daily 6am–10pm. Visitor center daily 8am–5pm.

El Paso Mission Trail ✿ First established in the 17th and 18th centuries, three historic Spanish missions provide a link to El Paso's colonial past. All three are among the oldest continually active missions in the country, and warrant a visit for their architectural and historic merit. But if you only have time to hit only one, drive out to San Elceario; unlike Ysleta and Socorro, it's removed from the modern urban development and still feels like it's from a simpler time. San Elceario was the personal highlight, from the surrounding village to the mission itself; it's a part of the U.S. that's from a totally different era and culture.

From I-10, exit Zaragosa Road (Exit 32) and head south 3 miles to **Mission Ysleta,** 9501 Socorro Rd. at Zaragosa Road, established in 1682 in what was then Mexico. The silver-domed chapel here was built in 1851 after floods shifted the Rio Grande and washed away all of the previous structure, save the foundation.

Heading southeast on Socorro Road for 3 miles takes you to **Mission Socorro** (© **915/859-7718**), established in 1682, 1 day after Mission Ysleta. The original adobe chapel (1692) was washed away by a flood in the 1740s, rebuilt, destroyed again in 1829, and finally replaced in 1843 by the current structure. The mission is in the midst of a major restoration project, slated for completion in August 2003.

Presidio Chapel San Elceario (© **915/851-2333**), established at its present location in 1789 as a Spanish military outpost, sits 6 miles south of Mission Socorro on Socorro Road. Parishioners built the present-day church in 1877 as the centerpiece of the village plaza, which retains its historic charm to this day. This structure is the largest of the three missions, and an excellent example of the merging of American Indian and Spanish architectural styles with majestic arches and a pressed tin ceiling. The surrounding village has been gaining fame in recent years as the site of "The First Thanksgiving," said to have taken place in 1598, 23 years before the Plymouth Thanksgiving.

Visitors are welcome to tour the missions on their own; expect to spend at least 3 hours if you visit all three. Bus tours are offered on occasion by the **El Paso-Juárez Trolley Company** (© **915/544-0062**).

An 8-mile stretch of Zaragosa and Socorro Rds., southeast of downtown El Paso via I-10. © **915/534-0677**. www.missiontrail.com. Free admission.

 ## El Paso's Public Art

El Paso is home to a variety of distinctive works of public art, sculptures that are at once reflections of the contemporary city and reminders of days gone by:

In El Paso's downtown San Jacinto Plaza, the **Plaza de los Lagartos,** a fiberglass fountain comprised of snarling alligators, basks in the sun. The lively 1993 piece by pop artist (and El Paso native) Luis Jimenez harks back to the gators that called the plaza home from the 1880s to the 1960s, first deposited by the mayor as something of a joke, then thriving there amid the hustle and bustle of the growing city. (Located in San Jacinto Plaza, bordered on the east and west by Mesa and Oregon sts., and north and south by Main and Mills sts.)

The **Buffalo Soldier Monument** honors the black U.S. Army infantry soldiers who served on the Southwestern frontier in the Indian Wars of the late 19th century. They received the name "Buffalo Soldiers" from American Indians, who thought their hair resembled that of a buffalo. The 8×11×5-foot bronze statue, which guards the Robert E. Lee entrance gate to Fort Bliss, depicts a black soldier on horseback, turning to fire his rifle. (Located at Robert E. Lee Rd. and Airport Rd. on the southeast corner of Fort Bliss.)

Mt. Cristo Rey looms over western El Paso from an 800-foot peak in Sunland Park, New Mexico. Since Spanish sculptor Urbici Soler carved the 33-foot statue of Christ out of blocks of limestone in the 1930s, thousands annually hike the 1.5-mile trail to the statue to pray. (Located on the west side of McNutt Rd. in Sunland Park, New Mexico.)

For maps and directions, contact the **El Paso CVB** (© **915/534-0696**).

El Paso Museum of Art ★★   Once regarded as lacking a regional focus, the El Paso Museum of Art has recently turned that criticism on its head: The stunning landscapes and personal portraits on display here evoke the region's look, and more importantly, its feel. Of the five permanent galleries, three are dedicated to the cultures that have commingled in El Paso for the last 400 years: One is dedicated to Mexican art of the 17th to 19th centuries, one to European art from the 13th to 18th centuries, and one to American works dating from 1800 to the mid-1900s. There are also seasonal exhibits that often feature edgier contemporary works. The museum begs for an unhurried hour of your time.

1 Arts Festival Plaza. ℂ 915/532-1707. www.elpasoartmuseum.org. Free admission. Tues–Sat 9am–5pm; Sun noon–5pm.

MORE ATTRACTIONS

Ascarate Lake City Park   Centered on a 44-acre artificial lake, this municipal park consists of 400 acres of undeveloped terrain crisscrossed by trails. While swimming in the lake is prohibited, recreational opportunities include fishing (the lake is stocked with channel catfish and rainbow trout) and golfing at the park's 27-hole golf course. There's also an aquatics center with an indoor Olympic-size pool and ball fields.

Delta Dr., between Alameda Ave. and Border Hwy. ℂ 915/772-3941. Free admission to park, although some attractions have fees, including the golf course and Western Playland Amusement Park. Open daily dawn–dusk.

Concordia Cemetery   El Paso's "Boot Hill," Concordia is the final resting place of numerous infamous outlaws who met their maker in the city's wilder days. The gravestones here, which mostly date to the second half of the 19th century, remain haunting reminders of El Paso's storied past. Near the northern gate, the most notable grave is that of notorious John Wesley Hardin, known as "The Fastest Gun in the West." After his 1895 assassination in downtown El Paso, Hardin was put to rest here alongside other gunslingers (including Hardin's killer) and a generation of law-abiding citizens. Hardin's grave is said to be El Paso's most-visited attraction.

Copia St. and I-10. ℂ 915/562-7062. Free admission. Daily 24 hr. Immediately north of I-10 via Copia St. (Exit 22A).

El Paso Zoo ★ *Kids*   Home to 600 animals from 175 different species in natural habitat exhibits, the El Paso Zoo is one of the state's best. The focus is on American and Asian wildlife, with a monkey island, reptile house, Asian Grasslands exhibit, and Americas Aviary. Among the crowd favorites (and our favorites as well) are sun bears, black jaguars, tigers, and Asian elephants. There is also a restaurant, gift shop, and a replica of a "Paraje," the 16th-century equivalent of a rest stop on the Camino Real. Allow at least 1 hour.

4001 E. Paisano Dr. (across from the El Paso County Coliseum). ℂ 915/544-1928. www.elpasozoo.org. Admission $4 adults, $3 seniors 62 and over, $2 children ages 3–12, free for children under 3. Mon–Fri

---

Fun Fact **Live by the Gun . . .**

Notorious gunslinger John Wesley Hardin, who claimed to have killed 40 men, was shot in the back of the head in a saloon in 1895. At the time, Hardin was planning to embark on a law career (he had even gone as far as printing business cards), despite the fact that he spent more than three-quarters of his last 20 years in prison.

> (*Tips* Scenic Drive Park
>
> Located high above downtown atop the cliffs of the Franklin Mountains, this municipal park (on Scenic Dr. between Rim Rd. and Alabama Ave.) offers amazing views of the El Paso area. With the naked eye or coin-op telescopes, you can see from the University of Texas at El Paso to downtown, across the Rio Grande to Juárez, and even parts of New Mexico.

9:30am–4pm year-round (open at 8am Fri summer); Sat–Sun 9:30am–4pm winter, 9:30am–6pm summer. Closed Thanksgiving, Dec 25, and Jan 1.

Magoffin Home State Historic Site   Built in 1875 for Joseph Magoffin, a pioneer leader who helped guide the city through its chaotic Wild West days, this is El Paso's only historical house museum open to the public. A recommended hour-long stop for the history buff, the house is a prime example of Territorial architecture, with an adobe structure and Greek Revival accents. Many rooms have been meticulously preserved to reflect pioneer life, with their original furnishings still in place: The Victorian parlor is unique due to its Mexican accents, the oldest part of the home still sports a viga ceiling (thatched and exposed), and one bedroom is outfitted with a 13-foot half-canopy bed and furnishings purchased at the 1884 World's Fair in New Orleans.

1120 Magoffin Ave. ⓒ 915/533-5147. www.magoffinhome.com. Admission $2 adults, $1 students, free for children under 6. Daily 9am–4pm.

National Border Patrol Museum   The only museum dedicated to the U.S. Border Patrol, this facility does a good job presenting displays on all aspects of the federal agency, founded in El Paso in 1924. Allow about a half-hour to peruse such highlights as the "Lady Liberty" exhibit, a Statue of Liberty replica and text and diaries about the immigrant experience; and two former Border Patrol aircraft: a Piper Super Cub plane and a Hughes OH-6A helicopter. There are also exhibits on Border Patrol dogs, electronics, and ground vehicles, a seasonal display, and a good selection of souvenirs.

4315 Transmountain Dr. ⓒ 915/759-6060. www.nationalbpmuseum.org. Free admission (donations accepted). Tues–Sun 9am–5pm. Closed major holidays.

ESPECIALLY FOR KIDS

Insights Science Museum ⚡ *(Kids*   This downtown museum is a winner for young minds curious about the inner workings of nature. There are more than 60 interactive exhibits here, on topics ranging from energy and optics to health and biology. Kids get a big jolt of fun out of the Tesla coil that courses with 500,000 volts several times a day. Another favorite is the exhibit on sound, with an "Echo Tube" and displays on sonic waves. A comprehensive tour requires about an hour. There's an on-site observatory, open to the public ($3.50) for night sky viewing on the first Saturday of every month, from 8 to 10pm.

505 N. Santa Fe St. ⓒ 915/534-0000. www.insightsmuseum.org. Admission $5.50 adults, $4.50 students, seniors, and military, $3.50 children ages 2–5, free for children under 2. Mon 9am–2pm; Tues–Fri 9am–5pm; Sat–Sun noon–5pm.

Western Playland Amusement Park *(Kids*   El Paso's only amusement park, Western Playland is home to the El Bandito roller coaster, three water rides (including "Tsunami!" with a 50-ft. drop), carnival games, a miniature golf course, a go-cart track, and a kiddie playland. Concession stands and picnic areas fill the needs of the hungry and thirsty.

6900 Delta Dr. in Ascarate Lake City Park. ℂ **915/772-3914.** Admission $15 for a pass for unlimited rides, or $5 admission plus $2 ride tickets. Mar–Apr and mid-Aug to mid-Oct Sat 2–9pm, Sun 2–8pm; May Fri 6:30–10pm, Sat 2–9pm, Sun 2–8pm; June to mid-Aug Wed–Fri 6:30–10pm, Sat–Sun 3–10pm.

ORGANIZED TOURS

The **El Paso–Juárez Trolley Company** ⚡ (ℂ **915/544-0061;** www.border jumper.com) offers trolley tours that venture into Mexico, New Mexico, and historic El Paso for $10 to $20, depending on the package. Juárez tours depart hourly from One Civic Center Plaza from 10am to 4pm year-round. Call for information on other tours, which are offered seasonally.

The **El Paso CVB** (ℂ **915/534-0696**) can provide travelers with informative brochures that detail self-guided historic walking tours of both El Paso and Ciudad Juárez.

OUTDOOR ACTIVITIES

At nearly 24,300 acres, **Franklin Mountains State Park** is the largest urban wilderness park in the United States and a favorite destination of El Pasoans looking to hike, bike, or climb. Rugged and speckled by cacti and ocotillo, the mountains are populated by small mammals, birds, reptiles, deer, and the occasional mountain lion. At 7,192 feet, the summit of North Franklin Mountain is about 3,000 feet higher than the city below.

The mountains, the final southern ridge of the geological phenomenon that created the Rockies, are home to about 40 miles of developed hiking and mountain biking trails, with work underway on a trail extension that will link together a 118-mile network by the time you read this. The hikes are primarily moderate to difficult; try the 1.2-mile round-trip to the Aztec Caves or the more difficult 9.2-mile round-trip to the peak of North Franklin Mountain.

If you don't want to break a sweat, take the **Wyler Aerial Tramway** (ℂ **915/566-6622**) to the summit of Ranger Peak ($7 adults, $4 children 12 and under). Beyond the trails and the tram, the park is also a renowned rock-climbing spot and home to an outdoor amphitheater (see "The Performing Arts," later in this chapter).

It takes about 20 minutes to reach the park by car from downtown El Paso. There are numerous primitive campsites, but no water or electricity in the park. Fees are $3 for day use (free to children under 13) and $8 for camping, and the park is open from 8am to 5pm year-round (campers receive a combination to the gate so they can come and go after day-use hours). For more information, contact Franklin Mountains State Park, 1331 McKelligon Canyon Rd., El Paso, TX 79930 (ℂ **915/566-6441**).

Hueco Tanks State Historic Site, located 30 miles northeast of El Paso via U.S. 62/180 and Ranch Road 2775, is another popular rock-climbing destination. It is a world-class bouldering site, among the best on the planet. Centered about three small, rocky outcroppings that loom above the surrounding desert, the park gets its name from the *huecos* (depressions) that catch rainwater and attract life. Many of the rocks are marked by lively pictographs, the work of native tribes over the last 10,000 years. Tours of these fragile sites are offered at 9am and 11am in the summer and 10am and 2pm in the winter; reservations are recommended.

Other than climbing, hiking and camping are popular activities at the park. There are 6½ miles of trails and a campground with 20 back-in sites (3 with water only, 17 with water and electricity) and showers. Campsite availability is dependent on volunteers; call ahead to see if the campground is open. The park charges $4 for day use and $10 to $12 for campsites. Bikes are not permitted. For more information, contact Hueco Tanks State Historic Site, 6900 Hueco Tanks Rd. #1, El Paso, TX 79938 (© **915/857-1135**).

GOLF   The 27-hole **Painted Dunes Desert Golf Course,** located 9 miles northeast of I-10 via U.S. 54 at 12000 McCombs St. (© **915/821-2122**), is one of the top municipal courses in the entire country. Nonresident greens fees range from $32 to $35 and carts are $10. El Paso native Lee Trevino began his illustrious professional golf career at **Emerald Springs Golf and Conference Center,** 20 miles east of town at 16000 Ashford St. (© **915/852-9110**). Greens fees are $29 to $34, cart included. There is also **Ascarate Golf Course** in Ascarate Lake City Park (© **915/772-7381**), with greens fees of $13 to $16 (carts: $10) and **Cielo Vista Golf Course,** 1510 Hawkins Blvd. (© **915/591-4927**), with greens fees of $19 to $24 (carts: $10).

HIKING   The top hiking areas in and around El Paso are at **Franklin Mountains State Park** and **Hueco Tanks State Historic Site** (see above).

HORSEBACK RIDING   **Rio Grande Valley Ranch,** 300 Farm Rd. 259 (© **915/877-4447**), is a full-service equestrian facility, offering trail rides ($15 for an hour), stabling, and riding lessons. Additionally, about 20 miles of horse-friendly trails will open at **Franklin Mountains State Park** (see above) by the time you read this.

MOUNTAIN BIKING   **Franklin Mountains State Park** (see above) is by far the most popular mountain biking destination in the El Paso area. About 20 miles of trails are open to bikers now, and there will be more than 50 miles of bike-accessible trails in the park once a trail extension is completed in 2003.

SPECTATOR SPORTS
BASEBALL   The **El Paso Diablos,** the AA Texas League affiliate of the Arizona Diamondbacks, play an April-to-August schedule at 10,000-seat Cohen Stadium, 9700 Gateway Blvd. N. The stadium is one of the country's more colorful ballparks—sluggers hold out their batting helmets to the crowd for donations after home runs. Single-game tickets are $5 to $7. Call © **915/755-2000** or visit www.diablos.com for schedules.

BASKETBALL   The University of Texas at El Paso (UTEP) fields a Western Athletic Conference (WAC) team, the **Miners,** that plays from December to March at the Don Haskins Center, 2801 N. Mesa St. Tickets range from $5 to $15 for single games. Call © **915/747-5234** to purchase tickets or for more information.

FOOTBALL   The **UTEP Miners** football squad plays a WAC schedule from September to December on campus at the Sun Bowl. Single-game tickets are $6 to $15. Also, the stadium hosts the second-oldest New Year's bowl game in the nation. Call © **915/747-5234** for schedules or to purchase tickets.

Fun Fact
El Paso is the most populous American city that is not home to a major-league sports franchise (MLB, NHL, NFL, or NBA).

HOCKEY The **El Paso Buzzards** (www.elpasobuzzards.com) compete in the Western Professional Hockey League, winning the league's first two titles in the late '90s. The schedule runs from October to March with single-game tickets from $8 to $15. The team's home ice is at the El Paso County Coliseum, 4100 E. Paisano Dr. Call ✆ **915/533-7825** for tickets.

HORSE RACING There are live horse races just outside of western El Paso (actually in New Mexico) at **Sunland Park Racetrack and Casino,** 1200 Futurity Dr. (✆ **505/874-5200**). The racing season runs from November to April (simulcast racing from around the country is featured year-round). There are also three restaurants, five lounges, and a casino with 300 slot machines.

RODEO The **PRCA Southwestern International Livestock Show and Rodeo** is held every February at the El Paso County Coliseum, 4100 E. Paisano Dr. Call ✆ **915/532-1401** for schedules and ticket information.

SHOPPING

El Paso's main shopping district is downtown—targeting both Mexican and American shoppers—and there are several enclosed malls scattered around the city. The area is known for Western wear, Southwestern art, and Mexican imports.

The three-story **Galeria San Ysidro,** 801 Texas Ave. (✆ **915/544-4444**), is more than just an antiques store, housing an impressive selection of art, furniture, and decor from all over the world. Renowned for the talent that it represents, **Adair Margo Gallery,** 415 E. Yandell Dr. (✆ **915/533-0048**), specializes in sculpture and paintings by local and regional artists, including Tom Lea and James Magee. **Cowtown Boots,** 11451 Gateway West (✆ **915/593-2929**), claims to be the world's largest Western wear store, with 40,000 square feet of boots (alligator to ostrich), jeans, clothing, and accessories. For tongue-searing delicacies, we love the **El Paso Chile Company,** 1909 Texas Ave. (✆ **888/4-SALSAS** or 915/544-3434) for its sauces (with fiery names like "Hellfire & Damnation") and all things spicy.

The top shopping center is **Sunland Park Mall,** 750 Sunland Park Dr. (✆ **915/833-5595**), anchored by Dillard's, Sears, and Mervyn's. Located where Pancho Villa and General Pershing once negotiated, **Placita Santa Fe,** 5034 Doniphan Rd., features 20 quaint shops, specializing in art, designer clothing, antiques, and jewelry.

WHERE TO STAY

You'll find a plethora of hotels and motels in El Paso, but little in the way of B&Bs and resorts. Most of the accommodations are chain franchises, with a few exceptions, located either near the airport or adjacent to I-10. The city's room taxes add about 14% to lodging bills.

In addition to the properties described below, there are numerous hotels and motels located off I-10 near El Paso International Airport, including **Best Western Airport Inn,** 7144 Gateway East (✆ 800/295-7276 or 915/779-7700); **Comfort Inn,** 900 Yarbrough Dr. (✆ 800/228-5150 or 915/594-9111); and the **El Paso Airport Hilton,** 2027 Airway Blvd. (✆ 800/742-7248 or 915/778-4241). Downtown, there is the **Travelodge City Center** at 409 E. Missouri St. (✆ 800/578-7878 or 915/544-3333). In the Sunland Park area, the pick of the litter is the **Holiday Inn Sunland Park,** 900 Sunland Park Dr. (✆ 800/678-2744 or 915/833-2900).

EXPENSIVE

Camino Real Hotel ★★   El Paso's finest hotel—and one of a handful down-town—is the only Camino Real hotel or resort outside of Mexico. However, it's just 6 blocks north of the border, adjacent to the El Paso Convention and Performing Arts Center and within easy walking distance of all of the downtown attractions. Listed on the National Register of Historic Places, the hotel effort-lessly meshes El Paso's past and present.

Formerly known as the Hotel Paso del Norte, the property first opened in 1912, awing guests with its lavish marble and cherrywood lobby under a stun-ning glass dome from Tiffany's in New York. While the dome remains in place, almost everything else has changed in the time since as a result of numerous ren-ovations. In 1986, a modern 17-story tower was built next to the old Paso del Norte, expanding the lobby and more than doubling the hotel's capacity.

Tastefully decorated with reproductions and contemporary furnishings, the oversized rooms have two doubles, two queens, or one king-size bed, the decor punctuated by massive mirrored armoires and great views of downtown. The selection is rounded out by a wide variety of elegant suites with Victorian and Southwestern motifs.

101 S. El Paso St., El Paso, TX 79901. (℃ **800/722-6466** or 915/534-3000. Fax 915/534-3024. www.camino real.com. 359 units. $99–$150 double; $160–$990 suite. AE, DC, DISC, MC, V. Underground parking $5 daily. **Amenities:** 3 restaurants; bar; outdoor heated pool; exercise room; sauna; concierge; courtesy car; business center; 24-hr. room service. *In room:* A/C, TV w/pay movies, dataport, coffeemaker, hair dryer, iron.

El Paso Marriott ★   After a major renovation in 2000, this modern chain property is a solid lodging option for those flying in or out of El Paso. The lobby, centered about a large comfortable seating area, was stylishly refurbished in the renovation, not to mention the thick-walled rooms, which are reliable and con-temporary, embellished with a nice range of amenities. The place is aimed at the business traveler, but it more than fills the needs of tourists and it's a bargain on the weekend.

1600 Airway Blvd. (¼ mile south of El Paso International Airport), El Paso, TX 79925. (℃ **800/228-9290** or 915/779-3300. Fax 915/779-4591. 296 units. $149–$169 double ($69–$79 on weekends); $300 suite. AE, DC, DISC, MC, V. **Amenities:** Restaurant; bar; 2 pools (1 indoor, 1 outdoor); exercise room; fitness center; Jacuzzi; sauna; concierge; courtesy car; business center; limited room service; coin-op laundry and laundry service; dry cleaning; executive level. *In room:* A/C, TV w/pay movies, coffeemaker, hair dryer, iron.

MODERATE

Cliff Inn *Finds*   Located on the slope of the Franklin Mountains above downtown El Paso, the Cliff Inn is an unusual midpriced hotel with a distinct personality of its own. From the entrance, shaded by palm trees, to the Art Deco interior, almost everything here veers off the traditional path. The tiled lobby, elegant with a touch of eclectic kitsch, is brimming with antiques, tapestries, and furnishings from all over the world. The halls, adorned with murals of a hedge-maze with topiary sculptures, lead to the rooms, which are comfortable and well maintained, albeit a bit dated. Some of the rooms have kitchenettes and great city views.

1600 Cliff Dr. (adjacent to the El Paso Medical Center), El Paso, TX 79902. (℃ **800/333-2543** or 915/ 533-6700. Fax 915/544-2127. 80 units. $60 double; $60–$80 suite. Rates include continental breakfast. AE, DC, DISC, MC, V. **Amenities:** Restaurant; bar; concierge; courtesy car; limited room service. *In room:* A/C, TV w/pay movies, kitchenette in some units, fridge, coffeemaker, hair dryer, iron, safe.

Sunset Heights Bed & Breakfast Inn   Named for the historic district in which it resides, Sunset Heights is El Paso's only B&B, a stately three-story Victorian inn shaded by palm trees and guarded by wrought iron fencing.

Beyond the rich parlor (stained glass, crystal chandeliers), the guest rooms are comfortable and romantic, with natural woods accented by a red-and-blue color scheme and period furnishings. The Oriental Room, with a private balcony, claw-foot tub, and city view, is our pick, but every choice has its merits. The crowning touches: the backyard, with a nice pool surrounded by gardens; and breakfast, multiple-course events with a regional flair.

717 W. Yandell Ave., El Paso, TX 79902. ⓒ 800/767-8513 or 915/544-1743. Fax 915/544-5119. 4 units, including 1 suite. $75–$120 double; $165–$200 suite. Rates include full breakfast. AE, DISC, MC, V. **Amenities:** Outdoor pool; Jacuzzi. In room: A/C, TV, no phone.

Travelodge Hotel—La Hacienda Airport ⭐ *Kids* *Value* Some roadside motels surprise you with their attention to detail—this is definitely one of them. Situated northeast of downtown off busy Montana Avenue, the grounds here are a world apart, centered about a shady courtyard surrounding a heated pool. The rooms are housed in 10 different brick buildings, with exterior entry through hand-painted wooden doors. Some of the accommodations in the older buildings are on the small side, albeit well maintained and comfortable, while the larger rooms in the newer structures are a notch above the norm, with blue-and-white decor and exposed wooden-beamed ceilings. We like the eight Jacuzzi rooms, featuring a picture window that separates the tub from the bedroom, and the family suites, amusingly decorated with plenty of room.

6400 Montana Ave., El Paso, TX 79925. ⓒ 800/772-4231 or 915/772-4231. Fax 915/779-2918. www. the.travelodge.com/elpaso05473. 91 units. $49–$62 double; $85 suite; $75 Jacuzzi room. Rates include continental breakfast. AE, DC, DISC, MC, V. Pets accepted with $10/night fee. **Amenities:** Restaurant; bar; outdoor heated pool; exercise room; business center; limited room service. In room: A/C, TV w/pay movies, dataport, fridge, coffeemaker, hair dryer, iron, safe.

INEXPENSIVE

Gardner Hotel/El Paso International Youth Hostel *Value* A downtown mainstay since 1922, the Gardner Hotel has a storied history—infamous gangster John Dillinger stayed here in the 1930s while on the run. The public areas are well kept, especially the attractive lobby, which has been restored to its original condition with a marble staircase, mauve carpeting, and historic photographs. There are two shared hostel rooms—one for males and one for females—each with two bunk beds and desks. There is also a wide range of private accommodations—some with no frills, some with the original antique furnishings. Hostel guests share bathrooms and an equipped kitchen, and also have access to a television, pool table, and a pay Internet kiosk. The private rooms have private bathrooms.

311 E. Franklin St., El Paso, TX 79901. ⓒ 915/532-3661. www.gardnerhotel.com. 50 units. $15 dormitory bunk (plus a one-time linen fee of $2); $20–$64 private rooms. MC, V. In room: A/C.

CAMPING

Several primitive campsites are available at Franklin Mountains State Park, and there are also tent and RV sites at Hueco Tanks State Historic Site; see "Outdoor Activities," above.

El Paso–West RV Park Located just west of the Texas–New Mexico state line, this clean campground is nicely treed (for the desert, that is), with laundry facilities, a dump station, handicap-accessible showers, and a small store with groceries and RV supplies. An 18-hole golf course is located right across the street.

1415 Anthony Dr., Anthony, NM 88021. ⓒ 800/754-1543 for reservations or 505/882-7172. 100 sites with full hookups, including 70 pull-throughs. $20 nightly. MC, V. 10 miles west of El Paso city limits (I-10, Exit 162 in New Mexico).

WHERE TO DINE

Note: In 2002, a smoking ban went into effect for all of El Paso's restaurants and bars.

VERY EXPENSIVE

Café Central ★★ CONTEMPORARY ECLECTIC   Worth the splurge, Café Central is an anomaly in a town dominated by Tex-Mex: a sleek urban bistro serving sophisticated international cuisine. There are three seating areas—a gracious dining room, a lounge with jet-black tables and faux leopard skin chairs, and a breezy patio out front. The menu changes daily, but always offers a wide range of standout fare (most notably the creative Southwestern interpretations of traditional continental dishes). On a given night, you might start with Dos Equis steamed clams with tomatoes, garlic, jalapeños, and cilantro; follow with a cup of cream of green chile soup; and then enjoy a tantalizing main course of sautéed calamari and shellfish on a capellini bed; a grilled white veal chop with a revelation of a side dish in the green chile risotto; or possibly luscious guyamas shrimp with a zesty tequila-cilantro sauce. The wine list is one of the city's best, with nearly 300 bottles, and the desserts include the best *leches* (Mexican milk cakes) in all of Texas.

109 N. Oregon St., in the lobby of the Texas Tower (One Texas Court). © 915/545-2233. Reservations recommended. Main courses $7–$28 lunch, $13–$35 dinner. AE, DC, DISC, MC, V. Mon–Thurs 11:30am–10pm; Fri–Sat 11:30am–11pm. Closed major holidays.

Dome Restaurant ★★ CONTINENTAL   In a room adjacent to the lavish Tiffany dome in downtown's Camino Real Hotel (p. 327), the Dome Restaurant is as highly regarded for its sumptuous dinners as it is for its regal atmosphere—replete with European chandeliers, marble floors, and meticulous table settings. The offerings begin with classic appetizers (including top-notch escargots) and continue with gourmet soups and salads. The creative entrees, however, are the main attraction: You'll be hard pressed to find another El Paso menu with duck (with tequila-chile-cactus coulis), veal osso buco, and grilled rack of lamb every night. Many of the dishes draw from regional influences; however, the chefs are not constrained by any one school of cuisine.

101 S. El Paso St., in the Camino Real Hotel. © 915/534-3000, ext. 3010. Reservations recommended. Main courses $17–$29. AE, DC, DISC, MC, V. Mon–Thurs 6–10:30pm; Fri–Sat 5:30–11pm.

EXPENSIVE

Indian Cliffs Ranch Cattleman's Steakhouse ★ *Kids* STEAKS   Established in 1973, this steakhouse feels like a city unto itself, a desert outpost dedicated to the consumption of enormous cuts of beef. In the main building, there are seven themed dining rooms—ranging from tropical to the kitschy to the authentically Western—as well as a patio with a spectacular view of nearby Sand Cliff Lake. Also on the property: a mini-zoo with goats, ostrich, buffalo, and a rattlesnake pit; a movie set used by several Hollywood productions; and a pair of children's play areas. With all of the activity, it's a surprise the food ever gets any notice, but the thick, flavorful steaks here are tough to top. Perpetually voted the best in the El Paso area, they range in size from the 6-ounce Lady's Filet to the hearty-beyond-belief Cowboy, a 2-pound porterhouse. There are also barbecue and seafood dishes, but if you're a vegetarian, you're out of luck.

Fabens Rd., 5 miles north of I-10, Exit 49 (29 miles east of El Paso via I-10 and Fabens Rd.). © 915/544-3200. Reservations not accepted. Main courses $8–$26. AE, DC, DISC, MC, V. Mon–Fri 5–10pm; Sat 4–10pm; Sun noon–9pm.

MODERATE

La Hacienda *Overrated* MEXICAN A Rio Grande institution since 1940—located on the spot where conquistador Don Juan de Oñate first crossed the river in 1598—La Hacienda serves up respectable tacos *carne asada,* chiles rellenos, and chicken mole. Colorfully decorated with longhorn skulls, hand-painted chairs, and a stained-glass portrait of Pancho Villa, the restaurant features three seating areas: an airy dining room, a festive cantina with wrought-iron barstools, and a patio with a view of Ciudad Juárez across the river. Although it's popular, the place has a bit of a manufactured feel, and the food and the margaritas are just average in comparison with some of the more authentic, *familia*-owned restaurants in town.

1720 W. Paisano Dr. ℂ 915/533-1919. Main courses $6–$13. AE, DISC, MC, V. Mon–Thurs 11am–9pm; Fri–Sat 11am–10pm; Sun 11am–8:30pm (bar open later).

The State Line BARBECUE So named because it straddles the Texas–New Mexico border, the State Line is where El Paso heads for barbecue, and with good reason. The platters of delectable slow-cooked barbecue—ribs, beef, pork, chicken, sausage, and turkey, all served with potato salad, coleslaw, and baked beans—make for a sure cure for hunger. Expect a heavy dose of nostalgia with your meal, in the form of an antique "love tester" and weathered wooden walls plastered with collages of RC Cola ads, cigar box covers, and apple crate labels. There are also "Blue Plate Specials" with steak or seafood, a couple of all-you-can-eat options, and sandwiches at lunch.

1222 Sunland Park Dr. ℂ 915/581-3371. Reservations accepted for large parties only. Main courses $5–$21 lunch, $10–$21 dinner. AE, DISC, MC, V. Summer daily 11:30am–10pm; winter daily 11:30am–9:30pm.

INEXPENSIVE

Beyond the options listed below, you can't go wrong grabbing a quick breakfast or lunch at **Cacique,** at the Tigua Cultural Center on the El Paso Mission Trail (p. 316–317), 305 Ya Ya Lane (ℂ **915/859-5287**). Taking its cues from native tradition, this colorful diner dishes out a terrific red chile stew and standout breakfast burritos stuffed with peppers, eggs, cheese, and potatoes. For coffee or a plump sandwich, hit the Seattle-themed **Pike Street Market,** 207 Mills St. (ℂ **915/545-1010**), a downtown hangout popular with suits and slackers alike.

H&H Car Wash and Coffee Shop ★ *Finds* TEX-MEX/COFFEE SHOP A dinky coffee shop straight out of the 1960s, the H&H is a bit weathered, noisy, and not much to look at. It doesn't matter—the place is home to some of the best inexpensive Tex-Mex in town. The place is packed with locals from open to close, scarfing down specialties like *carne picada* (diced sirloin with jalapeños, tomatoes, and onions), huevos rancheros, and chiles rellenos. Proprietor Kenneth Haddad does one heck of a job, using only the freshest ingredients and sticking with tradition. For hungry road-trippers with dirty cars and tight budgets, you can't get any more convenient than the H&H: Gas up, get your car washed, and have a bite to eat, all in one fell swoop. The car wash operates from 9am to 5pm during the week and from 9am to 3pm on Saturdays, charging $10 to $15 for a complete hand cleaning, inside and out.

701 E. Yandell Dr. at Ochoa St. ℂ 915/533-1144. Reservations not accepted. Main courses $4–$7. AE, DISC, MC, V. Mon–Sat 7:30am–3pm.

L&J Café ★★ TEX-MEX Nicknamed "The Old Place by the Graveyard" because of its proximity to the Concordia Cemetery (p. 322), the L&J has been an El Paso landmark since it first opened its doors in 1927, and the rowdy bar and the checkerboard-floored dining room are both now legendary. For Tex-Mex fanatics like us, the chicken enchiladas, overflowing with fluffy meat and buried under chunky green chile and Jack cheese, approach perfection. Fiery and addictive, the chile con queso and *caldillo* (spicy and strong beef and potato stew with a green chile and garlic kick) are as good as you'll find anywhere. There are also healthy versions of many entrees, prepared with less cheese and tortillas that aren't fried. It doesn't hurt that the salsa is spicy, the beer is cold, and the service is quick and friendly, even when the place is filled to capacity—as it is most of the time.

3622 E. Missouri St. (✆ **915/566-8418.** Reservations not accepted. Main courses $5–$10. AE, DC, DISC, MC, V. Mon–Fri 10am–8pm; Sat 10am–6pm (bar open later).

EL PASO AFTER DARK

El Paso's entertainment scene is spread throughout the city, and remarkably diverse. The El Paso Performing Arts Center, the McKelligon Canyon Amphitheatre, the outdoor and indoor stages at Chamizal National Memorial, and the facilities at University of Texas at El Paso all host regular performances. Fans of rock, country, Tejano, and jazz will likely find what they're looking for at the city's bars and clubs.

The free, monthly *El Paso Scene* and its online counterpart, **www.epscene.com**, are the best places to start for exploring arts-and-entertainment opportunities. The Friday *El Paso Times* also features performance listings, as does *The Prospector*, UTEP's student newspaper. Tickets for many events are available through **Ticketmaster** (✆ **915/544-8444;** www.ticketmaster.com).

THE PERFORMING ARTS

El Paso Opera, 1035 Belvidere St., Suite 100 (✆ **915/581-5534;** www.epopera.org) produces spring and fall shows annually, with a Thursday and Saturday performance of each held at the El Paso Performing Arts Center. Spanish and English subtitles are projected for every performance. Tickets run $10 to $70 for a single event. **El Paso Pro-Musica,** 6557 N. Mesa St. (✆ **915/833-9400;** www.elpasopromusica.org) presents several concerts a year, including the El Paso Chamber Music Festival every January. Concerts are held at the First Baptist Church, 805 Montana Ave., and the Fox Fine Arts Center on the campus of UTEP, with ticket prices of $10 to $20. **El Paso Symphony Orchestra,** 1 Civic Center Plaza (✆ **915/535-3776;** www.epso.org), puts on about a dozen different concerts annually. Most events are held at the El Paso Performing Arts Center. Tickets for single performances are $7.50 to $25, with discounts for children and seniors.

At Franklin Mountains State Park, the outdoor **McKelligon Canyon Theatre,** 2 McKelligon Canyon Rd. (✆ **800/915-8482** or 915/565-6900; www.viva-ep.org) annually wows audiences with two excellent productions. Thursday through Sunday in September, **Shakespeare on the Rocks** features a dozen outdoor performances of four Shakespeare plays. There are Renaissance-style dinners before the 8pm shows, and tickets range from $16 to $22 with dinner and $5 to $14 without. From late May to late August, **Viva! El Paso** takes over. One of the nation's best-attended outdoor dramas, performances are held Thursday through Saturday at 8pm, integrating dance, music, and costumes from Spanish, Mexican, and American Indian cultures in telling El Paso's 400-year history. Barbecue dinners are served at 6:30pm before each performance; tickets run $16 to $26 for adults with dinner ($11–$16 for children), $8 to $19 for adults without dinner ($6–$13 children).

The **El Paso Playhouse,** 2501 Montana Ave. (© **915/532-1317;** www.elpaso playhouse.org) stages a new production almost every month. There's also a children's company, Kids-N-Co., which produces timeless fairy tales and other light fare. Tickets are usually under $10. The **University of Texas–El Paso Dinner Theatre,** Union Ballroom on the UTEP campus (© **915/747-6060** or 915/747-5234; www.utep.edu/udt) is a tradition, producing student musicals since 1983. Today, the theater presents plays Wednesday through Sunday at 7pm during the school year. Dinner might include prime rib, baked potato, and a cookie sundae. Recent productions have included *Chicago, Victor/Victoria,* and the Who's *Tommy.* Tickets run about $28, except for Sunday matinees (2:30pm), which are around $15, but don't include dinner.

THE CLUB & LIVE MUSIC SCENE
Going strong for more than a decade, **Club 101,** 500 San Francisco St. (© **915/ 544-2101**), is a downtown alternative hotspot featuring DJs and local and national rock acts. **Stampede,** 5500 Doniphan Rd. (© **915/833-6397**), is an El Paso country-and-western institution that features recorded and live music Thursday through Saturday. **Xcape,** 209 S. El Paso St. (© **915/542-3800**), caters to the young and hip with shows ranging from Latin to techno. Located in a century-old theater renovated for the new millennium, it's open Friday and Saturday.

THE BAR SCENE
Serving cayenne-spiced Cajun dishes and daily $1 beer specials, **Crawdaddy's,** 212 Cincinnati St. (© **915/533-9332**), is a cozy-but-rowdy haunt favored by the UTEP crowd. It's located amid a strip of bars and restaurants on Cincinnati Street, one of the city's livelier blocks at midnight. One of the most regal places in the Southwest to sip a cocktail, **Dome Bar,** 101 S. El Paso St. in the Camino Real Hotel (© **915/722-6466**), is light years beyond a typical hotel bar. **Wildhare's Booze & Adventure,** 4025 N. Mesa St. (© **915/532-3589**), is a west-side standby that attracts a young, energetic crowd with its live rock and blues shows. It features Shiner Bock on tap and touts its Bloody Marys as the best in town.

A SIDE TRIP TO CIUDAD JUAREZ
El Paso's sister city, Ciudad Juárez, is the fourth-largest city in Mexico with approximately 1.7 million residents. Together, the cities form the largest binational population in the world. Juárez is a regional manufacturing center, due to cheap, abundant labor, and companies like General Motors and Sony have facilities in the city. Juárez is seedy in the same way as other border cities like Nogales and Tijuana, but it is more of a real Mexican city, not one that is built on tourism alone. Juárez's history and authenticity, in our opinion, make it an interesting stop for an afternoon, or even an entire day. If you're headed specifically to Marfa or Big Bend, however, it probably isn't worth the diversion, but for those who have more of an interest in Mexican culture and history, it definitely merits a stop.

Like El Paso, Juárez's modern history begins with Spanish conquistador Juan de Oñate crossing the Rio Grande in 1581. The oldest structure on the border, La Misíon de Nuestra Señora Guadalupe (Our Lady of Guadalupe Mission), was completed in 1668 and remains in remarkably good condition today. The city played important roles in the Mexican-American War and the Mexican Revolution, and was once frequented by Pancho Villa.

Today, the city's booming manufacturing industry is complemented by tourism, with many visitors crossing the border to take in the colorful outdoor

Tips **A Note About Safety**

Although most visitors to Juárez have an enjoyable time without incident, the city sees more than its fair share of drug trafficking, pickpocketing, and gang violence. The recent gruesome discovery of mass graves filled with female factory workers was especially disconcerting; tourists have not been targeted by violence, but are commonly the victims of theft. It is especially important to remain aware of your surroundings when visiting the city.

markets, historic missions, and lively nightlife. Tourists often drive across the five bridges scattered around El Paso, park in downtown El Paso and walk across, or else take a taxi or a trolley tour. The bridges, aside from the "Free Bridge" (or Cordova Bridge) south of I-10 via U.S. 54, all charge nominal tolls, even to pedestrians, of 25¢ to $2. The most convenient points of entry are the two downtown bridges, at Stanton Street and Santa Fe Street. U.S. currency is welcome practically everywhere in Juárez.

ESSENTIALS

VISITOR INFORMATION Contact **Fiprotur Chihuahua,** Ave. de las Americas No. 2551, Ciudad Juárez, Chihuahua, Mexico (© **888/654-0394** or 011-52/16-11-31-74). The **El Paso Convention & Visitors Bureau,** One Civic Center Plaza, El Paso, TX 79901 (© **800/351-6024** or 915/534-0692) can also provide information and advice on trips across the border. If you're on foot, pick up the excellent *Downtown Historic Walking Tour of Juárez* brochure.

TROLLEY TOURS We strongly recommend taking one of the tours offered by the **El Paso–Juárez Trolley Company** (© **915/544-0061;** www.border jumper.com). Riders board in front of the El Paso Convention and Performing Arts Center downtown and can leave the train to shop or eat at any of eight different stops, then catch another trolley later in the day to return to El Paso. The trolleys run daily from 10am to 4pm year-round. Tickets cost $13 for adults, $9 for children ages 4 to 12, and free for kids under 4.

WHAT TO SEE & DO

See the "El Paso" map on p. 316 to locate these attractions.

The Top Attractions

Juárez Museum of Art This contemporary, cone-shaped concrete structure is a worthwhile stop for people particularly interested in Mexican art, but its location begs for a visit via trolley. The museum has three main galleries, with the main gallery surrounded by a moat and connected to the others via bridges, and visitors should expect to spend a little less than an hour exploring them. Exhibits change about six times annually, and include historic and contemporary pieces by local artists with a special emphasis on plastic arts.

Ave. Lincoln and Ave. Ignacio Mejia, in the PRONAF Center area. © **011-52/16-13-17-08.** Tues–Sun 11am–7pm. Admission 75¢.

La Misíon de Nuestra Señora Guadalupe Originally built between 1662 and 1668 by Mexican, Spanish, and Indian labor, this is the oldest surviving church in the area and remains an active chapel today. It is considered a prime example of Indian baroque architecture, influenced by Arab tradition, and is

The Copper Canyon

El Paso is often a jumping-off point for trips to the Copper Canyon in northwestern Mexico. If you are interested in seeing a rugged and beautiful land; if you're interested in taking one of the most remarkable train trips in the world; if you're interested in hiking or riding horseback through remote areas to see an astonishing variety of flora and fauna; or if you're curious about a land still populated by indigenous people living pretty much the way they have for centuries, the Copper Canyon is the place to go.

Most often, when people say "Copper Canyon," they are referring to a section of the Sierra Madre known commonly in Mexico as the Sierra Tarahumara (after the Indians who live there). The area was formed through violent volcanic uplifting, followed by a slow, quiet process of erosion that carved a vast network of canyons into the soft volcanic stone.

Crossing the Sierra Tarahumara is the famed **Chihuahua al Pacífico (Chihuahua to the Pacific)** railway. Acclaimed as an engineering marvel, the 390-mile railroad has 39 bridges (the highest is more than 1,000 ft. above the Chinipas River) and 86 tunnels. It climbs from Los Mochis, at sea level, up nearly 8,000 feet through some of Mexico's most magnificent scenery—thick pine forests, jagged peaks, and shadowy canyons—before descending again to its destination, the city of Chihuahua.

It's easier than ever to get to the region, but it's trickier than ever to travel through it on your own—hotel rooms can be hard to come by,

adorned with 18th-century sculptures and oil paintings. Next door is a contemporary cathedral; behind the mission is a bronze statue of the founder, Fray Garcia of San Francisco.

Ave. 16th de Septiembre, 2 blocks west of Ave. Juárez.

Monumental Bullring At Mexico's fourth-largest bullring (with 17,000 seats), the traditional bloody spectacles are held April through September. Each match lasts about 2 hours. The crowd is mostly locals, with pockets of El Pasoans, students, and tourists. It's not a particularly rowdy event—there is more of an air of tradition.

Paseo Triunfo de la Republica #4630. (C) **011-52/16-13-11-82** or 011-52/16-13-16-56. Bullfights are held sporadically on Sun in spring and summer. Tickets $4–$25.

Shopping

Browsing the outdoor markets and specialty stores in Juárez is a favorite pastime of the city's visitors.

Prices are rock bottom for the usual Mexican knickknacks—tapestries, sculptures, and souvenirs—and a bit less than their U.S. counterparts for liquor and food. I personally bought a hand painted plaster of Paris bust of Elvis here are $14. (I don't know if you'd considered that a good deal, but I thought it was outstanding.) Bargaining is part of the game at almost every shop in Juárez—it's not bad form to haggle at all. The markets are open daily from morning to evening, but exact hours are up to individual shopkeepers.

and there have been numerous changes in the operation of the Copper Canyon train. Consequently, this is not the place to do casual, follow-your-nose traveling. A number of tour operators and packagers book trips to the Copper Canyon. The easiest thing is to contract with an agency that will plan your trip from El Paso. **Southwest Shuttle & Tours** (© 800/605-1257; www.tourcoppercanyon.com) sets up trips for any number of people using regular bus service and the Copper Canyon train. Or, you can take a bus to Chihuahua and contact a travel agency there that will book a trip into the canyon. This would be the cheapest and most flexible way to do it. I recommend **Turismo al Mar** (© 614/410-9232, dial 001-52 from the U.S.; www.copper-canyon.net).

Another option is to go with a custom tour operator; travel through these companies generally allows you more time in the canyon and a better experience. The best of the bunch is **Columbus Travel** (© 800/843-1060; www.canyontravel.com), which is pretty much in a class by itself. It has lined up some beautiful small lodges in the canyons and staffed them with talented local guides. Another operator that provides good service is the El Paso–based **Native Trails** (© 800/884-3107; www.nativetrails.com).

For more information on traveling in the Copper Canyon, pickup a copy of *Frommer's Mexico.*

—*David Baird*

The **Juárez City Market,** at Agustin Melgar Street and Avenida 16th de Septiembre, is a fun—although not particularly upscale—shopping spot. The two-story building is loaded with an endless array of velvet paintings, plaster of Paris statues, jewelry, and other standard-issue Mexican souvenirs. If your tastes tend towards posh, try **Decor,** at the intersection of Avenida Ignacio Mejia and Avenida Lincoln, a three-story retail standout chock-full of furniture, glass, ceramics, and jewelry. Other popular shopping spots include the **duty-free stores** at Avenida Juárez #378 and Avenida 16th de Septiembre #531 for liquor, porcelain, crystal, and perfumes; and **Avenida Juárez,** just south of the Santa Fe Street Bridge, lined with street merchants, souvenir shops, and pharmacies.

WHERE TO DINE

Our tried-and-true pick is Nuevo Martino (see below), but **Los Arcos,** Avenida las Americas (© 011-52/16-16-69-35), offers a solid selection of Baja-style seafood dishes, and **Ajuua!,** 162 N. Efren Ornelas, (© 011-52/16-29-01-56) is a festive eatery serving in authentic Mexican cuisine.

Nuevo Martino ⭐ CONTINENTAL/MEXICAN   The atmosphere is thick at Nuevo Martino, straight from the jet-set days of the 1940s. A favorite of tourists and well-heeled locals, this intimate downtown cafe is dimly lit with red leather booths, a fully stocked bar, and mirrored walls. White-jacketed waiters serve a full Continental menu, with dishes ranging from quail to octopus to chateaubriand (prepared table side), as well as a selection of authentic Mexican entrees. Our favorites: the filet *tampiqueño,* a tender cut of beef covered with green chiles and soft Jack cheese, served with soup, salad, beans, tacos, and an enchilada; and the black bass medallions Mexicana with mini-spuds in a rich and spicy red pepper sauce. The prices beat what you'll find north of the border, and the potent margaritas are not to be missed.

Ave. Juárez #643. © **011-52/12-33-70**. Main courses $10–$20. MC, V. Sun and Tues–Thurs noon–11pm; Fri–Sat 11am–midnight.

CIUDAD JUAREZ AFTER DARK

Juárez is a popular after-dark destination for El Pasoans, and there are numerous bars geared toward tourists on Avenida Juárez downtown and, to the east, Avenida Lincoln. Many of the bars are actually strip clubs, although there are sports bars and nightclubs as well. The can't-miss nightspot is the **Kentucky Club,** 629 Av. Juárez, swank in a Juárez sort of way. You can't do any better if you're looking to spend an afternoon over margaritas—legend has it that the drink was invented here in 1946 by an elderly gent who still tends the bar. And Hollywood types once frequented this bar: Marilyn Monroe bought the bar a round after a quickie divorce from Arthur Miller.

2 Small Towns of Central West Texas ⟨★⟩

Travelers crossing West Texas pass through a smattering of communities where they'll find a variety of roadside motels and restaurants. But those who only grab some Zs or a quick bite to eat will be missing out on some fun things to see and do. While most of the areas discussed in this section would not be our choice as a vacation destination in and of themselves, they are definitely worth a stop, and one could easily spend anywhere from a few hours to a few days in each place.

FORT DAVIS & DAVIS MOUNTAINS STATE PARK

205 miles SE of El Paso; 23 miles NE of Alpine; 110 miles NW of Big Bend National Park

A charming small town surrounded by dramatic scenery and steeped in Old West lore, Fort Davis is one of those rare places that can please both city and country types. The town itself is teeming with boutiques and B&Bs, and to the north, outdoors buffs will appreciate Davis Mountains State Park.

The town's origins are tied to Fort Davis, the identically named U.S. Army post that was active beginning in 1854. The town was initially a ranching center, but the 1891 abandonment of the fort and the railroads' decision to bypass the community led to an economic bust. Many plans to turn the town into a tourist destination failed in the first half of the 20th century, but, after the fort was designated a National Historic Site in 1961, traffic increased and helped create the tourism-heavy landscape in place today.

ESSENTIALS
Getting There

Fort Davis is located on Tex. 17 between Balmorhea and Marfa. From the north, the town is accessed via I-10 by taking either Exit 192 or Exit 206 and driving south on the highway for about 40 miles. Tex. 118 also runs through the town, from Kent (on I-10) to the northwest and to Alpine to the southeast. The nearest major commercial airports are 170 miles north in Midland and 205 miles to the northwest in El Paso.

Getting Around

Fort Davis is centered on the town square and historic courthouse. Most of the businesses, lodging establishments, and restaurants are located on **Main Street**

(**Tex. 118**), which runs north-south through the town square. You can stroll around town, but not to any of the attractions discussed below.

Visitor Information

The **Fort Davis Chamber of Commerce,** 4 Memorial Square (Box 378), Fort Davis, TX 79734 (© **800/524-3015** or 915/426-3015; www.fortdavis.com) provides brochures, advice, and other information.

FAST FACTS   **Big Bend Regional Medical Center,** 2600 Tex. 118 North in Alpine (© **915/837-3447**) has 24-hour emergency services. The **post office,** located on the town square on Main Street, is open Monday through Friday from 8am to 4pm.

WHAT TO SEE & DO
The Top Attractions

Fort Davis National Historic Site ⭐   One of the best remaining examples of a frontier military post, Fort Davis was established in 1854, named after then-secretary of war Jefferson Davis. Surrounded by geological formations that offered natural defense as well as beauty, six companies of the Eighth U.S. Infantry first occupied the fort to battle hostile Comanches, Kiowas, and Apaches. Confederate soldiers then commandeered the fort in 1861, only to be forced out by Union forces the following year. The fort sat vacant until 1867, when it rose again as a stronghold in the Indian wars of the late 19th century, pitting the African-American 10th U.S. Cavalry and other soldiers against the Apaches. It was abandoned once and for all in 1891. Ten structures have since been restored for public display (five are furnished with period antiques). Most of the Texas forts are either run-down or sitting in the middle of a barren plain, so this one—well manicured with a stunning rocky backdrop—is a standout. Expect to spend a little more than an hour if you tour all 10 structures.

Tex. 17/118, 1 mile north of Fort Davis. © 915/426-3224. www.nps.gov/foda. Admission $3 adults, free for children under 17. Memorial Day to Labor Day daily 8am–6pm; rest of year daily 8am–5pm.

McDonald Observatory ⭐ *Kids*   Operated by the University of Texas and free from urban light pollution, McDonald Observatory is one of the word's leading astronomical research facilities. Start at the visitor center and take in the 12-minute orientation video: It will provide you with perspective both historical and interstellar. Guided tours depart the center several times daily and last about an hour. Twice daily, the visitor center hosts solar-viewing activities, where guests can get a glimpse of sunspots, flares, and other solar activity. If your schedule allows, visit during a nighttime "Star Party," held Tuesday, Friday, and Saturday at times determined by the season. These events allow guests to view celestial objects and constellations through the observatory's high-powered telescopes.

Tex. 118 North, 16 miles northwest of Fort Davis. © 877/984-STAR (7827) for recorded information, or 915/426-3640. www.as.utexas.edu. Admission $5 adults, $4 children under 13, $15 maximum per family; guided tours $7 adults, $6 children under 13, $22 maximum per family. Daily 9am–5pm. Guided tours are conducted at 11:30am and 2pm daily.

Outdoor Activities

Fort Davis's outdoor recreation is centered on **Davis Mountains State Park,** located 4 miles northwest of town via Tex. 118 (© **915/426-3337**). The second-highest range in all of Texas, the Davis Mountains reach their pinnacle at the peak of the 8,382-foot Mount Livermore. Hiking is our activity of choice here; try the moderate, 8-mile round-trip that leads to the Fort Davis National

Historic Site. On or off the trails, the park is a great place for wildlife viewing and bird-watching. It's one of the few places in the United States that you might spot a Montezuma quail, and javelinas (the wild boars that roam the Southwest), tarantulas, horned frogs, and pronghorn antelope also live in the park. The entrance fee is $3 for adults, $2 for seniors, and free for children under 13. Campsites run $15 for full hook-ups, $12 for water and electric hook-ups only, and $6 to $8 for tent and primitive sites.

WHERE TO STAY

Fort Davis has a full range of lodging options, from roadside motels to guest ranches to country inns. For those itching for the cowboy lifestyle, mosey on over to the **Prude Guest Ranch,** 6 miles northwest of town on Tex. 118 (© **800/ 458-6232** or 915/426-3502; www.prude-ranch.com), with double rates of $58 to $75. Other options include the **Butterfield Inn,** at State and 7th streets (© **915/ 426-3252**), with quaint cottages for $70 nightly; and the **Fort Davis Motor Inn and RV Park,** on the north side of town on Tex. 17 (© **800/803-2847** or 915/426-2112), with double rates of $55 to $60.

Hotel Limpia ★   Spread out over six historic buildings, the individually decorated rooms at the Hotel Limpia are outfitted with quilted queen-size beds, rocking chairs, and modern bathrooms. The gorgeous 1,100-square-foot master suite in the vine- and stone-clad main building opens from a glassed veranda into a delightful garden area, but if you're looking for privacy, try one of the secluded cottages, located nearly a mile away from the main buildings. (Some of the units have kitchenettes.) There's also a great gift shop with Texas-flavored curios, books, and decor, the county's only bar, and a top restaurant (see "Where to Dine," below).

101 Memorial Square (P.O. Box 1341), Fort Davis, TX 79734. © **800/662-5517** or 915/426-3237. Fax 915/ 426-3983. www.hotellimpia.com. 39 units. $89–$99 double; $109–$190 suite. AE, DISC, MC, V. **Amenities:** Restaurant; bar. *In room:* A/C, TV, kitchenette in some units, hair dryer.

Indian Lodge   Located at the base of a gentle slope adjacent to Davis Mountains State Park, this hotel is actually a state park in and unto itself—Indian Lodge State Park. Built in the 1930s by the Civilian Conservation Corps, Indian Lodge's architects drew inspiration from Indian pueblos, resulting in 18-inch thick adobe walls and thatched viga ceilings fashioned from river cane and wooden beams. The original rooms are decorated the same as the day the place opened—with hand-carved cedar chairs, dressers, and bed frames, all with engraved petroglyphs, as well as decorative fireplaces and ornate stonework. A 1960s-era annex houses 24 motel-style rooms that lack the character of the originals. All of the rooms are set off from a sunny central patio with a wishing well and rock gardens.

Tex. 118 North, at Davis Mountains State Park (P.O. Box 1858), Fort Davis, TX 79734. © **915/426-3254**. Fax 915/ 426-2022. 39 units. $65–$85 double; $90–$100 suite. DISC, MC, V. **Amenities:** Restaurant; outdoor heated pool. *In room:* A/C, TV.

Old Schoolhouse Bed and Breakfast   Situated in a shady grove of 32 pecan trees at the foot of Sleeping Lion Mountain, this B&B served as Fort Davis's schoolhouse from 1904 into the 1930s. It was then a private residence until 1999, when Carla and Steve Kennedy converted it into a charming inn where guests come from Texas's big cities to "decompress." The quaint rooms are scholastically themed: The spacious Reading Room has a king-size bed, a sleeper sofa, and a private entrance; the smaller 'Riting and 'Rithmetic rooms share a bathroom and feature antique furnishings. You won't want to skip the breakfasts here; you'll miss tempting home-cooked entrees like corn tortilla quiche, apple-baked oatmeal, or baked eggs with ham and three cheeses.

401 N. Front St. (P.O. Box 1221), Fort Davis, TX 79734. ℂ 915/426-2050. Fax 915/426-2509. www. schoolhousebnb.com. 3 units, 2 with shared bathroom. $85–$95 double. Rates include full breakfast. MC, V. *In room:* A/C, no phone.

Old Texas Inn ☆   The rooms at this inn are on the second floor of an old-fashioned drug store/gift shop/restaurant on Fort Davis's main drag downtown. With great views from two public balconies and a spacious common room with satellite TV, there are plenty of reasons to leave your room. There are also plenty of reasons not to leave your room: Homey and cozy, they're veritable galleries for local artisans. All of the rooms have handmade quilts on their beds, hardwood floors, handmade lamps, and small private bathrooms with Western touches.

Main St. (P.O. Box 56), Fort Davis, 79734. ℂ 877/426-3784 or 915/426-3118. Fax 915/426-2368. www. oldtexasinn.com. 6 units. $65 double. AE, DISC, MC, V. *In room:* A/C, coffeemaker, hair dryer, iron, no phone.

WHERE TO DINE

If you're looking for a quick bite, your best bet is **Murphy's Pizzeria & Café,** at the junction of Tex. 17 and Tex. 118 on the south end of town (ℂ 915/462-2020), serving up better-than-expected pizzas ($8–$18), as well as pasta, sand-wiches, and salads.

Hotel Limpia Dining Room AMERICAN   With gracious white tables and chairs, floral carpet, and an understated country atmosphere, the Hotel Limpia offers Fort Davis's most intimate dining. You might start your dinner with "Texas Cheesecake," a baked-then-chilled concoction of cheeses with layers of colorful bell peppers, onions, olives, and parsley; then move on to an entree of grilled eggplant, pot roast, or a 12-ounce rib-eye steak; and finish up with a slice of homemade pie or cake. Upstairs, there's Sutler's Club, the only watering hole in the traditionally dry Jeff Davis County. Memberships, which cost $3 for 3 days, are required.

100 State St., in Hotel Limpia. ℂ 915/426-3241. Reservations accepted. Main courses $9–$20. AE, DISC, MC, V. Daily 5:30–9:30pm; brunch Sun 11:30am–2:30pm.

BALMORHEA STATE PARK ☆☆
185 miles E of El Paso; 32 miles N of Fort Davis

One of the lesser-seen jewels of the Texas State Park system (and one of the smallest, at 45 acres), **Balmorhea State Park,** 9207 Tex. 17 South (ℂ 915/375-2370), is centered around a massive, 1.75-acre swimming pool that is fed by San Solomon Springs. It holds 3.5 million gallons of water at a fairly constant 74°F (23°C). Size aside, this is no ordinary pool: Its water teems with fish, its floor laden with rocks. The Civilian Conservation Corps built the V-shaped pool in the 1930s, surrounding it with shady trees and a 200-foot circle of lime-stone and flagstone. Swimming is popular, as are snorkeling and scuba diving. You might see the occasional (nonpoisonous) water snake or turtle in it. A canal system crosscuts the park, leading from the pool to other areas, and providing a habitat for many native fish species, two of which—the Comanche Springs pup-fish and Pecos Gambusia—are endangered. There are changing areas with show-ers and two diving boards at the pool, which is open daily from 8am until a half-hour before sunset. Next door, the **Toyahvale Desert Oasis,** 9225 Tex. 17 South (ℂ 915/375-2572; www.toyahvale.com), provides swimwear, snorkel rentals, and scuba equipment rentals and air fills from 10am to 6pm daily.

A reconstructed *cienega* (desert wetland) is another notable attraction in Balmorhea State Park. Located near the campground, the San Solomon Cienega is a good spot to look for native wildlife: You might see a Texas spiny softshell turtle, a blotched watersnake, or a green heron from the raised wooden platform, or spot a channel catfish through the underwater viewing window. A path system allows viewing of the fish, reptiles, and amphibians in the canals.

The park has 34 campsites (14 pull-through, 14 back-in, and 6 tent sites) with water and electrical hook-ups available, for $8 to $13 a night, in addition to the $3 entrance fee. Additionally, there is a small motel on the park's grounds, with standard double rooms for $50 to $55 and kitchenettes for $60 nightly. For groceries, you'll need to head into town, as the gift shop at the visitor center stocks mainly souvenirs and books. The park is located 5 miles south of the town of Balmorhea on Tex. 17.

MARFA
115 miles NW of Big Bend National Park; 193 miles SE of El Paso; 21 miles S of Fort Davis

Named after a character in Dostoevski's *The Brothers Karamazov* by a railroad exec's wife, this town of 2,500 residents is on the brink of one of the last American frontiers. Surrounded by rugged terrain, Marfa is, to say the least, remote. Once an Old West saloon-and-casino outpost, the town has surprisingly evolved into a haven for contemporary artists, its nucleus being the avant-garde Chinati Foundation. This phenomenon makes for some interesting contrasts: 10-gallon hats and berets, wine bars and feed stores, cowboys and intellectuals, all coexisting in the same small town.

ESSENTIALS
Getting There
Marfa is located at the junction of U.S 67, U.S. 90, and Tex. 17, just 50 miles north of Big Bend National Park. If you're arriving from the east, take I-10, Exit 248, and proceed 82 miles on U.S. 67 through Alpine. From the west, Marfa is located 78 miles southeast of Van Horn on U.S. 90; from the north, it's 60 miles south of I-10, Exit 206, on Tex. 17. The nearest major commercial airport is nearly 200 miles away in El Paso.

Getting Around
Tex. 17 (Lincoln St.) is the main north-south artery and U.S. 90 (San Antonio St.) is the main east-west route. The town square and Presidio County Courthouse are located at Lincoln and Highland streets. You can stroll around downtown Marfa, but in general, a car is necessary to check out the Marfa lights and other attractions.

Visitor Information
The **Marfa TX** website (www.marfatx.com) includes general visitor information and travel tips, local news links, and a calendar of events. You can also contact the **Marfa Chamber of Commerce,** P.O. Box 635, Marfa, TX 79843 (© **800/ 650-9696** or 915/729-4942; www.marfachamberofcommerce.com) for additional information.

FAST FACTS The nearest hospital is 35 miles west in Alpine, the **Big Bend Regional Medical Center,** 2600 Tex. 118 North (© **915/837-3447**). The **post office,** 100 N. Highland St., is open Monday through Friday from 8am to 4:30pm.

The Marfa Mystery Lights

In 1883, an illumination flickered on the horizon east of Marfa, spooking a young cowhand by the name of Robert Ellison. Fearing the lights were Apache campfires, Ellison left behind the cattle he was herding and searched the terrain on horseback. He found nothing.

Ever since, the "Marfa Ghost Lights" have puzzled thousands of eyewitnesses, as they appear, disappear, and reappear in an area where there are no roads, no houses, and no human inhabitants. Some observers insist the lights are the work of supernatural beings or visiting aliens, while others point to electrostatic discharge or phosphorous as the real cause. Regardless, no one has definitively proven what lies behind the phenomenon.

The Texas State Highway Department built a viewing area 9 miles east of Marfa on U.S. 90 to get the growing horde of onlookers off the road. The lights are best viewed between 2 and 4 hours after sundown: Look to the northeast, just to the right of the mountains, along the horizon for the sporadic flickers of light. There's often quite a crowd, a scene straight out of *Close Encounters of the Third Kind*. The **Apache Trading Post** on U.S. 90 in Alpine (© **915/837-5506**) shows a free video on the lights, and Mystery Lights souvenirs are available throughout Marfa. If the lights really pique your interest, don't miss the annual Marfa Lights Festival, a Labor Day weekend celebration with a parade, street dances, a 5K run, concerts, and arts and crafts sales.

THE TOP ATTRACTIONS

Chinati Foundation ★★ *Finds* Housed in 15 buildings at a former U.S. Army post, this decidedly different arts facility is the centerpiece of Marfa's fertile contemporary arts scene. Founded in 1985 by the late Donald Judd, the permanent collection consists of hundreds of works of minimalist and avant-garde art in mediums ranging from steel to paper to concrete. Defying artistic expectations, these pieces are all about context, as each is strongly tied to its indoor or outdoor setting. There are also several temporary displays each year, as well as exhibitions by a very international group of artists-in-residence. Guided tours last about 3 hours. The foundation hosts a major open house every October with concerts, poetry readings, and special exhibitions, most of which are free and open to the public. But the population of Marfa momentarily doubles during the event, so every hotel within a 100-mile radius quickly sells out.

U.S. 67 (½ mile south of Marfa). © 915/729-4362. www.chinati.org. Admission $10 adults, $5 students and seniors. No public admission except by guided tours, which are offered Thurs–Sat at 10am and 2pm or by appointment.

Marfa and Presidio County Museum Housed in the historic Victorian adobe Humphris-Humphreys House, this museum focuses on the area since 1883, with exhibits on ranching, mining, and military history. We recommend it mainly for the excellent collection of black-and-white photographs shot by

Frank Duncan in the first half of the 20th century, and a natural history exhibit on the surrounding Chihuahuan Desert. Allow 1 hour.

110 W. San Antonio St. ℂ **915/729-4140**. Free admission, donations accepted. Mon–Fri 2–5pm or Sat by appointment.

Presidio County Courthouse   Built in 1885 for $60,000, this courthouse is one of West Texas's most impressive, with its magnificent domed roof and classical Victorian woodwork. The architectural style is Second Empire with Italianate details such as overhanging eaves, decorative brackets, and windows that delineate the floors. A "Statue of Justice" stands atop the dome, sans the traditional scales. According to local legend, a convicted cowboy shot the scales out of the statue's hands in the 1890s, proclaiming, "There is no justice in this country." If you have the time, climb to the fifth floor for the view of Marfa and the surrounding countryside.

Lincoln and Highland sts. ℂ **915/729-4942** for information. Free admission. Building open Mon–Fri 9am–5pm; grounds open 24 hr.

WHERE TO STAY

Housed in a beautiful Victorian adobe (1886), the **Arcón Inn,** 215 N. Austin St. (ℂ **915/729-4826**), is a six-room B&B with double rates of $65 to $95. For the budget-minded, there's the basic **Holiday Capri Inn,** 512 W. San Antonio St. (ℂ **915/729-4326**), with double rates of $48. A luxury option for those who can afford the $350 room rates is the self-contained **Cibolo Creek Ranch** (ℂ **866/496-9460** or 915/229-3737; www.cibolocreekranch.com), which is 30 miles away in Shafter. Overall, I'd recommend that Chinati-oriented visitors stay in Marfa.

The Hotel Paisano ★★ *Finds*   After years of semi-hibernation, this glorious 1930s-era hotel was rescued in 2001 by the proprietors of the Hotel Limpia in nearby Fort Davis. A comprehensive restoration later, the property has reclaimed its former status as the premiere hotel between El Paso and San Antonio. The building itself is stunning, a renowned hybrid of prairie and mission architecture that's listed on the National Register of Historic Places. Inside, the rooms balance history and modernity, with comfortable new furnishings and a myriad of arches, stained glass windows, and other subtle details. And there's some serious Hollywood lore: The cast and crew of the epic *Giant* stayed here during production during the 1950s. James Dean's onetime room is the most popular, but Rock Hudson's corner suite, with a full kitchen and a massive balcony overlooking the courtyard pool, is our favorite.

Texas and Highland sts. (P.O. Box Z), Marfa, TX 79843. ℂ **866/729-3669** or 915/729-3669. Fax 915/426-3983. www.hotelpaisano.com. 40 units, including 9 suites. $79–$89 double; $99–$170 suites. AE, DISC, MC, V. **Amenities:** Restaurant, bar; outdoor pool. *In room:* A/C, kitchen, no phones.

WHERE TO DINE

There are a few good restaurants in Marfa, including **Jett's Grill** at the Hotel Paisano, Texas and Highland streets (ℂ **915/729-3838**). Named after James Dean's character in *Giant,* the restaurant serves dinner and Sunday brunch only and features Continental fare spiced with a south-of-the-border twist (from a recent menu: grilled salmon with ancho chile butter sauce, black bean polenta, or pork medallions with apricot chipotle nectar). Main courses run $9 to $24. Another upscale option is **Maiya's,** 103 N. Highland Ave (ℂ **915/729-4410**), offering a creative selection of Northern Italian fare Wednesday through

Saturday evenings, with most dishes between $13 and $20. **Mando's,** 1601 W. San Antonio St. (© **915/729-8170**), is a weathered greasy spoon that serves inexpensive-but-respectable Mexican dishes and burgers for $5 to $9.

3 Midland-Odessa

300 miles E of El Paso; 135 miles S of Lubbock

Welcome to oil country, where the ups and downs of the petroleum industry have long defined these twin cities, 21 miles apart on I-20. Midland-Odessa sits in the geographic center of the Permian Basin, the home of the country's richest oil fields—22% of the United States' reserves. Today, only Alaska produces more oil than the Permian Basin.

The area saw the first of several oil booms in the 1920s. However, less than a decade later, the Great Depression brought on the first of several busts. Production increased during World War II, but foreign competition brought on another bust by 1970s. The pendulum again swayed in the boom direction during the Arab oil embargo era of the 1970s. In 1982, the bottom suddenly fell out of the oil market: Wells were capped, new houses went unsold, and three banks ultimately failed in the city. In the time since, the economy has diversified and recovered, but Midland-Odessa remains the heart and soul of the Permian Basin's oil industry. As it goes, so does Midland-Odessa.

The onetime home of two presidents—George H. W. Bush and his son George W.—the cities are home to a handful of noteworthy attractions (including a replica of London's Globe Theatre and a meteor crater), and the area offers an interesting peek at the rewards and the ravages of a volatile, oil-heavy economy. But Midland-Odessa is by no means a destination—it's really an overnight stopover on the dusty and dry West Texas plains.

ESSENTIALS
GETTING THERE

Midland is located on the north side of I-20, accessible via exits 136 and 138. Tex. 349 runs north-south through the city. Odessa is located 21 miles west of Midland on the north side of I-20, accessible via exits 112 through 121. U.S. 385 (Grant Ave.) bisects the city north-south, through downtown and to I-20.

Midland International Airport, located between Midland and Odessa at 9506 La Force Blvd. (© **915/560-2200;** www.midlandinternational.com), is the primary commercial airport in the Permian Basin. All of the major car-rental companies are represented here.

GETTING AROUND

Laid out on a fairly standard grid that parallels I-20, Midland is a relatively easy city to navigate by car. Most of the accommodations are located on the west side of town on **Wall Street (Business 20),** which continues east through downtown. **Loop 250** circumnavigates the city.

Odessa's busiest street is **Grant Avenue (U.S. 385),** which runs north-south through the middle of downtown. **42nd Street** becomes **Tex. 191** and continues east to Midland. **Loop 338** circles the city.

VISITOR INFORMATION

The **Midland Convention and Visitors Bureau,** 109 N. Main St. (P.O. Box 1890), Midland, TX 79702 (© **800/624-6435** or 915/683-3381; www.visit midlandtx.com) and the **Odessa Convention and Visitors Bureau,** 700 N.

Midland's Famous Son

Don't call President George W. Bush an Ivy Leaguer or even an easterner. Although originally from Connecticut, and an alumnus of Yale and Harvard, the 43rd president of the United States will always be a Texan. He made that point clear as he and wife Laura were leaving Texas for his inauguration in January 2001, when he said they didn't expect to feel at home in Washington.

"In a way, Laura and I will never quite settle in Washington. Because while the honor is great, the work is temporary. I'm leaving Texas, but not forever. This is my home."

Born in New Haven, Connecticut on July 6, 1946, George Walker Bush—also known as "Dubya"—was on the plains of West Texas by the time he was 2 years old. His father (and our 41st president), George H. W. Bush, moved the family west to seek fortune in the oil business. First stop was Odessa, but in 1950 the family moved to nearby Midland, where they lived until 1959.

It was this time in Midland—young George's formative years—that made the biggest impression on this president-to-be, and in 1975 he returned as an adult to make Midland his home and make his own name in the oil business. To this day, he still considers Midland home, and for those who want to see some of the forces that molded our 43rd president, Midland is the place to start.

Childhood friends remember Bush not for any business or political ambitions but for his love of baseball—he was the catcher. Bush recalled, "We were always organizing a game, we played for hours until our mothers would pull us away." One of their favorite fields was at

Grant Ave., Suite 200, Odessa, TX 79761 (✆ **800/780-4678** or 915/333-7871; www.odessacvb.com) can provide additional information on the cities.

FAST FACTS **Midland Memorial Hospital,** 2200 W. Illinois Ave. (✆ **915/685-1111**), has a 24-hour emergency room; Midland's **downtown post office** is at 100 E. Wall St. **Medical Center Hospital,** 400 W. 4th St. (✆ **915/640-2400**), is Odessa's largest full-service hospital; the **main post office** is located at 200 N. Texas St.

WHAT TO SEE & DO
THE TOP ATTRACTIONS

American Airpower Heritage Museum ✪ With a "Ghost Squadron" of more then 130 planes and choppers, this museum is home to the world's largest collection of vintage World War II aircraft. It's worth an hour or two for aviation and history buffs. The planes are housed in an adjacent 60,000-square-foot hangar, with about 15 on display at any given time. There are also multimedia exhibits and nice collections of war artifacts and aviation nose art. The museum's operators sponsor the annual AirSho each October, featuring dramatic re-creations of World War II events.

9600 Wright Dr. at Midland International Airport. ✆ 915/563-1000. www.airpowermuseum.org. Admission $9 adults, $8 teens and seniors, $6 children 6 to 12, free for children under 6. Mon–Sat 9am–5pm; Sun and holidays noon–5pm.

Cowden Park, just south of one of the Bush family's Midland homes at 2703 Sentinel Ave. Look for the old baseball backstop, pretty much all that remains of the field. In addition to the Sentinel Avenue house, the family home from 1957 until 1959, the Bushes lived at 1412 W. Ohio Ave. (1951–55) and 405 E. Maple Ave. (1950–51).

Most locals love Dubya in and around Midland, where he took nearly 80% of the vote in the 2000 presidential election. All over town, bumpers are plastered with a MIDLAND, TX IS BUSH COUNTRY sticker. As we went to press, a local nonprofit was raising funds to restore the Ohio Avenue home to its 1950s appearance and open it to the public as the **George W. Bush Childhood Home.** The target date for the project's completion is fall 2004. For current information, contact the **Midland CVB,** 109 N. Main St. (© **800/624-6435;** www.midlandtxchamber.com). Additionally, the **Presidential Museum** in Odessa (© **915/363-7737**) owns a pair of former Bush family homes (one each in Midland and Odessa), and plans to relocate one of them to the museum's grounds and open the other as an educational center. The museum can also provide a map to Bush-related sites in the Midland-Odessa area.

Since occupying the White House, George and Laura Bush haven't spent too much time in Texas. But when they are back home, they head straight to their 1,600-acre ranch near tiny Crawford, Texas, about 20 miles west of Waco. Although the Secret Service will certainly keep you off the ranch property, local businesses can direct you to where you can get a glimpse of the ranch.

The Globe of the Great Southwest *(Finds* A replica of London's Globe Theatre (William Shakespeare's old haunt), this venue's existence was initially spurred in the 1940s by a student diorama at Odessa High School. From the octagonal design to the way in which the stage juts out, surrounded by seating, painstaking care was taken in the theater's construction. The resident company produces about eight plays annually; the emphasis is on Shakespeare, with two or three of his works staged yearly. The theater also hosts touring productions.

2308 Shakespeare Rd., Odessa. © **915/332-1586.** www.globesw.org. Admission $5; tickets for performances $8–$10. Mon–Sat 9am–5pm. Tours available by appointment only.

Museum of the Southwest *(Kids* Occupying the stately Turner Mansion (1934), this museum does a nice job displaying art and archaeological artifacts. We were impressed by the quality of the museum's permanent collection, with pieces by several Taos Society members and a wide range of indigenous art. Also on-site: the Fredda Turner Durham Children's Museum, with interactive exhibits on art and science and an armadillo-themed slide, and the Marian Blakemore Planetarium. Shows are usually held on Friday nights at 8pm. Expect to spend an hour here, more if you're stopping in with kids.

1705 W. Missouri Ave., Midland. © **915/683-2882.** www.museumsw.org. Free admission (donations welcome). Planetarium shows $3 adults, $2 children ages 12 and under. Tues–Sat 10am–5pm; Sun 2–5pm.

Odessa Meteor Crater and Museum   The second-largest meteor crater in the United States (bested only by Sunset Crater near Flagstaff, Arizona) is about 50,000 years old, born when a flaming hunk of asteroid collided with the West Texas plains. A National Natural Landmark, the crater was once 550 feet wide and 100 feet deep, but erosion and sediment have since obscured it substantially. It's still big enough to encompass a short nature trail, marked with several interpretive signs that detail the initial impact and the subsequent study. The museum here houses chunks of the actual meteorite that created the crater, as well as a smattering of meteor-themed displays. The museum and crater can easily be covered in 45 minutes.

Meteor Crater Rd. (9 miles southwest of Odessa via I-10, Exit 108). © **915/381-0946.** Free admission. Tues–Sat 9am–6pm; Sun 1–6pm.

The Permian Basin Petroleum Museum   Midland, being the center of both the Permian Basin (geographically) and the American oil business (economically), is the ideal location for a museum dedicated to "black gold." Requiring a little more than an hour of time to investigate, the displays here are a tad dated and often come off as propaganda for the Texas oil industry. Nonetheless, the museum is informative and thought provoking, detailing the prehistoric basis for the rich oil field—West Texas was a tropical sea 230 million years ago— and the modern history of petroleum from technological, cultural, and economic perspectives.

1500 I-20 West (Exit 136), Midland. © **915/683-4403.** www.petroleummuseum.org. Admission $5 adults, $4 students and seniors, $3 children 6–11, free for children under 6. Mon–Sat 9am–5pm; Sun 2–5pm.

The Presidential Museum ⭐   Whereas many museums detail the life and times of one president, this is one of a few museums dedicated to the office of the U.S. presidency. For our money, it's the best, worth an hour or two of your time if you choose to visit. The permanent collection of campaign memorabilia is exhaustive and fascinating, with scores of buttons, posters, and stickers bearing the names of candidates from every imaginable party. Don't miss the posters from the 1976 campaign that depict Jimmy Carter with a flowing mane and angelic halo ("J. C. Will Save You!") and its counterpart, Gerald Ford done up as *Happy Days*'s Arthur Fonzarelli ("Fordzie!").

4919 E. University Blvd., Odessa. © **915/363-7737.** Free admission (donations accepted). Tues–Sat 10am–5pm; Sun 2–5pm. Closed major holidays.

OUTDOOR ACTIVITIES & SPECTATOR SPORTS

Midland has two public golf courses: the 27-hole **Hogan Park Golf Course,** 3600 N. Fairground Rd. (© 915/685-7360), and the 18-hole **Nueva Vista Golf Club,** 6101 W. Wadley Ave. (© 915/520-0050). Greens fees range from $12 to $18. In Odessa, **Ratliff Ranch Golf Links,** 7500 N. Grandview Ave. (© 915/550-8181), and **Sunset Country Club,** 9301 Andrews Hwy. (© 915/366-1061), are both 18-hole courses open to the public year-round. Greens fees at each are $13 during the week and $18 on weekends and holidays.

Baseball fans can get their fix in the form of the **Midland RockHounds** (© **915/520-2255;** www.midlandrockhounds.org), the AA Texas League affiliate of the Oakland Athletics. The RockHounds play 70 home dates from April to August at the new First American Bank Ballpark, Loop 250 and Tex. 191. Tickets cost $4 to $8. The Central Hockey League's **Odessa Jackalopes** (© **915/552-7825;** www.jackalopes.org) play an October-to-March schedule at the Ector County Coliseum, 42nd Street and Andrews Highway. Tickets run $13 to $23.

WHERE TO STAY

Thanks to its status as an oil industry hub, there are numerous chain hotels and motels in Midland-Odessa. Options in Midland include **Comfort Suites,** 4706 N. Garfield St. (© 915/620-9191); and **Holiday Inn,** 4300 W. Wall St. (© 915/697-3181). In Odessa, accommodations include the **Best Western Garden Oasis,** 110 W. I-20 (© 877/574-9231 or 915/337-3006); and **Days Inn,** 3075 E. Business Loop 20 (© 915/335-8000).

Hilton Midland and Towers ⚓ If you're looking for luxury at a reasonable price, look no further than this full-service hotel, located at ground zero of the American oil business in downtown Midland. The hotel consists of two 11-story towers on either side of a courtyard pool. Graced with a three-level atrium and several palm trees, the lobby is relaxing and inviting, and the guest rooms are spacious and comfortable. Every room has plush chairs, a pair of two-line phones, and a 27-inch television. The rooms on the concierge level have more extravagant furnishings, and some have balconies.

117 W. Wall St., Midland, TX 79701. © 800/445-8667 or 915/683-6131. Fax 915/683-0958. www. midland.hilton.com. 249 units. $69–$119 double; $140–$225 suite. AE, DC, DISC, MC, V. **Amenities:** Restaurant; bar; outdoor heated pool; exercise room; 2 Jacuzzis; concierge; courtesy car; limited room service; laundry service; dry cleaning; executive level. *In room:* A/C, TV w/pay movies, dataport, coffeemaker, hair dryer, iron.

MCM Elegante This former Radisson reopened as an independent in 2002 under the tag, "tropical elegance in the desert." With a lobby boasting multi-hued floral carpeting, stained glass chandeliers, and a large aquarium, the hotel is a bit over the top, but it hits the mark more often than not. With nice city views from wall-length windows, crown molding, and red-hued wood furnishings, the rooms go beyond what you'd expect in a chain, with plenty of perks. (One example: The smallish baths are stocked with bottled water—guests readily pay the $2.50 price tag once they get a taste of what's on tap.) The recreational facilities are dynamite, including a jogging track, putting/chipping green, seasonally domed pool area, and several sports fields.

5200 E. University Blvd., Odessa, TX 79762. © 866/368-5885 or 915/368-5885. Fax 915/362-8958. www.mcm elegante.com. 249 units, including 4 suites. $69–$99 double; $149–$225 suite. AE, DC, DISC, MC, V. **Amenities:** Restaurant; bar; indoor/outdoor heated pool; exercise room; spa; Jacuzzi; car-rental desk; courtesy car; limited room service; dry cleaning; executive level. *In room:* A/C, TV w/pay movies, dataport, coffeemaker, hair dryer, iron.

WHERE TO DINE

Our pick for a quick bite in the area is **Manuel's Crispy Tacos,** 1404 E. 2nd St., Odessa (© 915/333-2751), a fun family joint known for its namesake dish. Main courses are $5 to $16.

The Barn Door *Kids* STEAKHOUSE A local favorite, the Barn Door resides in an expansion of the old 1892 Panhandle–Santa Fe railroad depot. There's a copious country atmosphere about the place, with red-and-white checkered tablecloths, well-placed wagon wheels, and the twang of country music oozing from the sound system. The food is the main attraction and, as is the case at so many other Texan eateries, that means big, juicy steaks. You can't go wrong with a slab of slow-roasted prime rib, cut to order and served with au jus and creamy horseradish, or, if you've got a really empty belly, the 24-ounce sirloin. The steaks come with a side dish; the selection runs the gamut from onion rings to mashed potatoes to cheese enchiladas. If you're burnt out on steaks, there's

seafood, chicken, and Mexican fare. What used to be the depot is now an inviting lounge with—what else?—a railroad theme.

2140 N. Grant Ave., Odessa. ℂ **915/337-4142.** Main courses $6–$9 lunch, $9–$22 dinner. AE, MC, V.
Mon–Thurs 11am–9:30pm; Fri 11am–10:30pm; Sat 4 –10:30pm; Sun 11am–3pm.

Wall Street Bar and Grill ☆ BISTRO   With a stock ticker over the front
entrance, this restaurant caters to the wheelers and dealers of Midland's business
community, but history buffs will find other things to gawk at while they dine.
The 1910 building, originally a saddle shop, still features the original pressed tin
ceiling, and the cherry-stained mahogany bar and back bar received a commen-
dation from the Texas Historical Foundation for their restoration. The menu,
conversely, is contemporary, with tastily creative offerings like seafood rellenos
with chipotle-tomatillo sauce, pecan-crusted trout, and charbroiled pork chops
with ancho chile sauce. The crawfish étoufée, rich and thick, is just about as
good as it gets.

115 E. Wall St., Midland. ℂ **915/684-8686.** Main courses $7–$24 lunch and dinner. AE, DC, DISC, MC, V.
Mon–Fri 11am–2:30pm; Sun–Thurs 5:30–10pm; Fri–Sat 5:30–11pm; Sun brunch 10:30am–2:30pm.

DUNE SLEDDING IN MONAHANS SANDHILLS STATE PARK
30 miles W of Odessa

When Spanish explorers first stumbled upon these sand hills in the mid–16th
century, they labeled them "perfect miniature Alps of sand." Perpetually changing geologic and geometric wonders, the 3,840 acres of dunes at **Monahans
Sandhills State Park,** I-20 Exit 86 (ℂ **915/943-2092**), represent the only public access to a 200-mile range of dunes that stretches from eastern New Mexico
into the Permian Basin of West Texas.

Start at the visitor center, where you can watch a short orientation video,
check out exhibits on all things sandy, and trek through the dunes on a ¼-mile
interpretive trail. The center rents plastic disks ($1 an hour) for West Texas–style
sledding, down dune-slopes that top out at 70 feet in height. Besides sledding
them, you can explore the dunes on foot or horseback. (You'll need to bring your
own horse to the 600-acre equestrian area; no stables are on-site.)

The dunes are far from barren. Many plants thrive here, including the shin
oak, an unusually small oak with unusually large acorns that comprise a
"Liliputian Jungle" in the park. Other native inhabitants are deer, coyote, pos-
sum, and bobcats. For the human guests, there are 24 back-in campsites with
water and electricity for $9 a night; the day-use fee is $2 (free for children under
13). The park is open daily from 8am to 10pm.

If you're a Coca-Cola fanatic, stop in at **Big Burger,** 1016 Stockton St. in
Monahans (I-20 Exit 80; ℂ **915/943-5655**), an all-American burger joint plastered with every imaginable piece of Coke memorabilia. Menu items range from
$4 to $7; the fried catfish dinners merit a detour.

4 San Angelo
224 miles NW of Austin; 111 miles SE of Midland; 64 miles N of Sonora

First known as "the town over the river" from Fort Concho, San Angelo was the
prototypical rollicking, gun-slinging Wild West outpost during the late 1860s
and 1870s. During these early days, the soldiers from the fort and cowhands
from the field would cross the Concho River to get to the brothels, casinos, and
saloons that dominated the town on the other side.

A city of about 95,000 residents, modern San Angelo is a more than adequate stopover on a cross-Texas road trip. Its rowdy past can be revisited in the form of Historic Concho Avenue, now lined with boutiques and jewelers instead of casinos and bordellos, and old Fort Concho, now a National Historic Landmark. The city is also one of the few oases of West Texas, with the Concho snaking through town and five reservoirs within 40 miles, and the home of a burgeoning arts scene.

ESSENTIALS
GETTING THERE

The largest city in Texas not located on an interstate, San Angelo lies at the junction of three U.S. highways: 67, 87, and 277. U.S. 87 crosses I-20 at Big Spring, and U.S. 67 and U.S. 277 are both accessible from I-20 near Abilene. From the south, U.S. 67 diverges from I-10 at Fort Stockton and U.S. 277 crosses the interstate at Sonora.

San Angelo Regional Airport/Mathis Field, located about 8 miles south of the city at 7654 Knickerbocker Rd. (© 915/659-6409), is the only commercial airport in the Concho River Valley. Car rentals are available at the airport from **Avis, Budget,** and **Hertz.**

GETTING AROUND

With the confluence of the north and south forks of the Concho River marking the city center, bridges seem to be everywhere and can often make navigation by car a bit tricky. **Bryant Boulevard** (U.S. 87/277) is the major north-south street, but it splits into two one-way streets (the northbound **Koenigheim St.** and southbound **Abe St.**) in the middle of the city. **Chadbourne Street,** just a few blocks east of Bryant Boulevard, runs through the historic part of the city, skirting downtown and **Historic Concho Avenue** en route to Fort Concho and other attractions.

The **civic bus system** (© 915/655-9952), operates five routes from the Historic Santa Fe Depot at 703 S. Chadbourne St., from 6:30am to 6:30pm Monday through Friday and from 9:30am to 6:30pm Saturday. Fare is $1 for adults, 50¢ for students and seniors, and free for any accompanying children under 5.

VISITOR INFORMATION

The **San Angelo Convention and Visitors Bureau,** 500 Rio Concho Dr., San Angelo, TX 76903 (© 800/375-1206 or 915/653-1206; www.sanangelo-tx.com), operates a visitor center, open Monday through Friday from 8:30am to 5pm.

FAST FACTS   San Angelo has two 24-hour emergency rooms: **San Angelo Community Medical Center,** 3501 Knickerbocker Rd. (© 915/949-9511); and **Shannon Medical Center,** 120 E. Harris Ave. (© 915/653-6741). The **main post office,** 1 N. Abe St., is open Monday through Friday from 8am to 5:30pm, Saturday from 9am to 4:30pm.

WHAT TO SEE & DO
THE TOP ATTRACTIONS

Fort Concho National Historic Landmark   Established in 1867 as a means of pioneer defense, Fort Concho provided the impetus for San Angelo's original development. Originally 40 buildings on 1,000 acres, this U.S. Army post, once commanded by William "Pecos Bill" Shafter, was active until 1889, with black Buffalo Soldiers making up a considerable portion of the men stationed here. The post is now one of the jewels of the old Texas forts, with 17 restored buildings and five rebuilt structures. Some of the buildings are fully furnished with period artifacts, including a barracks outfitted to an 1870s T, down to the last checker on the board. There are exhibits in two of the restored officers' quarters (one is a small museum on telephony, featuring one of Alexander Graham Bell's originals) and the old post headquarters. Expect to spend a little more than an hour here.

630 S. Oakes St. © **915/481-2646.** Admission $2 adults, $1.50 seniors, $1.25 students, and free for children under 6. Tues–Sat 10am–5pm; Sun 1–5pm.

River Walk ⭐ Thanks to the River Beautification Project, which kicked off in 1986, the Concho River is now a splendid centerpiece for the entire city of San Angelo. Sporting a 4-mile, walking/jogging trail, bountiful outdoor gardens and water displays, and even a 9-hole golf course (© 915/657-4485) on the River Walk's acres (greens fees $6–$8). Celebration Bridge crosses the river behind the San Angelo Museum of Fine Arts (see below), right past a bronze statue of a mermaid, "Pearl of the Conchos." Between the bridge and the old downtown plaza (El Paseo de Santa Angela) sits the Bill Aylor, Sr. Memorial RiverStage, an outdoor venue that is a focus of San Angelo's performing arts scene. The River Walk provides easy access to the San Angelo Museum of Fine Arts, Historic Concho Avenue, and Fort Concho.

Along the banks of the Concho River.

San Angelo Museum of Fine Arts ⭐ From its eye-catching home on the Concho River, this standout museum is a must-see for lovers of art and architecture, demanding a stop of 45 minutes or more. The permanent collection focuses on contemporary American ceramics, with 150 such pieces, and every year from April to June, the museum features the country's top ceramics show, with a national competition in even-numbered years. Another nice perk: The museum has an open back office that allows visitors to see how the facility is managed and get a glimpse into the storage areas. The award-winning building is a work of art in itself, consisting of native limestone, in-grain mesquite flooring, and a curving, copper-clad roof. Under the same nonprofit umbrella is a **children's art museum** at the Cactus Hotel, 36 E. Twohig Ave. (© 915/659-4391).

1 Love St. on the Concho River. © **915/653-3333.** http://web2.airmail.net/samfa. Admission $2 adults, $1 seniors, and free for students and children. Tues–Sat 10am–4pm; Sun 1–4pm. Closed major holidays.

⌐ Fun Fact The Concho Pearl

The word *concho* pops out from every other corner in San Angelo, from Concho Avenue to Fort Concho to the Concho River. If you're not from the area, it probably doesn't mean much, but if you're a San Angelo jeweler, it means a great deal. The Concho River Valley is home to a dozen species of freshwater mussels in the *Unionacea* family that produce the rare concho pearl, tinted luminous pink, deep purple, or rich lavender by Mother Nature. Some of the earliest known examples of the pearls were Spanish crown jewels in the 16th century. If you want to try to harvest one yourself, you'll need a permit from the **Texas Parks and Wildlife Department** (© **800/792-1112**). You can avoid wading in the river, however, if you're willing to plunk down some cash at a local jeweler.

OUTDOOR ACTIVITIES

When it comes to outdoor recreation, San Angelans are blessed with the Concho River, two reservoirs, and an excellent civic park system. The highlight is **San Angelo State Park** 🏃🏃, 3900-2 Mercedes St. (© **915/949-4757**), at O. C. Fisher Lake on the city's northwest side, attracting mountain bikers, hikers, boaters, anglers, and equestrians. The park sits at the nexus of four distinct geographical areas—Hill Country, Trans-Pecos, the rolling plains to the east, and the high plains to the north—in an area that has been inhabited by humans for over 10,000 years. Admission to the park is $2 per adults, $1 for seniors, and free for children under 13. The day-use hours are from 8am to 10pm.

The park's trail system is one of the best in all of West Texas, with more than 50 miles of multiuse trails (hiking, biking, horseback riding). Certain trails provide access to the only ride-in, equestrian campsites between El Paso and San Antonio. The trails connect the north and south shores of the reservoir and range from flat and smooth to rocky and rugged; a detailed map is available at the entrance. There are ample opportunities for birding and wildlife watching, with 300 avian and 50 mammal species (including pelicans, cormorants, Texas longhorn cattle, and buffalo), and a significant population of horned lizards. In season, hunters target deer and wild turkey and anglers try to hook crappie, bass, and catfish.

On guided tours, visitors can take a look at the petroglyphs in the park, go on a 3-mile hike to fossilized footprints, or learn about the history of buffalo and Texas longhorn. The tours are informative, engaging, and offered on demand ($2 for adults, $1 for seniors, 50¢ for students, and free for children under 13).

There are 79 campsites with water and electric hook-ups here, and over 100 primitive tent camping areas. The campground on the north shore, shaded by massive pecan trees, is especially isolated and attractive, while the southern campgrounds are closer to the reservoir and playground. Nightly camping fees, in addition to park entrance fees, are $10 for the developed sites and $6 for the undeveloped sites. There are also a few simple cabins that can accommodate six guests for $35 a night.

Six miles south of downtown via Knickerbocker Road, the city-owned **Lake Nasworthy** is a fishing, hiking, and boating hotspot. Below the nearly 1,600 surface acres of fresh water, two nonnative saltwater species (hybrid trout-corvina and red drum) have thrived alongside native bass and catfish. **Spring Creek Marina and RV Park,** 45 Fisherman's Rd. (© **800/500-7801** or 915/944-3850), has campsites with full hook-ups ($24 nightly), boat rentals, and a convenience store. Hourly rental fees range from $10 for nonmotorized paddleboats to $50 for motorboats.

The **San Angelo Nature Center** at Lake Nasworthy, 7409 Knickerbocker Rd. (© **915/942-0121**), is a small museum with a garden, library, and 8-mile interpretive trail system. Most of the trails are located on the 260-acre Spring Creek Wetland, which is only open for self-guided tours on the second and third Saturdays of each month from 9am to noon. However, a 1-mile trail through a very active wildlife habitat (armadillos, owls, bobcat, and deer) is open during daylight hours year-round. The center itself is open Tuesday through Saturday from noon to 5pm.

The **Pictographs of Painted Rocks,** called a "museum, library, and art gallery" of ancient American Indians, is another noteworthy excursion near San Angelo. Located 22 miles southeast of the city near the town of Paint Rock, the site features a natural limestone wall adorned with more than 1,600 pictographs. On the

Winter Solstice, rays of light reflect off of an ornate, otherwise invisible painting known as "Sun Dagger." For information on tours, call © **915/732-4376.**

The municipal park system in San Angelo is a cut above average, with the **River Walk** (p. 350) and **Civic League Park,** W. Beauregard and Park Streets, featuring the International Water Lily Garden. This garden displays lily species from all over the globe that bloom both day and night during the spring and summer. Call **San Angelo Park Headquarters** at © **915/657-4279** for additional information on the city's 313-acre park system.

BOATING & FISHING   In addition to O. C. Fisher Lake and Lake Nasworthy (see above), there are three other reservoirs within a 40-mile radius of San Angelo: **Twin Buttes Reservoir** (© **915/481-2617**), located immediately west of Lake Nasworthy; **Lake E. V. Spence** (© **915/453-2061**), known for its striped bass, situated 35 north of San Angelo via Tex. 208 and Tex. 158; and **Lake O. H. Ivie** (© **915/357-4886**), the largest body of water in the region at 25,000 surface acres, located 40 miles east of the city via Farm Roads 765 and 2134. All three are fishing and boating destinations with adjacent commercial campgrounds.

GOLF   The 7,171-yard **Quicksand Golf Course,** 2305 Pulliam St. (© **915/ 482-8337**), is one of Texas's best (and toughest) 18-hole courses, with greens fees around $20 to $35, cart included. There's also the 18-hole **Riverside Golf Course,** 900 W. 29th St. (© **915/653-6130**), with greens fees of $14 to $26.

HIKING   The top hiking area in the region is **San Angelo State Park,** with 50 miles of trails. The trails are easy to difficult, with the loops between the north and south shores and the hike to the **Highland Range Scenic Lookout** (less than a mile) being the most popular.

LLAMA TREKS   **Jordan Llamas** (© **915/651-7346** or 916/655-0968) offers guided llama treks in San Angelo State Park, along the Concho River, and elsewhere in the area. The trips cost $35 per person for a half day with one meal or $50 per person for a full day with two meals.

MOUNTAIN BIKING   The most popular mountain biking spots in the San Angelo area are the trails at **San Angelo State Park** and around **Twin Buttes Reservoir.** Bike rentals are not available in town.

SPECTATOR SPORTS

The **San Angelo Colts** (© **915/942-6587;** www.sanangelocolts.com) play in the AA Central Baseball League from early May to early September at Colts Stadium, 1600 University Ave. Single-game tickets are $4 to $8. The local Central Hockey League franchise, the **San Angelo Saints** (© **915/944-6253;** www. sanangelosaints.com) plays at the San Angelo Coliseum, 50 E. 43rd St., October through March. Single-game tickets run $5 to $16. The **San Angelo Stock Show and Rodeo Association** (© **915/653-7785**) organizes several annual roping and rodeo events.

SHOPPING

Historic Concho Avenue, downtown between Oakes and Chadbourne streets, is a melting pot of boutiques, jewelers, and antiques shops. Among its highlights are **J. Wilde's,** 20 E. Concho Ave. (© **915/655-0878**), a boutique with fashions and furnishings best described as Western chic (which doesn't quite do them justice); and **Legend Jewelers,** 18 E. Concho Ave. (© **888/655-4367** or 915/653-0112), purveyors of the luminous concho pearl. The top shopping center is **Sunset Mall,** 4001 Sunset Dr., at Loop 306 (© **915/949-1947**), with Dillard's and Sears among its 85 stores.

San Angelo is home to a vibrant arts community, typified by the Texas hippie vibe at the **Old Chicken Farm Art Center,** 2505 N. Martin Luther King Blvd. (© **915/653-4936**), a local landmark since 1971. Formerly an abandoned chicken farm, this funky artist's compound (adorned with the likes of longhorn skulls, steel cutouts of chicken and cacti, and an old phone booth) is home to 12 studios that are open at various times, displaying a wide range of pottery, metalwork, and paintings. The main **StarKeeper Gallery** houses the contemporary handmade ceramics of Roger Allen, the center's founder and proprietor, open Tuesday through Saturday from 10am to 5pm. Allen, whose creative StarKeeper and Dancing Ladies dishes are in high demand throughout the Southwest, lives in a cozy house on-site and will spin you a tale if you've got the time. The Art Center hosts resident artist's openings on the first Saturday of each month. Additionally, there's an on-site B&B, the **Inn at the Art Center** (see below).

WHERE TO STAY

There is a nice variety of lodging available in San Angelo, with a handful of B&Bs and numerous chain motels and hotels. Most of the properties are located along Bryant Boulevard or near the convention center on Rio Concho Drive. Among the chain properties are the new **Clarion Inn & Suites,** 333 Rio Concho Dr. (© **915/655-8000**); **Hawthorn Inn & Suites,** 1355 Knickerbocker Rd. (© **915/653-1500**); and **Howard Johnson's Inn of the West,** 415 W. Beauregard Ave. (© **915/653-2995**). Of the independents, we recommend **Inn of the Conchos,** 2021 N. Bryant Blvd. (© **800/621-6041** or 915/658-2811), with double rates of $45 to $69.

Holiday Inn Convention Center ★ _(Kids)_   This property is our pick for a night in San Angelo for several reasons: a quiet location, surrounded by trees and parkland near the banks of the Concho River and the River Walk; reliable rooms with mild decor and powerful air-conditioning; and a full range of amenities. It's a good bet for families, with a kid's menu in the restaurant, in-room video games, small indoor pool, and outdoor volleyball court. As far as Holiday Inns go, this one is right up there, a solid property that's well managed and nicely maintained.

441 Rio Concho Dr., San Angelo, TX 76903. © 800/HOLIDAY or 915/658-2828. Fax 915/658-8741. 148 units. $79–$109 double; $169 suite. AE, DC, DISC, MC, V. **Amenities:** Restaurant; bar; indoor heated pool; exercise room; Jacuzzi; courtesy car; limited room service; laundry service; dry cleaning. _In room:_ A/C, TV w/ Sony PlayStation, dataport, coffeemaker, hair dryer, iron.

Inn at the Art Center ★ _(Finds)_   If you like your B&B a bit on the unusual side, look no further. In place of Victorian architecture and antiques, you'll find rooms in what once were chicken coops and feed silos at the Old Chicken Farm Art Center (see "Shopping," above). Our favorite: the Artist's Loft, situated between two cylindrical silos (the bedroom in one, and a sitting area, bathroom, and huge closet in the other) connected with an arched doorway. Resident and visiting artists contribute to a mural above the queen-size bed, a continuous "work in progress." There's also the themed Santa Fe and French rooms in the old coop. Outside, you can get a firsthand look at artists at work or relax in one of the many shady nooks and crannies on the property, including a sculpture-laden courtyard and a covered patio with a fountain. The restaurant, the Silo House, serves prix-fixe dinners on Thursday, Friday, and Saturday evenings.

2503 Martin Luther King Blvd., San Angelo, TX 76903. © 866/557-5337 or 915/658-3333. Fax 915/658-3333. www.chickenfarmartcenter.com. 3 units. $75–$100 double. Rates include full breakfast. AE, DISC, MC, V. **Amenities:** Restaurant. _In room:_ A/C.

CAMPING

The best campgrounds are at **San Angelo State Park** (© **915/949-4757**) and **Spring Creek Marina and RV Park** (© **800/500-7801** or 915/944-3850) at Lake Nasworthy. See "Outdoor Activities," above.

WHERE TO DINE

For a quick breakfast or lunch, hit the **Cactus Café,** 36 E. Twohig Ave. in the lobby of the Cactus Hotel (© **915/659-1470**). The strong coffee and fresh baked goods lure the commuters, and the plump sandwiches ($4–$6) are the best lunch deal downtown.

Armenta's *Finds* TEX-MEX   The proprietors of this festive eatery did not hold back one iota when it came to decoration, transforming a once-standard diner into a feast for the eyes with an armada of colorful parrot sculptures, strings of chile pepper lights, and Mexican pottery. They don't hold back with the first-rate food, either, which is every bit as spicy as the scenery. You can't miss with the fiery *guizo*—sautéed beef with onions, tomatoes, and peppers—or the *camarones a la diabla*—shrimp spiced for the most inflammable of taste buds. There are some good combination plates, gorditas, chalupas, and quesadillas, as well as burgers and chicken-fried steaks.

1325 S. Oakes St. (1 mile south of downtown). © **915/653-1954.** Main courses $1–$3 breakfast, $4.50–$8 lunch and dinner. AE, DISC, MC, V. Mon–Sat 8am–10pm. Closed major holidays.

Mejor que Nada MEXICAN/STEAKS   The name, Spanish for "better than nothing," is certainly true, but also a gross understatement. This place is a whole lot better than nothing. In fact, it gets better—and bigger—almost every single year. Opening as a small convenience store in 1986, demand for its homemade Mexican food sent the establishment into expansion mode. First came picnic tables, then an enclosed patio, then an addition to the front room, and so on. Now the place is a big, bustling restaurant, dishing out enticing Mexican fare and thick, juicy steaks. Our personal favorite is Mejor's chicken enchilada, jammed with onions and peppers and covered in a zesty, sweet-hot tomatillo salsa. Carnivores will delight in the steaks, ranging from a 6-ounce filet to a 16-ounce Kansas City sirloin. Calorie watchers can order a "poquito" plate (with reduced portions) or "Karla"—Mexican stir-fry with mushrooms, onions, peppers, zucchini, broccoli, and cabbage.

1911 S. Bryant Blvd. © **915/655-3553.** Main courses $5–$14. AE, DISC, MC, V. Mon–Thurs 11am–9:30pm; Fri–Sat 11am–10:30pm; Sun 11am–3pm.

Miss Hattie's Café and Saloon STEAKS/SEAFOOD   Named after the infamous proprietor of one of San Angelo's now-defunct bordellos, Miss Hattie's is one of the city's culinary standouts. Housed in a brick edifice that dates from 1884, the dining room is full of Victorian frills and antiques, with lace-sheathed tables under the original pressed-tin ceiling. The cuisine is a nice match for the atmosphere: tender steaks, daily seafood specials, salads, and pastas. Our recommendation: Start with the chicken and corn fritters as an appetizer and move on to the "Southwestern Carpetbagger" (a rib-eye stuffed with spiced crabmeat) for the main course. The lunch menu sports a nice selection of gourmet sandwiches and salads and heartier fare like meatloaf and chicken with dumplings. Two doors down is **Miss Hattie's Bordello Museum,** 18½ E. Concho Ave. The restored brothel offers tours Thursday through Saturday every hour from 1 to 4pm; admission is $5 per person.

26 E. Concho Ave. © **915/653-0570.** Main courses $6–$11 lunch, $10–$27 dinner. AE, DISC, MC, V. Mon–Thurs 11am–9pm; Fri–Sat 11am–10pm.

SAN ANGELO AFTER DARK

San Angelo has a strong performing arts culture for a city its size. The **San Angelo Symphony** performs about a half-dozen classical and pops shows a year at various venues (© **915/658-5877;** www.sanangelosymphony.org). Single tickets are $4 to $6 for children and students and $15 for adults. The **Angelo Civic Theater,** 1936 Sherwood Way (© **915/949-4400**), billed as the oldest community theater in all of Texas, produces about five musicals, comedies, and dramas a year at its 230-seat playhouse. Tickets run $8 to $15. The city is also home to the **Cactus Jazz Series** (© **915/653-6793;** www.sanangeloarts.com) at the historic Cactus Hotel, 36 E. Twohig Ave., culminating in the annual Cactus Jazz and Blues Festival in September.

A SIDE TRIP TO THE CAVERNS OF SONORA

Hidden in the middle of nowhere, some 75 miles from San Angelo, are the delightful **Caverns of Sonora.** Designated a Registered Natural Landmark by the National Park Service in 1966, these truly magnificent caves are privately owned and can be explored only on guided tours. You'll see glistening draperies, miles of fluffy looking popcorn, millions of helictites and soda straws, reflecting pools, plus all the usual stalagmites and stalactites in a wildly fascinating collage of formations. The caverns signature formation is a delightfully unusual helictite shaped like a butterfly.

Two walking tours are offered. The Horseshoe Lake Tour is 1¼ miles and takes about 1 hour and 15 minutes; cost is $15 for those 12 and older, $12 for children 4 to 11, and free for children under 4. The Crystal Palace Tour is 2 miles long and takes about 1 hour and 45 minutes; price is $20 for those 12 and older, $16 for children 4 to 11, and free for children under 4.

The caverns are open daily from 8am to 6pm March through Labor Day, and from 9am to 5pm the rest of the year, except Christmas Day. From San Angelo, go south on U.S. 277 64 miles to the small town of Sonora, then 8 miles west on I-10 to Exit 392, then follow signs south to the caverns. For additional information, contact **Caverns of Sonora,** P.O. Box 1196, Sonora, TX 76950 (© **915/ 387-3105;** www.cavernsofsonora.com).

Camping in an attractive tree-shaded campground is available at the Caverns, at $10 for tent sites and $14 for pull-through RV sites. Sites have water and electric hook-ups, but not sewer, and there is no RV dump station. There are bathhouses with hot showers, and pet kennels available free for campers. Other than that, the nearest lodging, dining, and other services are in Sonora. For information, contact the **Sonora Chamber of Commerce,** 707 N. Crockett Ave., P.O. Box 1172, Sonora, TX 76950-1172 (© **915/387-2880**).

5 Del Rio & Amistad National Recreation Area

246 miles S of Abilene; 154 miles W of San Antonio; 268 miles NW of Corpus Christi; 392 miles SW of Dallas

For our money, this pleasant little city of about 35,000 people is one of the nicest border towns you'll find from Texas to California. Situated along the U.S.–Mexico border across the Rio Grande from Ciudad Acuña, Del Rio is a great base for watersports enthusiasts visiting Amistad National Recreation Area, and also has an excellent museum where you can learn about Judge Roy Bean, one of the most colorful judges in the history of the American West, who became both famous and infamous as "The Law West of the Pecos."

The site of Del Rio was originally called San Felipe del Rio by Spanish missionaries, who unsuccessfully tried to start a mission here in 1635 but were thwarted by hostile American Indians. The name survived, however, and was in use in the mid-1800s when the reliable water source of San Felipe Springs helped the area begin to develop as a farming community. The springs also were a watering stop for the short-lived U.S. Army Camel Corps, in which camels imported from North Africa were used on the Western frontier as a substitute for horses. The name of the community was shortened to Del Rio in 1883.

In the late 1960s a dam was built on the Rio Grande near Del Rio, creating a 67,000-acre lake that provides flood protection and irrigation water, as well as a huge water playground in what is generally an arid and rocky land of cactus and sagebrush.

ESSENTIALS
GETTING THERE
Del Rio is located at the junction of U.S. highways 90 and 277/377, along the U.S.–Mexico border. The nearest major **airport** is in San Antonio (see chapter 7). The **Amtrak** station (© **800/872-2745**) is at 100 N. Main St. along the route of the Sunset Limited.

VISITOR INFORMATION
The **Del Rio Chamber of Commerce,** 1915 Ave. F, Del Rio, TX 78840 (© **800/889-8149** or 830/775-3551; www.drchamber.com), operates a visitor center and can also mail information to you before your trip.

FAST FACTS   Val Verde Regional Medical Center, 801 Bedell Ave. (© **830/ 775-8566**), has a 24-hour emergency room. The **post office,** 2001 N. Bedell Ave., is open Monday through Friday from 8:30am to 4:30pm, Saturday from 9am to 11am.

AMISTAD NATIONAL RECREATION AREA ⊛
A beautiful spot for boating, fishing, water-skiing, scuba diving, and swimming, this is a rare international recreation area, created by the United States and Mexico with the construction of a 6-mile-long dam across the Rio Grande at the international border. Amistad Reservoir—*amistad* is Spanish for friendship— provides electric generation, water storage, flood control, and most important to anglers and water sports enthusiasts, a huge lake.

The water here is a beautiful blue color, caused by the lake bed's limestone character and lack of loose soil. The 67,000-acre lake is actually at the confluence of three rivers, and runs 74 miles up the Rio Grande, 24 miles up the Devils River, and 14 miles up the Pecos River. Shoreline measures 890 miles: 540 miles in Texas and the rest in Mexico.

There are about a dozen boat ramps spread throughout the recreation area, with three developed boat launching areas. **Diablo East** is 10 miles northwest of Del Rio via U.S. 90, **Rough Canyon** is 23 miles north of Del Rio via U.S. 90 and U.S. 277/377, and **Pecos** is 44 miles northwest of Del Rio via U.S. 90. Boat and slip rentals and sales of supplies are available at Diablo East and Rough Canyon. Motorized boat use passes cost $4 per day or $40 per year.

At Diablo East, **Lake Amistad Marina,** HCR-3 U.S. 90, P.O. Box 420635, Del Rio, TX 78842 (© **830/774-4157;** www.foreverresorts.com), rents a variety of boats, ranging from three- or six-person fishing boats and runabouts costing $70 to $125 per 8-hour day to luxurious 59-foot houseboats that sleep 10 and rent for $2,500 for a 3-day/2-night weekend in summer, with lower rates Monday through Thursday and fall through spring. Boat rentals are also available at similar rates at **Rough Canyon Marina,** P.O. Box 420845, Del Rio, TX 78842 (© **830/775-8779**).

There is a swimming area (no lifeguards) at Governors Island, and swimming is permitted in most undeveloped areas. Water temperatures range from a chilly 54°F (12°C) in winter to a pleasant 86°F (30°C) in summer. Water-skiing is permitted in open water (away from mooring areas, channels, and swimming beaches) during daylight hours only.

Forty-pound catfish have been pulled from the lake, and a record 45-pound striped bass, a whopping 44 inches long, was caught in the lake in May 1990. Among other species caught are largemouth bass, yellowbelly and bluegill sunfish, white and black crappie, and alligator gar. Fishing is permitted from boats and from shore anywhere except in marinas, at boat ramps, and designated swimming beaches. There are also fishing docks and fish-cleaning stations at several locations. A Texas fishing license (available at recreation area headquarters) is required on the U.S. side of the border, and a Mexican fishing license is required in Mexican waters. A list of licensed fishing guides is available at the headquarters.

Among the wildlife you're likely to see are white-tailed deer, javelina (also called collared peccaries), black-tailed jackrabbits, rock squirrels, and nine-banded armadillos. Campers might also see ringtails, which usually only venture out at night. The recreation area is also home to poisonous snakes including several species of rattlesnakes and copperheads, plus poisonous scorpions, spiders, and stinging insects. Birds to watch for include white-winged doves, scaled quail, northern mockingbirds, sandpipers, great blue herons, great egrets, American coots, ring-necked ducks, killdeer, roadrunners, black vultures, ravens, and an occasional bald or golden eagle. One particularly good spot to see desert birds, as well as wintering and migratory species, is the San Pedro Campground, where you're also likely to see a lot of butterflies.

American Indian peoples are believed to have come to this area about 12,000 years ago, but it was not until about 4,000 years ago, when a different group inhabited the area, that the creation of the spectacular rock art we can see today in several areas in and near the recreation area began. These pictographs— designs painted on rocks using colors created from ground iron ore and other minerals mixed with animal fat—are difficult to get to, but well worth the effort.

One of the best rock art sites is **Panther Cave,** at the confluence of the Rio Grande and Seminole Canyon, which is usually accessible by boat and a steep climb up stairs. It has numerous figures that resemble humans or animals, including what looks like a 9-foot panther. Another good site, accessible by boat at average lake levels and by a strenuous hike through tall brush at low water levels, is **Parida Cave,** located on the Rio Grande. See also the section on Seminole Canyon State Park & Historic Site, below.

The recreation area has four campgrounds, with a total of about 60 primitive sites. Campgrounds are generally open, with brush and some low trees, but little shade, and have vault toilets, covered picnic tables, and grills. **Governors Landing Campground,** with 15 sites overlooking the lake, is the only campground with drinking water (water is also available at the recreation area headquarters and along the Diablo East entrance road, where there is also an RV dump station). **San Pedro Campground** has 21 sites and **Spur 406** and **277 North** campgrounds each have about a dozen sites. There is also a dispersed camping area at Spur 406 with rooms for about a dozen sites. Camping is first come, first served, and is limited to 14 consecutive days, or 60 days in a 12-month period. Backcountry camping from boats is permitted along the lakeshore, except at marinas and other developed areas. Camping costs $4 per night.

Rangers present a variety of programs November through March, including evening programs at the amphitheater at Governors Landing Campground; and kiosks with displays on natural history, recreation, and water safety are scattered throughout the recreation area. Pets are permitted, but must be leashed at all times. Rangers warn that limestone, which is abundant along the shore, can cut the pads of dogs' feet, and they add that pets need to be protected from fleas, ticks, and heartworm (spread by mosquitoes) at the lake.

Facilities in the Mexican part of the lake include a swimming beach and a boat ramp near the west end of the dam. Boaters who touch land in Mexico are required to pass through U.S. Customs (in Del Rio) when they return to the United States.

Admission to the park, which is open 24 hours, is free. The park headquarters, with information, a small bookstore, and a few displays, is open Monday through Friday from 8am to 5pm, except Thanksgiving, Christmas, and New Year's. It's located just west of Del Rio along U.S. 90. The first lake access is about 6 miles west of the headquarters on U.S. 90. The Amistad Dam Exhibit Center has displays on the dam's construction and the recreation area's flora, fauna, and cultural resources, and is open daily from 10am to 6pm. For information, contact the **Amistad National Recreation Area,** HCR-3, Box 5J, Del Rio, TX 78840-9350 (© **830/775-7491;** www.nps.gov/amis).

SEMINOLE CANYON STATE PARK & HISTORIC SITE

Adjacent to Amistad National Recreation Area, about 45 miles northwest of Del Rio via U.S. 90, this state park provides opportunities to take guided hikes to see what many consider the best pictographs in North America, possibly 4,000 years old. In addition, Seminole Canyon offers a short nature trail, camping, hiking through a rugged limestone terrain, wildlife viewing and bird-watching, and a museum.

Although it is believed that humans lived in this area at the end of the last Ice Age, some 12,000 years ago, they left few signs of their presence. Then, about 7,000 years ago, a different culture arrived, and within 3,000 years of their arrival they began to paint designs on sheltered rock walls. State park rangers lead hiking tours to several of the rock art sites.

The **Fate Bell Cave Dwelling Tour** is offered Wednesday through Sunday at 10am and 3pm. Cost is $3 per person, $1 for children ages 6 to 12, and reservations are not required. This is a moderately rated 2-mile round-trip hike that leads into Seminole Canyon to a huge rock shelter where participants will see hundreds of pictographs. The state park also has two guided tours that are offered only about a half-dozen times a year, by advance reservation through the park office (see below). The 1¾-mile round-trip **Upper Canyon Tour,** which costs $10 per person and takes 2 hours, leads to a normally closed area of the park in the upper section of the canyon to see pictographs and some railroad sites from 1882; and the 8-mile round-trip **Presa Canyon Tour,** which costs $25 per person, is an all-day hike into the lower canyon to see rock art sites that are normally off-limits to the public.

The park has a 6-mile round-trip **hiking/biking trail** along the top of the canyon that leads to a bluff from which you can see Panther Cave, and its namesake painted panther, across Lake Amistad (see the section on Amistad National Recreation Area, above). The trail has little elevation change, but is rocky with little shade. No one is allowed to go down into the canyon except on guided tours.

The **Windmill Nature Trail,** just behind the visitor center/museum, is an easy, although unshaded and therefore hot ⅓-mile loop. It meanders through a harsh environment of ocotillo, cacti, yucca, juniper, Texas mountain laurel, and other desert plants to its namesake windmill—actually the remains of two windmills, one from the 1890s and one from the 1920s.

The species of birds and animals to watch for in the park are much the same as at the adjacent Amistad National Recreation Area, and include birds such as great blue herons, black and turkey vultures, scaled quail, killdeer, white-winged and mourning doves, greater roadrunners, and northern mockingbirds. Also watch for great-tailed grackles, northern cardinals, pyrrhuloxia, ash-throated flycatchers, ladder-backed woodpeckers, and black-chinned hummingbirds. Mammals here include desert cottontails, black-tailed jackrabbits, coyotes, raccoons, white-tailed deer, striped skunks, and javelina.

The small campground, with 31 sites, sits on an open knoll covered with mesquite, creosote bush, yucca, cacti, and other desert plants. There are hot showers and a dump station. Sites with water only cost $8 per night and those with water and electricity cost $11 per night. Campsites can be reserved, with a credit card, by contacting **Texas State Parks** (✆ 512/389-8900; www.tpwd.state.tx.us).

The park is open 24 hours a day year-round, except for 2 weeks in December when it is open only to properly licensed hunters. The visitor center, with its excellent museum containing exhibits on the area's ancient inhabitants as well as its more recent history, is open daily from 8am to 5pm. Admission to the park costs $2 per person, free for children under 13. For information, contact **Seminole Canyon State Park & Historic Site,** P.O. Box 820, Comstock, TX 78837 (✆ 915/292-4464).

MORE TO SEE & DO IN DEL RIO

In addition to the attractions discussed below, there are a number of handsome **historic buildings** in Del Rio. A free brochure that describes and locates some three dozen buildings constructed between 1869 and 1929 is available at the chamber of commerce's visitor center (see "Visitor Information," above). Also, many visitors to Del Rio take an excursion across the border to **Ciudad Acuña,** a small Mexican city where you'll find a main street lined with shops offering a variety of leather goods, pottery, woven items, jewelry, and other products, plus a number of good restaurants. As with most border towns, American currency is welcome at practically all businesses in Ciudad Acuña.

Val Verde Winery   Established in 1883 by Italian immigrant Frank Qualia, Val Verde Winery, the state's oldest bonded winery, is now the pride and joy of third-generation vintner Thomas Qualia. Using grapes from the adjacent vineyards and other Texas vineyards, the winery produces from six to eight varieties of wine including its award-winning Don Luis Tawny Port, which is aged in white French oak barrels for 5 years. Short, informative guided tours are available at no charge, followed or substituted by free tastings. Wines are available by the bottle (usually $7.75–$25, with a 10% discount for purchases of 12 or more bottles), and a well-stocked gift shop sells wine paraphernalia, cookbooks, kitchen gizmos, and the like. Credit cards are not accepted. Allow 20 minutes for your visit.

100 Qualia Dr. (near its intersection with Hudson St.) ✆ 830/775-9714. Fax 830/775-5394. Free admission. Mon–Sat 10am–5pm.

Whitehead Memorial Museum ★★ (Kids)   This above-average small-town museum really does have something for everyone. Covering more than 2 acres, exhibits range from a replica of the Wild West saloon/courtroom of the infamous Judge Roy Bean to a wide variety of pioneer memorabilia and antiques. There's a complete mercantile store with upstairs living quarters from the late

Roy Bean

Judge Roy Bean, the self-styled "Law West of the Pecos," was by all accounts an eccentric character, and definitely the stuff of which legends are made. Born Phantly Roy Bean in Kentucky, probably around 1825, as a teenager he followed his two older brothers west, to California and then New Mexico. Although his brothers were mostly successful and respectable, Roy seemed to always be in trouble, usually related to gambling and women, and occasionally would leave town just a few steps ahead of the hangman.

During the Civil War, Bean reportedly smuggled supplies from Mexico to Confederate troops in Texas. After the war he ended up in San Antonio, where he gained a somewhat dubious reputation by selling firewood of questionable ownership. There he married 18-year-old Virginia Chávez, and they had four children before Bean abandoned them about 16 years later, when he followed a railroad construction crew west to the settlement of Vinegarroon, where it's believed he opened a saloon in a tent. Somehow, Bean got appointed as justice of the peace there in the summer of 1882.

Several years later Bean moved north to a small settlement along the railroad tracks that came to be called Langtry. Bean claimed he had named the town after the beautiful English actress of the day Lillie Langtry, with whom he was quite infatuated, although officials of the Southern Pacific Railroad stated that before Bean's arrival the town had received its name for a construction foreman. Bean wrote to Miss Langtry several times, asking her to visit the town "named in her honor," and it is believed that Bean may have seen her performonce in San Antonio. However, there is no evidence that they ever met.

Bean was elected and reelected as justice of the peace on and off for about 20 years—he reportedly was briefly thrown out of office when it became evident that he had received more votes than there were eligible voters. Bean's Langtry courtroom, which he called the Jersey Lilly after Miss Langtry, was also his saloon and home, and he often chose his juries from the saloon's customers.

Numerous stories about Bean's sometimes bizarre rulings have been told, and it's often difficult to tell fact from fiction. One fairly

1800s, a furnished log cabin, a blacksmith shop, an old caboose, a 1919 American LaFrance fire engine, and the early-20th-century office of Dr. Simon Rodriguez, the community's first Hispanic physician, who is credited with delivering more than 3,000 babies in the area. The graves of Roy Bean and one of his sons are also on the property. Among our favorite exhibits is the bizarre tin hand-powered washing machine, and we also enjoyed meeting "Pepe," a parrot that greets visitors at the door.

The star of the museum, however, is the fantastic Cadena Nativity—a 32-by-20-foot nativity scene that contains more than 600 figurines of people and animals plus another 600-plus miniature buildings, trees, bushes, and the like. The nativity scene was created over about 30 years by Beatriz Rodriguez Cadena, a well-documented story is the case of the murdered Chinese man. Bean was known for his racism, and when a railroad worker was charged with killing a Chinese laborer, Bean said that although it was definitely against the law to kill your fellow man, he could find no law against killing a "heathen Chinaman," so the case was dismissed. The killer was, however, required to pay for the dead man's funeral.

Another generally accepted story is the case of a man who had apparently fallen off a bridge and died. The dead man was found to have a gun and gold coins worth about $40 in his pockets, so Bean promptly fined the corpse $40 for carrying a concealed weapon. Bean gained perhaps his greatest notoriety for staging a heavyweight championship fight in 1896. At the time, prizefighting was illegal in Texas as well as in Mexico, just across the Rio Grande from Langtry. Bean staged the fight, between Bob Fitzsimmons and Peter Maher, on a sandbar in the Rio Grande, in a no-man's land between the United States and Mexico. Fitzsimmons won in about a minute and a half, and Bean made a tidy profit at his saloon selling drinks to the spectators.

Although there are also stories of Bean being a "hanging judge" there is no proof that he ever sentenced anyone to hang. But then, Bean kept no records at all of what transpired in his courtroom. Bean died in his saloon on March 16, 1903, supposedly after a binge of heavy drinking in Del Rio. Several months later, Lillie Langtry, who was performing in the western United States, spent 30 minutes in Langtry during a train stopover. She reportedly visited Bean's saloon and talked with the townspeople, and later, in her autobiography, she wrote that her visit to Langtry was "a short visit, but an unforgettable one."

To learn more about Bean, and visit his grave, stop at the Whitehead Memorial Museum (p. 359) or drive out to Langtry (60 miles west of Del Rio via U.S. 90) to Bean's restored saloon at the **Judge Roy Bean Visitor Center** (© **915/291-3340**). Dioramas and displays in this official state visitor center next to the saloon tell the story of Bean's life, and a motion-activated voice tells visitors to the saloon about the judge. The visitor center and saloon are open daily from 8am to 5pm and admission is free. Allow about an hour.

native of Mexico who emigrated to the United States and lived in Del Rio until her death in 1969. Most of the figurines were purchased in Mexico; some were handmade. The museum also has a small wedding chapel, built to honor the 300 years of Spanish influence on Christianity in the area (and available for ceremonies with advance notice), and a gift shop. Allow 1 to 2 hours.

1308 S. Main St. © **830/774-7568.** Fax 830/768-0223. www.whitehead-museum.com. Admission $4 adults, $3 seniors, $2 youths 13–18, $1 children 6–12. Tues–Sat 9am–4:30pm; Sun 1–5pm; check for possible holiday closures.

WHERE TO STAY IN DEL RIO

Avenue F, the main drag through town (which is U.S. highways 90, 277, and 377) is lined with chain motels. Choices here include **Best Western Inn of Del**

Rio, 810 Ave. F (© **800/336-3537** or 830/775-7511); **Days Suites,** 3808 Ave. F (© **800/329-7466** or 830/775-0585); **La Quinta Inn,** 2005 Ave. F (© **800/ 531-5900** or 830/775-7591); and **Ramada Inn,** 2101 Ave. F (© **800/272- 6232** or 830/775-1511). Room tax adds 13%.

Villa del Rio Bed & Breakfast ★★   For anyone who appreciates the old-world ambience of a historic mansion, a bit of pampering, and a creative and tasty breakfast, Villa del Rio is the place to stay while visiting the Del Rio area. This luxurious bed-and-breakfast is a Mediterranean-style villa—actually a mix of Italian and Mexican styles—built in 1887 that still has the beautiful original hand-painted Italian tile floors. You'll also find a series of small hand-painted murals that depict the area's rich history, and a large circular leather couch and big screen TV in the living room/lobby. Outside is a delightful sitting area around a Mexican-tile fountain and two acres of grounds covered with subtropical vegetation, including palm, magnolia, and century-old pecan trees.

There are three rooms on the second floor of the main house (no elevator), all with queen-size beds, cedar closets, and decorated with a mix of new and antique furnishings. The spacious and colorful Peacock Suite, which has a private bathroom, has a small screened sun porch and a small sitting room with a day bed that sleeps two. The other two somewhat smaller rooms—Yellow Rose of Texas and Southern Comfort—have white wicker furniture and share a connecting bathroom. Behind the main house and across a lawn is the Adobe Cottage. Originally the servants' quarters, this pleasant small house has 1½ bathrooms, a fully equipped kitchen, washer and dryer, and sleeps seven. The homemade breakfasts are hearty, Southwest-style cooking, such as jalapeño crepes served with a thick slice of baked ham, fruit, and cinnamon rolls. The inn is entirely nonsmoking.

123 Hudson Dr., Del Rio, TX 78840. © **800/995-1887** or 830/768-1100. Fax 830/775-2691. www.villadelrio. com. 4 units. $85–$175 double. Rates include full breakfast. AE, MC, V. Well-behaved older children welcome in the main house; children of any age are welcome in the cottage. *In room:* A/C, no phone.

WHERE TO DINE IN DEL RIO

As with lodging, you'll find most national restaurant chains, including Burger King, Kettle, McDonald's, Sirloin Stockade, and Subway located along Del Rio's Avenue F.

But you'll be better served (in more ways than one) by seeking out one of Del Rio's locally-owned restaurants, such as the **Avanti Authentic Italian Restaurant** ★★, 600 E. 12th St., at the intersection of 12th Street and Avenue G (© **830/775-3363;** www.avantidelrio.com). Although West Texas doesn't usually come to mind when you think of great Italian food, it will after a visit to Avanti. It offers genuine homemade lasagna, ravioli, and other Italian specialties—mostly northern Italian—prepared with fresh ingredients and cooked to order. We especially recommend the Venetian Chicken—a chicken breast rolled in cheese, with a sauce of heavy cream and Marsala wine. Those who want to experiment might opt for the Taste of Italy, a sampler of three different Italian dishes, and there's an excellent selection of northern Italian wines. Avanti is open Monday through Thursday from 11am to 9pm, Friday from 11am to 10pm, Saturday from 4 to 10pm, and Sunday from noon to 7:30pm. Main courses range from $6.95 to $16.

Big Bend & Guadalupe Mountains National Parks

by Don & Barb Laine

You'll find Texas's most spectacular mountain scenery, as well as absolutely wonderful opportunities for hiking and other forms of outdoor recreation, at Big Bend and Guadalupe Mountains National Parks. These parks also have an abundance of wildlife and both prehistoric and historic sites. Big Bend National Park is bounded by the Rio Grande, as it defines the U.S.–Mexico border, while Guadalupe Mountains National Park boasts the highest peak in Texas and a canyon that we believe has the prettiest scenery in the state, especially in the fall.

In addition to these two national parks in Texas, a third, Carlsbad Caverns National Park, is just over the state line in New Mexico. This easy side trip from Guadalupe Mountains National Park offers some of the world's most beautiful cave formations, and, if you're so inclined, the thrill of a true caving experience, as you crawl belly-to-rock through dirty, narrow, and dark underground passages.

1 Big Bend National Park ★★

Vast and wild, Big Bend National Park is a land of extremes, diversity, and a few contradictions. Its rugged terrain harbors thousands of species of plants and animals—some seen practically nowhere else on earth—and a visit here can be a hike into the sun-baked desert, a float down a majestic river through the canyons, or a trek among high mountains where bears and mountain lions rule.

Geologists tell us that millions of years ago an inland sea covered this area. As it dried up, sediments of sand and mud turned to rock, and then came the creation of mountains and roar of volcanoes until, finally, millions of years of erosion produced the delightful canyons and rock formations we marvel at today. These rock formations—with their wonderful hues of red, orange, yellow, white, and brown—have created a unique and awe-inspiring world of immensity and rugged beauty. This is not a fantasyland of delicate shapes and intricate carvings, like Bryce Canyon National Park in Utah, but a powerful and dominating landscape. Although the greatest natural sculptures are in the park's three major river canyons—the Santa Elena, Marsical, and Boquillas—throughout Big Bend you'll find spectacular and majestic examples of what nature can do with this mighty yet malleable building material we call rock.

Visitors to Big Bend National Park encounter not only a geologic wonder, but also a wild, rugged wilderness, populated by myriad desert and mountain plants and animals, ranging from box turtles and black-tailed jackrabbits to funny-looking javelina and powerful black bears and mountain lions. The park is considered a birders' paradise, with more bird species than at any other national park. It's also a wonderful spot to see wildflowers and the delightfully colorful display of cactus blooms.

For hikers, there's a tremendous variety of trails, from easy walks to rugged backcountry routes that barely qualify as trails at all. There are also opportunities to let the Rio Grande do the work as it carries rafts, canoes, and kayaks among canyons carved through 1,500 feet of solid rock. Drivers of 4×4s enjoy exploring the backcountry roads, and history buffs find a number of historical attractions and cultural experiences. Because of the vastness of this park, you'll need to schedule at least 2 full days here, and 3 or 4 would be better.

ESSENTIALS

GETTING THERE   Big Bend National Park is not really close to anything except the Rio Grande and Mexico. There is no public transportation to or through the park, so to get to the park you'll need a car. Park headquarters is 108 miles southeast of Alpine via Tex. 118, and 69 miles south of Marathon via U.S. 385. From El Paso, 328 miles northwest of the park, take I-10 east 121 miles to Exit 140, follow U.S. 90 southeast 99 miles to Alpine, then turn south on Tex. 118 for 108 miles to park headquarters.

There is train and bus service to Alpine, where the nearest hospital is located. For information contact the **Alpine Chamber of Commerce** (© **800/561-3735** or 915/837-2326; www.alpinetexas.com).

The nearest commercial airport is **Midland International** (© **915/560-2200;** www.midlandinternational.com), 235 miles north. From the airport, located between Midland and Odessa, take I-20 west about 50 miles to Exit 80 for Tex. 18, which you follow south about 50 miles to Fort Stockton. There take U.S. 385 south 125 miles through Marathon to park headquarters. Car rentals are available at the airport.

VISITOR INFORMATION   For advance information, contact the **Superintendent,** P.O. Box 129, Big Bend National Park, TX 79834 (© **915/477-2251;** www.nps.gov/bibe). For information on nearby attractions, as well as places to stay and eat, contact the **Big Bend Area Travel Association** (© **877/244-2363;** www.visitbigbend.com).

Books, maps, and videos are available from **Big Bend Natural History Association** (© **915/477-2236;** www.bigbendbookstore.org). The free park newspaper, *The Big Bend Paisano,* published seasonally by the National Park Service, is a great source of current information on special programs, suggested hikes, kids' activities, and local facilities, with telephone numbers inside and outside the park.

There are four visitor centers in the park: **Panther Junction Visitor Center** (open year-round) is centrally located at park headquarters; **Persimmon Gap Visitor Center** (open most of the year) is at the North Entrance to the park on U.S. 385; **Rio Grande Village Visitor Center** (open Nov–Apr) is on the river in the eastern part of the park; and **Chisos Basin Visitor Center** (open year-round) is in the Chisos Mountains in the middle of the park, at 5,401 feet in elevation. All visitor centers provide information, backcountry permits, books, and maps, and also have exhibits; there is a particularly impressive display on mountain lions at Chisos Basin. At **Castolon,** near the river in the southwest end of the park, there is a visitor contact station. Bulletin boards with schedules of ranger programs, notices of animal sightings, and other visitor information are located at each of the visitor centers and the contact station.

FEES, REGULATIONS & PERMITS   Entry into the park for up to a week costs $10 per passenger vehicle, and $5 per person on foot or bicycle. A free

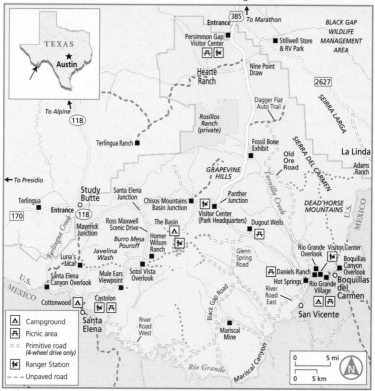

camping permit, available at any visitor center, is required for all backcountry camping; and free permits are also required for all river-float trips (see "Camping" and "River Running," later in this chapter).

Wood or ground fires are prohibited in the park, and caution is advised when using camp stoves, charcoal grills, and cigarettes. Smoking is prohibited on all trails. Check at the visitor centers for current drought conditions, and any special restrictions that may be in effect when you visit. Horses are not permitted on any paved roads in the park.

WHEN TO GO   Weather here is generally mild to hot, although because of the vast range of elevations—from about 1,800 feet at the eastern end of Boquillas Canyon to 7,825 feet on Emory Peak in the Chisos Mountains—conditions can vary greatly throughout the park at any given time. Essentially, the higher you go, the cooler and wetter you can expect it to be, although no section of the park gets a lot of precipitation.

Summers are hot, often well over 100°F (38°C) in the desert in May and June, and afternoon thunderstorms are common July through September. Winters are usually mild, although temperatures occasionally drop below freezing, and light snow is possible, especially in the Chisos Mountains. Fall and spring are usually warm and pleasant.

Average annual visitation is just over 300,000. Although the park is relatively uncrowded much of the year, there are several periods when lodging and campgrounds are full: college spring break (usually the 2nd and 3rd week in Mar), Easter weekend, Thanksgiving weekend, and the week between Christmas and New Year's Day. Park visitation is generally highest in March and April, and lowest in August and September.

Although the park's visitor centers, campgrounds, and other developed facilities may be taxed during the busier times, visitors can still be practically alone simply by seeking out lesser-used hiking trails. Those seeking solitude should discuss their hiking skills and expectations with rangers, who can offer advice on the best areas to get away from the crowd.

SAFETY   Watch for wild animals along the roads, particularly javelina, deer, and rabbits, especially at night when they may be blinded by your vehicle's headlights and stunned into standing still in the middle of the road. Of course, feeding wildlife is prohibited, not only to minimize the risk of injuries to park visitors, but also because it's bad for the animals.

The Basin Road Scenic Drive into the Chisos Mountains has sharp curves and steep grades and is not recommended for trailers longer than 20 feet or motor homes longer than 24 feet. The **Ross Maxwell Scenic Drive** to Castolon is okay for most RVs and trailers but can present a problem for those with insufficient power to handle the steep grade. These roads require extra caution by all users—drivers of motor vehicles, pedestrians, and bicyclists.

Desert heat can be dangerous. Hikers should carry at least 1 gallon of water per person per day; wear a hat, long pants, and long sleeves; and use a good sunscreen. Don't depend on springs as water sources, and avoid hiking in the middle of the day in summer. Early mornings and evenings are best. Talk to rangers about your plans before heading out; they can help you plan a hike in accordance with your ability and time frame. They can also advise you on expected weather conditions—sudden summer thunderstorms are common and can cause flash flooding in usually dry washes and canyons.

Swimming is not recommended in the Rio Grande, even though it may look tantalizingly inviting on a hot summer day. Waste materials and waterborne microorganisms have been found in the river, and can cause serious illness. Also, strong undercurrents, deep holes, and sharp rocks in shallow water are common.

RANGER PROGRAMS & SPECIAL EVENTS   Park ranger naturalists offer a variety of programs year-round. Illustrated evening programs take place at the 5,400-foot **Chisos Basin amphitheater** in summer. From November to April, evening programs are offered regularly in the amphitheater at **Rio Grande Village** and occasionally at Cottonwood Campground. Subjects include the park's geology, plants, animals, and human history. We especially like the ranger-led **nature walks** ⭐⭐, and rangers also occasionally lead driving tours. Workshops are also planned, on subjects such as adobe construction or photography. Look for weekly schedules on the bulletin boards scattered about the park.

The park has a **Junior Ranger Program** for children of all ages. Kids learn about the park through a variety of activities, and earn stickers, certificates, badges, and patches. Pick up Junior Ranger Activity Books ($1) at any visitor center.

The **Big Bend Natural History Association** (see "Visitor Information," above) offers a variety of seminars. Cost is about $50 per day and most seminars are for 1 or 2 days. Subjects could include black bears, archaeology, bats, birds, cacti, photography, and wildflowers.

The **International Good Neighbor Day Fiesta,** annually on the third Saturday in October, is designed to promote international friendship and understanding with music, dancing, food, and cultural demonstrations.

WHAT TO SEE & DO
EXPLORING THE HIGHLIGHTS BY CAR

There are several paved roads in the park—one goes through and others take you to different parts of the park. In addition, there are several unimproved roads requiring high clearance or 4×4 vehicles.

There are two scenic drives in the park, both with sharp curves and steep inclines and not recommended for certain RVs and trailers (see "Safety," above).

The 7-mile **Chisos Basin Drive,** which takes at least a half-hour, climbs up Green Gulch to Panther Pass before dropping down into the Basin. Near the pass there are some sharp curves, and parts of the road are at a 10% grade. The views are wonderful any time of the year, and particularly when the wildflowers dot the meadows, hills, and roadsides. The best month for wildflowers is usually October, after the summer rains.

When you've breathed your fill of clear mountain air, head back down and turn west toward the **Ross Maxwell Scenic Drive** through the Chihuahuan Desert and finally to the Rio Grande. This drive, which will take an hour or so plus stops, winds through the desert on the west side of the Chisos Mountains, providing a different perspective. Afterward, it passes through Castolon, and then continues along and above the river to **Santa Elena Canyon.** Here you should park and hike the trail, which climbs above the river, offering great views into the steep, narrow canyon (see "Hiking," below).

Another worthwhile drive, recommended for all vehicles, begins at **Panther Junction Visitor Center** and goes to Rio Grande Village. Allow a half-day. From the visitor center head southeast through the desert toward the high mountains that form the skyline in the distance. The first half of the drive passes through desert grasses, finally making a comeback after severe overgrazing in the decades before the establishment of the park in 1944. Recovery is slow in this harsh climate, but it is beginning to revegetate.

As the elevation gradually decreases, you progress further into the desert, and the grasses give way to lechugilla and ocotillo, cacti, and other arid-climate survivors. Off to the south is the long, rather flat **Chilicotal Mountain,** named for the chilicote, or Mescal-bean bushes, growing near its base. The chilicote's poisonous red bean is used in Mexico to kill rats. Several miles further the River Road turns off and heads southwest toward Castolon, more than 50 miles away. This is a primitive road for high-clearance vehicles only.

If you feel adventurous, take the **Hot Springs** turnoff about a mile beyond the Tornillo Creek Bridge. It follows a rough wash to a point overlooking the confluence of Tornillo Creek and the Rio Grande. A trail along the riverbank leads to several springs. The foundation of a bathhouse is a remnant of the town of Hot Springs, which thrived here about 20 years before the park was established, and continued as a concession for another 10 years.

Back on the paved road, you'll soon pass through a short tunnel in the limestone cliff, after which is a parking area for a short trail to a view point overlooking **Rio Grande Village.** It's just a short drive from here to Rio Grande Village, your destination, where you can take a ¼-mile nature trail ending at a high point above the Rio Grande, offering terrific views up and down the river.

HISTORIC SITES

There is evidence that prehistoric American Indians and later Apaches, Kiowas, and Comanches occupied this area. Throughout the park you can find **petroglyphs, pictographs,** and other signs of early human presence, including ruins of **stone shelters.** There are pictographs along the Hot Spring Trail (see "Hiking,"

> (*Tips* **Don't Cross the Rio Grande!**
>
> Increased national security following the September 11, 2001, terrorist attacks has put a stop to the once popular informal trips to Mexico that many visitors to Big Bend National Park used to make. Although there are no authorized border crossing points within the national park, for years Mexican citizens would use rowboats to ferry park visitors across the Rio Grande to several small Mexican villages, where the Americans could shop and eat genuine Mexican food. But Park Service officials have announced that those informal border crossings are no longer permitted, and anyone entering the United States from Mexico in the park is subject to a fine of up to $5,000 and imprisonment of up to 1 year.

---

below), and along the river. Watch for **mortar holes** scattered throughout the park, sometimes a foot deep, where Indians would grind seeds or mesquite beans.

Also within the park boundaries are the remains of several early-20th-century communities, a mercury mine, and projects by the Civilian Conservation Corps.

The **Castolon Historic District,** located in the southwest section of the park just off the Ross Maxwell Scenic Drive, includes the remains of homes and other buildings, many stabilized by the National Park Service, that were constructed in the early 1900s by Mexican American farmers, Anglo settlers, and the U.S. Army. The first is the **Alvino House,** the oldest surviving adobe structure in the park, dating from 1901. Nearby is **La Harmonia Store,** built in 1920 to house cavalry troops during the Mexican Revolution, but never actually used by soldiers because the war ended. The building was then purchased by two civilians, who converted it into a general store, calling it *La Harmonia* for the harmony and peaceful relations they hoped to encourage among area residents. The store continues to operate, selling snacks, groceries, and other necessities.

The village of **Glenn Springs,** located in the southeast section of the park and accessible by dirt road off the main park highway, owes its creation to having a reliable water source in an otherwise arid area. It was named for rancher H. E. Glenn, who grazed horses in the area until he was killed by Indians in the 1880s. By 1916 there were several ranches, a factory that produced wax from the candelilla plant, a store, a post office, and a residential village divided into two sections—one for the Anglos and the other for the Mexicans. But then Mexican bandit-revolutionaries crossed the border and attacked, killing and wounding a number of people, looting the store, and partially destroying the wax factory. Within 3 years the community was virtually deserted. Today, the spring still flows, and you can see the remains of several adobe buildings and other structures.

Remains of a small health resort can be seen at the **Hot Springs,** accessible by hiking trail or dirt road, along the Rio Grande west of Rio Grande Village in the park's southeast section. Construction of the resort was begun by J. O. Langford in 1909, who was forced to leave during the Mexican Revolution. However, Langford returned and completed the project in the 1920s, advertising the Hot Springs as "The Fountain of Youth that Ponce de León failed to find." Today you'll see the ruins of a general store/post office, other buildings, and a foundation that fills with natural mineral water, at about 105°F (41°C), creating an almost natural hot tub.

To get to the **Marsical Mine** you will likely need a four-wheel-drive or high-clearance vehicle. Located in the south-central part of the park, it is most easily accessed by River Road East, which begins 5 miles west of Rio Grande Village.

The mine operated on and off between 1900 and 1943, producing 1,400 76-pound flasks of mercury, which was almost one-quarter of the total amount of mercury produced in the United States during that time. Mining buildings, homes, the company store, a kiln, foundations, and other structures remain, in what is now a National Historic District.

Also in the park you can see some excellent examples of the work done by the **Civilian Conservation Corps** in the 1930s and early 1940s. These include stone culverts along the Basin Road, the Lost Mine Trail, and several buildings, including some stone-and-adobe cottages that are still in use at the Chisos Mountains Lodge.

OUTDOOR ADVENTURES

Local companies that provide equipment rentals and a variety of guided adventures both in the park and the general area include **Desert Sports** (© **888/ 989-6900** or 915/371-2727; www.desertsportstx.com), located on FM 170, 5 miles west of the junction of FM 170 and Tex. 118.

Bird-Watching & Wildlife Viewing ★★

There is an absolutely phenomenal variety of wildlife at Big Bend National Park. About 450 species of birds will be found here over the course of the year—that's more than at any other national park and nearly half of all those found in North America. At latest count there are also about 75 species of mammals, close to 70 species of reptiles and amphibians, and more than three dozen species of fish.

This is the only place in the United States where you'll find the Mexican long-nosed bat, listed by the federal government as an endangered species. Other **endangered species** that make their homes in the park include the black-capped vireo and a tiny fish—the Big Bend gambusia, which we hope prospers and multiplies because its favorite food is mosquito larvae.

Birders consider Big Bend National Park a key bird-watching destination, especially for those looking for some of America's more unusual **birds.** Among the park's top bird-watching spots are Rio Grande Village and Cottonwood campgrounds, the Chisos Basin, and the Hot Springs. Species to watch for include the colorful golden-fronted woodpecker, which can often be seen year-round among the cottonwood trees along the Rio Grande; and the rare colima warbler, whose range in the United States consists solely of the Chisos Mountains at Big Bend National Park. Among the hundreds of other birds that call the park home, at least part of the year, are scaled quail, spotted sandpipers, white-winged doves, greater roadrunners, lesser night-hawks, white-throated swifts, black-chinned and broad-tailed hummingbirds, acorn woodpeckers, northern flickers, western wood-pewees, ash-throated flycatchers, tufted titmice, bushtits, cactus and canyon wrens, loggerhead shrikes, Wilson's warblers, and Scott's orioles.

Mammals you may see in the park include desert cottontails, black-tailed jackrabbits, rock squirrels, Texas antelope squirrels, Merriam's kangaroo rats, coyotes, gray foxes, raccoons, striped skunks, mule deer, and white-tailed deer. There are occasional sightings of mountain lions, usually called panthers here, in the Green Gulch and Chisos Basin areas. Three attacks on humans have occurred. Black bears, which were frequently seen in the area until about 1940, were mostly killed off by area ranchers who saw them as a threat to their livestock. However, with the protection provided by national park status, they began to return in the mid-1980s, and have now established a small population.

There are a number of **reptiles** in the park, including some poisonous snakes, such as diamondback, Mojave, rock, and black-tailed rattlesnakes, plus the trans-pecos copperhead. Fortunately, it is unlikely you will see a rattler or copperhead, since they avoid both the heat of the day and busy areas. You are more apt to encounter nonpoisonous western coachwhips, which are often seen speeding across trails and roadways. Sometimes called "red racers," they're reddish, sometimes bright red, and among America's fastest snakes. Other nonpoisonous snakes that inhabit the park include Texas whipsnakes, spotted night snakes, southwestern black-headed snakes, and black-necked garter snakes.

Among the **lizards** you may see scurrying along desert roads and trails is the southwestern earless lizard—adult males are green with black and white chevrons on their lower sides, and often curl their black-striped tails over their backs. You'll also see various whiptail lizards in the desert, but in the canyons and higher in the mountains, watch for the crevice spiny lizard, which is covered with scales and has a dark collar. Although rare, there are also **western box turtles** in the park, as well as several types of more common water turtles.

Hiking ★★★

Big Bend National Park is a wonderful park for hikers, with a wide variety of trails, most of which are easy or moderate. There are a number of short, easy interpretive nature walks, either with booklets available at the trail heads or signs along the trail. One example is the **Panther Path,** which is 50 yards round-trip, outside the Panther Junction Visitor Center, that offers a walk through a garden of cacti and other desert plants. We also enjoy the **Window View Trail,** which is 0.3 miles round-trip, and which is accessible via the Chisos Basin Trailhead. This level, paved, and wheelchair-accessible self-guided nature trail runs along a low hill and offers beautiful sunset views through the Window, a V-shaped opening in the mountains to the west. The **Rio Grande Village Nature Trail** ★, 0.75 miles round-trip, which starts at the southeast corner of Rio Grande Village Campground across from site 18, is a good choice for sunrise and sunset views. It climbs from the surprisingly lush river floodplain about 125 feet into desert terrain to a hilltop that offers excellent panoramic vistas.

Those who want to see historic structures should try the easy 1-mile **Hot Springs Trail,** which is at the end of an improved dirt road to Hot Springs, off the road to Rio Grande Village. An interpretive booklet available at the trail head describes the sights, including a historic health resort and homestead (see "Historic Sites," above), along this loop. Fairly substantial ruins remain of a general store/post office, other buildings, and a foundation that fills with natural mineral water, at about 105°F (41°C), creating an inviting hot tub. Also along the trail are pictographs left by ancient Indians, and panoramic views of the Rio Grande and Mexico.

Among other easy hikes is the **Tuff Canyon Trail,** 0.75 miles round-trip, which is accessed from the Ross Maxwell Scenic Drive, 5 miles south of the Mule Ears Overlook access road. This walk leads into a narrow canyon, carved from soft volcanic rock called tuff, with several canyon overlooks. The 1.6-mile **Chisos Basin Loop Trail** (access at the Chisos Basin Trailhead) is a fairly easy walk that climbs about 350 feet into a pretty meadow and leads to an overlook that offers good views of the park's mountains, including Emory Peak, highest point in the park at 7,825 feet. The easy **Grapevine Hills Trail,** which is 2.2 miles round-trip, begins about 6 miles down the unpaved Grapevine Hills Road. It has an elevation change of about 240 feet as it follows a sandy wash through the desert, among massive granite boulders, ending at a picturesque balancing rock.

Among shorter moderately rated trails, we heartily recommend the 0.8-mile one-way **Santa Elena Canyon Trail** ★★★, which you'll find at the end of Ross

Maxwell Scenic Drive. You may get your feet wet crossing a broad creek on this trail, which also takes you up a series of steep steps. But it's one of the most scenic short trails in the park, leading along the canyon wall, with good views of rafters on the Rio Grande, and down among the boulders along the river. Interpretive signs describe the canyon environment. Beware of flash flooding as you cross the Terlingua Creek, and skip this trail if the creek is running swiftly. Another good moderate hike is the **Boquillas Canyon Trail** ✯, which is 1.4 miles round-trip and starts at the end of Boquillas Canyon Road. This hike begins by climbing a low hill and then drops down to the Rio Grande, ending near a shallow cave and huge sand dune. There are good views of the scenic canyon and the Mexican village of Boquillas, across the Rio Grande.

Among longer trails, we suggest the moderately rated 3.8-mile round-trip **Mule Ears Spring Trail** ✯, which you'll find at the Mule Ears Overlook Parking Area along the Ross Maxwell Scenic Drive. This relatively flat desert trail crosses several arroyos and then follows a wash most of the way to Mule Ears Spring. It offers great views of unusual rock formations, such as the Mule Ears, and ends at a historic ranch house and rock corral. At 4 miles round-trip the moderate **Pine Canyon Trail** takes you from desert grasslands dotted with sotols into a pretty canyon with dense stands of piñon, juniper, oak, and finally bigtooth maple and ponderosa pine. At the higher elevations (it climbs 1,000 ft.) you'll also see Texas madrones—evergreen trees with smooth reddish bark that is shed each summer. At the end of the trail is a 200-foot cliff, which becomes a picturesque waterfall after heavy rains. This trail is located at the end of unpaved Pine Canyon Road (check on road conditions before going).

Horseback Riding

Horses are permitted on most dirt roads and many park trails (check with rangers for specifics), and may be kept overnight at many of the park's primitive campsites, although not at the developed campgrounds. The **Government Springs Campsite,** located 3½ miles from Panther Junction, is a primitive campsite with a corral that accommodates up to eight horses. It can be reserved up to 10 weeks in advance (© **915/477-2241**). Those riding horses in the park must get free stock use permits, which should be obtained in person up to 24 hours in advance at any of the park's visitor centers.

Although there are no commercial outfitters offering guided rides in the park as of this writing, there are opportunities for rides just outside the park on private land, at nearby Big Bend Ranch State Park, and across the river in Mexico. **Big Bend Stables** (© **800/887-4331** or 915/371-2212), and **Lajitas Stables** (© **888/508-7667** or 915/424-3238; www.lajitasstables.com), offer a variety of guided trail rides, lasting from 1 hour to all day to 5 days. Some trips follow canyon trails; others visit ancient Indian camps, ghost towns, or abandoned mines. They can also take you to see pictographs, fossils, and petrified wood. Both stables are under the same management, and the company also has access to facilities in Mexico. Typical rates are $25 for 1 hour, $58 for 4 hours, and $110 for a full day; multiday trips are usually about $135 to $160 per day, and include all meals and camping equipment, as well as the horse. Novice riders and children 4 years and up are welcome.

Mountain Biking

Bikes are not permitted on hiking trails, but are allowed on the park's many established dirt roads. Mountain bikes are available for rent from **Desert Sports** (see above), at a cost of $25 per day, $125 for 5 to 7 days, and $15 for each additional day after 7 days. The company also offers 1-day and multiday guided trips, including a combination mountain-biking and float trip in the park—3 days for $350.

River Running ★

The Rio Grande follows the southern edge of the park for 118 miles, and extends another 127 miles downstream as a designated Wild and Scenic River. The river offers mostly fairly calm float trips, but does have a few sections of rough white water during high-water times. It can usually be run in a raft, canoe, or kayak. You can either bring your own equipment, or rent equipment near the park (none is available in the park), but for novices it's safest to take a trip with one of several river guides approved by the National Park Service.

Those planning trips on their own must obtain free permits at a park visitor center, in person only, no more than 24 hours before the trip. Permits for the lower canyons of the Rio Grande Wild and Scenic River are available at the **Persimmon Gap Visitor Center,** when it's open, and a self-serve permit station located at **Stillwell Store and RV Park,** 7 miles from the park's North Entrance on FM 2627. Permits for the section of river through Santa Elena Canyon can also be obtained at the **Barton Warnock Environmental Education Center** 1 mile east of the community of Lajitas, Texas, about 20 miles from the park's west entrance. Park rangers, however, strongly advise that everyone planning a river trip check with them beforehand to get the latest river conditions. A river-running booklet, with additional information, is available at park visitor centers and from the **Big Bend Natural History Association** (see "Visitor Information," above).

Rafts, inflatable kayaks, and canoes can be rented from **Desert Sports** (**888/989-6900** or 915/371-2727; www.desertsportstx.com). Rafts cost $20 per person per day (3-person minimum) with discounts for trips longer than 4 days; inflatable kayaks cost $30 per day for one person and $40 per day for two people; and canoes cost $40 per day, with discounts for multiday rentals. The company also provides shuttle services, and offers guided 1-day and multiday canoe and raft trips, where you can either grab a paddle and take an active role, or sit back and let your boatman and the river do the work. Typical prices are $250 per person for 2 days on the river through Santa Elena Canyon; and $425 per person for 3 days on the river through Marsical Canyon, considered the most remote canyon in the national park. Desert Sports also offers trips that combine a float trip with hiking or mountain biking. Also see "Mountain Biking," above.

Another company that provides guided trips on the Rio Grande is **Big Bend River Tours** (© **800/545-4240** or 915/371-3033; www.bigbendrivertours.com), which has raft trips daily year-round. Trips range from a delightful half-day float for about $62 per person to 10-day excursions for about $1,550 per person. Among the company's most popular trips is the 21-mile float through beautiful Santa Elena Canyon, which offers spectacular scenery and wonderful serenity, plus the excitement of a challenging section of rapids called the Rockslide. There are often opportunities to see javelinas, coyotes, beavers, wild burros, golden eagles, and peregrine falcons. The canyon can be explored on a day trip (about $130 per person), a 2-day trip (about $285 per person), or a 3-day trip (about $425 per person), with rates varying based on the number of people making the trip. The longer trips include a stop in a side canyon with waterfalls and peaceful swimming holes. Big Bend River Tours also offers guided canoe and inflatable kayak trips, provides a shuttle service, and rents equipment.

Also offering raft trips year-round, at similar rates, is **Far Flung Adventures** (② **800/359-4138;** www.farflung.com); **Rio Grande Adventures** (② **800/343-1640;** www.riograndeadventures.com); and **Texas River Expeditions** (② **800/ 839-7238** or 915/371-2633; www.texasriver.com).

WHERE TO STAY & DINE

This is an isolated area, and you won't find your favorite chain motel or restaurant right around the corner. Make lodging reservations well in advance, especially in winter, the high season here when rates are highest.

IN THE PARK

Chisos Mountains Lodge ⚡ The best place to stay while exploring Big Bend, Chisos Mountains Lodge offers a variety of accommodations ranging from simple motel rooms to our choice, the historic stone cottages. Built by the Civilian Conservation Corps in the 1930s, the six delightful cottages have a rustic feel that seems right in a national park setting. They have stone floors, wooden furniture, three double beds, and covered porches. Book as far in advance as possible.

The lodge units, which are also a bit on the rustic side, have one double and one single bed, wood furnishings, and painted brick walls with Western and/or Southwestern art. The lodge's motel rooms are small and simply decorated, with two double beds and terrific views of the Chisos Mountains. The Casa Grande Motor Lodge, also part of the Chisos Mountains Lodge, offers spacious and more modern motel rooms, attractively furnished, with two beds and private balconies.

Chisos Basin, Big Bend National Park, TX 79834-9999. ② **915/477-2291.** Fax 915/477-2352. www.chisos mountainslodge.com or www.foreverresorts.com. 72 units. $79–$84 double. AE, DC, DISC, MC, V. Pets accepted. *In room:* A/C in motel and Casa Grande units, no phone.

Chisos Mountains Lodge Restaurant AMERICAN Splendid views from the dining room's large windows are a big plus at this lodge restaurant, which offers good food at reasonable prices. The menu generally includes steak, pork chops, roast turkey, baked trout, and sandwiches, plus specials such as chicken fajitas, and a vegetarian dish. There's a good breakfast buffet ($6.95), and an all-you-can-eat soup and salad bar at lunch and dinner ($6.95). Hikers and others on the move can order a "traveler's lunch" to be picked up the next morning.

Chisos Basin, Big Bend National Park. ② **915/477-2291.** Main courses $6.25–$16. AE, DC, DISC, MC, V. Daily 7am–8pm.

THE STUDY BUTTE–TERLINGUA AREA

Just outside the national park's west entrance, this is the closest community to the park with lodging and other services. Here you'll find the **Big Bend Motor Inn,** at the junction of Tex. 118 and FM 170 (P.O. Box 336), Terlingua, TX 79852 (② **800/848-BEND** or 915/371-2218), offering simple but comfortable and well-maintained modern motel rooms, with rates of $75 to $85 double and $125 to $145 for suites with kitchens. Under the same management, the **Mission Lodge** across the street has slightly smaller rooms (although they were renovated in 2002) and rates of $65 to $75 double. The **Chisos Mining Co. Motel,** on FM 170 about ¾-mile west of Tex. 118 (P.O. Box 228), Terlingua, TX 79852 (② **915/371-2254;** www.cmcm.cc), is an attractive, well-maintained property. It has standard motel units (some with TVs), and cabins, which have fully equipped kitchens but no TVs.

The **Big Bend Motor Inn Restaurant & Convenience Store,** at the Big Bend Motor Inn discussed above (② **915/371-2483**), serves basic Mexican and

American fare such as sandwiches and burgers, burritos and tacos, and an excellent breakfast—try the breakfast burrito or biscuits and gravy. You can also get full dinners such as chicken fried steak as well as Mexican combination plates. It's open daily from 6am to 10pm and main courses cost $4 to $12.

CAMPING

A free camping permit, available at any visitor center, is required for use of the primitive backcountry roadside and backpacking campsites. All are open year-round.

In the Park

There are three developed campgrounds run by the National Park Service (no showers, laundry facilities, or RV hook-ups; $8 per night), and an RV park run by a concessionaire. All are first-come first-served.

Rio Grande Village Campground is the largest, with 100 sites, flush toilets, running water, and a dump station. It has numerous trees, many with prickly pear cacti growing up around them, and thorny bushes everywhere. Sites are either graveled or paved and are nicely spaced for privacy. Sites are often taken by 1pm in winter (the busy season). One area is designated a "No Generator Zone." Separate but within walking distance is **Rio Grande Village Trailer Park,** a concessionaire-operated RV park with 25 sites with full hook-ups. It looks like a parking lot in the midst of grass and trees, fully paved with curbs and back-in sites (no pull-throughs). Cost is $15 per night. Tents are not permitted. A small store has limited camping supplies and groceries, a coin-operated laundry, showers for a fee, propane, and gasoline.

Chisos Basin Campground ★★, although not heavily wooded, has small piñon and juniper trees and 65 well-spaced sites. The highest-elevation campground in the park, at 5,401 feet, it's nestled around a circular road in a bowl below the visitor center. There is a dump station, flush toilets, and running water. The access road to the campground is steep and curved, so take it slowly. The campground is not recommended for trailers over 20 feet or motor homes over 24 feet.

Cottonwood Campground is named for the huge old cottonwood trees that dominate the scene. The 31 sites in this rather rustic area are gravel and spacious, within walking distance of the river. There are pit toilets, and generators may not be used.

Near the Park

About 7 miles east of the park's North Entrance on FM 2627 is **Stillwell Store and RV Park,** HC 65, Box 430, Alpine, TX 79830-9752 (© and fax **915/376-2244**), a casual RV park in desert terrain that's open year-round. There are two areas across the road from each other. The west side has full hook-ups, while the east has water and electric only, but the east side also features horse corrals and plenty of room for horse trailers. There are 80 RV sites ($14–$16 per night) plus almost unlimited space for tenters, who are charged $5 per person. There's a dump station, showers, a self-serve laundry, and a public phone. The park office is at the Stillwell Store, where you can get groceries, limited camping supplies, and gasoline. There is also a small museum (donations accepted), with exhibits from the Stillwell family's pioneer days.

About 3 miles from the West Entrance to the park is **Terlingua Oasis RV Park,** part of the Big Bend Motor Inn complex at the junction of Tex. 118 and FM 170 (P.O. Box 336, Terlingua, TX 79852; © **800/848-BEND** or 915/371-2218). This park, which is open year-round, offers pull-through and back-in RV sites and grassy tent areas. There are pay showers, a laundry, gas and diesel fuel, a convenience store, recreation room, planned activities, and a gift shop, but no dump station. Cost is $9 for tent sites, $16 for water and electric hookups, and $21 for water, electric, and sewer hookups.

2 Guadalupe Mountains National Park

Once a long reef poking up through the ocean, then a dense forest, Guadalupe Mountains National Park is today a rugged wilderness of tall Douglas firs and lush vegetation rising out of a vast desert. Here you will find varied hiking trails, panoramic vistas, the highest peak in Texas, plant and animal life unique in the Southwest, and a canyon that many believe is the prettiest spot in all of Texas.

As you approach from the north, the mountains seem to rise gradually from the landscape, but seen from the south they stand tall and dignified. El Capitan, the southern tip of the reef escarpment, watches over the landscape like a sentinel. In the south-central section of the park, Guadalupe Peak, at 8,749 feet the highest mountain in Texas, provides hikers with incredible views of the surrounding mountains and desert.

The 86,416-acre park has several separate sections. Park headquarters and the visitor center are at Pine Springs, along the park's southeast edge, where you'll also find a campground and several trail heads, including one with access to the Guadalupe Peak Trail, the park's premier mountain hike. Nearby, a short dirt road leads to historic Frijole Ranch, with a museum and more trail heads. A horse corral is nearby. The McKittrick Canyon section of the park, near its northeast corner, gets our vote as the most beautiful spot in Texas, especially in fall, when its oaks, maples, and other trees produce a spectacular show of color. A day-use area only, McKittrick Canyon has a delightful although intermittent stream, a wide variety of plant and animal life, several trail heads, and historic buildings. Along the park's northern boundary, practically in New Mexico, is the secluded and forested Dog Canyon.

Particularly impressive about Guadalupe Mountains National Park is its vast variety of flora and fauna. You'll find species here that don't seem to belong in west Texas, such as the maple and oak that produce the wonderful fall colors in McKittrick Canyon. Scientists say these seemingly out-of-place plants and animals are leftovers from a time when this region was cooler and wetter. As the climate changed and the desert spread, some species were able to survive in these mountains, where conditions remained somewhat cooler and more moist. At the base of the mountains, at lower elevations, you'll find desert plants such as sotol, agave, and prickly pear cactus; but as you start to climb, especially in stream-nurtured canyons, expect to encounter ponderosa pine, ash, walnut, oak, and ferns. Wildlife abounds, including mule deer, elk, and all sorts of birds and snakes.

It takes several days to fully explore this park, but just a half-day trip to McKittrick Canyon would be well worth your time.

ESSENTIALS

GETTING THERE Located on the border of New Mexico and Texas, the park is 55 miles southwest of Carlsbad, New Mexico, along U.S. 62/180. From El Paso drive northeast 110 miles on U.S. 62/180 to the Pine Springs Visitor Center.

Air travelers can fly to **Cavern City Air Terminal** (© 505/887-1500), at the south edge of the city of Carlsbad, which has commercial service from Albuquerque with **Mesa Airlines** (© 505/885-0245), plus Hertz car rentals. The nearest major airport is **El Paso International** (© 915/772-4271) in central El

Paso just north of I-10, with service from most major airlines and car rental companies; see chapter 9 for more information.

VISITOR INFORMATION Contact **Guadalupe Mountains National Park,** HC 60, Box 400, Salt Flat, TX 79847-9400 (© **915/828-3251;** www. nps.gov/gumo). Books and maps can be ordered from the **Carlsbad Caverns Guadalupe Mountains Association,** 727 Carlsbad Caverns Hwy., Carlsbad, NM 88220 (© **505/785-2232, ext. 481;** www.ccgma.org). *The Capitan Reef,* a free seasonal publication available at the visitor center, contains pertinent current information.

Park headquarters and the main visitor center are located at Pine Springs just off U.S. 62/180. There are three other access points along this side of the park: Frijole Ranch, about 1½ miles east of Pine Springs and a mile north of the highway; McKittrick Canyon (day use only), about 7 miles east and 4 miles north of the highway; and Williams Ranch, about 8 miles south of Pine Springs and 8 miles north of the highway on a four-wheel-drive road.

The **Pine Springs Visitor Center,** open daily year-round except Christmas, has natural history exhibits, a bookstore, and an introductory slide program. **McKittrick Canyon** has a visitor contact station with outdoor exhibits and an outdoor slide program on the history, geology, and natural history of the canyon. On the north side of the park is **Dog Canyon Ranger Station,** at the end of N. Mex. 137, about 70 miles from Carlsbad and 110 miles from park headquarters. Information, restrooms, and drinking water are available.

FEES, REGULATIONS & PERMITS Entry into the park is free. Backcountry camping is free, but a permit is required. Corrals are available for those who bring their horses to ride in the park; although use is free, permits are required. All permits are available at the Pine Springs Visitor Center and Dog Canyon Ranger Station, and must be requested in person, either the day before or the day of use. Horses are prohibited in the backcountry overnight.

Visitors to McKittrick Canyon, a day-use area, must stay on the trail; entering the stream is not permitted. The McKittrick Canyon **entrance gate** opens at 8am daily, and closes at 4:30pm Mountain Standard Time and at 6pm Mountain Daylight Time. Neither wood nor charcoal fires are allowed anywhere in the park.

WHEN TO GO In general, summers in the Guadalupe Mountains are hot (highs in the 80s and 90s and lows in the 60s) and winters are mild (highs in the 50s and 60s and lows in the upper 20s and 30s), but there can be sudden and extreme changes in the weather at any time. In winter and spring, high winds can whip down the mountain slopes, sometimes reaching 100 mph; on hot summer days, thunderstorms can blow up quickly. The sun is warm even in winter, and summer nights are generally cool no matter how hot the afternoon. Clothing that can be layered is best, comfortable and sturdy walking/hiking shoes are a must, a hat and sunscreen are highly recommended, and plenty of drinking water is essential for hikers.

Overall, Guadalupe Mountains National Park is one of America's lesser-visited national parks, with attendance of only about 225,000 each year. This is partly because it is primarily a wilderness park, where you'll have to tackle rugged hiking trails to get to the best vistas, and also because of its isolation. The only time the park might be considered even slightly crowded is during spring break time at Texas and New Mexico colleges, usually in March, when students bring their backpacks and hit the trails. There are also quite a few families visiting during summer, although the park is not usually crowded even then, and visitation drops considerably once schools open in late August.

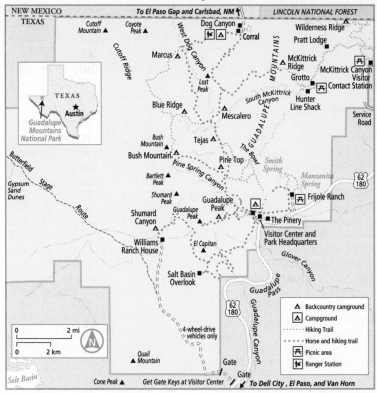

An exception is McKittrick Canyon, renowned throughout the Southwest for its beautiful fall colors, at their best in late October and early November. The one road into McKittrick Canyon will be a bit busy then, but once you get on the trails you can usually walk away from the people.

SAFETY   This is extremely rugged country, with sometimes unpredictable weather, and hikers need to be well prepared, with proper hiking boots and plenty of water. Because the park's backcountry trails often crisscross each other and can be confusing, rangers strongly recommend that hikers carry topographical maps.

RANGER PROGRAMS   On summer evenings, rangers offer programs at the campground amphitheater.

WHAT TO SEE & DO
EXPLORING THE HIGHLIGHTS BY CAR
This is not the place for the vehicle-bound. There are no paved scenic drives traversing the park; roads here are simply means of getting to historical sites and trail heads.

HISTORIC SITES
The Pinery was one of 200 stagecoach stations along the 2,800-mile Butterfield Overland Mail Coach Route. The stations provided fresh mules every 20 miles and a new coach every 300 miles, in order to maintain the grueling speed of 5

mph 24 hours a day. John Butterfield had seen the need for overland mail delivery between the eastern states and the West Coast, so he designed a route and the coaches, and acquired a federal contract to deliver the St. Louis mail to San Francisco in 25 days. In March 1857 this was a real feat, and the remaining rock walls at the ruins of the Pinery, which you can see on The Pinery Trail (see "Hiking," below) commemorate Butterfield's achievement.

Located in McKittrick Canyon, **Pratt Lodge** was built by Wallace E. Pratt in 1931 and 1932, of stone quarried from the base of the Guadalupe Mountains, using heart-of-pine from east Texas for rafters, collar beams, and roof supports. Pratt, a geologist for the Humble Oil Co. (now Exxon), and his family came for summer vacations when the heat in Houston became unbearable. He finally retired here in 1945. In 1957, the Pratts donated 5,632 acres of their 16,000-acre ranch to the federal government to begin the national park. In addition to the grand stone lodge, there are several outbuildings, stone picnic tables, and a stone fence. These can be seen on the McKittrick Canyon Trail (see "Hiking," below).

Williams Ranch House rests at the base of a 3,000-foot rock cliff on the west face of the Guadalupe Mountains. The 7.3-mile access road, navigable only by high-clearance 4×4s, follows part of the old Butterfield Overland Mail Route for about 2 miles. The road crosses private land and has two locked metal gates, for which you must sign out keys at the visitor center.

History is unclear on exactly who built the house and when, but it's believed to have been built around 1908, and it is fairly certain that the first inhabitants for any significant period of time were Henry and Rena Belcher. For almost 10 years, they maintained a substantial ranch here, at times with close to 3,000 head of longhorn cattle. Water was piped from Bone Spring down the canyon to holding tanks in the lowlands. James Adolphus Williams acquired the property around 1917, and with the help of an Indian friend, ranched and farmed the land until moving to New Mexico in 1941. After Williams's death in 1942, Judge J. C. Hunter bought the property, adding it to his already large holdings in the Guadalupes.

Another historic site is **Frijole Ranch,** which was a working ranch from when it was built in the 1870s until 1972. Inside the ranch house is a museum with exhibits on the cultural history of the Guadalupe Mountains, including prehistoric Indians, the later Mescalero Apaches, Spanish conquistadors, and ranchers of the 19th and 20th centuries. On the grounds are several historic buildings, including a schoolhouse.

OUTDOOR ADVENTURES
Hiking 🎿🎿
This is a prime hiker's park, with more than 80 miles of trails that range from easy walks to steep, strenuous, and sometimes treacherous adventures. Among shorter trails, try the **Indian Meadow Nature Trail** 🎿, with access from Dog Canyon Campground (walk south from the water fountain). This exceptionally easy 0.6-mile round-trip stroll follows a series of numbered stops keyed to a free brochure, available at the trail head. You'll learn about the native vegetation and cultural history of the area as you ramble along this virtually level dirt trail. The name comes from early settlers, who told of seeing Indian tepees in this lovely meadow. The **McKittrick Canyon Nature Trail** 🎿, rated easy to moderate, is 0.9 mile round-trip, and begins at the McKittrick Canyon contact station. A great way to discover the variety of plants and animals that inhabit the canyon, this trail, which has some steep climbs, has numerous interpretive signs along the path telling you why rattlesnakes are underappreciated and how the cactus supplies food and water for wildlife.

The easy 0.75-mile round-trip **Pinery Trail** (paved and accessible by wheelchair) gives visitors a brief introduction to the low-elevation environment at the park. Interpretive signs discuss both the plants along the trail and the history of the area. About 0.25 mile from the visitor center the trail makes a loop around the ruins of an old horse-changing station, left over from the Butterfield Stage Route (see "Historic Sites," above). The trail head is by the Pine Springs Visitor Center; or from the parking area on U.S. 62/180, located 1 mile north of the visitor center entrance road.

Among the park's longer trails our favorite is the moderate-to-difficult **McKittrick Canyon Trail** ★★★, which is 5.1 miles one-way, with access at the McKittrick Canyon Trailhead. McKittrick Canyon is the most beautiful spot in Texas, and this trail explores the length of it. The first 2.3 miles to the Pratt Lodge are easy; the following 1.2 miles to the Grotto gain 340 feet in elevation and are considered moderate; and the strenuous climb to the Notch rises 1,300 feet in 1.6 miles. Even so, this is one of the most popular hikes in the park, though not everyone makes it to the Notch.

The canyon is forested with conifers and deciduous trees. In fall the maples, oaks, and other hardwoods burst into color, painting the world in bright colors set off by the rich variety of the evergreens. The stream in the canyon, which appears and disappears several times in the first 3 miles of the trail, is a permanent stream with reproducing trout. Hikers may not drink from, wade in, or disturb the stream in any way.

The first part of the trail is wide and seems quite flat, crossing the stream twice on its way to Pratt Lodge, which is wonderfully situated at the convergence of North and South McKittrick canyons. About a mile from the lodge a short spur veers off to the left to the Grotto, a recess with odd formations that look like they belong underground in a cave. This is a great spot for lunch at one of the stone picnic tables. Continuing down the spur trail to its end, you reach the Hunter Line Cabin, which served as temporary quarters for ranch hands of the Hunter family. Beyond the cabin, South McKittrick Canyon has been preserved as a Research Natural Area with no entry. Return to the main trail and continue toward the Notch, or head back down the canyon to your car. In another 0.5 mile, the trail begins switchbacking up the side of South McKittrick Canyon for the steepest ascent in the park, until it slips through the Notch, a distinctive narrow spot in the cliff. Sit down and rest while you absorb the incredible scenery. The view down the canyon is magnificent, and quite dazzling in autumn. You can see both Hunter Line Cabin and Pratt Lodge in the distance. Remember to start down in time to reach your car well before the gate closes (see "Fees, Regulations & Permits," above).

To stand at the highest point in Texas, hike the strenuous **Guadalupe Peak Trail** ★★, which goes 4.2 miles from the trail head in Pine Springs Campground to the top of 8,749-foot high Guadalupe Peak, where the magnificent views make the almost 3,000-foot climb worthwhile. If you have only 1 day to explore this park, and you are an average or better hiker, this is the hike you should choose. Start early, take plenty of water, and be prepared to work. When you've gone about halfway, you'll see what seems to be the top not too far ahead, but beware: This is a false summit. Study the changing life zones as you climb from the desert into the higher-elevation pine forests—this will take your mind off your straining muscles and aching lungs. A mile short of the summit, a campground lies in one of the rare level spots on the mountain. If you plan to spend the night, anchor your tent strongly since the winds can be ferocious up here, especially in spring.

From the summit, the views are stupendous. To the north are Bush Mountain and Shumard Peak, the next two highest points in Texas, with respective elevations of 8,631 and 8,615 feet. The Chihuahuan Desert stretches to the south, interrupted only by the Delaware and Sierra Diablo Mountains. This is one of those "On a clear day you can see forever" spots—sometimes all the way to 12,003-foot-high Sierra Blanca, near Ruidoso, New Mexico, 100 miles north.

Horseback Riding

About 60% of the park's trails are open to horses for day trips, but horses are not permitted in the backcountry overnight. There are **corrals** at Frijole Ranch (near Pine Springs) and Dog Canyon (see "Fees, Regulations & Permits," above). Each set of corrals contains four pens that can accommodate up to 10 horses. There are no horses or other pack animals available for hire in or near the park. Park rangers warn that horses brought into the park should be accustomed to steep, rocky trails.

Wildlife Viewing

Because of the variety of habitats here, and also because these canyons offer some of the few water sources in west Texas, Guadalupe Mountains National Park offers excellent wildlife viewing and bird-watching possibilities. **McKittrick Canyon** and **Frijole Ranch** are considered among the best wildlife viewing spots, but a variety of species can be seen throughout the park. Those spending more than a few hours will likely see mule deer, and the park is also home to a herd of some 50 to 70 elk, which are sometimes seen in the higher elevations or along the highway in winter. Other **mammals** include raccoons, striped and hog-nosed skunks, gray foxes, coyotes, gray-footed chipmunks, Texas antelope squirrels, black-tailed jackrabbits, and desert cottontails. Black bears and mountain lions also live in the park, but are seldom seen.

> (*Tips* **Leaf Peepin'**
>
> McKittrick Canyon's beautiful display of fall colors usually takes place between early October and mid-November. It varies, though, so call before going.

About two dozen varieties of **snakes** make their home in the park, including five species of rattlesnakes. There are also numerous **lizards,** which are usually seen in the mornings and early evenings. These include the collared, crevice spiny, tree, side-blotched, Texas horned, and marbled whiptail. The most commonly seen is the prairie lizard, identified by the light-colored stripes down its back.

More than 200 species of **birds** are known to spend time in the park, including peregrine falcons, golden eagles, turkey vultures, and wild turkeys. You are also likely to encounter rock wrens, canyon wrens, black-throated sparrows, common nighthawks, mourning doves, rufous-crowned sparrows, mountain chickadees, ladder-backed woodpeckers, solitary vireos, and western scrub jays.

WHERE TO STAY & DINE

There are no accommodations or restaurants within the park. The closest communities offering lodging and dining are in New Mexico: **White's City,** 35 miles from the park, and **Carlsbad,** 55 miles from the park, which are discussed below.

CAMPING
In the Park

There are two developed vehicle-accessible campgrounds in the park. Both are open year-round, cost $8 per night, have restrooms and drinking water, but no showers or RV hookups. **Pine Springs Campground** ✿ is near the visitor center and park headquarters just off U.S. 62/180. There are 19 spaces for RVs, 20 very attractive tent sites, and two group campsites (call park headquarters for information). About 0.5 mile inside the north boundary of the park is **Dog Canyon Campground,** accessible from N. Mex. 137. Here there are nine tent sites and four RV sites. Although reservations are not accepted, you can call ahead to check on availability of sites (✆ **915/828-3251**). Camp stoves are allowed, but wood and charcoal fires are prohibited.

The park also has 10 designated **backcountry campgrounds,** with from two to eight sites each. Be sure to pick up free permits at the Pine Springs Visitor Center or Dog Canyon Ranger Station the day of or the day before your backpacking trip. Water is available at trail heads, but is not available in the backcountry. All trash, including toilet paper, must be packed out. Fires are strictly prohibited; use cook stoves only. You can only camp in designated campgrounds.

Near the Park

Nothing is actually nearby, but you'll find commercial camping in New Mexico at **White's City RV Park** in White's City (35 miles from the park), which is discussed below in the section on Carlsbad Caverns National Park.

3 A Side Trip to Carlsbad Caverns National Park

One of the largest and most spectacular cave systems in the world, Carlsbad Caverns National Park comprises more than 90 known caves that snake through the porous limestone reef of the Guadalupe Mountains. Fantastic and grotesque formations fascinate visitors, who find every shape imaginable (and unimaginable) naturally sculpted in the underground—from frozen waterfalls to strands of pearls, soda straws to miniature castles, draperies to ice-cream cones. Plan to spend a full day.

Formation of the caverns began some 250 million years ago, when a huge inland sea covered this region. A reef formed, and then the sea disappeared, leaving the reef covered with deposits of salts and gypsum. Eventually uplifting and erosion brought the reef back to the surface, and then the actual cave building began. Rainwater seeped through cracks in the earth's surface, dissolving the limestone and leaving hollows behind. With the help of sulfuric acid, created by gases released from oil and gas deposits further below ground, the cavern passageways grew, sometimes becoming huge rooms.

Once the caves were hollowed out, nature became artistic, decorating the rooms with a vast variety of fanciful formations. Very slowly, water dripped down through the rock into the caves, dissolving more limestone and absorbing the mineral calcite and other materials on its journey. Each drop of water then deposited its tiny load of calcite, gradually creating the cave formations we see today.

Although American Indians had known of Carlsbad Cavern (the park's main cave) for centuries, it was not discovered by settlers until ranchers in the 1880s were attracted by sunset flights of bats emerging from the cave. The first reported trip into the cave was in 1883, when a man supposedly lowered his 12-year old son into the cave entrance. A cowboy named Jim White, who worked for mining companies that collected bat droppings for use as a fertilizer, began to explore the cave in the early 1900s. Fascinated by the formations, White shared his discovery with others, and soon word of this magical belowground world spread.

Carlsbad Cave National Monument was created in October 1923. In 1926, the first electric lights were installed, and in 1930 Carlsbad Caverns gained national park status.

Underground development at the park has been confined to the famous Big Room, one of the largest and most easily accessible of the caverns, with a ceiling 25 stories high and a floor large enough to hold 14 football fields. Visitors can tour parts of it on their own, aided by a state-of-the-art CD-ROM portable audio guide, and explore other sections and several other caves on guided tours. The cave is also a summer home to about 250,000 Mexican free-tailed bats, which hang from the ceiling of Bat Cave during the day, but put on a spectacular show each evening as they leave the cave in search of food, and again in the morning when they return for a good day's sleep.

ESSENTIALS

GETTING THERE   The main section of Carlsbad Caverns National Park, with the visitor center and entrance to Carlsbad Cavern, the park's main cave, is located about 35 miles from Guadalupe Mountains National Park. From Guadalupe Mountains National Park take U.S. 62/180 northeast to White's City, and turn left onto N. Mex. 7, the park access road. You enter the boundary of Carlsbad Caverns National Park almost immediately and reach the visitor center in about 7 miles. From the city of Carlsbad, head 30 miles southwest on U.S. 62/180 and then 7 miles on N. Mex. 7 to the visitor center.

For airport information, see the "Getting There" section under Guadalupe Mountains National Park, above.

VISITOR INFORMATION   Contact **Carlsbad Caverns National Park,** 3225 National Parks Hwy., Carlsbad, NM 88220 (© **505/785-2232;** www.nps.gov/cave). Books and maps can be ordered from the **Carlsbad Caverns Guadalupe Mountains Association,** 727 Carlsbad Caverns Hwy., Carlsbad, NM 88220 (© **505/785-2232, ext. 481;** www.ccgma.org).

The visitor center is open daily from 8am to 7pm from Memorial Day to late August; and self-guided cave tours can be started from 8:30am to 5pm. The rest of the year the visitor center is open from 8am to 5pm, with self-guided cave tours from 8:30am to 3:30pm. Tour times and schedules may be modified during slower times in the winter. The park is closed on Christmas Day.

At the visitor center are displays depicting the geology and history of the caverns, bats and other wildlife, and a three-dimensional model of Carlsbad Cavern. You can also get information about the tours available and other park activities, both below- and aboveground. There is also a well-stocked bookstore, a restaurant, and a gift shop.

FEES   Admission to the visitor center and aboveground sections of the park is free. The basic cavern entry fee, which is good for 3 days and includes self-guided tours of the Natural Entrance and Big Room, is $6 for adults, $3 for children ages 6 to 15, and free for children under 6. Holders of Golden Eagle, Golden Age, Golden Access, and National Parks passes, plus their immediate families, are admitted free.

A general cave admission ticket is required in addition to tour fees for all guided cave tours except those to Slaughter Canyon Cave and Spider Cave. Reservations are required for all guided tours. Holders of Golden Age and Golden Access passports receive 50% discounts on tours. The King's Palace guided tour costs $8 for adults, $4 for children ages 6 to 15, and is free for children aged 4 and 5 with an adult—younger children are not permitted. Guided tours of Left Hand Tunnel, limited to those 6 and older, cost $7 for adults and $3.50 for children 6 to 15. Guided tours of Spider Cave, Lower Cave, and Hall of the White Giant are limited to those 12 and older, and cost $20 for adults

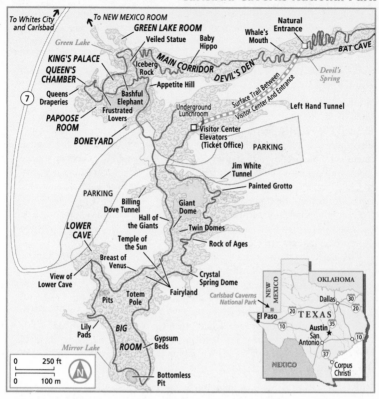

and $10 for youths 12 to 15. Slaughter Canyon Cave tours, for those 6 and older, cost $15 for adults and $7.50 for children 6 to 15

You can make reservations for cave tours up to 3 months in advance by phone or Internet (© 800/967-CAVE or 301/722-1257; www.nps.gov/cave).

REGULATIONS & PERMITS   As you would expect, damaging the cave formations in any way is prohibited. What some people do not understand is that they should not even touch the formations, walls, or ceilings. This is not only because many of the features are delicate and easily broken, but also because skin oils will both discolor the rock and disturb the mineral deposits that are necessary for growth.

All tobacco use is prohibited underground. In addition, food, drinks, candy, and chewing gum are not allowed on the underground trails. Those making wishes should not throw coins or other objects into the underground pools.

Cave explorers should wear flat shoes with rubber soles and heels, because of the slippery paths. Children under 16 must remain with an adult at all times while in the caves. Although strollers are not allowed for younger children, child backpacks are a good idea, but beware of low ceilings and doorways along the pathways.

Flash photography is not permitted at the evening Bat Flight programs.

Pets are not permitted in the caverns, on park trails, or in the backcountry, and because of the hot summer temperatures pets should not be left unattended in vehicles. There is a kennel (© 505/785-2281) available at the visitor center.

It has cages in an air-conditioned room, but no runs, and is primarily used by pet owners for periods of 3 hours or so while they are on cave tours. Pets are provided with water, but not food, and there are no grooming or overnight facilities. Reservations are not necessary; cost is $4 per pet.

Free permits, available at the visitor center, are required for all overnight hikes into the backcountry.

WHEN TO GO   The climate aboveground is warm in the summer, with highs often in the 90s and sometimes exceeding 100°F (38°C), and evening lows in the mid-60s. Winters are mild, with highs in the 50s and 60s in the day and nighttime lows usually in the 20s and 30s. Summers are known for sudden intense afternoon and evening thunderstorms; August and September see the most rain. Underground it's another story entirely, with a year-round temperature that varies little from its average temperature of 56°F (13°C), making a jacket or sweater a welcome companion.

Crowds are thickest in summer, and on weekends and holidays year-round, so visiting on weekdays between Labor Day and Memorial Day is the best way to avoid them. January is the quietest month.

Visiting during the park's off-season is especially attractive because the climate in the caves doesn't vary regardless of the weather on top, where the winters are generally mild and summers warm to hot. The only downside to an off-season visit is that you won't be able to see the bat flights. The bats head to Mexico when the weather starts to get chilly, usually by late October, and don't return until May. There are also fewer guided cave tours off-season, although those tours will have fewer people. The best time to see the park might well be September, when you can still see the bat flights but there are fewer visitors than during the peak summer season.

RANGER PROGRAMS   In addition to the cave tours, which are discussed below, rangers give a talk on bats at sunset each evening from mid-May to October at the cavern's Natural Entrance (times change; check at the visitor center). Rangers also offer a variety of demonstrations, talks, guided nature walks, and other programs daily. Especially popular are the climbing programs, where rangers demonstrate caving techniques. In recent years there have also been a series of stargazing programs presented by graduate students from New Mexico State University. The park also offers a **Junior Ranger Program,** in which kids can earn badges by completing various activities. Details are available at the visitor center.

On the second Thursday in August (usually), a "bat flight breakfast" from 5 to 7am encourages visitors to watch the bats return to the cavern after their night of insect-hunting. Park rangers prepare breakfast for early morning visitors for a small fee and then join them to watch the early morning return flight. Call the park for details.

WHAT TO SEE & DO
EXPLORING THE HIGHLIGHTS BY CAR
No, you can't take your car into the caves, but it won't be totally useless here, either. For a close-up as well as panoramic view of the Chihuahuan Desert, head out on the **Walnut Canyon Desert Drive,** a 9½-mile loop. You'll want to drive slowly on the one-way gravel road, both for safety and to thoroughly appreciate the dramatic scenery. Passenger cars can easily handle the tight turns and narrow passage, but the road is not recommended for motor homes and cars pulling trailers. Pick up an interpretive brochure for the drive at the visitor center bookstore.

CAVING ADVENTURES ★★★

Carlsbad Cavern (the park's main cave), Slaughter Canyon Cave, and Spider Cave are open to the general public. All guided tours must be reserved and have individual fees in addition to the general cave entry fee (see "Fees," above). Guided tours are popular and are sometimes fully booked weeks in advance, so reserve early.

Most park visitors head first to Carlsbad Cavern, which has elevators, a paved walkway, and an Underground Rest Area. A 1-mile section of the Big Room self-guided tour is accessible to those in wheelchairs (no wheelchairs are available at the park), though it's best to have another person to assist. Pick up a free accessibility guide at the visitor center.

The Big Room Tour, Natural Entrance Route, and King's Palace Guided Tour are the most popular trails, and all of them are lighted, paved, and have handrails. However, the Big Room is the only one of the three that's considered easy. The formations along these trails are strategically lit to display them at their most dramatic. This also means that today's visitors can see much more of the cave than early explorers, who were limited by the weak light produced by their lanterns.

The **Big Room Self-Guided Tour** ★★★ is an easy 1-mile loop that you get to by taking the visitor center elevator to the Underground Rest Area or via the Natural Entrance Route (see below). Considered the one thing that all visitors to Carlsbad Caverns National Park must do, this easy trail meanders through a massive chamber—it isn't called the Big Room for nothing—where you'll see some of the park's most spectacular formations and likely be overwhelmed by the enormity of it all. Allow about 1 hour.

The **Natural Entrance Route,** also 1 mile, is considered moderate to difficult, and is accessed outside the visitor center. This fairly strenuous hike takes you into Carlsbad Cavern on the same basic route used by its early explorers. You leave the daylight to enter a big hole, and then descend more than 750 feet into the cavern on a steep and narrow switchback trail, moving from the "twilight zone" of semidarkness to the depths of the cave, which would be totally black without the electric lights conveniently provided by the Park Service. The self-guided tour takes about 1 hour and ends near the elevators, which can take you back to the visitor center. However, we strongly recommend that from here you proceed on the Big Room Self-Guided Tour, which is described above, if you have not already been there.

The **King's Palace Guided Tour** ★★ is a moderate 1-mile loop that you get to by taking the visitor center elevator to the Underground Rest Area. This 1½-hour ranger-led walk wanders through some of the cave's most scenic chambers, where you'll see wonderfully fanciful formations in the King's Palace, Queen's Chamber, and Green Lake Room. Watch for the delightful Bashful Elephant formation between the King's Palace and Green Lake Room. Along the way, rangers discuss the geology of the cave and early explorers' experiences. Although the path is paved, there is an 80-foot elevation change.

Ranger-Led Cave Tours

In addition to the popular self-guided and guided tours discussed above, there are a number of ranger-led tours to less-developed sections of Carlsbad Cavern that provide more of the experience of exploration and genuine caving than the above tours over well-trodden trails. These caving tours vary in difficulty, but all include a period of absolute darkness or "blackout," which can make some people uncomfortable. Because some tours involve walking or crawling through tight spaces, people who suffer from claustrophobia should discuss specifics with rangers before purchasing tickets.

The 0.5-mile (one-way) **Left Hand Tunnel** starts in the visitor center near the elevator. The easiest of the caving tours, in this one you actually get to walk (rather than crawl) the entire time! Hand-carried lanterns (provided by the Park Service) light the way, and the trail is dirt but relatively level. You'll see a variety of formations, fossils from Permian times, and pools of water. Open to those 6 and older, this tour takes about 2 hours. The moderate **Lower Cave Tour,** which is 1 mile round-trip, starts at the visitor center near the elevator. This 3-hour trek involves descending or climbing over 50 feet of ladders, and an optional crawl. It takes you through an area that was explored by a National Geographic Society expedition in the 1920s, and you'll see artifacts from that and other explorations. In addition, you'll encounter a variety of formations, including cave pearls, which look a lot like the pearls created by oysters and can be as big as golf balls. This tour is open to those 12 and older only. Four AA batteries are required for the provided headlamp; sturdy hiking boots and gloves are recommended.

The **Hall of the White Giant Tour,** which starts at the visitor center, is only ½-mile one-way, but is strenuous and will take 3 to 4 hours as you crawl through narrow, dirty passageways and climb up slippery rocks. The highlight is, of course, the huge formation called the White Giant. Only those in excellent physical condition should consider this tour; children must be at least 12. Four AA batteries for the provided headlamp and sturdy hiking boots are required; and kneepads, gloves, and long pants are strongly recommended.

More Cave Tours

It takes some hiking to reach the other caves in the park, so carry drinking water, especially on hot summer days. All children under age 16 must be accompanied by an adult; other age restrictions apply as well. Each tour includes a period of true and total darkness or "blackout."

The **Slaughter Canyon Cave Tour** ★★ is 1.25 miles round-trip (plus half-mile hike to and from the cave entrance), and is considered moderate. The parking area is about a 45-minute drive from Carlsbad and is reached via U.S. 62/180, going south 5 miles from White's City to a marked turnoff that leads 11 miles to the parking lot. Discovered in 1937, this cave was mined for bat guano (used as fertilizer) until the 1950s. It consists of a corridor 1,140 feet long with many side passageways. This highly recommended guided tour lasts about 2 hours, plus at least another half-hour to hike up the steep trail to the cave entrance. No crawling is involved, although the smooth flowstone and old bat guano on the floor can be slippery, so good hiking boots are recommended. You'll see a number of wonderful cave formations, including the crystal-decorated Christmas Tree, the Teardrop, the 89-foot-high Monarch, and the menacing Klansman. Open to children 6 and older. Participants must take D battery flashlights.

The 4-hour tour of **Spider Cave** is a very strenuous 1-mile loop (plus half-mile hike to and from cave). Meet at the visitor center and follow a ranger to the cave. This tour is ideal for those who want the experience of a rugged caving adventure as well as some great underground scenery. Highlights include climbing down a 15-foot ladder, squeezing through very tight passageways, and climbing on slippery surfaces—all this after a fairly tough half-mile hike to the cave entrance. But it's worth it. The cave has numerous beautiful formations—most much smaller than those in the Big Room—and picturesque pools of water. Children must be at least 12 years old. Participants need four AA batteries for the provided headlamps and good hiking boots. Kneepads, gloves, and long pants are strongly recommended.

BATS, BIRDS & OTHER WILDLIFE VIEWING

At sunset, from mid-May to October, a crowd gathers at the Carlsbad Cavern Natural Entrance to watch hundreds of thousands of **bats** take off for a night of insect hunting. An amphitheater in front of the Natural Entrance provides seating, and ranger programs are held each evening (exact times vary, check at the visitor center) during the bats' residence at the park (the bats winter in Mexico). The most bats will be seen in August and September, when baby bats born earlier in the summer join their parents, along with migrating bats from the north, on the nightly forays. Early risers can also see the return of the bats just before dawn. Flash photography is not permitted, as it may disturb the bats.

However, bats aren't the only wildlife at Carlsbad Caverns. The park has a surprising number of **birds**—more than 300 species—many of which are seen in the Rattlesnake Springs area. Among species you're likely to see are turkey vultures, red-tailed hawks, scaled quail, killdeer, mourning doves, lesser nighthawks, black-chinned hummingbirds, vermilion flycatchers, canyon wrens, northern mockingbirds, black-throated sparrows, and western meadowlarks. In addition, each summer several thousand cave swallows usually build their mud nests on the ceiling just inside the Carlsbad Cavern Natural Entrance (the bats make their home further back in the cave).

Among the park's **larger animals** are mule deer and raccoons, which are sometimes spotted near the Natural Entrance at the time of the evening bat flights. The park is also home to porcupines, hog-nosed skunks, desert cottontails, black-tailed jackrabbits, rock squirrels, and the more elusive ringtails, coyotes, and gray fox. These are sometimes seen in the late evenings along the park entrance road and the Walnut Canyon Desert Drive.

WHERE TO STAY & DINE

There are no accommodations within the park, but there are two concessionaire-operated restaurants (② 505/785-2281). A family style full-service restaurant at the **visitor center** serves three meals daily—mostly American standards plus a few Mexican items—in the $3 to $8 range. The restaurant is open from 8:30am to 4:30pm most of the year, with extended hours from Memorial Day to mid-August and on Labor Day weekend. The **Underground Rest Area,** located inside the main cavern 750 feet belowground, has a cafeteria-style eatery offering fast food such as sandwiches and burritos, with prices from $3 to $7. Its hours are coordinated with cave hours.

The closest lodging properties are at White's City, which contains a variety of businesses under one management, including two motels, restaurants, shops, a museum, gas station, and an RV park. The **Best Western Cavern Inn,** 17 Carlsbad Cavern Hwy. at N. Mex. 7 (② 800/228-3767 or 505/785-2291), plus its sister property across the street, offer spacious rooms with southwestern decor. Most folks dine and drink at the complex's **Velvet Garter Saloon and Restaurant,** a family-style restaurant offering American dishes in the $8 to $14 range, or pick up a quick burger, sandwich, and the like at nearby **Fast Jack's,** with most prices from $3 to $6. The White's City arcade contains a post office, a small grocery store, a gift shop, a museum, and a theater for weekend melodramas. Between the Cavern Inn and its neighbor properties, there are two swimming pools, two Jacuzzis, and a tennis court.

The next closest services are in and near the city of Carlsbad. Here you'll find several chain and franchise motels and a number of independent and chain restaurants. Motels on the southwest edge of the city, on the road to Carlsbad Caverns, include **Best Western Stevens Inn,** 1829 S. Canal St. (② 800/730-2851 or

505/887-2851), which also has a good restaurant, **The Flume,** with American dishes and main course prices of $4 to $8 at lunch and $8 to $20 at dinner. Also in this area is the **Comfort Inn,** 2429 W. Pierce St. (© 800/228-5150 or 505/887-1994); **Days Inn,** 3910 National Parks Hwy. (© 800/325-2525 or 505/887-7800); **Quality Inn,** 3706 National Parks Hwy. (© 800/321-2861 or 505/887-2861); and **Super 8 Motel,** 3817 National Parks Hwy. (© 800/800-8000 or 505/887-8888).

Lodging tax adds about 11% to room bills. For additional information, contact the **Carlsbad Chamber of Commerce,** P.O. Box 910, Carlsbad, NM 88220 (© **800/221-1224** or 505/887-6516; www.chamber.caverns.com), or stop at the chamber's visitor center at 302 S. Canal St. in Carlsbad.

CAMPING

There are no developed campgrounds or vehicle camping of any kind in the national park. Backcountry camping, however, is permitted in some areas; pick up free permits at the visitor center.

The closest camping is **White's City RV Park,** 17 Carlsbad Cavern Hwy. at N. Mex. 7 (© **800/228-3767** or 505/785-2291), located in the White's City complex at the east edge of the park boundary, about 7 miles east of the visitor center. In addition to RV sites with hook-ups and shade shelters, the campground has practically unlimited tent camping in a grassy area with picnic tables and some trees. There's a dump station and a clean bathhouse. Because the campground is part of the White's City complex, with its motels, restaurants, and other services, campers have access to the motel pools, an ATM, convenience store, liquor store, post office, and gift shop. It's open year-round and rates for both RVs and tents are about $23 per night.

11

The Panhandle Plains

by Eric Peterson

A wide-open sea of prairie, the high plains of northern Texas might well be the nation's crossroads: The small-town charm of the Great Plains, the spice of the Southwest, and the polite twang of the South are all present in equal measures. Beyond this cultural intersection, highways have crisscrossed the region since the 1930s, fostering a brood of cheap motels and kitschy roadside Americana.

Inhabited by nomadic tribes for much of the last 12,000 years, the Panhandle Plains are distinguished by a high mesa—3,000 feet above sea level—that tapers downhill to the south and east, bordered by spectacular canyons and unique geological formations. In 1541, when Vásquez de Coronado ventured north in his quest for the fabled Seven Cities of Gold, he pounded stakes into the ground to claim the land for Spain—as well as mark his route for a return trip through the mostly featureless flatlands. Thus, the "Llano Estacado," Spanish for "staked plains," was born. Today, Lubbock inhabits the center of the mesa that Coronado staked out; Amarillo sits on its northern edge.

The late 19th century brought significant change to the area: Ranchers began to graze cattle here, railroads crisscrossed the mesa in all directions, and agriculture took hold as the predominant industry. Million-acre ranches became the norm. During the fall and winter of 1874–75, the indigenous tribes battled the U.S. Army in the Red River War, culminating with the dispersal of Comanches, Kiowas, and Southern Cheyennes to reservations in Oklahoma.

The landscape was irrevocably altered again by the discovery of oil in the 1920s, when ranchers found themselves sitting on "black gold" mines. The Dust Bowl days of the 1930s dampened development, but the area recovered and saw tremendous growth following World War II.

At first glance, the Panhandle Plains might strike the passerby as drab and monotonous, but the region is actually worth a closer look than you'll get from behind the wheel. The magnificent palette of Palo Duro Canyon, the lively nightlife in Lubbock, and Amarillo's ranching heritage—from cattle to Cadillacs—are unexpected diversions that make this area a worthy stopover on a cross-country trek.

1 Amarillo

122 miles N of Lubbock; 267 miles E of Albuquerque, New Mexico

The commercial center of the Texas Panhandle, Amarillo arose when the Fort Worth and Denver City Railway started laying track in the area in 1887, a decade after ranchers began to graze their cattle on the buffalo grass–speckled plains. When the town was formally incorporated, the name Amarillo—meaning "yellow" literally and "wild horse" figuratively—was adopted from a nearby lake. In a little over a decade, the combination of the railroad and the ranchland led to the establishment of Amarillo's long-standing status as a cattle-shipping capital. To this day, the city "smells like money" most when the Amarillo Livestock Auction is in full swing.

While its agricultural roots remain the cornerstone of the local economy, Amarillo's location on a major east-west highway—Route 66 until 1970 and I-40 thereafter—has long made it a popular stopover for tourists, with a plethora of motels and restaurants catering to the cross-country crowd. Amarillo is fairly low-key and nondescript at first glance, but it's a pleasant, inexpensive spot for an overnight stay. Several of its attractions are worth a closer look, namely the roadside kitsch of Cadillac Ranch and the Big Texan steakhouse. As a destination, however, Amarillo itself will likely hold a visitor's attention for a day or two at most.

ESSENTIALS
GETTING THERE

BY PLANE   More than 50 commercial flights take off or land daily from **Amarillo International Airport** (© 806/335-1671), off I-40 Exit 76 (Lakeside Drive), 7 miles east of downtown. Airlines serving Amarillo include **American Eagle** (© 800/433-7300), **Continental Express** (© 800/525-0280), **Delta Connections** (© 800/221-1212), **Southwest** (© 800/435-9792), and **Great Lakes Aviation** (© 800/554-5111). Car rentals are available from **Avis** and **Hertz; Advantage** and **Enterprise** will deliver cars to the airport.

BY CAR   Coming from east or west, Amarillo can be accessed via I-40, exits 62 (Hope Rd.) through 75 (Lakeside Dr.). The primary downtown exit is 70 (Taylor/Buchanan sts.) and the airport is located northeast of Exit 75. Coming from the north by car, you'll likely enter Amarillo via U.S. 87/287, which takes you through the heart of downtown and continues south to Canyon and Lubbock as I-27. If you are coming from the northwest, Texas FM 1061 can be used as a shortcut from U.S. 385; it becomes Tascosa Road as it enters metro Amarillo. U.S. 60 is the primary route northeast to Pampa and southwest to Hereford, and U.S. 287 veers east beyond the city, to Childress, and, beyond that, Wichita Falls and Dallas.

ORIENTATION

I-40 cuts through the heart of Amarillo, skirting the south side of downtown. The city's primary north-south artery is U.S. 87, which splits into four one-way, north-south streets in the downtown area. (From the west, these streets are Taylor, Fillmore, Pierce, and Buchanan.) South of I-40, U.S. 87 becomes I-27, which leads to Canyon and Lubbock. The northern boundary of downtown is 1st Avenue, the southern boundary I-40. The Route 66 Historic District begins at 6th Avenue and Georgia Street and continues west along 6th Avenue for a mile to Western Street. Amarillo Boulevard is a major east-west route through the northern stretch of the city. Along with Georgia Street, Ross-Mirror and Washington streets are among the busiest north-south roads in Amarillo. Loop 335 is comprised of four roads (Soncy Rd., FM 1719, Lakeside Dr., and Hollywood Rd.) that circumnavigate the city.

GETTING AROUND

Aside from some one-way streets downtown, Amarillo is a snap to navigate by car, with relatively little traffic. (Instead of a rush hour, Amarillo locals like to say they have a "rush minute.")

Amarillo City Transit (© **806/342-9144** or TDD 806/372-6234) operates a bus system Monday through Saturday from 6:15am to 6:45pm. The main transfer point is located downtown at 3rd Avenue and Fillmore Street. There are

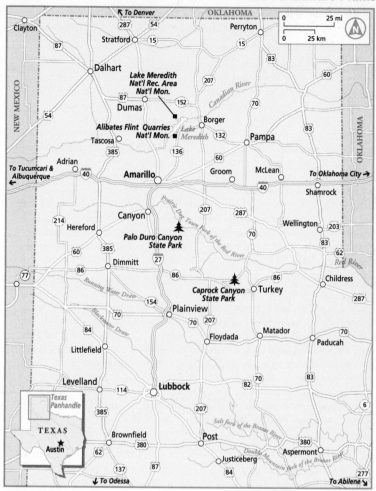

eight different routes that run from downtown to the major shopping centers and Harrington Regional Medical Center. Ride tickets are 75¢ for adults, 60¢ for children ages 6 to 12 and students, and 35¢ for seniors and travelers with disabilities.

Taxi service is provided by **ABC Taxi Service** (© 806/379-9393), **Yellow Cab** (© 806/374-8444), and **Bob & Son Taxi Service** (© 806/373-1171).

VISITOR INFORMATION

The **Amarillo Convention & Visitor Council** maintains an information center in the historic Bivins Mansion, 1000 S. Polk St. (© 800/692-1338 or 806/374-1497; www.amarillo-cvb.org). For statewide information, visit the **Texas Travel Information Center** on the city's east side; it's located on the south frontage road just west of I-40 Exit 75.

FAST FACTS The **Northwest Texas Hospital** is at 1501 S. Coulter Dr. (© 806/354-1000), just north of I-40 on the Harrington Regional Medical

Center campus. The main **post office** is located at 2301 S. Ross St. and is open Monday through Friday from 7:30am to 6pm and Saturday from 9am to 2pm.

WHAT TO SEE & DO
THE TOP ATTRACTIONS

American Quarter Horse Heritage Center & Museum *Kids*   Dedicated to the history of the equine breed named for its speed when racing a quarter-mile, this facility offers a comprehensive look at the animals and the culture surrounding them. The museum is geared towards horse lovers and kids—who will no doubt be delighted by the interactive exhibits and a fiberglass quarter horse replica you can climb aboard—but it has limited appeal for others. If the subject matter piques your interest, expect to spend an hour or so here. Start with the orientation show in the modern Theater of America's Horse. Next, investigate the three galleries, featuring an engaging chronological history of the American Quarter Horse and other equine-specific exhibits. There are also live demonstrations at an actual stable on-site.

2601 I-40 East at Quarter Horse Dr. (✆ 888/209-8322 or 806/376-5181. www.aqha.org. Admission $4 adults, $3.50 seniors 55 and over, $2.50 children ages 6–18, free for children under 6. Mon–Sat 9am–5pm; Sun noon–5pm.

Cadillac Ranch ★   One of the more recognizable and bizarre roadside attractions in the country, Cadillac Ranch consists of 10 vintage Cadillacs (dating 1949–64) buried up to their backseat in a wheat field west of Amarillo, rising out of the earth at the same angle as Cheops Pyramid in Egypt. Conceived and funded by Amarillo's Stanley Marsh 3, the eccentric grandson of one of the Panhandle's most successful oilmen, Cadillac Ranch was constructed in 1974 by the Ant Farm, a San Francisco–based art collective, and relocated west in 1997 to its present site to escape the shadow of Amarillo's growth. Cadillac Ranch is also interactive: Marsh freely allows visitors to add their creative touches with spray paint, a marker, or a key. (For more on Stanley Marsh 3's artistic exploits in the Amarillo area, see "Unanticipated Rewards" on p. 395.)

I-40 West, on the south frontage road between exits 60 (Arnot Rd.) and 62 (Hope and Holiday roads). Free admission. Daily 24 hr.

Route 66 Historic District   This colorful area west of downtown Amarillo preserves about a mile of old Route 66, aka the "Mother Road." Once a suburb accessible by trolley car, the district has evolved into a hub for the city's nightlife and shopping. Buildings that once housed drugstores and theaters are now home to eateries, antiques stores, and specialty shops. The area is a bit run-down in spots, but it's not all that touristy and it's fun as a glimpse of the glory days of Route 66. The surrounding neighborhood, known as Old San Jacinto, might have once been a suburb, but, in many ways, it is now the heart of the city. During the summer, the district hosts several festivals, with street dances, live entertainment, and art displays.

6th Ave. between Western and Georgia sts. Call the Amarillo CVB at (✆ 806/374-1497 for additional information.

MORE ATTRACTIONS

Amarillo Botanical Gardens   Dedicated to the art, science, and enjoyment of horticulture, these outdoor gardens feature displays on flora indigenous to the high plains region and offer a pleasant, if unremarkable, spot to take a 30-minute break from the road. Of special note is a "scent garden" designed for

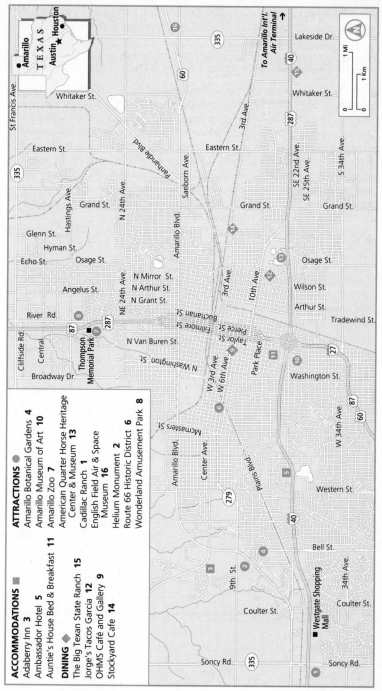

patrons with sight impairments. Temporary exhibits on regional horticultural subjects are housed indoors here, and groundbreaking for a new tropical greenhouse was slated for mid-2003.

1400 Streit Dr., at Harrington Regional Medical Center. ℭ **806/352-6513**. Free admission. Outdoor gardens daily dawn–dusk; indoor exhibits Tues–Fri 10am–5pm year-round; also Sat–Sun 1–5pm June-Sept.

Amarillo Museum of Art   The only accredited art museum within a 260-mile radius, this institution houses a worthwhile collection of paintings, photographic exhibits, and sculptures in its galleries. Requiring about 30 minutes to peruse, the permanent collection includes a good deal of regional 20th-century art and a nice Asian exhibit, due to a local patron with a passion for Far Eastern works. The museum hosts nearly 20 changing exhibits annually in its six galleries; recent programs included works by Georgia O'Keeffe, a former area resident, and displays that used art as a lens to explore the area's colorful history.

2200 S. Van Buren St., on the campus of Amarillo College. ℭ **806/371-5050**. www.amarilloart.org. Free admission. Tues–Fri 10am–5pm; Sat–Sun 1–5pm. Closed major holidays.

Amarillo Zoo   This accredited zoo is small and generally unspectacular, although it excels at preserving and displaying the High Plains' indigenous animals, termed "Texotic." The highlight is a 20-acre range populated by grazing bison; the mustang, the feral horse of the American West, is also in the collection, as are mountain lions, Texas longhorns, and spider monkeys. In all, the zoo is a good half-hour stop for families with children who've been cooped up in the backseat for far too long.

Thompson Memorial Park, about 1 mile north of downtown on U.S. 287. ℭ **806/381-7911**. Free admission (donations accepted). Tues–Sun 9:30am–5:30pm. Closed major holidays.

English Field Air & Space Museum   A must-see for aviation buffs (and a ho-hum for others), this museum features an impressive array of historical aircraft and missiles; a tour takes a bit less than an hour. Of special interest is a Mars Lander: It is one of three in existence and the only one on Earth. (The other two reside on Mars's red surface.) There is also an extensive collection of nuclear ordnance from the Cold War era, several airplanes and helicopters, and the third longest concrete runway in the world, which, at 13,600 feet, is an alternate landing site for the space shuttle.

2014 English Rd. ℭ **806/335-1812** or 806/622-0433. Free admission (donations accepted). Sat–Sun noon–5pm or by appointment.

Helium Monument   Being that Amarillo is the helium capital of the United States, it is a perfectly natural location for this monument to the lighter-than-air element. Erected in 1969 to commemorate the 100th anniversary of the discovery of helium in the sun's spectrum, the monument is comprised of four helium-filled steel columns, each housing a time capsule packed with artifacts and predictions from 1968. Fans of space-age kitsch will love the structure, but it's not a must-see by any means. The monument is located in front of the Don Harrington Discovery Center, a children's science museum that was closed at press time, with hopes of reopening in 2004.

1200 Streit Dr., at the Don Harrington Discovery Center. ℭ **806/355-9547**.

Wonderland Amusement Park *(Kids)*   An Amarillo landmark since the glory days of Route 66, Wonderland is the Panhandle's top amusement park, featuring more than 25 different nostalgic rides on a 15-acre chunk of Thompson Park. The amusements include three roller coasters, six water rides, a carousel, and

Unanticipated Rewards

Cadillac Ranch (see p. 392) is just the tip of Amarillo's public art iceberg, which is in large part the product of the fervent imagination of Stanley Marsh 3 (he favors the Arabic '3' over the Roman 'III').

The grandson of an early Texas oil millionaire, Marsh is also the man behind 200 signs on display at Amarillo homes and businesses. Looking very much like colorful municipal signs, they don't dispense traffic or parking rules, instead offering a variety of offbeat slogans. One reads "Strong drink." "What is a village without village idiots?" asks another. "'Either the well is very deep,' thought Alice, 'or I'm falling very slowly,'" reads yet another. While the signs are spread out around Amarillo and the surrounding towns, Old San Jacinto is the neighborhood where you'll see them in the highest concentration. The ever-enigmatic Marsh explained the signs, saying, "They are to be looked at. The signs are just there, like the Rock of Gibraltar or the Statue of Liberty. They are a system of unanticipated rewards."

Beyond Cadillac Ranch and the signs, Marsh's eccentric public art vision extends south, to the junction of I-27 and Sundown Lane, where a sculpture of a pair of disembodied legs greets passerby. There's also "Floating Mesa," hundreds of sheets of plywood painted the color of a blue sky on the side of a mountain. Unless it is overcast, the resulting impression is that the summit is floating. It is located about 8 miles northwest of Amarillo via Tascosa Road.

While many are amused by the creations of Stanley Marsh 3, not every Amarillo resident finds them in good taste. Those disgusted by their presence have decried them as eyesores with little or no artistic value. In response, Marsh was once quoted as saying, "Art is a legalized form of insanity, and I do it very well."

several kiddie rides. My favorite: The double-loop "Texas Tornado" coaster and the "Shoot the Chutes" water ride. There is also a mini golf course and an arcade.

2601 Dumas Dr., at Thompson Memorial Park. © 806/383-3344. www.wonderlandpark.com. Individual rides $1.50 each plus a $3 gate admission fee. Unlimited rides $11 weeknights, $17 weekends. Apr–Labor Day Sat–Sun 1–10pm; May Tues and Thurs–Fri 6:30–9:30pm; June to mid-Aug Mon–Fri 7–10:30pm. Closed Labor Day–Mar.

OUTDOOR ACTIVITIES
Amarillo offers many opportunities for outdoor recreation, in the form of in-city golf courses, pools, and parks, as well as several lakes, reservoirs, and state parks in the surrounding area. The best recreation spot is **Palo Duro Canyon State Park** (see "Canyon & Palo Duro Canyon State Park," later in this chapter), about 27 miles southeast of the city.

The **Lake Meredith National Recreation Area** (© 806/857-3151; www.nps.gov/lamr), located 38 miles northeast of Amarillo via Texas 136, is another outdoor hot spot, featuring opportunities for boating, fishing, hunting, horseback riding, camping, hiking, swimming, wildlife and bird viewing, and four-wheeling. The site is also home to **Alibates Flint Quarries National Monument,** the point of origin for a significant percentage of arrowhead points found throughout the Great Plains. While the monument is closed to most recreational activity, guided tours are offered at 10am and 2pm during the summer and at other times of the year by reservation. Aside from boat-launching fees, access to Lake Meredith is free to the public.

Wildcat Bluff Nature Center, located 3 miles north of I-40 on Loop 335 (*©* **806/352-6007;** www.wildcatbluff.org) is the best spot for hiking and wildlife viewing in the city itself, offering about 2 miles of moderate trails on its 600 acres of cottonwood-shaded hills. Guided hikes are available with advance notice. The center's wildlife population includes mule deer, horned toads, coyotes, and turkey vultures.

The major city parks in Amarillo include: **Thompson Memorial Park,** at Dumas Drive and 24th Avenue, home to Wonderland Amusement Park and the Amarillo Zoo, as well as a 36-hole golf course, 1 mile of jogging/walking trails, a heated outdoor pool (open seasonally), ball fields, picnic sites with grills, and fishing ponds; **John S. Stiff Memorial Park,** at SW 48th Avenue and Bell Street, with ball fields, three indoor and eight outdoor tennis courts, an outdoor heated pool, and picnic sites; and **Southeast Regional Park,** at SE 46th and Osage Street, with an outdoor heated pool, ball fields, fishing ponds, and picnic areas. For more information on Amarillo's city parks, contact the Parks and Recreation Department at *©* **806/378-3036.**

BOATING **Lake Meredith National Recreation Area** is the Panhandle's top watersports destination. The main lake occupies 12,000 of the area's 46,000 acres and draws in boaters, windsurfers, water-skiers, and even scuba divers. Boat rentals (from personal watercraft to houseboats) are available from **Forever Resorts** (*©* **800/255-5561** or 806/865-3391) at the marina at Lake Meredith National Recreation Area. To launch a boat of any size into Lake Meredith, a $4 day-use fee is required.

FISHING Catfish and bass are the fish of choice for anglers in the Texas Panhandle and there are several spots in and around Amarillo that are quite popular. For no fee outside of the cost of a Texas state fishing license, visitors can fish in several ponds in Amarillo's city park system, including **Thompson Memorial Park** at Dumas Drive and 24th Avenue, **Martin Road Park** at NE 15th Avenue and Mirror Street, **Southeast Regional Park** at SE 46th Avenue and Osage Street, and **Harrington Regional Medical Center Park** at SW 9th Avenue and Wallace Street. **Lake Meredith National Recreation Area** is another popular fishing spot for the Panhandle. At the lake's **marina** (*©* **806/865-3391**), there are basic fishing supplies, concessions, and a fishing hut ($4 for 12 hr.).

GOLF The City of Amarillo Parks and Recreation Department manages two 36-hole golf courses: **Comanche Trails,** 4200 S. Grand St. (*©* **806/378-4281**), and **Ross Rogers Golf Course,** 722 NE 24th Ave. in Thompson Memorial Park (*©* **806/378-3086**). Greens fees for each of these civic courses runs $12 to $16 for 18 holes during the week and $14 to $18 on weekends.

HIKING Aside from the hiking opportunities at **Wildcat Bluff Nature Center,** there are two hiking trails at **Lake Meredith National Recreation Area.** The Devil's Canyon Trail is a moderate one-way trail that leaves from Plum Creek on the north side of the lake and continues into the canyon for 1½ miles. There are also numerous foot trails at **Palo Duro Canyon State Park** (see "Canyon & Palo Duro Canyon State Park," below).

HORSEBACK RIDING There are several horse-friendly trails in **Lake Meredith National Recreation Area,** in McBride Canyon and alongside Plum

Creek on the Lake's north side. The National Park Service provides corrals at the Plum Creek and Mullinaw campgrounds, but riders need to bring their own horses. There are also horse trails and stables in **Palo Duro Canyon State Park** (see "Canyon & Palo Duro Canyon State Park," below).

MOUNTAIN BIKING   The closest mountain biking trails to Amarillo are 27 miles away in **Palo Duro Canyon State Park** (see "Canyon & Palo Duro Canyon State Park," below). The 3-mile Devil's Canyon Trail at **Lake Meredith National Recreation Area** (see "Hiking," above) is also accessible to mountain bikers.

SPECTATOR SPORTS

BASEBALL   The **Amarillo Dillas** have been the city's Texas Louisiana Baseball League team since 1922. Named for the region's omnipresent armadillos, the team's schedule runs from early May to August at the 5,500-seat Potter County Memorial Stadium, aka the "Dilla Villa," 3rd Avenue and Grand Street (*©* **806/ 342-3455** for ticket information; www.dillas.com). Tickets cost $5 to $8.

HOCKEY   The **Amarillo Gorillas** play in the Central Hockey League at the Amarillo Civic Center (the "Jungle"), 401 S. Buchanan St. in downtown Amarillo (*©* **806/242-7825** for ticket information; www.amarillogorillas.com). The schedule runs from mid-October to late March with single game ticket prices ranging from $9 to $15.

RACING   Motor-sports enthusiasts can get a fix of racing action at **Route 66 Motor Speedway,** located about 10 miles east of downtown Amarillo at 3601 E. Amarillo Blvd. (*©* **806/383-7223;** www.route66motorspeedway.com). The oval dirt track is ⅜ mile long. Races are held on Saturdays from mid-April to October.

RODEO   The Working Ranch Cowboys Association (WRCA) holds its annual **World Championship Ranch Rodeo** in Amarillo during the second week of November. Real working cowboys compete in events like wild cow milking, bronco riding, and team penning at the Amarillo Civic Center, 401 S. Buchanan St. (*©* **806/378-3096** for tickets; www.wrca.org).

SHOPPING

Amarillo's biggest enclosed shopping center is the **Westgate Shopping Mall,** 7701 I-40 West, between the Coulter Drive and Soncy Road exits (*©* **806/358-7221;** www.westgatemalltx.com). The mall's stores include Dillard's, The Gap, and Sears, and there is also a movie theater and several restaurants. Westgate is open Monday through Saturday from 10am to 9pm, and Sunday from noon to 6pm. The **Historic Route 66 District** is an antiques buff's dream, with more than 100 stores on W. 6th Avenue between Georgia and Western streets. Western wear is also big in Amarillo; head to **Cavender's Boot City,** 7920 I-40 West at Coulter Drive (*©* **806/358-1400**) for a huge selection of boots, along with hats, belt buckles, jeans, jewelry, and practically every other Western wearable on the market.

WHERE TO STAY

Amarillo's location on I-40 makes it an ideal stopping point on cross-country trips. There are also several inexpensive mom-and-pop motels on Amarillo Boulevard (Loop 335) in northern Amarillo, but finding a good room in that area is a hit-or-miss proposition. A better bet is the I-40 corridor: You'll find dozens of chain motels located just off the interstate, including **Best Western Amarillo Inn,** 1610 Coulter Dr. (*©* 800/528-1234 or 806/358-7861); **Best Western Santa Fe Inn,** 4600 I-40 East at Exit 73 (*©* 800/528-1234 or

806/372-1885); **Comfort Suites,** 2103 Lakeview Dr. (℗ 800/228-5150 or 806/352-8300); **Holiday Inn,** 1911 I-40 East at Exit 71 (℗ 800/HOLIDAY or 806/372-8741); **Motel 6,** 3060 I-40 East at Exit 66 (℗ 800/466-8356 or 806/359-7651); **La Quinta Inn,** 1708 I-40 East at Exit 71 (℗ 800/531-5900 or 806/373-7486); and **Quality Inn and Suites,** 1803 Lakeside Dr. (℗ 800/847-6556 or 806/335-1561). Room taxes in Amarillo add about 15% to lodging bills.

Adaberry Inn ★★ *Finds* Constructed from scratch in 1997, the Adaberry Inn rose to national prominence when it served as Oprah Winfrey's home for 2 months in 1999 while she fought a defamation lawsuit brought on by Amarillo-area cattle ranchers. One look inside this thoroughly modern B&B and it's easy to see why the TV talk show star chose to stay here. The uniquely decorated rooms are each themed after a particular city: Missoula features a Western motif, with cowboy hats, barn doors under the sink, and a mountainous mural on one wall; and Key West offers a more tropical setting with aquatic artwork, a latticed ceiling, and yellow walls. The best, though, is the Aspen suite (Oprah's room), which features a rock fireplace, a Jacuzzi for two, and ski-themed decorative touches.

Seven of the rooms have private balconies or patios. There's also a game room with a putting green and a pool table downstairs, adjacent to a state-of-the-art home theater. The inn's main balcony is an ideal place to watch sunsets over the Lost Canyon, a quiet wildlife refuge with walking trails right in the Adaberry's backyard. Smoking and pets, aside from the caged doves in the parlor, are not permitted inside of the inn.

6818 Plum Creek Dr., Amarillo, TX 79124. ℗ **806/352-0022.** Fax 806/356-0248. 9 units. $109 double; $195 suite. Rates include full breakfast and complimentary snacks and beverages. AE, DC, DISC, MC, V. Children over 11 accepted. **Amenities:** Exercise room; game room; dry cleaning. *In room:* A/C, TV/VCR, dataport, hair dryer.

Ambassador Hotel ★★ The 10-story Ambassador is Amarillo's tallest hotel. It's also the city's best, a pleasant touch of class in cowboy country. The beige-and-blue guest rooms—with either a king-size bed or a pair of queens—are spacious and nicely furnished. The 10th floor is the concierge level, with brass fixtures, minibars, and complimentary breakfast and cocktails. Many of the upper rooms have great views of the pleasantly treed cityscape below—those facing east are the best in this regard. The lobby is striking—a five-story atrium with a sloping glass enclosure over an excellent cafe and a small pool—and the service and amenities are the best in town.

3100 I-40 West (Exit 68B on Georgia St.), Amarillo, TX 79102. ℗ **800/817-0521** or 806/385-9869. Fax 806/385-9869. www.ambassadoramarillo.com. 265 units, including 2 suites. $99–$129 double; $399 suite. AE, DC, DISC, MC, V. **Amenities:** 2 restaurants; bar; indoor heated pool; privileges at a nearby health club; exercise room; indoor Jacuzzi; concierge; courtesy car; business center; limited room service; laundry service; dry cleaning; executive level. *In room:* A/C, TV w/pay movies and Nintendo, dataport, coffeemaker, hair dryer, iron.

Auntie's House Bed & Breakfast ★ This 1912 Prairie Craftsman home, now on the National Register of Historic Places, is one of the Panhandle's top urban B&Bs. The white shingles and green trim sheath a charming country home with comfortable guest rooms. "The Master's Bedroom" features such macho nostalgia as antique football helmets and fishing poles, deep red wallpaper, and a queen-size bed dating from the 1880s. On the other side of the spectrum, the "Ede Mae Rose Room" is a frilly, floral space, loaded with antique dolls and photos. "Sadie's Suite" has separate sleeping and sitting areas decorated with antiques from the 1920s.

The 800-square-foot "Enchanted Cottage" out back dates from 1995 and is decorated with dozens of cherubs and a queen-size bed with a 10-foot headboard. The bathroom is spacious and modern, with a large shower with two heads, a two-person Jacuzzi, and a bidet. Also in the backyard: a big hot tub and a barbecue for everyone. Breakfast at Auntie's includes innkeeper Corliss Burroughs's gourmet biscuits—butterscotch, strawberry cream cheese, and peach are just a few of the possibilities.

1712 S. Polk St., Amarillo, TX 79101. (✆ 888/661-8054 or 806/371-8054. Fax 806/373-2979. www.aunties house.com. 4 units, including 1 suite and 1 guest cottage. $89 double; $129 suite; $225 cottage. Rates include full breakfast. AE, DISC, MC, V. Children over 12 accepted. **Amenities:** Outdoor Jacuzzi. *In room:* A/C, TV, no phone.

CAMPING

There are several camping options in and around Amarillo, with numerous RV campgrounds in the city as well as primitive camping opportunities at Lake Meredith National Recreation Area (see "Outdoor Activities," above). The recreation area does not have RV hook-ups, but there is no fee. See also "Canyon & Palo Duro Canyon State Park," below.

Amarillo KOA   Located in a secluded spot near the airport on Amarillo's eastern fringe, this campground is well maintained and reliable. Facilities include a pet walk, a heated outdoor pool, playground, game room, and gift shop with sundries and RV supplies. Also, a chuck wagon dinner is served nightly during the summer and the operators offer a free shuttle to the musical *Texas Legacies* in Palo Duro Canyon State Park.

1100 Folsom Rd., Amarillo, TX 79108. (✆ 800/562-3431 or 806/335-1792. Fax 806/335-3702. 123 sites, including 50 pull-throughs, 45 back-ins, 23 tent sites, and 5 cabins. $20–$28 campsites; $35–$45 cabins. DISC, MC, V. Located east of Lakeside Dr. (I-40 Exit 75) via Texas Hwy. 50.

WHERE TO DINE

The Big Texan Steak Ranch ★ *Kids* STEAK   It is next to impossible to miss the Big Texan when you drive across the Panhandle on I-40: You'll see the first billboards touting the legendary deal—"Eat a 72-ounce steak dinner in an hour and get it for free!"—hours before the restaurant. Beyond the hype, the Big Texan is a unique attraction in itself, with a gift shop, motel, old-fashioned shooting gallery, and extensive collection of taxidermy and kitsch. There are costumed cowboy musicians performing every night, as well as a full-blown opry showcasing local talent each Tuesday.

With so much going on, you might forget that the Big Texan is a restaurant, but its legendary steaks are what put the place on the map: They're actually quite good. Beyond the 72-ouncer (which, not so incidentally, sports a $72 price tag if you don't finish it), the restaurant also serves juicy prime rib, rib-eye, New York strip, and other steaks in a dinner that includes salad, bread, and two side dishes. There's also a smattering of seafood and barbecue dishes. Breakfast and lunch are comparable: all-American and ultra-hearty.

For the record, some 40,000 people have tried to eat the 72-ounce steak since its introduction in 1959, and nearly 7,000 have succeeded. One—a wrestler named Klondike Bill—inhaled two of the dinners in the 1-hour time limit.

7701 I-40 East. (✆ 800/657-7177 or 806/372-6000. Reservations accepted for large parties only. Main courses $5–$16 breakfast, $7.50–$30 lunch and dinner. AE, DC, DISC, MC, V. Daily 7:30am–10:30pm.

Jorge's Tacos Garcia TEX-MEX   Jorge's proprietor, George Veloz II, dreamed of opening a Tex-Mex restaurant since he was in middle school. Fittingly, Jorge's

Tacos Garcia is the spitting image of his childhood vision, right down to the stained-glass windows, century-old wrought-iron chandeliers, and the fountain out front. The "West Texas Tex-Mex" recipes are time-tested at Jorge's, from a family that has been in the restaurant business for half of a century. I like the batter-free rellenos, the *enchiladas de chile verde*, made with blue corn tortillas and topped with green chile, and the *taquitos de barbacoa*, grilled tacos loaded with "Mexican barbecue." Fans of the Mexican specialty *menudo* can indulge themselves with Jorge's special recipe at any time the restaurant is open. There are also a dozen combination plates, daily specials, and a kids' menu.

1100 S. Ross St. ℂ 806/371-0411. Reservations not accepted. Main courses $5–$8. AE, DISC, MC, V. Mon–Sat 10:30am–10pm; Sun 10:30am–3pm.

OHMS Café and Gallery ✶ ECLECTIC   My pick for a lunch spot, the chalkboard menu changes daily at this pleasant downtown eatery, which doubles as a gallery for local artists. (Incidentally, OHMS stands for "On Her Majesty's Service," so named by the former owner, a native of the United Kingdom.) Lunch is served cafeteria-style, with such regular offerings as a very British—and very good—shepherd's pie, linguine with fresh basil and Brie, and herbed baked chicken, all with soup or salad (with tasty homemade dressings) and fresh bread. Dinner is a bit pricier and healthier than the Amarillo norm; likely selections are baked salmon, rosemary-mustard pork loin, Prime rib, and lasagna. The art on display changes monthly, and there is live acoustic music on a regular basis.

619 S. Tyler St. ℂ 806/373-3233. Main courses $7 lunch, $10–$18 dinner. AE, DC, DISC, MC, V. Mon–Fri 11:30am–1:30pm; Fri–Sat 6–9pm.

Stockyard Cafe *Finds* AMERICAN   Whereas the Big Texan is kitschy and Disney-esque, the Stockyard Cafe is the real deal: Diners just don't get any more cowboy than this. Tucked away at the site of one of the largest livestock auctions in the world, this restaurant is smoky, old-fashioned, and furnished with cowhides, burlap, and the requisite taxidermy. But it's the food that keeps those cattlemen coming, from the simple and fresh American breakfasts to the steaks, hamburgers and sandwiches at lunch. Dinnertime in Amarillo means more steaks, and the Stockyard Cafe is no exception, serving the chicken-fried variety and 8-ounce sirloins. Everything on the menu is fresh and Texas-sized.

100 S. Manhattan St., in the Amarillo Livestock Auction Bldg. ℂ 806/374-6024. Reservations not accepted. Main courses $4.50–$10 lunch, $6–$10 dinner. AE, DISC, MC, V. Mon–Sat 6:30am–2:30pm; Fri–Sat 5–9:30pm.

AMARILLO AFTER DARK
THE PERFORMING ARTS

Amarillo Little Theatre, 2019 Civic Circle (ℂ 806/355-9991; www.amarillo littletheatre.org), produces 10 plays annually at two theaters southwest of downtown. The Little Theater focuses on musicals and lighter fare, whereas the new A.L.T. Adventure Space produces edgier, adult-oriented fare. Recent productions have included *Chicago, Buddy: The Buddy Holly Story,* and *How I Learned to Drive.* Ticket prices range from $12 to $18.

The **Amarillo Opera,** 2223 S. Van Buren St. (ℂ 806/372-7464; www. amarilloopera.com), produces two main stage operas annually, one each in the fall and spring, and an annual spirituals concert on the first weekend of every February. The performances take place at the Amarillo Civic Center, 401 S. Buchanan St., and tickets are priced from $12 to $40. The **Amarillo Symphony** (ℂ 806/376-8782; www.amarillosymphony.org) performs classical and pops concerts year-round also at the Amarillo Civic Center; tickets for most concerts cost between $15 and $25.

Lone Star Ballet (© **806/372-2463;** www.lonestarballet.org) presents a season of local and guest performances from September to March at the Amarillo Civic Center. The local company produces *The Nutcracker* annually on the second weekend of December, and occasionally performs joint performances with the Amarillo Symphony. Tickets are $12 to $32.

NIGHTCLUBS & BARS

The two main nightlife districts in Amarillo are the **Historic Route 66 District** and **South Polk Street** downtown, between 7th and 8th avenues. **Brewster's Pub,** 715 S. Polk St. (© **806/342-0782**), is a good bet: a big sports bar with a game room and live music 4 nights a week. Rough and raw, the **Golden Light Cafe,** 2908 W. 6th Ave. (© **806/374-9237**), is a Route 66 landmark, open since 1946 with a grill and oodles of nostalgia. For country-and-western fans, there's **Midnight Rodeo,** 4400 S. Georgia St. (© **806/358-7083**), featuring a gargantuan dance floor centered about an oval bar. Another good venue for live music—primarily country—is the hubcap-laden **Route 66 Roadhouse,** 609 S. Independence St. (© **806/355-7399**), which also has pool tables and dartboards.

2 Canyon & Palo Duro Canyon State Park ★

16 miles S of Amarillo; 103 miles N of Lubbock

Founded as Canyon City in 1889, Canyon takes its name from the spectacular Palo Duro Canyon, which lies 12 miles to the west. The nomadic pre-horse tribes of Apaches first inhabited the region, but by the 18th century Comanche and Kiowa horsemen used the canyon as a major campground. By the late 19th century, white ranchers began grazing cattle in the area: Charles Goodnight, the inventor of the chuck wagon, drove a herd into Palo Duro Canyon in 1876 and established the JA Ranch.

Today a city of 13,000 residents, Canyon is known primarily as the gateway to Palo Duro Canyon State Park and the home of West Texas State A&M University. The town is a good base camp for those who want to explore Palo Duro Canyon but don't want to spend their nights in a tent. The community also has a charming small-town vibe, and much of its colorful history is presented at the excellent Panhandle-Plains Historical Museum.

ESSENTIALS

GETTING THERE & AROUND

Canyon is located immediately south of the junction of I-27 and U.S. 87, about 16 miles south of downtown Amarillo. Once entering town, U.S. 87 becomes 23rd Street, one of Canyon's main commercial thoroughfares. Texas 217, which runs east-west, becomes 4th Avenue in town and is accessible via I-27, Exit 106; head west 2 miles to get to Canyon proper or east 10 miles to get to Palo Duro Canyon State Park.

Canyon's small size makes it impossible to get lost. The streets run north-south and begin at 1st at the west side of town. The avenues run east-west and begin numerically in the north.

VISITOR INFORMATION

Open from 9am to 4:30pm weekdays, the **Canyon Chamber of Commerce,** 1518 5th Ave. (© **806/655-1183;** www.canyonchamber.org), can provide visitors with information and maps.

FAST FACTS   The closest hospitals are located 16 miles north in Amarillo, including **Northwest Texas Hospital,** 1501 S. Coulter Dr. (© **806/354-1000**). The **post office** is at 1304 4th Ave., open Monday through Friday from 9am to 4:30pm.

WHAT TO SEE & DO
THE TOP ATTRACTIONS

Palo Duro Canyon State Park ★★ *Moments*   The 60-mile Palo Duro Canyon, sculpted by the Prairie Dog Town Fork of the Red River over the last 90 million years, presents a grand contrast to the ubiquitous treeless plains of the Texas Panhandle. Its 800-foot cliffs, striped with layers of orange, red, and white rock and adorned by groves of juniper and cottonwood trees, present a stark beauty that make this the preeminent state park in all of Texas. Simply put, it is the one "can't miss" natural attraction in the region. Palo Duro, which is Spanish for "hard wood," is a geology buff's dream: The base of the canyon is walled by red shales and sandstones from the Permian period (ca. 250 million B.C.); these are topped by colorful Triassic shales and sandstones; and the top of the canyon is made of a pastiche of stones only a few million years old. Of the 200 species of animals that venture into the canyon, you're most likely to see mule deer and wild turkeys. There's also the famed Pioneer Amphitheatre; the venue for the musical drama *Texas Legacies;* several hiking, biking, and horseback riding trails; and a visitor center/museum/bookstore with interpretive exhibits on the canyon's formation, history, and wildlife.

Route 2 (P.O. Box 285), Canyon, TX 79015. © **806/488-2227.** www.palodurocanyon.com. Day use $3 adults, $2 seniors, free for children ages 12 and under. Additional fees for campsites (see "Camping," below). Gates open daily 8am–10pm. 12 miles west of Canyon via TX 217.

Panhandle-Plains Historical Museum ★★ *Finds*   The largest history museum in the entire state, the Panhandle-Plains Historical Museum is anything but a dusty collection of spurs and bits. Well thought out, engaging, and informative, the facility stands out as the top museum in the Panhandle (and all of West Texas, for that matter) because it comprehensively covers so many subjects under one roof. A new permanent exhibit, entitled "People of the Plains," is a comprehensive history of the Panhandle's inhabitants, offering a glimpse into how people have adapted to the past and present challenges of water, food, and climate. The museum is largely hands-on and interactive: You can sit in a Mustang and listen to Buddy Holly tunes or try out a sidesaddle. Other wings

---

Tips **Texas Legacies**

More than 3 million people attended the musical drama *Texas* since performances began in 1966, making it the nation's biggest outdoor drama. It's been updated as *Texas Legacies,* a spectacle of choreography and song covering the Panhandle's storied past. Staged at Pioneer Amphitheatre in Palo Duro Canyon State Park, the 2-hour play takes place Thursday through Tuesday from early June to mid-August at 8:30pm. For tickets, call © 877/588-3927 or 806/655-2181 or visit **www.epictexas.com**. Adult tickets range from $10 to $25; those for children under 12 are slightly cheaper. For an extra $7.50 ($6 for children), attendees can partake of a barbecue dinner at 6:30pm. The admission fee to Palo Duro Canyon State Park is waived at 5:30pm for all *Texas Legacies* ticket holders.

cover the region's history in terms of petroleum, art, transportation, Western heritage, and paleontology/geology. Allow 1 to 2 hours.

2401 4th Ave., on the campus of West Texas State A&M University. ℂ 806/651-2244. www.panhandle plains.org. $4 adults, $3 seniors, $1 children ages 4–12, free for children under 4. Sept–May Mon–Sat 9am–5pm; June–Aug Mon–Sat 9am–6pm; year-round Sun 1–6pm. Closed major holidays.

OUTDOOR ACTIVITIES

GOLF   Palo Duro Creek, 50 Country Club Dr. (ℂ **806/655-1106**), is an 18-hole course open to the public 365 days a year. Greens fees are $18.

HIKING   With 25 miles of trails, Palo Duro Canyon State Park is the best hiking spot in the entire Texas Panhandle. The most popular hike is to see the **Lighthouse,** an impressive "hoodoo" rock formation so named because of its towering appearance. The Lighthouse is accessible by two trails: Lighthouse Trail, a moderate 5¾-mile round-trip; or Running Trail, a more strenuous 11-mile round-trip that runs through gullies and flats, and over a ridge. Both trail heads begin near the Hackberry Camp Area.

HORSEBACK RIDING   Many of the trails in Palo Duro Canyon State Park are horse-friendly, including the aforementioned Lighthouse Trail. There are also several equestrian campsites in the park. For those who do not have a horse of their own, **Old West Stables,** located inside the park (ℂ **806/ 488-2180**), offers 1-hour guided tours on horseback for $20 and wagon rides for $8 per adult (free for accompanying children 8 and under).

MOUNTAIN BIKING   Mountain bikes are permitted—and quite popular— on the myriad trails in **Palo Duro Canyon State Park.** However, there are no bike rentals available in Canyon or Amarillo, so bringing your own is a prerequisite.

WHERE TO STAY

There are a number of mom-and-pop motels and a few B&Bs in Canyon. For reliability and convenience, I like the **Holiday Inn Express,** 2901 4th Ave. (ℂ **800/ 465-4329** or 806/655-4445), Canyon's only chain, with an indoor pool, Jacuzzi, and exercise room.

Hudspeth House ✦   This three-story B&B was a "kit home" ordered from Sears and Roebuck and assembled in 1909, then relocated to its present location in 1913. The inn takes its name from a teacher at the college that became West Texas State A&M University, Miss Mary Elizabeth Hudspeth, a friend of Georgia O'Keeffe who also taught at the school in the 1910s. Miss Hudspeth even hosted many dinner parties at the house that the famed artist attended.

Outside, a shady wraparound porch and colorful gardens invite guests into a lively and elegant parlor. The uniquely decorated and themed rooms are quaint and comfortable, each with its own private bath. My favorites: the second-story Americana room (with an American flag, antique banks, board games, and building blocks); and the Empire room, spacious with a four-poster queen-size bed, and decorated with such classical touches as an antique violin and a bust. There are also two cozy loft rooms on the third floor.

1905 4th Ave., Canyon, TX 79015. ℂ **800/655-9809** or 806/655-9800. www.hudspethinn.com. 8 units. $85–$150 double. Rates include full breakfast. AE, DISC, MC, V. **Amenities:** Restaurant. *In room:* A/C, TV.

CAMPING

Palo Duro Canyon State Park   The park offers a wide variety of camping options, from primitive backpacking sites accessible only by foot to standard RV sites with water and electrical hook-ups. There are showers and restrooms at

Old Route 66

The ghosts of speed demons behind the wheels of phantom hot rods, torching the highway between Chicago and Los Angeles, still cruise northern Texas's stretch of the fabled "Mother Road." However, the construction of I-40, completed in 1984 on a similar course as Route 66, irrevocably changed the landscape of cross-country travel. What was once Route 66 is now a patchwork of service roads, two-lane highways, and inaccessible stretches of dirt. As the interstate defined the course of the last several decades of development, many of the towns through which Route 66 once snaked lost a fair share of commercial traffic, but hordes of nostalgic travelers have given many of the old and offbeat roadside landmarks a much-needed boost in recent years. Contact the **Texas Route 66 Association (℗ 806/373-7576)** for more information.

OLD ROUTE 66 HIGHLIGHTS

Established in 1890 by an Irish sheep rancher, **Shamrock,** 100 miles east of Amarillo via I-40, is home to the **U Drop Inn,** located at the junction of U.S. 83 and Old Route 66. Built in 1936, this service station/coffee shop is one of the earliest examples of Art Deco architecture on the Texas plains. At press time, it had been donated to the city and was being restored as a tourist center; the target date for opening was fall 2003. Aside from the U Drop Inn, the **Pioneer West Historical Museum,** 204 N. Madden St. (℗ 806/256-3941), is the prime tourist stop, with 28 rooms in the restored Reynolds Hotel (1925) devoted to historical artifacts and other displays, including objects on loan from NASA's Houston Space Center. It's open Tuesday through Friday from 1 to 5pm, although hours are somewhat erratic; admission is free, but donations are accepted. Also, come March 17, Shamrock hosts a lively St. Patrick's Day celebration, with a street fair, parade, and other festivities. Shamrock has a number of restaurants and motels, including the **Irish Inn,** 301 I-40 East (℗ 806/256-2106), with double rates from $57 to $72.

several of the camping areas, as well as a dump station. For more substantial supplies, you'll want to hit a grocery store in Canyon, such as **Lowe's,** 900 23rd St. (℗ 806/655-2171). The two rustic, mission-style cabins were built in the 1930s, and since renovated. They can sleep four people and have full bathrooms; they have no kitchens, but have grills out front. Pets are permitted at all of the sites, but they must remain leashed at all times.

Route 2 (P.O. Box 285), Canyon, TX 79015. (℗ 512/389-8900 or 806/488-2227 for reservations. 100 sites, including 7 pull-throughs, 75 back-ins, and 18 tent sites. Additional primitive sites, equestrian sites, and 2 cabins available. $9–$12 campsites; $65 cabins. DISC, MC, V. Located 12 miles east of Canyon via Tex. 217.

WHERE TO DINE

A local favorite, **Pepito's,** 408 23rd St. (℗ 806/655-4376), is a charming little Tex-Mex restaurant with tiled, landscape-adorned tables and regional art. The

In the small town of **McLean,** 16 miles west of Shamrock, you'll find the Devil's Rope Museum, at the Junction of Old Route 66 and Kingsley Street (© **806/779-2225**), a converted Sears bra factory now home to displays on the history and evolution of both barbed wire and Route 66. From April to mid-December, it's open Tuesday through Saturday from 10am to 4pm and Sunday from 1 to 4pm with admission by donation. It's closed from mid-December to March.

The town of **Groom,** 25 miles west of McLean, is the home of the largest cross in the Western Hemisphere: **the Cross of Our Lord Jesus Christ,** located off of I-40, Exit 119 (© **806/665-7788**). With about 1,000 visitors stopping daily, the 190-foot, 1,250-ton cross is truly monolithic. If for nothing else, cross-country travelers should stop to admire its sheer size.

Just east of Groom is another Route 66 landmark: **The Leaning Tower of Texas,** a water tower intentionally built to slant with one set each of short and long legs and the subject of many a souvenir since. Like the cross in Groom and Cadillac Ranch in Amarillo, the tower gives Old Route 66 a jolt of quirky personality. If you're a fan of roadside attractions, stopping for this peculiar photo op is a must.

By far the biggest Texas city on Old Route 66, **Amarillo** still houses a nicely preserved stretch of the restored highway in its Historic Route 66 District, between Western and Georgia streets on West 6th Avenue (see p. 392).

About 45 miles west of Amarillo is the tiny town of **Adrian,** known as the "Midpoint of Route 66." The appropriately named **MidPoint Café** on Route 66 (© **806/538-6379**), a favorite of tourists, cowboys, and bikers alike, is a friendly diner open for three meals daily in the summer (7am–9pm) and breakfast and lunch in the winter (8am–2:30pm). Bedecked with Route 66 memorabilia and shelves of souvenirs, the menu includes hearty American breakfasts, burgers with the works, and steaks, with most main courses coming in at under $5 for breakfast and under $10 for lunch and dinner.

specialties are fajitas and the restaurant is open for lunch and dinner Mondays through Saturdays. **The Bistro,** 1905 4th Ave. in the Hudspeth House Inn (© **806/655-9800**), offers a nice selection of salads and sandwiches for lunch and gourmet dinners by reservations only.

A unique dining experience can be had with **Cowboy Morning/Cowboy Evening** (© **806/944-5562** or 800/658-2613) in Claude, about 40 miles east of Canyon. The meals include a horse-drawn wagon ride to a canyon overlook and authentic chuck wagon cuisine. Cowboy Morning includes sourdough biscuits, eggs, sausage, cowboy coffee, and orange juice and is priced at $19 for adults, $15 for children ages 4 to 12, and free for children 3 and younger. Cowboy Evening includes rib-eye steaks, Texas red beans, salad, and campfire cobbler for $25 adults, $15 children ages 4 to 12, and free for children 3 and under.

3 Lubbock

122 miles S of Amarillo; 100 miles SE of Clovis, New Mexico

When Capt. Randolph Marcy, one of the first Anglo explorers to happen onto the site of modern-day Lubbock, arrived, he was something less than impressed. "It was the dreaded Llano Estacado," he wrote, "a land where no man, either savage or civilized, permanently abides a treeless, desolate waste of uninhabited solitude, which has always been and must continue uninhabited forever."

Certainly, Marcy would be in for a shock if he were able to see Lubbock today: a city of about 200,000, the home of a major university in Texas Tech, and the economic and cultural center of the surrounding South Plains. Self-labeled as "the nursery" for Austin's music scene, its musical heritage is legendary: Buddy Holly still reigns as the local king, but Tanya Tucker, Waylon Jennings, and Natalie Maines (of the Dixie Chicks) have also called the city home.

Named after Col. Thomas Lubbock, a Confederate officer, Lubbock was established in 1890 and grew rapidly, its economy built on cotton and cattle, and, later, oil and gas. The city has long been a regional hub; hence the nickname, "Hub City." Look at a map and the moniker's appropriateness becomes crystal clear: Lubbock is surrounded by dozens of small agricultural towns.

A bit rough around the edges, Lubbock is a fun stopover for a night because of its lively dining scene, college-town vibe, and happening nightlife with plenty of good music.

ESSENTIALS
GETTING THERE
BY PLANE **Lubbock International Airport,** 5401 N. Martin Luther King Blvd. (© 806/775-3126; www.flylia.com), sees 70 arrivals and departures daily. Just four airlines serve the airport: **American** (© 800/433-7300), **Continental** (© 800/523-3273), **Delta** (© 800/282-3424), and **Southwest** (© 800/435-9792).

All the major car-rental agencies, including **Avis** and **Hertz,** have desks at the airport. **Royal Coach Towne Car Service** (© 806/795-3888) offers airport transportation in Lincoln Town Cars into the city for $10 to $17.

BY CAR Lubbock sits at the intersection of three major highways on the "Port to Plains" route. I-27 enters the city from the north and becomes U.S. 87 south of Lubbock. Cutting down from Clovis, New Mexico, northwest of the city, U.S. 84 continues southeast to I-20 near Abilene. U.S. 62/82 is the third major highway that runs through Lubbock, entering town from the southwest, where it is the primary route to and from Carlsbad and Roswell, New Mexico, and continuing through the plains to the east.

GETTING AROUND
Getting around Lubbock is fairly stress-free: It is laid out on a standard grid with few anomalies, with I-27 bisecting the city north-south and Loop 289, a major highway, circling it. Downtown is located just west of I-27, accessible via either Exit 3 (19th St.) or Exit 4 (4th St.). The east-west streets in central Lubbock are numbered, beginning with 1st in the north, and the north-south streets surrounding I-27 are arranged alphabetically, from Avenue A on the east side of the highway and continuing to Avenue Z on the west side of I-27.

CitiBus (© 806/767-2380; www.citibus.com), Lubbock's mass transit system, operates 14 routes Monday through Friday from 5:45am to 7:15pm and

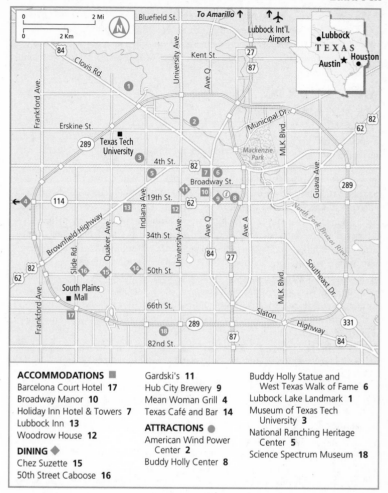

ACCOMMODATIONS ■
Barcelona Court Hotel **17**
Broadway Manor **10**
Holiday Inn Hotel & Towers **7**
Lubbock Inn **13**
Woodrow House **12**

DINING ◆
Chez Suzette **15**
50th Street Caboose **16**

Gardski's **11**
Hub City Brewery **9**
Mean Woman Grill **4**
Texas Café and Bar **14**

ATTRACTIONS ●
American Wind Power
Center **2**
Buddy Holly Center **8**

Buddy Holly Statue and
West Texas Walk of Fame **6**
Lubbock Lake Landmark **1**
Museum of Texas Tech
University **3**
National Ranching Heritage
Center **5**
Science Spectrum Museum **18**

Saturday from 6:45am to 7:35pm. No service is offered on Sunday. The main downtown transfer station is located at the intersection of Broadway and Buddy Holly Avenue (Ave. H). Fares are $1 for adults, 75¢ for children ages 6 to 12, 50¢ for seniors and those with disabilities, and free for children under 6. A $2 day pass allows for unlimited rides.

Taxi service is offered by **Yellow Cab** (© 806/765-7777) and **City Cab** (© 806/765-7474).

VISITOR INFORMATION

The **Lubbock Convention and Visitors Bureau,** 1301 Broadway, Suite 200 (© **800/692-4035** or 806/747-5232; www.lubbocklegends.org), can provide visitors with local maps and information on lodging, dining, and attractions. Another good regional resource is the **Llano Estacado Tourism Society** (© **806/632-6530;** www.llanoestacado.com), which can provide you with tons of good information on Lubbock and the surrounding area.

FAST FACTS **Highland Medical Center,** 2412 50th St. (© **806/788-4100**), and **Covenant Medical Center,** 400 24th St. (© **806/725-6000**), both south-west of downtown, operate 24-hour emergency rooms. The main **post office** is located downtown at 1515 Avenue G and is open Monday through Friday from 8:30am to 5pm.

WHAT TO SEE & DO
THE TOP ATTRACTIONS

Buddy Holly Center ★★ Named for Lubbock's legendary rock pioneer, this gem of a museum is a must-visit if you're a rock 'n' roll fan, and at least worth a quick look if you're not. The permanent exhibit about the life and music of Buddy Holly is the centerpiece of this facility, which also houses an art gallery and the Texas Musicians Hall of Fame. Though Holly died in a plane crash at the age of 23, his impact on the development of rock is undeniable—he influenced everyone from Elton John to the Grateful Dead. The center's collection includes such memorabilia as Holly's trademark horn-rimmed glasses (the pair recovered from the crash site) alongside his guitars, personal mementos, and interactive exhibits. Visitors should also view the 20-minute Holly documentary, if time allows. The Lubbock Fine Arts Gallery features rotating exhibits of all kinds, and the Texas Musicians Hall of Fame gives perspective on Lubbock's deep musical heritage. Acting as a regional arts center, the B.H.C. also hosts numerous courtyard concerts, classes, and "Cultural Conversations" on topics of regional artistic interest. The museum's breadth almost dictates that guest spend a bit more than an hour here.

1801 Ave. G, in the Depot District. © **806/767-2686.** www.buddyhollycenter.org. $5 adults, $3 seniors, free for children 12 and under. Tues–Fri 10am–6pm; Sat 11am–6pm. Closed major holidays.

Museum of Texas Tech University ★ Housing some 2 million objects and artifacts, this museum is a well-rounded facility that covers a diverse, if not terribly focused, mix of subjects: Visual arts, natural and social sciences, and the humanities are all represented with both permanent and regularly rotating exhibits. The 100,000-item ethnology and textiles collection is among the best you'll find anywhere, comprised of objects made by people living in Texas, the Southwest, and the Great Plains. There are also galleries filled with Taos and sub-Saharan art, exhibits on wildlife, and full-size dinosaur skeletons. The temporary exhibits are routinely excellent—in 2002, the museum hosted an exclusive, one-time-only exhibit of art on loan from the Vatican. Also on-site is the Moody Planetarium (public shows are held daily for $1 adults, 50¢ for students, free for seniors and children under 5). Expect to spend between 1 and 2 hours here if you want to scratch the museum's surface.

4th St. and Indiana Ave. © **806/742-2490.** www.museum.ttu.edu. Free admission. Tues–Sat 10am–5pm (till 8:30 Thurs); Sun 1–5pm. Closed major holidays.

National Ranching Heritage Center As some of the country's largest and most storied ranches originated in the Panhandle area in the early 1900s, Lubbock is a natural for the home of a museum dedicated to preserving the history of ranching in the United States. However, the history buff short on time might skip this in favor of the more comprehensive Panhandle-Plains Historical Museum in Canyon (p. 402). The outdoor displays consist of 40 relocated historic buildings; visitors can tour such structures as a *vaquero* corral (1783), a log cabin (1850), a "dugout" dwelling (1890), and the Victorian-style Barton House (1909). The center hosts several annual events, including a chuck wagon dinner and concert in the spring, fiddle dances in the summer, and "Candlelight at the Ranch" in December. Allow a half-hour to an hour.

3121 4th St. at Indiana Ave. © **806/742-0498**. www.ttu.edu/ranchingheritagecenter. Free admission. Mon–Sat 10am–5pm; Sun 1–5pm. Closed major holidays.

MORE ATTRACTIONS

American Wind Power Center *Finds*   Between 1850 and 1920, over 700 American companies manufactured windmills, but today there are a mere two U.S. businesses making these iconic machines. Such statistics provided an impetus for this unique and worthwhile museum, which displays a collection of 200 water-pumping windmills. Windmills of every size, shape, and color are displayed in the main gallery and outside on the museum's grounds, including a rare twin-wheel windmill, with a pair of 12-foot wheels on a single tower and two of the largest existent windmills on the continent. The center opened a new exhibit space in 2001, a cavernous barn-like building that houses 75 unusual windmills, an art gallery, and a gift shop. Allow 1 hour.

1701 Canyon Lake Dr. © **806/747-8734**. www.windmill.com. Guided tour $3; self-guided tour: $2 adult, free for children under 5. Tues–Sat 10am–5pm. Closed major holidays. Located 1 mile west of I-27 via 19th St.

Buddy Holly Statue and West Texas Walk of Fame   This shady urban isle just west of the Lubbock Civic Center pays tribute to Lubbock's most famous son, Buddy Holly, with an oversized statue of his likeness, guitar in hand. In 1979, Holly became the first inductee into the West Texas Walk of Fame that surrounds the statue. Other inductees include actor Barry Corbin (TV's *Northern Exposure*) and musicians Roy Orbison, Tanya Tucker, and Waylon Jennings. It's a pleasant spot to sit on a bench, enjoy the gardens, and reflect on the fleeting life and times of an American original.

Between 7th and 8th sts. at Ave. Q.

Lubbock Lake Landmark   A unit of the Museum of Texas Tech University, the Lubbock Lake Landmark consists of a 300-acre archaeological and natural history preserve, believed to be the only site in North America where a complete record of 12,000 years of human history has been uncovered. The nicely presented interpretive center features chronological displays on each group that has inhabited the region, from the nomadic hunters of the Paleo-Indian period to the pioneers of the late 1800s. The facility requires about 45 minutes to tour, and, if it's fresh air you're after, take an extra hour to explore 4 miles of nature trails and an outdoor sculpture garden with life-size bronzes depicting animals that once roamed the area, including a mammoth and a giant armadillo. Additionally, Lubbock Lake Landmark is home to an active archaeological program during the summer and children's programs throughout the year.

2401 Landmark Dr. at Loop 289 and Clovis Rd. (U.S. 84). © **806/742-1115**. www.museum.ttu.edu/ LLL/index.html. Free admission (donation requested). Tues–Sat 9am–5pm; Sun 1-5pm.

Science Spectrum Museum *Kids*   This museum aims to educate children about science and technology, and hits the bull's-eye more often than not. With three floors and 200 exhibits that take 1 to 2 hours to explore, the subject

---

Fun Fact

"At least the first 40 songs we wrote were Buddy Holly–influenced."
—Former Beatle Paul McCartney

A Different Kind of Texas Tea

The images of herds of longhorn, oil pumps on the horizon, and endless cotton fields might be the enduring images of the northwestern Texas plains, but if the area's burgeoning wine industry has anything to do with it, the vineyard could just become another regional icon. The climate is close to ideal for the cultivation of grapes, with its moderate elevation, warm days, and cool nights. Within a 15-minute drive of Lubbock, there are three wineries that open their doors to tours.

Emerging from a grape-growing experiment on a shady Lubbock patio in 1976, **Llano Estacado Winery,** located 5 miles southeast of Lubbock on Tex. 1585 between U.S. 84 and U.S. 87 (✆ **806/745-2258;** www.llanowine.com), is now one of the largest and best wineries in Texas: Its wines have won more awards than any other winery in the state. Free tours that end in an elegant tasting room are available from 10am to 4pm Monday through Saturday and from noon to 4pm Sunday. **Cap*Rock Winery,** 4 miles south of Lubbock at U.S. 87 South and Woodrow Road (✆ **806/863-2704;** www.caprockwinery.com), uses vinifera grapes to produce chardonnays, cabernet sauvignons, and other wines. Free tours and samples are available from 10am to 5pm Monday through Saturday and from 1 to 5pm Sunday. **Pheasant Ridge Winery** on Route 3, 12 miles northeast of Lubbock via I-27 (✆ **806/746-6033;** www.pheasantridgewinery.com), is located on the site of one of Texas's oldest vineyards and offers tours and tastings Friday and Saturday from 10am to 5pm and Sunday from 1 to 5pm.

For more information on Texas wineries, call the **Texas Wine Market Research Institute** at Texas Tech University at ✆ **806/742-3077.**

matter runs the gamut from animals and aquariums to space and flight, and many of the displays are interactive. The big news for 2003 was the splashy debut of the "Brazos River Journey," a permanent aquarium/terrarium exhibit detailing how the regional river ecosystem interacts with the hand of man. The facility is also home to the Omnimax Theatre—with a 55-foot dome screen—and an excellent gift shop.

2579 S. Loop 289 (between Indiana and University aves.). ✆ 806/745-6299. www.sciencespectrum.com. $5.50 adults, $4.50 seniors and children ages 3–12, free for children under 3. Additional tickets necessary for the Omnimax Theatre. Mon–Fri 10am–5pm; Sat 10am–6pm; Sun 1–5pm. Closed Mon late Sept to Mar.

OUTDOOR ACTIVITIES

Within the city limits of Lubbock, the 248-acre **Mackenzie Park,** located east of I-27 at 4th Street (✆ 806/775-2687), is the largest recreation area, with two golf courses—one traditional and one Frisbee—walking, jogging, and equestrian trails, and Prairie Dog Town, one of the few active colonies in the urban United States.

Caprock Canyons State Park and Trailway (✆ 806/455-1492) is a 2½-hour drive from Lubbock, located to the northeast near Quitaque off Tex. 86. Like Palo Duro Canyon to the northwest, this 13,906-acre park offers a startling contrast to the plains in its jagged formations of red rocks and diverse vegetation. An abandoned railroad line was converted into a 64-mile trail system that travels along a canyon floor, through a one-time railroad tunnel, and up a steep incline onto the mesa of the High Plains. Hikers, bikers, and horses are permitted on the trail. There are several other hiking opportunities in the park. There are primitive backcountry campsites for $7 nightly as well as campsites with partial RV hook-ups for $12. Additionally, boaters and fishers can take advantage of Lake Theo, located on the south side of the park. The park charges a $2 day-use fee per person (free for kids 12 and under).

BOATING   There are two boat ramps at the spring-fed **Buffalo Springs Lake,** Texas 835, 5 miles east of Loop 289 (© **806/747-3353**). Gate fees are $2 adults, $1 seniors and children under 11, and $3 per watercraft. Rentals are not available. Boating is also allowed at **Lake Alan Henry** (© **806/775-2592**), 65 miles southeast of Lubbock via U.S. 84 and FM 2458, a rugged-looking reservoir surrounded by a wildlife habitat area with about 10 miles of hiking trails.

GOLF   There are several public 18-hole golf courses in Lubbock, including **Elm Grove Golf Course,** 3202 Milwaukee St. (© 806/799-7801), with greens fees of $23 to $27 with a cart or $12 to $17 on foot; **Shadow Hills Golf Course,** 6002 3rd St. (© 806/793-9700), with greens fees of $25 to $30 with a cart and $15 to $20 without; and **Meadowbrook Golf Course,** 601 Municipal Dr. in Mackenzie Park (© 806/765-6679), with greens fees of $17 to $36 for a day pass of unlimited holes. Nearby, **The Mackenzie Disk Golf Course** is free, although you'll need your own Frisbee. It is a 21-hole course that includes a 470-yard shot over the Brazos River from a cliff.

HIKING   There are 4 miles of nature trails at **Lubbock Lake Landmark** (p. 409), as well as the 64-mile trail at **Caprock Canyons State Park.** There are also several miles of walking and jogging trails, many of which are horse-friendly, within the city limits at **Mackenzie Park,** 4th Street and I-27 (© **806/775-2687**).

MOUNTAIN BIKING   There are a few trails at **Buffalo Springs Lake,** Texas 835, 5 miles east of Loop 289 (see "Boating, above), but Lubbock's hard-core mountain bikers head north to **Palo Duro Canyon State Park** (see "Canyon & Palo Duro Canyon State Park," earlier in this chapter) and **Caprock Canyons State Park.**

SWIMMING   Lubbock is home to four municipal pools, all outdoor and open from late May to early August: **Clapp Municipal Swimming Pool,** 4500 Ave. U; **Mae Simmons,** 2300 Weber Dr.; **Maxey,** 4007 30th St.; and **Rogers,** 3200 Bates St. In season, each is open from 1 to 6:30pm daily with an admission fee of $2 adults, $1.50 children 17 and under. For further information, call © **806/ 775-2673**. There are also two beaches at **Buffalo Springs Lake** (see "Boating," above) that are open to swimmers year-round. Aside from the admission fee ($2 adults, $1 children 11 and under), there is no additional fee to swim. A year-round indoor pool is located at the **YWCA,** 3101 35th St. (© **806/792-2723**). A day pass is $5.

SPECTATOR SPORTS

The Lubbock home crowd roots for the **Texas Tech Red Raiders,** who compete in Big 12 football, baseball, and men's and women's basketball. Call © **888/GO-BIG12** or 806/742-4412 for schedules and ticket information. A Central Hockey League team, the **Lubbock Cotton Kings** (© **806/747-7825;** www.cottonkings.com), plays 32 home games at Lubbock Municipal Coliseum between October and March. Tickets are $3.50 to $6.

SHOPPING

Lubbock is home to the region's largest mall, **South Plains Mall,** 6002 Slide Rd. at South Loop 289 (© **806/792-4653**), which houses more than 150 stores, including The Gap, Abercrombie & Fitch, and many other department stores, specialty shops, and restaurants. The mall's hours are from 10am to 9pm Monday through Saturday and from 1 to 6pm Sunday. The **Antique Mall of Lubbock,** 7907 W. 19th St. (© **806/796-2166**), offers West Texas's largest selection of antiques, open daily from 10am to 6pm.

WHERE TO STAY

You'll find Lubbock's greatest concentration of hotels and motels in three areas: downtown; off of I-27 between 50th Street and Loop 289; and in the city's southwest corner, off Loop 289 near Quaker and Indiana avenues. Among the city's chain properties are: **Four Points By Sheraton,** 505 Ave. Q, (© **800/749-0171** or 806/747-0171); **La Quinta Inn,** 601 Ave. Q (© **800/687-6667** or 806/763-9441); and **Motel 6,** 909 66th St. (© **800/466-8356** or 806/745-5541).

The **Lubbock Inn,** 3901 19th St. (© **800/545-8226** or 806/792-5181), is a first-rate independent, with double rates of $69 to $79 and suites for $90 to $100. **Broadway Manor,** 1811 Broadway (© **877/504-8223** or 806/749-7407), is a good Victorian B&B, with rooms from $85 to $150. Room taxes in Lubbock add about 13.5% to lodging bills.

Barcelona Court Hotel   A solid mid-price option, this Lubbock mainstay is centered around a striking three-story atrium with tropical flora, red Spanish tile, and a triple-tiered fountain. The rooms are large and comfortable, a value for road-trippers in dire need of space. Each unit is a true two-room suite with a king-size bed or two doubles, a hideaway sleeper sofa, and a fully furnished kitchen, as well as two phones and two televisions. Some rates include such special perks as a complimentary full breakfast, airport shuttle, and an evening reception with complimentary cocktails, for $5 to $10 more per night.

5215 S. Loop 289, Lubbock, TX 79424. © 800/222-1122 or 806/794-5353. Fax 806/798-9398. www. barcelonacourt.com. 158 suites. $75–$79 double. AE, DC, DISC, MC, V. **Amenities:** Indoor heated pool; privileges at a nearby health club; indoor Jacuzzi; sauna; dry cleaning. *In room:* A/C, TV/VCR, dataport, kitchen, coffeemaker.

Holiday Inn Hotel & Towers 🟊   The cream of the Lubbock hotel crop, this early 1980s–era Holiday Inn is the city's largest lodging option, located adjacent to the Civic Center smack-dab in the middle of downtown. Well-maintained and comfortable, the rooms are pleasant if unremarkable, with off-white walls and beige furnishings. I like the east tower, six stories of rooms surrounding a wide-open atrium. The suites with north-facing windows are the best—you'll be greeted every morning by the Buddy Holly statue on the West Texas Walk of Fame below. Other rooms overlook a treed central courtyard.

801 Ave. Q, Lubbock, TX 79401. © 800/HOLIDAY or 806/763-1200, Fax 806/763-2656. www.holiday-inn. com/lubbock-civic. 295 units. $99 double; $129 suite. AE, DC, DISC, MC, V. **Amenities:** Restaurant; bar; small indoor pool; exercise room; indoor Jacuzzi; courtesy car; limited room service; coin-op laundry; dry cleaning. *In room:* A/C, TV w/pay movies, dataport.

Woodrow House 🟊🟊   The Southern Colonial architecture (complete with white pillars and a redbrick exterior) of this urban bed-and-breakfast belies its age: Built in 1995, the Woodrow House combines Texas tradition with modern amenities. The suite here—a retrofit Santa Fe caboose in the backyard—is a real eye-catcher, and my favorite room in town. It has a queen-size bed framed by wrought iron and a foldout futon, as well as a kitchenette. The old engineers' seats are now great spots to sit and read.

Inside, there's an elegant parlor and seven themed rooms. The Lone Star Room is a lot of fun: a framed Republic of Texas dollar, longhorn skulls, a Texas flag, and a four-poster queen with patchwork quilt. But if your nostalgic leanings are a bit more modern, book the '50s Room, where images of Buddy Holly and Elvis abound.

2629 19th St., Lubbock, TX 79410. (℗ **800/687-5236** or 806/793-3330. Fax 806/793-7676. www.woodrow house.com. 8 units. $95 double; $115 suite. Rates include full breakfast. AE, DISC, MC, V. **Amenities:** Game room; babysitting; laundry service. *In room:* A/C, kitchenette in suite, fridge, coffeemaker, iron.

CAMPING

Buffalo Springs Lake, Texas 835 ((℗ **806/747-3353**), has one of the most scenic campgrounds in the area, with 33 shady sites and three tent areas. Camping fees are $10 for tents and $18 for full hook-ups. **Caprock Canyons State Park** ((℗ **806/455-1492**) is another popular camping destination, with primitive backcountry sites ($7) as well as sites with partial RV hook-ups ($12). See "Outdoor Activities," above, for complete information on both parks.

WHERE TO DINE

Chez Suzette ★★ *Finds* FRENCH/ITALIAN   Almost hidden in a strip mall, Chez Suzette is Lubbock's most romantic dining spot. Black-and-red checkerboard floors, lattice, and dim lighting give the dining room a Continental feel, which carries over to the menu. Start with escargot or carpaccio and a salad, then move on to the main course: coq au vin; veal medallions topped with blue cheese and garlic sauce, served with zucchini pancakes; or ahi tuna with a balsamic reduction. Lighter selections include pastas and vegetarian plates. Lunches are similar but smaller, and the mouthwatering desserts—crème brûlée, bananas Foster, crepes, and pastries—are all made from scratch.

4423 50th St., in the Quarter Square Shopping Center. (℗ **806/795-6796.** Reservations recommended. Main courses $8–$18. AE, DC, DISC, MC, V. Tues–Fri 11:30am–2pm; Mon–Thurs 5:30–10pm; Fri–Sat 5:30–10:30pm.

50th Street Caboose *Kids* MEXICAN/AMERICAN   A hit with kids because of its massive game room (complete with Skee-Ball!), the Caboose is also quite popular with the local grownups because of its late hours and good vittles. The "fajitaladas," beef or chicken fajitas rolled in tortillas and topped with queso, are something else; other favorites include the "Awful, Awful Burger" ("It's awful big and awful good," says the menu), pizza, and the West Texas specialties: grilled catfish, barbecue, and steaks. There are two dining areas to choose from: a large central bar and a family-friendly room with decor best described as "Main Street meets the Southwest."

5027 50th St., in Pyramid Pointe shopping center. (℗ **806/796-2240.** Reservations accepted for large parties only. Main courses $4–$10 lunch, $6–$12 dinner. AE, DISC, MC, V. Sun–Thurs 11am–11pm; Fri–Sat 11am–midnight.

Gardski's AMERICAN   A favorite of both students and suits, this landmark eatery near the campus of Texas Tech University is actually a converted Victorian home, abandoned by its residents after a close call with a tornado in 1970. The place serves some mighty mean sandwiches—I can't resist the Smokin' Mad Jack, plump with smoked ham, brown sugar bacon, pepper jack, and red onions, with jalapeños on the side. There are also good burgers, and a more upscale dinner menu of lighter chicken and seafood plates, pasta, and some down-home favorites: meatloaf, catfish, and chicken-fried steak.

2009 Broadway. (℗ **806/744-2391.** Reservations not accepted. Main courses $5.50–$7.50 lunch, $7.50–$13 dinner. AE, DC, DISC, MC, V. Daily 11am–10pm.

Hub City Brewery ⟨★⟩ PUB FARE   A good spot to start an evening of bar hopping in the Depot District, this hip microbrewery attracts a cross-section of Lubbock to its long copper bar, which sits directly in front of the glass-enclosed brewing area. It serves some interesting twists on traditional bar food, like my favorite, the bratwurst club: a sliced brat on a French roll with Swiss cheese, bacon, sauerkraut, and hot mustard. The menu also offers pizzas, calzones, steaks, and seafood. But the terrific beers are the main attraction: Hub City won "Brewpub of the Year" and "Brewmaster of the Year" at the 2002 Great American Beer Festival. The Red Raider Amber Ale and the Yellowhouse Wheat are some of the best suds in the west.

1807 Buddy Holly Ave., in the Depot District. ℂ 806/747-1535. Main courses $6–$14. AE, DISC, MC, V. Daily 11am–11pm (bar open later).

Mean Woman Grill ⟨★⟩ *Finds* BURGERS/AMERICAN   The Mean Woman Grill is one of those places you have to see to believe: a burger joint that looks as if it were the brainchild of Salvador Dalí and Andy Warhol. The menu is basic, with burgers—the green chile cheeseburgers are tops—sandwiches, and Frito pies, but the decor is anything but. The walls are plastered with rock 'n' roll posters, Christmas lights, Mexican Day of the Dead cutouts, cowboy memorabilia, oddball toys, and painted cow skulls; the salad bar is an old watermelon cooler; the baked potato bar, an old Nehi box. Says co-proprietor Miz Ayn, "Some stuff is just not meant to be thrown away." Live music accompanies dinner Thursday through Saturday, with performances by an eclectic mix of singer-songwriters, rock bands from Austin, and local notables.

209 E. Texas 114 in Levelland, 25 miles west of Lubbock. ℂ 806/897-0006. Reservations accepted for large parties only. Main courses $3–$6. No credit cards. Tues–Sat 11am–9pm. Closed 1 week in July and late Dec.

Texas Café and Bar ⟨★⟩ BARBECUE   This rowdy, smoky roadhouse, affectionately called "The Spoon" by locals, is pure Texas, from the local color seated at the bar and weathered tables to the Lone Star neon signs, longhorn skulls, and politically incorrect wooden Indian. The menu, too, is 100% Texan: spicy beef chili with Texas-shaped cornbread; barbecued turkey, ribs, beef, and sausage; Texas beans; and big, juicy burgers. If you want something that's a little different, try the "fajitas a la brisket," barbecued beef brisket wrapped in a tortilla and served with pico de gallo salsa. Everything here is spicy, hearty, and just plain good. There's a pool room in the back, and live music on weekends.

3604 50th St. ℂ 806/792-8544. Reservations not accepted. Main courses $4.50–$11. AE, MC, V. Daily 11am–10pm (bar open later).

LUBBOCK AFTER DARK
THE PERFORMING ARTS

Built in 1938, the beautifully restored **Cactus Theater,** 1812 Buddy Holly Ave. (ℂ 806/762-3233 for information; www.cactustheater.com), is now the centerpiece of Lubbock's performing arts scene. On Friday through Sunday, it features regular doo-wop and nostalgia shows, as well as other concerts and musicals. Popular productions have included *Always: Patsy Cline* and *Buddy: The Buddy Holly Story.* Tickets run $15 to $25.

   Lubbock Symphony Orchestra, 1313 Broadway, Suite 2 (ℂ 806/762-1688; www.lubbocksymphony.org), performs 10 classical concerts and one pops concert every year at the Lubbock Civic Center Theater (at 6th St. and Ave. O), often featuring guest conductors and musicians from around the world. Ticket prices range from $10 to $30.

Established in 1926, the **Texas Tech University Theatre,** on the Texas Tech campus on 18th Street between Boston and Flint avenues (© **806/742-3603;** www.theatre.ttu.edu), has produced over 1,000 plays in the time since. Recent productions include *Damn Yankees, Angels in America,* and *The Laramie Project.* The theater also hosts ballets, experimental plays, and one-act play festivals. Tickets are $8 to $12.

NIGHTCLUBS & BARS

Lubbock has a bustling nightlife, primarily due to the presence of 25,000 Texas Tech students. The vibrant **Depot District,** located between Buddy Holly Avenue and I-27 around 19th Street, is where you'll find the highest concentration of clubs, including **The Blue Light,** 1806 Buddy Holly Ave. (© **806/ 762-1185**), known for its live music and hip, young crowd; and **Bleachers Sports Café,** 1719 Buddy Holly Ave. (© **806/744-7767**), a huge sports bar/music venue. You can line dance and two-step to live and recorded country music at **Midnight Rodeo** ★, 7301 University (© **806/745-2813**). **Cricket's Grill and Draft House,** 2412 Broadway (© **806/744-4677**), is a rowdy Texas Tech hangout with nearly 100 beers on draft. Many restaurants morph into bustling nightspots after sundown, including the **Texas Café and Bar** (p. 414) with live rock and blues on weekends and the **Hub City Brewery** (p. 414), with live acoustic music and jazz 5 nights a week.

Appendix:
Texas in Depth

by Neil E. Schlecht

The history of Texas is laced with events and heroes large and legendary, many of which have catapulted into state and national lore. In many ways Texas has come to symbolize the nation's westward expansion, its complicated struggle for independence, and the dearly held mystique of a land of opportunity and wide-open spaces. Texas's complex settlement pattern—the territory was claimed by Spain, France, and Mexico before becoming an independent republic and then the 28th state in the Union in 1845—support its mythic status. "Six flags" really did famously fly over the state from the 16th to the 19th century, during which time there were eight changes of government. Even though the state has increasingly become one of immigrants from other states and other nations south of the border, Texans continue to exhibit a fiercely independent streak. The pages that follow explain the state's history and provide a primer on its unique culture.

1 History 101

EARLY NATIVE AMERICANS

In prehistoric times, central parts of the state were once submerged underwater, and about a hundred million years ago, massive dinosaurs, some of them unique to Texas, roamed the plains.

The first human occupation of the land dates from about 10,000 B.C. Traces of a prehistoric people today referred to as the Paleo-Indians have been found, though very little is known of these early hunters. Tribal groups emerged around 8,000 B.C., leaving behind murals of daily life and religious ceremonies in caves in what is now West Texas. As many as 30,000 different Native American tribes—including the Caddos, Coahuiltecans, Tonkawans, Apache, and Comanche—occupied the land before the arrival of European settlers in the 16th century. Agriculturally oriented Indians grew crops that would become modern mainstays, such as cotton, corn, beans, squash, tomatoes, and potatoes. Even the name "Texas" can be traced to

Dateline

- **10,000 B.C.–A.D. 1500** Prehistoric and Native American tribes occupy the territory between the Rio Grande in the south and the Red River in the north.
- **1519** A Spanish explorer, Alonso Álvarez de Piñeda, explores and maps the Texas coastline.
- **1528** Cabeza de Vaca shipwrecks on Galveston Island and spends the next few years exploring Texas.
- **1682** Spanish missionaries establish the first two missions in present-day Texas, near El Paso.
- **1685** The Frenchman LaSalle establishes Fort St. Louis on the coast and lays claim to Texas for France.
- **1716–89** Spain establishes Catholic missions in Texas and the new towns San Antonio, Goliad, and Nacogdoches.
- **1821** Stephen F. Austin receives a grant from the Mexican government to begin colonization in Texas, and many thousands of Americans settle over the next 2 decades.
- **1835** Texans turn back Mexican troops at the Battle of Gonzales, instituting the Texas Revolution.

Native American tribes: *Tejas* is the Spanish pronunciation of the Caddo word for "friend."

ARRIVAL OF THE SPANIARDS

Unfortunately, the arrival of the Spaniards was hardly friendly. Many of the Native American tribes were quickly wiped out, killed either by disease or land-grabbing conquistadors. Along with opportunists in search of gold, glory, and land were missionaries in search of souls. Their objective was the Christianization of native tribes.

The first European to reach Texas shores is believed to have been Alonso Álvarez de Piñeda. In 1519, the Spanish explorer made a map of the Texas coast, establishing the basis for the first claim to the land and Spanish rule. Alvar Núñez Cabeza de Vaca landed in Galveston in 1528 in search of cities of gold, eventually finding his way several years later to Mexico City, where he told stories of seven such cities that lay just north of where his expeditions took him. His tall tales—the first of many that would emanate from Texas—prompted fellow explorer Coronado to venture north through Texas all the way to Kansas. Of course, he never found those elusive cities of gold, the so-called Seven Cities of Cíbola, but his explorations did fortify Spain's land claims.

In 1598, Juan de Oñate formally claimed Texas for Spain, though the first permanent settlement and official mission, Corpus Christi de la Isleta (near El Paso), didn't come for another 84 years. Spain held Texas for 300 years, and its influence, perhaps filtered through its Latin American colonies, is strongly felt, though in reality Spain did little more than raise a few missions and settlements along the coast.

UNDER THE FRENCH FLAG

The French claimed Texas based on a visit from Rene-Robert Cavelier, Sieur

1836 The Texas Declaration of Independence is signed and an interim government for the Republic of Texas is formed. A small Texan army is overwhelmed by the Mexican army during a 2-week siege at San Antonio's Battle of the Alamo. Nearly 400 Texans are executed by the Mexicans at the Goliad Massacre, under order of Santa Anna. Texans decisively defeat Mexican forces at the Battle of San Jacinto and win independence.

1845 U.S. president James Polk annexes Texas and signs legislation making Texas the 28th state.

1846 The Mexican-American War erupts over boundary disputes, establishing Texas's southern boundary at the Rio Grande River.

1861 Texas secedes from the Federal Union and joins the Confederate States of America.

1870 The U.S. Congress readmits Texas into the Union.

1883 The University of Texas is inaugurated in Austin.

1888 The present state capitol in Austin, larger than the U.S. Capitol, is dedicated.

1925 Texas becomes the second state to elect a woman governor, Miriam Ferguson.

1963 Pres. John F. Kennedy is assassinated in Dallas. Texan Lyndon B. Johnson is sworn in as president.

1964 The Space Center in Houston (now named for Lyndon B. Johnson) becomes permanent home to NASA.

1966 A gunman atop the tower at the University of Texas at Austin opens fire on students and faculty below, killing 17 before being killed by police.

1970s Unprecedented population growth as "Sun Belt" seekers flood the state; oil industry is catalyst behind booming economy.

1980s Bust hits the oil and gas industry; real estate prices plummet.

1993 A Waco cult, the Branch Davidians, enters into a 2-month standoff with federal officials from the Bureau of Alcohol, Tobacco and Firearms.

1994 Texas becomes the second most populous state in the nation.

continues

de la Salle, who sailed the Mississippi River down to the Gulf of Mexico in 1682. Back in France, La Salle received a royal commission to establish a French empire in the southwestern territories of North America. When he returned in 1685, the Frenchman miscalculated and landed 400 miles west of the mouth of the Mississippi, on the Texas coast near Matagorda Bay. Undaunted, he established Fort San Louis and raised the French flag. The French settlement lasted only a few years, victim of both disease and Indian attack (which felled the fort), and La Salle himself was killed by his own men.

- **2000** After a prolonged and disputed election, Texas Gov. George W. Bush is ushered into the presidency of the United States by the U.S. Supreme Court.
- **2001** Houston-based energy giant Enron—formerly the world's largest energy trading company—files for bankruptcy.
- **2002** Enron's demise erupts into a scandal of improper accounting practices and fake "shell companies," prompting Justice Department inquiries, arrests, and the suicide of at least one former executive. Texan Lance Armstrong wins his fourth consecutive Tour de France, the world's most difficult cycling competition.

Spaniards quickly responded to the French settlements in Texas and Louisiana, establishing their own new mission, San Francisco de los Tejas, in East Texas in 1690. Three decades later, the Mission of San Antonio de Valero—the Alamo—led to the founding of the city of San Antonio (which became the seat of Spanish government in Texas in 1772). Spain established missions across Texas, but its colonization of the territory proceeded slowly.

MEXICO'S TURN

Mexico won independence from Spain in 1821 and turned its sights to the immense territory north. The Mexican government granted authorization to Stephen F. Austin, who would become known as the "Father of Texas," to settle in southeast Texas with a colony of 300 families (the "Texas Original 300"). The Austin settlers weren't the first Anglo-Americans in Texas, but the new colony, made up mostly of Tennesseans, marked the official beginning of Anglo-American colonization. Just 15 years later, nearly 50,000 people had settled in Texas.

American settlers had to accept Mexican citizenship and Roman Catholicism to remain in Texas. Mexico had a republican form of government, but states' rights, including those of Texas, were not defined, and the Mexican government did little to protect its colony. As more Americans settled there, Texas took on the shape of a U.S. outpost, despite the Mexican flag flying over it. Stephen Austin organized a militia, which would become the famous Texas Rangers, to protect the colony. Tensions grew, and Mexico denied the entry of additional American settlers in 1830. Other religious, political, and cultural clashes between Texans and the Mexican government ensued, and the self-proclaimed president of Mexico, Gen. António López de Santa Anna, bolstered his troops in Texas. Texans then requested the status of independent Mexican state. When their diplomatic initiative failed, Texans declared independence from Mexico on March 2, 1836.

War was imminent. Texas forces attacked San Antonio. In response, Santa Anna and his troops vastly outnumbered and then ruthlessly crushed the valiant Texans, led by Davy Crockett and Jim Bowie, at the Alamo in a 2-week battle in March 1836. Mexican troops slaughtered more than 300 Texas prisoners at Goliad only days later, unwittingly giving rise to the battle cry of independence: "Remember the Alamo! Remember Goliad." (Though only the first defeat is now generally remembered.) Six weeks later the Texans, led by Gen. Sam

Houston's army, rebounded with a stunning and decisive victory over Santa Anna at the Battle of San Jacinto, winning their independence from Mexico on April 21, 1836.

THE REPUBLIC OF TEXAS & THE CONFEDERACY

The Lone Star flag flew triumphantly for nearly a decade, from 1836 to 1845, over the Republic of Texas, a nation that was officially recognized by the United States and Europe but not Mexico. Six different sites served as the Texas capital until the town of Austin finally won out in 1839. The government, based on the U.S. model, had a president, a senate, and a house of representatives, army, navy, and militia. Yet the new republic faced some daunting problems, such as boundary disputes, debt, and concerns about Mexican attack. Unable to solve those by itself, the republic accepted U.S. annexation, and Texas became the 28th state in 1845, ceding some western lands (parts of modern-day Oklahoma, New Mexico, and Colorado) to the Union. Mexico terminated diplomatic relations with the United States; the Mexican War ended with Mexico's surrender to the United States in 1848 and the Treaty of Guadalupe Hidalgo, which rejected Mexican claims on Texas and the southwest.

But there was more tumult to come. Texas joined the Confederate States of America, seceding from the United States in January 1861. Texas sided with the Confederacy during the Civil War, though support was not unanimous among leaders. Gov. Sam Houston chose to resign rather than back the Confederate states. About 90,000 Texans saw military service, and the Texas economy was left in shambles. After the end of the Civil War, Texas—after ratifying the 13th, 14th, and 15th Amendments—officially rejoined the Union in March 1870.

THE WILD WEST TO TODAY

Texas was still the Wild West and most of its settlers lived the frontier life. The dismal economy after the war and abundant longhorn cattle in southern Texas led to the great Texas trail drives to northern markets in the 1860s. The drives north from Texas to Kansas City, such as the famous Chisholm Trail, brought prosperity to ranchers and particularly the city of Fort Worth, the site of cattle auctions and shipping companies, which grew as the railroads reached Texas at the end of the 19th century. The free-for-all, boomtown aspect of life in Texas became a natural haven to all sorts of opportunists and outlaws, among them Wild Bill Hickok, John Wesley Hardin, and Billy the Kid (and later, Bonnie Parker and Clyde Barrow).

In 1901, the Texas oil and gas boom exploded with the discovery of the Spindletop oil field near Beaumont, transforming the agricultural economy and bringing riches to many other Texans. The discovery of "black gold" produced a spate of new Texas boomtowns, with an influx of workers—known as wildcatters and mavericks—hoping that a little hard work in the oil fields would translate into rapid wealth.

Texas celebrated its centennial in 1936 with the Texas Centennial Exposition in Dallas at Fair Park. But the next real watershed event in Texas was a tragic one. On November 22, 1963, President John F. Kennedy was assassinated as his motorcade passed through downtown Dallas. Kennedy's vice-president, Texas's own Lyndon B. Johnson, was sworn in as the 36th president aboard the presidential plane at Dallas's Love Field airport.

The urban areas of Texas have continued to grow, with Houston, San Antonio, and Dallas among the 10 largest cities in the United States. These cities and fast-growing, formerly suburban communities have successfully attracted firms that have relocated their headquarters from around the country. Texas has recently become a leader in the technology industry, and the capital, Austin, has been transformed from a government and university town to one of the nation's most important clusters of high-tech corporations and computer chip makers.

2 Talk Like a Texan

It may be true that Texans talk differently, but it's tough to pin down a true Texas accent—a reality evident in virtually any Hollywood picture about the place. Most Texans don't speak with the southern drawl of the Deep South. It's more of a Western twang. And because Texas is such a big place, influenced by the language of adventurers heading west and newly arrived immigrants (Yankees from the north, Mexicans from south of the border), Texans have adopted a rich vocabulary and colorful manner of speaking.

It's not just how they say it, but what they say that makes Texans stand out. Their folksy language and homespun hyperbole seems to come effortlessly. While tracking the most recent barnburner of a presidential election, CBS news anchor Dan Rather, a native of Wharton, described a candidate who "tore through Dixie like a big wheel through a cotton field." The former Texas governor Anne Richards was especially given to colorful phrases like, "That dawg don't hunt."

Another tried-and-true method of talkin' Texan is to sprinkle in Spanish words and Anglicize the Spanish names of towns and streets. Even non-Hispanic Texans liberally toss around phrases like "Hola," "Qué pasa?" and "Adiós, amigo" in their everyday patter. Keep an ear out for things like "Guada-loop" (for Guadalupe) and "Man-shack" (for Manchaca).

Here's some help to getting on linguistically in the Lone Star state.

GLOSS'RY

All the fixins Accompaniments—beans, mashed potatoes, gravy, and the like—to go with your chicken-fried steak. The plate should groan under their weight.

Awl Texas's largest industry. As in, awl 'n' gas.

Big ol' Large. Esteemed.

Buffalo chip What cowboys kick around out in the fields—cow dung.

Coke Generic term for soft drink. Dr. Pepper, Pepsi, RC Cola—they're all just "Coke" to Texans.

Dadgummit and **dadburnit** Common expletives.

Fixin' to A general state of preparedness or intent to carry out an act. ("I'm fixin' to eat that chicken-fried steak of yours.")

Gimme cap Freebie baseball caps, with logos of awl 'n' gas and other companies on the bill. Redneck uniform to be worn as an alternative to cowboy hat. The name is derived from the frequent request, "Gimme one them thar caps."

Give a holler A plea to call, write, or e-mail.

Good ol' boy A true Texan.

Gussied up The look necessary for going out in public: dolled up 'n' pretty.

Hook 'em The cry and hand signal (index finger and pinkie raised like horns) of UT graduates everywhere. As in, "Hook 'em, horns."

Howdy, y'all The one-size-fits-all greeting—singular, plural, who cares? Y'all is a contraction of "you all," but is actually just Texan for "you." Howdy is pronounced "high-dee."

I reckon The act of thinking out loud.

Kicker Cowboy who puts his pointy-toed boots to good use.

Over yonder Where you'll likely be when you give a holler.

Yankee A northerner. Outsider. Opponent of Texas statehood.

Yes ma'am The polite way to respond to any woman over 20.

Yessir and **nossir** The polite way to respond to a Texan man.

3 Texan Style

When my editor suggested I contribute a few words on Texan style to this section, she laughingly added, "If that's not an oxymoron." It's true, Texans are probably better known as world-class shoppers than arbiters of taste, so a Yankee could be forgiven for thinking that "Texan style" might be a contradiction in terms. But style? Texans have plenty of that.

Beyond oil, championship sports teams, and roots music, Texas's greatest export is the classic Western cowboy style that the state seems to embody for people around the world. Everybody from Ralph Lauren to Madonna seems to have adopted cowboy duds as the very symbol of American cool and rugged independence. Outsiders may not pull it off with as much natural ease as Texans, but the basics of cowboy style aren't hard to master.

There's the fundamental **ranch hand style,** which depends on clothes tough enough to withstand the demands of life on the range: long, snug-fitting boot-cut jeans (preferably Wrangler or Lee) that bunch up at the bottom, worn with a belt featuring a big ol' buckle, scuffed-up calfskin cowboy boots, crisp Western shirt, and a cowboy hat (straw in summer, felt in winter). Taking the basic elements, you can gussy up the look as much as you wish. The **drugstore cowboy** or **rodeo queen** look adopts fun and fancy embellishments like embroidered yokes and sterling silver collar tips. **Urban cowboys** in oil and banking simply throw more money at the basics, and don boots and hats with their pinstripes for business (and ranch-style gabardine twill pants in place of jeans on the weekends). The boots aren't made of regular old calfskin leather, but of an exotic skin like alligator, ostrich, or eel, preferably handmade and with elaborate uppers. The hat will be a top-of-the line number from a classic Western outfitter like M. L. Leddy's in Fort Worth. The belt buckle (along with the tip and keeper) is sterling silver.

For a certain kind of woman in Texas—the kind that will only wear a Western shirt if it is expensively studded with rhinestones and rubies—the classic look has long been the one created by upscale Dallas and Houston shopping mavens: big salon-coifed and frosted hair, a wide pearly smile, and an overly precious designer outfit, accented by a cornucopia of fur and jewelry. The Robert Altman film *Dr. T & the Women* got the Dallas upper-class look of professional shoppers down to a tee.

⌐ *Fun Fact* **Texas Types**

The Wildcatter. An independent oilman, a gambler at heart whose fortunes rise and fall with the oil and gas industry.

The Roughnecks. Laborers who operate the oil rigs. Often itinerant or immigrant—down and dirty and flush with cash. Texas sailors.

The Maverick. Originally denoted an unbranded calf, but came to be understood as a Texas archetype: the nonconformist, independent-thinking man (or woman!).

BOOTS   Cowboy boots date from the riding boots the Spanish conquistadors and *vaqueros* wore. They're the most fundamental element of the cowboy look, and almost everyone in Texas owns at least one pair. President Bush delights in showing his off to reporters. Real cowboys have everyday boots and dress-up or dance-floor boots. The basics are plain old black or brown calfskin boots, with either a roper (low heel) or a riding or semiwalking (high heel) style. The toes can be pointed, squared off, or gently rounded. The sharp pointed toe is the most authentic, though today many younger ropers go with the rounded style. The tops, which are generally calf-high, can be either V-shaped or straight, but should always have stitched-on pull straps. Boot stores stock a bewildering array of leathers: Besides basic (but smooth, rugged, and inexpensive) calfskin, you'll find showy and more delicate (and often vastly more expensive) exotic skins, such as lizard, eel, alligator, ostrich, snake, stingray, water buffalo, and kangaroo. Generally the most expensive boots a shop will stock are horned-toe crocodile; a pair of those babies will set you back a couple of grand. Boot design can be no-nonsense or elaborately styled, with contrasting uppers, fancy stitching, and piping.

Even more important than look, though, is fit: A boot has to fit properly. It should be snug, requiring you to pull on with both straps and yank off with a touch of difficulty, but not tight. Your heel should snap into place but allow for a little movement. A good boot seller can help you determine the right fit. Don't buy unless you're sure. Texas brands to look for include Lucchese, Nocona, Justin, and Tony Lama.

HATS   Cowboy hats are serious business. They're worn at all times and not taken off indoors; if you don't think so, check out a Western dance hall on a Friday night, where you'll find cowboys twirling about the dance floor with their best hats firmly in place. The classic Stetson, like the one LBJ wore on the ranch, dates from the 1850s. A cowboy's proper "beaver" dress hat can run $1,000 or more. The key to your new hat is getting it formed, or creased, for that perfect range or courthouse look. A real-life roper retires his white straw hat at the end of summer, opting for a sturdy felt sombrero for autumn and winter—a seasonal fashion dictum not unlike the one that demands that New Englanders banish white from their wardrobes after Labor Day.

WESTERN SHIRTS   Most traditional and urban cowboys go for heavy, pressed cotton Western shirts in plaids or solids. Fancy Western swing shirts with pearl snaps, contrasting yokes, and little "smile" or "arrow" pockets aren't that easy to find these days. If you want a singing cowboy or fancy honky-tonk shirt, you'll either need to go vintage or shell out big bucks for a high-end designer, like Manuel of Hollywood (who dressed Dolly Parton and other flashy country music stars). At its most basic, though, the Western shirt should have a reinforced Western yoke, flap pockets, a full cut, and snapped cuffs. The shirt-tail is always worn tucked in.

ACCESSORIES   The most important Western accessories are belt buckles, belts, hatbands, bolo ties, and bandannas. For the Texan man, hand-tooled belts (often with the wearer's name embossed), hatbands, and especially buckles—which range from obscenely large Texas state seals, oil derricks, and Jack Daniels emblems to simple, elegant silver buckles, tips, and keepers—allow him to express himself. A real Texan never buys a leather belt that comes stock with a buckle. Bolo ties, though still worn in some parts, are a little passé for the average Joe trying to adopt the cowboy look.

4 Texan Music

Neither country and western nor the blues originated in Texas, but both genres of roots music have been indelibly shaped by talented Texans. The state ranks alongside Tennessee or Louisiana for contributions to the Americana music scene, and the number of individual music greats that Texas has spawned is astonishing. They've come from the big cities like Houston, Austin, and Dallas, of course, but most remarkable is how many have rolled out of Lubbock. The barren lands of West Texas have proved incredibly fertile for the creation of homespun music. Texas has spawned so many musicians that a museum honoring their contributions to pop culture is in the works, most likely to be housed in Houston (check www.americanmusichistory.org for updates).

Most listeners think of country music when they think of Texas sounds, and the state was certainly instrumental in the form's early development, a product of cowboy songs and folk contributions from new immigrants. **Bob Wills and the Texas Playboys,** who emerged from Lubbock in the 1920s, introduced Western swing (or Texas swing), a combustible mix of hillbilly tunes, fiddle music, jazz, polka, cowboy ballads, and Mexican ranchero music. Texas artists like **George Jones** in the 1950s popularized honky-tonk, characterized by steel guitars, fiddles, and plaintive vocals. Jones, one of country's finest voices, later became a balladeer and top-10 hit maker. Like **Kenny Rogers** of Conroe, Texas, he was more closely identified with Nashville than with Texas.

With characteristic independence, Texas musicians developed their own kind of country. Progressive and outlaw country fused hard-core honky-tonk, folk, rock, and blues. With country music reaching a national audience in the 1970s with the blandly orchestrated Nashville Sound, a gang of Texas outlaws, led by **Willie Nelson, Waylon Jennings, Jerry Jeff Walker** (not a native Texan but closely identified with the scene), and **Kris Kristofferson** seized the stage with a gritty, maverick rejection of the slicker country being produced in Nashville. Waylon and Willie's "Luckenbach, Texas," a song about a town with two dozen people, became a state anthem. Nelson, the braided, bandanna-wearing iconoclast of Texas country, evolved into one of Texas's most beloved contemporary figures. He began his career as a songwriter of hits for Patsy Cline ("Crazy") and others before positioning himself as a cult artist and finally a crossover country star, daring to dabble in all genres, from traditional country to ballads ("Blue Eyes Cryin' in the Rain") and potent country poetry.

Other Texas singer-songwriters, such as **Guy Clark** and **Townes Van Zandt,** less prone to the outlaw lifestyle but still resolutely independent, mined a territory of lyrical country-folk music. These unjustly overlooked artists lay the foundation for the current generation of Texas songwriters, including **Lyle Lovett, Jimmie Dale Gilmore,** and **Steve Earle,** musicians as at home in country as they are in rock, gospel, and the blues. Western swing has undergone a couple of rounds of revival, in the 1970s and again in the early 1990s. **Asleep at the Wheel,** a multipiece band that has gone through innumerable lineup changes, has been present for both. Current stars among Texas singer-songwriters with a touch of twang include **Nanci Griffith, Michelle Shocked,** and **Kelly Willis.** Expanding the horizons of Texas music are Dallas-area rockabilly barburners **Reverend Horton Heat** and Texas polka aficionados **Brave Combo,** originally from Denton.

Texas blues began with legendary figures like **Blind Lemmon Jefferson** (whose "Black Snake Moan" struck quite a chord in the 1920s) and **Blind**

Willie Johnson, both of whom played the area around Deep Ellum in Dallas. **Robert Johnson** may have been from Mississippi, but he made his only known recordings in Dallas and San Antonio in the 1930s. **Sam "Lightning" Hawkins,** of Houston, created a blistering blues guitar style that influenced generations of rockers. Other notable Houston blues musicians include **B. B. King, Albert Collins,** and **Clarence "Gatemouth" Brown.**

Port Arthur's **Janis Joplin**'s raw vocals and blues-inflected rock (not to mention her heroin overdose and posthumous hit, "Me and Bobby McGee") made her an icon of the 1960s. **Stevie Ray Vaughan,** an incendiary guitar wizard from south Dallas, also became a blues-rock star before his light went out prematurely in a helicopter crash in 1990. Austin club regulars **Angela Strehli** and **Lou Ann Barton** continue the Texas blues tradition.

Texas has produced its share of rock 'n' roll pioneers, too. Lubbock's **Buddy Holly,** the bespectacled proto-rocker who with his band, the Crickets, influenced Elvis, the Beatles, and countless new-wavers with tunes like "Peggy Sue" and "That'll Be the Day," went down in a 1959 plane crash after just a couple of years at the top. **Roy Orbison,** from Vernon, Texas, began his career in rockabilly, but his high, haunting voice propelled a number of memorable mainstream hits in the 1960s, like "Only the Lonely" and "In Dreams." **ZZ Top,** from Houston, started out in swaggering blues-rock territory, singing about "Tush" and "LaGrange" before their belly-length beards and songs like "Legs" and "Tube Steak Boogie" made them MTV darlings. Current Texas faves on the alternative scene include **Spoon** (from Austin) and **Slobberbone** (Dallas).

With its Latino roots and large Hispanic population, Texas has given rise to yet another genre that reflects cross-cultural fertilization, Tex-Mex border sounds. Conjunto, *norteña,* and Tejano are all slightly different takes on this definitive Tex-Mex style, anchored by the accordion and 12-string Mexican guitar. The megastar **Selena** (yet another Texas music star to burn out early rather than fade away) brought Tejano to national Latino audiences before her death, and reached a wider audience through films and books about her life. **Flaco Jiménez** is the leading conjunto proponent today. Another cross-cultural musical phenomenon in Texas is zydeco, a creole stew that combines Afro-Caribbean, blues, and Cajun rhythms, and is especially popular in the Houston and Galveston areas (as well as Louisiana).

In large part, Texas has proved such fecund musical ground because of its strong tradition of live performance. For a couple of decades now, Austin has immodestly declared itself the "Live Music Capital of the World," and its rollicking clubs have presented nightly diverse lineups of homegrown and imported live music acts. From Armadillo World Headquarters to Club Foot and Liberty Lunch, Austin has embraced a disproportionate share of legendary, beloved, and now-defunct live music venues. **Gilleys** and **Billy Bob's,** two huge, slick honky-tonks still going strong in Houston and Fort Worth, are important national showcases for traditional country and redneck rock bands, while classic small-town Texas dance halls such as **Gruene Hall** (in Gruene, pronounced "green," located south of Austin) keep the flame burning. Dancing to country music is a true Texas art, and while the popularity of individual dances—the Two-Step, Cotton-Eyed Joe, and line dancing (a kind of kickers' aerobics)—rises and falls with the latest hits, in Texas they have amazing staying power. The dance floors of local honky-tonks pack in young Billy Ray Cyrus look-alikes and single rodeo queens in tight jeans as well as nimble older folks boot-scootin' like there's no tomorrow.

5 Texan Cuisine

Texans are famous for their love of artery-clogging steaks the size of Volkswagens. Amarillo's Big Texan Steak Ranch restaurant features a 72-ouncer (eat it in under an hour and get it for free). Locals are rabidly fond of **chicken-fried steak.** This oddity is a thick slab of inexpensive beef beaten until tender and dipped in batter, deep-fried like chicken, buried under a puddle of cream gravy, doused with pepper, and served with a glob of mashed potatoes (skins on). Other home-style veggies like okra and black-eyed peas are also worthy accompaniments. A good chicken-fried steak—crisp, light, and tender—is weirdly enjoyable, but an inferior one can be like gnawing on an old tire. Note to Yankees who don't want to get laughed out of town: Don't specify "medium" or "medium rare" when ordering a chicken-fried steak. It comes only one way: cooked.

But steak—whether broiled or chicken-fried—is only part of the story. The real holy trinity of Texas eats consists of three down-home staples no true Texan can do without for long: chili, barbecue, and Tex-Mex.

CHILI A bowl of Texas red, hot, or hotter than hell, is often thought of as Mexican or Tex-Mex. But it's as Texan as they come, with its origins in San Antonio in the late 1800s. Chili (not *chile,* which is Spanish for pepper) should be thick, meaty, and spicy, and served unadorned. Real Texas chili is made with beef (or occasionally rabbit or venison) but not beans. This standard has been relaxed, though, and plenty of Texans like pinto beans (never kidney beans) in their chili. There are annual chili cook-offs across the state; the most famous is held in the border town of Terlingua. Degrees of fire are usually designated as one-, two-, or three-alarm or indicated by an X, XX, or XXX. Four X's means that bowl of devil's soup is guaranteed to scorch your tongue, lips, and entire digestive tract.

Weird food item: **Frito pie,** which is meaty chili, cheese, and diced onions poured over a plate of (or into a bag of) Frito's corn chips. Frito pie is a staple in Texas school cafeterias (or at least it was when I was growing up).

BARBECUE (BBQ) Vying with chili and chicken-fried steak for the honor of state dish is barbecue (even though Texans didn't invent it; the word comes from the Spanish, *barbacoa,* and the style originated in Spain and evolved in the Caribbean and Latin America). Still, the art of roasting meats over an open fire distinguishes Texans from, say, lesser humans. Texans slow cook (smoke) beef brisket and ribs (and to a lesser extent, pork, chicken, sausage, and *cabrito,* young goat) in pits over mesquite or hickory wood. The slow roasting and wood give it its unique, revered flavor. Texas barbecue, unlike its worthy regional competitors in places like Memphis and the Carolinas, is almost wholly focused on beef, and it tends to be tangier and spicier than the sweeter pork popular in those places. A plate of brisket or ribs is served with heaps of tangy barbecue sauce (which is often also employed as a basting sauce), and side dishes like potato salad, pinto beans, and coleslaw. A proper Texas barbecue will either be a down-and-dirty, ramshackle joint like Sonny Bryan's in Dallas and Angelo's in Fort Worth, or a rustic place in the country with long picnic tables and a huge barbecue pit in full view, like the Salt Lick in Buda, outside of Austin.

TEX-MEX Neither identifiably Mexican nor strictly Texan, Tex-Mex is, as the name indicates, a hybrid menu of simple dishes. A Texan gets homesick for authentic Tex-Mex cooking just as fast as she does for barbecue or chili. No Texan has ever had good Tex-Mex except in Texas; both barbecue and chili seem a bit easier to reproduce over state lines. Not spicy or intricate like authentic Mexican food, Tex-Mex is greasy, filling, tasty, and cheap, a step above addictive junk food. There is little distinction between dishes and ingredients. Almost all involve corn or flour tortillas, lots of white and yellow cheese, chili, hot sauce, and rice and refried beans—meaning that a good plate of Tex-Mex will lack for color. It will be essentially a uniformly muddy yellow-brown hue. Tex-Mex dishes can be spiced up with Tabasco sauce or scorcher jalapeño peppers, which young Texans learn to gobble up like pickles.

All Tex-Mex meals begin with tortilla chips and salsa (hot sauce) and guacamole for dipping. Enchiladas, chile rellenos, *tacos al carbón,* and burritos have long been the standard bearers for Tex-Mex but in the past couple of decades, **fajitas,** grilled beef or skirt steak rolled in flour tortillas and dolled up with guacamole, pico de gallo, and cilantro, have become the most popular dish. Less than authentic, but wildly popular, is the substitution of strips of barbecued chicken breast for beef.

BEVERAGES   Texans wash down chili and barbecue with plastic glasses of **ice tea** (it's the rare Texan who says *iced* tea) the size of small oil drums and **Texas beer,** preferably longnecks of Lone Star, Pearl, and Shiner Bock, drunk straight from the bottle. Beverage choices shift slightly in Tex-Mex restaurants. While pitchers of ice tea are fine, the beer should be ice-cold *cerveza,* Mexican beer like Corona, Tecate, Dos Equis, or Bohemia, usually served with a wedge of lime squeezed into the bottle or can. And the number-one libation for washing down a plate of Tex-Mex is the **margarita,** a tart concoction of tequila, lime juice, and triple sec, either served on the rocks or frozen. Most margaritas use cheap well tequila, but connoisseurs opt for "top-shelf" margaritas (served on the rocks), made with 100% blue agave tequilas. And the connoisseurs of connoisseurs drink aged tequilas—called *reposado* or *añejo*—straight, followed by a "tequila chaser," like the one served at Javier's restaurant in Dallas: a shot glass of orange juice, lemon juice, V8, pepper, salt, and Tabasco.

Texas also has a surprisingly robust roster of **wineries,** many in the Central Texas Hill Country around Fredericksburg and the High Plains near Lubbock. Llano Estacado and Pheasant Ridge are national award winners.

Index